STRAGEATH

EXCAVATIONS WITHIN THE ROMAN FORT 1973–86

STRAGEATH

EXCAVATIONS WITHIN THE ROMAN FORT 1973–86

BY

S.S. Frere and J.J. Wilkes

With contributions by Anne Anderson, S. Butler, C. Cartright, R. Clough, C. Dickson, N. Gale, A. Grant, F. Grew, B.R. Hartley, K.F. Hartley, M. Henig, J. Macdonald, A.J. Price, R. Reece, A.S. Robertson, F. Roe, R. Welander and Marion Wilson

Britannia Monograph Series
No. 9

Published by the Society for the Promotion of Roman Studies

31 GORDON SQUARE, LONDON, WC1H OPP

1989

BRITANNIA MONOGRAPH SERIES NO. 9

Published by the Society for the Promotion of Roman Studies
31–34 Gordon Square, London WC1H OPP

Monograph Series Editor: Professor S.S. Frere

This Monograph was published with the aid of grants from the Scottish Development Department (Historic Buildings and Monuments) and from the Administrators of the Haverfield Bequest.

Copies may be obtained from the Secretary of the Roman Society.

British Library Cataloguing in Publication Data

Frere, Sheppard, *1916–*
Strageath: excavations within the Roman fort, 1973–86. –
(Britannia monograph series; no.9).
1. Scotland. Tayside Region. Perth and Kinross
(District). Roman Empire forts. Excavation of remains
I. Title II. Wilkes, J.J. (John Joseph), *1936–*
II. Society for the Promotion of Roman Studies
936.1'28

ISBN 0-907764-11-8

Produced by Alan Sutton Publishing Ltd., Gloucester
Printed in Great Britain

CONTENTS

PART I: THE EXCAVATIONS

PART II: THE FINDS

BRIEF DESCRIPTION OF CONTENTS

Excavation took place at the Roman fort at Strageath, Perthshire, annually between 1973 and 1986, and three periods of military occupation were distinguished. The first fort was built in the late first century (Flavian period) and is attributed to the governorship of Julius Agricola. The second (Antonine I) was built on the re-occupation of Scotland c. A.D. 142, and the third (Antonine II) after a short evacuation some sixteen years later. On each re-occupation the defences were completely remodelled and a quite different garrison installed: in the Antonine I period the fort seems to have been held by a quingenary cohors equitata, but in both the Flavian and Antonine II periods the garrison was more powerful, consisting of elements of two cohortes equitatae on each occasion. Apart from an Antonine bath-building partly constructed in masonry, all structures were half-timbered. The Flavian fort was provided with exceptionally large granaries.

Although aerial photographs show a complicated system of fortified annexes outside the fort to the west, excavation was confined to the interior of the fort and to a partial examination of its defences with the aim of throwing as much light as possible on the internal buildings and on the character of the units in garrison. The results have shed new light on the archaeology of Roman forts and on the frontier problems of Roman Scotland.

After a first chapter describing the site and its characteristics, and a second recording work on the defences, the report provides details of the excavation of the various areas of the interior (Chapter III-VII) in each of their three periods. This arrangement was necessary in order to keep the plans and drawn sections of the various areas in as close a relationship as possible for ease of reference. But in the final descriptive chapter (VIII) these details are summarised and brought together in a general discussion of each fort as a whole. Part II describes the pottery, metal objects and other small finds.

LIST OF PLATES

LIST OF FIGURES IN THE TEXT

LIST OF TABLES

ABBREVIATIONS

Arch. Ael.[4,5]	*Archaeologia Aeliana*, fourth or fifth series. Society of Antiquaries of Newcastle upon Tyne.
Arch. Journ.	*The Archaeological Journal*, Royal Archaeological Institute, London
BAR	British Archaeological Reports
C.G.	Central Gaulish
CIL	*Corpus Inscriptionum Latinarum*
D.	*see* Déchelette, J., 1904.
Derbys. Arch. Journ.	*Derbyshire Archaeological Journal*
Glasgow Arch. Journ.	*Glasgow Archaeological Journal*
Journ. Chester Arch. Soc.	*Journal of the Chester Archaeological Society*
JRS	*The Journal of Roman Studies*, London
O.	see Oswald, F., 1936-7
P.S.A.S.	*Proceedings of the Society of Antiquaries of Scotland*, Edinburgh
RCAHMS	Royal Commission on the Ancient and Historical Monuments of Scotland
RIC	*The Roman Imperial Coinage*, London (quoting the second edition of vol. I)
S.G.	South Gaulish
Trans. Glasgow Arch. Soc.[2]	*Transactions of the Glasgow Archaeological Society*, second series
S&S 1958	*see* Stanfield, J.A. and G. Simpson

BIBLIOGRAPHY

Anderson 1979: S.T. Anderson, "Identification of wild grass and cereal pollen', *Danm. Geol. Unders. Yearbook 1978*, 69–92. Copenhagen.

Atkinson 1914: Donald Atkinson, 'A Hoard of Samian Ware from Pompeii', *JRS* iv (1914), 27–64.

Biddle, M. 1967: 'Two Flavian burials from Grange Road, Winchester', *Antiquaries Journal*, 47, 224–50.

Boon, G.C. 1966: 'Roman window glass from Wales', *Journal of Glass Studies*, 8, 41–5.

Boyd, W. 1984: 'Environmental change and land management in an area of the Antonine Wall, Central Scotland = a summary.' *Glasgow Arch. Journ.* xi, 75–81.

Boyd, W. 1985: 'The problem of the time-span represented by pollen spectra in podsol turves . . . ' In N.R.J. Fieller *et al.* (eds.), *Palaeobiological Investigations*, BAR Int. Series No. 266, 189–96.

Bushe-Fox, J.P. 1926: *First report on the excavation of the Roman fort at Richborough, Kent.* Reports of the Research Committee of the Society of Antiquaries of London No. VI, Oxford.

Bushe-Fox, J.P. 1932 J.P. Bushe-Fox, *Third Report on the Excavations of the Roman Fort at Richborough, Kent.* Reports of the Research Committee of the Society of Antiquaries of London No.X, Oxford.

Charlesworth, D. 1959a: 'Roman glass from northern Britain'. *Archaeologia Aeliana* (fourth series), 37, 33–58.

Charlesworth, D. 1959b: 'Roman glass in the Tullie House museum'. *Transactions of the Cumberland and Westmorland Antiquarian Society* (second series), 59, 32–40.

Charlesworth, D. 1972: 'The glass', in S.S. Frere, *Verulamium excavations.* vol.i. Reports of the Research Committee of the Society of Antiquaries of London 28, 196–215.

Charlesworth, D. 1975: 'Glass', in Hobley, B. 'The Lunt Roman fort and training school for Roman cavalry, Baginton, Warwickshire. Final report, excavations (1972–73) with conclusions'. *Transactions of the Birmingham and Warwickshire Archaeological Society*, 87, 38–40.

Charlesworth, D. 1979: 'Glass', in Hanson, W.S. *et al.*, 'The Agricolan supply-base at Red House, Corbridge'. *Archaeologia Aeliana* (fifth series), 7, 58– 61.

Curle, J. 1911: *A Roman frontier post and its people: the fort of Newstead in the parish of Melrose* (Glasgow).

Curle, J. 1931–32: 'An inventory of objects of Roman and provincial Roman origin found on sites in Scotland not definitely associated with Roman constructions'. *Proceedings of the Society of Antiquaries of Scotland* 66, 277–397.

Déchelette, J. 1904: *Les Vases céramiques ornés de la Gaule remaine.* Paris.

Dimbleby, G.W. 1985: *The Palynology of Archaeological Sites.* Academic Press.

Domaszewski/Dobson 1967: *Die Rangordnung des Römischen Heeres.* Köln/Graz.

Dore, J. and & Greene, K. 1977: *Roman Pottery Studies in Britain and Beyond.* BAR Supplementary Series 30. Oxford.

Fox, C. 1923: *The Archaeology of the Cambridge region.* Cambridge.

Frere, S. 1972: *Verulamium Excavations* i. Repts. Res. Comm. Soc. Antiqs. London, No.XXVIII. Oxford, 1972.

Frere, S. 1984: *Verulamium Excavations* iii. Oxford Univ. Comm. for Arch. Monograph I. Oxford, 1984.

Gage, J. 1834: '. . . the Bartlow hills, Ashdon, Essex, with an account of Roman sepulchral remains recently discovered in the lesser barrows'. *Archaeologia* xxv, 1–23.

Gage, J. 1836: '. . . the recent discovery of Roman sepulchral relics in one of the greater barrows at Bartlow, in the parish of Ashdon, Essex'. *Archaeologia* xxvi, 300–17.

Gazda 1981: E.K. Gazda, 'A marble group of Ganymede and the eagle from the age of Augustine', in J.H. Humphrey, *Excavations at Carthage 1977 conducted by the University of Michigan (Carthage VI)* (Ann Arbor), 125–78.

Gercke 1970: P. Gercke, 'Die Gemmensammlung im Archäologischen Institut der Universität Göttingen' in P. Zazoff, *Antike Gemmen in Deutschen Sammlungen* iii (Wiesbaden), 63–176.

Guido, M. 1978: *The glass beads of the prehistoric and Roman periods in Britain and Ireland.* Reports on the Research Committees of the Society of Antiquaries of London 35.

Guiraud 1974: H. Guiraud, 'Cultes champêtres sur des intailles d'époque romaine', *Pallas* xxi, 111–7.

Guirand 1982: H. Guiraud, 'La Terre et les Paysans dans l'Antiquité Classique', *Pallas* xxix, 39–56.

Hanson, W.S. *et al.* 1979: 'The Agricolan supply base at Red House, Corbridge', *Arch. Ael.*[5] vii, 1–97.

Harden, D.B. 1962: 'Glass in Roman York'. *Eburacum – Roman York.* RCHM (London), 136–41.

Harden, D.B. 1967: 'The glass jug', in Biddle 1967, 238–40.

Harden, D.B. 1974: 'Window glass from the Romano-British bath-house at Garden Hill, Hartfield, Sussex'. *Antiquaries Journal*, 54, 280–81.

Harden, D.B. and Price, J. 1971: 'The glass'. In Cunliffe, B.W., *Excavations at Fishbourne 1961–1969. Volume 2, the finds.* Reports of the Research Committee of the Society of Antiquaries of London 27, 317–68.

Harden, D.B. *et al.* 1987: *Glass of the Caesars* (Milan).

Hartley, B.R. 1972: 'The Samian Ware' in Sheppard Frere, *Verulamium Excavations*, Vol.I. Reports of the Research Committee of the Society of Antiquaries of London No.XXVIII, 216–262, Oxford.

Hartley, B.R. 1972a: 'The Roman Occupations of Scotland: the Evidence of Samian Ware.' *Britannia* iii, (1972), 1–55.

Hartley, B.R. 1985: Chap.32 'The Samian Ware' in Lynn F. Pitts and J.K. St Joseph, *Inchtuthil: The Roman Legionary Fortress*, 314–22. Britannia Monograph No.6. London.

Hartley, K.F. 1977: 'Two major potteries in the first century A.D.', in Dore and Greene 1977, 5–17.

Hartley, K.F. and Webster, P.V. 1973: 'Roman-British Pottery kilns near Wilderspool, *Arch. Journ.* cxxx, 77–103.

Haverfield, F. and Taylor, M.V. 1908: 'Romano-British Shropshire', *Shropshire* volume 1. Victoria County History, 205–78.

Henig, M. 1978: *A Corpus of Roman Engraved Gemstones from British Sites.* BAR 8, 2nd edition, Oxford.

Henig in Rodwell 1980: M. Henig, 'Art and Cult in the Temples of Roman Britain', in W. Rodwell, *Temples, Churches and Religion in Roman Britain.* BAR 77, 91–113, Oxford.

Horster 1970: G. Horster, *Statuen auf Gemmen* (Bonn).

Hull, M.R. 1963: *The Roman Potters' Kilns of Colchester.* Rep. Res. Comm. Antiq. London, No. XXI. Oxford, 1963.

Isings, C. 1957: *Roman Glass from dated finds* (Groningen).

Knorr, R. 1919: *Töpfer und Fabriken verzierter Terra-Sigillata des ersten Jahrhunderts.* Stuttgart.

Knorr, R. 1952: *Terra-Sigillata-Gefässe des ersten Jahrhunderts mit Töpfernamen.* Stuttgart.

Maaskant-Kleibrink, M. 1978: *Catalogue of the Engraved Gems in the Royal Coin Cabinet, The Hague.* The Hague.

MacIvor, I. *et al.* 1978–80: 'Excavations on the Antonine Wall fort of Rough Castle, Stirlingshire, 1957–61,' *P.S.A.S.* cx, 230–85.

Manning, B.M. *Cat.* W.H. Manning, *Catalogue of the Romano-British Iron Tools, Fittings and Weapons in the British Museum*, London, 1985.

Manning, Newcastle *Cat.* W.H. Manning, *Catalogue of Romano-British Ironwork in the Museum of Antiquities, Newcastle upon Tyne*, Newcastle upon Tyne, 1976.

Monkton, A. 1979: 'A Romano-British site at Lower Runhams, Lènham'. *Kent Archaeological Review*, 55, 118–21.

Oliver, A. 1984: 'Early Roman faceted glass'. *Journal of Glass Studies*, 26, 35– 58.

Oswald, F. 1936–7: *Index of Figure-types on Terra Sigillata* ('Samian Ware'). Liverpool.

Potter, T.W. 1979: 'The Roman fort at Ravenglass', in Potter, T.W., *The Romans in north-west England: excavations at the Roman forts of Ravenglass, Watercrook, and Bowness on Solway.* Cumberland and Westmorland Antiquarian and Archaeological Society Research series, 1, 1–138. Kendal.

Price, J. 1977: 'The Roman glass', in Gentry, A *et al.*, 'Excavations at Lincoln Road, London borough of Enfield, November 1974-March 1976'. *Transactions of the London and Middlesex Archaeological Society*, 28, 154–61.

Price, J. 1980: 'The Roman glass', in Lambrick, G. 'Excavations in Park St., Towcester'. *Northamptonshire Archaeology*, 15, 63–9.

Price, J. 1985: 'The Roman glass', in Pitts, L.F. and St. Joseph J.K., *Inchtuthil: the Roman legionary fortress.* Britannia monograph No.6 (London), 303–12.

Price, J. 1987: 'Glass from Felmongers, Harlow in Essex; a dated deposit of vessel glass found in an Antonine pit'. *Annales du 10 ème, Congrès de l'Association Internationale pour l'Histoire du Verre* (Amsterdam), 185–206.

Price, J. and Cool, H.E.M. 1985: 'Glass'. In Hurst, H.R., *Kingsholm.* Gloucester Archaeological Reports 1, 41–54. Gloucester.

Price, J. and Cool, H.E.M. forthcoming: 'The glass and evidence for Romano-British glass-making at Mancetter', in Hartley, K.F. *Excavations at Mancetter, Warwickshire.*

Richmond, I.A. and Birley, E.B. 1930: with a note by F. G. Simpson, 'Excavations on Hadrian's Wall in the Birdoswald-Pike Hill Sector, 1929,' *Trans. Cumb. & West. Antiq. & Arch. Soc.* xxx (2nd. Ser), 169–205.

Rogers: motif in G.B. Rogers, *Poteries sigillées de la Ganule Centrale. Gallia* suppl. xxviii (1974). Paris.

Sena Chiesa, G. 1966: *Gemme del Museo Nazionale di Aquileia.* Aquileia and Padua.

Stanfield, J.A. and G. Simpson 1958: *Central Gaulish Potters.* London.

Stead, I.M. 1976: *Excavations at Winterton Roman Villa.* London, H.M.S.O. 1976.

Stevenson, R.B.K. 1954–56: 'Native bangles and Roman glass' *Proceedings of the Society of Antiquaries of Scotland*, 88, 208–21.

Thomas, G. 198–: (Inveresk), *P.S.A.S.* forthcoming.

Thorpe, W.A. 1933–4: 'A glass jug of Roman date from Turriff, Aberdeenshire'. *Proceedings of the Society of Antiquaries of Scotland*, 68, 439–44.

Thorpe, W.A. 1939–40: 'A fragment of Roman glassware from Tealing, Angus'. *Proceedings of the Society of Antiquaries of Scotland*, 74, 134–5.

Turner, R.C. 1979: 'The identification of the game', in Potter, T.W., *The Romans in north-west England; excavations at the Roman forts of Ravenglass, Watercrook, and Bowness on Solway.* Cumberland and Westmorland Antiquarian and Archaeological Society Research series, 1, 76–9.

Ward, J. 1903: *The Roman fort at Gelligaer in the county of Glamorgan* (London).

Wheeler, R.E.M. and Wheeler, T.V. 1928: 'The Roman amphitheatre at Caerleon, Monmouthshire'. *Archaeologia* 78, 111–218.

Whiting, W. *et al.*, 1931: *Report on the excavation of the Roman cemetery at Ospringe, Kent.* Reports of the Research Committee of the Society of Antiquaries of London 8.

Zwierlein-Diehl, E. 1979: *Die Antiken Gemmen des Kunsthistorischen Museums in Wien ii.* Vienna

ACKNOWLEDGEMENTS

Thanks must be expressed to numerous bodies and persons for financial or practical help to the excavation. Funds were provided by the Society of Antiquaries of Scotland, the Scottish Development Department (Historic Buildings and Ancient Monuments Division), the British Academy, the Russell Trust, the Administrators of the Haverfield Bequest, and the Universities of Aberdeen, Dundee, Edinburgh, Glasgow, St. Andrew's and Strathclyde. Gratitude is expressed to Lady Jane Willoughby and to successive Factors of the Drummond Estates for permission to excavate, and to Mr. R.S. and Mr. R. Brown, tenants of Strageath Mains Farm, for much practical help and kindly tolerance. We thank Professor T.B. Mitford, Dr. K.A. Steer, Mr. D.B. Taylor and Dr. W.S. Hanson, successive chairmen of the School Committee, for their support; and Miss Charlotte Lythe, Secretary of the School for ten years, and her successor Mrs. Lorna Main for shouldering the heavy burden of administration which made the undertaking possible. Mr. W. McNichol and Mr. G.C. Mays, both of the Department of Civil Engineering at the University of Dundee, gave much help with surveying, and Mr. McNichol also gave practical classes on site. The loan of surveying and projection equipment is gratefully acknowledged from the Department of Civil Engineering and from the Department of Geography at Dundee University and from the Department of Archaeology at Glasgow University. Mrs. D. Lye, Mrs. Val Dean (Treasurer of the School) and Miss J.E.M. Comrie gave much help both on the site and with various local arrangements, and Dr. Lynn Pitts wrote first drafts of some sections of this report; these were revised, and the rest of Part I written, by S.S. Frere. Thanks are also expressed to Mrs. Anne Anderson for much help on site and to Dr. David Breeze for unfailing interest and support. The following acted as site supervisors in various successive years: Mr. and Mrs. A. Scott Anderson, Miss J.E.M. Comrie, Mr. R. Goodburn, Mr. F. Grew, Mr. M.W.C. Hassall, Mr. T. Hill, Mr. S. Heap, Mr. M. Hoadley, Miss C. Lythe, Mr. J. McLeish, Mr. R. Oram, Dr. Lynn Pitts, Professor J.J. Wilkes and Miss M.G. Wilson. The published versions of the plans and some sections were made by S.S. Frere but the majority of the published sections are by Marion Wilson. The drawings of pottery and small finds are mainly the work of Marion Wilson; others are acknowledged to Dr. A.J. Price, Mr. P.J. Crossman, Mr. Terry Shiers, as well as to the Drawing Office at the Institute of Archaeology at Oxford and to the Ancient Monuments Inspectorate and National Museum of Antiquities at Edinburgh. Thanks are due to Mr. B.R. Hartley for his work on the samian finds and to Mrs. K.F. Hartley for examining the mortaria; likewise to Dr. D.P.S. Peacock for examining some of the amphora sherds. We are also grateful to Mrs. Anne Anderson, for the report on the coarse pottery and to Mr. S. Butler, Miss C. Cartwright, Mr. R. Clough, Mr. T. Cowie, Miss C. Dickson, Dr. N.H. Gale, Miss A. Grant, Mr. F. Grew, Dr. M. Henig, Miss J. Macdonald, Dr. Jennifer Price, Mrs. Fiona Roe, Mr. J.C. Romans, Dr. R.S.O. Tomlin and Mr. R. Welander for their specialist reports, and to Professor Anne Robertson, Dr. R. Reece and Andrew Burnett for examining the coins found. The majority of the metal objects were conserved by Mrs. Sarah Pollard in the Laboratory at the Institute of Archaeology, Oxford; others were treated at the Ancient Monuments Laboratory, Edinburgh and at the National Museum of Antiquities.

The total cost of the 14 seasons of excavation was £80,278 of which £49,828 was contributed by the Scottish Development Department.

The finds and archive are deposited in the National Museum of Antiquities at Edinburgh.

Publication of this Report was made possible by generous grants from the Administrators of the Haverfield Bequest and the Scottish Development Department, Historic Buildings and Monuments Division. It is regretted that publication was greatly delayed by the failure of specialist contributors to meet generous deadlines, in one case by over nine months.

Finally, we record our grateful thanks to Lynda Smithson and Gail Davies for their careful typing of often difficult manuscript drafts.

S.S. Frere, J.J. Wilkes

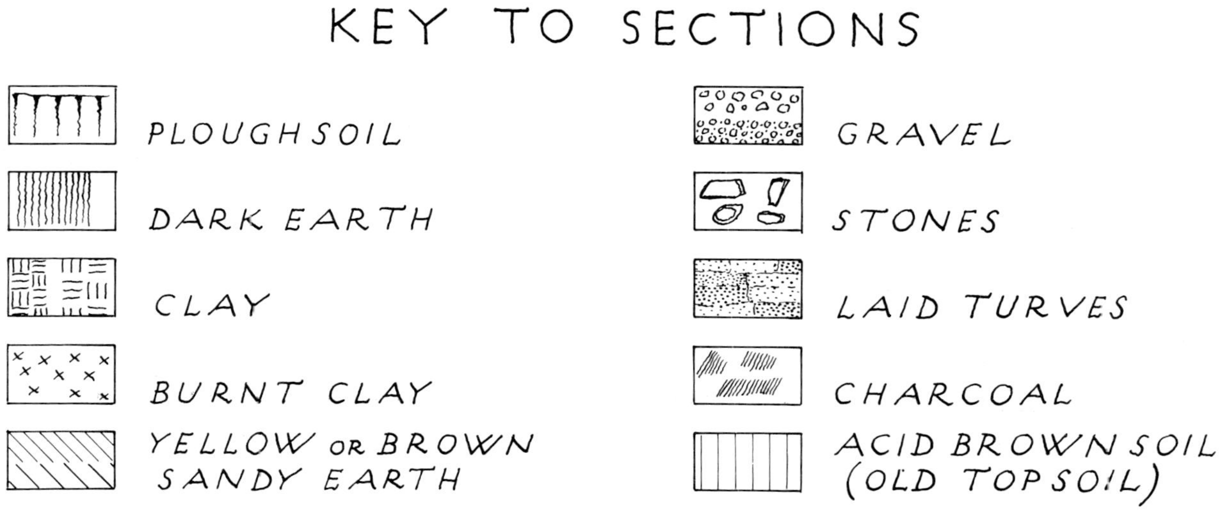

FIG. 1. Conventional indications used in the Sections.

INTRODUCTION

The Roman fort at Strageath (NN 898180) is situated in the county of Perthshire, in the Tayside Region of Scotland, at a point *c.* 5.2 km south-east of Crieff, and stands at an altitude of *c.* 36.6 m (120 ft.) above O.D. overlooking the river Earn on its right bank. Here excavation has been conducted annually from 1973 to 1986 by the Scottish Field School of Archaeology. The School was established to carry out programmes of training in methods of fieldwork and excavation for students of Scottish universities. For many years, under the direction of Professor Anne Robertson, work had been undertaken at the Roman forts of Birrens and latterly at Cardean. In 1972 Professor Robertson relinquished the directorship although continuing her own work at Cardean and, when Professor S.S. Frere was appointed to succeed her as director, the Roman fort of Strageath was chosen for continuing training-excavations by the School. There were several practical reasons for choosing another Roman fort; among them were the continuing slow destruction of the site by agricultural ploughing, the anticipation of a stratigraphical sequence of timber structures, and the likelihood that these would be associated with sufficient archaeological finds for training in their handling and conservation.

From the beginning, the aim of the excavation, as explained below (p.2), has been to throw as much light as possible upon the internal planning of the fort, in the hope that study of the buildings in successive occupations might provide information about the numbers and composition of the garrisons: these problems are discussed in Chapter VIII. Holding to this objective has meant that little work has been undertaken on the defences: only one gateway has been examined; and although the rampart has been sectioned we still have virtually no understanding, save by inference, of the complicated ditch-system visible on aerial photographs. Nor is much known of *intervallum* buildings save their bare existence. Such problems have had to be left for future workers; but even inside the fort the results of fourteen seasons are by no means conclusive. Within the ramparts the defended area amounts to 15,615 square metres, of which only 2942 square metres have been excavated (FIG.65, p.134) – a proportion of only 18.8%.

Work has taken place at Strageath for four weeks each summer or autumn; and as few of the students had had previous experience of excavation, its progress has been inevitably slow, not least because the features to be excavated were all of timber structures which were often hard to identify. In the event, excavations extended over fourteen years. In 1981 the directorship passed to Professor J.J. Wilkes. The present volume is a joint report.

During the first four seasons, excavation was entirely manual, one paid labourer being employed for the heavy work of de-turfing and removing the ploughsoil. In 1973–4 the excavation took place in July; but the dryness and hardness of the ground created difficulties, which were overcome when the work was switched in subsequent years to September. Experience also showed that the methods employed in these early years, when comparatively small trenches were dug in various parts of the north *retentura* and in the *principia*, did not result in an entirely satisfactory reconstruction of the building plans. In 1977 a new tactic was introduced; a trench 12 ft. (3.66 m) wide was cleared by machine across the whole length of the northern (right) *praetentura* at right-angles to the building-lines; and the following year a second trench was cut parallel but some distance away (FIGS.39–41, 65). Once the topsoil had been cleared, the area to be examined by hand was laid out in the bottom of the excavation. As the machine-cut trenches were always slightly wider than the archaeological trenches within them, lines of post-holes (particularly of the Antonine II period) could often be traced on the resulting berm when these did not fall within the trench itself. But indiscriminate search for features beyond the machine-cut trenches had to be avoided for fear of disturbing features of a different period. It proved possible from the remains found in these trenches to extrapolate the plans of barracks and other buildings with a fair probability of success, especially when subsidiary trenches were extended at right-angles to define the end-walls of the buildings. The method has subsequently been used in both the south (left) *retentura* and in the left *praetentura*, and gives a clearer idea of the successive fort-plans than was obtained in the right *retentura*. Similar trenches were cut across the central block each side of the *principia* in 1979 and 1986, but the presence of a root-crop prevented exploration of the full areas here in the former year; and in the event it is clear that, because their character is much less predictable than that of the barracks, full elucidation of the plans in these areas requires more excavation than has been undertaken. It has proved impossible, however, to raise the finance necessary to extend the activities of the School at Strageath; and for this reason some uncertainties remain about the buildings in the Central Range. Fortunately these do not affect interpretation of the history and garrisoning of the successive forts.

Until 1978 the excavation was run on a very small budget, money being raised from participating universities and supplemented by grants from the British Academy and from the Administrators of the Haverfield Bequest. In that year, however, the School was able to persuade the Ancient Monuments Inspectorate that real damage to the site was being caused by ploughing, and additional money was then made available from Rescue funds.

The excavation was recorded in feet and inches; in this report metric equivalents have been added.

The objectives of the excavation were to discover the periods during which the fort was occupied by Roman troops, and, by recovery of the successive plans of its internal arrangements, to contribute to our understanding of the nature and organization of the units which from time to time formed the garrison. There was reason at the outset to suspect that Strageath like Ardoch had been occupied three times, in the Flavian, Antonine I and Antonine II periods – namely in the fourth quarter of the first century, during the years *c.* 142–154 and in *c.* 158–163 on current dating; but there was an additional possibility that the fort might have been re-occupied as an outpost to Carpow under Septimius Severus in the early third century. Furthermore the complexity of the crop-marks seen on aerial photographs (FIG.4, PLS. I–IV) raised the question whether the first-century fort may not have lain west of its successors (p.5). In the event, the first season's work on the eastern defences and in an area within them solved the last question by demonstrating that three successive occupations were superimposed in the same area, and this and later results showed that there was no Severan occupation. These and other conclusions, together with the evidence on which they are based, are discussed in the pages which follow.

PART 1: THE EXCAVATIONS

I. THE FORT AND ITS SETTING

A. Early Accounts

References to Strageath in the works of the older antiquaries are less useful than for some other northern sites. Sibbald, *The Thule of the Ancients* (1695), after describing Ardoch, continues 'and five or six miles to the north-east of this, hard by the Water of Earn, near to Inch Paferay, is a lesser camp, the *castra exploratorum*, the camp of the Advance Guards, and a little eastward of this beginneth the Roman *via militaris* called by the common people the *Street Way*.' In his *Historical Enquiries* (1707) he gives similar information.

A. Gordon, *Itinerarium Septentrionale* (1726), p.42, writes 'The great Military Way . . . passes at the Foot of the Hill reaching towards *Innerpeffery*; near which Place, at a very small village called *Strageth*, there is another *Roman* Fort, the Area of which is sufficiently visible, as are three Rows of Ditches and Ramparts to the South-West; but on the other sides of the Fort, they are flat and demolished. Although the Dimensions of the Fort be much about the same with that of *Ardoch*, yet I have thought proper to give a Plate of it.' His plate is a plan showing a rectangular but nearly square outline, with four gates, the *Porta Praetoria* being marked in the north-east side.

William Roy in his *Military Antiquities of the Romans in Britain* (1793) published a very useful and substantially accurate plan (see our PL. V), but his text gives little further information. On p.82 he writes 'another [body of troops] might probably be sent to the passage of the Earn, at Strageth, about five miles distant, where there are the distinct vestiges of a station, though the camp is now ploughed down.' On pp.128–9 he writes that '[Strageath] consists of two parts, whereof the original work seems to have been that next the river; and to which the Romans had made, or intended, at least, an addition westward, divided again into two parts. From the style of these last works, and particularly from the abrupt manner in which they are broken off, it would seem as if the design had never been fully executed; but whatever degree of probability there may be in this conjecture, or whether it may not be wholly imaginary; the nature of the works in general, the course of the Roman Way, and the branch which it sends into the station, will be best conceived from the plan.'

Stuart in his *Caledonia Romana* (1845; 2nd edition, 1852, quoted here) has little to add. On p.203 he writes: 'The farm at Strageath is situated on the south bank of the Earn, distant eight and a-half miles from Dalginross and six miles from Ardoch. Many years have passed since its fields became almost entirely cleared of such encumbrances as the dykes and ditches of a Roman station. Time was, however, when the inquisitive wanderer could find attraction there, in the long preserved forms of both. The ridge of a moderate rising ground, abutting upon the river nearly opposite to Inverpeffry, was the site of these remains. In their most perfect condition of which we have any knowledge, the Roman works at Strageath comprised the shattered outlines of a permanent station, supplied with a *Procestrium* or addition on one side, somewhat resembling that at Birrens, and of a large camp adjacent, which covered an area of seventeen Scots acres. The interior of the former, including both its divisions, (that is, Station and *Procestrium*), measured

FIG. 2. Map showing Roman forts in Scotland.

nearly 750 by 400 feet. It was protected by a treble line of ramparts and trenches, and had a single *vallum* across the interior, which separated the two compartments. The latter lay to the north-west, on the direct line of the Military Way, which passed through it immediately before crossing the Earn.'

With Crawford's book *Topography of Roman Scotland north of the Antonine Wall* (Cambridge, 1949) we enter the modern era of the site's study, in which aerial photographs have supplemented the observations of fieldwork. In fact, Crawford has little to say of Strageath, but he does publish a valuable airphotograph (his pl. V), taken in 1939. He writes (pp. 40–41) 'The ramparts of the fort have been nearly levelled by cultivation . . . which had begun in Roy's time' [in fact much earlier, see Gordon's account above], 'but with the help of his plan, of the air-photo . . . and repeated efforts on foot, it is possible to restore the main outlines. The sides of the fort are about 430 ft. in length. There is a gap visible in the west side, and there must have been another in the north side, where a branch road (visible on the air-photograph in the next field) left it to join the main road. On the level ground west of the fort Roy's plan and the air-photo show a number of banks which cannot now be reduced to any order. We can only surmise that they must represent the defences of an earlier fort that was, as in other cases, superseded by a smaller one . . . The present name is Gaelic, meaning 'strath of the marsh' . . .'

In 1951 and 1958 St. Joseph published aerial photographs and short descriptions of Strageath (*JRS* xli, 1951, 63, pl. VII, 2; xlviii, 1958, 90, pl. XII, 2) and noted that in 1957 'a visit on foot to the site happened to coincide with the harvesting of the crop, and it proved possible to recognise the position of every ditch by the variation in growth in the belt of barley temporarily left standing by the reapers, and so to obtain a complete measured section from north to south across the fort and its defences.' In 1976 (*Glasgow Archaeological Journal* iv, 19–22) he published another air-photograph, one of several taken in 1962 'when crop marks were particularly distinct', together with a plan of what was visible. By that time the excavations described below had already begun.

B. The Site

The fort at Strageath lies north of the Forth-Clyde isthmus (FIG. 2). In the Flavian period it housed one of the garrisons guarding the road to Inchtuthil and beyond; in the second century it lay north of the Antonine Wall, outposted on the road to the Tay.

In both the first and second centuries one of the functions of the forts along this road is likely to have been the protection of the region of Fife, to the east of it, from Caledonian aggression.

The fort of Ardoch lies 9.5 km to the south-west; that at Bertha, on the Tay west of Perth, is situated 22.5 km to the north-east. Like many Roman forts, Strageath is placed at a river-crossing; one of its tactical purposes was to protect the bridge across the river Earn. Indeed, the need to protect the crossing of the Earn, which forms by far the most formidable obstacle between Ardoch and Bertha on the Tay, must be the reason for the great disparity of interval between these forts. There can be little doubt that a permanent wooden bridge existed for, although the river can be forded at various spots nearby when the water is low, in winter or after heavy rain this is impossible. The fort lies on a promontory of glacial sand above the river, at the eastern end of a small level plateau. The site is tactically strong, being protected by the small but significant valley of a tiny stream on the south side, by the ravine of the Earn's bend on the east, and by steep slopes down to the river's flood-plain on the north. Only to the west is the approach level, and on this side lay an area of fortified annexes (FIG. 4); across this level ground the Roman road from Ardoch approaches.[1] The fort itself, however, is served by a branch road passing through the annexes; the main road avoids the fort and its annexes by striking north-east towards the river across the face of the slopes. The plan suggests that originally, if only for a brief period, Strageath may have formed the terminal of the road. When William Roy studied the site in the middle of the eighteenth century,[2] he considered that the main road had turned northwards from the junction to cross the Earn north of Strageath Mains Farm at the now-disused Creel ford, and that it then followed the left bank of the river round to rejoin the main alignment near the Innerpeffray Library. This course is still shown on O.S. 6 inch Sheets NN 81 NE and 91 NW (FIGS. 3 and 4). But Roy's river-crossing is 480 m distant from the fort and cannot be supervised from it. Although much of the road has been ploughed away on the slope, the true course can be made out where indicated on FIG. 4, and can be clearly recognized on an aerial photograph taken

1. For a description of this road see O.G.S. Crawford, *Topography of Roman Scotland* (Cambridge, 1949) chapters 3 and 4.
2. W. Roy, *Military Antiquities of the Romans in Britain* (London, 1793), pl. XIX; for his plan of Strageath see pl. XXXII (our PL. V).

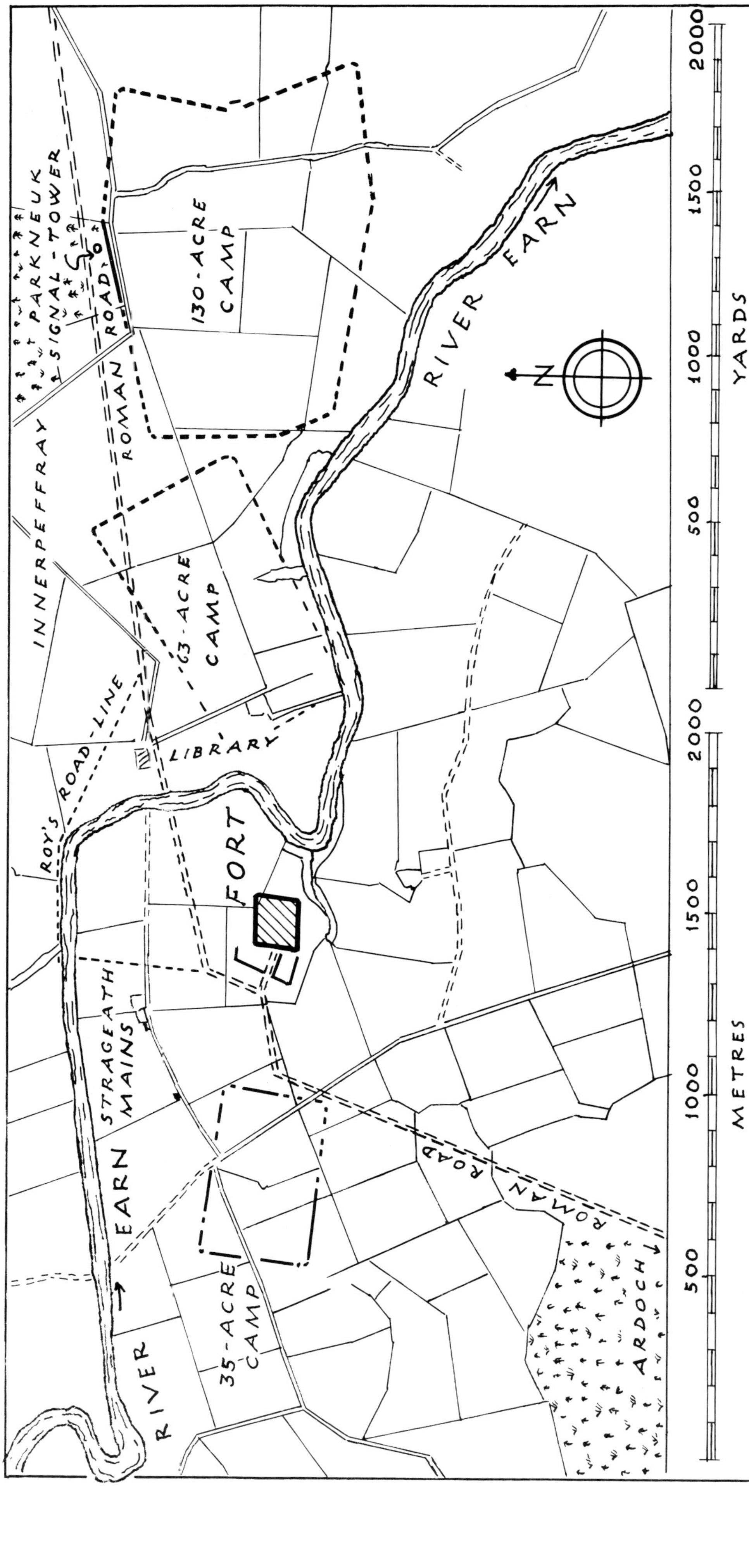

FIG. 3. Map showing the position of Strageath and nearby marching-camps. Scale, 1:16,220.(*Based on the 1863 edition of the six-inch map and information from G.S. Maxwell and J.K. St Joseph*).

by Crawford:[3] it is also seen on PL. I, a photograph taken by Dr Colin Martin. The road is aiming directly for the site of the former Innerpeffray ferry; but the reason for this precise course here is to avoid the head of a small bog (recently filled in) at the foot of the slope, after which the road probably swung slightly southwards to make directly for the Innerpeffray Library. This course would be on the alignment east of the river and, to confirm it, there exists, immediately south of the Library, an old cutting (now choked with bushes) leading down through the cliff to the river. Here must be the site of the bridge. This position is only 325 m distant from the fort and can be overlooked from it directly downhill. From the Innerpeffray Library the road led straight up to and along the Gask Ridge where, in the Flavian period, it was accompanied by the well-known chain of signal- or watch-towers. Other towers lie along the road back to Ardoch via the fortlet of Kaims Castle. The three towers between Kaims Castle and Ardoch were surrounded by twin ditches, while those further north-east to Strageath and beyond it along the Gask Ridge had only one; an independent construction may be deduced for the first group before the system was extended.[4] But the final result was a zone of surveillance at least 22.8 km long. The penetration of hostile elements towards Fife would easily be detected. It cannot be doubted that the manning of at least a large number of these towers was a responsibility of the Flavian garrison at Strageath, and the point may be relevant to interpretation of the plan of the fort (pp. 121–2).

The towers were not rebuilt in the Antonine period, but the road itself was then renewed as far as the crossing of the Tay at the fort of Bertha; and along the road, fifty years later still, advanced the armies of Severus, building two large camps at Innerpeffray, one in the 63 acre (25.5 ha), the other in the 130 acre (52.6 ha) series (FIG. 3). The emperor did not, however, re-garrison the fort. The passage of armies, indeed, along this corridor is further indicated by an earlier series of camps about 30 acres (12 ha) in size and of Flavian date. The known sequence starts at Dunblane; a second camp lies at Ardoch; and two more exist in the vicinity of Strageath. One of these lies on the north bank of the Earn at Dornock, 2.2 km to the north-west, implying a separate crossing-point of the river; but a second camp of about this size (33.5 acres, 13.4 ha) has recently been identified at Strageath itself on low ground only *c.* 410 m west-north-west of the fort (FIG. 4). The camp's relationship to the course of the road is perhaps suggestive of a context of road-building, and indeed it lies near enough to the fort itself to be considered as a possible construction-camp – although a different arrangement for housing the Flavian fort-builders is proposed on p. 117. In any case unless the camp is Antonine, as Maxwell has tentatively suggested,[5] its presence does strengthen the possibility that Strageath was the *Victoria* of Ptolemy, as Richmond was the first to propose.[6] The name is presumed to reflect the victory snatched by Agricola from the near-defeat of Legion IX Hispana at one of its camps, which the story (Tacitus, *Agricola* 26) shows to have been within a short night's march of another Roman camp. This (second) camp could have been at Dornock, or possibly at Dalginross. But Dalginross itself is another likely candidate for *Victoria*.[7] The name itself, of course, became attached to a fort; it is improbable that campaign-camps were endowed with lasting place-names.

In this part of its valley the river Earn has cut through glacial deposits. Many of these in the vicinity of Strageath carry a heavy well-wooded soil; but the plateau on which the fort stands consists of fine fluvio-glacial sand capable of supporting only a heathland vegetation. The soil sealed below the ramparts was examined by Mr J.C.C. Romans, and a report of his investigations has been published.[8] The soil is of the type known to soil-scientists as Acid Brown Soil. A difference was detected between the soil buried beneath the east rampart (1973 Trench I,

3. O.G.S. Crawford, *op. cit.* (note 1), pl. V.
4. See S.S. Frere and J.K. St Joseph, *Roman Britain from the Air* (Cambridge, 1983), 135–6.
5. *Britannia* xviii (1987), 36.
6. *P.S.A.S.* lvi (1921–2), 295–6; see also R.M. Ogilvie and I.A. Richmond, *De Vita Agricolae*, 243–4.
7. On this question see S.S. Frere, *Britannia* xi (1980), 421, where the suggestion of Rivet and Smith (*Place-Names of Roman Britain*, 499) that *Victoria* was Inchtuthil and reflects the presence there of *Legion XX Valeria Victrix* is refuted.
8. See J.C.C. Romans and L. Robertson in G.S. Maxwell (ed.), *The Impact of Aerial Reconnaissance on Archaeology* (C.B.A. Research Report No. 49, London 1983), 139.

FIG. 7) and that beneath the west rampart (1977 Trench A II–III, FIG. 9), which led Mr Romans to conclude that the former may indicate 'infield land under regular ard-cultivation prior to the Roman occupation. The indications below the west rampart suggest that this land was outfield grazing which, though occasionally cultivated, had lain fallow long enough to re-form a coherent surface turf.'

This conclusion is in accord with the results of excavation, which yielded no evidence of pre-Roman structures although flint flakes sparsely occurred together with a very few sherds of prehistoric pottery (pp. 269, 270). Thus the plateau on which the fort was built would have appeared as a comparatively open area on the edge of the forest, and for this reason will have caught the eye of the Roman commander. The deposit of sand, in places interleaved with lenses of very fine gravel, is very deep and it created difficulties for ditch- or pit-diggers; furthermore its grassy covering was not very suitable for rampart-construction in turf, for which thick cohesive sods are an advantage. It has been established that, for much of the circuit, the rampart-turves had to be fetched from a distance (pp. 17, 18, 272). But the advantages of the open site in a good defensible position outweighed this drawback. Only in one stretch, in the western rampart of the right *praetentura*, were turves from the immediate vicinity employed.

The sand subsoil was uniform below the fort save in one place; in Trench P XLIV beside the *principia* a very large glacial boulder was encountered (FIG. 22, Section M-N; PL. XX A). Although hopes were raised at first that this rock would prove to form part of some pre-Roman structure, it turned out to be entirely natural, firmly embedded in the surrounding sand, and can be classed as an erratic. It measured 3 ft. 4 in. by 1 ft. 8 in. by over 2 ft. deep (1.02 by 0.51 by at least 0.61 m). The sandy subsoil is acid, and has destroyed all bone except a few small fragments which had been burnt. The local absence of stone meant that boulders and gravel for the streets, and stones for packing post-holes, had to be brought from a distance. It is possible that the small bog mentioned above as lying beside the Roman road on the flood-plain of the river, 240 m north of the fort, may have originated as a Roman gravel-pit, for it forms a curious hollow in an otherwise flat area and extends below the level of the river. However, there can be little doubt that most of the boulders (which are water-rolled) and much of the gravel were collected from the river-bed itself.[9] An obviously ancient and overgrown terrace-way descends the steep spur above the river due east of the fort (FIG. 4), but leads to a point where the river cannot be crossed; and it was below the east gate (*porta decumana*) and below the adjacent rampart, not far from the head of this track, that a large spread of gravel was encountered on the old surface, suggesting the remains of a heap piled there for use as metalling (p. 27). Large river-boulders were employed in the foundations of streets and were capped by fine gravel; but as the gravel itself is also water-rolled it has very little binding-power; the surfaces are easily cut away by the plough, and are very difficult to clean even with a trowel without disturbance. It is true to say that only the presence of the boulders has prevented the plough from sinking deeply into the internal stratification. In 1977 part of the *via principalis* was encountered in Trench A I (FIG. 44), at a point where no boulders underlay it; the street had been reduced to a thickness of only 2 in. (0.05m). Despite this limited impediment to plough-damage, Antonine II floors and the demolition-layer which once covered them have almost entirely been removed, and the post-holes of this period are now shallow. There is no doubt that the plough is slowly but surely destroying the fort and its annexes.

The situation is even more serious in part of the north-west quarter of the northern (right) *retentura*, where a natural rise in the subsoil has left no stratification at all. Only the sockets of features cut into the sand survive, and these are being eroded.

Fortunately, apart from that removed by the action of wind, no soil can be eroded from within the fort because of the surrounding rampart. Even the gaps once occupied by the gates are closed, partly by plough-action but largely because of slipshod reconstruction in the Antonine periods (p. 30); turves which fell across the gap on the removal of the revetting timbers from the

9. In 1983, in the left *praetentura*, it was noticed that many of the packing stones used to support the uprights of the Antonine I buildings were of freshly split sandstone. This may imply that a quarry had been opened in this period, and if so it probably implies the building of the bath-house now (p. 102).

gate-passages were not cleared away before new metalling was laid down. In this respect the state of preservation at Strageath offers a notable contrast to that at Ardoch.

The fort at Strageath has been under plough since long before the middle of the eighteenth century, as William Roy's plan (PL. V) makes plain.[10] Material ploughed down from the rampart quickly formed a protective layer over the *via sagularis* and soon spread beyond this to cover the outer edges of adjacent buildings; further towards the centre, plough-damage is intense.

In all three periods of its existence (Flavian, Antonine I and Antonine II) the fort had turf ramparts and the buildings within were entirely timber-framed except for the Antonine bath-house. At some forts in Britain, for instance Great Casterton and Chester, the rampart was built with turf cheeks at front and rear to retain a core of other material dug from the ditches. At Strageath the Flavian rampart is entirely of turves, and the new work which was added to the front of the rampart in each of the Antonine periods is also entirely composed of the same material (PL. VIII). Hobley's experimental work at the Roman fort at the Lunt, Baginton,[11] has shown that a fort's turf ramparts could be built in as little as *c.* 12 days. The work is likely to have been undertaken in spring, or more probably after the campaigning season in autumn, when the turf is easy to cut and troops could be spared for the task. Certainly experience at Strageath in 1973–4 showded the extreme difficulty of cutting turf there in July, when the ground was too hard for easy work.

The great majority of Roman forts in Britain have ramparts at least partly built of turf. The front has a steep upward slope (p. 17) without a timber revetment. This method contrasts markedly with that used in most early forts on the Continent, which had ramparts boxed between timber revetments at both front and rear (the 'earth-and-timber' type). Different provincial armies would of course have developed differing traditions of craftsmanship. But it seems probable that the explanation of this widespread use in Britain of turf ramparts lacking timber facings is that the great majority of forts here were built quickly during or at the end of campaigning seasons for immediate tactical purposes, like those depicted on Trajan's Column. Turves were readily available almost everywhere, but timbers of the requisite size and quantity would have required time and effort to procure. On the Continent the majority of forts lie on frontiers, where they could have been built at leisure; they do not reflect the seasonal progress of conquest.

The surviving earthworks of the fort at Strageath measure *c.* 468 by 424 ft. (142.6 by 129.2 m), giving an area over the ramparts of 4.5 acres (1.82 ha).[12] The Flavian turf rampart was consistently 17–17½ ft. (5.18–5.33 m) wide at the base. The original height was probably *c.* 10 ft. (3.05 m) with added parapet (p. 25). Posts incorporated in the rampart supported the rear of the rampart-walk. The three main gates of the Flavian fort appear, on the evidence of aerial photographs and of that yielded by Trench 1978 B II (p. 20), to have been set back behind curving inturns of the rampart-ends, as at certain other Flavian forts in Scotland (p. 20); but in later periods the insets were eliminated. In each of the two Antonine periods the entire rampart was re-fronted with turf to provide a reliable rampart-walk, and this too was supported by posts.

On each occasion that the fort was re-occupied there was a total reconstruction, involving not only a rebuilding of the defences but also a completely new layout of internal buildings. There was also evidence for extensive and leisurely demolition at the end of each period. Short though the interval may have been between the Antonine I and Antonine II occupations, it is clear that they represent distinct historical episodes.

Except where disturbance had occurred, there was normally found, above the occupation-layers of each period, a demolition- or destruction-layer containing a considerable quantity of burnt daub. Had the various forts, or any of them, been destroyed by enemy action? As work continued it became obvious that no building in any of the superimposed forts had been burnt *in*

10. W. Roy, *Military Antiquities of the Romans in Britain* (London, 1793), pl. XXXII; cf. p. 3.
11. B. Hobley in S. Applebaum (ed.), *Roman Frontier Studies 1967* (Tel Aviv, 1971), 21–33; cf. *idem, Trans. Birmingham and Warwickshire Arch. Soc.* lxxxvii (1975), 20–3.
12. For more detailed estimates of the areas of the these successive forts see Chapter VIII (pp. 117, 126, 129).

situ: the contrast with the situation revealed at for instance Insula XIV at Verulamium[13] was complete. No burnt timbers were found *in situ*; where post-holes contained burnt daub, this was in small discrete fragments incorporated in an earth matrix; no post-hole showed edges scorched or baked by fire as would have happened if the standing uprights had been burnt down. The daub fragments had fallen into, or had been washed by rain into, the cavities left by posts withdrawn. No building was sealed by any bed of burnt wall-material. The burnt daub fragments were scattered, more in some places than in others, and were to be explained as the product of bonfires in which the smaller parts of timber-framed buildings, with some daub still attached, were burnt by demolition-parties; occasionally lumps of unburnt daub were found in the same demolition-deposits. Evidence was sometimes found for the deliberate withdrawal of timbers, in the form either of hollow post-pipes or of delvings in the upper parts of post-pits. In Trench 1976 H III a broken spade-blade was discovered in the top of a post-hole where it had been left during Antonine II demolition (p. 64).

Another feature of evacuation was the digging of so-called 'demolition-pits'. The stratification made clear that such pits had been dug after the demolition of buildings but before the erection of those of the succeeding period, for they sometimes destroyed the wall-lines but were sealed by the floors, streets or wall-lines of the succeeding period. The character of these pits differed from that of a few others which had been deliberately packed with turf or gravel; the latter had clearly been in use during the respective occupations and they can be interpreted as water-cisterns filled in at the evacuation (p. 12). The 'demolition-pits' were different, normally having a fill of earth mixed with stones or lenses of charcoal, and a consistent feature was the sinkage of the filling. The pits were sometimes as much as 6–7 ft. (2–2.2 m) deep. Superimposed floors or street-metalling of a later occupation were sometimes found sunk deep in the top filling of such pits (PL. XXXII). It was obvious that the pits must have been dug for a purpose, but the lower fillings never produced revealing finds, and certainly never any military equipment as did some of the pits at Newstead. The considerable subsidence of the filling suggested the deposition of organic matter, but none survived for recognition. Samples were taken in 1981 by Professor V.B. Proudfoot.[14] It may be supposed that the pits were dug to dispose of unwanted fodder or even such pieces of roofing- or wall-timbers as were not burnt in the bonfires. The acid soil would have destroyed such remains without trace. No baked clay or stone roofing-tiles were found at Strageath; the building were all roofed with thatch or shingles.

C. THE ANNEXES (PLS II–III, FIGS 4–5)

A large area of the flat ground west of the fort was occupied by successive defended annexes, which also extend onto sloping ground north of the E-W hedge-line; these provide a very complicated picture to the aerial camera. No excavation has been undertaken in this area; analysis of FIG. 4, a drawing based on one kindly provided by Professor J.K. St Joseph, suggests that the sequence may have been as follows (see FIG. 5): (i) a Flavian annexe placed in front of the left (southern) *praetentura* and confined to the area south of the approach-road. In this area the fort and annexe appear to have been separated by a single ditch (p. 15), wider than the two provided elsewhere; this difference confirms the association of this annexe with the earliest fort. In this period the annexe had a single ditch on its two outer sides connecting with the outer ditch of the contemporary fort; but along the approach-road it may have had only a bank. This annexe measures *c.* 330 by 188 ft. (100 by 57.3m) and covers an area of 1.42 acres (0.58 ha).
(ii) In the Antonine I period the annexe was more than doubled in size, extending now also across the front of the right *praetentura* and beyond it northwards to the edge of the plateau. This added *c.* 1.53 acres (0.62 ha) to the area previously enclosed, which now received a second ditch. The

13. S.S. Frere, *Verulamium Excavations* i (London, 1972), *passim*.
14. The samples have not yet been analysed; results will be published, so we are told, later as part of a wider project by Professor Proudfoot.

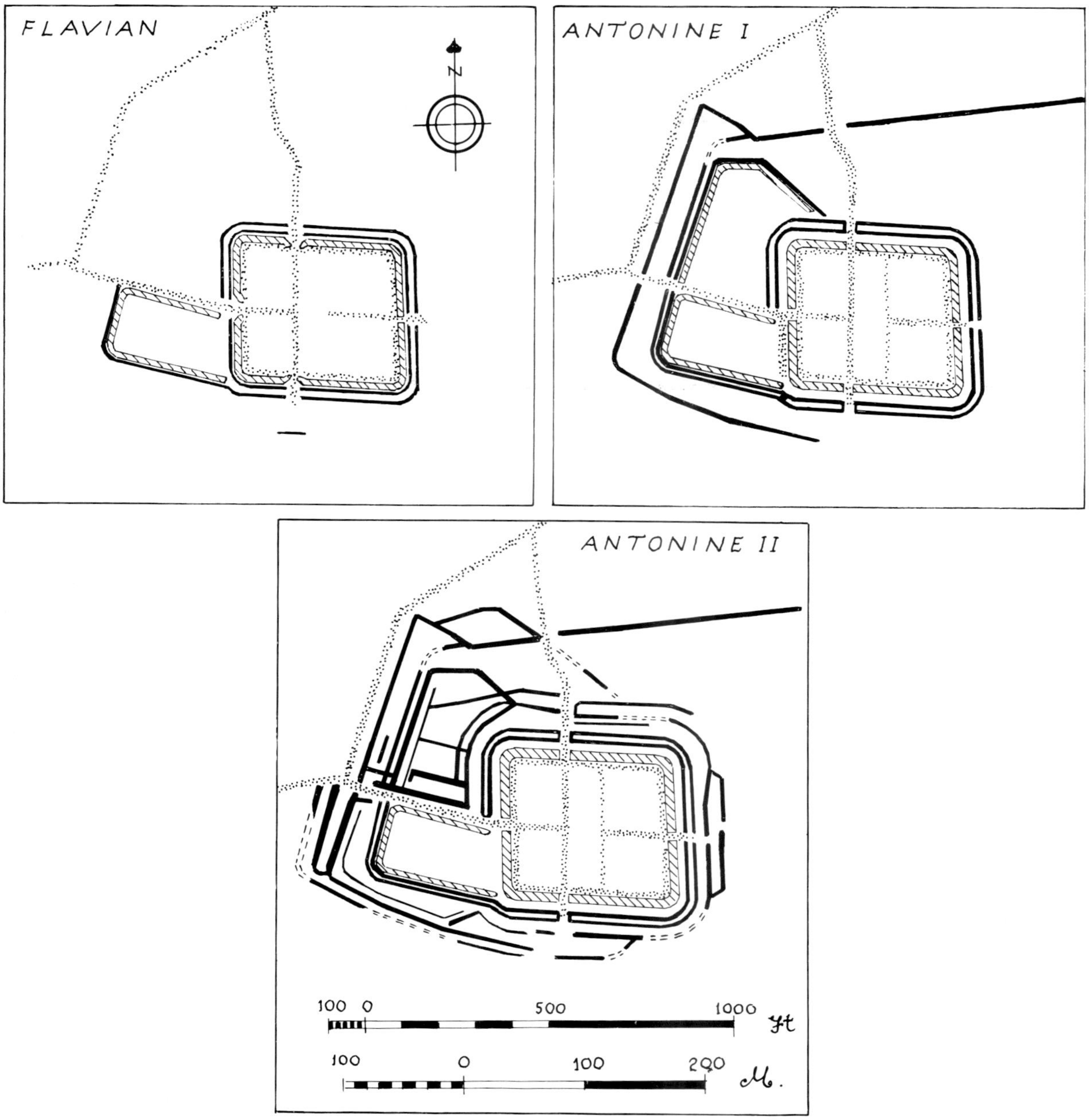

FIG. 5. Provisional analysis of the ditch-systems visible on aerial photographs or found in excavation.

addition was also accompanied by twin ditches, but larger and a little more widely spaced than those round the first annexe. On the west, across the level ground, the whole of the Antonine I annexe was additionally defended by an outer ditch lying some 50–60 ft. (15–18 m) beyond the inner pair.

(iii) In the Antonine II period the original small annexe south of the approach-road seems to have been retained, but the northern extension was given up and its site cut by a number of ditches giving extra protection to the north-west angle of the fort, and possibly also intended to define some small paddocks.

The photographs also show other ditches, including one west of the annexes which encloses a rectangular plot measuring *c.* 165 by 90 ft. (50.3 by 27.4 m) (FIG. 4); the purpose of this is unknown. Another large ditch runs obliquely downhill well to the north of the fort and seems to be linked to the Antonine I annexe; it cuts off direct approach from the river-crossing.

D. THE WATER-SUPPLY

Although the sand below the fort is too unstable for the digging of wells, water is available nearby. A small stream flows along the south side of the fort (though at too low an elevation to act as source for an aqueduct), while the Earn itself flows at the base of a steep slope only 150 m to the east. The old terrace-way, already mentioned, which runs down this slope could have been used by watering-parties equipped with barrels, but a small cliff at the bottom would have precluded its use for the watering of animals. Horses could, however, have been led down the extension of the northern *via principalis* and then along the main road to the river, where they could easily drink in the shallows. Such were perhaps the arrangements in the Antonine II period. However, in both the Flavian and Antonine I forts a pipe-line led in from the west through the *porta praetoria*. The remains are described on pp. 109, 125. Aerial photographs (PL. III) suggest that the pipe-line accompanies the approach-road at least from the junction with the main road. At a point 570 m west of the fort and not far from the Roman road (FIG. 4) a small spring exists (NN 892178), and this was possibly the source tapped by the aqueduct, although it rises at an elevation only a few feet above that of the fort. This is not a copious source, but calculations suggest that a 3-in. (7.6 cm) pipe (whether of wood or lead) could deliver a theoretical 15,300 gallons (69,550 litres) an hour, while a pipe of $2\frac{1}{2}$ in. (6.3 cm) could deliver 10,600 gallons (48,180 litres) an hour: both figures in practice would have been reduced by at least one third by friction. A second spring (NN 878174), used today as a water-supply, rises about 75 ft. (22.8m) above the level of the fort but at a greater distance (1.21 miles: 2.06 km) to the west-south-west.

It is probably no coincidence that in the two periods when the aqueduct was functioning large underground cisterns existed within the fort. In the Flavian period a tank holding at least 8,400 gallons (38,200 litres) lay in the *principia* (p. 35), and an even bigger tank holding perhaps as much as 10,650 gallons (48,450 litres) lay towards the south end of the central range (p. 53). A large cistern of Antonine I date was recognized inside Building I (p. 61), but the destination of the pipe-line in the front part of the fort has not been discovered. What may have been another tank, of unknown capacity, was found beside the Antonine II *via sagularis* in the northern (right) *retentura* (p. 63). How this was filled is unknown; perhaps it was supplied by barrel, or perhaps rain beating against the rear of the rampart was somehow collected.

E. THE DATES OF OCCUPATION

No dated inscriptions were found at Strageath, and accordingly the various occupations can be dated only in general terms. That the first occupation was Flavian is evident from the coins and samian. On the chronology proposed in *Inchtuthil*,[15] Agricola made his preliminary foray to the Tay in 80, but in 81 built a line of forts to secure the Forth-Clyde isthmus. It was only in 83 that he resumed his march to the north through Strathmore, an advance continued in 84 to culminate in the victory at Mons Graupius. The evacuation of his conquests north of the Forth occurred late in 86 or very early in 87. Thus, construction of the road to Ardoch, Strageath and Bertha, and of these forts themselves, would most naturally seem to belong to 83, the forts most probably having been built in the autumn of that year after campaigning had ceased.

Two other hypotheses have been put forward. The first, by Breeze and Dobson,[16] would place the construction of these forts after Agricola's recall which occurred in late 84. This leaves a very narrow margin of time before evacuation, especially if, as these writers have additionally suggested, the forts along the main road (such as Strageath) belonged to a *secondary* post-Agricolan phase, the first having seen only the construction of the advance forts at the mouth of the glens. This view of events cannot be disproved by archaeological evidence but only discounted by a judgement of historical and military possibilities such as those discussed in

15. L. Pitts and J.K. St Joseph, *Inchtuthil, The Roman Legionary Fortress* (London, 1985), 263 ff.
16. *Glasgow Arch. Journ.* iv (1976), 124–43.

Inchtuthil.[17] Yet the presence of pre- and early Flavian coins in some number, and of a samian vessel stamped by Carillus (p. 212) do hint that troops had occupied Strageath some years earlier than 85; while the exceptional capacity of the Flavian granaries here (p. 123) is best accounted for by close connection with the supply of Agricola's advancing army. Moreover, the course of the road approaching Strageath does suggest that the fort was briefly its terminus, before extension continued beyond the Earn (p. 5). Thus an Agricolan date of foundation is accepted here.

The second hypothesis was suggested by one of us in 1981,[18] namely that Ardoch and Strageath might have been established as early as 80, or at latest 81, as outposts beyond the Forth-Clyde line and for the protection of a friendly population in Fife, with whom relations will have been established during the advance to the Tay in the former year. The size of force involved in this march, if the camps at Dunning and Abernethy are correctly assigned to it, shows that the expedition was no mere hasty geographical reconnaissance. This hypothesis allows a usefully greater span of time for Strageath's occupation which will better accommodate the various signs of structural alteration (pp. 36, 59, 69f., 73f., 90f.), and it is satisfactorily consistent with two of the pieces of supporting evidence cited above: but it must be admitted that the large size of the granaries is better associated with the advance of 83.

As for the date of Flavian evacuation, the latest coin at Strageath, as at Stracathro, Cardean and Inchtuthil, is an As of 86. These coins appear to have been in mint condition when lost, suggesting the recent arrival of a pay-chest from the Mint of Rome; and since an As of 87 is known from Newstead and coins of both 84 and 85 were found at Strageath, there is a probability that such consignments arrived annually. If so, evacuation of the lands north of the Forth no doubt occurred at latest in early 87. The internal buildings were dismantled and unwanted woodwork burnt; but the defences themselves were not flattened.

The first Antonine re-occupation soon followed upon Lollius Urbicus's reconquest of southern Scotland, which had culminated in a victory won probably in 142; by that year work on the Antonine Wall had begun, as inscriptions from Balmiuldy suggest.[19] The establishment of the outpost forts to the north of it must have been contemporary or very soon subsequent, for they are integral to the functioning of the frontier. The fort of Strageath has yielded much pottery typical of Antonine I forms elsewhere, but nothing more closely datable; the finds include two coins of Trajan and at least six of Hadrian.

At the end of the Antonine I occupation the buildings were once again demolished and rubbish burnt, but as before the defences were left standing. It is regrettable that coin No. 40 (p. 139), from an Antonine I occupation-layer, is not closely datable within the reign of Antoninus Pius; but on general grounds the event may be dated within the period 155–158, and the cause was probably an outbreak of rebellion in the Pennines, necessitating concentration of forces from Scotland to suppress it.[20]

By the latter year Scotland had again been re-occupied and Strageath was rebuilt, though now occupied by a stronger garrison than before (p. 129). The Antonine II phase at Strageath is not closely dated at the site itself; much of the occupation-levels have been ploughed away; the pottery found is not easily distinguishable from that of Antonine I. Today, however, it is generally held that by 164 at the latest a final evacuation had occurred, with Roman troops withdrawn for a heavier policing of the Pennines behind Hadrian's Wall, which now in its Period Ib was reconstituted as the *limes*.

17. *op. cit.* (note 15).
18. S.S. Frere in *Scottish Archaeological Forum* No. 12, 89–97.
19. See A.R. Birley, *The Fasti of Roman Britain* (Oxford, 1981), 112–15.
20. See S.S. Frere, *Britannia, A History of Roman Britain* (3rd edition, 1987), 135–8.

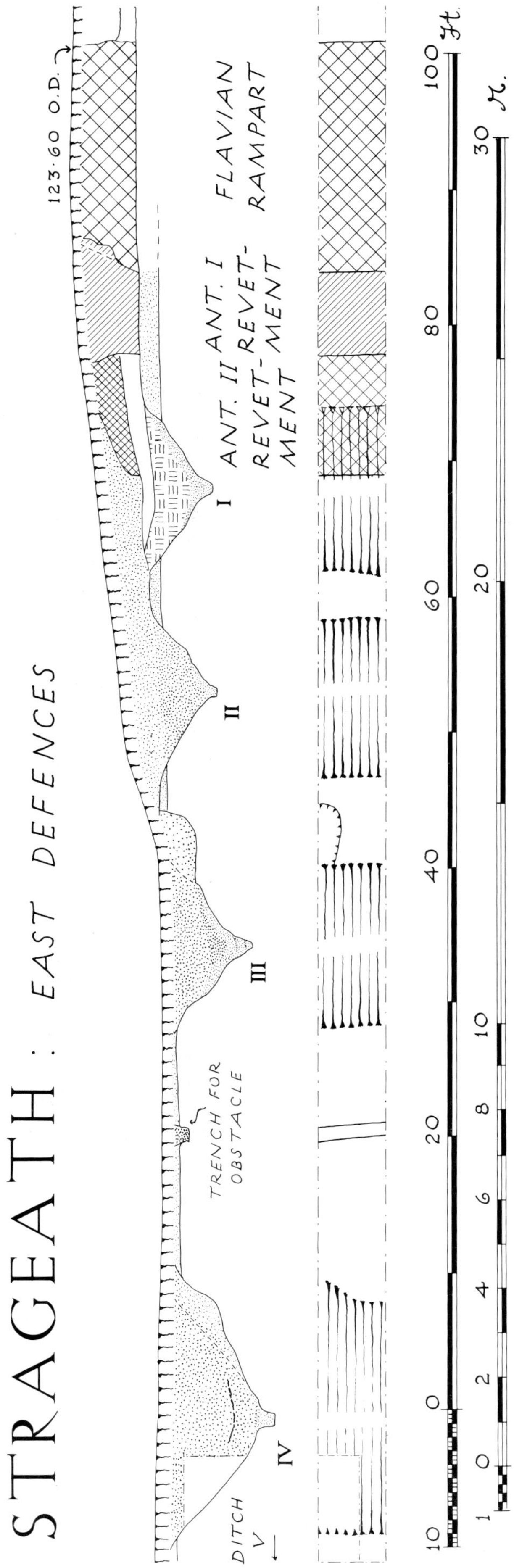

FIG. 6. The defences on the east side of the fort excavated in 1973. Scale, 1:144. (For position see FIG. 32 (p. 58) and FIG. 68).

II. THE DEFENCES

A. The Ditches (FIGS. 4–5 and 11)

Aerial photographs and the plan drawn from them by Professor J.K. St Joseph (cf. FIG. 4) show a complicated pattern of ditches at Strageath, which no doubt represents the cumulative results of refortification. The ditch-system has not been adequately explored by excavation; only on the east side in 1973 was a trench cut across it, and this trench did not reach the outermost ditch; in 1984 a Flavian ditch was discovered on the west side, to left of the *porta praetoria*.

On the east side there were five ditches in all. The innermost (Ditch I, FIG. 6) was buried beneath the Antonine II extension to the rampart-front and does not show on the aerial photographs. This and the next two ditches (II and III) were separated by berms of 4 and 5 ft. (1.22 and 1.52 m) respectively; all three were of uniform size, 12 ft. (3.66 m) wide and 5ft. (1.52 m) deep. Perhaps all three were Flavian; but more probably Ditches I and II were Flavian, and Ditch III was dug in the Antonine I period to replace Ditch I when this was filled in (p. 19). Only Ditch I yielded anything datable. An almost complete bowl of Dr. 18/31 stamped by the potter Carillus (p. 212) is assigned to the period A.D. 70–85; but as this bowl came from low down in layer 37 (FIG. 7), the lowest level of turf packing inserted when the ditch became redundant (either at the Antonine I refortification or later when the Antonine II rampart was extended over its site), the vessel does not, strictly speaking, have any relevance to the date of the ditch itself but only to that of the fort as a whole, for it reached its find-spot in the second century. Along the very bottom of Ditch I lay a number of fist-sized stones (eighteen in the 5-ft. length excavated); these must have rolled in, perhaps during demolition of the rampart-walk if this had been cobbled (p. 63). Ditches II and III contained a uniform brown sandy filling which yielded no finds, and they may have been open in all three periods. There had been a collapse of the inner face of Ditch III (FIG. 6). Indications were lacking that any ditch had been lined with turf or clay on this side of the fort.

Beyond Ditch III air-photographs show two wider ditches, of which only the inner (Ditch IV) could be excavated in the time available. This was 17 ft. (5.18 m) wide though now slightly enlarged on the inner slope on the south side of the trench (FIG. 6) by collapse of the soft sandy subsoil. The fill was a uniform brown sandy soil, differentiated only by a thin band of charcoal 3 ft. (1 m) above the bottom.

Ditches IV and V were perhaps additions of the Antonine period. Between Ditches III and IV lay a berm 18 ft. (5.47 m) wide, down the middle of which ran a square-cut trench 1 ft. 5 in. (0.43 m) wide and 1 ft. (0.10 m) deep, which is thought to have supported a fence or some other form of obstacle; and there were indications also of an oblique trench, though much disturbed by rabbits (PL. VI B). At a point 88 ft. (26.8 m) in front of Ditch IV, and approximately 40 ft. (12 m) in front of the unexcavated Ditch V, the digging of a rubbish-disposal pit in 1980 revealed a layer of yellow sand below the plough-soil and sealing an old turf-line; this proves the existence of an upcast mound. The product of the ditches, not having been used for rampart-construction, will have been spread beyond the ditches, as is known to have been done on Hadrian's Wall and the Antonine Wall.

In 1984 a machine-cut trench 8 ft. 6 in. (2.59 m) wide was cut through the west rampart south of the *porta praetoria*, and here a Flavian ditch was encountered beneath an Antonine I street belonging to the Annexe; the street itself was sealed by the Antonine II rampart-extension (p. 21, FIG. 11, Section 0-P; PL. XIV A). The ditch was not completely excavated and its outer lip could not be reached; nevertheless the width was seen to be *c.* 16 ft. (4.88 m) and there was a lining of sticky clay 6 in. (0.15 m) thick on both slopes. The upper filling (FIG. 11, layers 17, 18) was of clay and gravel damp enough to have preserved some twigs and bark; these layers were sealed by a thick demolition-deposit (20) containing burnt daub and charcoal. The ditch does not show on the aerial photographs; its unusual width may be the results of the conjunction of two elsewhere-separate ditches where they curve inwards towards the gate, but a more probable explanation is that in this stretch only one ditch instead of two was provided between the fort and its annexe, and this was accordingly made more substantial than the inner ditch elsewhere. What

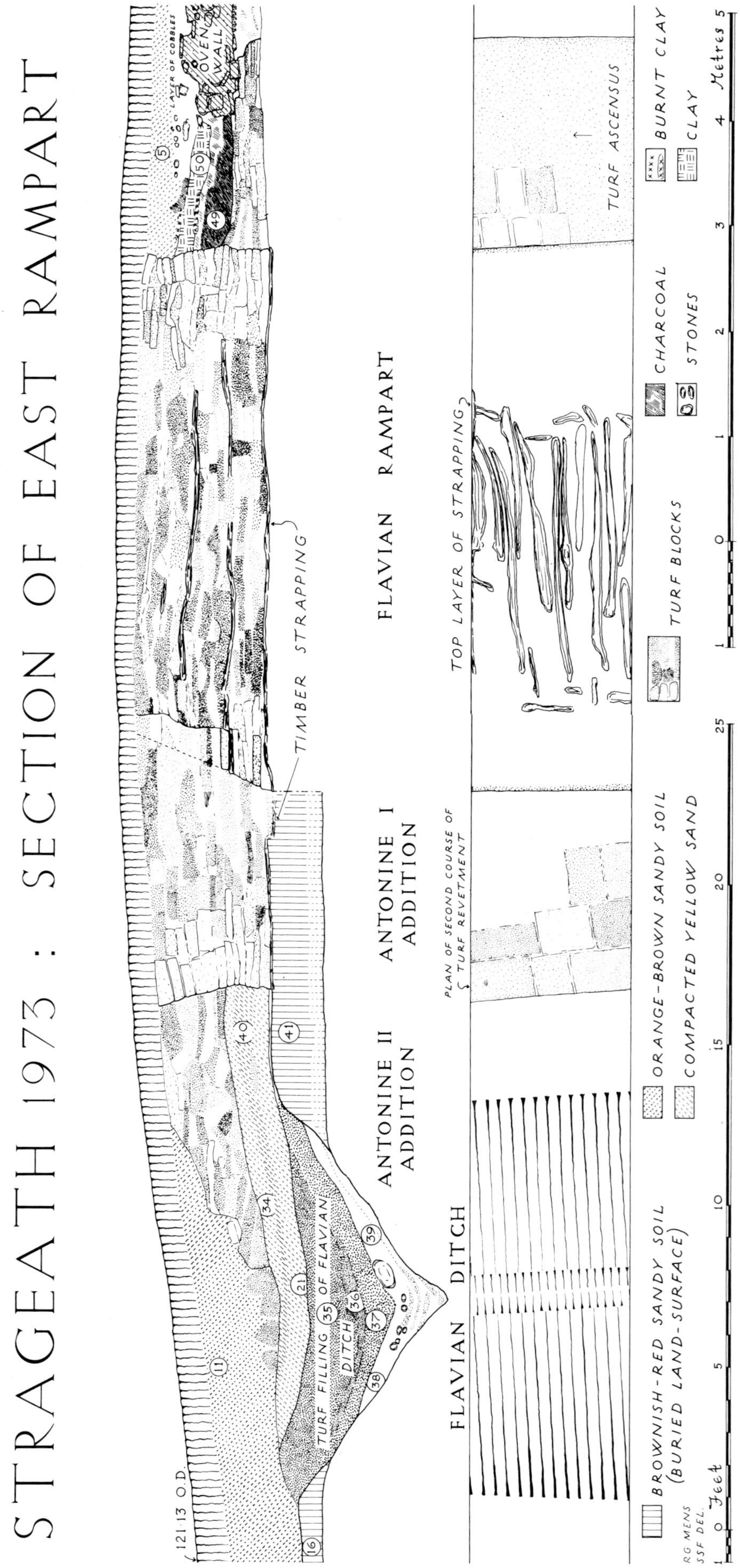

FIG. 7. The east rampart, section dug in 1973. Scale, 1:60.

appears in the section (FIG. 11, 22) as a narrow re-cutting was a local disturbance not extending across the trench.

B. **The East Rampart**, 1973 Trench I (FIG. 7)

The front of the Flavian rampart stood 9 ft. 6 in. (2.90 m) behind Ditch I; such a wide berm was perhaps a precaution against collapse of the soft sides of the ditch.[1] The Flavian rampart consisted entirely of laid turves, and was 17 ft. (5.18 m) wide at its base. The turves had been built on a timber strapping of small branches laid transversely on the old surface; additional layers of transverse branches were added at vertical intervals of just over 1 ft. (0.3 m) in order to bind the structure and impede collapse. The interval was no doubt formerly greater, but has been reduced by compaction. North of the *porta decumana* (p. 31, FIG. 15, Section E-F) the interval was 1 ft. 6 in. (0.46 m). The branches survived as stains or mineralized lines (PL. VII).

On the south side of the Trench there had been a partial collapse of the upper portion of the front of the rampart (FIG. 7), but on the north side the front could be seen rising sharply upwards at an angle of 67° (PL. X A). The back of the rampart, by contrast, rose vertically to a surviving height of 3 ft. 10 in. (1.17 m) (PL. X B). It is evident that the back could not have stood vertical much higher without danger of collapse and, although the angle to a more gentle slope did not survive, the probability exists that a profile such as was found at Chester[2] and has been restored for the Turf Wall of Hadrian[3] should be applied here. Thus the upper rear face will have sloped inwards at a more gentle angle of *c.* 50° from a height of 4 ft. (1.22 m) above the ground. The original top of the rampart can then be fixed at the height where the two lines of slope approach to within *c.* 6–7 ft. (1.8–2.1 m) to allow sufficient width for a rampart-walk. Such a calculation here gives the original height as 10 ft. (3.05 m), to which a parapet of 5 ft. (1.52 m) should be added (FIG. 13, p. 26). Additional evidence relevant to this question is quoted on p. 25. On Trajan's Column representations of rampart-walks made of transverse logs can be seen, and this may well have been the form used at Strageath. But, as already mentioned, a number of fist-sized stones found in the bottom of Ditch I, and more stones found over the Antonine II ovens behind the rampart (p. 63) suggest the possibility that cobbles may have been employed instead.

The purpose of the vertical rise of the lower part of the rear face was no doubt disciplinary; soldiers were not to scramble up the rampart at will, but must ascend to the rampart-walk at authorized places (*ascensus*) where steps or ramps were provided. On such place occurs in the 1973 section (FIG. 8; PL. X B), for behind the rear face of the rampart and distinct from it lies a turf platform 6 ft. 6 in. (1.98 m) wide and 1 ft. (0.3 m) high; this is presumed to be the base of a ramp or staircase leading to the rampart-walk. In view of the presumed profile of the rear face, the *ascensus* was no doubt aligned at right-angles to the line of the rampart. Where measurable the largest turves in this platform were 1 ft. 6 in. by 1 ft. (0.46 by 0.3 m); others were 11 in. (0.28 m) square. The thickness varied between 1 and 3 in. (0.025–0.076 m). The stratification in this Trench westwards of the *ascensus* is discussed on pp. 62–3. Part of a rather more extensive *ascensus* was found on the south side of the *porta decumana* (pp. 29, 87) and another in Trench V II north of the Central Range (pp. 26–7). A fourth possible example, but of Antonine I date, lay near the *porta praetoria* (p. 21).

The old soil buried beneath the Flavian rampart was of an orange-brown sandy texture, known to soil-scientists as Acid Brown Soil. When not under cultivation (pp. 7–8) this would carry a heathland vegetation, and it is evident that the thick clayey turves of the rampart could not have been stripped from the site of the fort itself. Mr J.C.C. Romans kindly investigated the problem of their source. The ground by the river Earn, on the flood-plain, had a subsoil of gravel and was

1. On the width of berms see M.J. Jones, *Roman Fort-Defences to A.D. 117* (BAR No. 21, Oxford, 1975), 105.
2. G. Webster, *Journ. Chester Arch. Soc.* xl (1953), 2 with figs. 2, 4 and 14; cf. F.H. Thompson, *Roman Cheshire* (Chester, 1965, fig. 5).
3. J. Collingwood Bruce, *Handbook to the Roman Wall* (13th edition by C.M. Daniels) (Newcastle upon Tyne, 1978), 17.

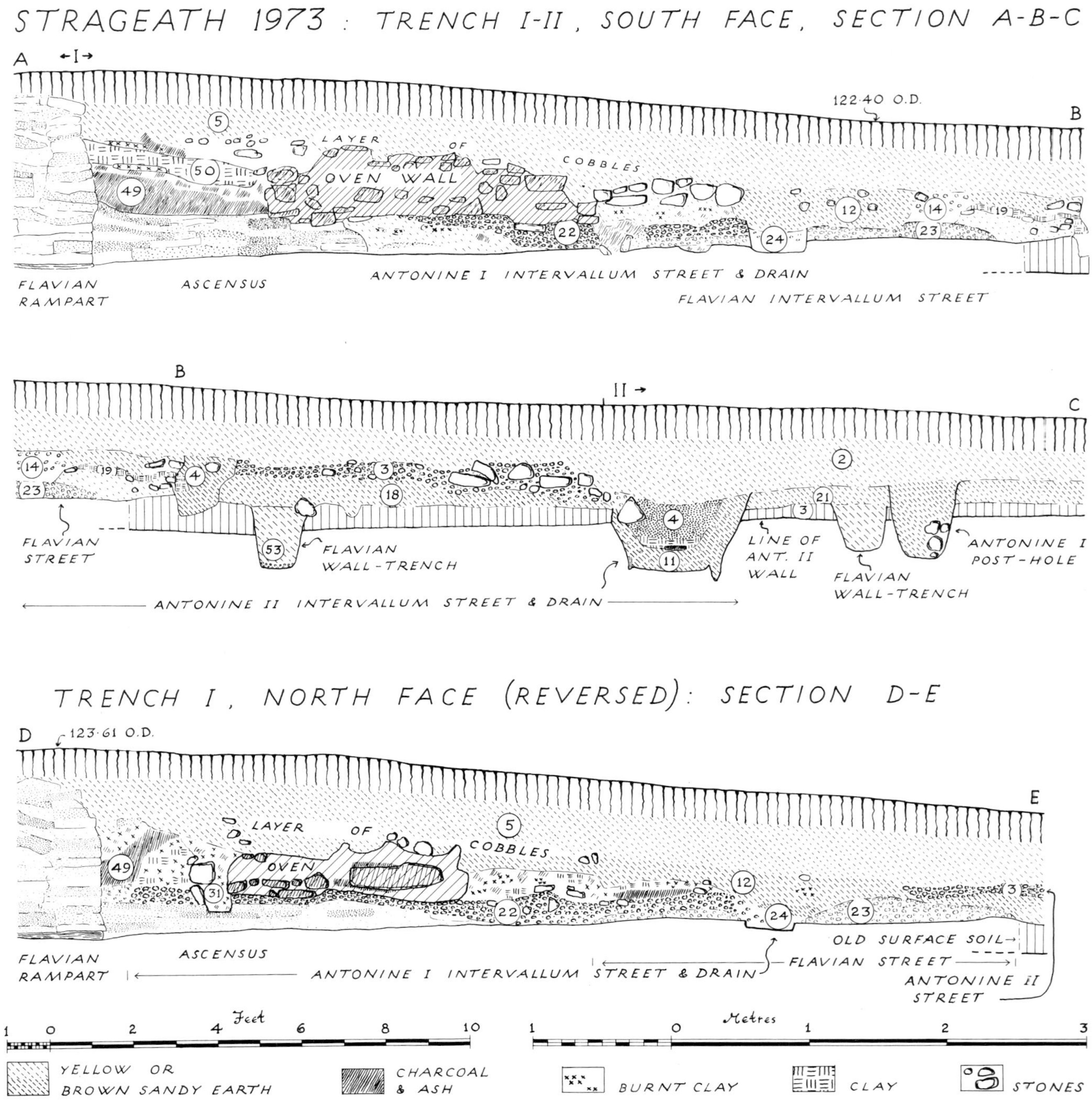

FIG. 8. Sections A–E behind the east rampart, 1973. Scale, 1:45. (For position see p. 58, FIG. 32).

too well-drained for the purpose. Eventually he found an area on the slope between the fort and the river, *c.* 270 m north-east of the east rampart, where drainage of the subsoil was sufficiently impeded for their growth. The work of carrying turves uphill this distance and delivering them unbroken must have been an exacting labour.

Turves of similar character were used round the south and part of the western perimeter as shown by sections cut in the south *praetentura* in 1983 and 1984 (pp.20–23). Only in the north *praetentura*, north of the *porta praetoria*, was a different kind of turf encountered (p. 20). Here in Trench 1977 A II the Flavian rampart was found to be built of almost black friable turves (PL. XII A) which Mr Romans considered to have been derived from the plateau itself.

At the outset of the Antonine I re-occupation, the defences were put in order once more. There was little or no sign that the Flavian rampart had been slighted in the interim. Although on the south side of the 1973 Trench I some of the turves had fallen away from the rampart-front above a height of 1 ft. 7 in. (0.48 m), the face was intact on the opposite side of the Trench. In both the 1977 and 1983 sections the front turves were similarly missing but the face of the rampart was intact to a height of 2 ft. 9 in. (0.84 m) on both sides of the 1984 trench. But nowhere was any trace found of fallen or silted material in front of the rampart. It might be argued that here it had been cleared away in preparation for reconstruction; another possibility is that the rampart had survived almost intact until *c.* 140, when the Antonine builders cut parts of it away at intervals in order to provide a better bonding for their addition. Equally, however, behind the rampart there was very little sign of turfy debris; its extent can be seen in FIG. 8, Section A–B, between the *ascensus* and the Antonine I *via sagularis*. Yet the Antonine I builders were not content to reuse or patch up the Flavian rampart. Instead they built a new front to it. In 1973 Trench I (FIG. 7) this was just over 6 ft. (1.8 m) wide, but at the *porta decumana* it had narrowed to 3 ft. (0.91 m) (FIG. 14), no doubt in order to make use of the old gate-position. As we shall see, the new fronts on the south and west sides were between 6 and 9 ft. (1.8–2.7 m) wide.

In the 1973 Trench, the new Antonine I front was built of turves on a layer of transverse branches laid directly on the old surface without any intervening silts (FIG. 7), but no higher levels of lacing were observed. Particular care had been taken over the selection of large thick turves for the new face (FIG. 7, PL. XI), which still stood to a height of 3 ft. 7 in. (1.09 m). These turves could be seen to be from 4 to 5 in (0.102–0.127 m) thick; in plan they measured 19 by 17 in., 21 by 13 in. or 24 by 15 in. (0.483 by 0.432, 0.533 by 0.330, or 0.610 by 0.381 m). In section the top of the new front is seen to slope forward beyond the vertical. This is clearly the result of later pressures; the original profile is probably more closely recognizable in the bottom five courses, which rise at an angle of 80°C. This is excessively steep, but the top was no doubt anchored back to the old rampart by the timbering of the rampart-walk. The new front lay only 3 ft. 6 in. (1.07m) from the lip of Ditch I, and it may have been now that this ditch was packed with turves to remove the danger of collapse. This would give a better context than the start of the Antonine II period for the deposition of the bowl of Carillus (p. 15), which would thus have been lying intact only during one intermission in the occupation. If so, Ditch III may have been an Antonine I substitute for Ditch I (see p. 14, FIG. 6).

At the beginning of the Antonine II re-occupation a second re-facing of the rampart was undertaken; this extended over Ditch I, which was now, if not earlier, packed with turf. The front of the new facing had entirely fallen away and the width is therefore uncertain; it was at least 8 ft. 9 in. (2.67 m) wide at the point sectioned and was 12 ft. (3.66 m) wide at the *porta decumana* (FIG. 14). Although the new structure consisted of turfy material, individual turves could not be so easily recognized. That this is a new front, and not just the tumbled top of the Antonine I rampart, is proved at the *porta decumana* (p.), where the Antonine II gateway is associated with this addition and not with the Antonine I gate-position behind it: moreover both at this gate and in Trench 1983 M I, on the south side of the fort, post-holes were associated with it.

The purpose of these additions was to create a basis for new rampart-walks which was both stable and reliable. By the Antonine II period the rampart had attained an overall width at the base of 31 ft. 9 in. (9.68 m), but only the front was truly functional. This statement is clearly proved by the fact that at the *porta decumana* (p. 30) the passage through the main body of the rampart was no longer revetted as it had been in the Flavian and Antonine I periods; the former passage-way must have been bevelled back at the angle of rest and so very probably was the back of the old rampart, which now allowed easy access to the rampart-walk without the need for special *ascensus*.

C. The West Rampart:

(i) North Praetentura, Trenches 1977 A II (FIG. 9) and 1978 B I

The inner face of the west rampart was encountered at the west end of Trench A II, and subsequently a small additional excavation was made to the west of it in order to establish the width of the rampart and the character of its front.

The Flavian rampart was 17 ft. 5 in. (5.31 m) wide at its base, 5 in. (0.13 m) wider than on the east side; but it was composed of black friable turves (PL. XII A) in great contrast to those of the Antonine extensions in front of it and to the turves in the east rampart. Mr J.C.C. Romans considered that they were derived from a context on the Acid Brown Soil of the plateau, perhaps under the annexes to the west. The rampart was seen to rest on transverse timber strapping (PL. XII A); the rear face stood vertical to a surviving height of 2 ft. 6 in. (0.76 m). The front stood to a height of only 1 ft. (0.31 m) above which it had fallen away. About 5 ft. (1.5 m) in front of the rampart and running obliquely across the Trench below the Antonine I extension was a scoop or shallow pit (FIG. 9, Section AA–BB); this was *c.* 5 ft. (1.5 m) wide and 1 ft. 4 in. (0.41 m) deep. In it were two layers of carbonized material separated by yellow sand, and across the top was a 6-in. (0.15 m) deposit of turfy material full of small fragments of red burnt daub which sealed some sherds of a large flagon in smooth reddish ware with a cream-white slip. The hollow represents some form of activity on the berm.

At the beginning of the Antonine I period a new front of turf was added to the rampart as on the east side. This was 6 ft. 5 in. (2.10 m) wide and the front survived almost vertical for 3 ft. (0.91 m) (FIG. 9, Section AA–BB); but the actual face was much more weathered than that in FIG. 7. The leading two or three inches of various turves had fallen away; this may perhaps be the result of this rampart facing the prevailing winds and heavy storms which so often accompany them. The Antonine I rampart was built of large yellow and grey turves from a source different from that which had provided the Flavian ones (PL. XII B).

At the start of the Antonine II period a further turf front had been added. This consisted of larger pieces of turf, some containing pebbles, and arranged less coherently. This new addition was at least 6 ft. (1.83 m) wide, but its front lay beyond the Trench and was not sought for lack of time and because it could be assumed to have fallen away.

In Trench 1978 B I the back of the Flavian west rampart was found 16 ft. (4.88 m) east of its expected line and sealed beneath the Antonine *via sagularis* (FIGS. 40; 47, Section P–Q (p. 83)). It is evident from this that the Flavian *porta praetoria* lay behind an inturn of the rampart which created a forecourt in front of the gate; this could be overlooked by defenders on the rampart as well as by those on the gate. The arrangement is closely paralleled at the Flavian forts at Oakwood, Bochastle and perhaps at Menteith and Cardean also,[4] and with other original planning of gateways at Newstead and Milton provides evidence for experimentation in fort-design under Agricola, perhaps even his own expressed interest in the subject (Tacitus, *Agricola* 22). In the Antonine period the rampart was straightened and the *porta praetoria* lay in the normal position. Close scrutiny of the aerial photographs suggests that both *portae principales* were also inturned in the Flavian period; only the *porta decumana* was different, perhaps because its position on the promontory above the river was thought to be sufficiently secure.

(ii) South Praetentura, Trenches 1983 L III, 1984 S IV (FIGS. 10, 11, Sections J–N, O–R)

The back of the west rampart was again encountered in Trench 1983 L III (FIG. 40), but here the rear face was badly preserved above a height of only a few inches. It rose at an angle of 46°, which

4. Oakwood: *P.S.A.S.* lxxxvi (1951–2), 81 ff. Bochastle: *Trans. Glasgow Arch. Soc.*[2] xiv (1956), 35 ff. Menteith: *Glasgow Arch. Journ.*. iv (1976), 23, pl. 7. Cardean: *ibid.* p. 22.

if original may perhaps have indicated a plinth offset from the vertical part of the face, here missing. At a distance of 6 ft. (1.83 m) forward of the rear edge of the rampart, and so *c.* 11–12 ft. (3.35–3.66 m) behind the probable position of the front, a large post-hole was encountered. This took the form of a void in the turf-work, approximately rectangular in shape and measuring 11½ by 8½ inches (29.2 by 21.6 cm); the short axis was slightly oblique to that of the rampart. The void descended to a depth of 4 ft. 10 in. (1.47 m), and thus the post must have been set in a large post-pit approximately 3 ft. (1 m) deep, sealed below the turves. Its relationship with the rampart, which had not been disturbed for its insertion, proves its Flavian date; proximity to the angle of the rampart and to the corner-tower which no doubt stood there (only *c.* 80 ft. = 24.3 m away) makes it unlikely that this post formed part of an interval tower, and its purpose is discussed below with that of a second similar post found in the south rampart (Trench 1983 M I). The turves of the Flavian rampart in Trench L III were yellow in colour and clayey in character.

In 1984 a machine-cut trench (S IV) 8 ft. 6 in. (2.59 m) wide, was dug through the west rampart as an extension of Trench S III. The cutting lies *c.* 17 ft. (5.2 m) south of the estimated south face of the gate-passage of the *porta praetoria* (FIGS. 10–11, Sections J–N, O–R). Here, as in the 1978 excavation, the Flavian rampart was found to turn inwards, to form the south side of the forecourt discussed above. Unlike the pattern seen at Oakwood,[5] however, the curve of the rampart resembled that of an internal *clavicula*, whose form suggests that the gate-house stood between the rampart-ends rather than behind them. If the gate was flanked by towers, these may have risen over the rampart-terminals and so have lacked a ground floor. The rampart itself was here only 15 ft. 3 in. (4.65 m) wide and lay 12 ft. (3.66 m) behind the ditch; it was constructed of laid turves with layers of transverse strapping visible at the base and at a height of 10 in. (0.25 m). The front face rose at an angle of 67° as on the east side of the fort, and the rear face was once again vertical for the surviving height of 3 ft. 2 in. (0.96 m) (FIG. 10, Section K–L).

In the Antonine I period a new rampart of turves was as usual laid against the front face of its predecessor. The extension was 8 ft. 6 in. (2.59 m) wide along the south face of the trench, but widened to 9 ft. 3 in. (2.82 m) on the north face because here the Flavian rampart behind it had begun its eastward curve (whereas the Antonine rampart continued straight). This implies that the Antonine I *porta praetoria* lay in front of the position of its predecessor. The lowest 18 in. (0.46 m) of the front of the rampart sloped up at an angle of *c.* 68°, but above that point it was distorted by forward pressure.

At the back of the Flavian rampart a block of laid turves (FIG. 10, Section K–L, 9) has been built over a layer containing charcoal and daub (11) evidently representing the Flavian demolition. The turves accordingly are of Antonine date and they appear to represent either an *ascensus* or else an attempt to fill the inturn, now no longer required. The block was 3 ft. 6 in. (1.07 m) wide (FIG. 41) and its inner face stood vertical for 1 ft. (0.3 m).

Immediately in front of the Antonine I rampart ran a N–S street of hard fine gravel 9 in. (0.23 m) thick, but deeper over the Flavian ditch; the metalling was 16 ft. (4.88 m) wide along the south face of the trench but narrowed to 14 ft. (4.27 m) at the north face. The outer edge was rutted. This street must be a feature of the Annexe which appears not to have been divided from the fort by a ditch south of the *porta praetoria* at this period (PL. VI A, where no ditch is visible outside the position of the street, whose line is faintly seen).

In the Antonine II period a fresh turf rampart was added in front of that of Antonine I. The front of this had as usual collapsed, but, exceptionally, in the north face of the trench it was possible to determine that the original width had been *c.* 16 ft. (4.8 m). This rampart was as usual poorly constructed of somewhat amorphous turf: the front, if correctly identified (FIG. 11, Section O–P), appeared to be countersunk at its base into the contemporary surface.

5. See note 4.

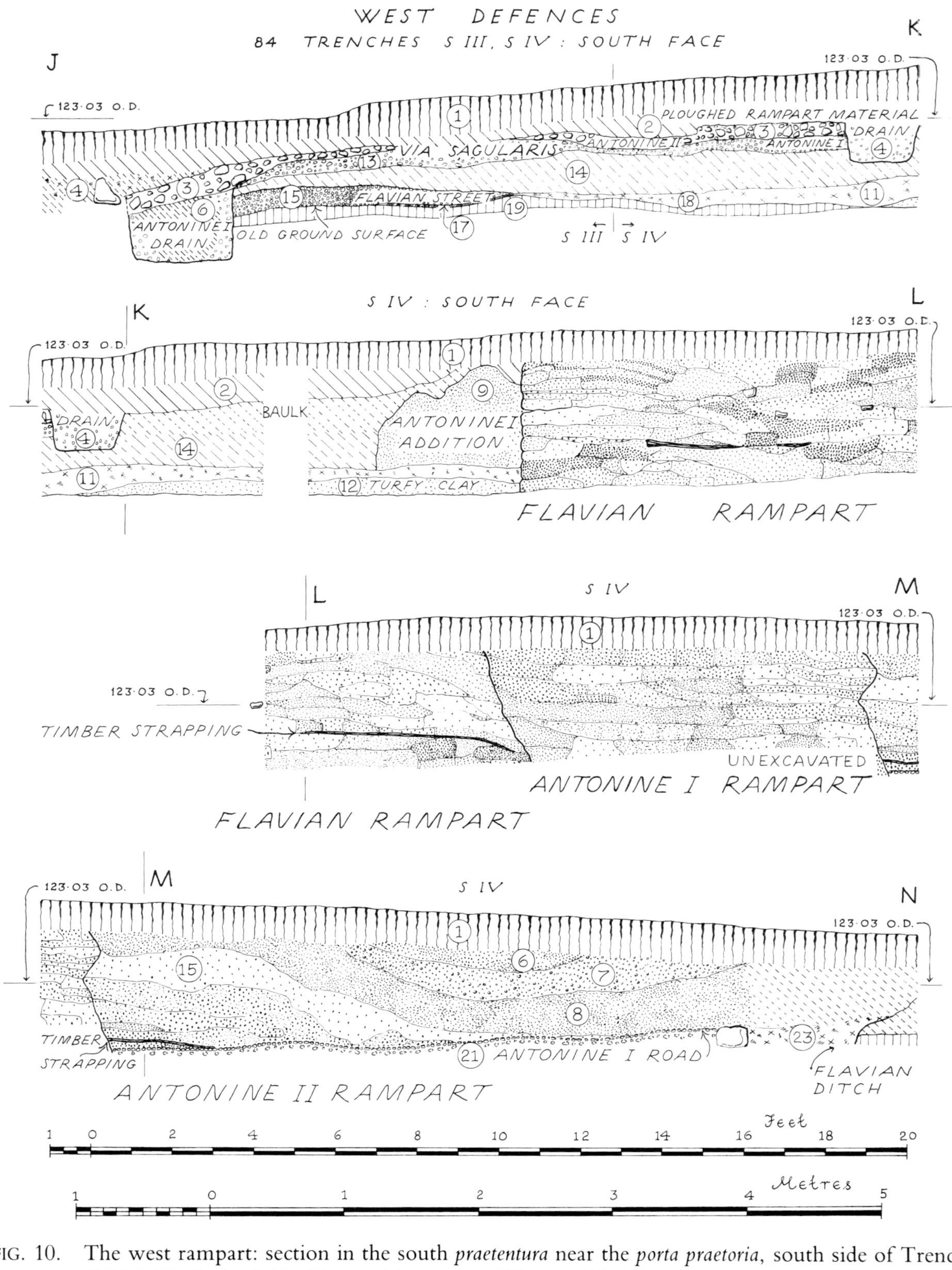

FIG. 10. The west rampart: section in the south *praetentura* near the *porta praetoria*, south side of Trench 1984 S IV. Scale, 1:45. (For position see p. 104, FIG. 58).

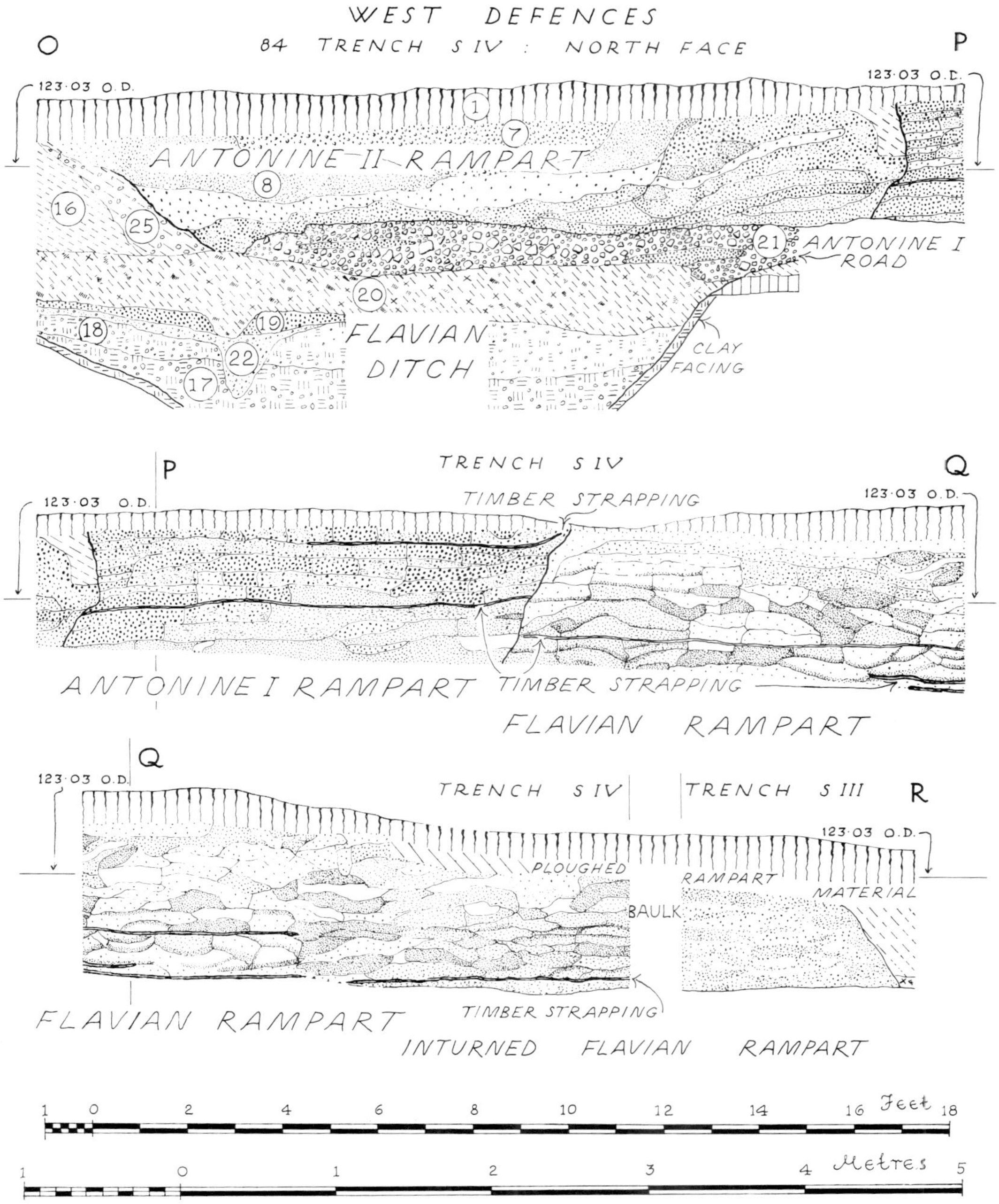

FIG. 11. The west rampart: north side of Trench 1984 S IV. Scale, 1:45. (For position see FIG. 58; for the rampart see p. 21, and for the ditch p. 15).

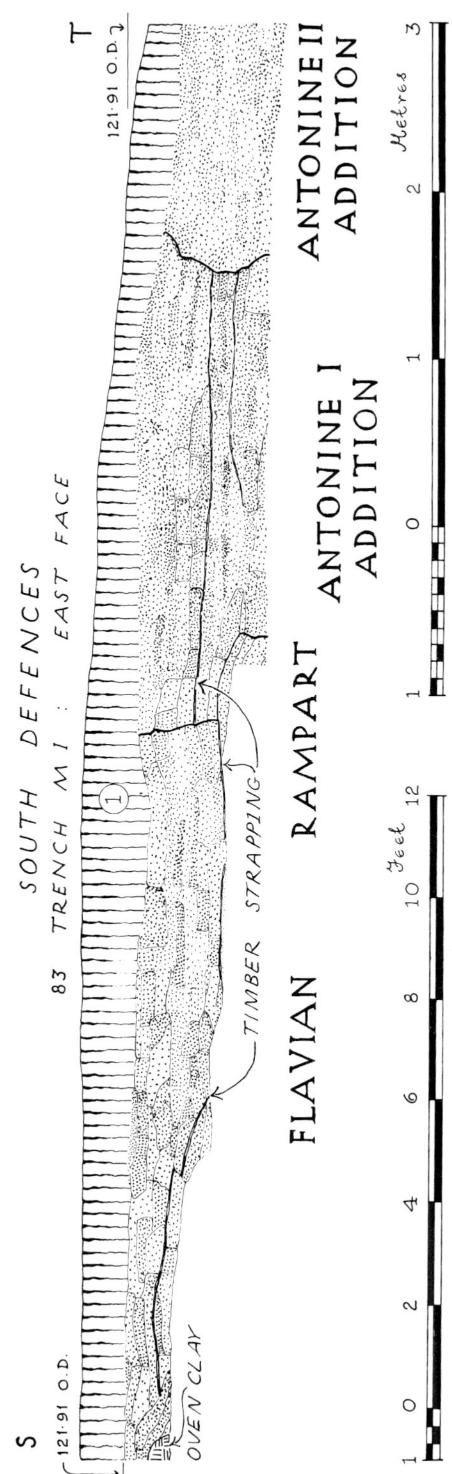

FIG. 12. The south rampart, section in Trench 1983 M I. Scale, 1:45. (For position see p. 104, FIG. 58).

D. The South Rampart:

(i) South Praetentura, Trench 1983 MI (FIG. 12)

The south rampart was also partially sectioned in 1983 (Trench M I) (FIGS. 40; 12, Section S–T). Here the rear face of the Flavian rampart had been largely cut away for insertion of an Antonine I oven, but the original width appeared to be 17 ft. 4 in. (5.28 m). The bottom 6 in. (0.15 m) of the front of this rampart was standing vertically, but the component turves had a forward tilt (Section S–T) as if there had been a collapse. Above 6 in., the front had been cut back as a shelf *c.* 9 in. (0.23 m) wide to seat a bonding for the new Antonine I front. In this Trench, as in L III, a large post-hole, here 14 in. (0.36 m) in diameter, was found embedded in the Flavian turves; the post-pipe was defined by a solid ring of iron pan. The post-hole was excavated to a depth of 3 ft. (1 m), but probing suggested that the post had descended at least 1 ft. (0.30 m) deeper, and this must imply a substantial post-pit below the rampart. The post lay 12 ft. (3.66 m) back from the front of the Flavian rampart, and since no corresponding post was found further forward it seems unlikely that part of an interval-tower is in question. If the profile of a standard turf rampart (p. 26) is applied, this post would support the rear edge of a rampart-walk 7 ft. 6 in. (2.28 m) wide at a height of 10 ft. 2 in. (3.1 m) above the ground (FIG. 13). The virtually identical position of the post in Trench L III suggests that it too had served this purpose.

The turves of the Flavian rampart were yellow and clayey. Except for those composing the actual front, the turves of the Antonine I addition were more sandy, but still very similar in appearance. The Antonine I new front lay 7 ft. 5 in. (2.26 m) beyond its predecessor. The addition was composed of yellow sandy turves which in the surviving section had been bonded by two layers of timber strapping 6 in. (0.15 m) apart. For just over 1 ft. (0.30 m) the face rose steeply at an angle of about 65° (FIG. 12), but higher up the face had been squeezed forward. If we assume a height of 10 ft. (3.05 m), the front of the rampart-walk would have lain 4 ft. 4 in. (1.32 m) behind the face at the bottom of the rampart, and a rampart-walk 7 ft. 6 in. (2.28 m) wide would have overlapped the Flavian front – a calculation which at first sight contradicts the thesis already put forward that the purpose of refronting the rampart was to provide a secure rampart-walk resting on new turfwork. However, the section (FIG. 12) shows that the front of the Flavian rampart had itself been cut back for the insertion of new turves; in what survives, the width of the new work is 9 ft. 6 in., and we may be sure that at the height of the top of the rampart the necessary width of 11 ft. 10 in. (3.61 m) of new turfwork would have been present. If this reasoning is correct, it would seem to follow that the recovery of so much of the front faces of the Flavian and Antonine I ramparts in the 1973 and 1984 Sections (pp. 17, 21) is exceptional.

A large stone-packed post-hole was found in the Antonine I rampart, immediately in front of the face of the Flavian rampart (FIG. 41). The post no doubt served as a support for the Antonine I rampart-walk. Excavation was hindered by bad weather; the packing stones appeared to have slumped into the post-pipe, but a void beneath them was at least 2 ft. 6 in. (0.76 m) deep.

In front of the Antonine I extension lay the turves of the Antonine II extension. As elsewhere, they formed an amorphous mass, perhaps very largely representing material flung down while cutting back the top of the Antonine I rampart to form a bonding. The Antonine II front, if it had survived, lay beyond the end of the Trench and was not sought. The width of the Antonine II addition exposed within the Trench was 4 ft. 6 in. (1.37 m).

Immediately in front of the Antonine I rampart-face, and thus associated with the Antonine II extension, lay a setting of packing-stones 3 ft. (1 m) in diameter, which very probably indicated the position of a post supporting the new Antonine II rampart-walk. Bad weather and lack of time prevented its examination in detail, but the reality of a supporting post in this position is strengthened by the discovery of similarly-placed post-holes near the Antonine II *porta decumana* (p. 30). The latter lay only *c.* 4 ft. (1.22 m) from the probable position of the front of the rampart, and the present post lay perhaps not more than 6 ft. (1.83 m) back from it, as certainly did the Antonine I post just described. None of these posts can therefore have supported the rear edge of their respective rampart-walks (as the corresponding Flavian posts have been taken to do), for they lay in a position where, because of the slope of the rampart-face, they would have

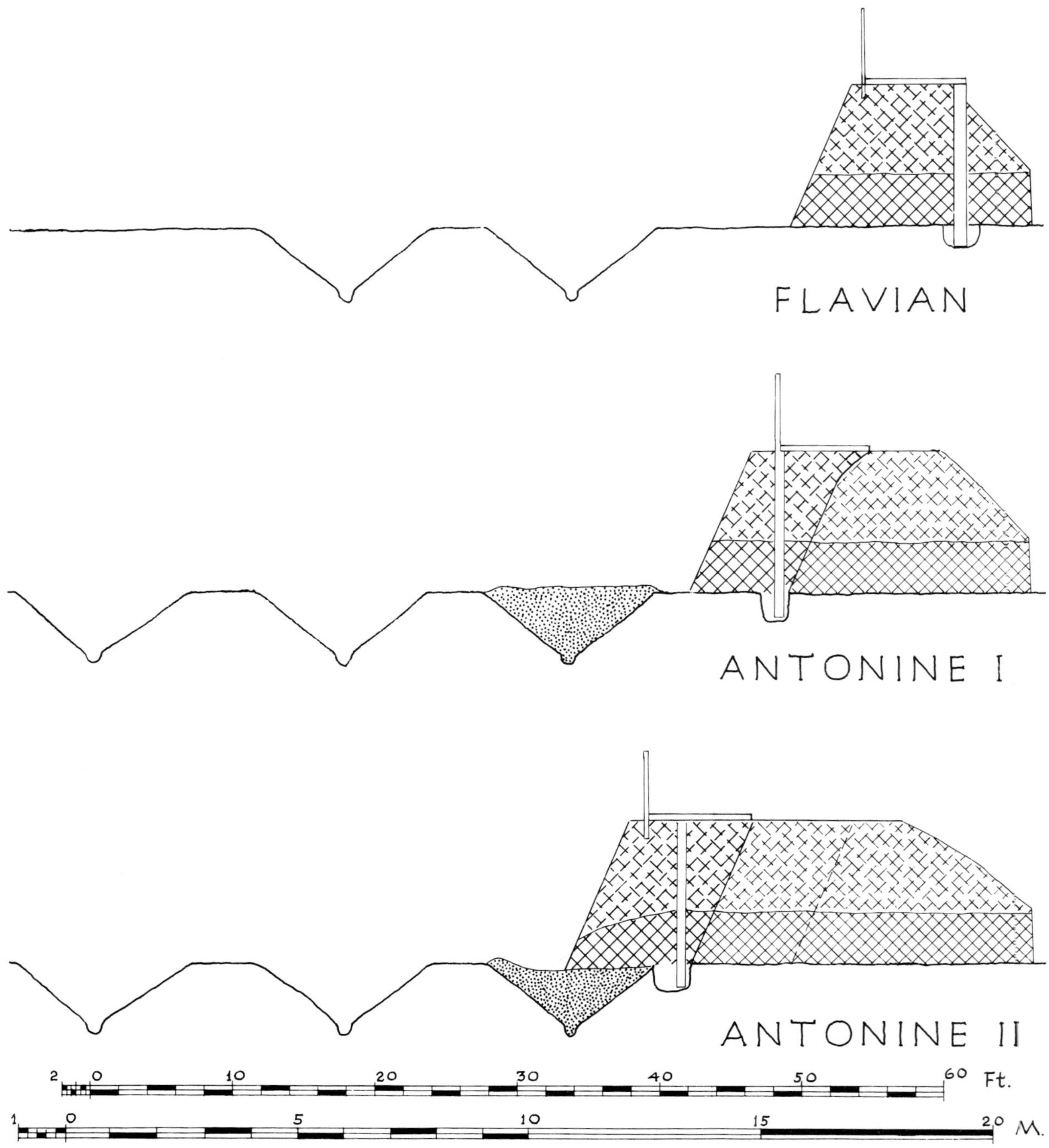

FIG. 13. Rampart section: composite reconstruction. Scale, 1:140.

emerged at the top of the rampart either at the breastwork or only a few feet behind it beneath the rampart-walk itself. But they could not have been placed further back without digging large holes through the earlier rampart. The purpose of these Antonine posts can be suggested as twofold: to decrease the possibility of a forward collapse of the new face, and to help support the weight of the rampart-walks or breastworks.

(ii) Central Range, Trench 1986 V II

A narrow extension southwards from Trench V II (FIG. 28, p. 52) was cut by machine to establish the line of the rampart. The front of the rampart was not reached but turfwork was found extending 23 ft. (7 m) back from the south end of the trench to within 7 ft. (2.13 m) of the south edge of the Flavian *via sagularis*, although here partly disturbed by a later stone-lined drain (p. 55). The inner face of the turfwork lay 9 ft. (2.74 m) north of the projected line of the rear face of the rampart and was taken to represent an *ascensus*. No line of division separated this from the rampart proper, and they must have been built in one operation – unlike the *ascensus* found in 1973 (p. 17).

A thin layer of gravel metalling, *c.* 7 ft. (2.13 m) wide, capped the *ascensus* just below the ploughsoil; it lay *c.* 2 ft. (0.61 m) above the base of the turfwork. In the space available it was not possible to decide whether the metalling represented a sloping ramp or a series of wide steps; but the latter seems to be the more likely explanation since there was no difference in the level of the metalling on either side of the Trench, which was 3 ft. 6 in. (1.07 m) wide.

The lower part of the *ascensus* seems therefore to have risen parallel with the vertical back of the rampart, for the metalling did not extend down the slopes to the base of the turves on the north side. But at a higher level the *ascensus* will probably have turned through 90° to climb the sloping upper portion of the rampart.

E. The North Rampart, TRENCH 1986 V I

The north rampart was encountered only in a machine-cut extension to Trench 1986 V I, where the back of the Flavian rampart was found 6 ft. 2 in. (1.88 m) beyond the northern edge of the contemporary *via sagularis* (FIG. 24, p. 46). Because of its location here on the crest of a steep slope northwards, the rampart was badly preserved. Only three courses of turves were found *in situ*, surviving to a height of 11 in. (0.28 m), and they did not show a vertical back but sloped upwards at an angle of only 56°. Possibly, therefore, these turves represented a plinth on which the vertical back had formerly rested. In the *intervallum* space, and partially sealing the Flavian *via sagularis*, lay much charcoal and fragments of burnt clay, suggesting the proximity of ovens.

The Porta Decumana

The rear gate of the fort was examined in 1974 and 1975. In all three periods there was a single-portalled timber gateway, which certainly carried a tower above it in the Flavian and Antonine I periods. These first two gates occupied exactly the same position and therefore some details of the Flavian arrangements especially on the north side were disturbed. The Antonine II gateway was built further forward.

(i) Flavian (FIG. 14)

The first structural episode was the deposition of a spread of gravel at the site of the gate; this also underlay the rampart on each side and probably represents the remains of a heap of gravel brought from the river and dumped here for use in the streets (PL. XVII). If so the implication is that work on the interior of the fort was underway before the rampart had been built at least in this sector (see p. 117). The transverse timber strapping on which the rampart was set was laid directly on this gravel; the voids created by the decay of the timbers yielded a large number of hazel-nut shells which had been imported by field mice in modern times and were accompanied by a few white grubs.

Through the layer of gravel the Flavian builders had dug two parallel post-trenches, 4 ft. (1.22 m) deep from the contemporary surface (FIG. 15, Section E–F) and 12 ft. (3.66 m) apart. The trenches were 15 ft. (4.57 m) long and 1 ft. 6 in. (0.46 m) wide, and they were laid out slightly oblique to the axis of the rampart. The inner ends ceased 3 ft. (0.9 m) in front of the rampart-back (FIG. 14). In the southern trench, and probably also in the northern one (where disturbance had been more severe), the bottom was paved with large flat slabs of stone (PL. XVIII), on which six

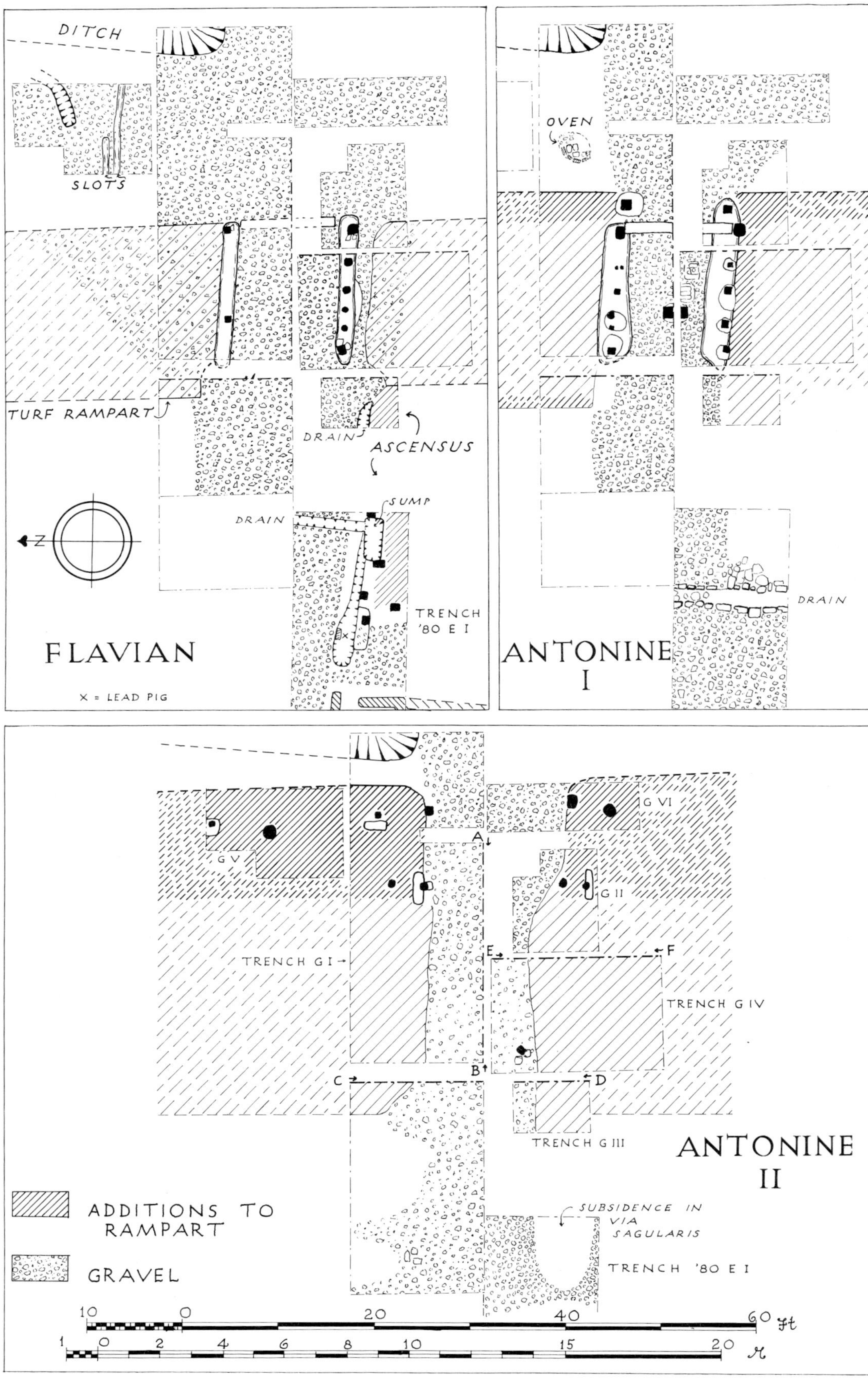

FIG. 14. The *porta decumana*: plan of successive east gates. Scale, 1:192.

upright posts were set and packed with earth (FIG. 15, Section E–F). The post-sockets where identifiable were 9 in. (0.229 m) in diameter.

One of the functions of the posts was to retain planks revetting the passage through the rampart; but such a depth of foundation and size of timber suggest that the structure also carried a tower above the bridge for the rampart-walk. The technical expertise shown by the remains of this structure was very impressive to see and suggests legionary work. The trenches were extremely narrow to have been dug so deep; there had been one small collapse of the side in the middle of the south edge of the southern trench. The use of deep trenches floored with slabs recurs in the small early granary in the right (northern) *praetentura* (p. 69).

The actual portal was indicated by a shallow slot for a wooden threshold inserted into the metalling flush with the front of the rampart (PL. XIX). Outside the gate on the north side part of a ditch-terminal was found. This lay 18 ft. (5.49 m) in front of the rampart and seemed to be swinging in; the distance is twice that separating the rampart from Ditch I in Trench 1973 I, 60 ft. (18.3 m) to the north, and it therefore seems likely that Ditch I did not enter the area excavated outside the gate and that the terminal is that of Ditch II, curving in to clasp the end of the other. The filling was a uniform pebbly brown soil yielding no finds. The ditch had been cut through the primary gravel spread.

Between the ditch-end and the rampart two small shallow slots were found cutting the gravel (FIG. 14) and sealed by the later Antonine II rampart-extension; nearby was the end of a more substantial trench 1 ft. 4 in. (0.41 m) wide and 9 in. (0.23 m) deep. These probably indicate fencing to block off the berm.

On the evacuation of the Flavian fort the removal of the timbers and plank revetment of the gate-passage resulted in a fall of turfwork over the street-metalling (FIG. 15, Sections A–B, E–F). This material was not removed by the Antonine I builders, who laid their own street over it. The repetition of the same sequence at the start of Antonine II resulted in the new street rising over a considerable hump before descending to the exterior (FIG. 15, Sections A–B, C–D; PL. XIV B).

At the east end of Trench E I, dug in 1980, a plank drain was found crossing the *via decumana* 16 ft. (4.88 m) from the rear portal of the gate-passage (see further p. 88). Together with another drain leading from the west it drained into a deep sump or soakaway pit beside the street (FIGS. 14, 50). Nearby were five large post-holes, the post-pit of one being cut by the east-west drain-trench and sealed by the metalling of the *via sagularis*. On the south side of Trench E I, in the area enclosed by the posts, were indications of laid turves. The most westerly post lies 23 ft. (7 m) from the rear of the rampart. Despite this distance the structure must be taken to represent part of an *ascensus* giving access to the gate-top. Further laid turves butting on to the back of the rampart were found in the south-west corner of Trench G III, and these too form part of the *ascensus*. In this area the Flavian rampart had subsided somewhat into an underlying hollow (Section C–D), probably where it no longer stood on the gravel spread. Between the *ascensus*-turves in Trench G III and the Flavian street was a length of timber-lined drain; this too presumably fed into the soakaway pit. Part of a charred plank, 8–9 in. (20–23 cm) wide and $\frac{3}{4}$. (1.9 cm) thick was found in this drain.

(ii) Antonine I (FIGS. 14, 15)

The 1973 Trench had shown that at the beginning of the Antonine I period the rampart had been given a new front 6 ft. (1.8 m) wide. At the *porta decumana*, 60 ft. (18.3 m) further south, the new front had narrowed to 3 ft. (0.9 m). A new gateway was built on the site of the Flavian gate, the old trenches being partially dug out and widened, and 4 ft. (1.2 m) of the rampart itself was cut back on the south side of the passage (FIG. 15, Section E–F) to facilitate the work. The southern trench was lengthened eastwards to reach the new front (PL. XIX), but on the north side a separate post-pit was dug instead. The revetted passage was now 16 ft. (4.88 m) long, and new turfwork was added at the inner end to give the rampart a width of 22 ft. 3 in. (6.78 m). In the middle of the gate-passage two post-holes were located, 8 ft. (2.44 m) back from the threshold. These perhaps served to support the rear of the bridge carrying the rampart-walk. They are too far back to have served as door-stops. The gate-position itself was indicated by a shallow trench (PL. XV A, XVI A) for the threshold; this lay 3 ft. (0.9 m) inside the gate-passage (which was 12 ft. (3.66 m) wide). The new foundation-trenches did not reach the bottom of the Flavian trenches (Section E–F), but were nevertheless 3 ft. 4 in. (1.02 m) deep from the surface of the contemporary street. The six posts in each were heavily packed in with large stones (PL. XVII). Once the revetment was in position the metalling was laid in the passage and new turf placed in the gap cut behind it. (Section E–F).

Just outside the gate a hearth was found on the berm, sealed by the Antonine II rampart-extension (PL. XVI B). It was *c.* 3 ft. 4 in. (1.02 m) in diameter and was made of flat stones and some (burnt) gravel with the remains of a kerb of stones set on edge. The probability is that this cooking-place, built in the lee of the rampart, was a temporary structure used by the gate-builders before proper facilities had been provided within the fort. During the later demolition of the gate, a good deal of burnt timber fragments accumulated on the Antonine I metalling; but there was no sign that the posts had been burnt *in situ*.

(iii) Antonine II (FIGS. 14, 15)

At the beginning of this period the rampart was again provided with a new front, which in the 1973 Trench was at least 8 ft. 9 in. (2.67 m) wide; the loss of the front turf revetment prevented discovery of the exact dimension. At the *porta decumana*, 60 ft. (18.3 m) further south, the extension was 12 ft. (3.66 m) wide, and may have reached this width here in order to accommodate the new gate-structure well clear of its predecessors (FIG. 14). The new gate contained a passage now 14 ft. (4.27 m) wide within two post-positions on each side, which were 8 ft. (2.44 m) apart. The post-holes varied between 12 and 15 in. (0.30–0.38 m) in diameter, with depths from the surface of the gravel spread of 15–18 in. (0.38–0.46 m); such shallowness seems to preclude the likelihood that a tower existed above the bridge. No attempt was made to revet the old passage through the rampart behind the gate, and this must have been bevelled off at the angle of rest. The new metalling was laid over fallen Antonine I turfwork (FIG. 15 Section C–D; PL. XIV B). The overall width of the rampart at the gate was now 34 ft. (10.36 m); but only the front, supporting the new rampart-walk, was really functional. A somewhat irregular line of post-holes north of the gate may have supported the parapet. In Trench 80 E I the *via sagularis* had seriously subsided over the Flavian sump, and had here been patched with extra cobbles.

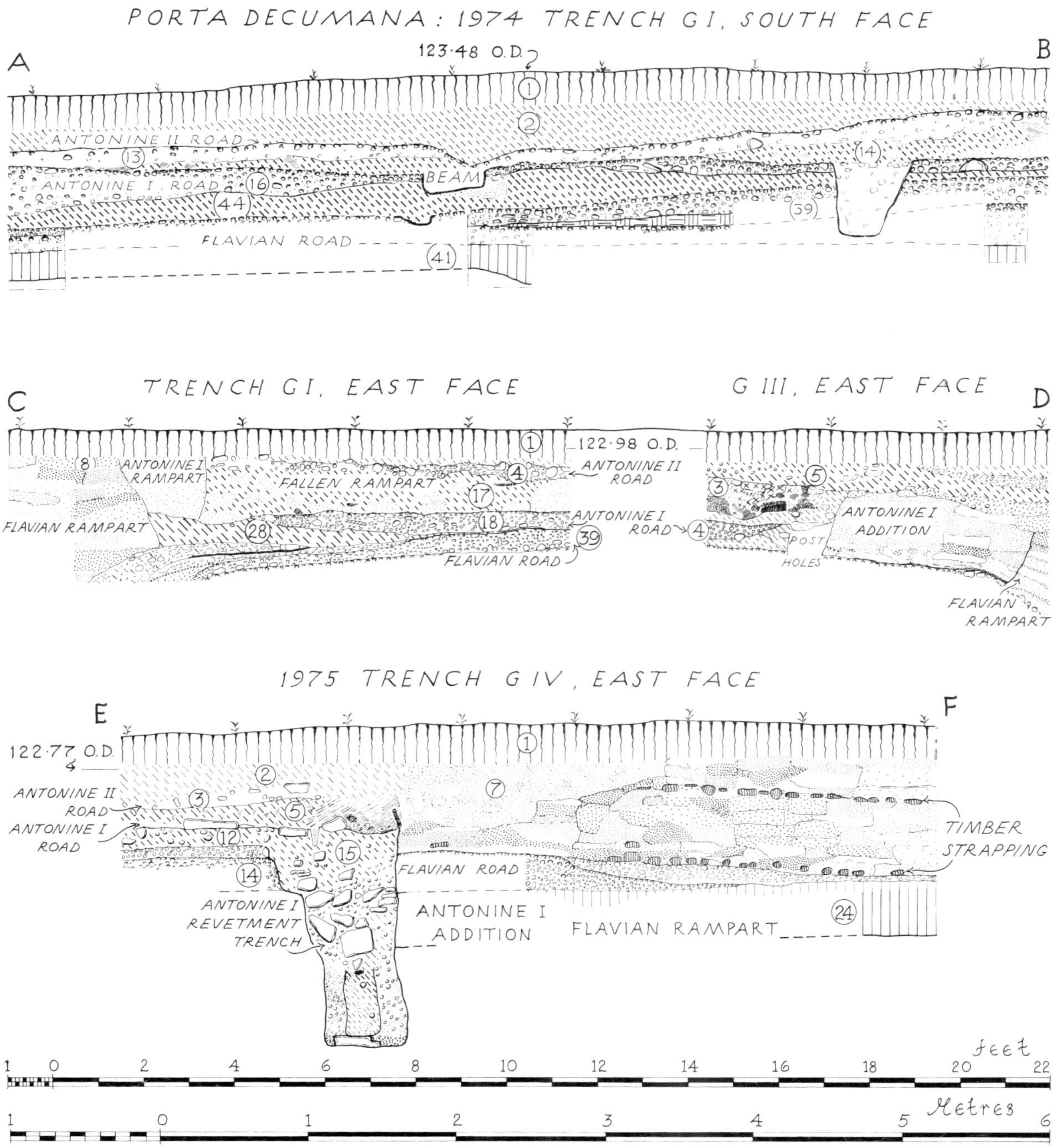

FIG. 15. *Porta decumana*: sections. Scale, 1:44.

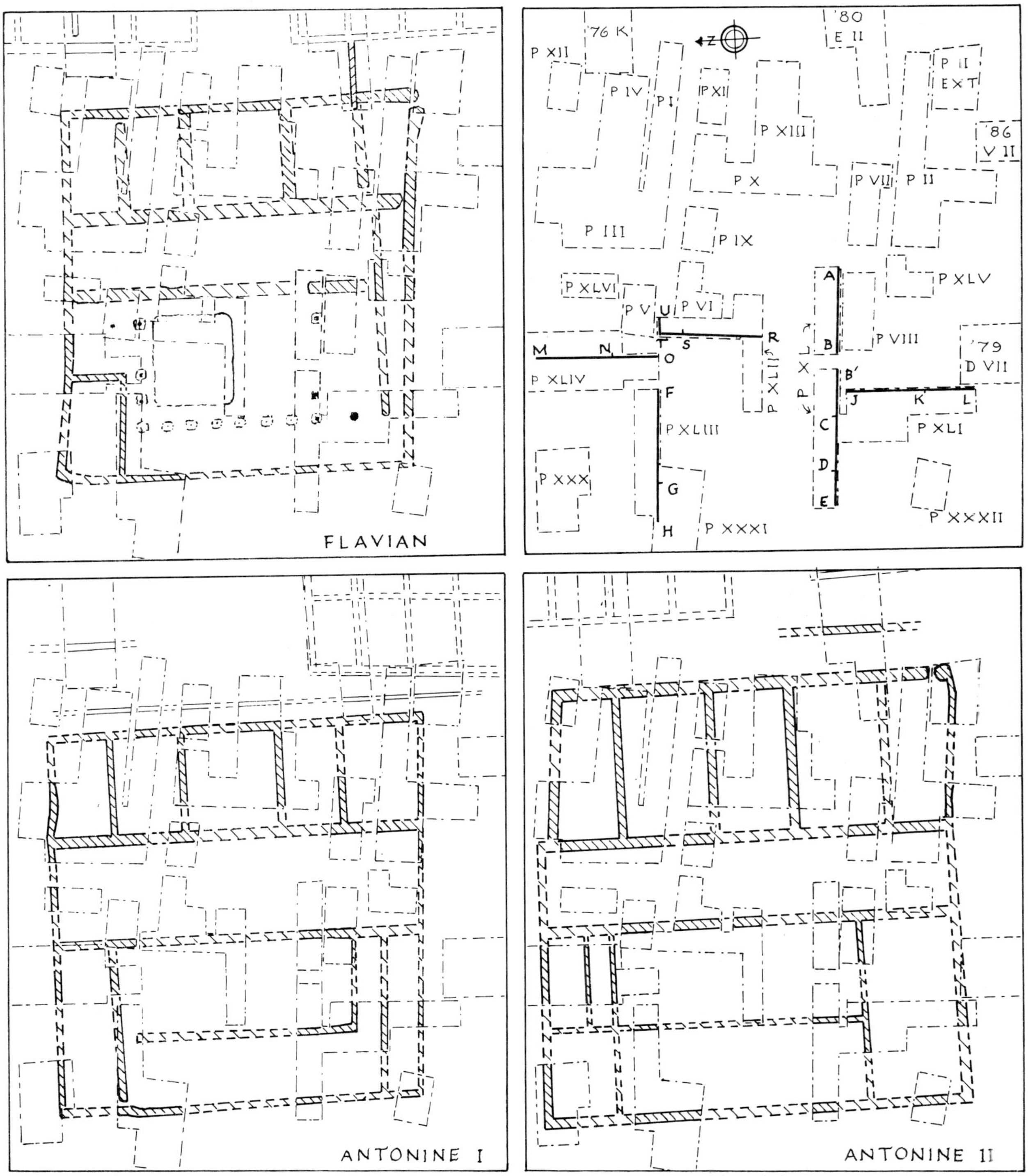

FIG. 16. Comparison of the three *principia* with trench-plan showing positions of published sections.

III. THE CENTRAL RANGE

Examination of the Central Range of the forts began in 1974 and 1975 with the excavation of the *principia*. The remaining areas, north and south of that building, were examined in 1979 and 1986. The results however are unsatisfactory; further work is required to produce fully comprehensible plans and this would have been undertaken had it not been for the unwillingness of the Ancient Monuments Branch of the Scottish Development Department to finance further excavation at Strageath after 1986.

In 1979 two north-south trenches, each 12 ft. (3.66 m) wide, were dug respectively north and south of the *principia*. That on the north side was divided into two lengths each of 50 ft. (15.24 m) named D I and D II for ease of supervision; the Trench south of the *principia*, 80 ft. (24.38 m) long, was divided into three lengths (D V, 28 ft. (8.53 m), D VI 22 ft. (6.70 m) and D VII 30 ft. (9.14 m) long) for the same reason. Because of the presence of root crops neither could be extended as far as the outer edges of the Range as had been intended (cf. FIGS. 24, 28).

Two small extensions (D I A and D IV) were made on the east side of D I–II, and *c.* 15 ft. (4.6 m) to the west of D I. Trench D VIII was dug to locate the edge of the *via principalis*.

In 1986 Trenches V I and V II were dug parallel with the earlier excavations and 33 ft. (10 m) further east. These did extend across the whole width of both blocks but were dug only 8 ft. (2.44 m) wide because of the lengths involved. Trench V I was 122½ ft. (37.34 m) long, and at its northern end a narrow extension was made by JCB to locate the back of the rampart. A small additional Trench (V I A) was also excavated 14 ft. (4.28 m) east of the northern end in order to seek the Antonine building-lines. South of the *principia* Trench V II was 138 ft. (42 m) long, and again a narrow extension was excavated mechanically in order to reach the rampart.

Unfortunately the result of this work left areas in the north-west and south-west corners of the respective blocks entirely unexplored, and because of the unpredictable character of the buildings each side of the *principia* it has not proved possible to extrapolate their plans with any pretence of credibility.

I. THE PRINCIPIA

In 1974 and 1975 excavations were carried out in the area covered by the three successive *principia*; these occupied approximately the same site and had the same basic internal layout, although the Antonine II *principia* was of slightly larger size than both its predecessors. A large number of hand-dug trenches of varying dimensions were laid out in order to establish the limits of the three superimposed buildings, their relationship to the streets and their internal layouts. In 1974 work was concentrated, in Trenches P I–XIII, on the rear half of the buildings and Trenches P XXX–XXXII established their front lines and corners. The dryness of the ground in 1974 made it difficult to identify the various elements. In 1975 work, in Trenches P XL–XLVI, was concentrated on the front half of the *principia*; in this year conditions were more favourable to the recognition of features. In 1980 Trench E II in the left *retentura* and its westward extension (pp. 91ff.) overlapped the southern end of the rear range of the *principia*. It confirmed the lines of the rear walls and some of the internal divisions. In addition new features were discovered at the rear of the *principia* of the Flavian and Antonine II periods; the street lines and the relationship of the *principia* to the buildings in the southern *retentura* were clarified.

(a) The Flavian *Principia* (FIG. 17)

The headquarters building at Strageath occupied the normal position in the centre of the fort facing the junction of the *viae principalis* and *praetoria*. As a result of the shape of the fort as a whole, the *principia* took the form of a parallelogram. The Flavian building measured 75 ft. (22.9 m) east-west by 70 ft. (21.3 m) north-south, an area of 5250 sq. ft. (487.8 m^2). The building was

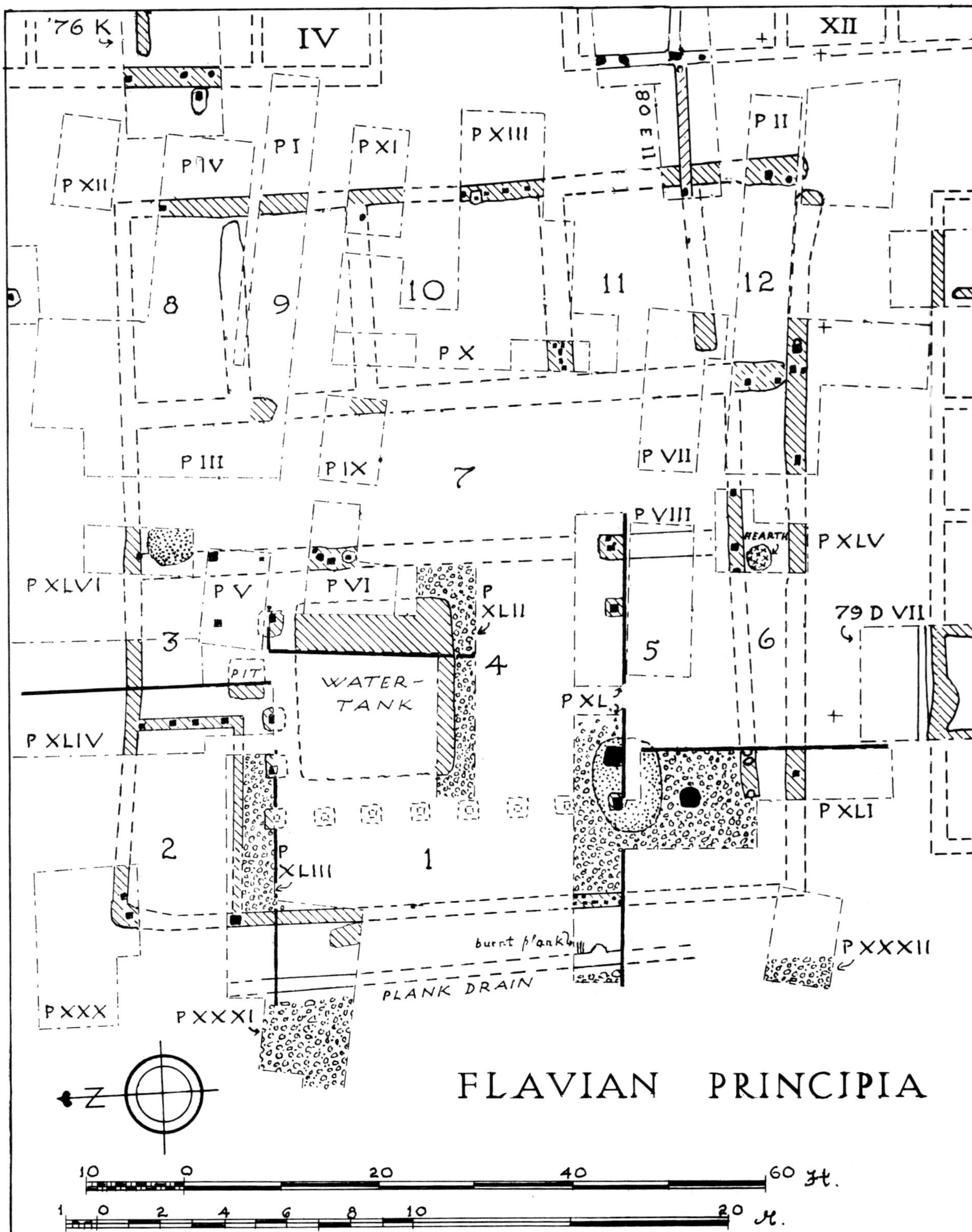

FIG. 17. The Flavian *principia*. Scale, 1:192.

thus smaller than *principia* in many other auxilliary forts, for example that of Fendoch (743 m^2).

A drain ran north-south along the *via principalis* in front of the building, some 5 ft. 2 in. (1.57 m) to the west. This drain was traced in Trenches P XXXI and P XL and was found to be *c.* 1 ft. (0.305 m) wide and 6 in. (0.15 m) deep. The drain was filled with burnt daub and charcoal and was sealed by the Flavian demolition layer (FIG. 20, Section D–E). Two pieces of charred plank were discovered on the Flavian ground-surface on either side of the drain in Trench P XL, suggesting that the drain had originally been lined and covered with planks. In Trenches P XXXI and XXXII the *via principalis* itself was seen to consist of gravel laid over a foundation of rocks up to 1 ft. (0.30 m) across packed in a layer of clay.

The building followed the standard plan for *principia* in auxiliary forts. This comprised three sections, a courtyard enclosed by porticoes and less frequently by side-rooms as well, a cross-hall or *basilica* and a rear range of rooms which included a centrally-positioned *aedes*, the shrine for the standards and the emperor's image. In auxiliary forts this range consisted of five rooms although in fortresses there were larger numbers. In all three periods the *principia* at Strageath followed this general pattern.

The courtyard (No. 4) measured 35 ft. (10.67 m) north-south by 24 ft. (7.3 m) east-west, creating an open area of 850 sq. ft. (77.9 m^2). The surface consisted of close-packed small pebbles and fine gravel which extended into the western portico (Room 1) and also into Room 5, although there the floor was seen only in Trench XLI (FIG. 21, Section J–K) and was missing in Trench VIII. This surface was observed in Trenches P XL, XLIII and XLIII in addition to Trench XLI; above it was a thin layer of earth, charcoal and burnt daub fragments from the Flavian demolition phase and then the cobbled floor of the Antonine I yard.

A large pit in the north-east corner of the courtyard was identified as a water-tank. This was first observed in Trench P XLII and its extent then established by extensions to the north and west. The pit measured 18 ft. (5.49 m) east-west by 16 ft. (4.88 m) north-south and was 4 ft. 8 in. (1.52 m) deep (FIG. 23, Section R–S); as a tank it would thus have had a capacity of 8,400 gallons (38,200 litres). The pit had almost vertical sides, which could not have stood unsupported in the soft sandy subsoil for more than a few days, and a flat bottom. There was no trace of a clay lining as in a second tank further south (p. 53), but the precision of the cutting suggested that there had formerly been a timber lining. The timbers will have been removed during the demolition of the fort at the end of the Flavian period; at that time the pit was filled with a sterile deposit of mixed turf, clay and gravel.

On its north, south and west sides the courtyard was enclosed by open colonnades, the post-holes for which were set at approximately 4-ft. (1.22-m) intervals. The southern row were deeply set in post-holes ranging from 2 to 2 ft. 8 in. deep (0.61–.81 m) (FIG. 20, Section A–C) but on the north side they were more shallow, and the corner one had been entirely removed by an Antonine I wall-trench (Section F–G) whereas its counterpart extended below the other end of this same Antonine I trench (Section B–C). The east end of the courtyard, however, was closed by the western wall of the cross-hall. To the west of the courtyard, adjacent to the *via principalis*, lay a portico (Room 1) facing inwards onto the yard. It measured 55 ft. (16.78 m) north-south by 8 ft. (2.44 m) east-west. To the north of the courtyard lay a narrow portico only 3 ft. (0.91 m) wide; this opened out at its eastern end into a larger open-sided room (No. 3), 14 ft. (4.27 m) square. West of Room 3, at the north-west corner of the building, lay Room 2 measuring 11 ft. (3.36 m) north-south by 19 ft. (5.79 m) east-west. The plan suggests that this room may have been an afterthought. On the southern side of the courtyard was a third portico (Room 5), measuring 24 ft. (7.32 m) east-west by 12 ft. (3.66 m) north-south. It was entered from the courtyard through a large opening, 14 ft. (4.27 m) wide, in the colonnade. To the south of this lay a long, narrow room (No. 6) which extended also across the southern end of the cross-hall. Room 6 measured 42 ft. (12.81 m) east-west and 5 ft. (1.53 m) north-south, narrowing to 3 ft. (0.915 m) towards its western end.

Room 3 recalls the two long narrow rooms found beside the courtyard in some *principia*, for instance at Fendoch, and long identified as *armamentaria*.[1] In the majority of auxiliary *principia* the courtyards were enclosed only by porticoes, as at Gelligaer, Housesteads or Chesters; but

1. The location of the *armamentaria* in or near the *principia* is suggested by *RIB* 1092 from Lanchester and argued in detail by Cagnat, *L'Armée Romaine d'Afrique et l'occupation militaire de l'Afrique sous les Empereurs* (Paris 1913, reprinted New York 1975) 491–6, in relation to Lambaesis; it is confirmed by the discovery of two hoards of weapons and armour close to the relevant rooms at Künzing (H. Schönberger, *Saalburg Jahrbuch* xxi (1963–4), 83 with Beilage 5; *JRS* lix (1969), 177; *Kastell Künzing-Quintana* (Berlin, *Limesforschungen* Bd 13, 1975), 47 with Beilage 7). For Fendoch, see *P.S.A.S.*. lxxiii (1939), 110–54; the *principia* at pp. 122–7.

occasionally there were other smaller rooms such as Room 2. The function of these extra rooms is uncertain; it seems that some at least served as weapon-stores, but some may have provided extra office-space (since they are not always present, there was not a uniform need for them in all *principia*). Extra offices were presumably necessary at Strageath in order to house the administration of the two units present in the fort, and as a weapon store Room 2 is rather small. Near the east end of Room 6, however, there lay an oval hearth of burnt clay, hollowed into the underlying soil. It measured 2 ft. 8 in. by 2 ft. 4 in. (0.81 by 0.71 m) and had a covering of charcoal and iron slag. This does suggest that the room may have been used by the armourer.

To the rear (east) of the courtyard lay the *basilica* (Room 7). This took the form of a long hall 61 ft. (18.6 m) north-south by 13 ft. 6 in. (4.1 m) east-west. The *basilica* usually ran the full width of the *principia* but here Room 3 extended across the southern end of the hall reducing its length. No internal features were noted. The position of the entrance is uncertain but it probably lay on the central axis of the building.

At the rear of the *principia*, beyond the cross-hall, lay the normal range of five rooms extending across the full width of the building for a depth of 18 ft. 6 in. (5.64 m) internally. In the centre of the range was Room 10; almost square, it measured 18 ft. (5.49 m) east-west. Room 10 can be identified as the *aedes*. No trace of a buried strong-box was found, despite search. Two rooms lay each side of Room 10; to the south Room 11 (12 ft. 6 in. (3.81 m) wide) and Room 12 (*c.* 9 ft. (2.75 m) wide), and to the north Room 9 (11 ft. (3.36 m) wide) and Room 8 (9 ft. (2.75 m) wide), all measurements being internal. The individual functions of the four rooms other than the *aedes* are uncertain; they will have housed the administration, pay- and personal records of the garrison.

In 1980 Trench E II, in the left (south) half of the *retentura* (p. 91), and its western extension revealed that Building XII there, a barrack, has been connected to the rear of the *principia*. A construction-trench extending the line of a *contubernium*-partition to the rear wall of the *principia* ran between the two buildings (FIGS. 17, 51). The dimensions of this construction-trench were greater than those of the barrack but similar to those of the *principia*. The intersection of this trench with that of the rear wall of the *principia* showed that it cut the latter and was therefore stratigraphically later, thus belonging to a second phase of construction. This is taken to indicate provision of an extra room behind the *principia*, which may have blocked the end of the *via decumana* as well as the *quintana*: excavation was not sufficiently extensive to locate the other wall or walls. The addition of rooms in this manner to the rear of a *principia* is rare, but may be paralleled in the third-century *principia* at Caernarvon.[2] The function of the room or rooms so created is unknown; no doubt extra office-space was required and the joining of the two buildings would have minimised the need for fresh construction. Circulation, however, within the fort would have been impeded; but the Flavian fort in any case lacked a metalled *via quintana*.

With the exception of the gravel in the courtyard and in Rooms 1 and 5, the floors of the Flavian *principia* were difficult to distinguish. A yellow sand floor was, however, observed in Trench P II, in Rooms 6 and 12.

Throughout the *principia* the construction-trenches were seen to have been dug down from the Flavian ground surface into the natural subsoil; they were sealed by a layer of Flavian demolition-material, earth mixed with charcoal and burnt daub, which underlay the Antonine I floors. In places the Flavian trenches had been cut by construction-trenches of the Antonine I period, for example the southern wall of Room 2 in Trench P XLIV and the northern wall of Room 6 in Trench P XLI, where the Antonine cutting had not been as deep as the Flavian (FIG. 21, Section J–K). Elsewhere, at the north-west corner of the courtyard, the position of a Flavian post-hole had been removed by a deep Antonine I construction-trench (Section F–G). At the base of the northern wall-trench of Room 6 (FIG. 21, Section J–K) two flat stones had been placed, clearly to act as base-plate for an upright. This trench, at 2 ft. 3 in. (0.69 m), was exceptionally deep. The north-eastern corner-post of the courtyard colonnade was set in a post-pit which had been dug too deep (FIG. 23, Section T–U); the post-socket was seen to rest on 9 in. (0.23 m) of

2. Cf. V.E. Nash-Williams, *Roman Frontier in Wales* (ed. 2 by M.G. Jarrett, Cardiff 1969), 61–3.

laid turf. The Flavian construction-trenches had a sandy yellow-brown content with an upper fill of burnt daub and charcoal from the demolition phase. Fragments of burnt daub had also been washed into some of the post-holes after the withdrawal of timbers, but no post-holes yielded evidence of timbers burnt *in situ*, nor were any of their edges burnt. It was clear that the signs of burning which were encountered came from deliberate demolitions rather than the firing of standing buildings. In Trench P II lumps of unburnt wall clay were also observed in the upper fill of the trenches. In general the fill of the construction-trenches contained few finds, but several sherds of a mica-coated beaker (p. 244, No. 10) were discovered in the trench of the southern wall of the *principia* in P XLI and appeared to form part of the original filling.

The construction-trenches of the *principia* varied in size but most were between 1 and 2 ft. (0.305 and 0.61 m) wide and deep and thus tended to be deeper than those of other buildings. The trenches for the outer walls were mostly 2 ft. (0.61 m) deep; some were shallower but had a deeper central slot as in the western external wall in Trench P XL (FIG. 20, Section C–D) or deeper post-holes as in Trench P X. The trenches for the internal walls were not always equally deep; those in Room 2 had a depth of only 1 ft. (0.305 m). The differences presumably reflect the structural function of individual walls and the load they carried. The post-holes for the main uprights and the intermediate stake-holes were observed within the construction-trenches in several places (Trenches P II, III, VI, X, XIII, XL and XLIV: see PL. XX A). In Trench P X the post-holes were found to be 6 to 7 in. (0.152–0.175 m) in diameter and the stake-holes 3 to 4 in. (0.076–0.102 m). In Trench P XIII it was observed that the posts were squared timbers measuring approximately 6 by 8 in. (0.152 by 0.204 m). Posts elsewhere in the building were of comparable size. The main uprights were set at approximately 2 ft. (0.61 m) intervals.

Several pits were dug during the demolition of the Flavian *principia*. A large one was found in Trenches P XL/XLI at the south-west corner of the courtyard; this measured *c.* 10 ft. (3.05 m) by *c.* 7 ft. (2.14 m) and extended into Rooms 1 and 5. It had truncated two of the post-holes of the colonnade, the bases of which survived beneath it (FIG. 20, Section B–C). The pit was filled with purple, red and yellow clay, presumably from the demolished walls, mixed with some earth and pebbles. Since the clay had not weathered or worn as much as the surrounding areas the pit was visible immediately below the topsoil but it was clearly of Flavian date, having been cut by a construction-trench in the Antonine I period. Another smaller pit *c.* 4 ft. (1.22 m) square was investigated in Trench P XLIV, Room 6 (FIG. 22, Section N–O); this was filled with earth, sand, charred wood, burnt daub and nails and was partly sealed by gravel (11) which seems to represent the metalling of the Antonine I courtyard.

(b) The Antonine I *Principia* (FIG. 18)

The Antonine I *principia* occupied the same position as the Flavian in the centre of the fort; indeed many of the walls were close to the lines of their predecessors. The building again took the form of a parallelogram because of the layout of the fort. It measured 75 ft. (22.86 m) north-south by 77 ft. (23.47 m) east-west and had a total area of 5,775 sq. ft. (536.5 m^2); it was thus larger than the Flavian *principia* by 48.7 m^2. Leading from the *via principalis* on the west, new metalled streets, composed of gravel over a foundation of larger stones, were laid immediately adjacent to the north and south walls of the building (PL. XX B). The full width of the south street was established as 10 ft. (3.05 m) in the southern extension to Trench P II, where the wall of the next building in the central range was also located. On the east side of the *principia* there was an unmetalled space 3 to 4 ft. (0.915–1.22 m) wide between the rear wall and the *via quintana*, which was also now metalled for the first time. This street was again observed in the western extension to Trench E II (p. 95); here the rear wall of the barrack in the southern *retentura* was *c.* 9 ft. (2.76 m) away from the rear of the *principia*, the street's metalling being only *c.* 4 ft. (1.22 m) wide. The corresponding barrack in the northern *retentura* was sited further away from the *principia* as Trench P I revealed. The *via quintana* was bordered by a gutter *c.* 10 in. (0.25 m) wide and 8 in. (0.20 m) deep, which was traced in Trenches P I, II, IV, XI and XIII. The shallow trench for the gutter was cut into the Flavian demolition-layer and was sealed by that of the Antonine I period;

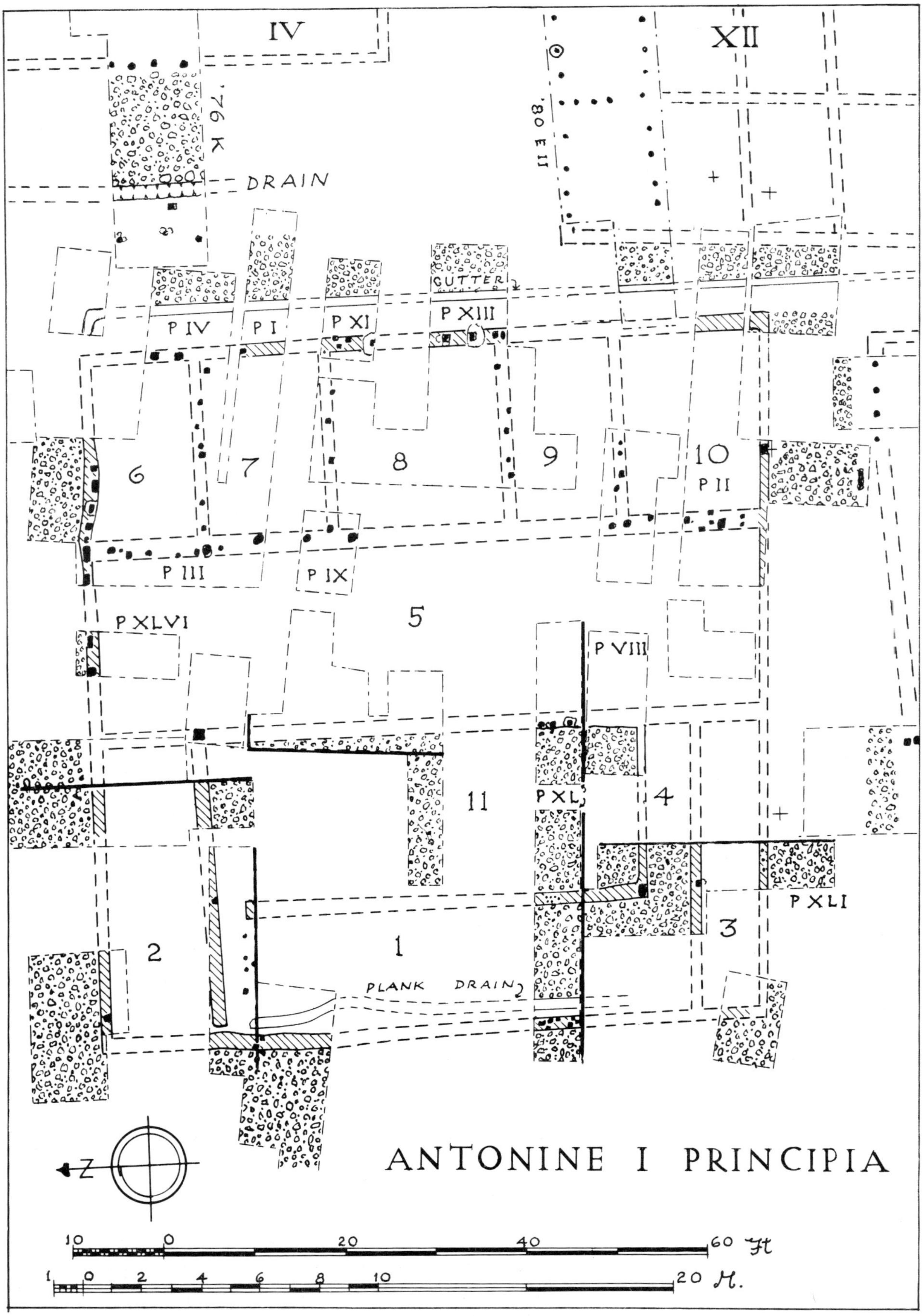

FIG. 18. The Antonine I *principia*. Scale, 1:192.

it was also cut by a stone-filled Antonine I demolition-pit in Trench P IV. The gutter had a lower fill of loose brown earth and an upper fill of burnt daub

The internal layout of the Antonine I *principia* conformed to the norm described on p. 35. The front range of the building was organized around a narrow courtyard (No. 11); this measured 47 ft. (14.34 m) north-south by 18 ft. (5.49 m) east-west and had an area of 846 sq. ft. (78.87 m^2). The courtyard, although of different shape, was thus similar in area to that of the Flavian *principia*. It had a metalling of gravel and pebbles 3 to 6 in. (0.076 to 0.152 m) thick laid over a make-up of earth and gravel; the surface lay directly beneath the metalling of the Antonine II courtyard. As in the Flavian period the gravel floor was observed to extend into the rooms lying south and west of the courtyard (Rooms 1 and 4), although at the north end of Room 1 the floor had changed to yellow sand. In both the floor was covered with a layer of brown earth containing burnt daub and charcoal from the demolition. Room 1, west of the court at the front of the *principia*, measured 51 ft. 6 in. (15.70 m) by 12 ft. (3.66 m), but the northern end was cut off 2 ft. 6 in. (0.76 m) from the wall by a row of stake-holes, which perhaps defined a passage to the courtyard.

An internal drain, running north-south, started near this partition and ran southwards in Room 1 *c*. 1 ft. inside the front wall. The trench for the drain was 11 in. (0.28 m) wide and about the same in depth (FIGS. 20, 21, Sections C–D, G–H). That it was once plank-lined is indicated by the discovery of several 2¼-in. nails pointing inwards horizontally from the sides of the trench. The presence of a drain in this position is unexpected; it perhaps implies a wide or even multiple entrance to the building, which faces the prevailing winds.

Room 4 measured 19 ft. (5.8 m) by 5 ft. (1.52 m), probably serving as a corridor. The similarity of the flooring of these rooms and of the courtyard suggests that they too saw much foot-traffic. The row of close-set stake-holes in the wall-trench on the west of the court noted in Trench P XL, however, indicates that Room 1 was separated from the courtyard not by an open colonnade but by a wattle and daub wall, through which there may have been a central entrance in addition to that at the north end. The two other rooms in the front were separate from the courtyard and would have had a more secluded function as stores or offices. They may be recognized as *armamentaria* (see p. 35, note 1). Room 2 to the north measured 32 ft. (9.75 m) by 10 ft. (3.05 m) and Room 3, probably entered from the corridor (Room 4), was 32 ft. (9.75 m) by 6 ft. (1.83 m). Both rooms had yellow sandy floors; the stratigraphical relationship of the floor was established in Trench P XLI (FIG. 21, Section J–L (13)), where it was observed to lie above the Flavian demolition-material and below that of the Antonine I period.

The cross-hall or *basilica* (Room 5) ran the full width of the building on the east side of the courtyard. The internal dimensions were 73 ft. (22.25 m) north-south by 20 ft. (6.1 m) east-west; no internal features were noted. The cross-hall floor was observed in Trenches P III, VIII, IX and XLVI, as a layer of coarse sand and fine gravel *c*. 2 in. (0.05 m) thick over a layer of pebbly earth make-up; the latter included patches of daub and charcoal, redeposited Flavian demolition material.

The rear range of the *principia* was divided as usual into five rooms, all 20 ft. (6.1 m) deep internally. The central room (Room 8) was almost square, being 18 ft. (5.49 m) wide; this is to be identified as the *aedes*. To the south were Rooms 9 and 10, 11 ft. (3.35 m) and 15 ft. (4.57 m) wide respectively, and to the north were Rooms 7 and 6, 13 ft. (3.96 m) and 11 ft. (3.35 m) wide. The floor of the *aedes* was identified in Trench P X; it consisted of a layer of yellow sand *c*. 1 in. (0.025 m) thick overlying a layer of earth and burnt daub and sealed by Antonine I demolition-material.

The Antonine I *principia*, in contrast to the contemporary barracks, was mainly constructed with posts set in construction-trenches rather than in post-pits. The construction-trenches were, however, frequently shallow with deeper post-holes dug into them, and they were difficult to trace during excavation. These trenches were dug into the Flavian levels, sometimes cutting Flavian features, for example the large pit at the south-west corner of the Flavian courtyard (Trench P XLI). The trenches were sealed by Antonine I demolition-material and their upper fill included charcoal and purple building-clay. The construction-trenches were of varying size, being 9 to 12 in. (0.23–0.30 m) wide and 8 in. to 1 ft. 6 in. (0.20–0.46 m) deep; in the shallower trenches the posts and stakes were driven deep, usually *c*. 1 ft. 6 in. (0.46 m) below the

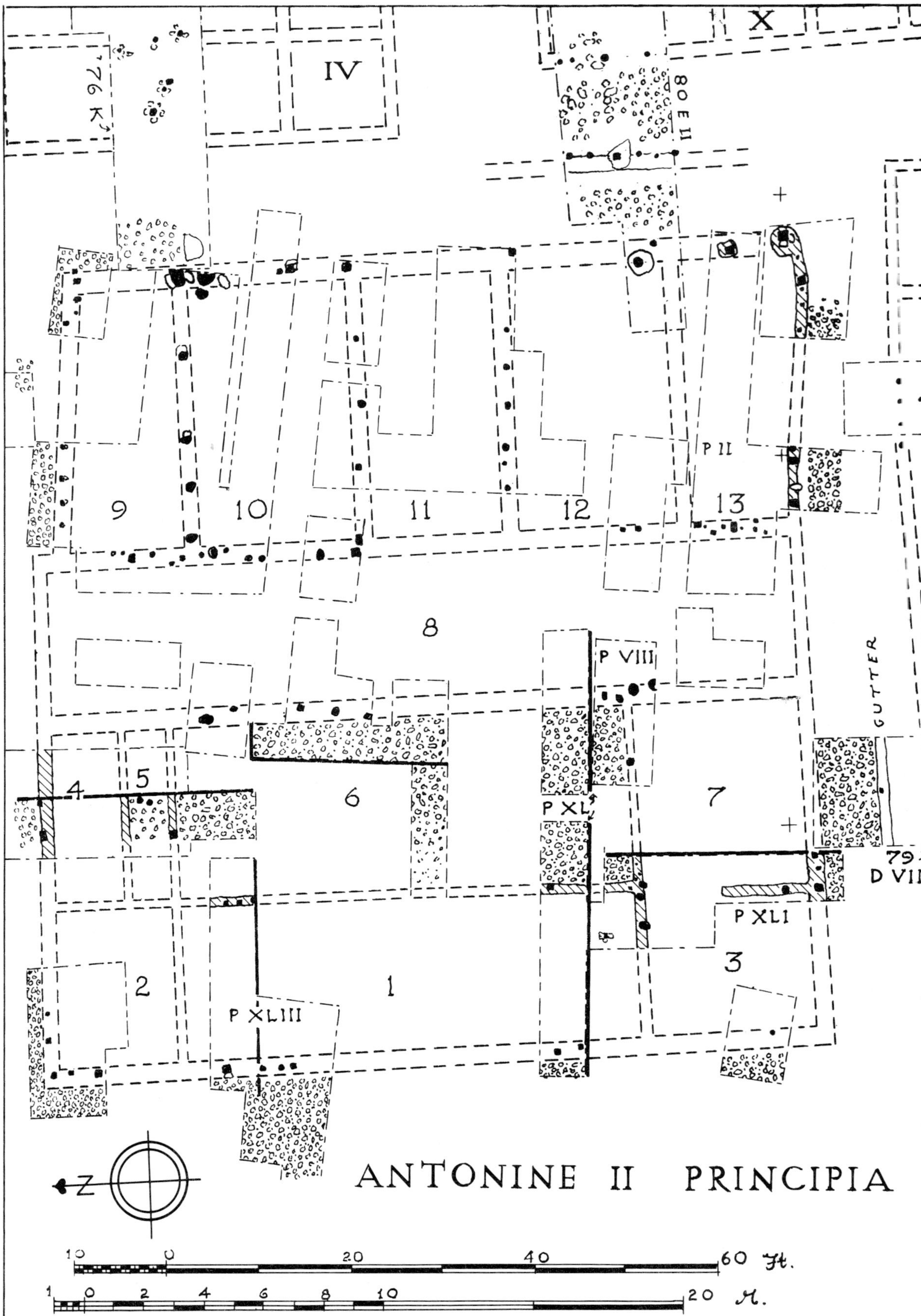

FIG. 19. The Antonine II *principia*. Scale, 1:192.

ground-surface. The stake- and post-pipes were easy to distinguish as they had a much darker fill than the rest of the trench. The main uprights were *c.* 8 in. (0.204 m) in diameter and these were held in place with stone packers, for example the corner post in Trench P XLI, which also rested on a stone plate. Between the posts were smaller stake-holes; in Trench P XL these were set close together in parallel rows presumably for interweaving of the wattles. There were signs that timbers were removed during demolition, perhaps for reuse; the delving around a post-hole in the east extension to P XL suggested that the post had been dug out.

(c) The Antonine II *Principia* (FIG. 19)

The Antonine II *principia* was larger and also more rectangular than its predecessors, encroaching onto the earlier adjacent streets on all four sides: the post-holes for its outer walls were dug through the metalling of these. Apart from the *via principalis*, the contemporary streets were very narrow and all lay immediately adjacent to the walls; their gravel surfaces had suffered plough-damage (PL. XX B). The widest, on the south side of the building, was 6 ft. 6 in. (1.98 m) wide in Trench 1979 D VII, but the metalling had narrowed to only 4 ft. (1.22 m) in the extension to Trench P II further east.

This *principia* was somewhat irregular in shape, but measured 85 ft. (25.91 m) north-south by 88 ft. (26.82 m) east-west and had a total area of 7480 sq. ft. (694.91 m^2). Except in the courtyard, the whole site had been covered with a layer of make-up, before the rebuilding, which sealed the Antonine I demolition-layer. This make-up was visible in all the trenches as a deposit of red-brown pebbly soil with many amphora sherds lying horizontally in it; the thickness of the make-up was variable, being 3 in. (0.08 m) in Trench P XL (FIG. 20, Section C–D (4)) and 8 in. (0.20 m) in Trench P XLIII (FIG. 21, Section F–H (3)). The make-up lay immediately below the ploughsoil and consequently the floors of the *principia*, except in part of the courtyard, have been lost.

The internal layout of the *principia* generally conformed to the norm for auxiliary forts. The front range was again organized around a narrow central courtyard (No. 6); this measured 49 ft. (14.93 m) north-south by 19 ft. (5.79 m) east-west and had an area of 931 sq. ft. (86.44 m^2). The gravel floor of the yard seen in all trenches cut there (FIGS 20–23, Sections B–C, F–G, N–O, R–S) had been laid immediately over the Antonine I metalling. Since the floor lay immediately below the topsoil, it had suffered plough-damage; deep plough-scores were visible in Trench P VIII and an iron ferrule from a modern plough was found embedded in the gravel.

The courtyard was enclosed on the north, south and west by a series of rooms of various sizes and not by open porticoes; the Antonine II *principia* thus showed greater resemblance to Continental rather than to British examples. The rooms are to be interpreted as vestibule, *armamentaria* and offices. The largest, Room 1, separated the courtyard from the *via principalis* and served as an entrance-hall, 49 ft. 6 in. (15.09 m) long by 16–17 ft. (4.88–5.18 m) wide. At the south-west corner lay Room 3 (18 ft. (5.49 m) by 15 ft. (4.57 m)), divided from Room 7 (18 ft. (5.49 m) by 20 ft. (6.1 m)) by a wall extending half way across their width. The wall dividing Room 2 (13 ft. (3.96 m) by 16 ft. (4.88 m)) from Room 1 was not located, but can be supposed to lie on the same line as the southern wall of Room 5. To the north of the courtyard lay Rooms 4 and 5; the latter was perhaps an open portico, being narrow, 18 ft. (5.49 m) by 4 ft. (1.22 m), and having a pebbly gravel floor similar to that of the yard; it gave acess to Room 4 which measured 18 ft. (5.49 m) by 7 ft. (2.13 m).

To the east of the courtyard lay the *basilica* (Room 8); this ran the full width of the building and was 81 ft. (24.69 m) long by 15 ft. 6 in. (4.72 m) wide. Again no internal features were noted and the floor above the make-up had been lost through ploughing. The rear range was, as usual, composed of five symmetrically-arranged rooms. The width of the building was slightly reduced in this range. All five rooms were 28 ft. (8.53 m) deep internally. The central room or *aedes* (Room 11) was 14 ft. (4.27 m) wide and was flanked on each side by a large room 17 ft. (5.18 m) wide (Rooms 10 and 12) and a small corner-room with a width of 11 ft. (3.35 m) (Rooms 9 and 13).

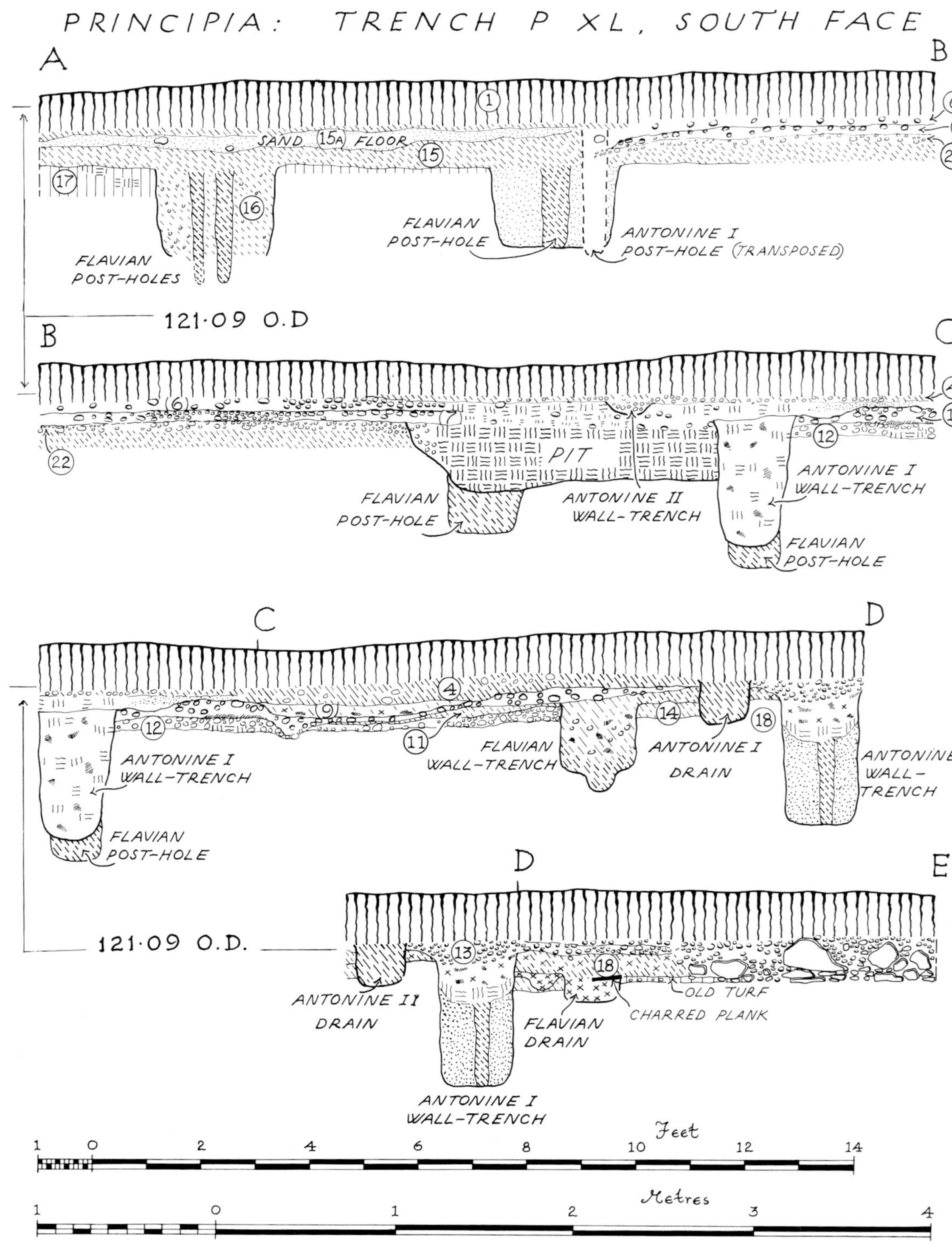

FIG. 20. The *principia*: Sections A-E. Scale, 1:35.

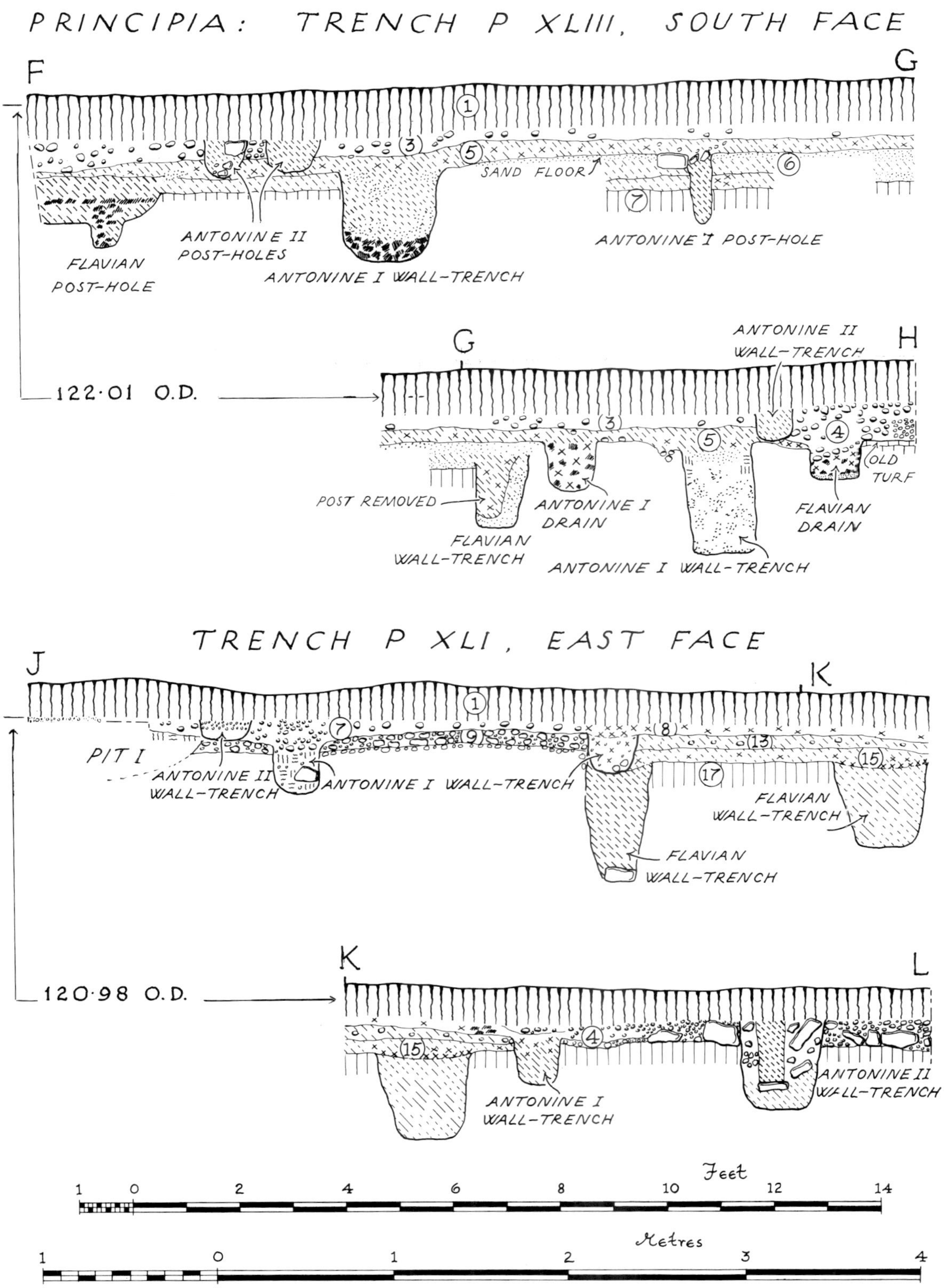

FIG. 21. The *principia*: Sections F-L. Scale, 1:35.

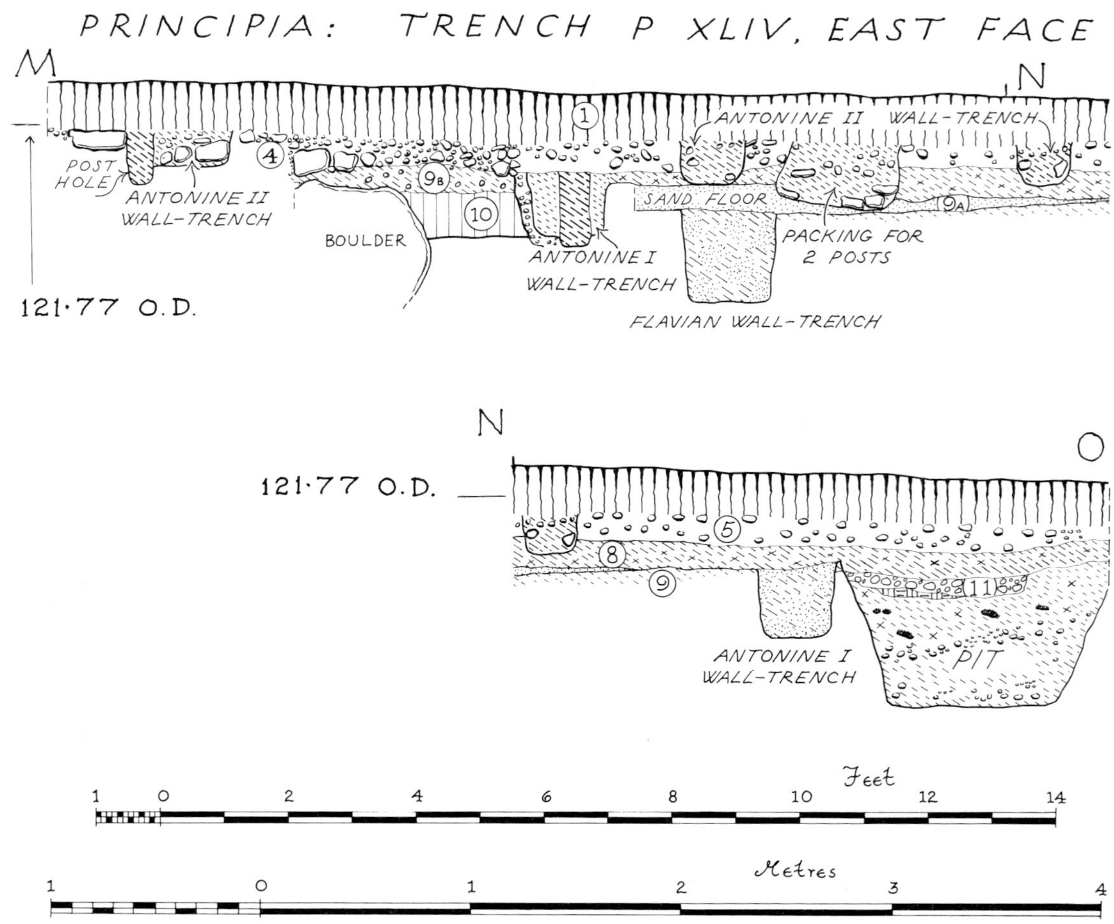

FIG. 22. The *principia*: Sections M-O. Scale, 1:35.

In 1974 it had been thought that the Antonine II *principia* was of post-in-pit construction as were the barracks of that period, since, on the whole, only post-holes and not trenches were observed; only in the south wall of Room 13 had a construction-trench been located; it was 1 ft. (0.305 m) deep. Then in the better conditions of 1975 it was observed that continuous trenches had been used, at least in the front range; unlike the construction-trenches of the Flavian period these were generally very shallow, ranging from 4 in. (0.10 m) in Trench P XLI (FIG. 21, Section J–K) to 6 in. (0.15 m) in Trench P XLIII (Section G–H); but the external south wall in Trench P XLI (Section K–L) was 1 ft. 8 in. (0.51 m) deep and the post there, near the junction of Rooms 3 and 7, had rested on a flat stone base-plate placed 5 in. (0.13 m) above the bottom of the trench; this arrangement may have been caused by the post being found too short to stand on the bottom of the trench. The shallower trenches may have been dug only as guides to the placing of the posts, which were then set in holes dug deeper at the appropriate points. Their shallowness and almost immediate backfilling, combined with the soil conditions during excavation and the fact that the trenches lay immediately below the ploughsoil, made them very difficult to locate. It is probable that they existed throughout the building despite inability to distinguish them during excavation in 1974. In contrast, the post-holes were easy to locate, having a dark brown fill with some charcoal accumulated during demolition; moreover large packing stones were almost always present. The post-holes varied between 8 in. (0.204 m) and 16 in. (0.408 m) in depth, the deepest being at the corners. The timbers themselves were also of various sizes ranging from 4 in. (0.102 m) across to 1 ft. (0.305 m) at the south-east corner of the building. Many posts were *c.* 8 in. (0.204 m) across with smaller posts between and larger ones at key structural points; the timbers appeared to have been squared. On demolition the timbers were removed and the holes became filled with demolition-material. Elsewhere the demolition-material had, however, been dispersed, and the Antonine II features were sealed by the lower ploughsoil.

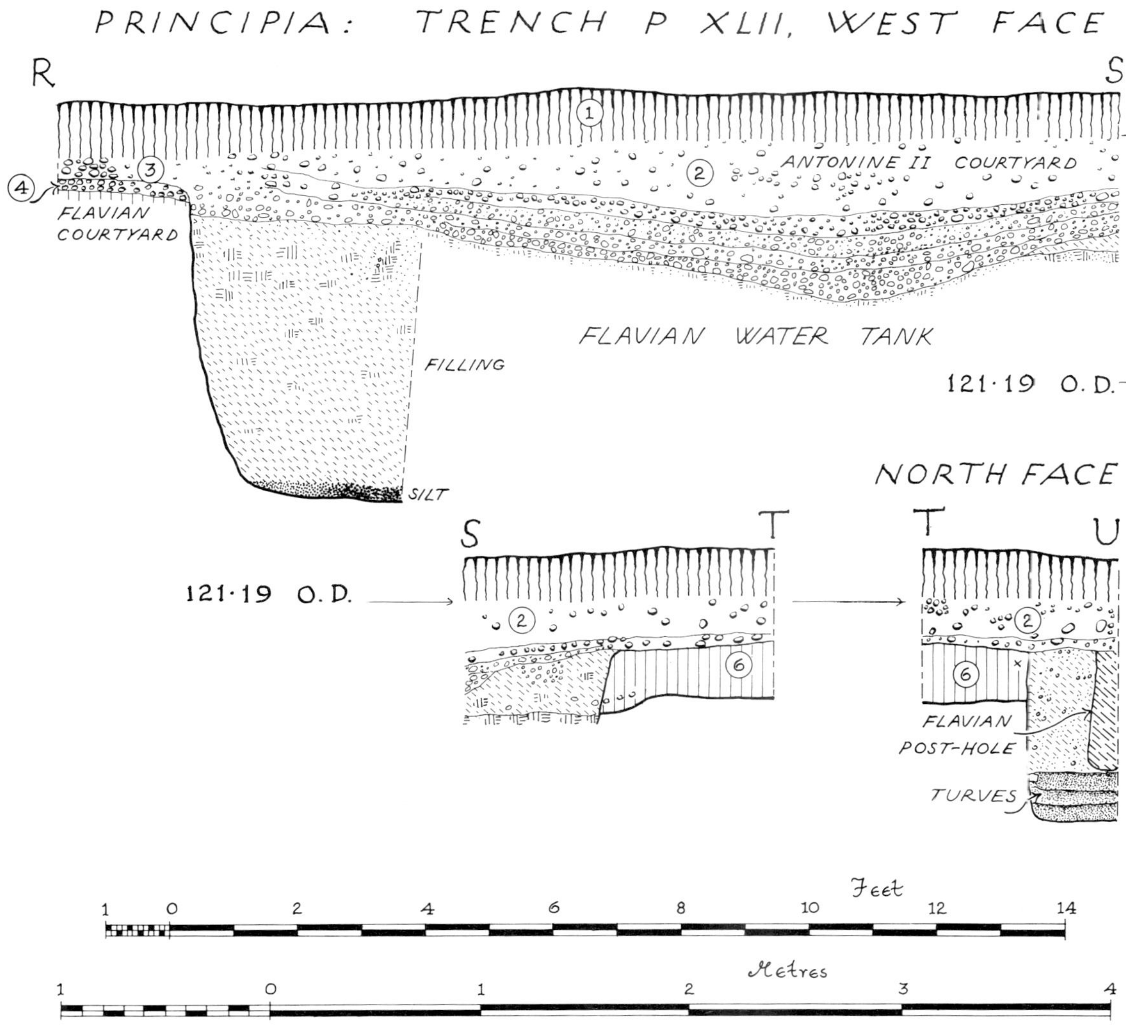

FIG. 23. The *principia*: Sections R-U. Scale, 1:35.

When Trench E II was dug in 1980 and extended across the area between Building X and the *principia* an additional wall-trench was found which is taken to indicate an extension to the rear of the latter (FIG. 19). The wall was inserted in the *via quintana*, reducing its width to 10 ft. (3.05 m) (p. 98). The post-holes associated with this trench lay not along its central line but at or in the eastern edge. The trench itself was 1 ft. (0.30 m) deep and 1 ft. 6 in. (0.46 m) wide, being cut through Antonine I and Flavian levels to natural subsoil, and it was sealed only by the ploughsoil. Thus its date was clearly in the Antonine II period and as it was cut through the *via quintana* of that date, the wall was presumably a secondary feature.

The trench had an upper fill of pebbly loam overlying a layer of loose gravel; a group of iron hobnails in the shape of the sole of a shoe (FIG. 91, No. 220) was discovered in this gravel; a secondary group of hobnails with a less definite outline was also noted. The line of post-holes was situated some 10 ft. (3.05 m) east of the rear wall of the *principia* as established in previous excavations, and two post-holes belonging to this latter wall were found in the extension to Trench E II. The outer row of post-holes should perhaps be interpreted as a corridor or enclosed portico bordering the street at the rear of the *principia* or as a simple extension to the normal plan called for by the extra administrative needs of two units in one fort.

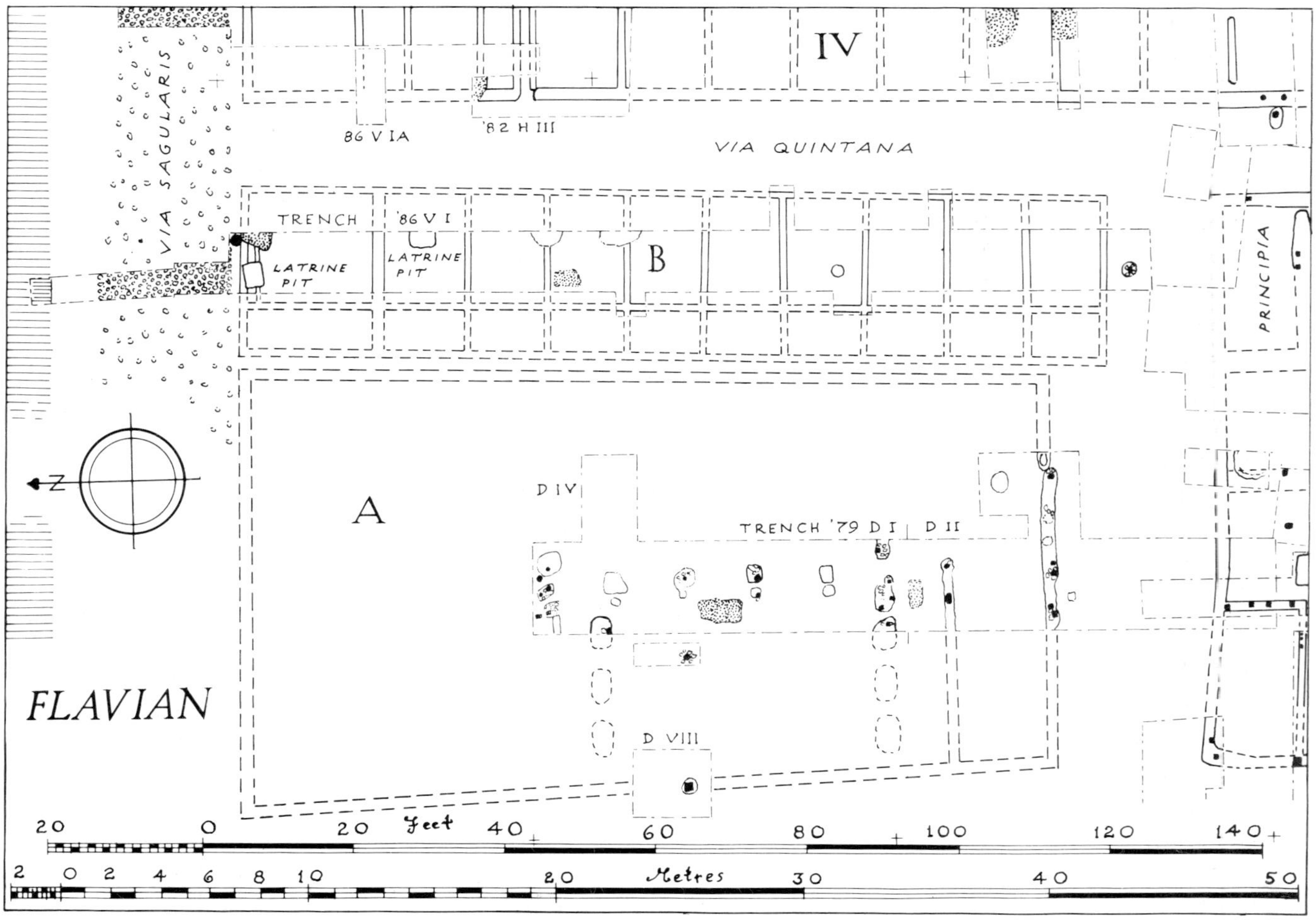

FIG. 24. The Central Range north of the *principia*: Flavian plan. Scale, 1:298.

II. NORTH OF THE PRINCIPIA (FIGS. 24–27)

Over the whole area of Trench V I, and particularly at its northern end, the stratification was very thin because of a rise in the natural sand below this part of the fort (p. 57); this caused considerable difficulty to the separation of Flavian from Antonine features and still more to the separation of the two Antonine levels.

Flavian (FIG. 24)

The northern *via sagularis*, separated from the rampart by a space of 6 ft. (1.83 m), was 17 ft. 6 in. (5.33 m) wide. Within it this part of the Central Range was occupied by two buildings, the Commander's house (*praetorium*, Building A) and a long block resembling a barrack (Building B). The whole length of the latter was revealed in Trench V I and the external east wall was located in two small extensions to the Trench. Two other extensions, on the west side of V I, revealed a parallel wall-trench across which the partitions continued, showing that the building consisted of two ranges of rooms.

The overall length of **Building B** in Trench V I is 115 ft. 3 in. (35.13 m), and it was divided into ten pairs of rooms. In the eastern row the depth of the rooms was 14 ft. (4.27 m); eight of them were 10 ft. (3.01 m) wide, but the ninth had a width of 10 ft. 6 in. (3.20 m), while the end room was larger still with a width of 16 ft. 6 in. (5.03 m). In this room a second construction-trench, only 8 in. (0.20 m) wide, ran parallel with the north wall of the building and only 14 in. (0.36 m) from it. This may have supported some item of furniture. At the eastern side of V I both walls had been destroyed by a large demolition pit, but the inner wall-trench had also been cut by what was taken to be a latrine-pit. This measured 3 ft. by 2 ft. 6 in. (0.91 by 0.76 m) and was 3 ft. deep, the sides being cut vertically in the soft sand and so clearly having been once timber-lined. The filling consisted of large lumps of red sandstone, no doubt cast in at the time of demolition. A second latrine pit was found in the next room to the south, but whether it is of Flavian or Antonine date is uncertain; it is marked on all three plans. The pit was 3 ft. 6 in. (1.07 m) wide by perhaps 2 ft. 6 in. (0.76 m), and had a depth of 2 ft. 11 in. (0.89 m). A large stone-packed post-hole was found 3 ft. (0.91 m) beyond the south end of the building; this may possibly represent a narrow portico along this side. It lay 10 ft. (3.05 m) from the north wall of the *principia*.

At the time of excavation Building B was taken to represent the rear range of the *praetorium*. But there are difficulties which make another interpretation preferable. First, if Building B was really part of the *praetorium* the area of the latter would amount to over 790 m^2, a figure larger by 160 m^2 than the area of the *praetorium* at Fendoch (629.9 m^2) and 192 m^2 larger than that at Pen Llystyn (598 m^2). Secondly, the south end of Building B does not align with the south wall in Trench D II, there assigned to Building A. And thirdly, whereas the construction-trenches on Site D were notably large, those in Trench V I (except in the most northerly room) were remarkably slight, being only 9 in. (0.23 m) wide and *c.* 4 in. (0.10 m) deep. This shallow depth, it is true, may be partly explained by the rise in the natural sand mentioned earlier and the consequent disturbance of Flavian levels by Antonine I occupation; but their narrow width cannot be so explained, and it suggests that (exceptionally at Strageath) this building may have rested on sleeper beams. The contrasted depths of sleeper-trenches and post-trenches at Corbridge was noted by J.P. Gillam.[3]

In the possession of ten pairs of rooms Building B resembles a barrack, although it is over 10 m shorter than other barracks at Strageath. But if the length (35.13 m) is compared with the figures given in TABLE III (p. 136) for the lengths of *contubernia* alone, excluding the lengths of their officers' quarters, there is a close resemblance. It is clear that no centurion was resident here, but the extra size of the end room suggests that the building was controlled by someone of lower rank such as an *optio* or *tesserarius*.

Similar buildings are not unknown in the central ranges of forts. The best parallels are in successive forts at Corbridge,[4] where J.P. Gillam termed them administrative blocks, explaining that the plan with up to 10 *contubernia* implied use by personnel, while location in the Central Range suggests some connection with administration. It was not implied explicitly that the building itself was used for administrative purposes, and perhaps Staff Quarters would be a more apt description.

It is, however, perhaps unlikely that as many as nine full *contubernia* amounting to 72 men, would be needed for administration in any normal auxiliary fort, and unless special circumstances can be shown to be present it may be preferable to see this building as housing transport vehicles or bulky stores such as tents, or even perhaps as stables.[5] Yet the need for additional administrative staff at Flavian Strageath cannot be ruled out, as is suggested on pp. 122–3.

Building B probably faced the *via quintana*, for there is hardly space for an alleyway between it and the *praetorium*. The rear rooms have been restored with an internal depth of only 5 ft. (1.52 m), in order to allow as much space for the *praetorium* as possible (see below). If this is correct, and if these rooms were sleeping-quarters, they would not accommodate more than two men

3. *Arch. Ael.*[5] v (1977), 51, 53–4.
4. *Arch. Ael.*[5] v (1977), 47–74, especially pp. 58, 62. Others exist at Pen Llystyn (*Arch. Journ.* cxxv (1969), fig. 19, building labelled 'hospital', and also at Housesteads (Building 7). Comparison should also be made with the ranges of rooms behind the *principia* in successive forts at Valkenburg (W. Glasbergen and W. Groenman-van Waateringe, *The Pre-Flavian Garrisons of Valkenburg Z.H.* (Amsterdam, 1974), fig. 9.
5. Compare the stables at Dormagen (G. Müller, *Ausgrabungen in Dormagen 1963–1977* (Koln/Bonn, 1979), Taf. 15) or those recently found at Krefeld-Gellep, both of which however were distinguished by large sump-pits.

each, whether drivers, grooms or store-keepers; if on the other hand the rooms were for equipment, their relative inaccessibility suggests that the *contubernia* concerned were detached from the fighting strength.

The *praetorium* (**Building A**) lay west of B. Its south wall in Trench D II lay 21 ft. (6.4 m) from the north wall of the *principia*, but was set back *c.* 7 ft. (2.13 m) from the south wall of Building B. Very little of the plan of the *praetorium* was recovered: the positions of the north and south walls is approximately fixed, but the E–W dimension depends on the width allowed to Building B. The outline as restored measures *c.* 109 ft. (33.22 m) north-south by *c.* 56 ft. (17.07 m) giving an area of 567 m^2. This compares with 629.9 m^2 at Fendoch, 598.3 m^2 at Pen Llystyn and *c.* 703 m^2 at Elginhaugh. The reason why the west range of Building B could not be restored at greater depth becomes apparent.

The south wall of Building A was marked by two slightly offset lengths of wall-trench: the width of these was 1 ft. 6 in. (0.46 m), widening at post-holes to 2 ft. (0.61 m); the normal depth was 1 ft. (0.3 m) but deepening to 1 ft. 7 in. – 1 ft. 10 in. (0.54–0.56 m) at post-positions. Twelve feet (3.66 m) further north ran a parallel but shallower wall-trench which ended in the excavated area, perhaps at a doorway. Beyond this lay a courtyard or garden surrounded on three sides by a portico 7 ft. (2.3 m) wide. This was represented by an arrangement of double post-holes set in large stone-packed pits, some 8 ft. (2.44 m) apart along the east side but more closely spaced on the others. The post-positions in these pits were (exceptionally) marked by fillings of green clay, which must have entered the sockets after the removal of the posts and have been derived from demolition of the neighbouring walls. A space of 39 ft. (11.89 m) between the courtyard and the north side of the building is unexplored, as is the space of *c.* 25 ft. (7.6 m) to the east wall. The front of the building is marked by a single post-hole at the edge of the *via principalis*.

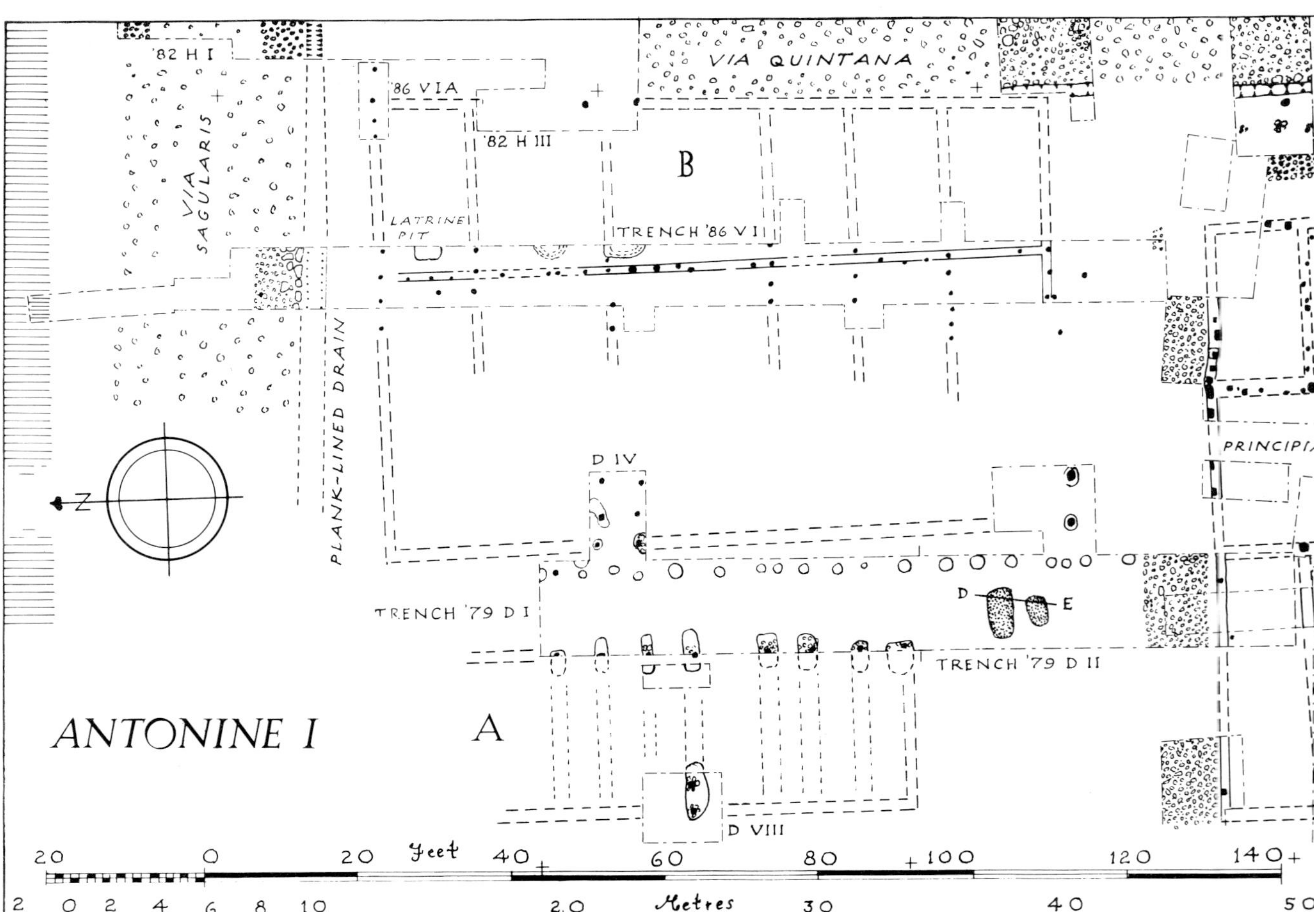

FIG. 25. The Central Range north of the *principia*. Antonine I plan. Scale, 1:298.

Antonine I (FIG. 25)

In this period the excavated area in Trench D I–II fell mainly within an open space between two buildings. The north wall of the *principia* was located near the south end of D II; outside it ran a metalled street 8 ft. (2.44 m) wide, consisting of a layer of gravel over a bedding of larger stones, in places 6 in. (0.15 m) thick in all.

Along the western edge of Trench D I–II ran a series of eight large stone-packed post-holes 1½–2½ ft. (0.46–0.76 m) deep, containing post-sockets *c.* 8 in. (0.20 m) in diameter. The discovery of a similar post-pit containing two post-holes in Trench D VIII showed that the building concerned (**Building A**) was 21 ft. (6.40 m) wide, and suggested that its form resembled that of a granary resting on parallel transverse rows of supports. The rows were 6 ft. (1.83 m) apart, but they were arranged in two groups of four separated by a gap of 8 ft. (2.44 m). It is possible that the more northerly group may have continued beyond the end of the Trench. Thus a building at least 46 ft. (14 m) long is represented, or possibly two buildings one of which is 18 ft. 6 in. (5.64 m) long and the other of identical length or longer. Building A seems likely to have been a granary, but further excavation is needed to confirm the identification: one difficulty is that no second pair of post-holes was found within Trench D VIII. The width (6.40 m) is narrow for a granary but not unparalleled. The other Antonine I granary at Strageath, Building XIII in the south *praetentura* (p. 110), has a width of 24 ft. (7.32 m). A granary at Hod Hill is 6.48 m wide, and two at Old Kilpatrick had widths of 5.49 and 6.10 m respectively.[6] It is tempting to compare the present building with the granaries of Group 2 at Usk;[7] these were each represented by two groups of post-holes with a space of 3 m between the two halves of the building, which is assumed to have been built with a central loading platform. The overall dimensions at Usk were 20.9 by 7.5 or 7.8 m, which is rather larger than the 14 by 6.4 m at Strageath.

A fairly uniform Antonine I occupation-layer 3–4 in. (0.08–0.10 m) thick was seen in Trenches D I–II and D IV, as well as a demolition layer containing quantities of burnt daub. Two large demolition-pits were found in D II. The larger (p. 56, FIG. 31, Section D–E) measured 6 by 3½ ft. (1.83 m by 1.07 m) and was 3 ft. (0.91 m) deep. Both yielded large amounts of burnt daub and charcoal. Burning of the sand at the base of the larger pit suggested that a bonfire had been lit in it during demolition. Some of the larger pieces of charcoal appeared to be from planks. Beside the street bordering the *principia* in Trench D II a small hoard of metal objects was found in the occupation-layer (6); it included an iron axe-head, hinged iron bars and a bronze object of uncertain function (p. 150, FIG. 75).

Building B. Along the east side of Trench D I–II ran a line of somewhat enigmatic features which was separated from Building A by a gap of 10 ft. (3.1 m). They first showed as a row of damp patches remaining after rain had elsewhere dried up, and showing through the thin Antonine II pebbly layer which sealed them – a phenomenon which has betrayed other deeply-cut features at Strageath. The tops of the features were thus clearly defined, as were their rounded bottoms cut into the yellow soil below; but the actual filling of brown loam was very difficult to differentiate either by colour or by texture from the surrounding layer: in this they differed from normal post-holes. Possibly they represented the seatings of stone pads for the support of uprights, the stones themselves having been removed. On the other hand the row is irregular for a colonnade and its function remains puzzling, especially as it extends further towards the *principia* than the apparent building-line behind it. Four to five feet (1.22–1.52 m) behind this line was found the normal post-holes of a building, but its nature is unknown.

Trench V I lay in the part of the fort where, as already mentioned, natural sand rises close to the surface; little stratification survived to differentiate the three periods of building. In this Trench the whole length of Building B was traced; both the south wall and a longitudinal wall

6. See Table of Dimensions in W.H. Manning, *Saalburg Jahrbuch* xxxii (1975), 116.
7. *Ibid.*, 123.

were marked by shallow construction-trenches into which posts had been driven; either side of the longitudinal wall lay rooms of varying widths.

The external east wall lay at the edge of the *via quintana* where two post-holes had previously been located in Trench 82 H III. A small Trench (V I A) was dug to trace the north-east corner. Here the natural sand was particularly close to the surface and somewhat disturbed; a line of post-holes was however seen on the expected line. The east wall is not parallel with the median wall, and the rooms here varied between 18 and 21 ft. (5.49–6.40 m) in depth.

Whether Building B extended as far west as the post-holes found in the eastward extensions to trench D I–II is uncertain. The latter were larger (8 in. = 0.20 m in diameter and set in post-pits 9–12 in. (0.23–0.3 m) deep) and are not quite in line.

The southern end of Building B yielded evidence that it had been an equipment store. Twenty-three fired-clay sling-bullets were found scattered here (FIG. 26), together with an iron spearhead, a horse's bit and a bronze cart-fitting (FIG. 74, No. 50). Towards the north end a demolition-pit in one room and a latrine-pit in another are not certainly of this period.

Building B was separated by a space of 7 ft. (2.13 m) from the plank-lined *intervallum* drain, here with its peg-holes clearly defined (PL. XXI A). It was 3 ft. (0.91 m) wide at the top and 1 ft. 7 in. (0.48 m) wide between the stakes: the depth was 1 ft. (0.3 m) and the base lay at 120.89 ft. (36.85 m) O.D. The stakes were spaced at 2-ft. (0.61-m) intervals. The outer edge of the drain had a kerb of flat stones, beyond which lay traces of the *via sagularis*, the outer edge of which had been ploughed away.

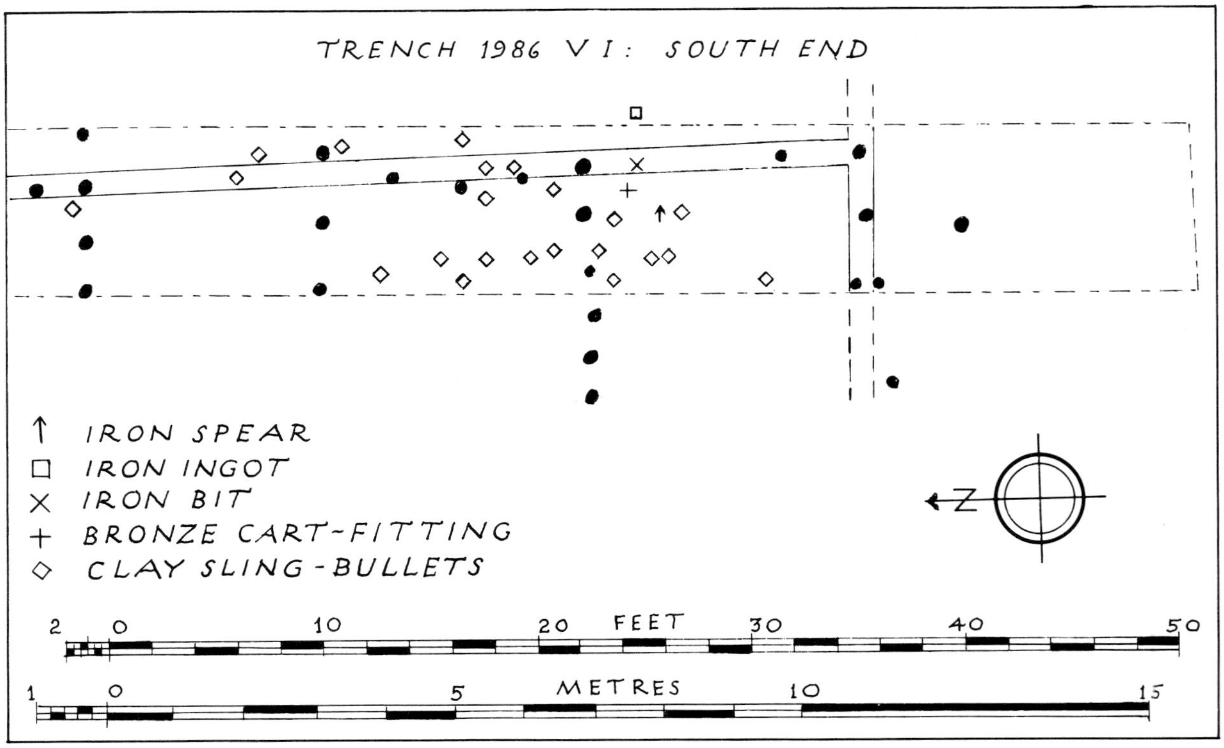

FIG. 26. Antonine I Building B: distribution of finds. Scale, 1:108. (For position see FIG. 25).

Antonine II (FIG. 27)

The area north of the *principia* in this period seems to have been entirely occupied by a large *praetorium* (**Building A**), so identified by the irregular arrangement of rooms; it measured 101–102 ft. (30.48–31.09 m) from north to south and *c.* 79–86 ft. (24.08–26.21 m) from east to west, giving an area of *c.* 778.5 m^2. The front wall was marked by post-holes in Trench D VIII along the edge of the *via principalis*, but the back wall was not located and is restored in line with

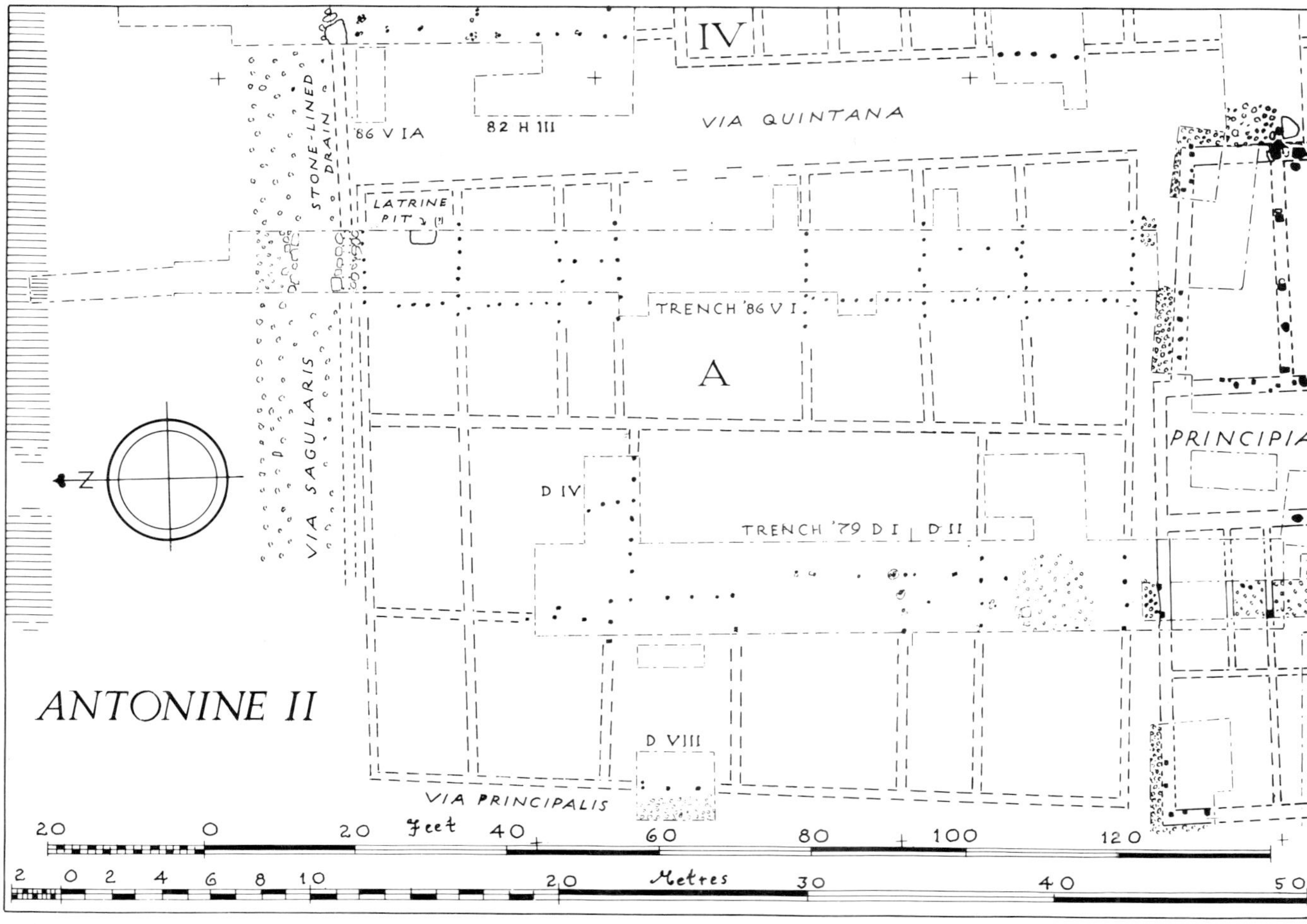

FIG. 27. The Central Range north of the *principia*. Antonine II plan. Scale, 1:298.

the rear of the *principia*. A very narrow but metalled alley, only *c.* 3 ft. (0.9 m) wide at its narrowest divided it from the latter building. The east end of the building, seen in Trench V I, consisted of two ranges, each three rooms wide, separated by a yard 25 ft. (7.62 m) wide. The contemporary occupation-layer had been entirely ploughed away in V I and only the bases of the post-holes survived. They were up to 6 in. (0.15 m) deep and normally 4–6 in. (0.10–0.15 m) in diameter, and (as often in the Antonine II buildings) seemed to have been driven in from above rather than set in post-pits. A bronze finial in the form of a gryphon (FIG. 74, No. 50) found in the base of the ploughsoil, though technically in an Antonine II position, may well have been ploughed up from the Antonine I layer below.

In Trench D II a thin scatter of pebbles seemed to represent the floor of the most southerly room; elsewhere a relatively hard-packed brown earth with pebbles up to 3 in. (8 cm) thick represented the remains of the flooring of this period.

At the north end of Trench V I a stone-lined drain 1 ft. (0.3 m) wide ran between the building and the *via sagularis* (PL. XXI A). Two rows of stake-holes in its floor showed that it had additionally been lined with planks. Stone-lined drains are unusual at Strageath; this one evidently continues the line of the stone-lined drain located in Trench 82 H I (p. 63). In V I the base of the drain lay at 120.33 ft. (36.68 m) O.D. In Trench H I the drain had been disturbed by a demolition-pit, and the level of the floor is uncertain. It is thought, however, to lie at *c.* 120.4 ft. (36.7 m) O.D., which gives a slight fall to the west, and the drain probably ran to an outlet at the *porta principalis dextra*.

Very little metalling of the *via sagularis* beyond the drain had survived the plough; the street appeared to be *c.* 11 ft. (3.35 m) wide, some four feet (1.22 m) wider than in Trench 85 N I further to the east (FIG. 35). Beyond it lay a wide *intervallum* space before the rear of the Flavian turf rampart was reached, 27 ft. (8.23 m) further north.

III. SOUTH OF THE PRINCIPIA (FIGS. 28, 29, 30)

Flavian (FIG. 28)

In the Central Range south of the *principia* lay two buildings separated by a largely empty space 34 ft. (10.36 m) wide, towards the west end of which, however, were found a large water-cistern and some traces of minor walls.

The Building furthest from the *principia* (**Building D**) was traced only in Trench V II, dug in 1986, for in 1979 when Trenches D V–VII were excavated this end of the field was inaccessible under a crop of beet. The Building, which adjoined the *via sagularis*, was 37 ft. 9 in. (11.51 m) wide externally and is restored with a length of 68 ft. (20.73 m), to which should probably be added the width of a veranda along its east front covering this part of the *via quintana*; the veranda was 8 ft. (2.44 m) wide, to judge by the single post-hole found. The building had a central longitudinal passage 9 ft. 3 in. (2.82 m) wide internally, flanked each side by ranges of rooms, one wider than the other. That on the south side had an internal width of 9 ft. (2.74 m) and that on the north 14 ft. 9 in. (4.50 m).

Building C, nearer the *principia* and lying some 9 ft. (2.74 m) south of it, was 45 ft. (13.72 m) wide and is restored with a length of 68 ft. (20.73 m). Like Building D it was divided longitudinally into three ranges, but here these were of almost equal width (13 ft. 3 in. – 13 ft. 6 in. = 4.04–4.11 m internally). The central section was unpartitioned at the east end and is taken to be a passage giving access to the rooms in the side ranges; but at the west or front end the passage had been partitioned to form perhaps two rooms at the entrance. The side ranges were divided into rooms 9–10 ft. (2.74–3 m) long, some of them subdivided. The construction-trenches had straight sides and flat bottoms, varying in width from 14 to 18 in. (0.36 to 0.46 m) and in depth

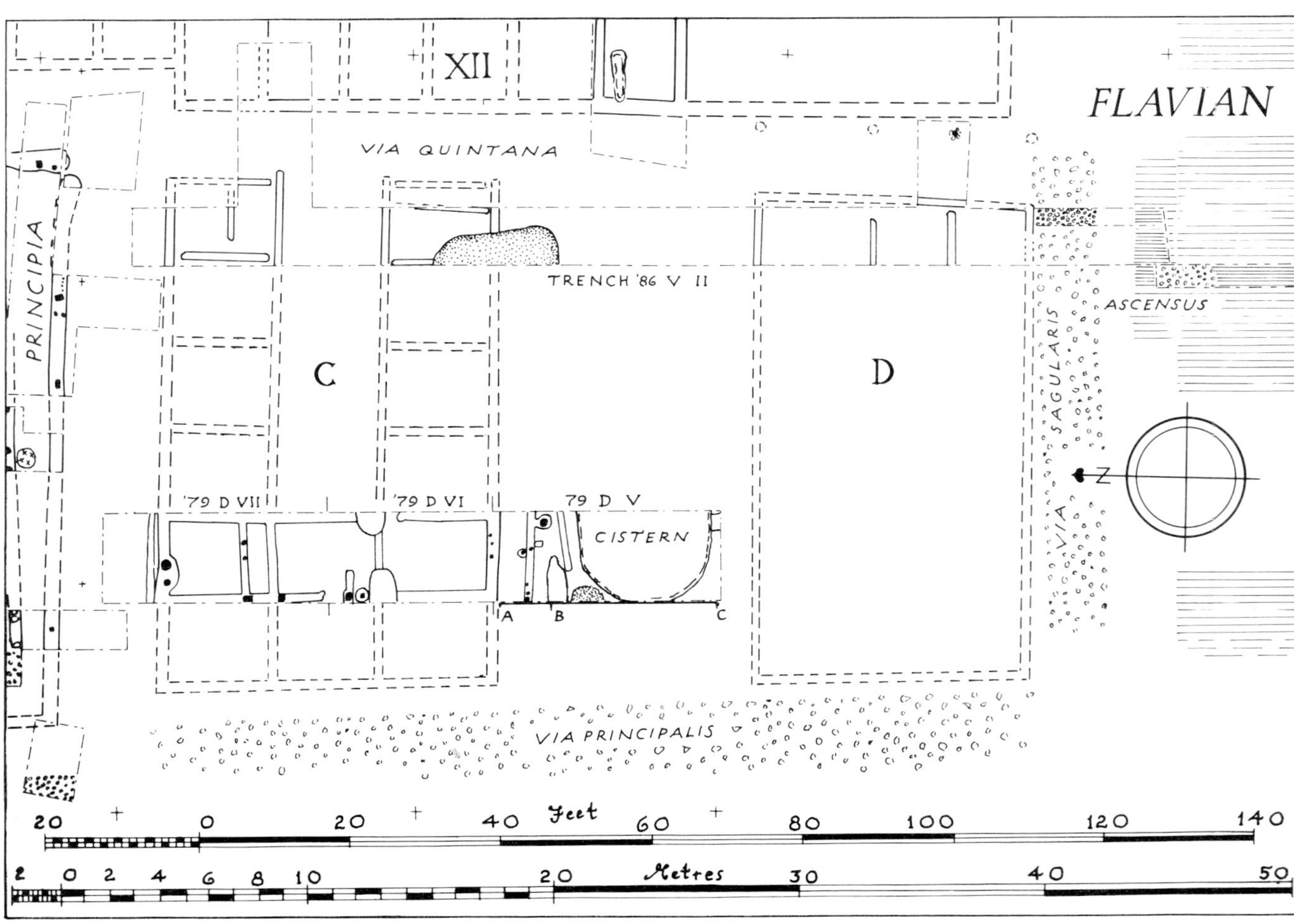

FIG. 28. The Central Range south of the *principia*. Flavian plan. Scale, 1:298.

from 8 to 12 in. (0.20 to 0.30 m), increasing to 2 ft. (0.61 m) where timbers had been set in deeper sockets. The filling was of light earth with some burnt daub at the top.

Building C is taken to be the hospital. In other examples of the type, at Fendoch[8] or Corbridge,[9] the central passage does not itself include rooms; but it is perfectly reasonable to see the front room at Strageath as a reception-room and the second room as a clinic or operating-room. It is true that the excavators of the Red House site at Corbridge[10] questioned the identification of such buildings as hospitals, but their grounds for so doing were not securely based. Building 10 at Red House was doubtless a *fabrica* as they argue, and as indeed the artefactual finds suggest; but the building bears little resemblance to the true hospital type identified at Fendoch or Corbridge, since it does not have three ranges extending the whole length of the building, nor does the central corridor extend even half-way along it.

At Strageath the south part of the Central Range of the fort was not needed for granaries because these were placed in the *praetentura*. Building D with its ranges of unequal width is not suitable either for a hospital or for stables and may be accepted as a *fabrica*. A second *fabrica* would seem to be unnecessary: the equal areas of the side rooms in Building C suit the planning of a hospital and it is noteworthy that there is space for 12 of these rooms, a total in agreement with the total of barracks in the Flavian fort. The dimensions of the buildings are similar to those found in some other hospitals (TABLE I).

TABLE I
DIMENSIONS OF HOSPITALS

Fort	Length (metres)	Width (metres)	Area of building (sq. metres)	Number of wards	Area of wards (sq. metres)
Fendoch	32.31	12.19	393.86	10	9.36
Corbridge IA	32.8	13.5	442.8	18	12
Corbridge IB	28	13.5	378	16	12
Corbridge 4 A	35	13	455	16	9
Pen Llystyn A[11]	27.3	13	354.9	12 (?)	12 (?)
Pen Llystyn B[12]	45.72	7.62	348.39	10	12.34
Strageath	20.72	13.72	284.28	12	10.85

Water-tank

Between the two buildings not far from the *via principalis* lay a large pit which was only partially excavated. It was sub-rectangular (almost octagonal) in shape, having straight almost parallel sides but with widely-rounded angles. The width was 17½–18 ft. (5.33–5.49 m) and the depth was 6 ft. 8 in. (2.03 m). The sides were cut vertically into soft sand (p. 56, FIG. 31, Section B–C) and must formerly have been timber-lined; there was also evidence for a clay lining *c.* 1 in. (2.5 cm) thick. This suggested that the pit was for holding water, as did the filling of clean turfy clay, sand and stones, a characteristic material found filling other cisterns at Strageath, but differing greatly from the filling of demolition-pits. A hollow in the top of the fill had been packed with boulders, presumably during the Antonine I construction-phase. On the assumption that the cistern was as long as it was wide, the capacity would be *c.* 1780 cubic feet (50.4 m^3) or 11,093 gallons (50,428 litres). For the water-supply of the fort and its problems, see pp. 125, 128, 130.

8. *P.S.A.S.* lxxiii (1938–9), 132–4.
9. *Arch. Ael.*[5] v (1977), 54, fig. 2.
10. *Arch. Ael.*[5] vii (1979), 18–19, 80–81.
11. This is the building attached to the *praetorium*.
12. This is the building identified as a hospital in the report.

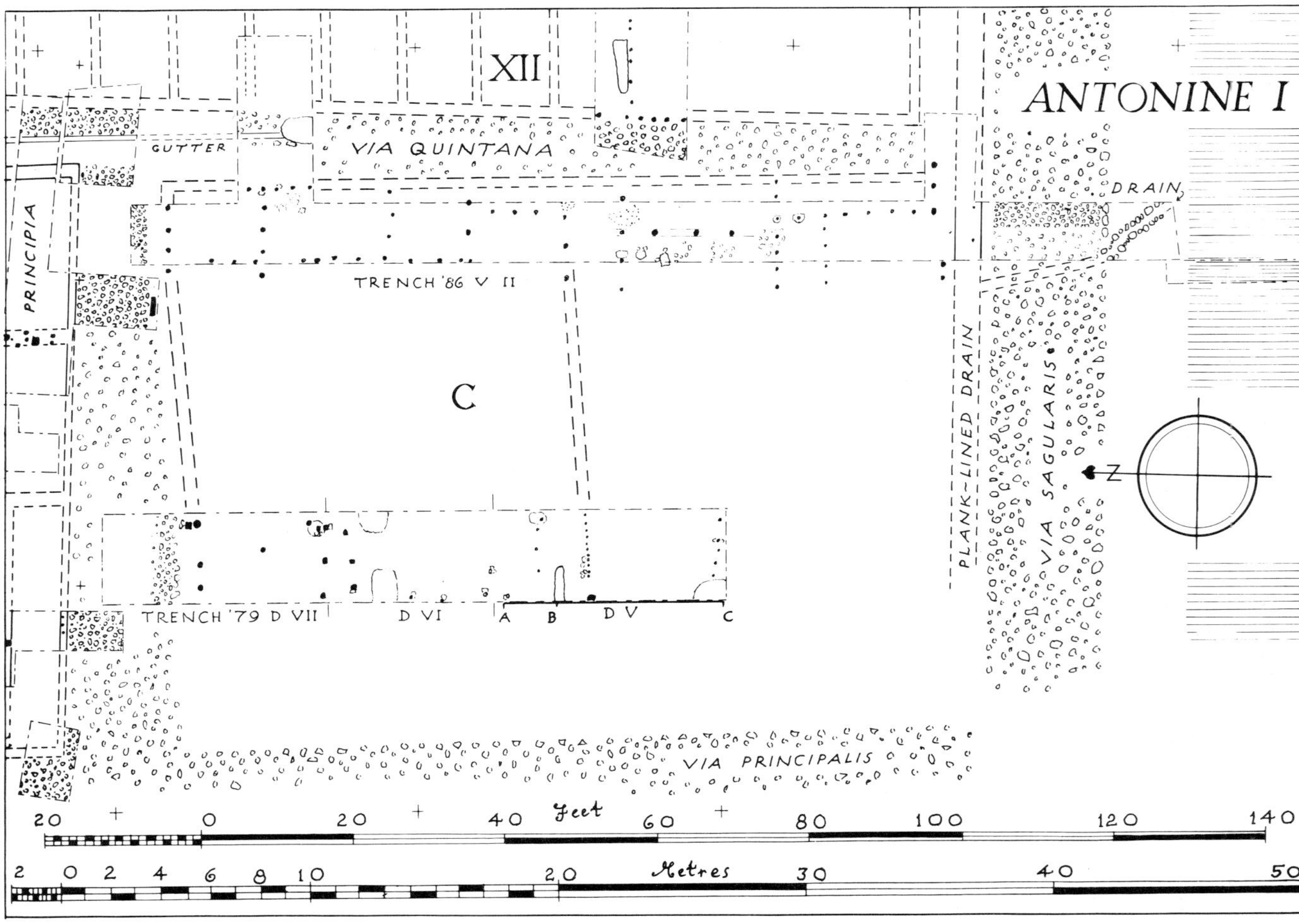

FIG. 29. The Central Range south of the *principia*. Antonine I plan. Scale, 1:298.

Antonine I (FIG. 29)

A metalled street 10–14 ft. (3.05–4.27 m) wide ran down the south side of the *principia*; as usual it was composed of a layer of fine gravel overlying a bedding of small boulders which were set in a layer of sandy soil 3 in. thick, sealing the Flavian demolition-deposit. Beyond this street in Trench V II the post-holes of two buildings were found with a space of 7 ft. (2.13 m) between them; it seems probable, however, that this space is really a corridor within the Antonine I *praetorium* (**Building C**), which should lie on this side of the *principia*. If so, the building measures 104 ft. (31.70 m) from north to south. The rear wall, adjacent to the *via quintana*, was traced in an extension to Trench V II. The front wall has not been located, but if it lies close to the *via principalis* the length of the building would have been between 72 and 75 ft. (21.95–22.86 m), giving an estimated area of *c.* 710 m^2. Unfortunately the internal arrangements are impossible to restore because of the inadequate area excavated. Most of the post-hole lines in Trench 79 D V–VII fail to correspond with those in V II, nor do they suggest anything coherent. The timber uprights had been *c.* 6 in. (0.15 m) in diameter and were set in post-pits between 6 and 12 in. (0.15–0.30 m) deep (FIG. 31, Section A–C). Traces of a gravel floor were noted in D V and there was a recognisable Antonine I occupation-level in which (in D VI) was found an As of Titus (of A.D. 77–8 (p. 000, No. 20).

At the south end of Trench V II there was deeper stratification and a better preservation of floors. These consisted of areas of sand or fine gravel which had been spread later than the erection of the walls; positions of the latter were marked by bands of clay between the areas of gravel; their widths varied from 8 to 26 in. (0.20–0.66 m). In one place, however, the line of post-holes lay beside rather than within the band of clay.

The south wall of the building, in which there was a 6 ft. (1.83 m) gap presumably marking an entrance from the *via sagularis*, ran close to the plank-lined drain bordering the inner edge of the southern *via sagularis*. This street was 15 ft. (4.57 m) wide, with a kerb of well-fitted large stones along the outer edge. Beyond it a large stone-lined drain ran obliquely out towards the rampart and, to judge by a line of dampness in the metalling, had crossed the street just west of our trench. This drain was certainly in use in the Antonine II period (p. 56) when its upper courses had been rebuilt in coarse rounded river boulders: but the original construction, in well-coursed blocks of red sandstone, was taken to be of Antonine I date (PL. XXI B). In this period it presumably gave relief to the main plank-lined drain.

Antonine II (FIG. 30)

In this period the *principia* was separated from the building on its south side by a metalled street 6 ft. (1.83 m) wide. In Trench V II there appeared to be four buildings aligned on an E–W axis. The most northerly (**Building B**) was $31\frac{1}{2}$ ft. (9.60 m) wide and consisted of two ranges of rooms, respectively 16 and 12 ft. (4.88 and 3.66 m) wide internally. Beyond a 6 ft. (1.83 m) gap **Building C** was $19\frac{1}{2}$ ft. (5.94 m) wide, also possessing two ranges of rooms with internal widths respectively of $7\frac{1}{2}$ and $8\frac{1}{2}$ ft. (2.29 and 2.59 m). A space of only 6 in. (0.15 m) separated it from **Building D**, which had a width of 20 ft. (6.10 m). Finally, beyond a gap of 18 in. (0.46 m) lay **Building E**, having a width of 30 ft. (9.14 m) and two ranges of rooms, respectively 11 and $15\frac{1}{2}$ ft (3.35 and 4.72 m) wide internally. The eastern wall of Building B was located in an extension to Trench V II on a line 6 ft. (1.83 m) east of the line of the rear wall of the *principia*. The east wall of Building D had been found previously in Trench 1981 F II (FIG. 58), where a fine sandy gravel floor was observed overlying the Antonine I demolition-layer in the end room.

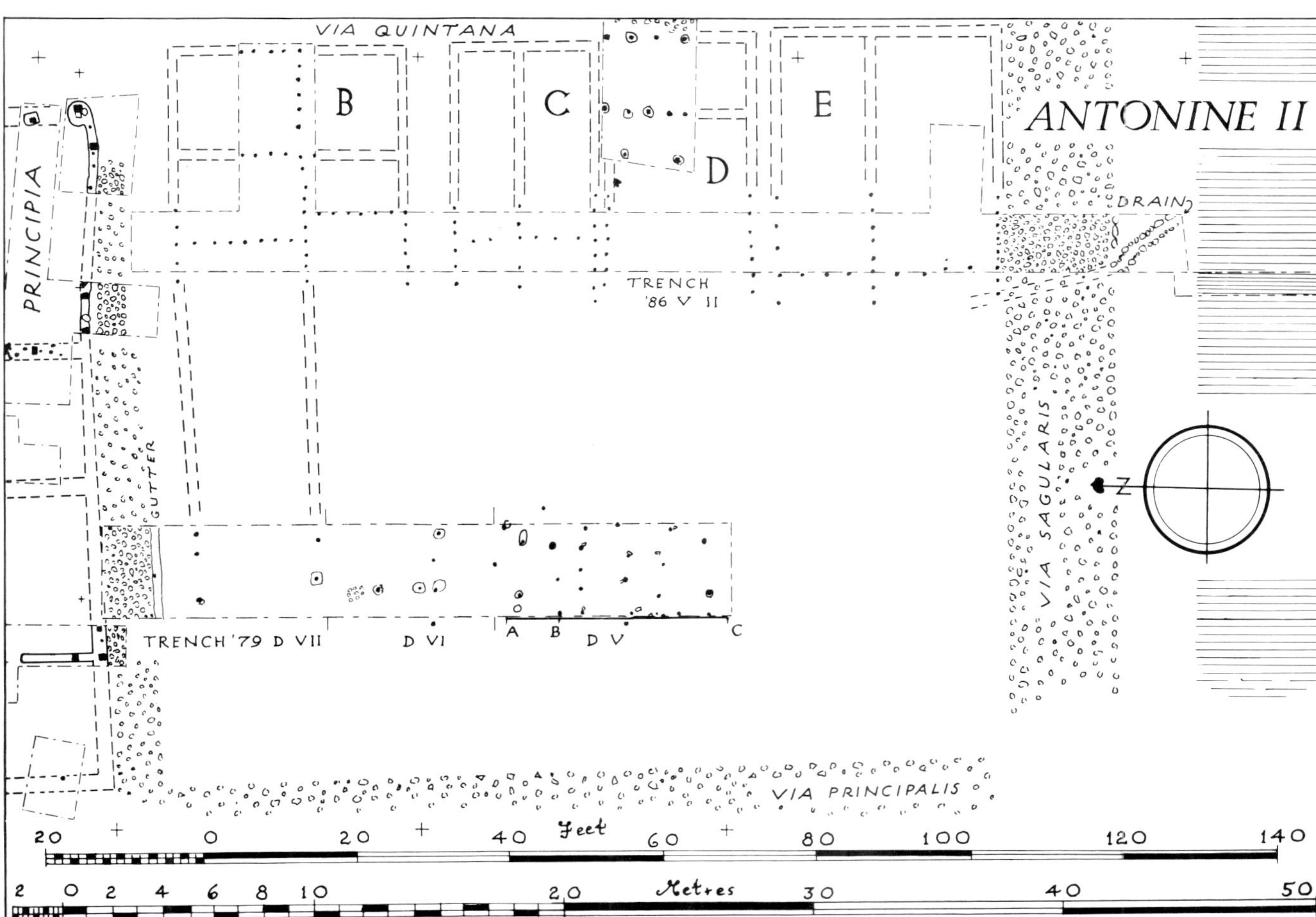

FIG. 30. The Central Range south of the *principia*. Antonine II plan. Scale, 1:298.

The south wall of Building E adjoined the *via sagularis*, which was here 15 ft. (4.57 m) wide, lying almost directly above its Antonine I predecessor. Outside this ran the oblique stone-lined drain already mentioned (p. 55): in its latest phase it had been rebuilt with rounded river-boulders over the lower courses of the original build formed of red sandstone slabs (PL. XXI B). That the drain crossed the street immediately west of Trench V II was apparent from a line of dampness showing through the metalling. In this period the drain presumably led from the interior of Building E, which may be taken to represent a workshop: the internal planning does not suit stables. In this context Dr. Henderson's report on two glazed pieces of stone (p. 188) should be noted.

It is unfortunate that once again in this period the remains found in Trenches D V–VII do not readily match those in V II. At the north end, in D VII, part of Building B can be recognised, here 32 ft. (9.75 m) wide; but south of this the plan shows an irregular collection of post-holes which at the time of excavation were taken probably to represent a badly-constructed granary. Further digging is required to clarify the arrangements. Beyond a gap of *c.* 10 ft. (3.05 m) there are six somewhat ill-aligned rows of post-holes running east-west; but the spacing is irregular, varying between 2 and 4 ft. (0.6 and 1.2 m) within the rows and between 3 and 6 ft. (0.9 and 1.8 m) from row to row. The contemporary occupation-layer had for the most part been removed by the plough, and in consequence the post-holes were only 6–9 in. (0.15–0.23 m) deep.

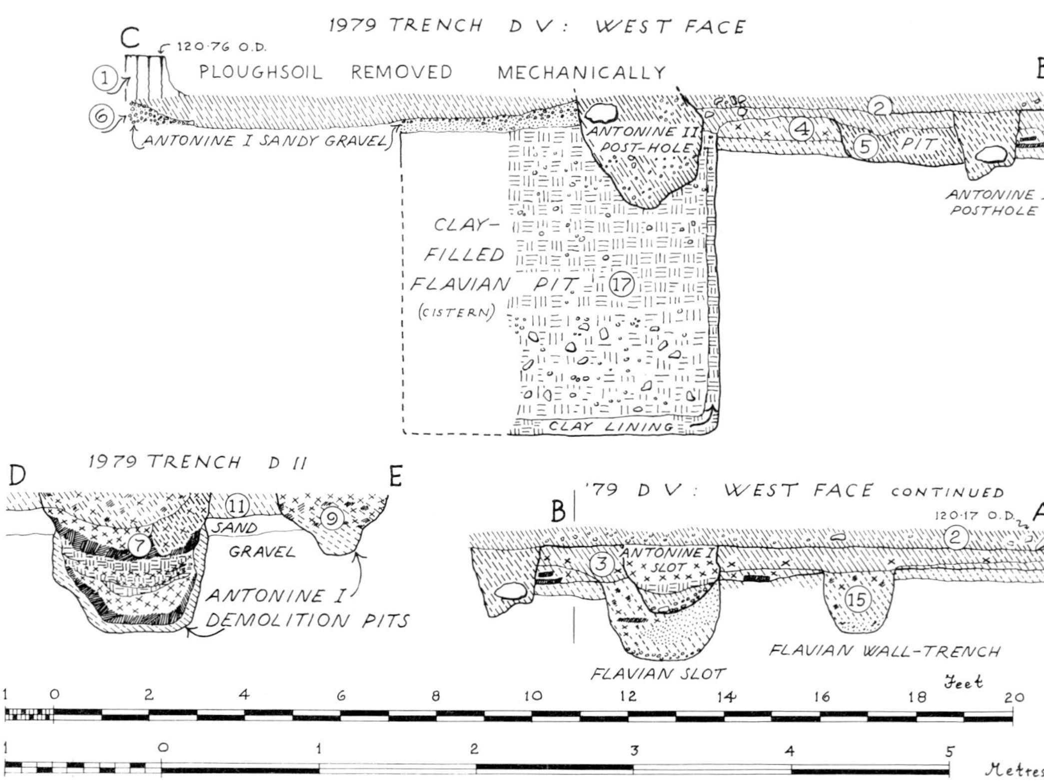

FIG. 31. The Central Range: Sections south (A-C) and north (D-E) of the *principia*. Scale, 1:48.

IV. RIGHT (NORTHERN) RETENTURA

The northern half of the *retentura* was examined in 1973, 1976, 1982 and 1985. In 1973 a trench (I + II), some 200 ft. (61 m) long and 5 ft. (1.53 m) wide, was cut across the eastern defences and was continued for some distance into the interior of the fort. Three large areas were opened up to the north of this (II, N. Extension; II, N. Extension 2; and II, N.W. Extension) to recover further details of the buildings adjacent to the three consecutive *intervallum* streets and if possible to locate the northern building-lines. In the same season Trench III established the southern building-line and was extended across the full width of the *via decumana*, while a small trench (IV), 6 ft. 6 in. (1.98 m) square, revealed an area of the Antonine II *intervallum* road near the north-east corner of the fort and a contemporary water-tank which had destroyed the outer wall of the Flavian barrack below it. This work showed that the east *intervallum* streets of the three forts were in separate and distinct positions. By the time this fact had been established, the presence of a large dump of excavated soil prevented full exploration of those parts of the Antonine I and Flavian buildings which lay under or east of the Antonine II *intervallum* street.

In 1976 the main trench, subdivided into H I and K, was cut on an east-west line some 30 ft. (9.15 m) to the south of Trench 1973 II; it covered an area 105 ft. (32 m) by 10 ft. (3.05 m). There were two additional trenches in this season, Trench H II, 40 ft. by 8 ft. (12.2 by 2.44 m), to the north of H I and Trench H III, 20 ft. by 10 ft. (6.1 by 3.05 m), to the south. These trenches were intended to identify the buildings in the *retentura* other than the barracks adjacent to the *intervallum* investigated in 1973. A further trench (B I), 18 ft. by 8 ft. (5.5 by 2.44 m), was dug in 1977 some 25 ft. (7.63 m) to the north of Trench 1976 H II. Its purpose was to verify that the officers' quarters in Buildings III and IV of the Flavian fort were not so long as those of Building I.

It was the somewhat unsatisfactory nature of the results yielded by these rather small-scale scattered trenches (which in the early seasons of the excavation were dug entirely by hand) that led to the strategy of exploring each of the other main areas of the fort by means of wide and well-separated trenches prepared by a JCB machine and extending across the entire width in each case.

In 1982 further work was undertaken to confirm the outlines and obtain more interior detail of the buildings identified in 1973 and 1976. An east-west trench (divided into G I and G II under separate supervisors), 140 ft. (42.7 m) by 12 ft. (3.6 m), was cut some 22 m in from the area of the northern rampart. In addition a trench (H I), 8 ft. (2.44 m) wide, was extended northwards from near the west end of Trench G II for some 40 ft. (12.2 m) to reveal the northern building-lines and successive *intervallum* streets. Four small trenches (H II, III, IV and V) were excavated as northern extensions of Trenches G I and II to confirm building-details. A further trench (J), 30 ft. (9.2 m) by 8 ft. (2.44 m), was dug some 50 ft. (15.25 m) south of Trench G II to confirm the line of the Antonine I *via quintana* and the internal layout of Building IV in all three periods.

Finally, in 1985, Trenches N I and N II, excavated close to the field fence, traced further details of the northern ends of some of the buildings, and established the lines of successive *intervallum* streets with greater certainty.

The combined results of these excavations, shown on FIGS. 33–35, leave some uncertainty about certain details of the layout. The plan of the Antonine I *retentura* is still somewhat confused; both in this period and in the Flavian there are indications of some possible reconstruction. In 1982 the interpretation of some features was made difficult because the subsoil rises to a crown of yellow sand and fine gravel only just below the ploughsoil in the areas of Buildings III and IV and all stratification had been removed.

(a) Flavian (FIG. 33)

The eastern *via sagularis* was found in Trench 1973 I (FIG. 8). It lay 6 ft. 7 in. (2m) from the inner face of an *ascensus* (p. 17) and 13 ft. 1 in. (3.99 m) from the back of the rampart. The metalling

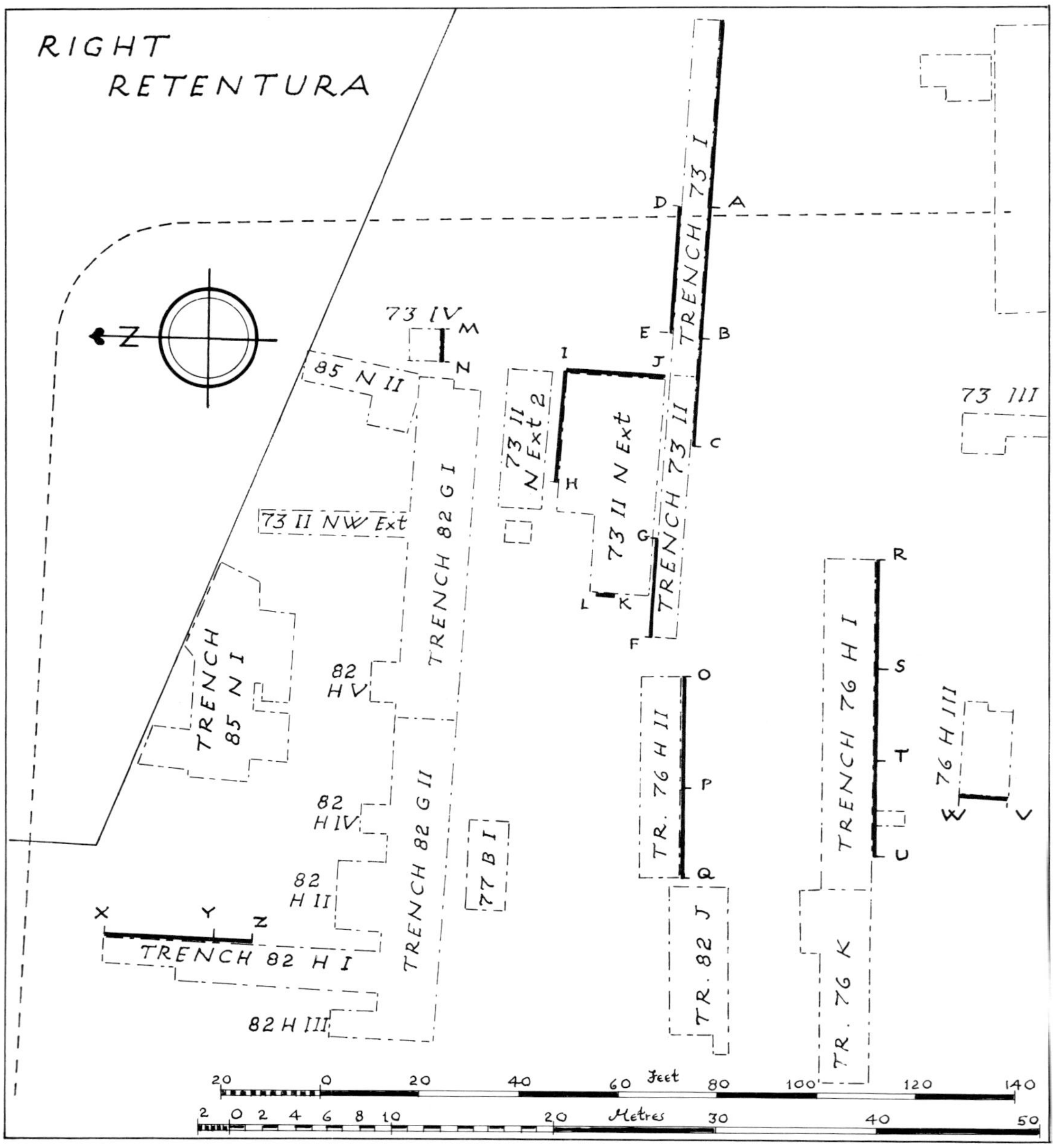

FIG. 32. The right (northern) *retentura*. Plan of Trenches with positions of published sections.

(FIG. 8, Section A–B) consisted of a layer of fine gravel, 4 in. (0.10 m) thick, without a bottoming of boulders; the street was 8 ft. 5 in. (2.56 m) wide and lacked any accompanying drain. The northern *via sagularis* was encountered in Trenches 1982 H I and 1985 N I and was similar in construction. It lay 2 ft. 2 in. (0.66 m) beyond the centurions' houses and was over 15 ft. (4.57 m) wide, the northern edge not having been found.

The *via decumana* was more firmly built with a foundation of boulders, over which lay a cambered surface of fine gravel up to 6 in. (0.152 m) thick. Later metallings had been removed by the plough.

This part of the Flavian fort contained four buildings. All four were of post-in-trench construction. The trenches had straight sides and flat bottoms and were normally about 1ft. to 1 ft. 3 in. (0.3–0.38 m) wide and between 1 ft. and 1 ft. 6 in. (0.3–0.46 m) deep (FIG. 8, Section B–C; FIG. 36, Section H–I; PL. XXIII A), and could be seen to have cut through the old surface soil. In several places it was possible to record the position of the posts themselves; these had been set into the natural sand below the bottom of the trench, as in Building III in Trench 1982 G I. An interesting constructional feature was noted in Buildings II and III; here the outer wall-trenches were continued across the gap between the end block and the main structure; this did not occur in Building IV.

Building I, parallel with and 3 ft. 8 in. (1.12 m) from the eastern *via sagularis* (FIG. 33), appears to have been a barrack with an extra large officers' block at its northern end. The building was 157 ft. (47.85 m) long overall; the northern end-wall was not located as it lies in a different field, but is assumed to be in line with that of Building II. The men's quarters were 28 ft. (8.54 m) wide and were divided into front and rear ranges of almost equal width by a median wall. The rear range had an internal depth of 12 ft. 6 in. (3.8 m); the front one of 12 ft. (3.66 m) (PL. XXII A). A sufficient number of east-west partition walls have been excavated to indicate division into eight *contubernia* each approximately 11 ft. (3.36 m) wide. These would provide accommodation suitable for two *turmae* of horsemen, as in the corresponding barrack (IX, p. 88) in the southern *retentura*; but there is reason to suspect that the occupants were in fact a century of legionaries (p. 119–20).

The officers' block was 64 ft. (19.5 m) long and 40 ft. (12.2 m) wide and projected to the west of the *contubernia*; no trace of a veranda fronting the *contubernia* in continuation of the western building line of the officers' quarters was found; those marked on an interim plan (*Britannia* iv (1973), 404, fig. 4) are now attributed to the Antonine I period. The longitudinal walls of the *contubernia* continued through the officers' block but the full internal layout of the latter has not been revealed. Two deep post-pits, packed with round cobbles and clean gravel, were discovered in the south-west corner-room of this block, perhaps belonging to some item of furniture or to a further partition. Building I faced west onto an unmetalled alley *c.* 20 ft. (6.1 m) wide; this alley was, however, blocked at the northern end by the projecting sections of Buildings I and II, leaving a gap of only 1 ft. (0.3 m). The lack of access to the *via sagularis* both to the east and north reinforces the suggestion that the occupants of Building I, whether legionaries or horsemen, had no direct concern with the defence of the rampart.

Building II was also 157 ft. (47.85 m) long; Trench 1982 H V (a northern extension of 1982 G I) revealed that it had a free-standing block at its northern end, 37 ft. (11.28 m) north-south by 28 ft. (8.54 m), corresponding to the end blocks in Buildings III and IV, where they were clearly centurions' quarters. The projecting officers' block of Building I, however, together with other rooms in Building II itself and the close proximity of Building III, prevented access to the end block of Building II except from the *intervallum* end; this and the unusual layout of the remainder of the building make Building II unsuitable for use as a barrack; it was perhaps a workshop, for the plan has some resemblance to von Petrikovits's 'Doppelhakenförmige Wirtschaftsbauten' or winged type of *fabrica*.[1] In the NW corner of the northern block was a latrine-pit. It measured 5 ft. by 3 ft. 6 in. (1.52 by 1.07 m) and was 3 ft. (0.9 m) deep with vertical sides. The base of the western and northern wall-trenches of the building showed as ledges along the sides of the pit. The main part of Building II was of an open-E plan *c.* 22 ft. (6.7 m) wide with wings 28 ft. and 29 ft. (8.54 and 8.84) wide. Trenches 1973 II and 1976 H I indicate either some rebuilding during the life of the building (with a new eastern wall-line on a somewhat oblique course) or else perhaps an original error in setting out. Some of the wall-trenches can be seen in FIG. 36, Section F–G and FIG. 37, Sections R–S, S–T.

Building III lay back-to-back with Building II, separated from it by a 2 ft. (0.61 m) gap, and facing Building IV. Building III occupied an area of 155 ft. 6 in. (47.4 m) north-south by 28 ft. 6 in. (8.69 m) and consisted of two separate blocks with an intervening gap of 2 ft. (0.61 m), as established by Trenches 1982 H IV and H V. To the north was a centurion's house measuring *c.* 35 ft. (10.7 m) by 28 ft. (8.54 m), no wider than the *contubernia*. The demolition-deposits

1. H. von Petrikovits, *Die Innenbauten römischer Legionslager während der Prinzipatszeit* (Opladen 1975), 92–3, Bild 25. The purpose of Building II is further discussed on pp. 124–5.

spreading over the *via sagularis* in Trench 1985 N I outside the north end of this contained several large sherds of a Dressel 20 amphora including a rim and handle; the layer was notably black with charcoal and contained much burnt and unburnt clay. The remainder of the building was divided into a front and rear range of rooms (each 12 ft. 6 in. (3.8 m) deep internally) by a median wall; this block contained ten *contubernia* each *c.* 11 ft. (3.36 m) wide, sufficient accommodation for a century of infantry. The southern end-wall was found in Trench 76 H III (FIG. 37, Section V–W). Just outside it ran a somewhat irregularly-cut gully (ibid., 10) which was taken to be a drain, although it might have been a miscutting of a wall-trench. The second *contubernium* from the south end contained a short length of trench 3 ft. (0.9 m) from its southern wall in the front room and a post-hole on the same line in the rear room. In both Trenches H I and H II the remains had been disturbed by a number of long narrow demolition-pits. One which is certainly of the Antonine I period is seen in FIG. 37, Section O–P.

Buildings III and IV were separated by a thinly gravelled street 8 ft. (2.44 m) wide.

Building IV was a mirror-image of Building III but probably faced west; it occupied an area of 156 ft. (47.54 m) by 28 ft. (8.54 m); the northern end wall-line was established adjacent to the *via sagularis* in Trench 1982 H I (FIG. 38, Section X–Y). It terminated a separate non-projecting centurion's house, 37 ft. (11.28 m) by 28 ft. (8.54 m),[2] south of which lay men's quarters divisible into ten *contubernia* each *c.* 11 ft. (3.36 m) wide; a complete *contubernium* was excavated in Trench 1982 G II and almost all another was found in Trench 82 J. In both, the eastern (rear) room had a depth of 13 ft. (3.96 m) and the western (front) room one of 11½ ft. (3.51 m). The line of the median wall of the men's quarters was continued north in the centurions' block; this and various east-west walls located in Trench 1982 H I indicate the complete arrangements of a centurion's house of typical plan. There was no trace of a veranda, but in Trenches 1982 G II and 1977 B I an eavesdrip was found to run along the eastern side of the *contubernia* and centurion's house – another indication that this was the back of the building. The eavesdrip was of shallow V-section 3 ft. (0.92 m) wide and 9 in. (0.23 m) deep; it did not extend to Trench 1982 J.

The earth floor of the barrack was seen in Trench 1976 K under a layer of demolition material. A Neronian As, dated to A.D. 66 (*RIC* 318) was found lying flat on its surface (1976 K I 13 A) and a Vespasianic *dupondius*, dated to 72–3 (*RIC* 740) was found embedded in it (1976 K I 23).

(b) Antonine I (FIG. 34)

In this period the **eastern via sagularis** was laid down further east than its Flavian predecessor. On the north side of Trench I (FIG. 8 (p. 18), Section D–E) the outer edge of the metalling now lay close to the back of the rampart; on the south side of the Trench the gap was wider since some metalling had been removed by the construction of Antonine II ovens (FIG. 8, Section A–B). The street was 14 ft. 6 in. (4.42 m) wide and consisted of a 4-in. (0.10-m) layer of river-gravel without a foundation of boulders. Along its western edge ran a drain, formerly plank-lined, which was 1 ft. 6 in. (0.46 m) wide and 10 in. (0.25 m) deep (PL. XXIII B; FIG. 8, Sections A–B, D–E). The base lay at 119.30 ft. O.D. (36.36 m). Later work (p. 92) showed that the fall was to the north. Along the **northern** *intervallum the* **via sagularis** was seen in Trenches 82 H I and 85 N I; the southern edge was 8 ft. (2.44 m) south of the edge of its predecessor, and it overlay the edge of the Flavian buildings; but in neither trench could its northern edge be reached. In H I up to 6 in. (0.15 m) of metalling survived over the southern half of the street, but north of this it had been ploughed away (FIG. 38, Section X–Y) save where a patch had sunk into a small Flavian demolition-pit. Here there were two thin layers of gravel, each 2– 3 in. (5–7.5 cm) thick and separated by a thin layer of sand; the position of the pit lies *c.* 16 ft. (4.88 m) north of Building IV and gives a minimum width for the street. There was no continuous drain along the north side of this part of the fort; instead, drainage was divided. A well-built, formerly timber-lined channel, 2 ft. (0.6 m) wide with good stone kerbs, began in Trench N I and ran eastwards along the inner side of the *via*

2. This compares well with the centurions' blocks at Fendoch, which had a length of 34 ft. (10.36 m).

sagularis, presumably to join the drain in the east *intervallum* and run out beneath the rampart. The fall was from 118.72 ft. O.D. (36.18 m) at the terminal to 117.77 ft. (35.90 m) in the length examined. In Trench H I there was U-shaped gully in the same position with a gravelly filling; it was *c.* 1 ft. 8 in. (0.51 m) wide and 10 in. (0.25 m) deep and presumably ran westwards to an exit at the *porta principalis dextra* (pp. 50, 132).

There was evidence (p. 63) that an Antonine I oven had been present somewhere north of Trench N I.

Between the drain of the eastern *via sagularis* and the *via quintana* post-holes belonging to four buildings have been located; these do not, however, provide enough information to characterise the buildings of this phase in the northern *retentura* in detail. Two (Buildings II and III) are too narrow for barracks and a third (Building IV), while having an overall width suitable for a barrack, possesses a tripartite longitudinal division, no two ranges of which are large enough for *contubernia* if the third were to be considered a veranda. Only Building I has an outline suitable for a barrack; but it is almost 1 m wider than Buildings X and XI, the two widest certain barracks elsewhere in the fort, and the details of its plan, so far as they are known, do not suggest division into *contubernia*. The probability is that the northern *retentura* in the Antonine I period contained a series of specialist buildings and was not used for the accommodation of troops.

Building I was 35 ft. (10.67 m) wide and *c.* 148 ft. (45.1 m) long. Two large stone-packed post-holes of its eastern wall were found in Trench I; they lay *c.* 1 ft. 6 in. (0.46 m) from the drain (PL. XXIII B). A median wall of similar post-holes (FIG. 8, Section B–C) divided the building into an eastern range 21 ft. (6.4 m) wide internally and a western range 10 ft. 6 in. (3.20 m) wide. Sufficient of the eastern range has been excavated (FIG. 34) to suggest that there were few if any cross partitions; only one partition was found in the western range and it is significant that this wall did not continue into the other part of the building. There is thus no sign of division into *contubernia*. Part of a very large pit *c.* 8 ft. (2.44 m) long was examined in the eastern range. It underlay the Antonine II *via sagularis* (PL. XXII A) and cut through a Flavian wall-trench; the pit (FIG. 36, Section I–J) was over 7 ft. 3 in. (2.20 m) deep and had a sterile fill of turves and gravel very different from the normal filling of a demolition-pit. The lower part had an almost vertical side, and the irregularity of the upper part may have been due to partial collapse when a timber lining was withdrawn. The pit most probably represents a water-tank, and if so the presence of such a large one suggests that Building I is a workshop.

Building II lay on the other side of a lightly metalled street 9–10 ft. (2.75–3m) wide. The building was of irregular shape, being 15 ft. (4.57 m) wide at the northern end but widening to 19 ft. (5.79 m) at the southern. The length is restored at 148 ft. (45.1 m). The post-holes of the eastern wall at the north end coincided with the line of a Flavian trench below and were difficult to distinguish in the dry conditions of 1973. Trench 76 H I did not extend far enough east to locate the eastern wall. A line of four post-holes in this trench were taken at the time to represent the eastern wall, but they must, in reality, represent some internal fitting, for otherwise the plan of the building would be impossibly irregular, with a width at the southern end of only 12 ft. (3.66 m). A median wall was traced in Trenches 1982 G I, 1973 I and 1976 H I; this divided the building into two narrow ranges with interior widths of 8 and 5 ft. (2.4 and 1.5 m) in G I and II and 11 and 4 ft. (3.35 and 1.2 m) in H I respectively. The median wall was interrupted by Pit 2 (FIG. 36, Section K–L). Although dug with exceptionally vertical sides this must be a demolition-pit; the date is indicated by the fact that it cut through walls of the Flavian and Antonine I period, but metalling of an Antonine II street had sunk into its filling. Building II is too narrow to serve as a barrack and will be shown to be unsatisfactory as a stable (p. 127); it must be interpreted as a store or workshop.

Building III was separated from II by an alleyway *c.* 10 ft. (3.05 m) wide, which had once been lightly metalled; the gravel survived only in Trench N I. Building III was 147 ft. (44.8 m) long, both end-walls being located; the main part was 18–19 ft. (5.5–5.8 m) wide but the northern end was widened to 23 ft. 6 in. (7.16 m) by a narrow corridor which also ran down the north side close to the kerb-stones of the drain. A median wall divided the building into two ranges each *c.* 8 ft. (2.44 m) wide, dimensions too narrow for anything but another store or workshop. Traces of the floor remained in Trenches 1976 H II and III as patches of yellow sand and gravel over the make-up (FIG. 37, Sections O–P, V–W). Some Black-burnished pot was embedded in the surface. A small area of flat stones showing marks of a fire in Trench 1982 G I may indicate the position of a hearth. Building III faced west onto a metalled alley 12 ft. (3.66 m) wide. Much of the metalling had been removed by the plough but patches of fine gravel and pebbles remained at the western end of Trench 1976 H I; a dupondius of Titus of A.D. 73 (p. 139, No. 18) was found lying flat on this gravel surface (1976 H I 12).

Building IV was *c.* 148 ft. (45.1 m) long. The northern end-wall had been destroyed by the Antonine II *intervallum* drain; the south wall is assumed to be in line with that of Building III. The width varied from *c.* 25 ft. (7.6 m) at the southern end to *c.* 29 ft. (8.8 m) at the northern. The building contained three ranges, divided by longitudinal partitions. The central range varied in width from 10 to 8 ft. (3–2.44 m) and seemed to be partitioned here and there; the side ranges were only *c.* 6–7 ft. (1.8–2.1 m) wide. Once again a store or workshop seems to be in question (p. 127).

The **via quintana** ran along the west side of Building IV; the metalling had been ploughed away in Trench 1982 G II, but survived in Trenches 1976 K and 1982 J. The street was *c.* 12 ft. (3.66 m) wide with a drain on either side; the drains were *c.* 9 in. (0.23 m) deep and varied between 9 in. and 1 ft. 6 in. (0.23 and 0.46 m) in width. The original metalling, which overlay the Flavian demolition layer and part of Flavian Building IV, was composed of a well-cambered layer of thin gravel; later the street had been relaid with gravel over large river boulders defined by large kerbstones; one of the latter in Trench 1982 J was a reused broken quernstone. In the same Trench the street had subsided into two large Flavian demolition pits. On the west side of the street some post-holes belonging to a building behind or attached to the *principia* were encountered (p. 38), buried below the Antonine II *via quintana*. In this period, as in Antonine II, the *via quintana* differed in position and width in the two halves of the *retentura*, because of the non-alignment of Buildings IV and XI. On the present site the west edge of the street lay 16 ft. (4.88 m) east of the main rear wall of the *principia*, leaving an area which was occupied either by a portico or possibly by some extension to the *principia* as indicated by the post-holes at the west end of Trench 1976 K.

All four buildings in the northern *retentura* were constructed with posts set in pits *c.* 2 ft. (0.61 m) in diameter and 1 ft. to 1 ft. 6 in. (0.30 to 0.46 m) deep, packed with large boulders (PL. XXII A). In places, especially in Trench 1982 G I, several of these pits interlocked to form an irregular construction-trench.

Several large demolition pits were noted during excavation. One of these, in the plot occupied by Building IV in Trench 1982 G II, contained much charcoal and burnt daub and was apparently the site of a bonfire; at the bottom of the pit the natural sand had been reddened by burning and was covered by a solid charcoal layer.

(c) Antonine II (FIG. 35)

In this period the eastern *via sagularis* lay further from the rampart than its predecessors; its outer edge lay 17 ft. (5.18 m) west of the Antonine I drain accompanying the inner edge of the contemporary street and the metalling, 14 ft. (4.27 m) wide, overlay a deposit of brown sandy soil representing the Antonine I demolition-layer possibly supplemented by wash from the rear of the rampart (FIG. 8 (p. 18), Section B–C, 18). Location of the street further from the rampart was probably mainly the result of a different general planning of the Antonine II fort; but it also allowed a wider *intervallum* space for bread-ovens and other activities. The space at Trench 73 I was 21 ft. (6.4 m) wide and segments of two successive ovens were encountered in this trench, built of clay and boulders (FIG. 8, Sections A–B, D–E), and there was a thick deposit of charcoal and wood-ash piled against the back of the rampart (Section A–B, 49) where it had been flung when the ovens were periodically cleared out (PL. X B). Sealing the remains of the ovens was a layer containing cobbles (FIG. 8, Section A–B). At the time of excavation these were taken to be the bottoming of yet another *intervallum* street; but no such street has been located in other Trenches and the cobbles are probably derived from the top of the back part of the rampart (p. 15). The eastern *via sagularis* was probably *c.* 14 ft. (4.25 m) wide, but its outer edge had been disturbed (FIG. 8, Section B–C). A rather ragged hole (Section B–C, 4) may possibly be part of an *intervallum* building, not otherwise attested in this area. On the north side of the fort there was little change in the position of the Antonine I and II *intervallum* streets, and the *intervallum* space was even wider than on the east side; it is estimated (FIG. 35) at *c.* 32 ft. (9.7 m). Here the Antonine II street was only 7 ft. (2.13 m) wide; it rested directly on its predecessor and was bounded on the north by a row of substantial post-holes which must indicate an *intervallum* building. More posts were found in Trench 82 H I. The second post-hole from the east in N I, which intruded on the Flavian latrine-pit beneath, had a substantial packing of re-used oven clay, indicating an Antonine I bread-oven nearby. A second row of slightly less large post-holes ran down the centre of the street itself and clearly bears some relationship to the more substantial row (FIG. 35). If a portico had been added thus to the *intervallum* building it would have blocked the street to all but pedestrian traffic. On both the east and north sides the Antonine II *via sagularis* had a bedding of large river boulders *c.* 1 ft. (0.3 m) in diameter supporting a gravel and pebble metalling (FIG. 8, Section B–C). In Trench 1973 IV a large pit intruded on the east side of the street. At the time of excavation it was taken to be a demolition-pit, cut through the metalling; but the sterile turfy fill of the pit together with its almost vertical sides and considerable depth (the bottom was not reached, but the pit was cut to a depth of over 3 ft. 8 in. (1.12 m) (FIG. 36, Section M–N) suggest that the pit may have been a water-tank. Demolition-pits are never turf-filled at Strageath: this filling indicates that the pit had been open during the occupation. A deep drain, once timber-lined, ran along the inner edge of the eastern *via sagularis*. The lining was indicated by the double row of stake-holes running along its sides and by the charred wood found at the bottom of the drain in Trench 73 II N. Extension. The drain, which was *c.* 2 ft. (0.61 m) wide and 1 ft. 6 in. (0.46 m) deep, was flat-bottomed. A levelling layer within the drain, *c.* 6 in. (12.5 cm) deep, yielded an almost complete Dr. 37 bowl stamped CINNAMI (FIG. 105), apparently a survival from the Antonine I period since it was obviously an old bowl, having been broken and riveted with lead, and the drain was presumably dug at the beginning of the Antonine II period. The destruction-layer filling the drain above this levelling layer in Trench 1973 II contained Black-burnished 2 pottery and an almost complete herringbone-stamped Colchester mortarium dated to the period A.D. 130–170. (FIG. 111, No. 34). The levels show that the drain flowed northwards (pp. 95–6), but it was not found round the corner beside the northern *intervallum* street in Trenches 73 II N.W. Extension or 85 N I, and probably discharged through a culvert beneath the rampart near the angle. Further west the remains of a similar drain were encountered on the inner edge of the *via sagularis* in Trench 82 H I. Unfortunately at this point the drain had been cut by a demolition pit, and it was not possible to be sure of the level at its base: it appeared to be at 120.4 ft. (36.7 m) O.D. This is 2.7 ft. (0.82 m) higher than the base of the drain in Trench 85 N II, and they clearly do not connect. The drain in H I connects with one found further west in Trench 86 V I (p. 51) and thus it appears that a new drain began its course north of Building IV and ran westwards to the *porta principalis dextra*. The demolition-pit in H I (FIG. 38, Section Y–Z) contained large stones, burnt daub, charcoal and a BB2 bowl; nearby a very large stone slab lay in the mouth of the drain which it may once have bridged.

Adjacent to the eastern drain lay **Building I**, on a north-south alignment. This measured 145 ft. (44.2 m) by 34 ft. (10.37 m), the end walls having been located in Trenches 1973 III and 1973 NW Extension. A longitudinal partition divided the building into a rear (eastern) range 16 ft. (4.88 m) deep and a front range 13 ft. (3.96 m) deep. The internal layout identifies the building as a barrack; the northern 62 ft. (18.9 m) formed the officer's quarters and the remainder is thought to have been divided into six *contubernia*, each *c.* 13 ft. (3.96 m) wide. A complete *contubernium* was uncovered in Trench 1973 N Extension 2. The longitudinal wall extended through the officer's quarters on almost the same alignment; the north-western room had a good gravel floor 17 ft. (5.18 m) wide, south of which another partition 10 ft. (3.05 m) away crossed both ranges. The small number of *contubernia* combined with their large area (see TABLE V, p. 138) and the large size of the officers' quarters suggest that Barrack I was occupied by horsemen rather than by infantry. The wall lines were established by the discovery both of post-holes and of the intervening stake-holes used in wattle-and-daub construction; the latter were most noticeable in Trench 1973 N Extension 2. The timber uprights in the southern part of the officers' quarters were set in construction-trenches rather than post-pits. Barrack I faced west onto a metalled street 10 ft. (3.05 m) wide which divided it from Building II.

Building II, which faced east, was 150 ft. (45.72 m) long and 23 ft. (7.02 m) wide. A longitudinal partition divided it into a front and rear range of rooms both *c.* 10 ft. (3.05 m) deep. The internal layout again allows identification as a barrack-block although an unusually narrow one. Two east-west partitions 9 ft. (2.75 m) apart were located in Trench 1982 G I; the rooms thus created at the northern end of the building probably formed part of the centurion's quarters, leaving space for ten *contubernia*, sufficient for an infantry unit. If this is so, the centurion's quarters were 45 ft. (13.7 m) long, and the *contubernia* were 9 ft. (2.74 m) wide.

In Trenches 1976 H I, II and III the make-up for the floor was identified; this consisted of flat sandstones approximately 6 in. (0.153 m) across set in gravel and red earth. In Trench 1976 H II this make-up was associated with a Hadrianic denarius (*RIC* 127a).

One of the post-holes adjacent to the *via decumana*, excavated in Trench 1976 H III, provided evidence of the systematic demolition of the fort at the end of the Antonine II occupation. A spade-shoe 7 in. (0.175 m) wide (FIG. 83, No. 121) was found in the stone-packed pit; it presumably broke off during the removal of the post.

Building III was separated from the rear of Building II by an unmetalled alley *c.* 5 ft. (1.52 m) wide. Building III was 151 ft. (46.02 m) long; it was a very narrow building, with a width of 15 ft. (4.57 m) in Trench 1982 G I widening to 17 ft. (5.18 m) in Trench 1976 H I. A north-south median wall divided the interior into two narrow ranges each 5–6 ft. (1.5–1.8 m) wide, and possible east-west partitions were indicated in Trenches 1982 G I and 1976 H I by a single post-hole in each place. The narrow character of the building rules out any attempt to restore it as a barrack, and the two ranges are too narrow for convenient use as stables; Building III should be interpreted as either a workshop or a store.

Building IV was separated from Building III by a metalled alley some 8 ft. (2.44 m) wide, narrowing at the northern end. Building IV measured 146 ft. (44.5 m) north-south, the northern end-wall being *c.* 2 ft. (0.6 m) from the *intervallum* drain described above. The differing lengths of Buildings I–IV are due partly to the shape of the fort and partly to the absence of a drain north of Buildings I–III. Building IV can be identified as a barrack by its internal layout. The building was L-shaped in plan since alone of the Antonine II barracks it possessed centurion's quarters which projected eastwards beyond the line of *contubernia*; an unexplained feature is that these quarters were also offset eastwards on the west side. They measured 44 ft. (13.41 m) by 26 ft. (7.9 m); the precise internal arrangement is uncertain but lines of post-holes in Trenches 1982 G II, H I and H II reveal a complex of interconnecting rooms and passages. The remainder of the building, *c.* 24 ft. (7.3 m) in width, was divided by a north-south median wall which in Trench 82 J gave two rooms each 10 ft. (3 m) deep; east-west partitions were located in Trenches 1982 J and 1976 K which suggest division into 10 *contubernia*, each 8–9 ft. (2.4–2.7 m) wide. In a northern extension to the latter Trench an area of rough heavy paving was encountered, covering an area of *c.* 5 by 4 ft. (1.5 by 1.22 m); it had once been more extensive before disturbance by the plough.

Two post-holes 8 ft. (2.44 m) west of Building IV, on the edge of the *via quintana*, were located in Trench 1976 K; these may perhaps represent a portico lining the street similar to that found on the other side of the *via quintana* further south (p. 45). The presence of this portico still further reduced the width of the *via quintana* in this half of the fort, already narrowed by the non-alignment of Building IV with its counterpart, Building X, in the southern *retentura*. The post-holes at the west end of Trench 76 K are only 5 ft. (1.52 m) from the rear wall of the *principia*

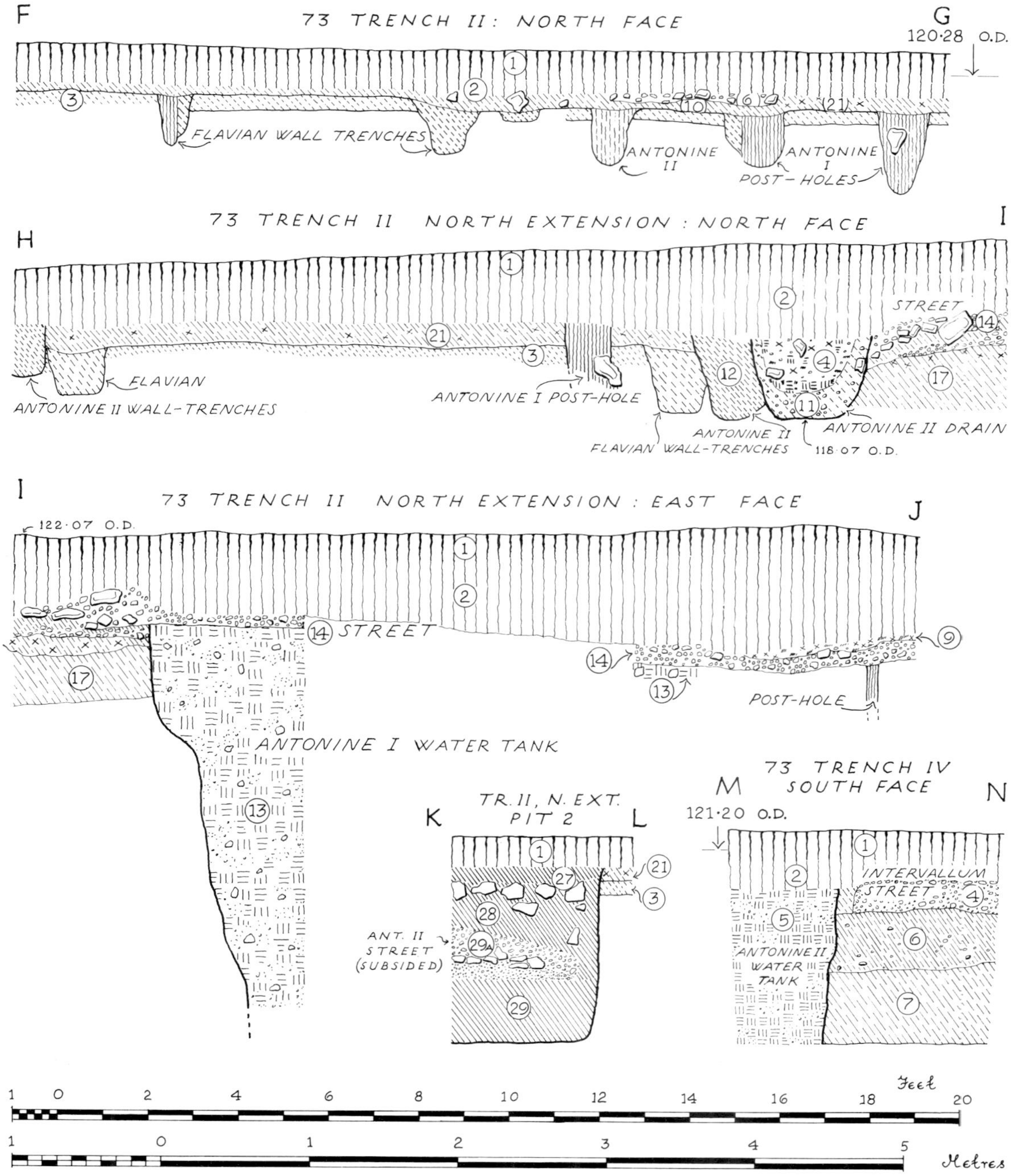

FIG. 36. The right (northern) *retentura*: Sections F-N. Scale, 1:45. (For sections A-E, see p. 18, FIG. 8).

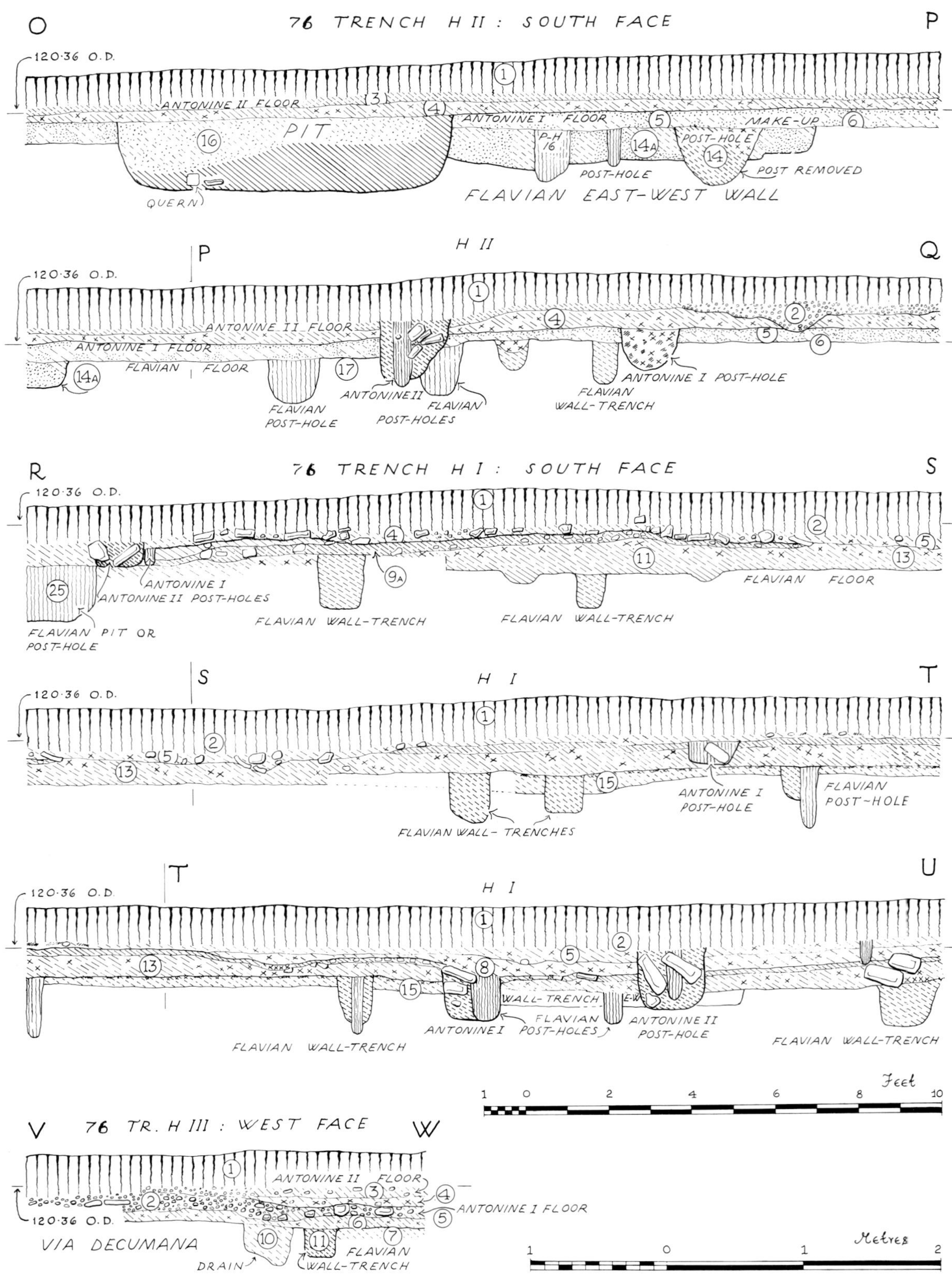

FIG. 37. The right (northern) *retentura*: Sections O-W. Scale, 1:45. (For positions see p. 58, FIG. 32).

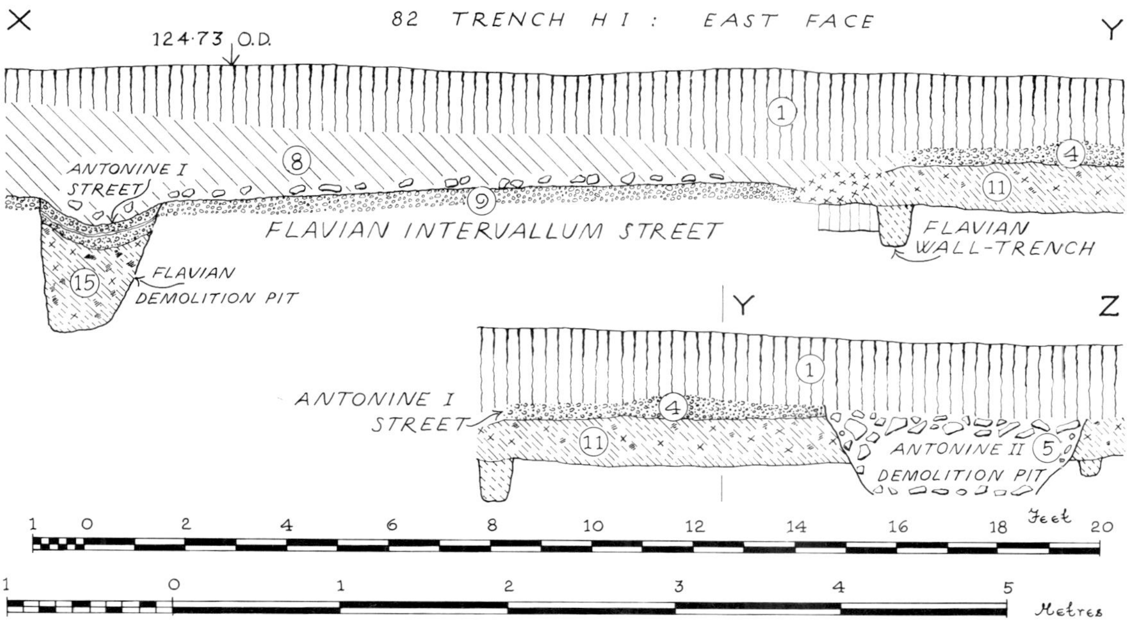

FIG. 38. The right (northern) *retentura*. Sections X-Z. Scale, 1:45. (For position, see FIG. 32).

and the metalling represents a mere path. The gravel surface of the *via quintana* had been removed by the plough but in Trench 76 K the foundation of river cobbles remained; sealed below the metalling was an Antonine I dish (FIG. 73, No. 137).

Buildings II, III and IV and parts of Building I were constructed with timbers many of which were set in post-holes and held in place with stone packers (FIG. 37, Section P–Q, T–U). The post-holes were often 6 to 10 in. (0.152–.0255 m) in diameter and 8 to 12 in. (0.204–.0305 m) deep, but a few were larger. The Antonine II occupation- and demolition-layers had largely been ploughed away, especially in Trenches 1982 G II and J. At the eastern end of Trench 1982 G I, however, they had been preserved by a thick layer of earth spread from the rampart by the plough. The demolition-layer below this contained a large amount of burnt and unburnt daub.

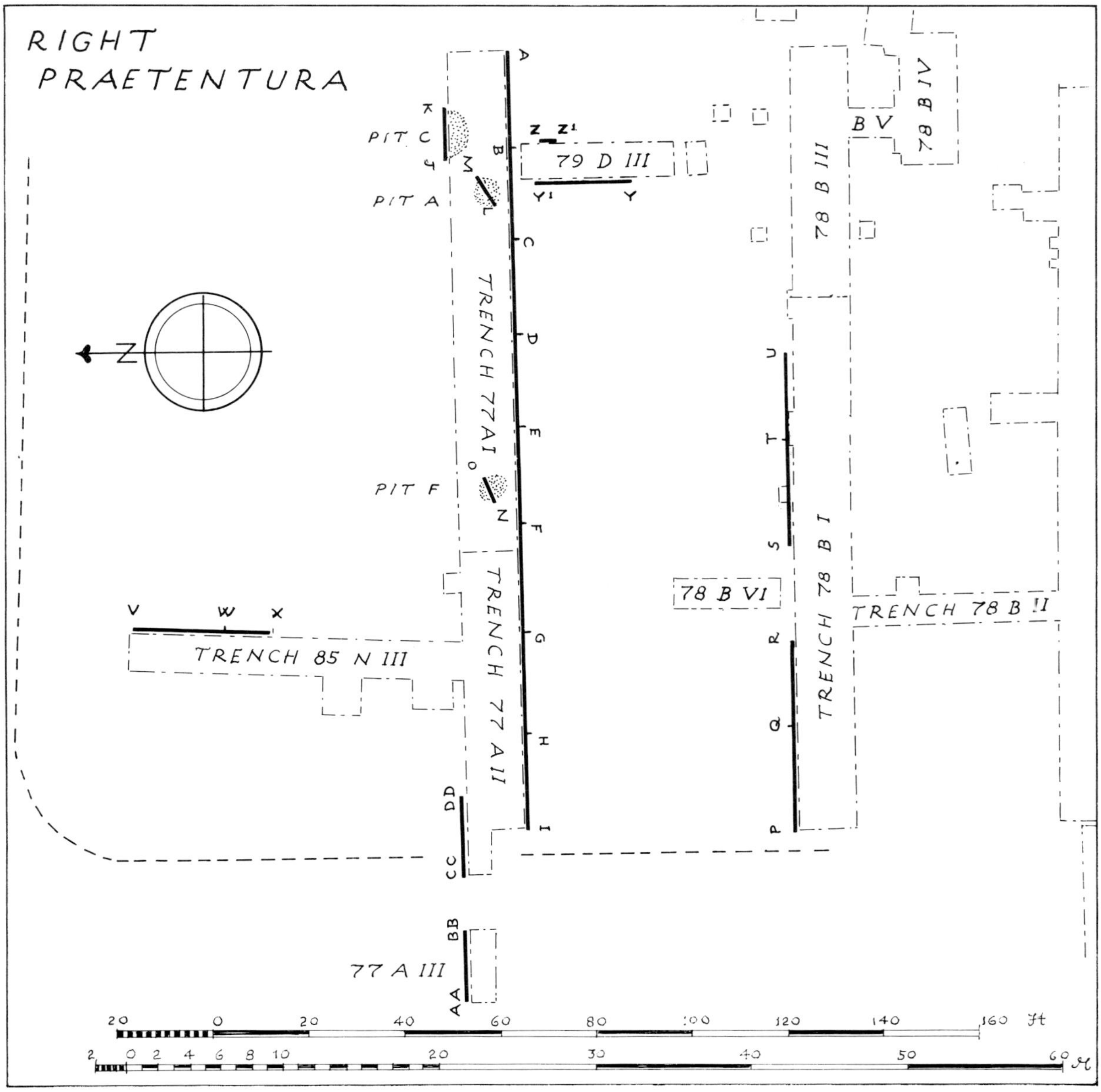

FIG. 39. The right (northern) *praetentura*. Plan of Trenches with positions of published sections.

V. RIGHT (NORTHERN) PRAETENTURA

In the years 1977–9 and 1985 excavation was carried out in the northern half of the *praetentura*. In 1977 a single trench (A I, A II, so divided because under two supervisors) was cut on an east-west alignment approximately 80 ft. (24 m) north of the *via praetoria*; this trench measured 160 ft. (48.77 m) by 12 ft. (3.66 m) and ran from the *via principalis* to the western rampart. An extension (A III), 15 ft. (4.57 m) by 5 ft. (1.53 m) was cut to the west of A II to locate the front and back of the western rampart. In 1978 a trench (B I, B III), measuring 160 ft. (48.77 m) by 12 ft. (3.66 m), was cut parallel to Trench A I–II but some 58 ft. (17.7 m) to the south; this trench also ran from the *via principalis* to the western rampart which in the Flavian period at this point was found to be turning inwards for the gateway. In addition subsidiary trenches were dug in this year as follows: B II (46 ft. (14 m) by 6 ft. (1.83 m)) was cut on a north-south axis between 42 ft. (12.8 m) and 48 ft. (14.6 m) from the western end of B I and at right angles to it; this trench extended across the *via praetoria* and a few feet into the southern *praetentura*. East of it an unnumbered trench marked on the plan in the line of the *via praetoria* was dug by machine in the preliminary stages of the excavation to define the area for Trench B I–III. It did not penetrate the metalling. Trench B IV (27 ft. (8.2 m) by 12 ft. (3.66 m)) was cut parallel to B III but some 10 ft. (3.05 m) to the south in order to examine the junction of the *viae praetoria* and *principalis*. B V (10 ft. (3.05 m) by 6 ft. (1.83 m)) was dug on a north-south axis to connect Trenches B III and B IV. B VI, measuring 22 ft. (6.7 m) by 6 ft. (1.83 m), was cut on a north-south axis some 3 ft. (0.92 m) to the north of B I and at right angles to it between 46 ft. (14 m) and 52 ft. (15.9 m) from the western end of B I in order to locate the front of the Flavian granary. Trenches B VII, VIII, X and XI, each approximately 4 ft. (1.22 m) square, were a series of sondages to the north and south of the eastern end of B III, dug to establish the position of the proto-Flavian granary. B IX was a small trial trench approximately 3 ft. (0.92 m) south of B III and 1 ft. (0.305 m) east of B V excavated in order to fix the corner of the Flavian building adjacent to the *via principalis*.

In 1979 a trench (D III), measuring 30 ft. (9.2 m) by 11 ft. (3.35 m), was cut on a north-south alignment between Trenches A I and B III; this trench lay approximately 8 ft. (2.44 m) to the west of the *via principalis* and was dug to test the extent of the proto-Flavian granary.

Finally, in 1985 Trench N III was dug by hand north of the western end of 77 A II in order to locate the building-lines along the northern side of the successive forts. Although only one building in each period was closely defined in this trench, the alignment of the northern *via sagularis* could be established from its position here and in the northern *retentura* at Trench 85 N I (p. 57), and thus a restoration of the other buildings can be proposed without too serious a margin of error.

(i) Proto-Flavian Granary (FIG. 40)

The normal sequence of three periods of occupation (Flavian, Antonine I and Antonine II), separated by demolition layers, was present; but in addition a fourth – earlier – period was identified in the south-east corner of the right *praetentura*. Here a small but exceptionally well-constructed granary was found to underlie the Flavian buildings. The granary is unique at Strageath; no other structures earlier than the main Flavian period have been noted elsewhere in the fort.

The proto-Flavian granary, the earliest structure in the right *praetentura*, was discovered in 1978. Two deep parallel foundation-trenches running east-west were discovered at the eastern end of Trench B III. The ends of a third were located *c.* 6 ft. (1.83 m) north of the *via praetoria* in Trenches B V and B VII and the ends of two more were found to the north of B III in Trenches B VIII, X and XI. The granary, however, extended no further north, for Trench D III, dug in 1979 to examine the question, failed to reveal further traces; the building thus possessed only five foundation-trenches. All contained a fill of soft dark brown soil mixed with charcoal and a few sherds, and they were easily distinguishable against the orange sandy subsoil.

The grid of parallel foundation-trenches conforms to the normal ground-plan of Roman military timber granaries,[1] which normally possess an uneven number of trenches. Each trench was *c.* 25 ft. (7.62 m) long and the five trenches were placed at intervals of approximately 6 ft. (1.83 m); the overall dimensions of the granary were thus 31 ft. 6 in. (9.6 m) by 25 ft. (7.62 m). The trenches all had straight well-cut sides and bow-ends; each trench was approximately 1 ft. 6 in. (0.45 m) wide and 3 ft. 6 in. (1 m) deep – about twice as deep as those in the other granary (Building VIII) in this half of the *praetentura*. Large flat stones were discovered *in situ* at the bottom of the trenches; these were certainly used as base-plates for the timber uprights which carried the raised platform of the granary. From the positioning of the stones the uprights can be assumed to have been placed at *c.* 4-ft. (1.22 m) intervals along the trenches while the distance between the timbers in adjacent trenches was *c.* 7 ft. 6 in. (2.3 m).

The foundation-trenches for the proto-Flavian granary were much deeper and more impressive than those of any other building so far excavated at Strageath except the Flavian *porta decumana* (p. 27), to the construction of which they bear a striking resemblance. The majority of the Flavian construction-trenches were only *c.* 1 ft. (0.3 m) wide and deep; even in the granary, Building VIII, they did not exceed 2 ft in depth and many were 3–6 in. shallower. The trenches of the proto-Flavian granary were also much more regular in outline and spacing that those of the Building VIII or indeed those of the other buildings of the Flavian fort. The granary-trenches represent the highest standards of military construction and are perhaps suggestive of legionary rather than auxiliary workmanship; at the very least they indicate the work of a unit other than that responsible for the rest of the Flavian buildings.

When compared to the majority of known military timber granaries in Britain,[2] the proto-Flavian granary at Strageath exhibits several unusual features. The most striking of these is its size; at 31 ft. 6 in. by 25 ft. (9.6 × 7.6 m), 788 sq. ft. (73 m^2), it is very much smaller than most known granaries; indeed its area is much less than half of that of many others. (Manning records only two military granaries of comparable size, those at Abergavenny and Crawford.) The small size of the granary indicates that it was not the main granary of an auxiliary unit. It may perhaps have been erected as a temporary measure (see p. 117) or may indeed never have been completed (and thus may represent a change of plan while construction-work was still in progress), for it is the length rather than width which is truly exceptional. Whilst the uprights were slightly closer set than normal along the trenches, the distance between the uprights in separate trenches was unusually great. The average distance between the uprights of the substructure of known timber granaries both longitudinally and latitudinally is *c.* 5 ft. (1.5 m). However, the foundation-trenches at both Crawford and Fendoch were placed at irregular intervals ranging at the former from 1.5 m to 3 m and at the latter from 1.5 m to 2.3 m. The timbers used in the wider-spaced trenches at Strageath would need to have been of larger dimensions than those used elsewhere if they were to carry a similar load. The unusually small number of foundation-trenches is paralleled at Crawford, a fort where the troops in residence were exceptionally few. The siting of the proto-Flavian granary at Strageath at the junction of the *viae principalis* and *praetoria*, presumably facing onto the latter, is also highly unusual. The normal position for the granaries in an auxiliary fort was in the central range or, less frequently, adjacent to one of the gateways. This unusual position is a further indication that the granary was not erected with the layout of a normal auxiliary fort in mind. Whether the granary was contemporary with the buildings in the *retentura* is impossible to decide; it was certainly demolished before those in the *praetentura* were erected. See p. 117 for a suggestion about its purpose.

(ii) Flavian (FIG. 40)

In the main Flavian period the right *praetentura* was occupied by four timber structures built on a north-south alignment, parallel with the *via principalis*; their posts were set in continuous

1. W.H. Manning, *Saalburg Jahrbuch* 1975, 105 f.
2. *ibid.*, 105–29.

construction-trenches. The easternmost two of these, Buildings V and VI, were observed to overlie the proto-Flavian granary. They therefore represent at least a partial replanning of the site. No trace of earlier buildings was noted in the rest of the northern *praetentura* (on a possible exception, there discounted, see p. 74): Buildings VII and VIII were the first erected on their plots. Moreover, all four excavated buildings (V–VIII) undoubtedly belong to one constructional phase; all the construction-trenches were of the type typical of the Flavian period at Strageath, being irregular in outline, roughly-cut and badly-aligned, and all except those of VIII measuring *c.* 1 ft. (0.3 m) in width and depth (PL. XXII B).

Building V lay adjacent to the *via principalis* (PL. XXVII B) and presumably faced onto it. The southern end-wall of the building was located in Trench B V; it was set back approximately 4 ft. (1.22 m) from the edge of the *via praetoria*. The building was 24 ft. (7.3 m) wide; it is restored with a length of 140 ft. (42.67 m) but could have been up to 5 ft. (1.5 m) longer. The construction-trench of a longitudinal partition was discovered in Trench A I (FIG. 44 (p. 81), Section B–C); this lay some 10 ft. (3.05 m) back from the front of the building, dividing it in two; the front range was 9 ft. (2.75 m) wide internally and the rear 12 ft. 6 in. (3.81 m). This construction-trench continued along Trench D III but was not present in Trench B III. There were also at least two east-west partitions in the rear division of the building; one, in Trench A I, lay 85 ft. (26 m) from the southern end of the building and the other, in Trench D III, at 42 ft. (12.8 m) (FIG. 49 (p. 84), Section Y–Y^1). Since the eastern wall bordered on the *via principalis*, Building V was not provided with a veranda.

The function of Building V is uncertain. The width is less than that of adjoining barracks and the depths of its wall-trenches are appreciably less than its neighbour's (FIG. 44, Section A–D). The lack of regular *contubernia* also supports the view that Building V was not a barrack. The presence of two cavalry barracks in the *retentura* might be thought to require complementary stables somewhere within the fort, but the existence of a partial and off-centre longitudinal partition in Building V reduces the likelihood of this identification. A store or workshop appears the more likely explanation, which is perhaps strengthened by the pit full of stiff clean pink clay with some large stones found within it in Trench A I (FIG. 44, Section A–B, 53). A second similar clay-pit was found just outside the south wall of the building in Trench B V. The position of the latter pit suggests use during building-construction.

Two other pits within the area of Building V merit mention; both support the workshop theory. Pit A in Trench 77 A I was *c.* 5 ft. (1.5 m) in diameter and 3 ft. (0.9 m) deep (FIG. 46, Section L–M). Over a thin band of loose sandy gravel on the floor of the pit (24) lay a deposit of sand containing much charcoal (23); this was sealed by 22, a layer containing burnt daub and charcoal. Above 22 the main part of the pit was filled with a demolition-deposit of dark soil and burnt daub. The pit is smaller than a normal demolition-pit and may have been in use during the life of Building V. For Pit C, a nearby demolition-pit of the Flavian period, see p. 83.

In Trench 79 D III a shaft was found, D-shaped in plan and measuring *c.* 5 by 5 ft. (1.5 by 1.5 m). The sides were vertical: excavation was abandoned at 8½ ft. (2.6 m) because of the danger of collapse (FIG. 49, Section Y–Y^1). The filling consisted of bands of dark brown sandy soil with some burnt daub in the lower levels. An Antonine I wall-trench crossed the top of the fill. This shaft was the only one of its kind to be found in the fort: in view of the local geology it seems unlikely that a well was being attempted, but it does recall certain shafts known at Bertha[3] and at Newstead,[4] many of which were extramural. It does not resemble a normal demolition-pit, and is likely to have been functional within the building.

Building VI was built back to back with Building V, with a space of *c.* 1½ ft. (0.46 m) between. The southern end-wall was not located but is restored in line with that of Building V on the evidence seen in Trench B VII. The northern part of the building has not been excavated but, like Building V, Building VI is known to have been at least 90 ft. (27.5 m) long and is restored on FIG.

3. H. Adamson, *The Muses' Threnodie* (Perth, 1774).
4. J. Curle, *A Roman Frontier Post and its People* (Glasgow, 1911), 116 ff.

40 with a length of 142 ft. 6 in. (43.43 m), to include a centurion's house 40 ft. (12.2 m) long. Building VI was 27 ft. (8.2 m) wide and faced west onto an unmetalled alleyway 4 ft. (1.2 m) wide, dividing its veranda from that of Building VII. The veranda posts stood at intervals of *c.* 3 ft. (0.92 m). The veranda itself was found to be 6 ft. (1.83 m) wide in Trench A I but narrowed to 4 ft. (1.22 m) in Trench B III. The building was probably divided internally into a double row of rooms forming *contubernia*, although the position of the partition walls is uncertain. A longitudinal construction-trench was excavated in Trench A I *c.* 5 ft (1.53 m) east of the front wall of the building and this appeared to continue to north and south of A I; in Trench B III, however, the longitudinal trench lay *c.* 10 ft. (3.05 m) east of the front wall. This construction-trench was cut by later demolition pits at both ends in Trench B III and thus it is not clear whether the trench continued on the same line to the north. Possibly it terminated at the northern edge of Trench B III at the intersection with an east-west partition wall. For the end-room of a barrack block to have an internal arrangement different from that of the rest of the block is not unknown; it would represent the quarters of the *principales*. The location of the partitions running east-west across the building is less certain. One was excavated along the northern edge of Trench B III. An end-room *c.* 17 ft. (5.18 m) wide was thus created; this is unusually wide for a normal auxiliary *contubernium* but is perhaps suitable for the *principales*. The front room of this *contubernium* was partially divided 11 ft. (3.35 m) from the end wall by a wall-trench which continued out across the veranda. Nor do the internal construction-trenches revealed in Trench A I fit the normal layout of *contubernia*. Two east-west trenches were excavated in the front section of the building approximately 5 ft. (1.53 m) apart; one of these continued across the veranda where it joined a veranda post-hole (PL. XXII B). Only a short length of east-west construction-trench was located in the rear section of the building. If the building were divided into *contubernia* *c.* 12 ft. (3.66 m) wide, there would have been a wall roughly on the line of this construction-trench. The extra internal division of the front room of one of the *contubernia* may perhaps be interpreted as a cupboard. The number of *contubernia* in this barrack is therefore probably seven, the quarters nearest the *via praetoria* being wider than the rest. All the construction-trenches excavated were somewhat irregular in outline and alignment; their dimensions varied but they were always a little less than 1 ft. (0.305 m) deep and not more than 1 ft. wide (Section B–D). In Trench A I some post-holes were located at the base of the construction trenches (PL. XXII B); they were between 1½ ft. (0.46 m) and 2 ft. (0.61 m) apart. The size of the posts themselves varied; they were on average 6 in. (0.15 m) across but were 9 in. (0.23 m) across at wall-junctions.

Building VII faced Building VI across the above-mentioned alleyway, as was normal for paired barrack-blocks. The line of the southern end-wall was established by means of small extensions to the south of Trench B I. The building was situated approximately 6 ft. (1.83 m) from the *via praetoria*. It is known to have been at least 85 ft. (25.9 m) long and, although the northern end has not been excavated, can be assumed to have had a length of 140 ft. (42.67 m) including a separate centurion's house 40 ft. (12.2 m) long. As a result of a notable discrepancy in the alignment of the rear (western) wall, the width of the building varied between 35 ft. (10.67 m) in Trench A I and 31 ft. (9.46 m) in Trench B I. The barrack was fronted by a veranda *c.* 5 ft. (1.53 m) wide supported by posts set at intervals of about 6 ft. (1.83 m). A construction-trench belonging to an internal longitudinal partition-wall was excavated in Trenches A I and B I; in both places this trench lay some 10 ft. (3.05 m) west of the front wall of the building, creating a front range of about 9 ft. (2.75 m) deep. The depth of the rear rooms of the barracks varied between 17 ft. (5.18 m) in Trench A I and 14 ft. (4.27 m) in Trench B I. An east-west partition was located in extensions to the north of Trench B I; this created an end *contubernium* approximately 12 ft. (3.66 m) wide. In Trench A I the east-west construction-trenches were not in line, but they were in roughly the right position to suit a row of *contubernia* 12 ft. (3.66 m) wide. The continuation of the partition-wall across part of the veranda in Trench A I reflects the same phenomenon in Building VI, but is probably without structural significance. As in Building VI, the number of *contubernia* appears to have been seven. The implications of these figures for the character of the garrison are discussed on pp. 119–20.

The construction-trenches here too were poorly aligned and irregular in outline; the width and depth were variable but very rarely more than 1 ft. (0.30 m). Moreover, the wall between the rear rooms of the *contubernia* in Trench A I was not indicated by a continuous trench; the uprights were set partly in a construction-trench and partly in individual post-pits. A series of relatively close-set post- and stake-holes were observed in the construction-trench which marked the rear wall of Building VII in Trench A II; these were at 6 in. (0.15 m) intervals and many had pointed profiles; the smaller stake-holes indicate the supports for wattle and daub between the main uprights.

For a Table setting out the various dimensions of these barracks, see p. 136.

The space between Building VII and the *intervallum* was not, as expected, occupied by a third barrack-block but by a granary (**Building VIII**). This lay adjacent to the *via sagularis* (PL. XXVI B), a street represented by gravel metalling 2½ in. (6.1 cm) thick laid, at least in Trench B I, on a turf bedding (FIG. 47, Section P–Q, 41). The road was 9½ ft. (2.9 m) wide and beyond it was an *intervallum* space of 18½ ft. (5.6 m). Building VIII was easily recognisable as a granary from the typical grid of roughly parallel foundation-trenches running east-west across its width. Two of these and parts of two more were excavated in Trench A II (PL. XXIV A), where the extreme west ends had been destroyed by the Antonine I drain. No trenches belonging to the grid were present in Trench B I but three more were discovered at the northern end of Trench B VI, which was dug to determine the position of the front of the building: its length was finally established in Trench 85 N III, in which the granary was found to extend to within 9 ft. (2.74 m) of the northern *via sagularis* (FIG. 48, Section V–W). It was thus 107 ft. (32.61 m) long with 23 transverse trenches, and was 29 ft. (8.8 m) wide;[5] these dimensions are smaller than those of the corresponding granary in the left *praetentura* (Building XVI, p. 107) but still imply a building far larger than the *horrea* normally found in auxiliary forts. The problems raised by this abnormal storage-capacity are discussed on p. 123

Building VIII lay *c.* 4 ft. (1.22 m) from the rear of Building VII and *c.* 3 ft. (0.92 m) from the *via sagularis.* The southernmost foundation-trench lay some 37 ft. (11.3 m) back from the *via praetoria.* In front of the granary lay a yard with a fine gravel floor, somewhat patchy but on average 4 to 6 in. (10–15 cm) thick, which was observed in both B I and B VI to lie directly on the old ground-surface (FIG. 47 (p. 83), Section Q–R, 17); this metalled area stretched some 34 ft. (10.4 m) northwards from the edge of the *via praetoria* but stopped *c.* 3 ft. (0.9 m) short of the end-wall of the granary. The lack of gravel here suggests that there was a loading area at this point with a raised wooden platform underneath which metalling would have been unnecessary. Post-holes for the timbers to support a roof-extension or platform were not located in Trench B VI but the area explored was too small to rule out their existence. This gravelled yard was bounded on the west by a fence marked by a trench over 1 ft. (0.3 m) deep, running parallel to and 5 ft. (1.5 m) west of Building VII, and on the west by a timber-lined drain (FIG. 47, Section Q–R) which separated it from the *via sagularis*, here inturning for the gate. Another fence-line, running obliquely from the south-east corner of the granary towards the *via praetoria*, was set in a trench cut through the gravel and may therefore be secondary. The uprights, visible in Trenches B I and B VI, stood in a series of interconnecting post-holes within the trench. Two large post-pits were found to the west of this fence some 20 ft. (6.1 m) south of the granary; three post-holes were observed in the easternmost of these and one in the other. These posts cannot belong to a gate into the yard from the *via praetoria*, since they are only 4 ft. (1.22 m) apart at most, leaving insufficient space for a waggon to pass between. They must, therefore, either be part of a later feature or belong to an east-west fence; the yard would thus have been enclosed on two sides and waggons could have entered it from the *via sagularis* alone.

The character of the grid of tranverse foundation-trenches is in strong contrast to that of the proto-Flavian granary described above, but is typical of the less regular layout found in auxiliary forts elsewhere. The individual trenches were irregular in alignment and outline and the spacing between them was variable (it ranged from 1½ ft. (0.46 m) to 5 ft. (1.52 m)). In the main, the foundation-trenches were *c.* 5 ft. (1.52 m) apart, as was the norm in Roman military timber

5. Or perhaps only 27 ft., see p. 74.

granaries (Manning, *S.J.* 1975, 108; chart 2); this spacing entails the assumption that there were a further five trenches in the unexcavated area between Trenches A II and B VI. The width and depth of the foundation-trenches were also variable, but they were normally 1 ft. 3 in. (0.38 m) wide and *c.* 1 ft. 6 in. (0.46 m) deep. These dimensions are very different from those of the trenches in the proto-Flavian granary (p. 70), which were unusually substantial. In both Trench A II and Trench B VI some of the post positions within the trenches were located. These posts were *c.* 4 ft. (1.22 m) apart (this corresponds to the norm as established by Manning); some, at least, had been driven in below the bottom of the trench.

An unusual feature, hard to explain, was found in Trench 77 A II at the west edge of the granary. Here the granary trenches were crossed by a north-south trench 14 in. (35.6 cm) deep, whose west side had itself been cut away by the Antonine I drain. Within the width of the excavation in A II this trench contained seven stakeholes (FIG. 40), *c.* 3 in. (7.6 cm) in diameter; these were pointed and had been driven down to a depth of 1 ft. (0.3 m) below the bottom of the trench itself (FIG. 45, Section G–H). Since the trench containing the stakeholes is cut by the Antonine I drain, it should be of Flavian date; yet it cuts off *c.* 2 ft. (0.6 m) from the original ends of the granary trenches (to judge by the alignment of the building as shown on FIG. 40). No trace of a similar feature was found in Trench N III, and indeed it is almost unknown for a timber granary to possess longitudinal trenches for earth-fast walls at the sides. The stakeholes are perhaps best seen as a local repair to the granary wall or perhaps as cladding to close off some of the space below the raised floor. If so the stakeholes should lie directly under the side wall of the granary and the building could not have extended to the end of the transverse trenches; it may thus have had a width of only 27 ft. (8.23 m) rather than the 29 ft. (8.84 m) suggested earlier. An alternative explanation might be that this feature, perhaps with the wall-trench mentioned above as running 5 ft. west of Building VII, indicates preliminary first steps in the construction of a third barrack-block before the decision to build the granary on this plot was taken. If so, the barrack would have been 32 ft. (9.75 m) wide, which is 2 ft. (0.6 m) wider than Building VI at its widest point, and about 5 ft. (1.5 m) wider than any other barrack in the *praetentura*; indeed, it would have been the widest barrack in the whole Flavian fort. These considerations suggest caution over this interpretation.

(iii) Antonine I (FIG. 41)

During the Antonine I period the right *praetentura* was again occupied by four timber structures aligned parallel with the *via principalis*. In the main, buildings were based on individual post construction and were, therefore, very different in character from the Flavian structures whose demolition-layer they overlay; posts set in continuous trenches were, however, used occasionally, as in Buildings V and VIII. The layout and construction of the Antonine I period was frequently even more irregular than that of the Flavian period.

Building V lay adjacent to the *via principalis* and *c.* 3 ft. (0.9 m) away from it; the southern end lay at approximately the same distance from the *via praetoria*. The building probably faced not onto the *via principalis* but onto an unmetalled alleyway, 8 ft. (2.4 m) wide, which separated it from Building VI. Like all Antonine I barrack-blocks at Strageath, Building V lacked a veranda, but the larger room in each *contubernium* is on the east side, which suggests that the barrack faces west.

The southern end-wall of Building V was located in Trench B V. The building is thus known to have been at least 92 ft. (28 m) long and, on the assumption that it extended as far as the northern *intervallum* street, will have had a length of *c.* 137 ft. (41.75 m); the width was 24 ft. (7.3 m). Building V was clearly identifiable as a barrack from the internal paritítions observed in Trenches A I, B III and D III. A longitudinal partition-wall, marked by a line of post-holes, was observed in all three trenches on the same north-south alignment and continued to the north of Trench A I; it divided the building into two sections, the eastern being 11 ft. (3.35 m) deep internally and the western 10 ft. (3.05 m). Excavation also revealed a series of transverse partitions dividing the *contubernia*. Only one of these walls was present in Trench A I but there were two in B III, thus yielding the full ground-plan of a *contubernium*, 8 ft. (2.44 m) wide internally. Four more partitions were located in Trench D III; both these and the single wall in A I were suitably positioned to fit *contubernia* commensurate with the one in B III. The block thus contained at least ten *contubernia*; the total number is unlikely to have been greater than this since the northern, unexcavated, section of the building can reasonably be assigned to the centurion's quarters and there is space for these to be 42 ft. (12.8 m) long. Ten is the normal number of *contubernia* required to house a full century of infantry. In Trench D III east-west lines of post-holes were discovered which ran parallel but only 2 to 3 ft. (0.61 to 0.92 m) apart; these were obviously too close together to represent the divisions of *contubernia*. In each case one of the lines must represent the wall between *contubernia* and the other some internal fixture such as a cupboard.

The main timber uprights of Building V were placed at intervals of 2 to 3 ft. (0.61–.092 m) (PL. XXVII B). The dimensions of the post-pipes were variable, ranging from 4 by 4 in. to 10 by 10 in. (0.10 by 0.10 m to 0.25 by 0.25 m); but the majority were *c.* 6 by 6 in. (0.15 by 0.15 m). The post-holes varied between 5 and 9 in. (0.12–.023 m) in depth, occasionally being deeper still. The posts were frequently held in place by substantial stone packers and in Trench D III two of the posts had basal stones in their pits. Some of the posts were set in large pits containing several post-holes (Trench A I) while others were set in exceptionally deep post-trenches (Trench D III) (FIG. 49, Section Y–Y[1]); these slots were less regular than the Flavian construction-trenches and were not always continuous for the full length of the wall.

Building VI lay on the western side of the unmetalled alleyway mentioned above, but the building may have been entered from the metalled street between it and Building VII. Neither end of the building has been located. However, if we assume that the southern end-wall was on line with the ends of Buildings V and VIII and that the building extended to the northern *intervallum*, the full length must have been *c.* 138 ft. (42.06 m). The building was only 18 ft. (5.4 m) wide and too narrow to have served as a barrack-block; moreover it lacked a longitudinal partition. A traverse partition occurred in Trench B I, some 16 ft. (4.9 m) from the southern end of the building; and in Trench A I a second line of post-holes, parallel to the eastern outer wall but 2 ft. (0.61 m) west of it, must mark some interior fitting. All the uprights were set in individual post-holes, some supported with stone packers; their dimensions were similar to those of Building V, most of the post-holes being 9 in. (0.23 m) deep.

Building VI corresponds closely in length and breadth with Building XV in the corresponding position in the southern *praetentura*. Building XV (pp. 110–11) showed signs of having been an arms-store and *fabrica*. It seems doubtful if there was need for another, and Building VI may be interpreted either as a store-building or stable. The presence of a separate room at the south end does not disprove a stable; on the other hand, it may be noted that, if the buildings were equally divided into storage-rooms 16 ft. (4.9 m) wide, the relevant partitions would lie outside Trench A I on either side. The problem of identification is further discussed on p. 127.

A metalled street ran north-south between Buildings VI and VII. This occupied 8 ft. (2.44 m) of the 12-ft. (3.66-m) space between the buildings. The street was best preserved in the northern half of Trench A I. There was some large stone bottoming but the street consisted mainly of smaller stones with a surface of fine gravel; the whole was 3 to 3½ in. (8–9 cm) thick. Some large kerb-stones were still in place on the western side of the street.

To the west of this street lay **Building VII**; the internal lay-out identified it as a barrack-block. Although neither end-wall has been located by excavation, a further *contubernium* to the south of that discovered in Trench B I would place the southern end of the building on line with the ends of Buildings V and VIII; the northern end has been placed *c.* 4 ft. (1.22 m) from the northern *via sagularis* in FIG. 41, giving an overall length of 140 ft. (42.67 m) and a centurion's block 42 ft. (12.8 m) long. The barrack-block was 26 ft. (7.9 m) wide and possessed no veranda. As in Building V, a complete *contubernium* was uncovered in Trench B I; its internal dimensions were as follows: western room 10 ft. by 8 ft. (3.05 by 2.44 m), eastern room 13 ft. by 8 ft. (3.97 by 2.44 m). That all the *contubernia* were *c.* 8 ft. (2.44 m) wide is substantiated by the position of the east-west wall located in Trench A II. (That this wall was not traced to the east of the central wall was probably due to the presence of intersecting Antonine I demolition-pits in this area.) A total of ten contubernia can be assumed with a centurion's quarters beyond. Once again there was sufficient accommodation for a full century of infantry. The building must face the metalled street despite the size of the front rooms, for there is little space for movement between it and Building VIII. The longitudinal partition-wall did not run parallel to the exterior walls, but Antonine I buildings were frequently irregular in plan. If the wall is correctly identified with the posts set in a construction-trench in Trench A II, the *contubernium* here would have been divided into a western room 8 ft. (2.44 m) deep and an eastern room 15 ft. (4.57 m) deep. In general the posts were set in post-holes *c.* 9 in. (0.23 m) deep and *c.* 2 ft. (0.61 m) apart and were often provided with large stone packers.

Buildings VII and VIII were separated by an alleyway surfaced with 3 in. (0.08 m) of fine gravel; this alleyway narrowed in width from 4 ft. (1.22 m) at the *via praetoria* to 2 ft. (0.61 m) in Trench A II.

The internal layout of **Building VIII** indicates that this too was a barrack-block, although much less regular in plan than Barracks V and VII. The southern end-wall was located in Trench B II adjacent to the *via praetoria* and the northern wall in Trench 85 N III, giving an overall length of 141 ft. (42.98 m). The width of the building varied from *c.* 23 ft. (7 m) in Trench B I to *c.* 25 ft. (7.62 m) in Trench A II. Again there was no veranda but the barrack faced west onto the *via sagularis*; between the barrack-block and the street-drain lay a strip of cobbles and gravel 30 in. (0.76 m) wide and 10 in. (0.26 m) deep, which could have formed a walkway along the front of the *contubernia*; no doubt, however, the street-drain was covered.

The longitudinal partition-wall was marked by a north-south line of post-holes observed in both trenches; this wall divided the *contubernia* into front and rear rooms which were 8 ft. (2.44 m) and 12 ft. (3.66 m) deep internally in Trench B I and 7 ft. (2.14 m) and 14 ft. (4.27 m) in Trench A II. The individual *contubernia* were much wider than those in Buildings V and VII, measuring *c.* 14 ft. (4.27 m) internally. The positions of the partition-walls for the southern three *contubernia* were established in Trenches B I, B II and B VI and a further east-west wall, suitably sited, was located in Trench A II. A total of seven *contubernia* thus existed, beyond which lay an officers' block 45 ft. (13.7 m) long and 24 ft. (7.3 m) wide; this was located in Trench 85 N III and consisted of two rooms 12 ft. (3.66 m) wide and an end one with a width of 15 ft. (4.57 m). The middle room here had been provided with a well-preserved floor of pebbles set in hard pink clay. Whether these three rooms were divided into six by a central partition could not be established. The suggestion that Building VIII may have accommodated two *turmae* of a *cohors equitata* is discussed on p. 126. The idea is supported by the large size of the *contubernia* and by the greater irregularity and different method of construction which suggests building and occupation by a different group. The uprights for the outer walls were set in very irregularly-cut trenches (FIGS. 45, 47, Sections F–G, Q–R) supported by stone packers; the posts were mainly 6 in. (0.15 m) across and were more closely spaced than in the other buildings, being frequently less than 1 ft. (0.305 m) apart. The unusual construction method was best illustrated by the western wall in Trench B I; here the post-holes for the uprights were located in widenings of a north-south trench 6 in. (0.15 m) deep (this trench was 10 in. (0.26 m) wide at the top but narrowed to 7 in. (0.18 m) at the bottom). Beneath the post-holes post-pits *c.* 1 ft. (0.30 m) deep were discovered; these contained very large stones used as packers beneath and around the timbers. In Trench 77 A II there was seen a trench cut in the wrong position on the east side of the building (FIG. 41). It was only 10 in. (25.4 cm) wide and 9 in. (22.8 cm) deep (FIG. 45, Section F–G, 44) and had been cut at an angle to the true wall-line.

The internal walls of the building were formed by posts driven into holes *c.* 8 in. (0.2 m) deep, sometimes supported by stone packers. These posts were found to be very irregularly placed, especially in Trench A II; they were not neatly aligned as those in Buildings V and VII. In addition traces of smaller-sized posts were discovered between the main post-holes.

For a Table setting out the various measurements of these barracks, see p. 137.

The **via sagularis**. In this period, unlike the Flavian, the rampart was not inturned at the *porta* *praetoria*; no Antonine I rampart-turves were found in Trench B I and the back of the rampart presumably lay further to the west as in Trench A III. The **western via sagularis**, which was found to be 15 ft. (4.6 m) wide, also ran straight north-south. It was well-preserved in Trench B I (FIG. 47, Section P–R, 10) where several kerbstones were found *in situ* on both sides of the street. The metalling was made up of large bedding-stones surfaced with a layer of fine gravel; the gravel ranged from 4 in. (0.1 m) thick near the kerb to 6 in. (0.15 m) at the centre, and there was a noticeable camber. The kerbs were *c.* 15 in. (0.38 m) wide. In Trench A II the street was flatter and less thick (FIG. 45, Section G–I, 27; see also PL. XXVI).

The **northern via sagularis** was located in Trench 85 N III, and its line could be reconstructed by linking it to a length recovered in the northern *retentura* in Trench 85 N I (p. 60). In N III the full width could not be examined: it was at least 14 ft. (4.27 m) wide and consisted of gravel metalling 8 in. (20.3 cm) thick; no kerb stones were present here (FIG. 48, Section V–W, 15)

The **intervallum drain**. Between the eastern kerb of the western *via sagularis* and the path in front of Building VIII ran an impressive drain (PL. XXVI A). In Trench B I (FIG. 47, Section Q–R) it was 16 in. (0.41 m) deep and narrowed from a width of 22 in. (0.57 m) at the top to 18 in. (0.46 m) at the bottom; in A II it reached a depth of 2 ft. 3 in. (0.68 m) and was 1 ft. 10 in. (0.56 m) wide (FIG. 45, Section G–H). It was flat-bottomed and certainly plank-lined although no peg-holes were detected in either of these lengths. At the angle the drain turned to continue running along the inner edge of the northern *via sagularis*, where it was found in Trench 85 N III (FIG. 48, Section V–W). In this section stakeholes for retaining the plank lining were recorded; they were at somewhat irregular intervals of between 1 and 1½ ft. (0.3–0.46 m) and the drain itself had evidently been originally 1 ft. wide. The fall was to the north, declining from 121.00 ft. O.D. in B I, 120.8 in A II, to 119.62 in Trench N III.

(iv) Antonine II (Fig. 42)

Above the Antonine I demolition-levels and immediately below the ploughsoil, which was *c.* 1 ft. (0.30 m) deep over the whole area, lay the Antonine II remains. The Antonine II layers had suffered much from plough-damage; no demolition-layer survived, the occupation-layer was contaminated by ploughsoil and the road-surfaces were damaged and even completely destroyed in places. Even so, sufficient archaeological evidence remained to formulate a clear plan of the Antonine II buildings and streets. In this period the right *praetentura* was occupied by three barrack-blocks separated by metalled streets. All three buildings were of individual-post construction; the post-holes were on average 6 in. (0.15 m) in diameter and between 6 in. and 1 ft. (0.15 m and 0.30 m) deep. Stone packers were sometimes discovered *in situ*; others had no doubt been displaced by the plough. None of the three barracks had been provided with a veranda; in each the front rooms of the *contubernia* opened directly onto the street as in the Antonine I period.

All three barrack-blocks, as in the two earlier periods, were aligned parallel with the *via principalis*. **Building V**, the most easterly of the three, lay immediately adjacent to this street; indeed the post-holes for the eastern wall of the building were found up against the kerb-stones. This was probably the rear wall of the building since the smaller rooms, probably to be identified with the front rooms, lay on the west of the block; the barrack would thus have faced west onto the narrow street which divided it from the next block, the two forming a facing pair in the normal manner. The line of the southern end-wall was located in Trench B IV, immediately adjacent to the kerbing of the *via praetoria*. The building is thus known to have been at least 95 ft. (29 m) long and, in FIG. 42 has been extended to within 4 ft. (1.22 m) of the line of the *via sagularis*, giving it an overall length of 151 ft. (46 m) including a centurion's block 48 ft. (14.6 m) long. The building was found to be 35 ft. (10.8 m) wide in both Trench A I and Trench B III, and a longitudinal partition-wall divided it into front rooms 12 ft. (3.66 m) deep internally and rear rooms 19 ft. (5.8 m) deep. Altogether seven of the east-west partitions between individual *contubernia* were located, two in Trench B III, four in D III and one in A I. These were placed at irregular intervals creating *contubernia* varying in width between 9 and 12 ft. (2.75 and 3.66 m). The *contubernia* were thus much larger than those of the Antonine I barracks as well as displaying much greater irregularity of size. Nine *contubernia* are known to have existed and it is unlikely that there was a tenth, which would have unduly reduced the space available for the centurion. Over Pit C in Trench 77 A I (FIG. 46, Section J–K) a thin gravel floor (43) in the rear room of a *contubernium* survived where it had sunk into the pit. In Trenches B III and B V two parallel rows of post-holes *c.* 1 ft. (0.30 m) apart were found dividing the rear rooms of the *contubernia*; these probably indicate the presence of some fixture such as a cupboard. In general the post-holes were not accurately aligned. The main timbers were usually set at 2 to 3 ft. (0.61–0.92 m) intervals but were occasionally much closer together. The building, as a whole, represents the general irregularity of layout and construction typical of the Antonine II period at Strageath.

The street which ran north-south between Buildings V and VI was approximately 8 ft. (2.4 m) wide. This street was metalled with a single layer of large stones *c.* 4½ in. (0.12 m) thick (PL. XXVII A). The metalling was reasonably well-preserved on the northern side of Trench A I but in the southern had sunk into a large Antonine I pit *c.* 6 ft. (1.83 m) across (FIG. 44, Section C–D, Pit B).

Building VI, as suggested above, probably faced east onto this street. The precise length of this block remains uncertain, neither of the end-walls having been excavated; but it has been restored on FIG. 42 with a length of 152 ft. (46.3 m) including a centurion's block 44 ft. (13.4 m) long. The width of the building was found to be *c.* 32 ft. (9.8 m). A longitudinal wall divided the building into a row of front (eastern) rooms 10 ft. (3.05 m) deep internally and a row of rear (western) rooms 18 ft. (5.5 m) deep internally. Only one east-west partition was located; this was in Trench B I approximately 16 ft. (4.88 m) north of the probable line of the end-wall of the building. Reconstruction of the internal layout of the barrack-block is, therefore, difficult since the width of individual *contubernia* is unknown. The fact that no east-west wall was discovered in Trench A I, itself 12 ft. (3.66 m) wide, suggests that each *contubernium* may have had a greater width than this. The reconstructed plan thus shows seven *contubernia* 12 ft. (3.66 m) wide and an eighth 16 ft. (4.88 m) wide at the southern end of the building. However, the width of the individual *contubernia* may have varied as was noted in Building V, and it is possible that nine was the real total as in V. Also as noted in Building V the post-holes were often found to be off-line and were unevenly spaced. In Trench A I, in addition to the lines of post-holes for the walls, two further post-pits were found surrounded by large stone packers; they were 5 ft. (1.53 m) apart and lay about 4 ft. (1.22 m) east of the rear wall of the building. Their purpose is unknown but they may represent the position of built-in bunks in the rear room of the *contubernium*.

A heavily metalled street, *c.* 13 ft. (4 m) wide, ran north-south to the west of Building VI; the metalling extended right up to the walls of the buildings on either side (FIG. 44, Section E–F; FIG. 47, Section S–T; FIG. 46, Section N–O). The street consisted of heavy bedding stones, mostly still in place, surfaced with smaller stones and coarse gravel which was completely ploughed out in places; the bedding stones measured up to 1 ft. 6 in. (0.46 m) across. In Trench B I several of the kerbstones on the eastern edge of the street were found *in situ*; the kerb was 6 to 8 in. (0.15–0.2 m) wide.

Between this street and the *intervallum* area lay the third (westernmost) barrack block, **Building VII**. Its eastern wall-line was close to the edge of the street and the post-holes for the southern end-wall, located in Trench B II, were set against the kerbstones of the *via praetoria*, in line with the south wall of Building V; the north end was located in Trench 85 N III, giving an overall length of 155 ft. (47.24 m). Building VII was the narrowest of the three, being only 30 ft. (9.15 m) wide. The line of the longitudinal partition-wall was established in Trenches A II and B I; it divided the building into an eastern range 15 ft. (4.57 m) deep internally and a western range 12 ft. (3.66 m) deep. The smaller rooms lay on the western side, and the building probably faced west despite the proximity of the *intervallum* drain (which was, however, doubtless covered). The individual *contubernia* ranged from 8 to 9 ft. (2.44 to 2.75 m) in width; the partitions between the end four were located in Trenches B I and B VI. No complete line of post-holes running east-west was located in Trench A II but one almost certainly existed roughly on the line of the east-west axis of the trench, and some post-holes were found in this position. The barrack thus held ten *contubernia*, beyond which lay a centurion's quarters 61 ft. (18.59 m) long, the start of which was marked by a small offset on the west side. The quarters consisted of six rooms if the longitudinal partition found at the north end of N III continued through the block. With an area of *c.* 187 m^2 it is the largest centurion-block in the northern *praetentura* and has exactly the same area as that suggested for the largest centurion-block in the southern *praetentura*, that of Building XI. The narrowness of the *contubernia* in this block gives credence to the suggestion made above that Building VI contained some equally narrow *contubernia*. The alignment and spacing of the post-holes showed the typical irregularity of the Antonine period. As in the central barrack-block, the positions of internal fittings, such as cupboards or bunks, were indicated by post-holes; in Trench A II a post-hole was found some 3 ft. (0.92 m) south of what was probably the partition-wall. Also in Trench A II some of the floor was found *in situ*, having survived the plough-damage suffered elsewhere; this floor was made up partly of a layer of earth mixed with pebbles (FIG. 45, Section G–H, 7) and partly of a group of flat 'paving' stones together with traces of fine gravel overall. Some flat stones and scattered gravel were also observed in the area of this barrack-block excavated in Trench B I, although much more distubed.

For a Table setting out the various measurements of these barracks, see p. 138.

The **intervallum** and **via sagularis**. To the west of Building VII lay the *intervallum*. As in the Antonine I period the back of the rampart ran in a straight line north-south with no inturn for the gateway. The *via sagularis* was found to be 13 ft. (4 m) wide in Trench A II widening to 18 ft. (5.5 m) in Trench B I where it approached the *via praetoria* and gateway. The space between the barrack and the road narrowed correspondingly from 6 ft. (1.83 m) in A II to 3 ft. (0.92 m) in B I. The road was well-preserved in Trench A II (FIG. 45, Section G–I, 6) where it was made up of small pebbles with traces of fine gravel over a foundation of close-set flat stones; in Trench B I only some of the bedding stones (for the most part no more than 6 in. (0.15 m) across) remained; the surfacing had been ploughed away. The kerb on the eastern side (FIG. 47, Section Q–R, beside the contemporary drain) was well-defined, being formed by large oval boulders up to 18 in. (0.46 m) long set at right angles to the line of the kerb; the kerb itself was about 6 in. (0.15 m) high.[6]

East of the *via sagularis*, between the barrack and the kerb, ran a north-south drain; in places this was less than 1 ft. (0.305 m) away from the barrack wall. The drain was found to have a flat bottom and straight sides and must originally have had a wooden lining; it was approximately 22 in. (0.56 m) wide. The water flowed northwards along the drain; in the northern section of Trench B I (FIG. 47, Section Q–R) the drain was *c.* 6 in. (0.15 m) deep but shelved to less than 2 in. (0.05 m) and petered out further south half way across the trench; in Trench A II the drain was at least 9 in. (0.23 m) deep (FIG. 45, Section G–H, 9), but the O.D. level at both was approximately the same (122.7 ft. = 37.40 m).

The edge of the northern *via sagularis* was encountered in Trench 85 N III, and its alignment could be linked with a stretch of the same street in the *retentura* in Trench 85 N I. In N III 4 ft. (1.2 m) of metalling 6 in. (0.15 m) thick (FIG. 48, Section V–W, 5) extended into the trench to within 2 ft. (0.6 m) of the northern wall of Building VII. The metalling consisted of loosely laid round cobbles. There was no drain in this space, so presumably the drain had been taken along the outer side of the street.

Along the west side of the *via sagularis* in Trench A II ran a V–shaped ditch 4 ft. (1.2 m) wide and 2 ft. (0.61 m) deep (FIG. 45, Section H–I). The lowest filling (29) consisted of lumps of pink clay in pebbly earth, above which was yellow-brown earth (22) capped by a spread of charcoal (14). The ditch presumably supplemented the drain on the other side of the street in preventing rainwater flooding back from the rear of the rampart. Beyond it lay a pit (FIG. 45, Section H–I,

6. On FIG. 42, this kerb lies to the east of a second row of large stones which represent the Antonine I kerb protruding through the metalling.

Pit 2) 1 ft. 6 in. (0.46 m) deep containing a thick bed of powdered charcoal over a deposit of dark earth.

A urinal was discovered in Trench A II set in the *via sagularis* near its western edge. This was formed by the lower half of a Spanish amphora (Dressel 20) (2 ft. (0.61 m) in diameter, FIG. 129) cut off at the base to leave a 4 in. (0.1 m) hole (PL. XXV); the amphora contained amphora- and Black-burnished 2 sherds presumably to aid drainage. A phosphate test of the soil immediately below the amphora and from a spot 3 m south-west of it, however, showed rather more phosphate at the latter spot.

A furnace was discovered in Trench A II cut into the soil piled against the back of the Antonine II rampart (FIG. 42); it lay approximately 5 ft. (1.53 m) from the outer edge of the *via sagularis*. This furnace consisted of a flue *c.* 1 ft. (0.305 m) wide and 4 ft. (1.22 m) long which led into a narrow Y-shaped chamber at its northern end (FIG. 43; PL. XXIV B). It was built from roughly-coursed stones fixed in clay burnt to a bright orange colour. The roofing stones had collapsed; amidst them was found the remains of an iron wall-cramp. Ovens used for cooking were frequently built into the back of the ramparts in Roman forts but this structure was too narrow for a bread-oven and may have been used rather as an armourer's furnace; a large and very fragile sheet-bronze object (tentatively identified during excavation as part of a bronze patera) was found at the very bottom of the flue channel; this may have been scrap intended for melting down and reuse. Some 64 ft. (19.5 m) to the south a small rectangular channel was excavated in Trench B I; this was cut into the top of the soil accumulated behind the Antonine II rampart and lay on the same line as the furnace, approximately 4 ft. (1.22 m) from the edge of the street. Although not so heavily fired, this feature was again distinguished by areas of burnt clay, but there were no stones or other traces of a fully-operational furnace such as that described above. The feature did, however, seem to form a channel *c.* 1 ft. (0.305 m) wide and 4 ft. (1.22 m) long, dimensions similar to those of the flue, and it may have formed part of some kind of oven.

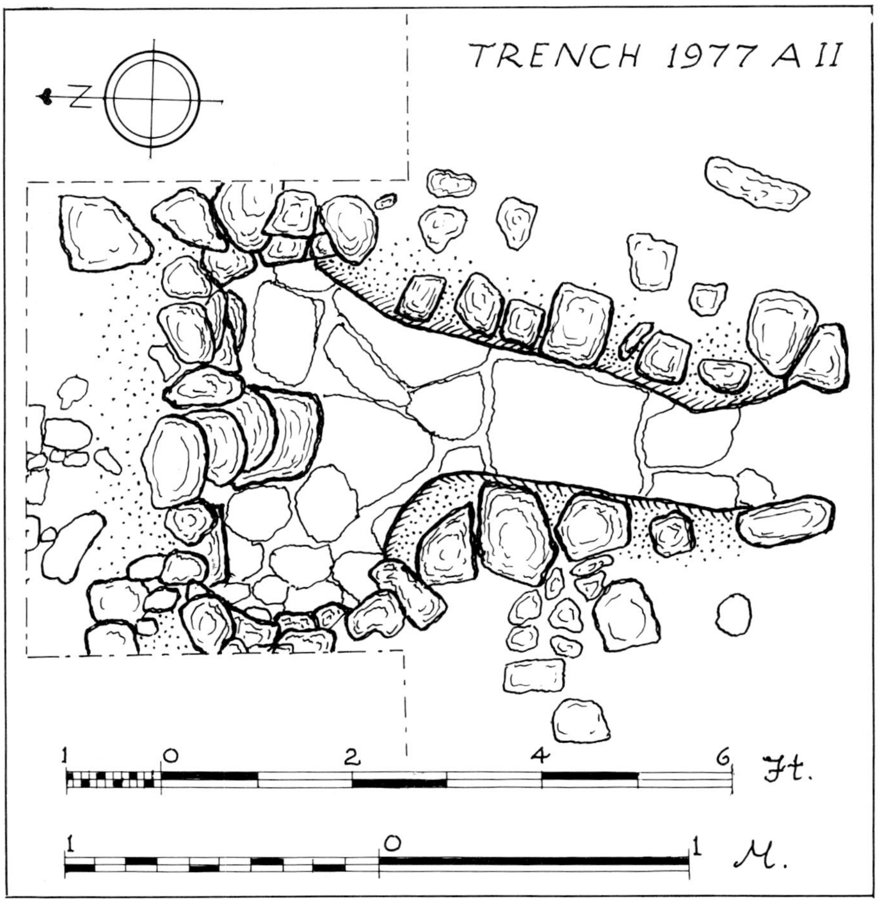

FIG. 43. Plan of Antonine II furnace in Trench 1977 A II. Scale, 1:24. (For position see FIG. 42).

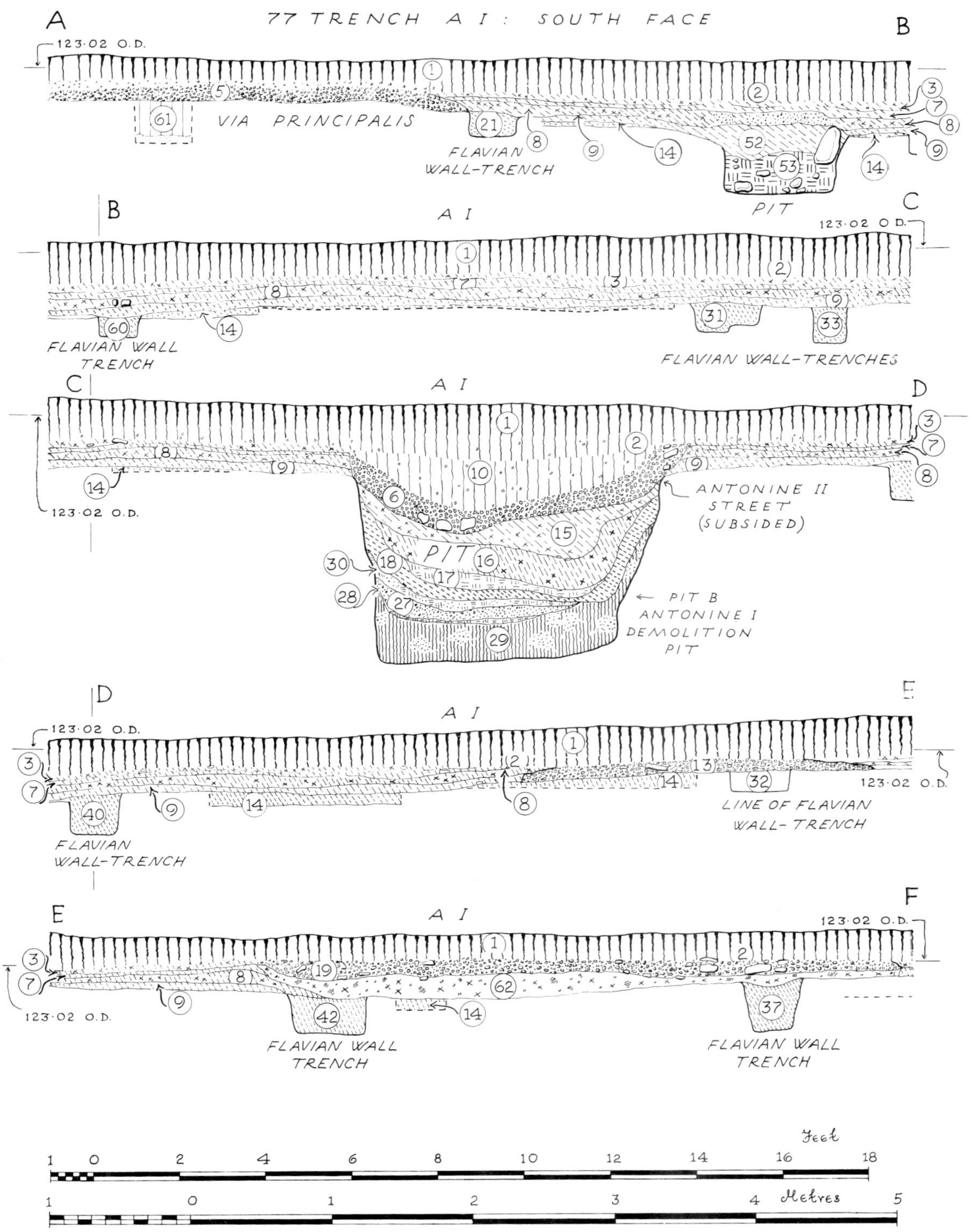

FIG. 44. The right (northern) *praetentura*: Sections A-F. Scale, 1:45. (For positions see p. 68, FIG. 39).

Demolition pits. Several of these were encountered in Trenches 77 A and 78 B, and they give a good idea of the character of such pits. Pit B interrupted the eastern wall of Antonine I Building VI but was sealed by Antonine II street-metalling, which had subsided into the top of the pit (FIG. 44, Section C–D; PL. XXVIII A). Below this, layers 15 and 16 contained varying amounts of burnt daub and charcoal, and both had obviously sunk into subsiding layers below. Layer 17, a light grey sandy soil, contained some light grey clay which may be unburnt daub from demolished walling, and 18, dark grey sandy soil, yielded a coin of (?) Hadrian (p. 139, No. 38). The main

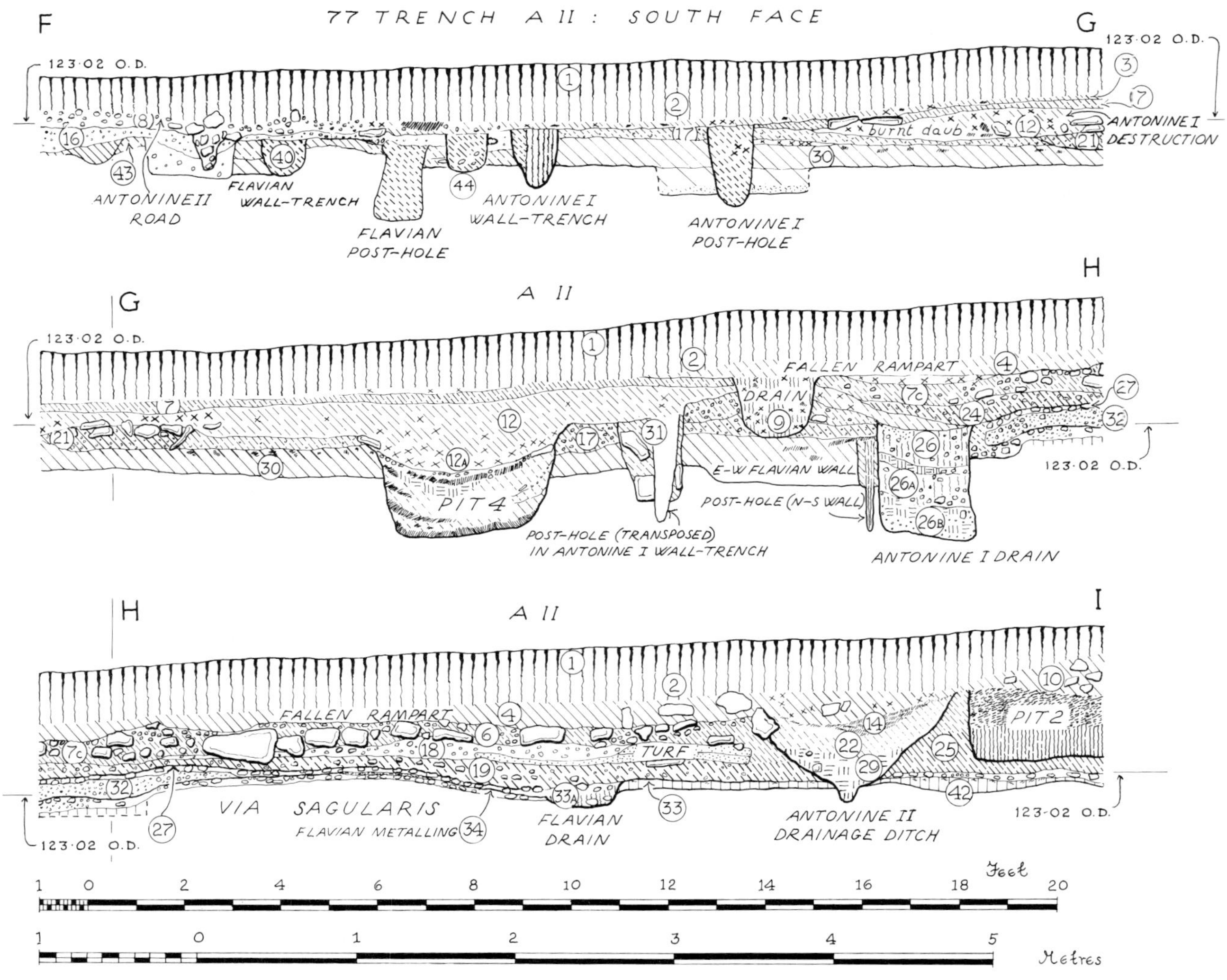

FIG. 45. The right (northern) *praetentura*: Sections F-I. Scale, 1:45. (For position see FIG. 39).

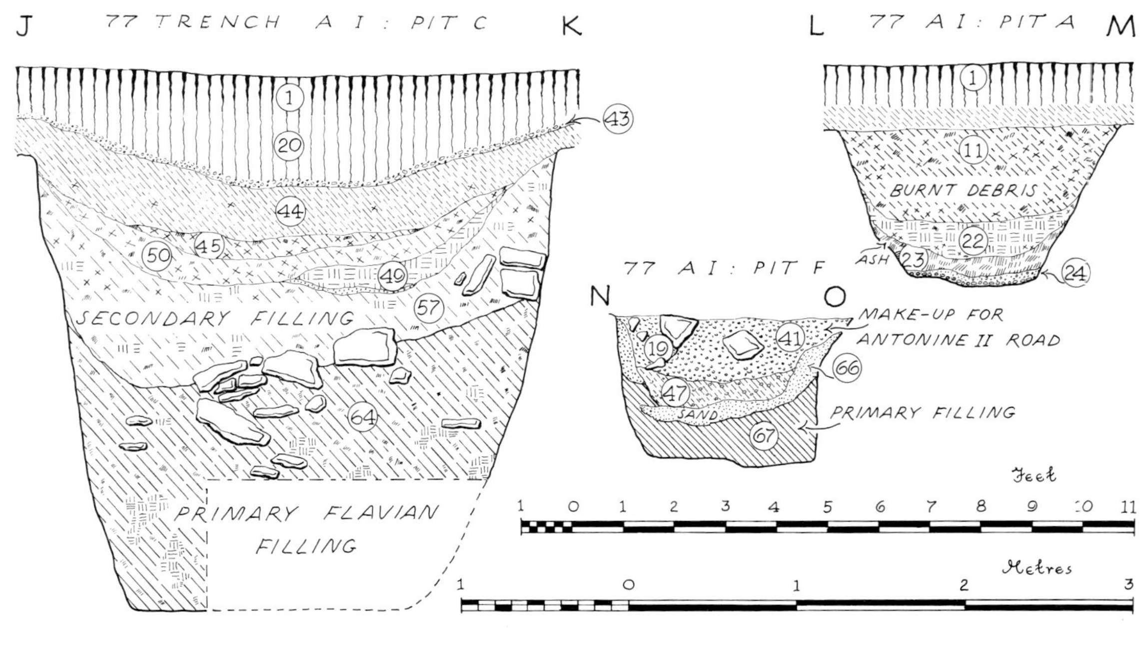

FIG. 46. The right (northern) *praetentura*: Sections J-O. Scale, 1:45. (For position see FIG. 39).

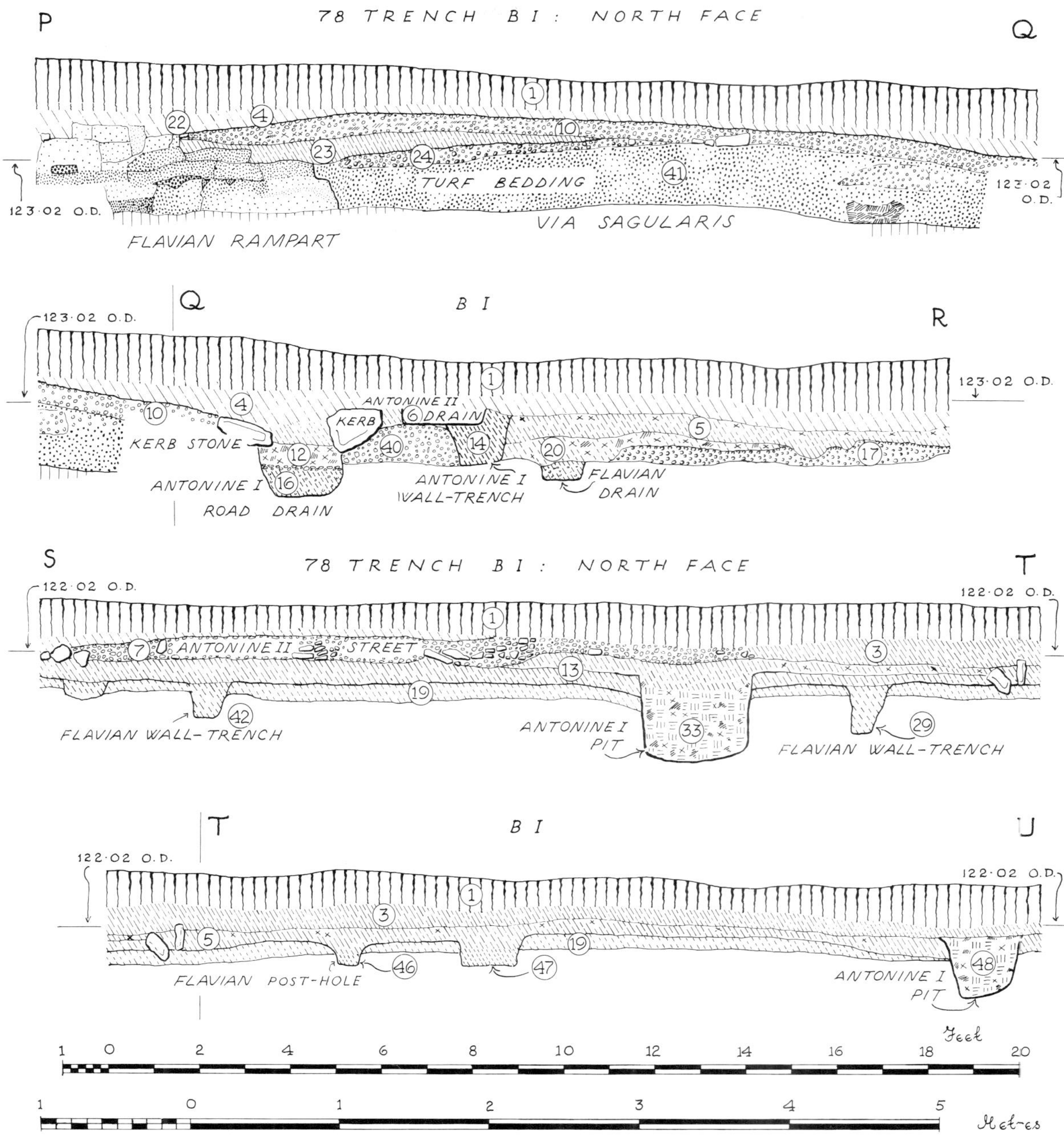

FIG. 47. The right (northern) *praetentura*: Sections P-U. Scale, 1:45. (For positions see FIG. 39).

original fill of the pit was probably represented by 29, which consisted of patches of sand with occasional stones and much black material resembling decayed turf.

Pit C (FIG. 46, Section J–K; PL. XXVII B) (some 10 ft. (3 m) in diameter and 9 ft. (2.7 m) deep), had been dug at the end of the Flavian occupation; it interrupted the longitudinal partition in Flavian Building V, and its lower fill (64) yielded an As of Vespasian (p. 139, No. 14) and two of Domitian minted in 84 and 85 respectively (Nos. 22, 23), together with first-century pottery. Layer 64 consisted of grey-brown clayey soil and scattered large stones. Above this came layers containing burnt and unburnt daub and brown sandy soil. The subsided floor-level of Antonine I Building V is probably represented by the top of layer 57, and the gravel floor of Antonine II Building V is layer 43, sealing the pit.

Pit F (FIG. 46, Section N–O) was one of a pair of demolition-pits in Antonine I Building VII. It measured 6 ft. 4 in. by 4 ft. 7 in. (1.93 by 1.39 m) and was only 3 ft. (0.9 m) deep. It encroached

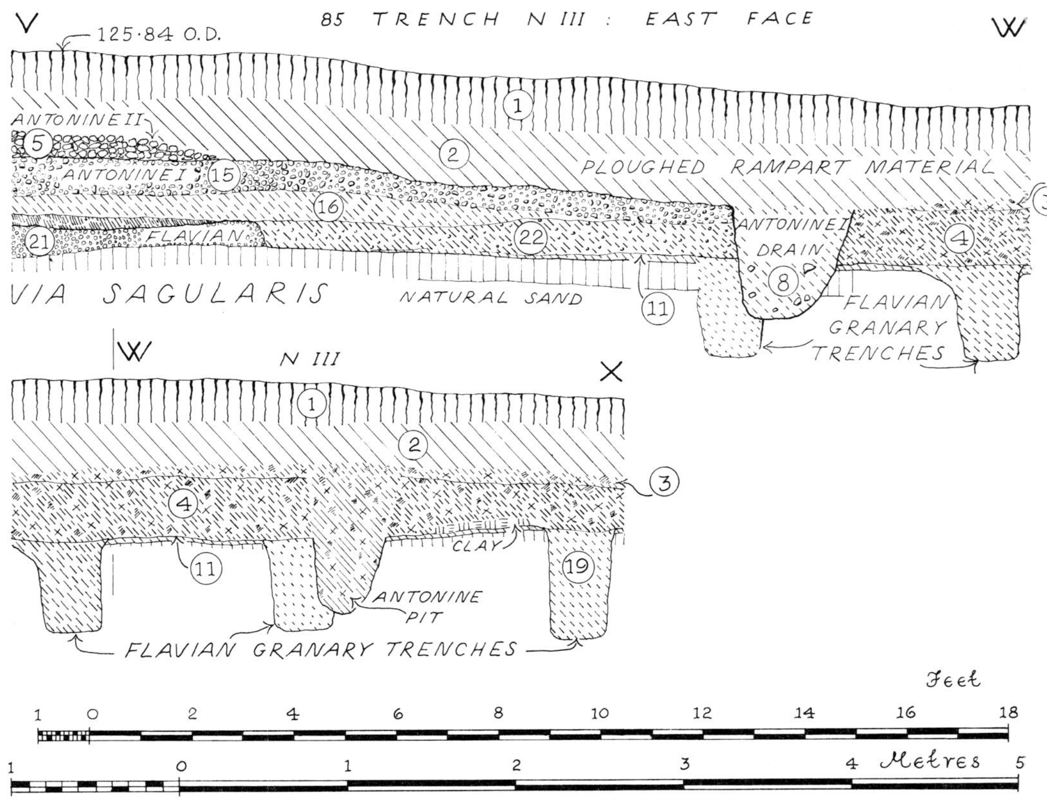

FIG. 48. The right (northern) *praetentura*. Section V-X. Scale, 1:45. (For position see FIG. 39).

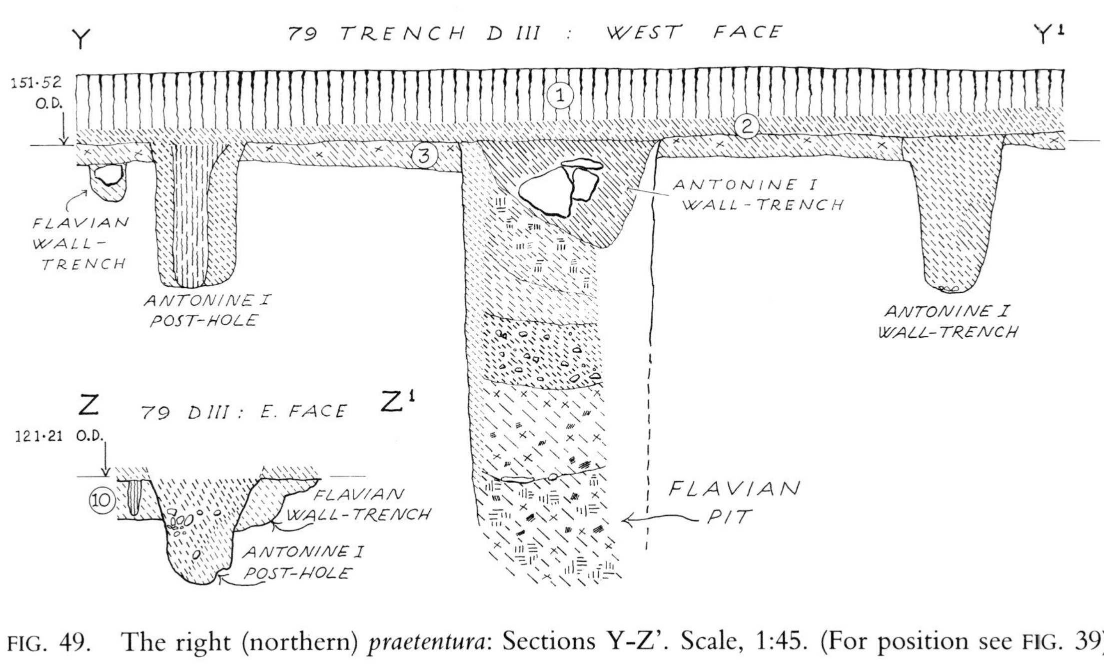

FIG. 49. The right (northern) *praetentura*: Sections Y-Z'. Scale, 1:45. (For position see FIG. 39).

upon a Flavian partition and was overlaid by the metalling of an Antonine II street. The primary filling was of sticky dark brown soil containing charcoal and clay which was sealed by a layer of sand (66) and one of dark brown stony soil (47).

Pit 4 (FIG. 45, Section G–H) lies in Antonine I Building VIII. It was almost 4 ft. (1.2 m) in diameter and 2 ft. (0.61 m) deep. The primary filling contained bands of charcoal and burnt clay, into which an upper layer of demolition-debris (12A) containing burnt daub had subsided. This sequence suggests that the pit may have been in use during the occupation of Building VIII.

A large demolition-pit occurred in Trench B I in Antonine I Building VII. It was of irregular shape and had interrupted one of the partitions. FIG. 47, Section S–T shows that the pit (33) is sealed by an Antonine II street; the filling was brown sandy soil with much charcoal and burnt daub.

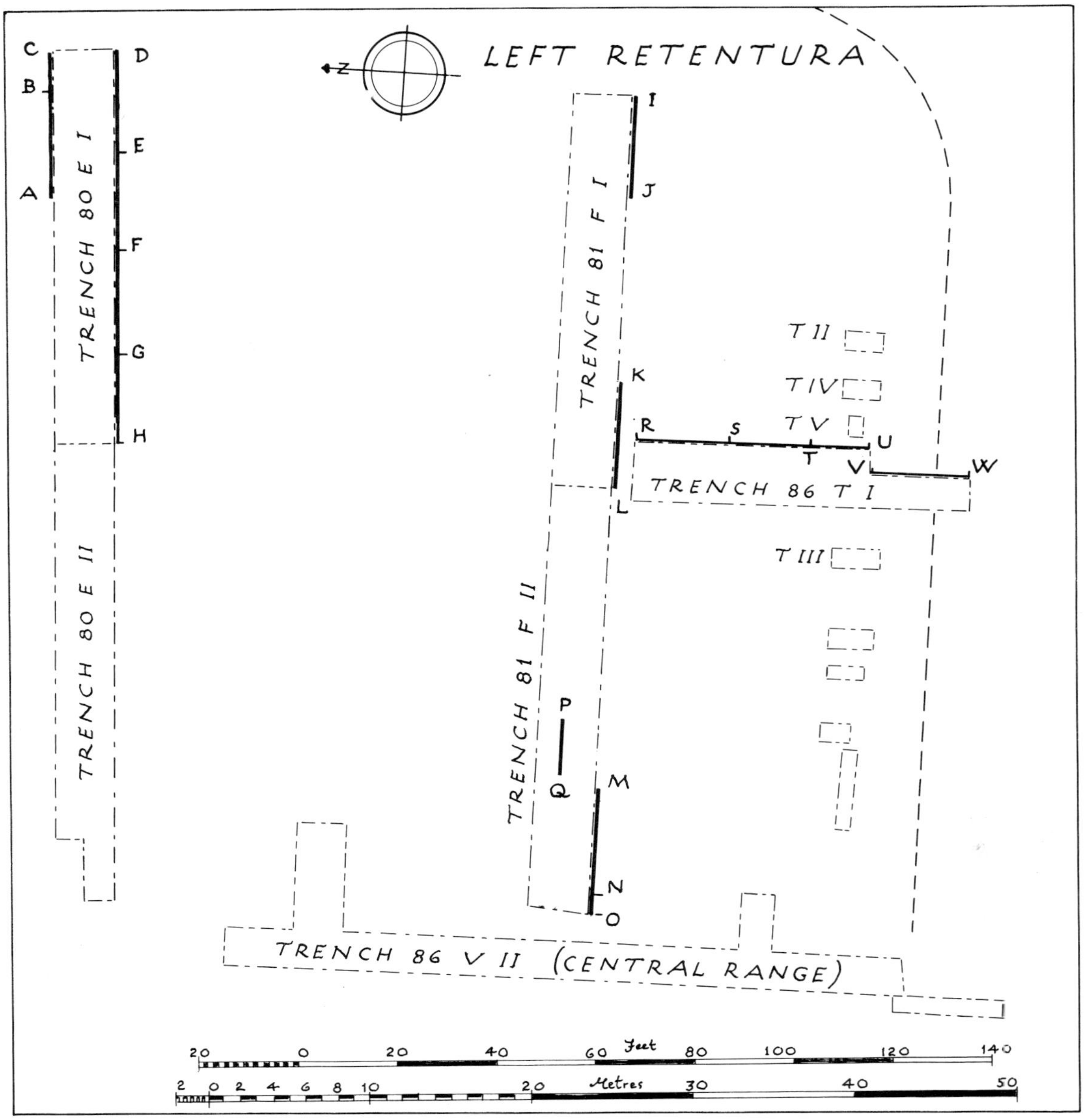

FIG. 50. The left (southern) *retentura*. Plan of Trenches with positions of published sections.

VI. THE LEFT (SOUTHERN) RETENTURA

The southern half of the *retentura* was examined in 1980, 1981 and 1986 (FIGS. 51–53). In 1980 an east-west trench E, 12 ft. (3.66 m) wide and 160 ft. (48.8 m) long was cut along the southern edge of the *via decumana*, extending from the vicinity of the *principia* to that of the east rampart just south of the *porta decumana*. The trench was supervised in two equal parts; E I to the east and E II to the west. An extension 12 ft. (3.66 m) long by 6 ft. (1.83 m) wide was dug at the south-west corner of E II in order to examine further details and to establish the relationship of the buildings of the *retentura* with the *principia*. In 1981 a second trench, F, 164 ft. (50 m) long and 12 ft. (3.66 m) wide was cut parallel to the 1980 trench but some 88 ft. (26.8 m) further south; like Trench E it extended from close to the Central Range as far as the eastern *intervallum* and was similarly supervised in two parts. F I, towards the east, was 80 ft. (24.4 m) long and F II, west of this, was 84 ft. (25.6 m). Finally in 1986 a trench (T I) measuring 48 ft. (14.63 m) by 12 ft. (3.66 m) (later extended southwards for 20 ft. (6.1 m) at a width of 7 ft. (2.13 m)) was dug from near the middle of Trench F towards the south rampart in order to establish the position of this and of the adjacent building-lines. Results here were complicated by the unexpected discovery of a second-century Bath-house. In all three seasons the topsoil, *c.* 10 in. (0.26 m) deep, was removed by machine to just above the surviving Antonine II levels.

(a) Flavian (FIG. 51)

Although neither E I nor F I reached the eastern rampart, the remains of what may be identified as an *ascensus* were discovered in the south-east corner of the former trench. The *ascensus* consisted of a series of laid turves (FIG. 55 (p. 100), Section D-E, 44) extending from the eastern end of the trench for at least 8 ft. (2.44 m) westwards, and probably originally for 9 ft. 6 in. (2.9 m). The turves were preserved to a height of more than 1 ft. (0.3 m) and were clearly visible in the south section (FIG. 55, Section D-E). Five large post-holes, all between 1 and 2 ft. (0.3 and 0.6 m) in depth, were associated with the turf mass (FIG. 51); presumably they held the uprights supporting timber cladding alongside the streets. The position of the *ascensus* shows that it gave access to the parapet at a point close beside the *porta decumana* (see also FIG. 14, p. 28) and also that the axis of the structure was probably at right-angles to that of the rampart: the western edge of the turves lies almost 24 ft. (7.3 m) from the back of the rampart – too far to represent the width of an *ascensus* built parallel with the rampart-line. The structure recalls the so-called *ballista*-platforms at Hod Hill, which also closely adjoin the gates: one of them was found to measure *c.* 20 ft. (6.1 m) from back to front.[1]

At its junction with the *via decumana* the **via sagularis** was laid on a turf make-up, probably debris left after the construction of the *ascensus*, and the street was at most only 8 ft. (2.44 m) wide, the width of the space between the *ascensus* and the rear wall of Building IX. In Trench F I, however, the street had a width of 11 ft. (3.35 m). Only patchy gravel survived in Trench E I, but in F I the metalling was well preserved, here overlying the natural subsoil from which the topsoil had been stripped. The street here was slightly cambered, being 6 in. (0.15 m) thick at the centre, and there were indications of a kerb on the outer side. (FIG. 56 (p. 101), Section I–J). Overlying the metalling and separating it from the Antonine I street above was a layer of loose dark soil probably representing accumulation during the period of disuse of the fort.

As a result of the angle of Trench E to the fort's orientation, a maximum width of 5 ft. (1.53 m) of the **via decumana** was exposed at the east end of E I, the width diminishing westwards along the trench. The street itself, *c.* 16 ft. (4.88 m) wide, consisted of a hard rammed gravel surface 1–1.5 in. (2.5–3.7 cm) thick over a make-up of fine gravel and large bedding stones 9 in. (0.23 m)

1. I.A. Richmond, *Hod Hill* ii (London, 1968), 73. For a re-interpretation of them as *ascensus* see D.B. Campbell, *Britannia* xv (1984), 81–3.

thick. The bedding here was laid directly on the old topsoil, which was 3 in. (7.6 cm) thick (FIG. 54).

Remains of burnt wooden planks (p. 271) were discovered on the surface of the *via decumana* at the east end of Trench E I beneath an 8 in. (20.4 cm) layer of turf. The turves had presumably fallen from the *ascensus* during its demolition or possibly from the rampart; they created a sterile layer between the Flavian and Antonine I levels. The planks lay east-west as they had been burnt, but their full length is unknown. Each plank was 9 in. (0.23 m) wide at the eastern baulk but widened to 1 ft. 10 in. (0.56 m) at its western end; they were between 0.5 and 0.75 in. (1.2–1.8 cm) thick. The planks had probably formed part of the timber cladding either of the passage through the gateway or, in view of their shape, perhaps more probably of the revetment of the *ascensus*.

Two Flavian **drains** were excavated at the eastern end of Trench E I. The larger of the two ran eastwards from the north-east corner of Barrack IX for a distance of *c.* 13 ft. (3.96 m); it was 1 ft. (0.30 m) wide and 1 ft. 6 in. (0.46 m) deep. This drain interrupted the Flavian *intervallum* street and must originally have been covered and lined with planks. It was filled with burnt and unburnt turves and charcoal from the Flavian demolitions. The drain debouched into a large rectangular pit adjacent to the *ascensus* which no doubt served as a soakaway. The pit measured 4 ft. (1.22 m) east-west by 2 ft. (0.61 m) north-south and was 4 ft. 10 in. (1.47 m) deep; it was filled with sandy soil interspersed with large amounts of charcoal. A second rather smaller drain coming from the north, but only 1 ft. (0.3 m) wide and 4 in. (10 cm) deep, also flowed into this pit. This drain ran across the *via decumana*, the metalling of which had been laid up to its edges, and it too much have been covered when in use. It has vertical sides and a flat bottom which lay at 120.88 ft. (36.84 m) O.D. (FIG. 54, Section B-C, 28). The filling was of dark brown silt mixed with quantities of charcoal and daub. During the Flavian demolition the larger of the two drain-trenches became enlarged at one point and in it had been deposited a lead pig (PL. XXVIII B), four iron ingots, an iron scythe-blade and an axehead (pp. 158–61, 174–6).

During the Flavian period the southern *retentura* was occupied by four timber structures (Buildings IX-XII) built on a north-south alignment, parallel with the *via principalis*; their main uprights were set in continuous construction-trenches in the manner typical of the Flavian period at Strageath.

Building IX lay adjacent to the *via sagularis*; it faced west on to an alleyway which separated it from Building X and can be identified as a barrack. The northern end-wall was located in Trench E I less than 1 ft. (0.30 m) away from the edge of the *via decumana*. The barrack is known to have been at least 112 ft. (34.2 m) long and on FIG. 51 is restored with an overall length of 151 ft. (46.02 m); this is 6 ft. (1.83 m) shorter than Building I, the corresponding barrack in the northern *retentura*.

In Trench E I Building IX was found to be 23 ft. (7 m) wide, while in Trench F I it had a width of 29 ft. (8.85 m). The greater width in Trench F I and internal division into various small rooms indicate that the structure here formed part of the officers' quarters, which extended beyond Trench F I to the north. In FIG. 51, the officers' quarters are restored with a length of 60 ft. (18.23 m), four feet (1.2 m) shorter and 11 ft. (3.35 m) narrower than that of Building I. The remainder of the barrack was probably fronted by a veranda *c.* 6 ft. (1.83 m) wide, for two post-holes were located in a suitable position in Trench E I.

A narrow room at the northern end of the building may have been used as a storeroom; this room was only 6 ft. (1.83 m) wide internally and was not divided into a front and rear room in the manner of *contubernia*. The room may have been fronted by an enclosed part of the veranda as indicated by an extension of the north wall and by a short length of construction-trench partly preserved below an Antonine I demolition-pit (FIG. 55, Section F-G, below 23).

Including this end room, the length of the men's part of the barrack is 91 ft. (27.74 m); it has a central longitudinal partition, noted in the edge of E I, and is restored with eight *contubernia* each with a front and back room of equal size, measuring *c.* 9 by 9 ft. 6 in. (2.74 by 2.89 m). This accommodation, taken with the large size of the officer's quarters, supports the idea that Building IX accommodated two *turmae* of horsemen.

The construction-trenches were all fairly regular with rectangular profiles except where disturbed by Flavian demolition or Antonine I pits and scoops. The western side of the eastern wall-trench in F I had been cut away by the Antonine II drain (FIG. 56, Section I-J, 27). All the construction-trenches varied between 9 and 12 in. (0.23 and 0.30 m) in width and depth. Those in Trench F I contained a clean sandy fill; in E I the filling was dark brown soil; the top of the construction-trenches sometimes contained a layer 1 to 2 in. (2.5–5 cm) thick containing burnt daub and charcoal, indicative of the Flavian demolition. The Flavian occupation-layer was, in general, difficult to differentiate as it had mostly been removed during the Antonine I reconstruction of the fort; but in places near the *via sagularis*, below the Antonine I levels, a layer of grey-brown stone-free soil may represent the Flavian occupation.

Building IX faced an unmetalled alleyway which divided it from Building X. The alley was only 3 ft. 6 in. (1.07 m) wide between the facing verandas at the *via decumana* end, increasing to 8 ft. (2.44 m) in Trench F I. A shallow gully, very irregular in outline, was seen in Trench F I; it ran north-south *c.* 1 ft. (0.30 m) away from the veranda posts of Building X. The gully had a clean sandy fill very similar to that of the Flavian construction-trenches. It may have served as an eavesdrip for Building X.

Building X faced east on to this alleyway. The northern end-wall was located in Trench E I and the south wall in Trench T I (FIG. 57, Section T-U), giving an overall length of 154 ft. (46.94 m). The width was 24 ft. (7.32 m) exclusive of a veranda *c.* 7 ft. (2.14 m) wide. Two post-holes for the veranda were located in Trench E I and two in Trench F I; the former were *c.* 10 in. (0.26 m) deep and the latter nearly 2 ft. (0.61 m); all four contained large sandstone blocks as well as river boulders for packers. The veranda posts were set at intervals of approximately 6 ft. (1.83 m).

All the construction-trenches were cut into the natural subsoil and were sealed by the Flavian demolition layers. They contained a fill of natural sand, with an admixture of gravel, burnt daub and charcoal in the top couple of inches. The trenches were fairly regular with rectangular profiles; as usual they varied between 10 in. (0.26 m) and 1 ft. (0.30 m) in width and 6 in. (0.15 m) and 1 ft. (0.30 m) in depth.

In Trench F I the construction-trenches for the front wall and part of the partitioning had been destroyed by a large Antonine I demolition-pit. The construction-trenches in E I and E II had also been badly disturbed by Antonine I pits. However, sufficient of the internal partitions remained for the building to be identified as a barrack.

The arrangement of rooms in Trench T I showed that the officers' quarters extended as far north as the partition in F I, giving them a length of 42 ft. (12.80 m), some 18 ft. (5.49 m) shorter than those in Building IX; but despite the disturbance caused by Pit 1 it was clear that this partition-wall had not extended into the veranda area to give an L-shaped outline to Barrack X similar to that of IX. Whether the veranda continued along the front of the officers' block is uncertain; the plan of Building XI suggests that it did not.

At the north end of the building lay two narrow rooms, only 6 ft. (1.83 m) wide internally; the front room had a depth of 6 ft. and the rear room 14 ft. (4.27 m). In this the barrack resembled Building IX. This pair is too narrow for a *contubernium* and is divided differently from the *contubernium* adjacent to the officers' quarters; like the corresponding space in Building IX it may be taken as a storeroom. Between these rooms and the officers' quarters lies a space of 104 ft. (31.69 m) which can be divided between 10 *contubernia* each 9 ft. (2.74 m) wide internally and consisting (as indicated by a central longitudinal partition in Trench F I) of two equal rooms 10 ft. (3.05 m) deep. The most southerly *contubernium*, however, must have been at least 10 ft. wide, since no second cross-partition was found in F I. The arrangements suggest accommodation for a century of infantry.

Buildings X and XI lay back to back, separated by a 5-ft. (1.53-m) gap. Of **Building XI** sufficient details of layout were established for it, too, to be identified as a barrack. The line of the northern end-wall was located in Trench E II, and if its southern end is restored in line with that of Building X an overall length of 153 ft. (46.63 m) is obtained. The width was constant at 28 ft. (8.54 m) in both E II and F II, and there was a veranda *c.* 7 ft. (2.13 m) wide along the west side.

Two post-holes for this were located in Trench E II and one in F II; the latter was 19 in. (0.48 m) deep, with stone packers still *in situ*. The alignment of the post-holes shows that the veranda belongs to Building XI rather than to XII; it is also clear that they cannot have extended as far as the south end of the building.

In Trench F II the part of the building uncovered to south of the east-west partition is taken as part of the officers' quarters since it is divided transversely into three rooms rather than the normal two of a *contubernium*; the E-W internal dimensions of these rooms are respectively 6 ft. (1.83 m), 7 ft. (2.14 m) and 10 ft. (3.05 m). The length of the officers' quarters is restored at 46 ft. 6 in. (14.17 m).

The westernmost of the two longitudinal partitions in Trench F II continued northwards beyond the Trench, dividing the area into two, the front one 9 ft. (2.74 m) deep and the rear 13 ft. 6 in. (4.11 m). This wall no doubt connected with the partition in Trench E II and, if so, runs at an angle slightly oblique to the axis of the building: in Trench E II it divided the block into two equal-sized rooms, each 12 ft. 6 in. (3.8 m) deep. An east-west partition wall was also located in Trench E II; this created an end *contubernium* 11 ft. (3.36 m) wide internally. Between this partition and the northern wall of the officers' quarters sufficient space was available for a further nine *contubernia* each *c.* 9 ft. (2.74 m) wide. Thus, in all there were probably ten *contubernia* in the block – suitable accommodation for an infantry century.

The construction-trenches of Building XI were as usual cut into the subsoil and were of normal rectangular profile. Those in Trench F II were wider than normal, varying from 1 to 2 ft. (0.30–0.61 m), but were still 10 to 12 in. (0.26–0.30 m) deep. Post-holes for the main uprights were found sunk *c.* 3 in. (7.6 cm) below the bottom of these trenches. Three such post-holes were located in the north-south partition in F II and two in the front wall in E II; they were placed at approximately 3 ft. (0.91 m) intervals. The construction-trench for the rear wall in E II had extra post-settings cut into its sides. This suggests the replacement of posts during the building's lifetime.

In Trench F II a layer of slightly stained pale orange-brown soil was identified as the Flavian occupation-level. This lay immediately below the Antonine I occupation level, indicating that the Flavian demolition material must have been removed or churned up during the clearance of the site for rebuilding.

Although there are irregularities in its plan, **Building XII** is clearly another barrack, forming a pair with Building XI, and despite the cramped conditions created by the veranda of the latter the smaller rooms of its *contubernia* on this side suggest that Building XII faced eastwards to the alley between the two. The north end-wall lay outside Trench E II; but on the assumption that it was aligned with the other buildings along the *via decumana*, there is space between this and the *via sagularis* for a building 151 ft. 6 in. (47.70 m) long. Of this, 40 ft. (13.72 m) is taken up by the officers' quarters, which are assumed to extend as far as the southern cross-partition in F II. Like the corresponding officers' quarters in Buildings X and XI they did not extend beyond the front wall of the *contubernia*.

In Trench F II the width of the building was 30 ft. 9 in. (9.37 m) overall; despite disturbance by a demolition-pit (Pit 2) and a clay-lined tank, both of the Antonine I period, the area could be seen to be divided into rooms whose internal dimensions were 9 ft. 3 in. (2.82 m) wide and 12 ft. (3.66 m) and 13 ft. (3.96 m) deep respectively. The median partition extended northwards from F II, no doubt connecting with that in E II.

In Trench E II the eastern front wall was not identified because of disturbance by Antonine I post-holes along the same line, but the positions of the central partition and the west wall were clearly visible, the latter yielding a number of post-positions. The most northerly *contubernium* was apparently 9 ft. 6 in. (2.90 m) wide, with a front room 10 ft. 6 in. (3.20 m) and a rear room 11 ft. (3.35 m) deep. The mens' quarters thus suggest division into 10 *contubernia* and occupation by a century of infantry.

The width of the building in E II is considerably less than in F II, being only 26 ft. (7.92 m) overall, a difference too great to be explained by poor alignment. It is more probable that the four northernmost *contubernia* were intentionally narrowed in order to leave adequate space between the barrack and the *principia* for the *via quintana*. Other evidence for overcrowding of buildings in this half of the *retentura* has already been noted in the alleyway between Buildings XI and XII.

However, if this was the original intention it was soon reversed when an east-west wall was built to connect Building XII with the *principia* some 12 ft. (3.66 m) away, thus blocking off access from the *via decumana* to the *quintana*.

It was first observed in Trench E II not quite on line with the *contubernium* partition-wall and was traced for its full length in the extension to Trench E II. The purpose of this connection of the two buildings is not clear, being unparalleled elsewhere. The wall appears to represent a second phase of Flavian construction, for examination of its intersection with the construction-trench at the rear of the *principia* revealed that it was stratigraphically later. It may perhaps represent the addition of extra office space or a storeroom to the *principia* (pp. 36, 125), making use of existing walls where possible.

Most of the construction-trenches of Building XII were of normal size and profile; but in Trench E II the median longitudinal trench showed as three short segments which were narrower and shallower than the others. In this Trench both the rear wall and that joining it to the *principia* showed a U-shaped profile and contained a darker filling than normal. This may imply that part of the rear wall of Building XII was reconstructed at the same time as the extension to the *principia* was built.

One of the partitions in Trench E II had been partly cut away by a small Flavian demolition-pit (Pit 1). This was only 2 ft. 6 in. (0.76 m) deep; it contained a primary filling of dark organic soil and charcoal which had been compressed to a thickness of only *c.* 6 in. (15 cm) beneath an upper filling of dark earth and large stones laid down to consolidate an Antonine I wall line; the pit yielded a denarius of Vespasian (p. 139, No. 15) together with a lump of slag. A deeper demolition-pit was cut through the east wall of Building X in Trench E I (Pit 2, cf. FIG. 55, Section G–H). This was 4 ft. (1.22 m) deep, and once again the Flavian filling (34), here of brown sandy earth mixed with grey sandy charcoal-stained soil, had subsided beneath large stones inserted to support an Antonine I post.

(b) Antonine I (FIG. 52)

In Trench F I the **eastern via sagularis** was found to be *c.* 12 ft. (3.66 m) wide. The outer edge was marked by a kerb of large sandstone and other boulders (FIG. 56 (p. 101), Section I–J) which may once have formed part of a stone-lined drain running from Trench E I; but in F I many of the stones had been disturbed for use as packers of two large Antonine II post-holes, and the existence of the drain here is uncertain.

The surface of the street was formed by medium-sized boulders and rounded pebbles set in fine gravel; there was a definite camber. This metalling overlay a layer of dark soil (FIG. 56, Section I–J, 14) which had accumulated over the Flavian street during the period of disuse or was make-up for the Antonine I street itself. For the most part the surface of the Antonine I *intervallum* street in this Trench lay immediately below the ploughsoil, the Antonine II street having been almost completely ploughed away.

In Trench E I the *intervallum* area presented a more complex situation; the eastern end of the trench contained the intersection of the *via sagularis* and the **via decumana**; the latter street was found to have two distinct phases. Since the *via decumana* ran at an angle to the axis of Trench E I, the width of metaling excavated decreased gradually along the trench. The first phase of the *via decumana* was observed only at the eastern end of Trench E I (FIG. 54 (p. 99), Section B–C, 35); in this phase the surface consisted of a layer of pink-brown gravel *c.* 2 in. (5 cm) thick. In the second phase the metalling was more substantial (11), consisting of fine gravel with occasional larger pebbles, up to 9 in. (0.23 m) thick in places. This latter was similar to the surface of the *via sagularis*. The **eastern via sagularis** was approximately 12 ft. (3.66 m) wide with a definite camber which can be clearly seen in the section on its western edge (FIG. 55, Section D–E). The Antonine I streets here overlay a layer of turves which had fallen from the Flavian *ascensus* and which formed a sterile layer between the two periods of occupation (FIG. 54). As in Trench F I, the Antonine I streets lay immediately below the ploughsoil, the Antonine II metalling having been almost entirely ploughed away.

A stone-lined **drain** was discovered in Trench E I which crossed the *via decumana*, here 15 ft. (4.57 m) wide, on a north-south alignment and continued along the eastern edge of the *via sagularis* (PL. XXVIII B); this drain continued to the north and south of the trench and was clearly a continuation of the drain discovered in the northern *retentura* (p. 60) where (because of the shape of the fort) it ran on the western side of the *via sagularis*. As explained above, the drain was not found in Trench F I, for here the area to the east of the *via sagularis* was much disturbed by Antonine II post-pits. However, like its Antonine II successor (p. 95), this drain appeared to have a watershed at the *via decumana*. The level of the base of the drain at the north face of Trench E I was 121.25 ft. (36.96 m) O.D.; at the south face it was 121.0 ft. (36.88 m) and thus appeared to be flowing south. But in the 1973 trench in the right *retentura* (p. 60) the level of the base was 119.3 ft. (36.36 m) O.D., indicating that in the right *retentura* the drain flowed north. The drain was contemporary with the first phase of the *via decumana*. It was cut through the turf layer and through the Flavian street-surface with its bedding (FIG. 54, Section B–C, 25), and overlay a Flavian demolition-pit. Within a construction-trench filled with soft brown earth the drain was lined with large stones, some more than 1 ft. (0.30 m) across, which were mostly still *in situ*. The channel was 1 ft. 6 in. (0.46 m) wide internally and *c.* 8 in. (0.20 cm) deep, and must originally have been covered. When the *via decumana* was resurfaced the drain was filled with pink-brown gravel (Section B–C, 25) and the new metalling (11) was laid over it.

The **southern via sagularis** was found to be 15 ft. (4.57 m) wide in Trench V II at the western edge of the Central Range and was at least 12 ft 6 in. wide at Trenches T II and IV; however, the insertion of the Bath-house (p. 102) narrowed it to only 4 ft. 9 in. (1.48 m) near the western end of that building, thus creating a considerable otstacle to circulation. The inner edge of the street was flanked by a deep plank-lined **drain** (FIG. 57, Section S–T), in which the usual peg-holes were distinguished. This drain had a fall to the east of 0.37 ft. (14.32 cm) between the two trenches, its base lying at 117.99 ft. (35.96 m) O.D. in Trench V II and 117.62 ft. (35.85 m) in Trench T I. The levels of the drain along the eastern *via sagularis*, given above, make it clear that the two drains had no direct connection; presumably both were led out of the fort beneath the rampart near the south-eastern angle.

During the Antonine I period the southern *retentura* was once again occupied by four buildings (IX–XII) laid out parallel with the *via principalis*. These were constructed with posts set in individual post-pits rather than in the continuous construction-trenches typical of the Flavian period. The post-holes, filled with loose dark earth and penetrated by roots, were clearly visible against the Antonine I occupation-layer of mid-brown soil 6 to 9 in. (0.15–0.23 m) thick. The Antonine I occupation-layer overlay the Flavian demolition deposit, a yellow sandy loam containing much charcoal and burnt daub; over the Antonine I occupation-layer was a deposit of darker clayey soil with dense concentrations of charcoal and burnt daub representing the Antonine I demolition; this was 2 to 3 in. (5–7.6 cm) thick.

Building IX, set back some 8 ft. (2.44 m) from the *via sagularis*, was traced in Trenches E I and F I. The northern end wall, discovered in Trench E I, lay some 6 ft. (1.83 m) to the south of the *via decumana*; however, a single post-pit located 4 ft. (1.22 m) north of the end wall might suggest a covered area alongside the street. This building was found to be 15 ft. (4.57 m) wide in Trench E I and 16 ft. (4.88 m) wide in Trench F I. No internal partition walls were seen in either trench. The building is obviously much too narrow to have served as a barrack. The possibility that it is a stable is considered on p. 127, but is dismissed on what seem to be sufficient grounds. The most likely interpretation is either as a shed for stores or as a workshop; the fragmentary remains of a hearth were noted in the occupation-layer in Trench F I. Also in Trench F I what may have been the sites of bonfires were identified in the demolition layer.

The post-holes indicate that the upright timbers were placed from 1 to 2 ft. (0.30–0.61 m) apart. The timbers themselves appear to have been *c.* 6 in. (15 cm) in diameter; they were set in post-pits which were mainly 1 ft. to 1ft. 4 in. (0.30 to 0.41 m) deep, although some were much shallower having a depth of only 6 in. (0.15 m). The line of the northern end wall was accompanied by stones presumably used as packers for the uprights.

Building X was separated from IX by an unmetalled alley 6 ft. (1.83 m) wide. The internal layout identifies Building X as a barrack. The northern end-wall was located in Trench E I adjacent to the *via decumana* and post-holes of the southern end-wall were located in Trench T I four ft. (1.22 m) inside the drain; the barrack thus has a length of 146 ft. (44.5 m). The width was 32 ft. (9.75 m) in Trench E I and 33 ft. (10.06 m) in Trench F I; like the rest of the Antonine I barracks it lacked a veranda.

A north-south line of post-holes in Trench E I marked the position of the longitudinal partition dividing the barrack into an eastern section 11 ft. (3.36 m) deep internally and a western section 17 ft. (5.18 m) deep internally. The narrower section was probably at the front of the building which, therefore, faced east. In Trench F I a similar line of post-holes divided a front section 11 ft. 9 in. (3.58 m) deep internally from a rear section 17 ft. (5.18 m) deep. No east-west partition was located in Trench E I; a *contubernium* 10 ft. (3.05 m) wide would have had a wall just south of the trench-edge. One east-west partition was located in Trench F I; and there was sufficient space between this and the northern end wall for ten *contubernia* each approximately 9 ft. (2.74 m) wide, thus providing accommodation suitable for a century of infantry. The cross-partition in Trench F I is taken to mark the northern end of the centurion's quarters; these had a length of 42 ft. 6 in. (12.95 m), a not untypical proportion.

In Trench E I the Antonine I floor was identified in the front room of the block beneath the demolition layer of burnt daub and ash 3 in. (7.6 cm) thick (FIG. 55, Section F–G, 15); the floor consisted of a fine gravel spread 3 in. (7.6 cm) thick but was bisected by the bottom of a post-medieval plough furrow. Most traces of the floor of the rear room had been removed by a large demolition pit (Pit 9, Section G–H, 12) measuring *c.* 10 ft. (3.05 m) across by 3 ft. (0.91 m) in maximum depth which contained a lower fill of ash and charcoal covered by gravel and then mixed earth and pebbles. Patches of a floor of loose gravel were also identified in the front rooms in Trench F I.

The post-holes for the uprights, mostly 6 to 8 in. (15 to 20.5 cm) deep, were set at approximately 2 ft. (0.61 m) internals. In Trench E I the posts for the end-wall had been driven into the bottom of a shallow trench; the precise lines of the trench had been destroyed by recutting during demolition but it was *c.* 7 in. (17.5 cm) wide and *c.* 5 in. (12.5 cm) deep. The post-holes for the median wall in Trench F I were similarly located in a shallow trench; the large stone packers for these posts were still in place. The top of a Flavian pit (Pit 2) underlying the median wall in Trench E I had been packed with gravel and stones to prevent further subsidence; one of these stones had been used as a base pad for one of the Antonine I posts. (FIG. 55, Section G–H).

Between the rear walls of Buildings X and XI lay an open space *c.* 9 ft. (2.75 m) wide; there was no evidence that it had ever been metalled. Two shallow pits were discovered here in Trench F II, roughly parallel and on an east-west alignment ; at most 9 in. (0.23 m) deep they were filled with a mixture of burnt daub, ash and charcoal together with sherds of Antonine pottery. These depressions were not related to any other feature and clearly belong to the demolition of the Antonine I fort.

Building XI was identifiable as a barrack by its internal layout. The northern end-wall was located close to the northern edge of Trench E II, adjacent to the *via decumana* which at this point ran outside the Trench. On the assumption that the south end-wall was not quite on the line of that of Building X because of the inclination of the *via sagularis*, Building XI was 144 ft. (43.89 m) long. It was 32 ft. 6 in. (9.91 m) wide and had no veranda. Lines of post-holes representing the north-south longitudinal partition were discovered in both trenches; this divided the building into an eastern range 18 ft. (5.5 m) deep in Trench E II and 19 ft. (5.8 m) deep in Trench F II and a western range 10 ft. 6 in. (3.20 m) deep in E II and 10 ft. (3.05 m) deep in F II. The fact that the smaller rooms lay on the west indicates that the barrack faced in that direction. An east-west partition was located in Trench E II which created an end *contubernium c.* 9 ft. (2.74 m) wide internally. Another east-west partition was located in Trench F II and there was space between this and the northern end-wall for ten *contubernia* each *c.* 9ft. 4 in. (2.84 m) wide, sufficient to accommodate a century of infantry. The median wall continued south of the partition in Trench F II; but this area, 37 ft. (11.28 m) long, must be assigned to the centurion.

The floor of the barrack was identified in Trench E II; it was represented by gravel patches in the Antonine I occupation layer, which was here dated by a Black-burnished 2 dish (FIG. 126, No. 174). The floor was not found in Trench F II where the occupation-material consisted of less than 1 in. (0.025 m) of silty soil under the demolition layer. However, two hearths were noted in the front and rear rooms of the *contubernium* in Trench F II, indicated by patches of compacted earth and large flat stones. The post-holes varied between 6 in. and 1 ft. (15–30 cm) in depth and were between 1 and 3 ft. (0.30–0.91 m) apart. Many stone packers were found *in situ*. Some of the post-holes for the northern end-wall were set in a very shallow gully with U-shaped profile filled with loose gravel and loam. The gully had an irregular outline and was very different from the construction-trenches of the Flavian period.

Buildings XI and XII faced each other across a metalled steet approximately 8 ft. (2.44 m) wide, the buildings themselves standing 10 ft. (3.05 m) apart. The street was surfaced with a layer of pebbles and loose gravel 3 in. (7.6 cm) deep over a bedding of larger stones. In Trench E II a possible kerbing of larger boulders lay on the western edge of the metalling. The street overlay the Flavian demolition layers and was sealed by Antonine I demolition material. In both Trench E II and F II a gully was traced running along the street some 3 ft. (0.915 m) east of the front wall of Building XII. This gully was about 1 ft. (0.30 m) wide and 3 to 4 in. (7.6–10.2 cm) deep; it appeared to have been cut through the metalling, previously uninterrupted, and was thus presumably a secondary measure to remove surface water. A layer of loose gravel had been washed into the bottom of the gully suggesting that it had acted as an open drain.

Building XII, like X and XI, was identified by its internal layout as a barrack. The northern end-wall was located in Trench E II adjacent to the *via decumana*; it is restored with a length of 139 ft. 6 in. (42.52 m), 38 ft. 6 in. (11.73 m) of which is assigned to the centurion's quarters. The building was found to be 31 ft. (9.45 m) wide in Trench E II and 32 ft. 6 in. (9.91 m) wide overall in Trench F II; there was no veranda but the building clearly faced east to the street described above, forming a pair with Building XI. Post-holes representing the longitudinal partition were located in both trenches; these divided the building into an eastern section 12 ft. (3.66 m) deep in E II and 15 ft. (4.57 m) in F II and a western section 14 ft. (4.27 m) deep in E II and 13 ft. 6 in. (4.11 m) in F II. An east-west line of post-holes in E II defined an end *contubernium c.* 9 ft. (2.74 m) wide. A second east-west partition was discovered in F II and between this and the northern end-wall there was space for ten *contubernia* 9 ft. (2.74 m) wide. The median wall of the building continued southwards into the presumed centurion's quarters.

The floor of the barrack was identified in Trench E II, under the make-up for the Antonine II *via quintana*, as a smooth surface of fine sandy loam with patches of unburnt daub. Both the Antonine I floor and occupation material (FIG. 56, Section M–N, 29) had been badly disturbed in Trench F II by the Antonine II street, but areas of patchy gravel were observed in the western half of the block. In Trench F II a large demolition-pit had destroyed part of the partition. This pit (Pit 2) was *c.* 9 ft. (2.74 m) in diameter and 4 ft. 5 in. (1.35 m) deep. The primary filling (FIG. 56, Section P–Q, 31) consisted of burnt daub and charcoal in a dark brown soil with some yellow sand (perhaps fallen in from the sides). As usual with such pits the original filling had subsided, here under the weight of an Antonine II street, despite a bedding of large boulders spread to counteract it. In this instance, at least, it is clear that subsidence was continuous during Antonine II, for the street had been repeatedly repaired as it sank. In Trench E II there had been a similar subsidence over a Flavian demolition pit (Pit 1); two of the post-holes of the median wall had been set in the upper filling of this pit.

An unusual feature was observed in the western room in Trench F II. Here a coffin-shaped and clay-lined trench ran on an E–W alignment close to the partition: it was 7 ft. (2.13 m) long and narrowed from 2 to 1 ft. 3 in. in width (0.61–0.38 m). The trench was 11 in. (0.28 m) deep at its eastern end dropping to 15 in. (0.38 m) at the other and there was a lining of pink and white clay 3 to 4 in. (7.6–10.2 cm) thick. The feature was cut into the Flavian occupation-layer and was sealed by a thick Antonine I demolition layer; the filling was gravel, which yielded a sherd of early Black-burnished ware and is thus securely dated to the Antonine I occupation. The lining suggests use as a water tank, but the siting within a *contubernium* poses a problem about its purpose.

The extension to Trench E II revealed the rear wall of the barrack and the rear wall of the *principia* some 9 ft. (2.76 m) to the west. Areas of metalling belonging to the *via quintana* had previously been found at the rear of the *principia*; patches of metalling were found in E II, but the street appeared to be only 4 ft. (1.22 m) wide, being bounded on the west side by a shallow gully (see p. 37). In Trench F II there was a layer of fine stones and gravel (12) laid on a bed of foundation-stones overlying the Flavian demolition material (FIG. 56, Section M–N, N–O) west of the rear wall of the barrack; this also formed part of the *via quintana*, here at the most only 7 ft. (2.13 m) wide.

(c) Antonine II (FIG. 53)

In Trench E I the surfaces of the **via decumana** and **eastern via sagularis** had been ploughed away leaving only patches of the bedding; the latter consisted of a layer of medium-sized pebbles, mainly 2 to 3 in. (0.05–0.08 m) thick but 7 to 8 in. (0.17–0.20 m) thick in places (FIG. 55, Section D–E, 10), for instance at the south-east corner of the Trench, where the cobbling had dramatically sunk into the top of a Flavian pit (PL. XXX). None of the gravel surfacing was found *in situ* but some had accumulated in the fill of the street drain. The southern edge of the *via decumana*, here 15 ft. (4.57 m) wide, ran along the northern side of Trench E I; the *via sagularis* appears to have been at least 25 ft. (7.63 m) wide, at any rate in Trench E I, although this exceptional width may have been the result of rounding the corner towards the gate. In Trench F I again only the bedding of the *via sagularis* survived plough-damage; here this consisted of large boulders laid directly on the Antonine I street-surface and extending over the Antonine I kerb (FIG. 56, Section I–J). The street in F I was at least 17 ft. (5.18 m) wide but its full extent is unknown.

In Trench F I two large post-pits were found cut through the street near its outer edge (FIG. 56, Section I–J), *c.* 14 ft. (4.27 m) east of the drain. These were first recognised at Flavian levels but the section showed them to be of Antonine II date; they cut through Antonine I and Flavian material, being sealed only by the lower ploughsoil. The Antonine II date is further supported by the re-use of the Antonine I kerbstones as packers. The post-pits were over 1 ft. (0.30 m) deep with post-pipes *c.* 6 in. (0.15 m) across and *c.* 6 ft. (1.83 m) apart. The post-holes lie *c.* 60 ft. (18 m) from the front of the contemporary rampart and *c.* 23 ft. (7 m) from the back of the Flavian rampart; clearly they form no part either of an interval tower or an *ascensus* and are best taken to indicate an *intervallum* building such as a cook-house. Indications of a similar building were found on the north edge of the northern *retentura* (p. 63).

In both the Trenches, F I and E I, the eastern *via sagularis* was bordered along its inner edge by a substantial **drain** which continued across the *via decumana* to connect with the drain in the same position in the northern *retentura*. The drain was *c.* 3 ft. (0.91 m) wide and deep with a stone kerbing at the top of its outer side (Sections E–F, I–J); small post-holes 6 in. (0.15 m) deep, were found at 1 to 2 ft. (0.30–0.61 m) intervals along the sides at the bottom (PL. XXXI A); these held stakes intended to retain a plank lining. In both Trenches, as in the 1973 Trench in the northern *retentura*, it was observed that the base of the drain-trench as dug was levelled with the insertion of make-up before the plank lining was inserted, so as to secure an even flow of water (FIG. 56, Section I–J). As with the Antonine I *intervallum* drain, there was a watershed at the *via decumana*, so that in the northern *retentura* it flowed to the north but in Trenches E I and F I to the south. The levels were as follows:

Trench E I,	south face	
	surface of make-up	120.08 (36.60 m)
	bottom of trench	119.58 (36.45 m)

Trench F I,	south face	
	surface of make-up	117.86 (35.92 m)
	bottom of trench	117.41 (35.79 m)
1973 Trench II (p.63)		
	surface of make-up	118.3 (36.06 m)
	bottom of trench	117.80 (35.91 m)
1985 Trench N II	bottom of drain	117.70 (35.87 m)

The drain had an upper fill of gravel, burnt daub and charcoal derived from the demolitions. The fill contained many pieces of amphora and potsherds, including part of a Cologne roughcast beaker, and also part of a lava quern, an iron blade and an iron finger-ring (pp. 251, 154). A subsidiary drain was discovered in Trench E I; this led from the north-east corner of Building VIII and emptied into the main drain. It was 1 ft. 3 in. (0.38 m) wide and 6 in. (0.15 m) deep, and was filled with loose earth and gravel interspersed with Antonine pottery.

An unmetalled space west of the main drain separated the *via sagularis* from the first of the buildings in the southern *retentura*; this space was 8 ft. (2.44 m) wide in Trench F I and 10 ft. (3.05 m) in Trench E I.

The **southern via sagularis** was found to be 15 ft. (4.57 m) wide in Trench V II near the SE corner of the Central Range. Further east its width had been reduced to 5 ft. (1.52 m) by the intrusive NW corner of the Bath-house (p. 98); east of this it gradually widened again, being up to 10 ft. (3.05 m) wide in Trench T I. No drain accompanied it along this side of the *retentura*, so the drain along the eastern edge must have been taken out beneath the rampart near the south-eastern angle.

In the Antonine II period the southern *retentura* was occupied by three barracks (Buildings VIII–X), all built on a north-south axis, parallel with the *via principalis*. The Antonine II occupation-layer was badly preserved; in places completely ploughed away, it was at most 2 in. (5 cm) thick and was consequently difficult to differentiate. This material was found immediately below the lower ploughsoil and overlay the Antonine I demolition-layer. The post-holes for the Antonine II buildings were also difficult to locate; they could be detected by their fillings of looser earth and by heavy penetrations of small roots. The post-holes were without post-pits. Presumably the posts had been hammered in from above, and although some stone packers were found *in situ* they were rare in comparison to those surrounding the Antonine I post-holes. The post-holes themselves varied between 4 and 6 in. (10–15 cm) in diameter and 8 and 16 in. (0.20–0.41 m) in depth.

Building VIII, adjoining the *intervallum* area, was identified as a barrack by its internal layout. The northern end-wall was located in Trench E I adjacent to the *via decumana*, and on the assumption that its southern end was approximately in line with that of Building IX the overall length was 151 ft. 6 in. (46.18 m). None of the Antonine I or Antonine II barracks at Strageath have verandas; Building VIII was found to be 26–27 ft. (7.92–8.23 m) wide in both Trenches. A longitudinal partition divided the block into an eastern range 8 ft. (2.44 m) deep internally and a western range 15 ft. 6 in. (4.72 m) deep. The arrangement suggests that the barrack faced on to the *via sagularis*. The median partition continued south of Trench F I into what is certainly the officers' quarters, so that there is no immediate clue to the length of the latter. The same Trench contained a complete *contubernium* 8 ft. (2.44 m) wide internally, but in E I the end *contubernium* must have had a width of at least 11 ft. (3.35 m). Between the two Trenches there is space for 9 further *contubernia* 8 ft. wide, giving eleven in all. It seems best to assume that the real total was ten and that the two rooms in Trench F I was part of the centurion's quarters, an assumption to some extent supported by the fact that a slight change of alignment affects the walls at that point. If this is accepted, the centurion's quarters will have had a length of 50 ft. (15.24 m), occupying almost exactly one third of the building. This proportion of 33% better suits the other evidence (p. 138, TABLE V) than the 27% given by the shorter length.

The floor within the barrack was observed in Trench F I as a patchy layer of pebbles set in dark loam; the layer was *c.* 2 in. (5 cm) thick and sealed Antonine I demolition material. In Trench E I a thin occupation-layer (FIG. 55, Sections E–F, F–G, 3) sealed the demolition-layer of Antonine I and was itself sealed only by the old ploughsoil (2).

A narrow metalled alley separated the rear wall of Building VIII from Building IX. The metalling was 6 ft. (1.83 m) wide in E I, and a few inches less in F I (Section K–L, 9), consisting of gravel over a foundation of larger stones; but as it lay directly below the lower ploughsoil it had suffered disturbance.

Building IX lay adjacent to the western side of this alley. The absence of traces of a median longitudinal partition in either E I or F I originally led to its interpretation as a shed or store-building. But discovery of a number of subdivisions in 1986 Trench T I which well suit a centurion's quarters, and the existence of cross-partitions in both E II and F II, suggest that it is after all a barrack, which the dimensions also support.

The position of both end-walls is known, giving an overall length of 151 ft. 6 in. (46.18 m); the width varies between 26 ft. (7.92 m) in Trench E I–II and 29 ft. 6 in. (8.99 m) in Trench F I–II, both measurements falling well within the range of other barrack-widths (p. 138, TABLE V). In Trench E a cross-partition created a room 10 ft. (3.05 m) wide and a second partition lay in Trench F; it is possible to restore ten *contubernia* each with a width of 9–10 ft. (2.74–3.05 m). The area south of the partition in Trench F is taken to be the centurion's quarters with a length of 44 ft. (13.41 m). Several of the rooms here were heavily metalled with gravel or cobbles (see FIG. 57, Sections R–S, S–T). This was particularly striking in Trench F I over Pit 1, an Antonine I demolition-pit whose original filling of burnt daub, clay, gravel and decayed organic material (FIG. 56, Section K–L, 29) had progressively subsided. Layer 21 represented the original Antonine II flooring, continuous with the metalling of the alley (9) but beyond its kerb, and consisting of very large river-boulders and blocks of sandstone covered with finer gravel; this had evidently subsided slowly, without distintegration. Later more stones and gravel (11) had been added to remake a level floor, but this too had sunk.

The absence of a median partition in Building IX may indicate that its construction was slighter than normal; but Antonine II post-holes were always very difficult to identify, since only their lower parts survived. Probing with a sharp survey-pin was normally the only sure way of finding them, and here they may have been missed. Those in external walls were normally 6 to 10 in. (15–25.5 cm) deep, but those in internal partitions were often no deeper than 4 in. (10 cm).

In Trench E II an area of gravel beside the northern wall was presumably the remains of the floor in that room, elsewhere ploughed out; it overlay Antonine I demolition-material. Remains of a metalled floor also survived in the southernmost *contubernium* in Trench F I (PL. XXIX B). Above it a contemporary occupation-layer 1 to 2 in. (2.5–5 cm) thick could be recognised in places.

A space of 14 ft. (4.27 m) separated Buildings IX and X. In Trench E II there were indications that it had been metalled, for despite plough-damage the top of the Antonine I demolition-layer showed an admixture of pebbles; no such traces survived in Trench F II.

Building X was identifiable as a barrack by its internal layout. Neither end of the building was located, but an overall length of 151 ft. (46.02 m) is restored on the plan (FIG. 53). The width of the building varied between 32 ft. (9.75 m) in Trench E II and 30 ft. (9.14 m) in F II. A longitudinal partition was found in both Trenches; this divided the barrack into an eastern range 16 ft. (4.88 m) deep in Trench E II and 13 ft. (3.96 m) deep in F II and a western range 12 ft. (3.66 m) deep in E II and 12 ft. 6 in. (3.81 m) deep in F II. The smaller size of the rooms on the west side suggests that the barrack faced on to the *via quintana*; this would imply that none of the barracks in this part of the *retentura* formed a facing pair.

An east-west partition was found in Trench E II; if the end-wall of the building lies in the expected position beside the *via decumana*, here outside the Trench, a *contubernium* only 8 ft. (2.44 m) wide is indicated. A complete *contubernium* 9 ft. (2.74 m) wide internally was located in Trench F II, and between this and the narrow *contubernium* in E II there is room for nine others 9 ft. (2.74 m) wide, giving a total of eleven. It is more likely, however, that the rooms in F II formed part of the centurion's quarters, allowing these a length of 51 ft. (15.54 m); if these quarters had ended on the south side of F II they would have had a length of only 40 ft. 6 in. (12.34 m); at only 26.8% of the overall length of the barrack this proportion would be abnormally small (p. 138, TABLE V).

In Trench E II the floor of the small end *contubernium* survived as a discontinuous layer of stone cobbling interspersed with gravel. The lower stone of a quern (p. 186, No. 15) lay *in situ* on this flooring (PL. XXIX A), strengthening identification of the room as part of a *contubernium* despite its small size. Flooring was also recognised in Trench F II where it consisted of patches of fine sandy gravel; in section these patches were observed to be in two layers separated by brown soil, which indicates that the floor was relaid at least once during the Antonine II occupation. Below this gravel a layer of clay which sealed the Antonine I demolition-material may represent make-up for the Antonine II floors.

The post-holes were normally similar to those of the other two buildings, but the northernmost east-west partition in Trench F II was represented by substantial post-holes with stone packers, roughly conjoined to form an uneven trench. Many of the post-holes in Trench E II were still surrounded by large stone packers.

Via quintana. To the west of Building X lay a heavily metalled street, the *via quintana*. In Trench F II it was 12 ft. (3.66 m) wide; in E II it seemed originally to have been 19 ft. (5.79 m) wide behind the *principia* but had later been narrowed to 10 ft. (3.05 m) when an additional room was added to the rear of the *principia* (p. 45). In Trench E II the bottoming of large boulders interspersed with gravel occurred immediately below the ploughsoil; two kerbstones were located *in situ* on the eastern edge of the street. There was a 2 in. (5 cm) layer of gravel beneath the boulders, apparently laid to support the street over underlying depressions. In Trench F II the surface of fine gravel was better preserved; this again overlay a foundation of large boulders varying from 3 in. (7.6 cm) to 1 ft. (0.30 m) in thickness in order to create a camber (FIG. 56, Section M–N, 3). The street had here partly subsided into an Antonine I demolition-pit (Pit 2) and had consequently been relaid several times over the depression; the metalling was thus 2 ft. 6 in. (0.76 m) thick over the pit (FIG. 56, Section P–Q; PL. XXXII).

The Bath-Building

A *reihentyp* bath-house was inserted during the Antonine period between the southern rampart and the *via sagularis*; its foundations were cut into the back of the Flavian rampart along the south side and they encroached on the metalling of the street along the north; but the axis of the building was parallel with neither (FIGS. 52, 53). The space available demanded a long narrow building, of the type found in similar positions at forts on the Antonine Wall, as at Bar Hill[2] or Balmuildy.[3]

The north wall was well preserved in Trench T I (PL. XXXIII B), less so elsewhere. It was built mainly of untrimmed red sandstone blocks, but with a few grey boulders as well, and was 3 ft. 6 in. (1.07 m) wide. The south wall, supported by the rampart, had a width of only 3 ft. (0.91 m). Both walls rested on a foundation of cobbles set in stiff clay and both were clay-bonded.

The robbed NE corner was found in Trench T V, and the building measured 79 ft. 9 in. by 21 ft. 3 in. (24.31 by 6.48 m) overall. To judge by the great quantity of red clay which enveloped the remains, the upper portions of the walls had been constructed of this material, for the deposit contained little stone and no tile. The building had been extensively robbed, for in many of the Trenches only the cobbled foundations survived: yet the overlying blanket of stiff red clay showed no indication of subsequent robber-trenches cut through it save only above a

2. *Britannia* x (1979), 276; G. Macdonald, *The Roman Wall in Scotland* (Oxford, 1934), 274.
3. Macdonald (*op. cit.* note 2), 314, 319.

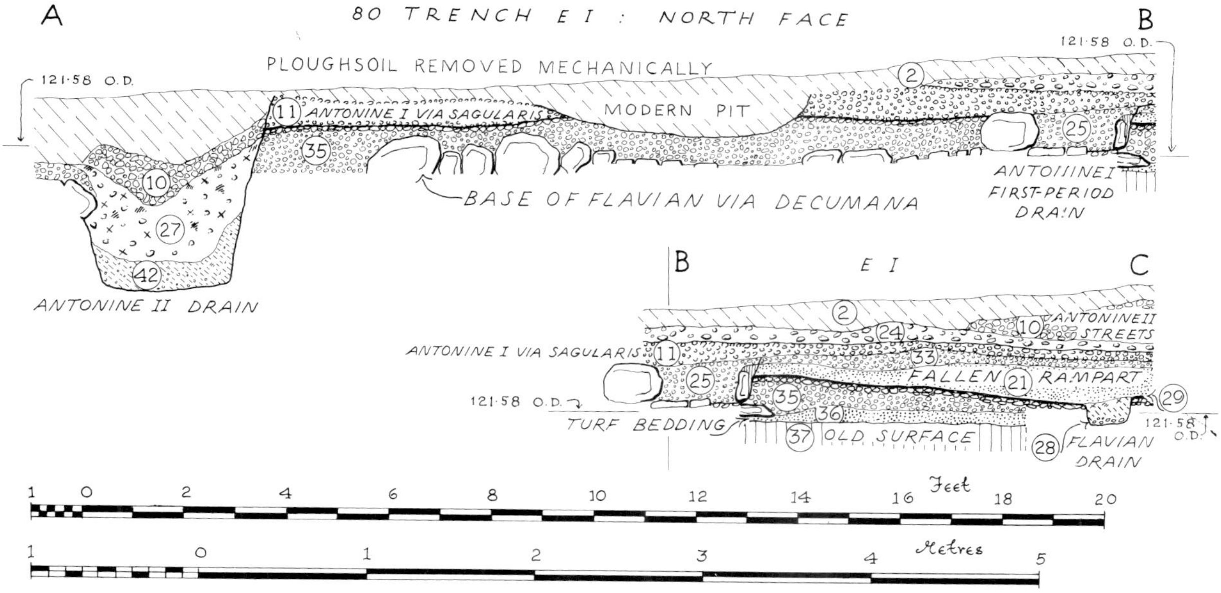

FIG. 54. The left (southern) *retentura*: Sections A–C. Scale, 1:45. (For position see p. 86, FIG. 50).

partition-wall in Trench T I itself (FIG. 57, Section V–W), and it must be concluded that the condition of the structure was the result of very thorough demolition at the end of the Antonine II period. The presence of the clay seriously impeded the speed of excavation despite the digging of a wide trench by JCB the length of the building, inside the north wall; and since it was only towards the close of the season that the building was identified as a bath-house, less of the plan was recovered than had been hoped.

The heated rooms lay at the eastern end; here the sub-floor was of substantial boulders set in heavy clay (PL. XXXIII). In Trench T I there were two *pilae* consisting of large rectangular stone blocks, and another larger one built of smaller stones; along the east side of the Trench ran the lower courses of a wall extending 7 ft. (2.14 m) northwards from the south wall (FIG. 57, Section V–W). This perhaps divided the hot plunge-bath from the *caldarium*. The heated rooms extended at least 38 ft. (11.6 m) from the eastern end, for another stone *pila* was found at that distance in a subsidiary trench.

At the west end of the building a 'floor' of fine plastic yellow clay extended from the end wall for more than 12 ft. (3.66 m) eastwards, and may have been laid as waterproofing below the flagged floor of a *frigidarium*.

No trace of tile was found anywhere on the site: the flues were built in recesses in the masonry of the wall or between the large stones blocks acting as *pilae* beside it. Here and there lumps of soft white sandy mortar were recovered from the ruins, none of it *in situ*: this may have served to bed a timber beam to the top of the masonry as a framework for the clay forming the upper walls.

Accompanying the outside of the north wall in T I was a trench 1 ft. 9 in. (0.53 m) wide, filled with turfy clay (FIG. 57, Section T–U, 7; PL. XXXIII B). This trench had been cut through the Antonine II *via sagularis*, but the section showed that it was not a construction-trench, for its bottom was separated from the foundations by a ridge of metalling; nor, with its vertical sides yet with a rounded bottom, did it show the character of a drain-trench (later filled in). The feature was probably constructed to provided water-proofing for the north end of the basement-rooms at a later phase in the Antonine II period.

An eaves-drip drain was, however, provided on the south side of the building: this had been cut into the surviving top of the turf rampart abutting the bath-house here (FIG. 57, Section V–W). The drain had two phases. The first consisted of a U-shaped trench 3 ft. 7 in. (1.09 m) wide and 13 in. (0.33 m) deep; it was lined with a thin layer of ash. After this had filled with a silt of turfy clay, a smaller channel 1 ft. 10 in. (0.20 m) wide by 6 in. (0.15 m) deep was dug; the filling of this contained a good deal of burnt matter as well as several large fragments of window

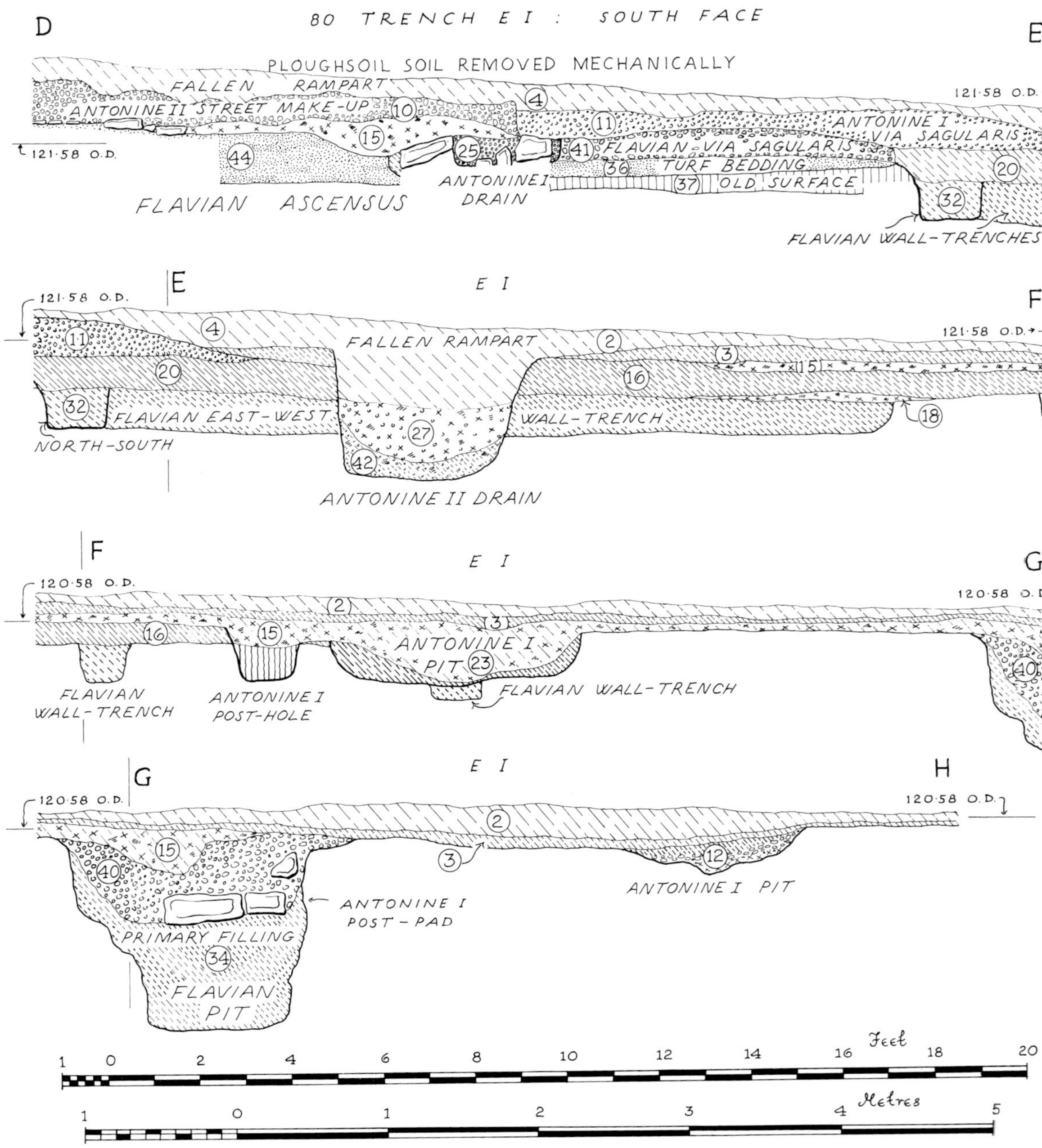

FIG. 55. The left (southern) *retentura*: Sections D-H. Scale, 1:45. (For position see FIG. 50).

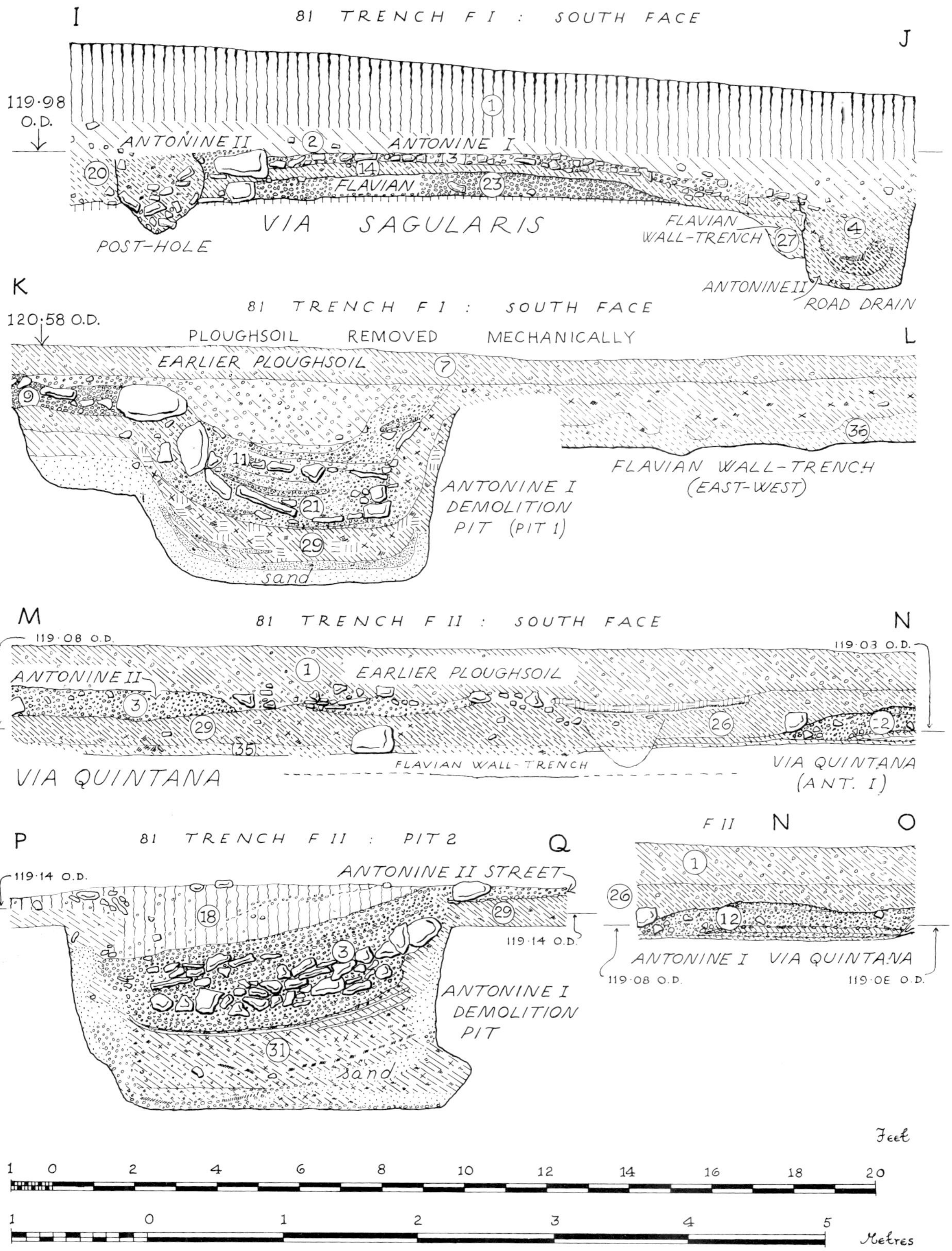

FIG. 56. The left (southern) *retentura*: Sections I-Q. Scale, 1:45. (For positions see FIG. 50).

glass. These successive drains have been attributed to Antonine I and Antonine II respectively on the plans.

To the east of the building and extending at least 20 ft. (6 m) from its wall (FIG. 53) lay a timber-framed stoking-room. The full extent of this was not discovered. A line of at least four large post-holes revetted the north edge of a shallow excavation (about 8 in. (0.20 m) deep) made through the Antonine II street-metalling down to the surface of the Antonine I *via sagularis* – or just possibly along the edge of an area left at the lower level when the Antonine II metalling was built up on their northern side. The filling of the hollow was of black soil with much burnt material. If a stoking-chamber had existed in the Antonine I period it must have been considerably smaller. Unfortunately time did not permit a full exploration.

The date of the Bath-building

The Bath-house had certainly been in use during the Antonine II period, and the presence of a stoking-chamber of that period, taken with the apparent absence of a predecessor, makes it possible to argue that the building was first erected then. But other arguments favour an original construction in the Antonine I period. One is the use of much red sandstone in the building; although occasional blocks of this stone have been found in Flavian contexts (pp. 47, 89), its appearance in quantity on the site as packers in post-holes has been noted as a feature of the Antonine I period, suggesting the opening of a quarry then: and if a quarry were opened, what other purpose could it have served but to provide stone for a bath-building? Stratigraphically also (FIG. 57, Section T–U) the north wall seems to conform suitably in level with the level of the Antonine I street. The fifteen or so years that the Antonine I occupation lasted provide a context in which the absence of such an amenity could call for comment. Yet, as already remarked, if the building is really of Antonine I origin, it must at that period have had a smaller stoking-chamber than the large shed provided in Antonine II.

The plan, however, suggests that the Bath-house was an afterthought rather than an original feature of the Antonine I fort (FIG. 52). The axis runs obliquely to the *via sagularis*, narrowing the street at the west end to a mere 4 ft. 9 in. (1.48 m); and even the Antonine II street (FIG. 53) was not laid out to make a better clearance: there is only a space of 5 ft. (1.52 m) between the bath-house and the corner of the Central Range. Although the south side does cut slightly into the rear face of the old Flavian rampart, and the surface of this had been reduced (as the level of the eaves-drip drains shows), it is curious that no larger incision was made in the turfwork so as to inset more of the structure; for it would have been possible to do this without affecting the contemporary defences. Evidently the obstacle caused to traffic-circulation was not considered sufficiently serious to warrant the extra work involved. This has a bearing on the purposes envisaged for the two Antonine forts (p. 135).

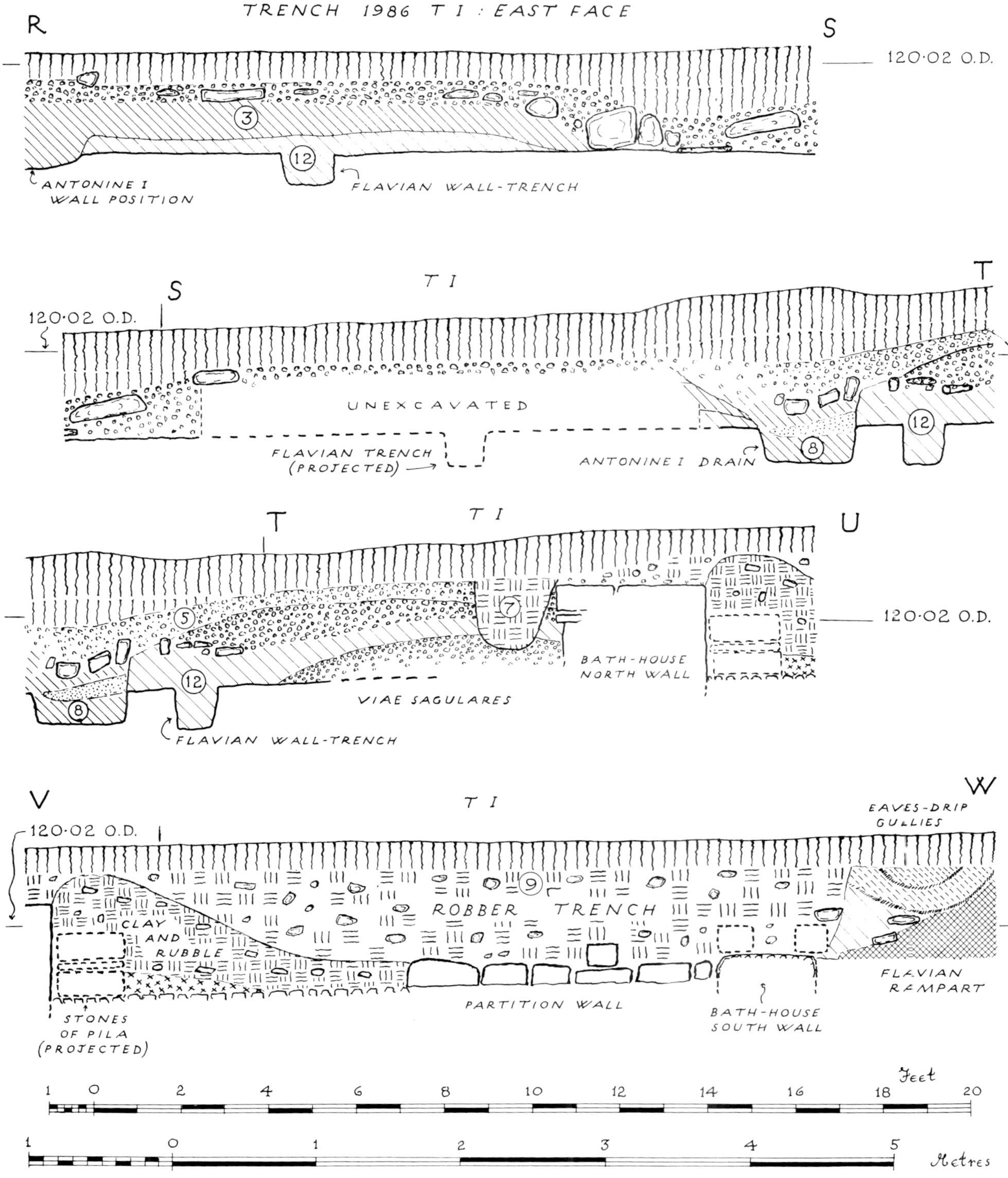

FIG. 57. The left (southern) *retentura*: Sections R-W. Scale, 1:42. (For positions see FIG. 50).

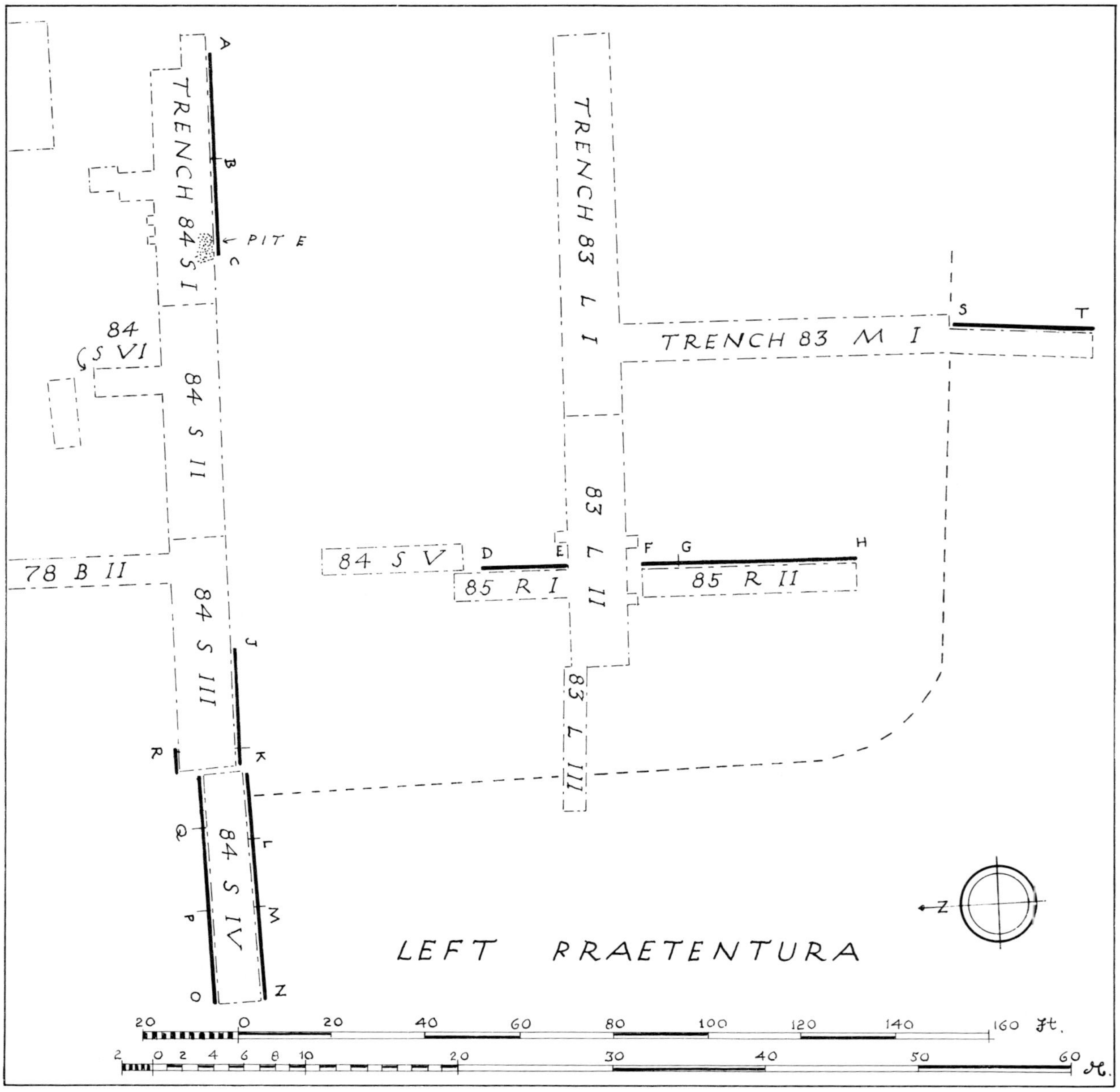

FIG. 58. The left (southern) *praetentura*. Plan of Trenches with positions of published sections.

VII. LEFT (SOUTHERN) PRAETENTURA

This part of the fort was examined in 1983–5. In 1983 a trench 135 ft. (41.15 m) long and 12 ft. (3.66 m) wide (L I–II) was dug east-west at a distance of 96 ft. (29.26 m) from the *via praetoria*; it ran from the edge of the *via principalis* to the *via sagularis* with an extension (L III), 30 ft. (9.14 m) long and 5 ft. (1.5 m) wide, cut by machine to make contact with the rear of the western rampart. Another trench (M I), 71 ft. (21.64 m) long and 8 ft. (2.44 m) wide was dug at right-angles to the first in order to discover the southern building-lines and *via sagularis*; this trench, too, was extended by machine to examine the southern rampart in a cutting 30 ft. (9.14 m) long by 5 ft. (1.5 m) wide, and the results have been described above in Chapter II. The weather in the last week of the excavation in 1983 was so continuously wet that efforts to complete the plan of the Flavian structures were seriously impeded.

In 1984 another trench 12 ft. wide was dug parallel with L I–II, but only *c.* 10 ft. (3 m) from the *via praetoria* (S I–III); it was 150 ft. (45.7 m) long. A machine-cut extension (S IV), 48 ft. (14.63 m) long by 8 ft. (2.44 m) wide, continued westwards to cut the western defences; the trench was near enough to the *porta praetoria* to reveal details of the inturn of the rampart which existed here in the Flavian period. Various smaller extensions were dug to make contact with the edges of the *viae principalis* and *praetoria* and to locate the building-lines against them. The main trench also cut across the southernmost 7 ft. (2.13 m) of Trench B II of 1978 which had sectioned the *via praetoria*. In addition Trench S V, 30 ft. (9.14 m) long by 6 ft. (1.83 m) wide, was dug at right-angles to S III to cut north-south across the area between S III and L II, with the primary aim of learning more about the Flavian granary in this area, and this investigation was extended in 1985 in Trenches R I and R II.

(a) Flavian

The area available for buildings was defined on two sides by the **via sagularis**. On the west side this street was found to be 8 ft. (2.44 m) wide in S III, but had formerly been slightly wider, for its inner edge had been removed by a deep Antonine I drain. The metalling was of fine hard-packed water-worn gravel up to 6 in. (0.15 m) thick (FIG. 10 (p. 22), Section J–K, 15) overlying the old surface soil (19), on which lay a small patch of burnt material (17), presumably from the Flavian clearance of the site. Some sherds of Antonine date lay on the metalling, which was then sealed by *c.* 6 in. of turfy material (14) as a basis for the Antonine I *via sagularis*; the latter had to rise a little here in order to be carried over the stump of the Flavian inturn.

The Flavian street was not seen in Trench 83 L III because bad weather prevented excavation to the necessary depth; nor was its line certainly identified on the south side of the fort in Trench M I for the same reason. Here the external wall of Building XV lay 26 ft. (7.92 m) from the rear of the rampart, so the margin of error in restoring the line (FIG. 59) is not large. In Trench 85 R II, however, the inner 6 ft. (1.83 m) of the southern *via sagularis* was located south of the granary. It consisted of fine gravel 6 in. (15 cm) thick (FIG. 64 (p. 115), Section G–H).

An important point was established when Building XV was found to possess a separate officers' block divided from the main structure by an alley 2 ft. 9 in. (0.84 m) wide. This recalled the similar separate blocks of Buildings II–IV in the right *retentura*, and was thought to justify similar restoration in Buildings XIII and XIV.

Building XIII was a barrack, as shown by its triple longitudinal walls. The east wall lay beyond the end of Trench 83 L I but was located in Trench 84 S I. Here the line of the wall-trench had later been re-used for an Antonine I pipe-line; but below the filling of the latter (FIG. 63, Section A–B, 9) there remained about 4 in. (10 cm) of the clean sandy filling characteristic of Flavian wall-trenches. There was no veranda, but the planning showed that the building faced the *via principalis*. The length of the *contubernia*-block was 113 ft. (34.44 m) and the width was 27 ft. (8.23 m) overall, a metre wider than the shed or stable, Building V, in the corresponding position across the *via praetoria*. The centurion's house is restored with a length of 40 ft. (12.19 m). Firm evidence of divisions between the *contubernia* was lacking except for one wall-trench in 84 S I; the next wall to the north of this may have lain just outside the north side of Trench S I; in this area there was much disturbance from the huge post-pits of an Antonine I granary. A cross-wall in that position would allow two *contubernia*, each *c*. 11 ft. (3.35 m) wide. At the south end of the building no cross-walls were seen in Trench 83 L I, so the final room here may have been as much as 14 ft. (4.27 m) wide, the remaining distance being divided into eight *contubernia* of 11 ft. (3.35 m) making nine in all. There is uncertainty also about the line taken by the median longitudinal wall; in Trench 83 L I a wall ran parallel with and *c*. 9 ft. (2.74 m) from the front wall, while in 84 S I the corresponding wall-trench was 14 ft. (4.27 m) from the front wall. The main median wall has been restored in the former position since this arrangement allows the main rear range of rooms a length of 14 ft. (4.27 m) each. The different arrangement in the two northernmost *contubernia*, where the rear rooms have a length of only 9 ft. 9 in. (2.97 m) may have been the result of these quarters being assigned to NCOs (*principales*). A parallel situation can be seen in Building VI in the right *praetentura* of the Flavian fort (FIG. 40).

The foundation-trenches were normally cut 14–16 in. (0.36–0.41 m) into the natural sand (FIG. 63, (p. 115), Section A–C); exceptionally the northern part of the median wall in Trench 84 S I and of the west external wall there were both cut to a depth of 23 in. (0.58 m). The fill of these Flavian trenches was as usual clean re-deposited natural sand with an admixture of soil, so that they often showed as slightly darker bands in the surrounding orange-coloured sand.

In the north-east corner of Trench 84 S I lay a small hearth of charcoal, 1 ft. (0.9 m) in diameter; associated with it were a fragment each of an iron axe(?) and a bronze steelyard (FIG. 78, No. 87), suggesting possible use for re-working metal.

Building XIV had the same length as XIII but was only 23 ft. (7 m) wide. It lay back to back with the latter, separated by a gap of only 1 ft. (0.3 m); on the west side it opened onto an alley 5 ft. (1.52 m) wide. The trenches of the adjacent back walls of XIII and XIV in Trench 83 L I were 17 and 14 in. (0.43 and 0.36 m) deep respectively (FIG. 63, Section B–C). Near the middle of Trench 83 L I they were crossed by a narrow trench only 8½ in. (0.22 m) deep; this is taken to represent an episode of demolition. In 1983 bad weather prevented excavation to sufficient depth to locate the front wall of the building in L I, but the internal arrangements seem to reflect those of Building XIII, with eight *contubernia* *c*. 11 ft. (3.35 m) wide and with a ninth at the south end rather wider (*c*. 14 ft. = 4.27 m). A median longitudinal wall gives a series of front rooms 5 ft. 6 in. (1.68 m) deep and back rooms measuring 13 ft. (3.96 m). A possible water-tank or latrine pit (Pit E) in Trench 84 S I is discussed below, under Antonine I Building XV (p. 111).

Building XV presents difficulties of reconstruction. The presence of a separate block at the south end suggests that the structure is a barrack (although this argument does not hold true for Building II (p. 39).) The officers' block at the south end measures 40 ft. 6 in. (12.34 m) from north to south and is restored with a width of 33 ft. (10.06 m) in order to leave space for the line of large post-holes (described below under Building XVI) which runs along the west side of the building; these are not regarded as representing a veranda (see below). The *contubernia* block has a length of 108 ft. 6 in. (33.07 m), but there are unusual arrangements at the north end where two suites, separated by a central passage 5 ft. (1.52 m) wide, have a length of *c*. 27 ft. (8.2 m). The western outside wall of the western suite runs within 2–2½ ft. (0.6–0.76 m) of the line of post-holes, leaving insufficient space for a veranda, which in any case would be expected to stop against projecting officers' quarters. The width of the main area of presumed *contubernia* is seen in Trench 83 L I–II, where the overall measurement is 27 ft. (8.23 m), divisible between two rooms one 5 ft. (1.52 m) and the other 17 ft. 6 in. (5.33 m) long. Because Trench 84 S II is occupied by an anomalous part of the building, there is little evidence for any confident reconstruction of *contubernia*; a possible division into 8 sets is indicated on FIG. 59. This has involved restoring a partition-wall within Trench 83 L I in an area incompletely cleaned during excavation because of bad weather. If the median wall in Trench 83 L I continues northward in the same line, the smaller rooms along the east side of the building would suggest that this was the front, facing Building XIV across the alley. This is another reason for rejecting a veranda on the opposite side. The unusual planning of Building XV, with eight *contubernia* and ample additional accommodation suitable for two *duplicarii* at the north end, might suggest that this barrack has intended for two *turmae* of horsemen in a *cohors equitata* (see pp. 119–20). The somewhat restricted space for equipment in the series of front rooms provides a contrary argument. These rooms have an area of 44.8 sq. ft. (4.16 m^2); on the other hand the suggested rear rooms of 161.6 sq. ft. (15.02 m^2) are notably more spacious than those in Building I with only 137.5 sq.ft. (12.8 m^2). That the officers' block of Building XV appears to be larger than that of XIV is in agreement with the principle defined by Baatz,[1] that in any facing pair of barracks the senior officer is on the right as one looks towards the officers' end of the block.

For a Table setting out the various dimensions of these barracks, see p. 136.

Building XVI. West of Building XV lay a massive *horreum* (granary). The line of large rather bowl-shaped post-holes between XV and XVI are taken to represent a fence, since reasons have been given for rejecting it as a veranda for Building XV. The post-holes were consistently *c.* 3 ft. (0.9 m) in diameter and between 18 and 24 in. (0.46–0.61 m) deep. Near the south face of 83 L II a cluster of three further post-holes adjoined the fence-line. They could not be differentiated in Sections, the filling of all being a uniform brown loamy soil with charcoal flecks. The most easterly was 28 in. (0.71 m) deep.

Granary XVI faces another granary (Building VIII) across the *via praetoria*, but is set back only 15 ft. (4.57 m) from the street instead of 37 ft. (11.28 m). A single foundation-trench beyond the north end, which was seen in Trench 78 B II (FIG. 59), lies 7 ft. (2.13 m) in front of Building XVI and perhaps indicates a loading platform. The spacing and the depth of only 9 in. (0.23 m) – less than half that of the true granary-trenches – show that this trench does not represent part of the sub-structure of the *horreum* itself. This began in Trench 84 S II–III, where two parallel trenches were found, 18 in. (0.46 m) wide at the top and up to 21 in. (0.53 m) deep; they were 30 ft. 6 in. (9.30 m) long and were spaced 56–60 in. (1.42–1.52 m) apart centre to centre. Six further trenches with similar spacing were located in Trench 84 S V, giving a total of twelve when allowance is made for four unexcavated examples between S III and S V.

Further south, in Trench 83 L II and its extensions, four more granary-trenches were located in which sparse indications of untrimmed rounded uprights *c.* 1 ft. (0.3 m) in diameter were seen. The spacing of the trenches, centre to centre, was a little less regular, being (from north to south) 4 ft., 5 ft. 6 in. and 5 ft. (1.22, 1.68, 1.52 m). The length of the trenches was also over 2 ft. (0.6 m) greater than those in S III, being 32 ft. 9 in.–33. ft. (9.98–10.06 m). The question therefore arose whether two separate granaries were present in this half of the *praetentura*. In 1985 Trenches R I and R II were accordingly dug to test the matter. The resulting plan shows that only one granary is present, although of unusual length. It is based on 27 transverse trenches, each 18–21 in. (0.46–0.53 m) deep (FIG. 64, Section D–E), giving a length of 129 ft. (39.32 m). The width is 30 ft. 6 in. (9.3 m) as given by the trenches at the north end; the longer trenches in L II must be assumed to be overcut. Few post-positions were identified in the lengths of trench examined. Two of them in L II were 10 ft. (3.05 m) apart; on the assumption that a third lay undetected between them, this gives a spacing of 1.52 m, a frequent figure in Manning's Table of Granary Dimensions.[2]

Although of almost identical width, Building XVI is over twice the length of the pair of granaries at Fendoch; but the presence of a second very large granary (Building VIII) in the right *praetentura* at Strageath (p. 73) shows that Building XVI is no mere substitute for the two smaller *horrea* normal in other forts. The problems raised by the exceptional store-capacity at Strageath are discussed on p. 123.

1. D. Baatz, *Kastell Hesselbach*, Limesforschungen xii (1973), 54–8.
2. *Saalburg Jahrbuch* xxxii (1975), 108.

At the south end Building XVI extends to within 8 ft. (2.44 m) of the *via sagularis*; 4 ft. beyond the final trench a single post-hole, 6 in. (15 cm) in diameter, was found in Trench 85 R II; it is possible that this formed part of the support for a loading-platform, although this end of the building is far less easy of access by carts than the north end beside the *via praetoria*, where a trench was found performing this function.

(b) Antonine I (FIG. 61)

In this period the **western via sagularis** was found to be 14 ft. (4.27 m) wide. The position of the street, which had large kerb-stones each side, was located both in Trench 83 L II–III and in 84 S III, giving an alignment not quite parallel with the back of the Flavian rampart. In Trench 83 L II–III the surface lay 1 ft. (0.3 m) below that of the Antonine II *via sagularis* and was not fully exposed (PL. XXXIV A); a layer of grey brown gritty soil, 6 in. (0.15 m) thick, separated the two streets. In Trench 84 S III the Antonine I street had a bottoming of some irregular boulders, but over much of the northern part of the trench its surface had been removed by the plough. The situation on the south face of S III can be seen in FIG. 10 (p. 22), Section J–K.

The **southern via sagularis** was found in Trench 83 M I. Here the width was reduced to 9 ft. (2.74 m). The extreme north edge of this street was encountered also at the south end of Trench 85 R II, where it appeared to be flanked by a small gully (FIG. 64, Section G–H), though this could equally well be an Antonine II feature.

The Oven. On the south side of the street in Trench M I lay a large cooking-oven (FIG. 60; PL. XXXVI B) with its flue on the north side leading from a small stoking-pit 7 in. (0.18 m) deep beside the *via sagularis* and its back built against the rear face of the Flavian rampart. The oven had an internal diameter of 7 ft. (2.13 m); the floor was of rough water-worn stones set in clay and the wall was constructed of clay-bonded slabs of red sandstone (2–3 courses surviving) within an

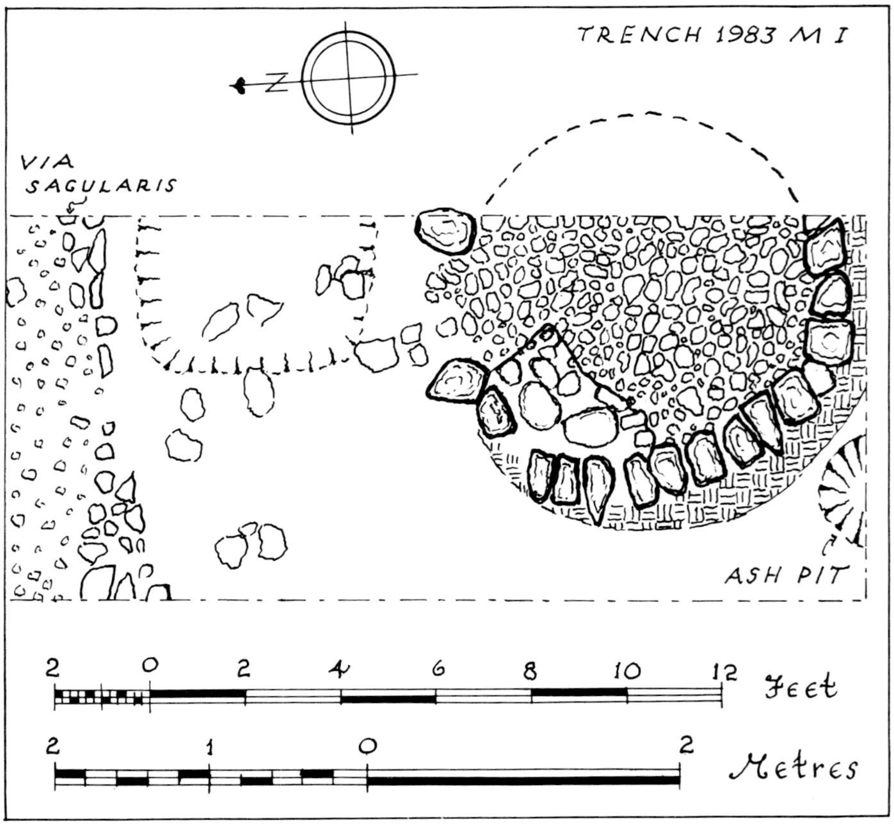

FIG. 60. Plan of Antonine I oven in Trench 1983 M I. Scale, 1:48. (For position see FIG. 61).

outer ring of clay. The whole interior was heavily burnt. Just inside the oven on the right (west) side of the flue-entrance was a 'shelf', 1 ft. 9 in. (0.53 m) wide and 3 ft. (0.9 m) long made of sandstone slabs; too little of this survived for certainty about its purpose.

A layer of ash, *c.* 1 ft. 6 in. (0.46 m) thick and containing bands of clean clay, covered the area surrounding and beneath the oven. These remains may be taken to indicate a succession of cleanings and re-linings of one or more earlier ovens which had occupied the same or a nearby site.

The **via praetoria** was widened southwards in this period by about 2 ft. (0.6 m).

The edge of the **via principalis** was located at the east end of Trenches L I and S I; it had been slightly widened in this period. There was a bottoming of river boulders over which fine gravel had been spread. The street was accompanied by a kerb-lined channel which was evidently a continuation of the water-pipe trench traced along the *via praetoria* to a corner in 1978 (FIG. 41). No iron colars were found, which suggests that the pipe, whether of lead or wood, had been taken out when the fort was evacuated. In Trench 83 L I the pipe-line trench was 9 in. (0.23 m) wide and only 6 in. (0.15 m) deep, its base lying at 119.95 ft. (36.56 m) O.D. In Trench 84 S I, however, the trench was 18 in. (0.46 m) wide and 13 in. (0.33 m) deep, the base being at 119.45 ft. (36.41 m) O.D. It was thought, however, that the Antonine water-pipe had been laid here in the upper filling of the front Flavian wall-trench; the trench did indeed contain two layers of fill (FIG. 63, Section A–B), and if so the Antonine pipe will have been at the same level (119.95 ft.) as in Trench L I.

The Intervallum Drain. In Trench 84 S III a substantial drain was found adjoining the eastern edge of the *via sagularis*, and its Antonine I date was demonstrated by the fact that the filling was sealed by surviving areas of undisturbed Antonine II metalling, preserved where they came down the sloping camber (PL. XXXVI A; FIG. 10 (p. 22), Section J–K). The drain-cutting was 2 ft. 8 in. (0.81 m) wide at the top, 1 ft. 10 in. (0.56 m) deep, and 2 ft. 5 in. (0.74 m) wide at the bottom; in the length of 7 ft. (2.13 m) excavated the filling was largely composed of gravel and stones from the Antonine I street, including dislodged kerb-stones. The flat bottom of the drain (119.68 ft. = 36.48 m O.D.) had a fall to the south; two lines of stake-holes 1 ft. 8 in. (0.51 m) apart along the base showed the position of a former lining, presumably of planks. The spacing of the stakes ranged between 11 and 18 inches (0.28–0.46 m).

A similar drain in a similar position was found in Trench 83 L II. It was 3 ft. (0.91 m) wide at the top, 1 ft. 11 in. (0.58 m) deep and 2 ft. (0.61 m) wide at the bottom; traces of stake-holes were once again encountered. The flat bottom lay at 119.47 ft. (36.41 m) O.D., that is 0.21 ft. (0.064 m) below that of the drain in Trench 84 S III, confirming a fall to the south. At the time of excavation the drain in 83 L III was taken to be an Antonine II feature, and indeed its relationship with the Antonine II *via sagularis* here does suggest that it was in contemporary use. Nevertheless, the stratification in 84 S III proves that there was a drain in this position in the previous period; the problem of the course of the Antonine II drain will be discussed in the next section. Here it should only be noted that if the drain in L III is an Antonine II reconstruction, the levels as they survive are those of the latter period.

The position of the Antonine I drain in the southern intervallum is uncertain because of insufficient excavation. It cannot have run south of the *via sagularis* because of the situation of the oven in Trench 83 M I. A large drain which was clearly of Antonine II date crossed this trench at the inner edge of the Antonine II *via sagularis* and cut through the Antonine I street which separated Buildings XV and XVI. It seems improbable that this drain was on the line of its predecessor, being 8 ft. (2.44 m) from the inner edge of the Antonine I *via sagularis*. Its base lay at 118.27 ft. (36.05 m) O.D., over a foot lower than that of the drain in Trench 83 L II, and thus could have been a continuation of it. At the east side of Trench M I (FIG. 62) this Antonine II drain curved southwards as if about to pass beneath the *via sagularis* towards an outfall at the *porta principalis sinistra*.

Thus the probability is that the Antonine I drain along the western *via sagularis* ran out through the rampart near the angle. The only indication of contemporary drainage along the southern *via sagularis* was a shallow gully, only 1 ft. (0.3 m) wide and 8 in. (0.20 m) deep (FIG. 64, Section G–H, extreme right), which accompanied the northern edge of this street where it just entered Trench 85 R II. This gully was not seen further east in Trench M I; but if the fall was westwards towards a junction with the main drain near the angle, it may have been too shallow in M I for recognition in the wet conditions of 1983. The Antonine I date of the gully, however, is not beyond doubt.

In the interior of this part of the fort the top surviving archaeological deposit was normally the demolition layer of the Antonine I fort. This consisted of a brown soil containing fragments of daub, sometimes yellow and unburnt but usually burnt red, together with small pieces of charcoal; the burnt daub was usually sparsely scattered but sometimes present in sufficient quantity to impart a reddish tinge to the soil.

Building XIII. The eastern end of Trench 84 S I was unexpectedly found to be occupied by three parallel rows of very large post-holes, the rows being *c.* 5 ft. 8 in. (1.73 m) apart centre to centre (FIG. 60, FIG. 63, Section A–B). As defined by their sockets, the posts, normally 1 ft. (0.3 m) in diameter, were untrimmed and stood in post-pits up to 3 ft. (0.9 m) in diameter and between 19 and 33 in. (0.48–0.84 m) deep (PL. XXXV A). The posts had been packed with large river-boulders and slabs of sandstone and occasionally with large sherds of amphora (Dressel 20). Each row consisted of 7 posts set *c.* 3 ft. 11 in. (1.19 m) apart centre to centre; the length of the rows was 24 ft. (7.31 m). The remains evidently represent part of a granary whose sub-structure was set in individual post-pits rather than in continuous trenches. Parallels for this form of construction exist at Fishbourne and Hod Hill in the first century, when it was much rarer than construction in continuous trenches. In the second century known timber granaries are in any case uncommon, but two continuous-trench granaries are known in the early Hadrianic period at Corbridge and a post-pit granary was found at Old Kilpatrick on the Antonine Wall. The latter building measured 25.91 m long by 6.1 m wide.[3] Building XIII faces the *via praetoria*, from which it stands back 9 ft. (2.74 m). The length of the granary is uncertain, but possibilities are restricted by the presence of Building XIV to the south. On FIG. 60 it has been restored with a ground-plan measuring 54 by 25 ft. (16.46 by 7.6 m), dimensions which closely resemble those of the granary at Hod Hill (16.76 by 6.48 m).

Building XIV was located in Trench 83 L I. Here it has a width of 24 ft. (7.32 m), divided between two rooms each 12 ft. (3.66 m) deep, one of which is 10 ft. (3.04 m) wide. The southern partition wall did not continue across the back room. The posts were set in stone-packed post-pits up to 2 ft. (0.61 m) in diameter and 18–22 in. (0.46–0.56 m) deep. On the assumption that the south end-wall is on the same line as that of Building XVI, the distance to the northern front wall of the granary is 145 ft. (44.2 m). Given a granary of the size suggested above, Building XIV cannot have been longer than *c.* 70 ft. (21.3 m). It may be interpreted either as a store-building or just possibly as accommodation for those administering the granary (*mensores* or *librarii horreorum*[4]). The absence of a partition on the south side of the rear room in Trench 83 L I suggests that this part of the building (shaded in FIG. 60) may perhaps have formed part of an officer's quarters, since the northern partition-wall aligns well with the north end of the centurions' quarters in Buildings XVI and XVII. If so, there is room for two *contubernia* beyond. Two small pieces of window-glass were recovered from the Antonine I demolition-layer above Buildings XIV and XV, implying that at least one had glazed windows.

Building XV was separated from XIV by an alley 5 ft. (1.52 m) wide, which in L I was lightly metalled in places with stone slabs. This building is *c.* 17 ft. (5.18 m) wide in L I, widening to 20

3. For these buildings see W.H. Manning, *Saalburg Jahrbuch* xxxii (1975), 105–129.
4. *Mensores*: von Domaszewski/Dobson, *Rangordnung*, 46: only legionary *mensores* are attested, but in principle there is no reason to exclude them from the *auxilia*. *Librarii horreorum: Digest*, 50, vi, 7.

ft. (6.1 m) in S I; the restored length is 140 ft. (42.67 m). The post-holes like those of Building XIV were set in stone-packed pits up to 2 ft. (0.6 m) in diameter and *c.* 12–17 in. (0.30–0.43 m) deep. A partition existed in L I *c.* 36 ft. (11 m) from the south end, and a room 13 ft. 6 in. (4.11 m) wide stood at the north end in 84 S I. The building evidently served as a weapon-store since a large number of fired-clay shot for slings or catapults were found in both areas examined – 45 in Trench L I and 16 in S I (FIG. 94). The presence of two small metal-working hearths in S I suggested use also as a *fabrica*. These remains consisted of adjoining circular patches of charcoal, one 16 in. (0.41 m) and the other 12 in. (0.30 m) in diameter, both yielding slag together with fragments of iron, bronze and lead. Broken bronze objects appeared to have been assembled for re-working (and cf. FIG. 80, No. 112).

Just south of the partition in Trench S I lay a sub-rectangular pit measuring *c.* 5 ft. 6 in. by 7 ft. (1.68 by 2.13 m) and 2 ft. 6 in. (0.76 m) deep (Pit E). The upper part had been filled with Antonine I demolition material including some sherds of BB1 ware; large stones had been flung into the bottom, while above the lowest filling was a layer of stones burnt red and covered by about 1 in. (2.5 cm) of gravel (FIG. 63, Section B–C), over which had been deposited a layer up to 1 ft. (0.3 m) thick of brown soil mixed with much burnt daub. It is possible that the pit had originally been dug as a water-tank or even as a latrine-pit, since it had a level bottom and very steep sides (perhaps once therefore plank-lined), and there was a sloping 'inlet' a foot wide and long on the north edge. The date of the original pit is not quite clear. It lies in the corner of both an Antonine I and a Flavian room (FIGS. 59, 60), and although it has destroyed parts of the Flavian walls this damage may have happened during the Flavian demolition process. If the pit is Flavian, the burnt stone 'floor' will be a consolidation over it contemporary with the Antonine I *fabrica*, sunk through gradual compression of the Flavian filling (the lowest levels, below the burnt stones, consisted of sand and brown earth). On the other hand, since latrine pits are not otherwise known in barracks at Strageath (save in Building B, p. 47) and a water-tank would be unnecessary there, it is perhaps more satisfactory to regard the pit as a water-tank within the Antonine I *fabrica*, later filled with demolition-material. An Antonine II partition crossed the pit-filling.

Building XVI was divided from XV by a metalled street of fine gravel 8 ft. (2.44 m) wide, which continued southwards along Trench 83 M I to join the *via sagularis*. Building XVI was 140 ft. (42.67 m) long. In Trench L I–II the width was 28 ft. (8.53 m), widening to 30 ft. (9.14 m) in S I. At the north end post-holes of the east wall were missing except for one very large post-pit in Trench S VI; this absence was probably the result of a rise in the natural sand in this area causing abnormal erosion in the layers above when ploughing takes place. At the south end abnormalities in the pattern of walls show that the centurion's quarters (shaded in FIG. 60) extended to the north edge of Trench L I–II, a distance of 44 ft. (13.41 m). North of this, in the remaining 96 ft. (29.26 m) of the building there is room for 7 *contubernia* each 14 ft. (4.27 m) wide. This calculation is based on the assumption that two post-holes in S II mark the line of the final partition-wall. The more easterly of these was substantial, marking a post 1 ft. (0.3 m) square set 28 in. (0.71 m) deep in a stone-packed pit 2 ft. 6 in. (0.76 m) in diameter; the other had a depth of only 14 in. (0.36 m) and held a post only 6 in. (0.15 m) square. There is no evidence for the position of the median longitudinal wall; we may perhaps assume that it was anchored to the more substantial of the two partition-posts, and if so the barrack will have faced east onto the street, with a row of front rooms *c.* 12 ft. (3.66 m) and back rooms *c.* 15 ft. (4.57 m) deep. A circular hearth, 3 ft. (0.9 m) in diameter, lay in the northernmost *contubernium*; it consisted of a hollow cut in the sand, 5 in. (12.7 cm) deep and filled with charcoal and small broken pieces of sandstone slabs (PL. XXXV B).

In Trench 83 L I lay an oval pit 4 ft. 10 in. by 5 ft. 3 in. (1.47 by 1.6 m) and 3 ft. (0.9 m) deep with straight sides (FIG. 60, Pit A). The filling was of dark soil containing daub and charcoal together with some large stones. The pit was possibly in use during the occupation and filled during the demolition since there was some suggestion of a former wooden lining.

A small piece of window-glass was recovered from the demolition-layer over Buildings XVI and XVII, suggesting that the centurion's quarters here had been glazed.

Building XVII had a length of 140 ft. (42.67 m) but its width was only 24 ft. (7.32 m) like that of Building XIV; it is taken to be a barrack, pairing with XVI. The absence of any sign of a median longitudinal wall in Trench 83 L II suggests that this area falls within the centurion's quarters, which may have terminated in a transverse corridor 8 ft. (2.44 m) wide in the north half of the trench. This arrangement would allow a length of 45 ft. (13.72 m) overall for the centurion's end (shaded on FIG. 60), leaving 96 ft. (29.26 m) for the *contubernia*. The most southerly room of the centurion's quarters contained a rather ruined succession of three small smithing furnaces. Stratigraphically the earliest, of which little survived, was the most northerly; unlike the others it had an east-west axis with flue to the west; the walls were mainly of burnt clay and the floor was pear-shaped and *c.* 1 ft. (0.3 m) wide at the maximum. The other two were stone-built and lay side by side with flues to the north, the more westerly furnace being the later and the better preserved. It had a roughly rectangular floor measuring *c.* 4 ft. (1.22 m) long by 1½ ft. (0.46 m) wide. Some large pieces of Dressel 20 amphora newly smashed were found in the demolition-layer (85 R II 5) above the ovens and more large fragments came from further north in R I 5 (FIG. 64, Section D–E); many more fragments, from at least two amphorae, came from the demolition-layer over the adjacent *via sagularis*.

The northern wall of Building XVII was seen in Trench 78 B II, 2 ft. (0.61 m) from the *via praetoria*, and the northernmost *contubernium* had a width of 14 ft. (4.27 m). A large stone-packed post-hole in the north-west corner of Trench 84 S V suggests the line of another partition, and if so the three most northerly *contubernia* will each have been 14 ft. wide. Two post-holes of another partition occurred 30 ft. (9.14 m) further south in Trench 85 R I, leaving a distance of 22 ft. (6.7 m) to the wall of the officer's corridor. These dimensions suggest either two more *contubernia* 14 ft. wide and then two only 10 ft. (3.05 m) wide, giving a total of seven, or else five *contubernia* only 9–10 ft. (2.74–3.05 m) wide in the central part of the building, as restored in FIG. 60, giving a total of eight. A hearth of flat sandstone slabs occurred at the south end of Trench 84 S V, up against one of the partitions.

What were evidently post-holes belonging to the median longitudinal wall were also found in SV. They were *c.* 18 in. (0.46 m) deep, two of them being cut into the filling of the Flavian granary trenches below. This line gives the rooms each side respective lengths of 5 ft. and 15 ft. 6 in. (1.52 and 4.72 m). Normally the smaller rooms mark the front of a barrack; but since Building XVII can hardly have been approached through the narrow gap between it and Building XVI, a gap which narrows from 6 ft. (1.83 m) at the south to only 2 ft. (0.61 m) at the north, we must assume that in this instance the arrangement was reversed and that Building XVII was entered from the *via sagularis*.

For a Table setting out the various measurements of these barracks see p. 137.

Demolition Pits. Pit B in the gap between Buildings XVI and XVII was a demolition pit which was incompletely excavated. It contained large stones and dirty grey soil. Pit C, within the centurion's quarters of Building XVII, was another demolition pit, 5 ft. 6 in. long by 2 ft. 6 in. wide (1.68 by 0.76 m) and 14 in. (0.36 m) deep. It was filled with black ash and burnt daub. A further demolition pit (Pit D) lay in the north-east corner of Trench 84 S V; its base was dished, penetrating to a maximum depth of only 16 in. (0.41 m). The filling was largely charcoal and burnt daub, which yielded a group of pottery including a large samian sherd of Dr. 37 (FIG. 106, No. 34). The filling was sealed beneath the line of an Antonine II partition, but had interrupted the median wall of Building XVII and so clearly belonged to the Antonine I demolition phase. Pit F was a large pit in the intervallum area west of the *via sagularis* in Trench 83 L III; the filling of black ash and burnt daub was incompletely excavated.

(c) Antonine II (FIG. 62)

In this period the accommodation provided in the left *praetentura* for the first time exactly matched that in the right; in each area three barracks were built (FIG. 68). However, over the entire extent of the left *praetentura* all Antonine II demolition levels, occupation-layers and floors had been destroyed by the plough; only the bottoms of the post-holes survived. In most cases they lacked post pits and appeared to have been driven into the surface of the Antonine I demolition-deposits (the top surviving layer) by means of hammering.

The *viae praetoria* and *principalis* remained unaltered in width, save that the water-pipe trenches along them were disused and metalled over.

The **western via sagularis** was found in Trenches 83 L II–III and 84 S III. In the latter the metalling was 17 ft. 6 in. (5.33 m) wide, 3 ft. 6 in. (1 m) wider than its predecessor, having been extended on the west side over the previous drain (PL. XXXVI A; no metalling had survived the plough on the crown of the road, where only the Antonine I bottoming survived (FIG. 10 (p. 22), Section J–K). In Trench 83 S III three post-holes penetrated this bottoming 5 ft. (1.52 m) from its western edge and were taken to represent an intervallum building which recalls traces of a similarly-placed structure in Trench 81 F I in the left *retentura* and one in Trench 85 N I in the right *retentura* (pp. 95, 63). In Trench 83 L II–III (PL. XXXIV A) the street was reduced to a width of 14 ft. (4.27 m). West of the metalling a capping of heavy stones was laid over the top of Pit F, an Antonine I demolition pit.

The **southern via sagularis** was seen in Trenches 83 M I and 85 R II (FIG. 64, Section G–H). It was 12 ft. (3.66 m) wide and had kerb-stones along its inner edge. Here the street lay 21 ft. (6.4 m) from the inner face of the Flavian rampart, suggesting that space had been allowed for ovens, although none occurred within the areas excavated. In Trench R II there were large sherds of at least two amphorae (Dressel 20) in the demolition layer (3) overlying the street.

Intervallum Drain. In Trench 84 S III what appeared to be the shallow beginning of a drain ran along the outer side of the *via sagularis*; it descended southwards from a depth of 2 in. (0.05 m) at the north face to 11 in. (0.28 m) in the south face (FIG. 62, FIG. 10 (p. 22), Section J–K, 4) where its floor was at 122.0 ft. (37.18 m) O.D.; the filling was fine silty gravel from the street. The Antonine II drain in the right *praetentura* similarly began in a very shallow channel with a fall towards the north (p. 79). In Trench 83 L III, however, no comparable feature was identified on the west side of the street. This may have been because of insufficient excavation in Trench L III; on the other hand, the large drain on the east side of the street which, as shown above, must be of Antonine I origin was certainly used or re-made in the Antonine II period, for its channel was cut through the Antonine I demolition-layer on the east side and was associated on the west with the metalling of the Antonine II *via sagularis*. Perhaps, therefore, the drain in 84 S III crosses the street somewhere in the intervening area. Alternatively this drain may have served a local purpose, perhaps within the suggested intervallum building, and ended in a soakaway pit; and the large Antonine II drain on the east side of the street may have started at a point south of Trench 84 S III. That this is likely is shown by the fact that in the right *praetentura* the corresponding Antonine II drain begins in Trench 78 B I at a point 18 ft. 6 in. (5.64 m) north of the north edge of the *via praetoria*; a corresponding point south of the south edge would lie *c.* 6 ft. (1.8 m) to the south of Trench S III.

On the south side of the fort the drain was found accompanying the north edge of the Antonine II *via sagularis*. Here in Trench M I it was 2 ft. 6 in. (0.76 m) wide with almost vertical sides and flat bottom, and was 2 ft. (0.61 m) deep from the surface of the street. In Trench R II (FIG. 64, Section G–H, 7) the dimensions were similar. There was a consistent fall eastwards in the direction of the *porta principalis sinistra*, from 119.47 ft. O.D. in Trench L III, 118.45 in R II, to 118.27 in Trench M I. There the filling consisted largely of gravel, but the upper part contained a dark brown sticky silt which yielded many sherds of a Dressel 20 amphora including its complete neck and rim together with some sherds of a second vessel, including part of a handle. In Trench M I the drain appeared to swing to the south as if to pass under the *via sagularis* to its outer edge. Stake-holes along the bottom once again indicated a former lining.

The Barracks. Buildings XI–XIII are barracks. In all three of them anomalies in the arrangement of walls within Trench 83 L I–II show that the centurions' quarters extended at least as far as the north face of this trench; in all three buildings entry to the centurions' quarters was by a corridor from the adjacent street. In Buildings XI and XIII these quarters might be thought to end on the north side of the corridor, at the partition nearest the north side of the trench; but in Building XII the corridor lies beyond a continuous partition and gives access to a rear room to the north of it. This fact shows that the centurions' quarters, at least in Building XII, extended to a wall lying north of the trench. Accordingly in all three barracks the centurions' quarters (shaded in FIG. 62) have been extended to a comparable position, beyond which lies space for eight *contubernia*.

Building XI is 33 ft. (10.06 m) wide. It has been restored with a length of 139 ft. (42.37 m) overall, of which the southern 52 ft. (15.85 m), shaded on FIG. 62, represent the centurion's quarters. A corridor 4 ft. (1.22 m) wide and 15 ft. (4.57 m) long (PL. XXI B) gave access to the latter from the *via principalis*, and led to a back (western) range of three or perhaps four rooms each 16 ft. (4.88 m) long. There remain 87 ft. (26.52 m) for the *contubernia*. In Trench 84 S I a complete *contubernium* was uncovered; it was 10 ft. (3 m) wide with one room 18 ft. (5.49 m) long and the other, west of it, 13 ft. 6 in. (4.11 m). As with some of the Antonine I barracks described in the previous section, the smaller rooms lie here at the back; the building could be entered only from the *via principalis*. There is space for another *contubernium* of the same dimensions at the north end of the building, and the planning suggests eight such *contubernia* altogether. The post-holes were normally *c.* 6–10 in. (0.15–0.25 m) in diameter and *c.* 5–8 in. (0.13–0.20 m) deep. None stood in surviving post-pits or had packing stones; they could be detected by their soft dark filling and by the absence of daub fragments therein, which contrasted with the texture and colour of the Antonine I demolition-layer into which they had been driven. The posts seemed to have been hammered into the soil.

Building XII was separated from XI by a gap of 4 ft. (1.22 m). The width of the building in Trench 83 L I was 38–39 ft. (11.58–11.89 m), but in 84 S I–II had narrowed to 36 ft. (10.97 m). The southern end of the barrack lay 10 ft. (3 m) from the *via sagularis*, and the north end was traced in Trench 84 S VI immediately adjacent to the *via praetoria*. The length accordingly is 138 ft. (42.06 m) overall, with a centurion's quarters at the south end (shaded on FIG. 62). These quarters were divided into two ranges of rooms by means of a median longitudinal wall on a line different from that dividing the *contubernia* (PL. XXXIV B). This is a feature of all three buildings. The suite was entered from the west by means of a corridor 4 ft. (1.22 m) wide which gives access to a room in the rear range extending further to the north – an arrangement which suggests that there was also a small room in the front range north of the corridor itself. Accordingly the front (western) range in the centurion's quarters contained four rooms in addition to the corridor, all 16–16½ ft. (4.88–5.03 m) long; the back or eastern range contained three or perhaps four rooms each 20 ft. (6.10 m) long. The length of the centurion's quarters is restored at 48 ft. (14.63 m) overall.

The remaining 90 ft. (27.43 m) of the building was divided into *contubernia*. In Trenches 84 S VI and S I–II two *contubernia* were identified, each 10 ft. (3 m) wide and divided between a front (west) room 19 ft. (5.79 m) and a rear (east) room 15 ft. (4.57 m) deep. Once again the smaller rooms are at the rear, for the barrack faces west onto a metalled street. As in the two other barracks, the total of *contubernia* appears to be eight.

Building XIII lay west of a space 16 ft. (4.88 m) wide in Trench 83 L II and 15 ft. (4.57 m) wide in 84 S II, down which ran a metalled street with a width in L II of 7 ft. (2.13 m) (PL. XXXI B). As usual it was of fine gravel laid over a foundation of large river-boulders; but in Trench L II most of the fine gravel had been ploughed away while in Trench 84 S II even the boulders had been removed except for a patch on the north side of the trench. Here the metalling, near the *via praetoria*, had an increased width of 10 ft. (3 m).

The northern end wall of Building XIII had been recorded in Trench 78 B II, lying 6 ft. (1.83 m) from the *via praetoria*. The southern end-wall aligns with that of Building XII, and the barrack has an overall length of 134 ft 6 in. (41 m), of which 46 ft. (14.02 m) is occupied by the centurion's quarters (shaded in FIG. 62); the building has an overall width of 30 ft. (9.14 m). The centurion's quarters were entered from the *via sagularis* by a corridor 5 ft. (1.52 m) wide and 10 ft.

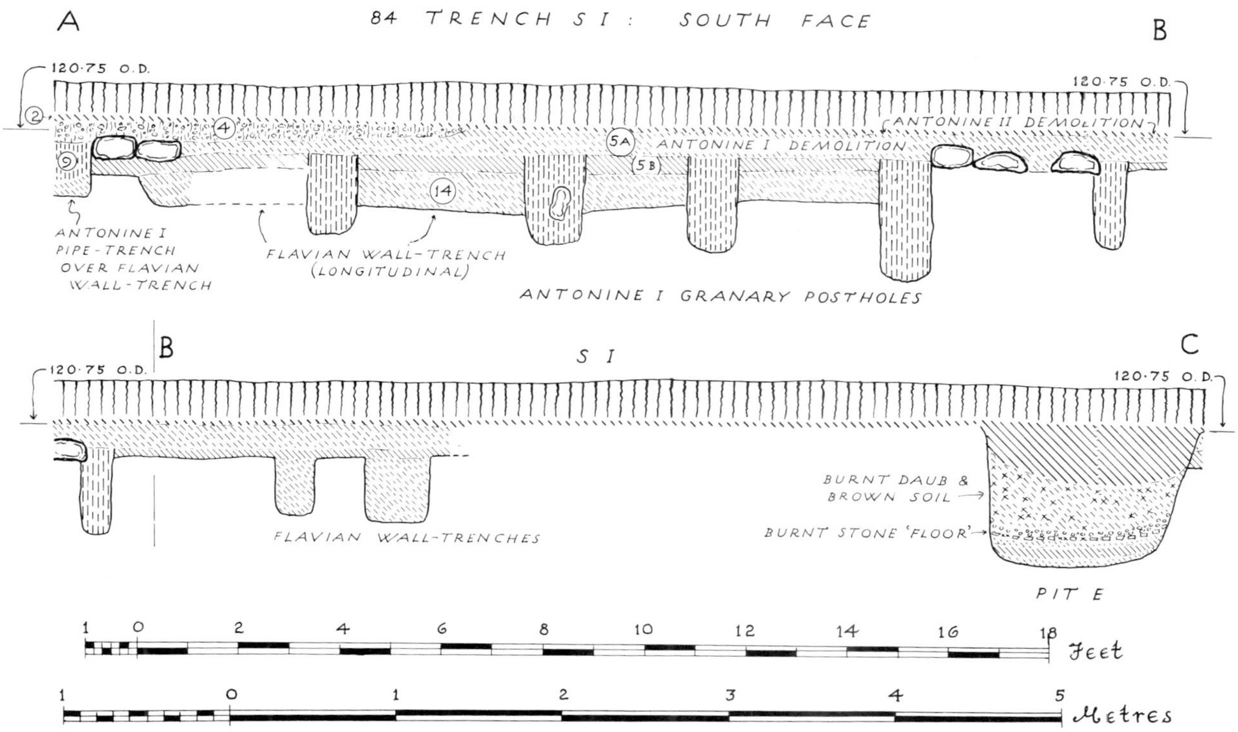

FIG. 63. The left (southern) *praetentura*: Section A-C. Scale, 1:45. (For position see p. 104, FIG. 58).

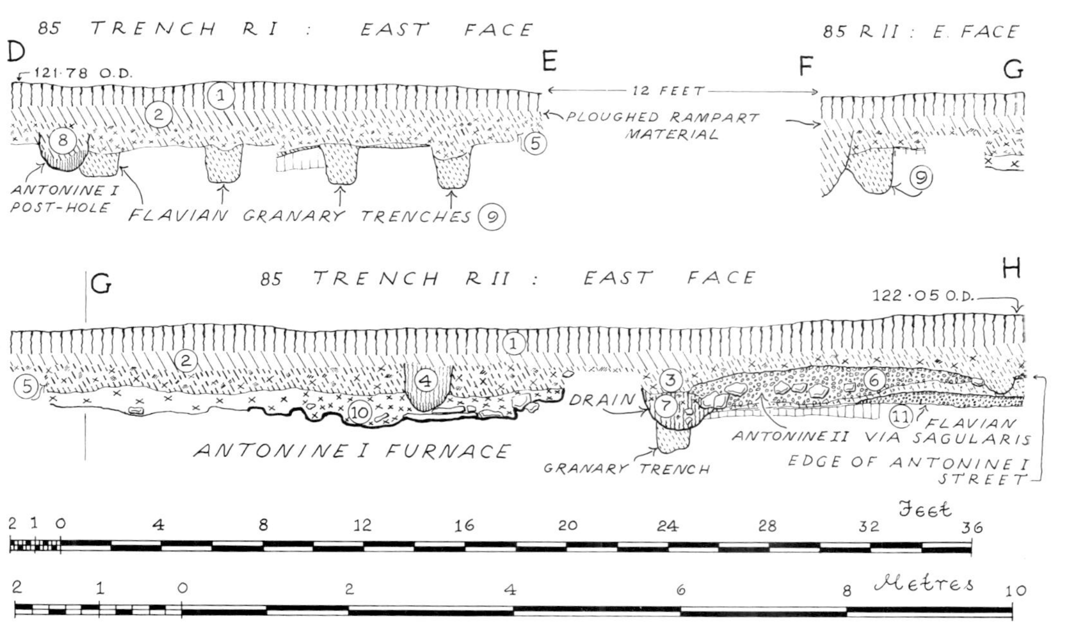

FIG. 64. The left (southern) *praetentura*: Sections D-H. Scale, 1:90. (For position see FIG. 58).

(3 m) long, flanked by rooms and leading to a rear range of rooms each 16 ft. (4.88 m) deep, in one of which was found a small hearth of flat stones, 18 in. (0.46 m) in diameter.

The area available for *contubernia* had a length of 88 ft. (26.82 m). At the north end two of these were identified with widths of 10 and 11 ft. (3 and 3.35 m) respectively, and a median longitudinal wall divided each into front (west) rooms 12 ft. (3.66 m) and back (east) rooms 14 ft. (4.27 m) deep. The median wall was found again in Trench 84 S V and further partitions at the same spacing were seen both in this trench and in 85 R I, so that the total of eight *contubernia* is here well authenticated. The post-holes were normally *c.* 4–6 in. (0.10–0.15 m) in diameter and 5–10 in. (0.13–0.25 m) deep and were spaced *c.* 2 ft. (0.61 m) apart.

On the measurements given above, the centurion in Building XII would appear to be the most senior and that in Building XIII the most junior. All three buildings are arranged back to back, so that Building XII does not strictly speaking pair with either of the others.

For a Table setting out the various measurements of these barracks, see p. 138.

VIII. SUMMARY
THE FORTS AND THEIR GARRISONS

The plans of the three successive forts at Strageath are shown on FIGS. 66–8. These are, of course, restored plans; the evidence for the restorations has been set out in detail in Chapters III–VII. In this chapter the evidence which the plans present is taken to represent the actual position. Elements of uncertainty admittedly still exist over certain details such as the total number of *contubernia* in some of the barracks; but in outline the restorations offered are thought to be reasonably secure, and discussion is necessarily based upon the best efforts at reconstruction, which have been drawn after much consideration of alternative possibilities.

The fort is in the form of a parallelogram rather than a rectangle, a fact which affected the internal planning at all periods. It is hard to see why a rectangular shape was not adopted, for there is plenty of space on the plateau. The reason seems to be that the fort was placed as near to the river as possible; its east front was accordingly forced into an area where the plateau narrows and the necessary length for the east rampart could be obtained only by taking a line oblique to the south rampart whose position was itself controlled by the side valley (FIG. 4, p. 7).

A. THE FLAVIAN FORT

The Flavian fort (FIG. 66) measured approximately 472 by 403 ft. (143.9 by 122.8 m), giving an area over the ramparts of 4.36 acres (1.77 ha),[1] a figure close to that of Fendoch (1.8 ha); the fort is therefore of a size which could have accommodated a milliary garrison. The true situation as revealed by excavation is not so simple.

All the Flavian buildings were of post-in-trench construction, the trenches (except in the granaries) being normally about 1 ft. (0.3 m) wide and deep or only a few inches larger.

An early phase of the Flavian occupation is indicated by the small granary which underlay Buildings V and VI in the *praetentura* (p. 69). This building (FIG. 40) was set in trenches dug with great precision to a depth of 1 metre, in which stone slabs at the bottom supported the weight carried by the uprights. The depth and careful cutting of these trenches differentiated the building from the other granaries in the *praetentura*, as did its small size; but the deep trenches with their stone slabs were closely comparable to those of the *porta decumana*, the only gate to be excavated. It would not be fanciful to recognise legionary craftsmanship in these constructions. There was no other certain sign of 'proto-Flavian' construction antedating the buildings elsewhere in the fort, for the theory (p. 74) that a barrack had been planned and partly built on the site later occupied by Building VIII, the main granary in the right *praetentura*, lacks convincing support. Nor is it probable that the proto-Flavian granary had been intended to be larger and was demolished before completion; for if so the other granaries, to which the building-party would have been diverted, might be expected to have been built in the same style. On the other hand, while it is not reasonable to picture a fort containing nothing else than this small granary, a context for it could well be the provisioning of a legionary detachment, itself living in tents while building the ramparts and gates of the fort. Legionaries are seen performing precisely these tasks on some of the scenes on Trajan's Column. The theory would imply that once the defences had been erected, the auxiliary garrison arrived to take over construction of the internal buildings, and the small legionary granary was demolished. The incoming garrison built twelve barracks, one possible *fabrica*, one store-building or stable, and two very large granaries. The archaeological evidence, on the other hand, suggests that (if this theory is correct) it was the legionaries who had laid out the streets of the fort, since gravel for this purpose had been assembled even before the construction of the east rampart (p. 27).

1. The area within the *via sagularis* measures 385 by 330 ft. (117 by 100.6 m), giving a usable area of 2.92 acres (1.18 ha).

Auxiliary units were of several types. The smallest was the *cohors quingenaria peditata*, consisting of six centuries of infantry (Hyginus, Chapter 28), each thought to have a nominal strength of 80 men. In the Flavian period milliary peditate cohorts began to make their appearance: these consisted of ten similar centuries (Hyginus, 28). Each size of cohort could alternatively be equitate (part-mounted); the exact composition of these, however, is not known for certain. For the *cohors milliaria equitata* we have what, at first sight, appear to be good figures from Hyginus (Chapters 26–7); he tells us that it consisted of 760 infantry and 240 horsemen, the infantry organised in ten centuries (under 10 centurions) and the horsemen in ten *turmae*[2] (each commanded by a decurion). We can be more sure of the 240 horsemen than of the 760 infantry, for a century of 76 men is not divisible equally into 10, 9, 8 or 7 *contubernia*; it appears that Hyginus did a quick sum substracting 240 (which should therefore be correct) from a round figure of 1000. It is preferable to follow R.W. Davies[3] and to assign a paper strength of 80 men (as in other types of unit) to the century, giving a total of 800 infantry and 240 horsemen – 1040 in all. Whether Hyginus is in error in assigning ten *turmae* (of 24 men each) – or six (of 40 men each) – rather than eight (of 30 men each) is undetermined but probable.

To a *cohors quingenaria equitata* Hyginus (Chapter 27) assigns six centuries and 'the rest half in proportion'. At first sight this looks like 480 infantry and 120 horsemen; the number of *turmae*, however was not five or three but in all probability four (to judge by the archaeological evidence).

In addition to these various types of *cohortes* the Roman army possessed cavalry units (*alae*), again nominally 500 or 1000 strong. Since Strageath was not large enough to hold an *ala*, or at any rate clearly did not do so,[4] discussion of these units may be omitted.

On the figures given above, a fort holding a *cohors quingenaria peditata* should show six barracks, and one holding a *cohors milliaria peditata* should show ten; a *cohors quingenaria equitata* would need six barracks for its infantry and two for its horsemen (two *turmae*, 60 men, being accommodated in a single barrack, but one with room for two decurions rather than one centurion). A *cohors milliaria equitata* would require ten barracks for infantry and either four or five for its mounted contingent. However, two tiresome problems of Roman military archaeology arise from the fact that few plans of the interior of forts are known in their entirety and that few of those known conform exactly to the expected patterns.

In the disorganisation of war, units could be split up: Hunt's *pridianum*[5] gives a good picture of the effect of this on the parent unit during Trajan's Dacian War. Even in more settled conditions, detachments from units could be outstationed, or units themselves could be divided between neighbouring small forts. Examples of such fragmentation are well known on the Antonine Wall and at first- and second-century Crawford.[6,7] A contrary effect could result from the concentra-

2. Lenoir emends this to six.
3. *Epigraphische Studien* iv (Koln, 1967), 110; *Historia* xx (1971), 751–63. However, even if Birley (*Corolla Memoriae Erich Swoboda Dedicata*, Graz-Koln 1966, 54) was correct in postulating that the centuries of a *cohors quingenaria equitata*, unlike those of its peditate equivalent, consisted of only 60 men, we may note that the basic assumptions of this chapter are not affected: the unit would still require six barracks for its infantry, each of ten *contubernia* (since 60 is not divisible by 9, 8 or 7). The alternative, that the barracks of its centuries might each contain only six *contubernia* (of 10 men each) is disproved by the extreme rarity of barracks with so small a total of *contubernia*; at Strageath there are only two possible examples, one in the Flavian and one in the Antonine II fort, and both can be accounted for otherwise. It would hardly be possible on archaeological grounds to decide whether a *contubernium* held six or eight men; but Davies's argument for a consistent century of 80 men in all units is very persuasive.
4. A quingenary *ala* would need 8 barracks for its 16 *turmae*. Of attested *ala*-forts in Britain only three are below 2.2 ha in area, and none is as small as Strageath.
5. *JRS* xlviii (1958), 102–16; R.O. Fink, *Roman Military Records on Papyrus* No. 63, 217–27; F.A. Lepper and S.S. Frere, *Trajan's Column* (Gloucester, 1988), 244–59.
6. *P.S.A.S.* civ (1971–2), 147–200; RCAHMS *Lanarkshire* (1978), 128–33.
7. Dr. Alan Bowman tells me that study (1988) of recent finds of writing-tablets at the fort of Vindolanda provides further startling evidence for the dispersal of large numbers of men of the milliary *cohors i Tungrorum* from their parent station at the fort there during the early nineties of the first century, long after the war in Scotland was over. He writes as follows: 'A writing-tablet from Vindolanda, probably dating to the first period of occupation

tion for strategic purposes of more than one auxiliary unit in a single large fort: examples in Scotland are the successive forts at Dalswinton.[8] Even the brigading together of a legionary vexillation and an auxiliary force was not unknown, witness Antonine Newstead.

The Flavian fort at Strageath, as already mentioned, contains twelve barracks, a total which does not identify with any of the units described above. Before further analysis can be attempted, we must examine the number of *contubernia* in each barrack and the respective sizes of the officers' quarters. If a block contains ten *contubernia* it is likely to be assignable to the 80 men of an infantry century; if eight, a barrack of two *turmae* may be in question.[9] Horsemen had more equipment than infantrymen and their quarters may therefore be larger; moreover an officers' block to accommodate two decurions may well be more ample than one for a single centurion.

Both the last two expectations are indeed sometimes, but by no means invariably, borne out in practice when the totality of excavated barracks is examined. It proves unfortunately impossible to rely unreservedly on larger-than-normal quarters for officers or on large-sized *contubernia* as criteria for the identification of barracks for *turmae*. However, when one or both criteria are present, they form useful clues.[10]

At Strageath the four Flavian barracks which have larger accommodation for officers than the rest[11] (see TABLE III, p. 136) each has other characteristics (such as eight (or less) *contubernia* or (in two cases) extra-large *contubernia*) which have prompted in the respective descriptions (pp. 59, 72, 88, 106–7) the suggestion of possible use by horsemen. Building VII has only seven *contubernia*, but they are of large size. Four barracks holding 8 *turmae* would be very suggestive; but, before we build on the identification, Building I (FIG. 33, p. 59) calls for further discussion because of the unusual size of its officers' block and because of the unparalleled ratio between the respective areas of this block and of the *contubernia*. The overall area of the officers' block is 237.9 m^2 (217 m^2 internally). These figures are outstandingly large in relation both to the other Flavian barracks at Strageath and also to auxiliary barracks of similar date elsewhere. Dr David Davison has supplied some *comparanda* of which the following are the highest figures for officers' quarters:

Corbridge:	180.0 m^2
Heddernheim, phase i:	180.95 m^2
Moos-Burgstall:	182.4 m^2
Rottweil, fort 3:	198.0 m^2
Echzell (type 1, left *retentura*):	172.5 m^2
(type 2, left *retentura*):	241.5 m^2

Except for the last and for decurions' quarters of 308 m^2 in the milliary *ala* fort of Heidenheim, the Strageath figure cannot be matched. The Echzell evidence does, of course, show that the Strageath figure is not impossible in a Flavian auxiliary context. But another difficulty is the percentage of the total barrack area taken by the officers' block. In Building I this is 49.6%, whereas elsewhere in Flavian forts it does not exceed 39%: in one rather small barrack at Claudian Hod Hill (IX) the figure rises to 43.26%. Likewise the percentage of the total length

(c. A.D. 90), contains a strength report of the cohors I Tungrorum milliaria which must have been stationed there at this time. It is remarkable in that it shows the extent to which the unit was fragmented at this time. The total strength of the cohort was about 740 men, of whom only about 270 remained at Vindolanda. The remainder (about 470 men) were absent on detached duties, with the governor, the procurator and (probably) at six other locations including London and Corbridge, the latter having a detachment of more than 300.'

8. Frere and St Joseph, *Roman Britain from the Air* (Cambridge, 1983), 123–6
9. It is worth remembering, however, that some barracks which seem certainly to have housed *turnae* are known to have had ten *contubernia*, as at Künzing (H. Schönberger, *Kastell Künzing-Quintana* (Berlin, 1975) and perhaps at Chesters (I.A. Richmond's 10th editiion of J. Collingwood Bruce, *Handbook to Hadrian's Wall* (Newcastle upon Tyne, 1947), 83. The problems over the housing of *cohortes equitatae* are further discussed by M. Hassall in B. Hartley and J. Wacher (eds.), *Rome and her Northern Provinces* (Gloucester, 1983), 96–131.
10. I have profited from the statistics assembled by Dr David Davison in his unpublished Oxford DPhil Thesis on *The Barracks of the Roman Army from the 1st to the 3rd centuries A.D.* (1987).
11. Building I, 237.90 m^2; Building VII, 130.20 m^2; Building IX, 161.68 m^2; Building XV, 124.10 m^2.

occupied by the officers' block is 40.75, far exceeding those found in the other barracks, which vary between 22.5% and 28.09% (see TABLE III, p. 136).

These difficulties suggest either that the plan incorporates some error, or that special circumstances existed. A change in the plan is not easy to support; if, for instance, the *contubernia* extended further north than shown, totalling ten, a partition between *contubernia* 9 and 10 should have been found within the south edge of Trench 82 G I (FIG. 33, p. 59), an area where *longitudinal* walls were indeed located but no transverse one. A wall in that position, moreover, would not have equally divided the space available, resulting in the tenth *contubernium* being larger than the rest.

If we assume, then, that the officers' block cannot be reduced in size, how can its exceptional area be explained? There is no precedent or reason for two of the four decurions of a *cohors equitata* being given quarters 38% larger than those allotted to their two colleagues. Was it perhaps occupied, not by decurions, but by a legionary centurion? The area is very comparable to the 234 m^2 given by Dr Pitts[12] as the internal area of a centurion's house at Inchtuthil. Perhaps, then, Building I housed a legionary century slightly under strength (8 *contubernia* instead of 10). So small a contingent would not have made much difference, perhaps, to the strength of the garrison of the fort; but it may well have had responsibilities connected with the construction of bridges and roads and of the Gask watch-towers, or with the movement of supplies.

The remaining barracks, apart from the four already discussed, have officers' quarters ranging between 83.7 and 120.96 m^2 (TABLE III, p. 136). Of these, five barracks in the *retentura* (III, IV, X, XI, XII) each have ten *contubernia* and are suitable for five of the six centuries of a *cohors equitata*, two of whose *turmae* may be assigned to Building IX. A glance at the plan of the Flavian fort (FIG. 66) shows a marked difference in appearance between these barracks and those in the *praetentura*, where division of space between the front and rear rooms of the *contubernia* is much less equal. The difference may suggest the work of a different unit. None of the barracks in the *praetentura* has as many as ten *contubernia*: VI has seven (or perhaps six plus quarters for a *principalis*); XIII has either nine *contubernia* or seven plus quarters for two *principales*, and XIV has nine *contubernia*. Buildings VII and XV, as already suggested, may have been for horsemen, thus housing the four *turmae* of a second *cohors equitata*, three of whose six centuries are represented (although under strength) by Buildings XV, XIII and XIV.

If this analysis is correct, Flavian Strageath held (a) a *cohors equitata* less one of its centuries and two of its *turmae* (which were presumably posted elsewhere); (b) four *turmae* and three centuries of a second *cohors equitata*; and (c) a legionary century. Of cohort B the 'missing' other three centuries were presumably posted elsewhere; but the three centuries present were under strength by perhaps as many as 8 *contubernia* or 64 men.

So far we have based conclusions solely on the building-plans; but evidence provided by the distribution of cavalry equipment of Flavian type is also relevant, although it raises some difficulties.

Pieces of such equipment from undoubtedly Flavian levels (pp. 142–7) occurred as follows:

Building III, four
Building IV, two
Building VII, one
Building IX, one
Buildings IX or X, one

A number of 'Flavian' pieces occurred in Antonine I levels, and the decision whether they may be added to the above figures depends partly on how firmly we believe that they were all undoubtedly of first-century manufacture and therefore were residual in Antonine I contexts, and partly on whether we can believe that Antonine I disturbance of the soil was insufficient to move them far from the original positions of their loss. The figures, so enlarged, are as follows:

12. L. Pitts and J.K. St Joseph, *Inchtuthil, the Legionary Fortress* (London, 1985), 174.

Building I(unstratified over the building), three
Building III, five
Building IV, two
Building V, one
Building VI, one
Building VII, one
Buildings V, VI or VII, two, plus one from an Antonine II context
Building IX, one
Building X, three
Buildings IX or X, one
Buildings X or XI, two, plus one from an Antonine II context
Building XI, one

The totals suggest that there has indeed been some dispersal or casual loss; but the figures for Buildings I, III and X are suggestive. Yet none of these were among those suggested on grounds of plan as cavalry barracks above, namely VII, IX, and XV. No cavalry equipment of any kind was associated with XV or its neighbourhood: this need not be significant. But it might be possible to assume that the five pieces from the area of Buildings VI, VII and V–VII had been dispersed from Building VII, and that the pieces from Buildings IX and X were originally associated with IX. This, however, is a very uncertain deduction. Building I remains so anomalous in an auxiliary context that the occurrence of only three cavalry pieces unstratified above its position cannot be taken to invalidate the conclusions reached on p. 120. Building III with five possible pieces remains. Despite the small size of the officers' quarters and the ten *contubernia*, this building should perhaps be assigned to horsemen. Davison has shown that cavalry barracks not infrequently have more than eight *contubernia*.[13]

If this is accepted, the revised garrison would have consisted of (a) a *cohors equitata* with its full complement of 4 *turmae* of troopers (in Buildings III and IX) but only 4 of its six centuries (in Buildings IV, X, XI and XII) and (b) four *turmae* and only three centuries of a second *cohors equitata*.

Other criteria for distinguishing the building-work of two units can be found; they result in alternative attributions, but make little difference to the analysis of the garrison figures.

In the first place, five barracks (VI, VII, IX, X, XI) appear to possess verandas, but seven (I, III, IV, XII, XIII, XIV, XV) do not (FIG. 66). In the second place, three barracks and one other building (III, IV, XV and II) were shown to have detached blocks occupied (except for II) by centurions: on reasonable grounds of symmetry this feature has been restored also in Buildings XIII and XIV, and with less assurance in Buildings VI and VII. Is there a relationship between the two sets of phenomena? If Buildings VI and VII, in fact, possessed attached quarters for the centurion, Building XII would be the only barrack with attached centurion's quarters to lack a veranda. However, its failure to have one undermines the credibility of a link between the presence of a veranda and the presence of a detached block. If a choice has to be made as to which phenomenon is significant, the importance of the veranda must be dismissed, for the pattern of distribution suggests that the provision of these depended only on the space available.

If a separate end-block is chosen as the hall-mark of a particular unit, then Buildings III (disregarding the cavalry equipment), IV, VI, XIII and XIV may represent five of the six infantry centuries of *cohors equitata* A and Buildings VII and XV may represent its four *turmae*. Buildings X, XI and XII will then represent half the infantry component of a second *cohors equitata* B, half of whose mounted contingent is represented by Building IX. Building I is still considered legionary. The remainder of cohort B – a contingent of 240 infantry and two *turmae* of horsemen – can be presumed to have been posted elsewhere as perhaps also can the single century from cohort A; but of the paper strength actually present at Strageath eight scattered *contubernia* are missing, a total of 64 men.

It is tempting, but may not be correct, to equate the shortfall in the fort with the occupation of towers along the Gask Ridge. Between Strageath and Bertha eleven signal-towers are known, of which all but two are nearer to Strageath than to Bertha and accordingly were in all probability

13. See notes 9 and 10 above (p. 119).

manned and administered from Strageath. Between Strageath and Kaims Castle one further tower is known and another is still to be located. Thus, at least eleven towers required manning. How many men would each require? When rotas of duty and the requirements of self-defence are taken into account, six men must surely be the minimum: and if so the 66 men required corresponds closely with the 64 available. Probably, however, it is more realistic to think of a *contubernium* of eight men being assigned to each tower. If so, 88 men would be needed, and we might consider the complete century which was missing from cohort A being assigned to this duty, and account for the reduced numbers in cohort B not by outstationing but by campaign casulaties (which would also seem to be the explanation of similar shortfalls in the Antonine forts).

The temptation to explain the shortfall in accommodation within the Flavian fort in terms of the need to hold the signal-towers is strong and this explanation has yielded suggestive results. But not all scholars are agreed that the towers were held for the entire duration of the Flavian occupation of this part of Scotland. If the towers were not garrisoned from the start of occupation at Strageath, another explanation for the shortfall in accommodation would have to be sought. When the accommodation in the Antonine forts at Strageath is considered (pp. 126, 129), it will be noted that there too the number of *contubernia* in barracks is irregular and does not conform to the theoretical norm. Such non-conformity is, in fact, wide-spread in both British and Continental forts of all periods, and therefore no unique explanations (such as garrisoning the towers) is needed. It is easy to see that at the moment of construction a unit may have been under strength, especially when forts were being built in the immediate aftermath of a campaign. It is less easy to understand why the newly-built accommodation should be planned to relate to present depleted numbers rather than to the establishment figure which fresh drafts might soon restore. There is no evidence that the establishment figure had been reduced in the second century – and if it was, we should still expect to see a (new) regularity in the numbers of *contubernia*. In the Antonine period there were no towers nearby to account for a 'missing' *contubernium*. To suppose that the regular complements of men in the *contubernia* was no longer formally maintained would be foolish, for this would overlook much first-century evidence for similar shortfalls in accommodation. The proper conclusion must surely be that accommodation was provided for the number of *contubernia* which each unit possessed at the moment of building, in the knowledge that numbers were unlikely to be brought up to full paper strength in the forseeable future, and that, if they were, the internal timber partitions could easily be adjusted. There is, however, little or no evidence that the internal arrangements of barracks were adjusted in this way.[14] It may be significant that comparable irregularity of *contubernia* totals are much less evident in stone-built barracks.

The question of accommodation at Flavian Strageath is complicated by the presence of Building B in the Central Range north of the *principia* (p. 46). This has the appearance of a barrack containing nine *contubernia* together with quarters for an *optio*; that the occupants were not general-duty soldiers is suggested by the *arma* of the barrack being sited at the rear rather than in front of the *papiliones*. The position of the building closely resembles that of similar structures in successive forts at Corbridge which Gillam assigned to administrative staff. As remarked earlier (p. 47), it is hard to see why a normal auxiliary fort should require so large an administrative staff as 72 men, or why they should be provided with accommodation other than in their centurial barracks. For that reason it was concluded that Building B was more probably used to house transport wagons or perhaps bulky stores such as tents. Nevertheless the correspondence between the total of nine *contubernia* in this building and the eight *contubernia* 'missing' from other barracks (p. 120) is sufficiently close to renew the questions whether Building B was after all used to accommodate men subtracted from their proper centuries, and if so for what purpose?

14. In this context attention might be drawn to the extra partitions which are taken in the text as indicating internal fittings in Buildings III (p. 60) and VI (p. 72). Others occur in Antonine I Building V (p. 000) and Antonine II Buildings V and VI (p. 78).

Three arguments can be found to support the need for additional administrative accommodation. First, the Flavian *principia* at Strageath is smaller than that at Fendoch by no less than 254 square metres, and so we may fairly claim that administrative space therein was cramped. Secondly the presence of elements of a second unit in the fort would have made extra administrative demands. Thirdly, as noted in the next paragraph, Flavian Strageath is mainly remarkable for the size of its granaries, which far exceed the normal provision in an auxiliary fort and so suggest a connection with Agricola's forward plans. It is possible, therefore, to conclude that a special staff may have been assembled to control the forwarding of supplies to the army in the field. Whatever the purpose of Building B, however, it need not imply the presence of extra men additional to the paper strength of the garrison already calculated (pp. 120–21).

A garrison equivalent to twelve centuries amounts to a force very little larger than that which occupied Fendoch. At this fort there were two granaries, each measuring 17.07 by 9.14 m (156 m^2), which may be assumed to have held sufficient stores for a year's supply. At Strageath the granaries have over twice that area. Building VIII measures 32.61 by 8.8 m, and Building XVI 39.32 by 9.3 m (286.97 m^2 + 365.67 m^2 = 652.6 m^2). It is evident that the *horrea* at Strageath were concerned with more than the supply of the immediate garrison. The fort should be regarded as one of the advanced bases housing supplies for Agricola's army in its advance further north; another was presumably the as-yet unlocated *Horrea Classis*. On the formula proposed by Manning[15] and allowing for gangways of 2.44 m, the total capacity of these granaries is 1632 man/year rations, or – if the gangways were only 1.8 m (6 ft.) – yearly rations for 1868 men. Either figure represents about double the probable size of the garrison.

We have calculated that this garrison included 180 horsemen. When officers' mounts and their spare horses are added there may have been about 200 horses at Strageath, without counting baggage-animals. The problem of the stables of the Roman army is as yet unresolved. Wells in a recent discussion[16] has emphasised the possibility that cavalry horses may often have been left out at grass in enclosures near their forts; but at least during the worst weeks of a Scottish winter it seems improbable that they were not placed under cover. Whether the necessary stabling lay within the fort or perhaps only within the annexe is another matter.

What should we expect the characteristics of a military stable to be? Virtually all that have been recognised or suggested are long narrow buildings, of similar length to the barracks for convenience of fort-planning, but not so wide. In them the horses might be arranged in short transverse rows with or without partitions forming horse-boxes, or else in either one or two longitudinal rows (depending on the width of the building), in which the animals stood at right-angles to the long axis.

Although most of the literature is obsessed with the height of the horses, measured in hands, the real problem concerns what allowance should be made for their length; while the capacity of the stable will depend on the allowance made for their widths.

At Ilkley[17] the third-century fort had a double stable, each half containing a longitudinal drain dividing a space for horses, 3.4 m deep, from a gangway 2.4 m wide. In the Flavian-Trajanic fort at the same site there was a possible stable 5.8 m wide internally, allowing almost exactly the same arrangement.

At Brough on Noe[18] there was a stable 3.96 m wide internally, with a longitudinal drain allowing *c.* 2.7 m for the length of the horse. The provision of drains in these buildings strengthens identification, although the presence or absence of a manger would affect estimation of the horse's length. Drains, however, are rare, and it is likely that a thick bed of straw or hay, mucked out at frequent intervals as one of the fatigues of service, was normally thought sufficient for the purpose. Permeability of the subsoil would also be a consideration.

15. *Saalburg Jahrbuch* xxxii (1975), 116–18.
16. *Limes: Akten des xi. Internationalen Limeskongresses* (Budapest, 1977), 659–665.
17. B.R. Hartley, *Proc. Leeds Philosophical and Literary Soc.* (Literary and Historical Section) xii, 2 (1966), 23–72.
18. G.D.B. Jones and J.P. Wild, *Derbys. Arch. Journ.* lxxxviii (1968), 89–93.

At Dormagen[19] stables were identified which consisted of stalls measuring *c.* 3.3 m square and containing roughly in the centre of each a long pit or sump 2.9–3.3 m long and 0.6–0.9 m wide. These are assumed to have had wooden covers and therefore their position (although at first sight seeming to imply a length-allowance of only *c.* 1.5 m per horse) is irrelevant to this question: each box probably held two horses, but there is insufficient evidence to establish the lengths of the animals. At Longthorpe[20] a building identified as a stable for two *turmae* had internal dimensions of 40.33 by 6.1 m; the width was thought sufficient to accommodate two rows of horses (each *c.* 2.3 m deep) and a gangway between of 1.5 m.

At Hod Hill[21] a length per horse of only 1.83 m was though sufficient and a width-allowance of 1.11 m; and in the 19th century horses were shipped to India in containers 2.13 m long and 0.69 m wide.[22] At Halton Chesters a building, reasonably identified as a double stable divided by a longitudinal wall,[23] measured 39.6 by 18.28 m. Granted two rows of horses divided by a gangway of 1.8 m in each half, a space of *c.* 3.5 m remains for the length of the horses.

TABLE II:

STABLES AND HORSES

	Length allowed per horse (m)	Width allowed per horse (m)	Gangway (m)
Hod Hill	1.83	1.11	1.81
P and O horse boxes	2.13	0.69	
Longthorpe	*c.* 2.3	1.11	1.5
Künzing	2.6	1.45	
Brough on Noe	2.74		1.22
Ilkley, Severan	3.43	1.14	2.4
Trajanic	2.9	1.15	
Halton Chesters	3.5		1.8
Maryport	2.25		
Gelligaer	2.58		
AVERAGE	2.63	1.11	1.75

Only two buildings in the Flavian fort at Strageath qualify as possible stables, namely Buildings II and V. Discounting the separate end-block and the projecting wings, Building II has a central chamber 35.2 m long by 4.1 m wide. This would suit a row of horses very well, but the total would amount to only 32, the mounts of a single *turma*. Moreover the accompanying veranda would have no clear function. Building V is internally 42.5 m long, with widths of 2.75 and 3.7 m on either side of a longitudinal partition for much of its length. The narrower chamber could indeed just take a row of horses, but would have no space left for service or manoeuvre, an impossible position. We are left with only the wider range as suitable, and it could accommodate only 38 horses at the most.

19. G. Müller, *Ausgrabungen in Dormagen 1963–77*, Rheinische Ausgrabungen Band 20 (Koln, 1979), 27 ff.
20. *Britannia* v (1974), 26–7 (Building vii).
21. I.A. Richmond, *Hod Hill* ii (London, 1968), 82–4.
22. For reference see note 20.
23. *Arch. Ael.*[4] xiv (1937), 164.

Since these buildings together can hold only about 70 horses, little over half those required for the four *turmae* of a single *cohors equitata* (whereas we have argued for the presence of six *turmae* in the fort), and since at the same time the buildings contain a great deal of space which is unaccounted for on this identification, we may conclude that neither is a stable.

Building II (FIG. 33) has some resemblance in plan to one of the types of military *fabrica* (p. 59); Building V can be suggested as a store for weapons and other materials. It contained a deep shaft which might have been intended for a well, and also a small pit containing stiff pink clay suitable for walling or for the manufacture of such objects as crucibles.

A demolition context in Trench 80 E I yielded four iron ingots (p. 176), a discovery which confirms that the manufacture and repair of weapons and equipment was carried out locally. A lead pig was found with them. This together with the frequent small pieces of melted lead found elsewhere in the fort show that this metal also was supplied in bulk and was presumably used mainly in construction, in pipes and roofs. Not much has survived; the greater part was no doubt removed at demolition, and the discarding of the ingot, virtually unused, should be taken to be unintended by the authorities.

Water supply to the Flavian fort

If the shaft in Building V was a well (p. 71), it was the only such feature found in any of the forts. The soft sand and the depth of the water-table made difficult the digging of wells. Instead a pipe-line was laid from a spring lying west of the fort (p. 12); the pipe ran along the road leading to the *porta praetoria* and then along the *via praetoria* to a T-junction in front of the *principia*. It can be assumed to have fed a number of subterranean water-tanks. Two were found, one in the courtyard of the *principia* (p. 35) and one near the southern end of the central range (p. 53). The estimated capacity of the former was 8,400 gallons (38,200 litres) and of the latter 11,093 gallons (50,428 litres). Although no iron junction-collars were found, so long a pipe-line is assumed to have been of wood. The presence of the pipe-line presupposes a drain to lead off surplus water; but this may have been quite a short length leading out of the South Gate, which was not excavated.

Drains in the Flavian fort.

See p. 131.

The Buildings of the Central Range in the Flavian fort

The Flavian *principia*, like its successors, was a parallelogram in plan rather than a rectangle, because of the shape of the fort itself. It measured 22.9 by 21.3 m, covering an area of 487.8 m^2 and consisted of the usual range of five offices behind the cross-hall (FIG. 17, p. 34); in front of this lay a courtyard surrounded on three sides by colonnades; but the NW corner was occupied by a room which had perhaps been provided to house the extra administrative staff necessitated by the presence of part of a second unit. The building itself is notably smaller than the *principia* at Fendoch (743 m^2), a fort of comparable size, and is only slightly larger than the Flavian-Trajanic *principia* at Bainbridge, a fort of only 1.06 ha, where the headquarters building measures 17.07 by 21.03 m (359 m^2).[24] These facts might imply that the size of the *principia* was calculated on the basis of its principal garrisoning unit only. However that may be, it is not surprising that the building was found to be too small. This must be the implication of the wall which was later inserted to block off the *via quintana* by joining the *principia* to Building XII behind it. The corresponding wall or walls further north were not located, but the purpose of the addition was evidently to supply extra administrative space at the back of the rear range of the *principia*. If Building B, north of the *principia*, also had an administrative function (pp. 47, 122), we can begin to glimpse the importance of one of the less obvious roles played by a forward fort on the main supply-route to the North under Agricola.

North of the *principia* along the *via principalis* lay the *praetorium*; but little of its plan is known.

24. *JRS* lix (1969), 206–7, fig. 29.

Part of a courtyard with surrounding timber colonnade was found (p. 48). The building is thought to have measured *c.* 33.2 by 17.1 m, giving an area of 567 m^2. This is smaller than the Fendoch *praetorium* by 62.9 m^2.

East of the *praetorium*, along the *via decumana* lay a second building (B), barrack-like in form but lacking a centurion's quarters (FIG. 24, p. 46); instead the end of the building was occupied by a room rather larger than the rest, suitable perhaps for an *optio*. The remainder consisted of nine *contubernia*. Similar buildings in the Central Range are known at Corbridge and elsewhere and have been thought to house administrative staff; the problems of this conclusion have been discussed on pp. 47 and 122–3.

South of the *principia* the Central Range was occupied by two buildings and a large cistern. Building C (p. 52) is taken to be the hospital. It seems to contain 12 equal-sized wards leading off a central corridor, in number corresponding with the 12 barracks in the fort, together with a reception-room and operating-room or clinic. The other building also possesses a central corridor, but the rooms on either side are not of equal width; it is probably a workshop, but little of its plan is known.

B. THE ANTONINE I FORT

The Antonine I fort (FIG. 67) was given new turf fronts to its ramparts which increased the overall dimensions to 480 by 424 ft. (146.3 by 129.2 m) and gave an area over the ramparts of 4.67 acres (1.89 ha). The area within the *via sagularis*, however, measures 375 by 321 ft. (114.3 by 97.84 m) and with the addition of a space of 1812 sq. ft. (168 m^2) in the right *retentura*, where the street is offset, gives a usable area of only 2.8 acres (1.13 ha) – slightly smaller than that of the Flavian fort (p. 117).

Unlike the buildings in the Flavian fort those of Antonine I were normally constructed with posts set in individual post-pits,[25] and they were secured in position by means of large packing stones. Though often coarse river-boulders, slabs of red sandstone were used much more frequently than in the Flavian period, a phenomenon suggesting the opening of a quarry somewhere for this material, no doubt with a view to erecting the bath-building. In a few places shallow and rather irregular post-trenches were dug instead of individual post-pits; but they were unusual.

The south *retentura* and the north and south *praetentura* all contain normal barracks – a total of eight; the north *retentura* has a series of buildings which are either too narrow or otherwise unsuitable to barracks; in this fort all the workshops and store-buildings (except the granaries) are concentrated in this section of the fort in a very unusual way.

The total number of barracks (FIG. 67) at first sight suggests provision for a *cohors quingenaria equitata*, but the total of *contubernia* is not quite typical. Five barracks – Buildings V, VII, X, XI and XII – have ten *contubernia* each, although two of them (X and XII) have unusually large blocks for centurions (TABLE IV, p. 137). Of the three remaining, one should be for infantry and two for horsemen, but selection is difficult. Building XVI, having both a large block for officers (114.40 m^2) and large *contubernia* of 35.14 m^2, should be one of the two for *turmae*. But choice between VIII and XVII for the other is not possible on the facts as known. Building VIII has *contubernia* with an average area of 26.21 m^2, but its officer's block at 100.01 m^2 is the smallest in the fort. Building XVII is similar, with *contubernia* at 26.00 m^2 and an officer's block of only 100.40 m^2. The fact that probably all these barracks contained only seven *contubernia* each need not be thought unduly disturbing, for similar anomalies are very common both in Britain and in the continent, however they are to be explained (p. 118).

Finds of cavalry equipment are not helpful. There were three pieces in Building X and two in

25. This is a technique not often previously used in military buildings in Britain, but was now being extensively used on the Antonine Wall.

XI (with a third from Street XI/XII): but all the pieces are typologically Flavian and are therefore probably residual in the Antonine I fort.

If the type of garrison has been correctly identified as a *cohors equitata*, it is worth seeing whether stabling can be found for 120–30 horses. Building III (43.58 m long) is divided (FIG. 34, p. 61) into two ranges respectively 2.74 m and 2.13 m wide. If we use the 'average' figure shown in TABLE II (p. 124) for the length allowed for a horse, 2.63 m, the wider of the two ranges in Building III could house about 39 horses (but with absolutely no room for manoeuvre or service); the other range is too narrow for the purpose, nor can it be interpreted as the service gangway, for a dividing wall would be unnecessary. Building II is even less possible as a stable, for both its ranges lack the necessary width (being only 1.83 m and 1.52 m wide at their southern ends). Building IV with its three ranges would have been plausible as a double stable had the widths been right; but the eastern range has a width of only 1.83 m and the western one is no wider at its northern end. Building VI, with internal dimensions of 41.1 by 4.8 m, and Building IX (41.76 m by 4.34 m) are thus left as the only suitable candidates for stables), for Building XV, companion to VI, has been shown to be an arms-store by the large number of baked clay sling-bullets which it yielded (p. 111). But VI has a capacity for only 37 animals, and Building IX for an equal number, in total only just over half of the presumed establishment. It must be concluded that the Antonine I fort, like its Flavian predecessor, lacked stables within the perimeter.

Building I, measuring 45.1 by 10.67 m, is rather wide for a barrack and its internal arrangements as far as they are known are dissimilar (FIG. 34). The only clue to its purpose is provided by the large water-tank in the centre of the building, which may have been as much as 4.88 m square and was over 2.2 m deep; its probable capacity is therefore *c.* 11,170 gallons (50,780 litres). Such a large tank suggests a workshop. Buildings II–IV may be taken as further workshops and store-buildings.

The Antonine I fort had no such ample provision of granaries as its Flavian predecessor. In the southern *praetentura*, in an unusual position beside the *via principalis* (p. 110), lay one granary (Building XIII) which was 7.6 m wide and perhaps 16.4 m long. If another similar granary exists somewhere in the central range the fort would possess the normal provision: a likely position for it is indicated by remains along the *via principalis* to north of the *principia* (p. 49). This might represent a *horreum* measuring 14 by 6.40 m with a central loading area 2.44 m wide.

Adjacent to Granary XIII along the *via principalis* lies a small barrack-like building. Its purpose is not known, but proximity to the granary and to the *fabrica* (XV) suggests that it may have accommodated specialist staff.

The Buildings of the Central Range in the Antonine I fort

The *principia* like its Flavian predecessor was a parallelogram in plan, measuring 22.86 by 23.47 m; it was thus (at 536.5 m^2) marginally larger than the latter and was rather more fully provided with rooms round the courtyard. Unlike the barracks, many of the walls of the *principia* were set in shallow wall-trenches with the posts themselves set in deeper holes along them.

Because of the layout of the fort the *via quintana* is offset in the northern half of the fort from its line in the southern portion, leaving a space 16 ft. (4.88 m) wide between the north-east corner of the *principia* and Building IV. It is possible that part of this space was occupied by an extension to the *principia*, for in Trench 76 K a line of three stone-packed post-holes (FIGS. 34, 67) was found running parallel with and 12 ft. (3.66 m) east of the rear wall of the building, leaving a space of 4 ft. (1.22 m) on the west side of the street-gutter. Unfortunately no more of this structure was located, but it may have extended as far as the *via decumana*. Additional accommodation for administration would appear to have been provided in the Antonine I period as it had been in the Flavian (p. 125); but here without the necessity of blocking the *via quintana*.

In this period the *praetorium* was built south of the *principia*. Little of the plan is known in detail but its size appears to be *c.* 22.5 by 31.7 m, giving an area of 713 m^2; this is over 145 m^2 larger than the Flavian *praetorium*.

North of the *principia* the area in the Central Range adjacent to the *via principalis* was occupied by a building running parallel with the street which, as already suggested, is best understood as a granary (p. 49). Behind it lay one or possibly two large buildings on a N–S axis; in the area explored most fully there was a somewhat irregular arrangement of rooms each side of a longitudinal wall, some at least of which had been used as an arms-store. Fired-clay sling, bullets, a spear and (?) part of a horse's bit were recorded from them.

The discovery of sling bullets in quantity, both here and in Building XV (and a single example each from a demolition layer in the *principia* and from Building XVII), attests the presence of *funditores* in the garrison; but no units solely specialising in this form of warfare are known in the Roman Army after Caesar's time, while Hadrian, in the section of his speech to the army at Lambaesis which was addressed to the *equites* of *cohors vi Commagenorum*[26] implies that the use of slings was part of general training. At Strageath there would seem to have been a group of specialist slingers within the cohort, or else the Commanding Officer was a particular believer in the value of general training in this weapon.[27]

The garrison of the Antonine I fort also included some archers armed with the composite bow, for an iron arrowhead of the triple-barbed type was found in a demolition-deposit in Building XI (p. 142, No. 18) and a second in Building VIII; a third arrowhead was recovered from the upper filling off a trench of Flavian granary XVI and is probably intrusive from the overlying Antonine I Building XVII. Although originally introduced in the West by specialist units from the eastern and North African provinces, this type of arrowhead is too frequent a find in auxiliary forts of the principate to justify the assumption that they always imply the presence of a cohort (or *ala*) of *sagittarii*, a conclusion confirmed by the similar wide distribution of the 'laths' or 'bow-stiffeners' from the bows themselves; most units will have contained at least some archers.[28] At Strageath the arrowheads and the sling-bullets merely emphasise the aggressive versatility of the force in garrison.

The Bath-Building in the Antonine I fort

A bath-house was constructed in the southern *intervallum* space of the south *retentura* (p. 98). Its attribution to the Antonine I rather than the Antonine II fort is not perfectly secure, but this seems to be the conclusion which best fits the known facts. The discovery came as a surprise, for the building is not really visible on the aerial photographs (PLS. IV, VIA). It was a long narrow structure measuring 24.31 by 6.48 m with solid stone foundations although the upper parts of the walls appeared to have been made of clay. The hot rooms lay at the east end. It is noteworthy that no fired-clay tiles were available to the builders, for no scrap of tile was found; the flues were formed of stone, at least in the bottom courses; above they were presumably hollowed in the clay superstructure.

The building had remained in use throughout the Antonine II period (p. 99) and had been very thoroughly demolished at the end of that occupation. Its construction appeared to be a secondary feature of the Antonine I fort, for the building did not lie parallel with the *via sagularis* but at the western end encroached upon it to such an extent that the street was reduced to a width of only 1.48 m.

Water supply to the Antonine I fort

The tank in Building I may have been filled with rainwater somehow collected on the western *intervallum* (south-westerly rainstorms would have beaten heavily against the rear of the rampart here), or else it was kept supplied from barrels brought up from the river. But the main water-supply was once again by pipe-line. The Flavian pipe-line trench (p. 125) was dug out and replaced; the new pipe-line has been traced along the *via praetoria* as far as the front of the

26. *CIL* viii, 18042 = *ILS* 2487.
27. On slingers in the Roman army see M. Mackensen, *Frükaiserzeitlichen Kleinkastelle bei Nersingen und Burlafingen an der oberen Donau* (Münchener Beiträge zur Vor- und Frügeschichte, Band 41, Munich, 1987) and the literature there cited. For British finds see S.J. Greep, *Britannia* xviii (1987), 183–200.
28. See E. Erdmann, *Saalburg Jahrbuch* xxxiii (1976), 5–10; J.L. Davies, *Britannia* viii (1977), 257–70; J.C. Coulston, 'Roman Archery Equipment' in M.C. Bishop (ed.), *The Production and Distribution of Roman Military Equipment* (B.A.R. International Series No. 275 (Oxford, 1985), 220–366, esp. pp. 224–34, 282–6; M. Mackensen (op. cit., note 27), 105, 113–15.

principia, where it turned south along the edge of the *via principalis*. The tank which must have been its destination has not been located: the aerial photographs (PLS. IV, VI A) show a large rectangular pit in the angle of the *viae principalis* and *sagularis* in the *intervallum* area south of the central range. This might be the tank, and if so it may have some association with the Bath-house.

Drains in the Antonine I fort

See p. 131.

C. THE ANTONINE II FORT

In the Antonine II period new fronts were once again added to the ramparts, so that the overall dimensions of the fort (FIG. 68) were increased to 508 by 450 ft. (154.8 by 137.1 m), giving an area of 5.26 arcres (2.12 ha). Within the *via sagularis*, on the other hand, the dimensions were now 368 by 326 ft. (112.2 by 99.3 m), which gives a usable area of 2.75 acres (1.11 ha), a little smaller than that of the Flavian fort (1.18 ha) and very slightly smaller than that of the Antonine I fort (1.13 ha).

The buildings in the Antonine II fort, like those of Antonine I, were built with posts individually aligned and not set in post-trenches. But although some could be seen to be set in post-pits, the great majority of wall-posts seem to have been hammered into position from above: they lacked packing stones as well as post-pits, and were correspondingly difficult to identify. Since almost everywhere the Antonine II demolition-levels, and the occupation- and floor-levels below them, have been destroyed by the plough, the possibility exists that shallow post-pits had existed at a higher level; but as the post-sockets were normally at least 15–20 cm deep this would still imply the use of some form of pile-driving equipment.

The layout of the Antonine II buildings was both different from and rather more regular than that of the previous period. The fort contained 12 barracks, of which at least one (No. 1) is thought to be for horsemen (although possessing only 6 rather than 8 *contubernia*). Of the remainder, six (Buildings II, IV, VII, VIII, IX and X) possess ten *contubernia*, the norm for infantry centuries; Building V has nine *contubernia* and the remaining four (VI, XI, XII and XIII) have eight.

This general pattern suggests that the garrison resembled that of the Flavian fort in being composite once more. If we attempt to discover the number of horsemen present, there are four barracks with eight *contubernia* thus satisfying one criterion for *turmae* barracks but not necessarily the decisive one. Reference to TABLE V (p. 138) shows that five barracks, I, V, VII, XI and XII, satisfy another criterion by having large quarters for officers at over 150 square metres;[29] but when the living-space of the constituent *contubernia* is examined, Barrack VII shows considerably less area than the rest; its *contubernia* each enclose only 21.32 m^2, whereas the *contubernia* of the others range between 35 and 28.80 m^2. Moreover Building VII is the only one of these five to have ten *contubernia*; it must accordingly be assigned to infantry. Building VI on the other hand, though having *contubernia* of 31.29 m^2, has an officers' block of only 131.30 m^2. Thus Buildings I, V, XI and XII are the most suitable for horsemen, and the garrison may be calculated to consist of one *cohors equitata* at almost full strength in Barracks I, II, IV and V–IX (two *contubernia* being missing from the *turmae* in Barrack I and two from the century in Barrack VI), together with part of a second *cohors equitata* consisting of four *turmae* in Barracks XI and XII and two infantry centuries in Barracks X and XIII, the century in XIII being under strength by two *contubernia*.

Outside the Central Range there were far fewer ancilliary buildings in the Antonine II fort than in its predecessor, and one less than the two provided in the Flavian fort. Building III is the sole store or workshop in either the *praetentura* or *retentura*. The deficiency was presumably made

29. In this period the percentage of the barrack acres occupied by officers' quarters is exceptionally large when compared with those of other forts.

good by Buildings C, D, E and F in the southern part of the Central Range, about which there is little information.

The Buildings in the Central Range in the Antonine II fort

The *principia* of the Antonine II fort was larger than its predecessors, measuring 25.91 by 26.82 m, giving an area of 694.9 m^2. This is still 48 m^2 smaller than the *principia* at Fendoch; nevertheless the building was provided with more ample administrative accommodation than in the earlier *principia* here. The rear range of the building was deeper and four additional rooms were also provided in the front part.

There was a large *praetorium* lying north of the *principia*; although not fully explored, it is thought to have had an area of 778.5 m^2, almost 81 m^2 larger than the *praetorium* of the Antonine I fort, which had lain on the other side of the *principia*.

At present no certain traces of *horrea* have been found in the Antonine II fort, but our knowledge of the area of the Central Range lying south of the *principia* is too slight to preclude the possibility that they lay there. The rear side of this part of the Range contained four buildings (C–F) which were perhaps workshops and stores. However, the fact that they are aligned east-west does suggest that they ran through to the *via principalis* and left no space for granaries.

The Bath-Building in the Antonine II fort

The bath-house, which had almost certainly been erected during the Antonine I occupation, was retained in use (p. 99). A large new cover-building for the stoke-hole was constructed in timber at the east end (p. 102) and a clay-filled trench was dug through the Antonine II *via sagularis* along the north side of the hot rooms, presumably to counter seepage of rainwater into the hypocaust basement. Even now the building continued to encroach upon the new *via sagularis*; the fact that this street was not laid out on a line to avoid it suggests that this part of the *via sagularis* was not expected to cater for vehicles. At the end of the occupation the Bath-house was thoroughly demolished, much of its stonework being removed down to the cobble-and-clay foundations and the site blanketed in a deep bed of heavy clay, which presumably derived from the upper portions of the walls.

Water Supply to the Antonine II fort

There was no sign of a piped supply to the Antonine II fort. A single water-tank was found; it lay in the *intervallum* space, east of the eastern *via sangularis* in the northern *retentura*, a location which suggests that it was supplied by barrels brought up from the Earn. The river would also seem to have been the only source of water for the Bath-house in this period unless the Antonine I pipe-line continued in use without having been replaced.

Intervallum Buildings

Apart from the stone-packed post-holes in the Flavian *intervallum* in the northern *praetentura* (FIG. 40, Trench A II) and the Antonine Bath-building (pp. 69, 98) the only indication of buildings in the *intervallum* occurred in the Antonine II fort; but others may have existed, for the area between the *via sagularis* and the rampart in the successive forts was little explored.

A substantial building, to judge by the size of its post-holes (5–8 in. (0.13–0.20 m) in diameter and 11 in. (0.28 m) deep) existed in the east *intervallum* of the south *retentura* (p. 95). Here a width of *c.* 22 ft. (6.7 m) was available for a building – more if the rampart had been cut back: but since only two post-holes, 6 ft. (1.8 m) apart were recovered, the nature of the structure is unknown.

In the north *intervallum* of the northern *retentura* rather more was uncovered of a second building (p. 63), but still insufficient for identification. Along the north edge of the *via sagularis* (FIG. 35) ran a shallow rounded gully 8 in. (0.20 m) deep and *c.* 21 in. (0.53 m) wide, filled with topsoil. Along this gully at intervals of 8 ft. (2.44 m) ran a series of substantial post-holes 8–14 in. (0.20–0.35 m) in diameter set in stone-packed pits. One of these, cut into the Flavian latrine-pit beneath, had a diameter of 3 ft. (0.91 m) and a depth of 4 ft. (1.22 m) and was packed with re-used oven-clay. A parallel row of posts had been set 4 ft. further south down the centre of the *via sagularis*; they were *c.* 12 in. (0.30 m) in diameter and up to 20 in. (0.51 m) deep.

The back of the Flavian rampart lay *c.* 31 ft. (9.45 m) north of the latter row of post-holes, but the building might have been wider if the rampart had been cut back.

Traces of a third building, lacking the southern row of post-holes, was seen further west in Trench 1982 H I (FIG. 35).

Little is known of the intervallum buildings in auxiliary forts. Possible uses include the latrines or cook-houses, but at Strageath the possibility that they were stables should be borne in mind.

Drains in the successive forts

Strageath today is subject to heavy storms of rain which normally beat down from the south-west, carried by the strong prevailing wind. It was not unusual, during excavations, for the site to become waterlogged or even partially flooded for 24 hours or more: the water ran back from the ramparts even in their present denuded condition, and it flooded into the interior. A much greater volume of water would have been caught by the ramparts standing to their original height of *c.* 3 m. Provision of drains to cope with these conditions would certainly be expected, even if in Roman times the climate had been less adverse. Of course, the modern surface is more impervious to water than it once was, because of the build-up of occupation-layers and of demolition deposits containing clay from half-timbered walls. Natural drainage through the sandy subsoil would certainly have been more effective in the Flavian fort than in those of the Antonine period. This may be the explanation for the very curious absence of a coherent system of drains in the Flavian fort. Nevertheless, the presence of an aqueduct would have necessitated some arrangement to cope with surplus water at its destination (p. 125).

Flavian

Except for one on the west side of the fort in Trench A II in the northern *praetentura*, no perimeter drains were located in the Flavian fort. The example in Trench A II (FIG. 40, FIG. 45 (p. 000), Section H–I, 33A) lay on the outer side of the *via sagularis* and was 18 in. (0.46 m) wide by 6 in. (0.15 m) deep, slight by comparison with later examples. It may have connected with a length of drain south of Granary VIII on the other side of the *via sagularis*, and the exceptional provision of such a drain may be a precaution taken to protect this granary from damp. Excavation in the southern *praetentura* was not sufficient to preclude the possibility of a similar drain beside Granary XVI there.

Apart from this drain and one in front of the *principia* (p. 34), the only attempt to deal with surplus water which was discovered was a group of two short drains leading into a soakaway pit (p. 88) in the NE corner of the southern *retentura* (FIG. 51). One led from the corner of the nearest building (IX). The other crossed the *via decumana*, but the source on the north side of this was not discovered; its purpose had probably been to prevent any water which accumulated in the space between the rampart and the *via sagularis* in the SE corner of the northern *retentura* from pouring out through the nearby gate, and to direct it instead into the soakaway.

Antonine I

In addition to whatever arrangements were made for the bath-house and for the tank at the end of the aqueduct, perimeter drains were now provided, except along parts of the north and south sides of the fort, so as to trap water pouring from the back of the rampart towards the interior. Substantial trenches up to 1 m wide and 0.6 m deep were dug and then normally were lined with planks held in position by pegs (PL. XXI A).

(a) In the northern *praetentura* (p. 77), on both the west and north sides, such a drain was traced along the inner edge of the *via sagularis* (FIG. 41). From the vicinity of the *porta praetoria* to that of the NW angle the fall was towards the north, and then eastwards along the north side. The levels at the base of the drain were 121.00 ft. O.D. (36.88 m) in Trench B I, 120.80 ft. (36.82 m) in Trench A II, and 119.62 ft. (36.46 m) in Trench N III. No doubt this drain continued to an outfall below the *porta principalis dextra*.

(b) In the southern *praetentura* (p. 109) a similar drain on the same alignment accompanied the inner edge of the western *via sagularis* (FIG. 60). In Trench S III the level of its floor (at 119.68 ft. = 36.48 m) was 1.55 ft. (0.47 m) below the drain in the northern *pratentura* and the fall was to the south;[30] however, in this quarter of the fort the drain did not turn eastwards along the south side and must have continued straight out below the rampart near the SW angle. No drain appears to have been provided in this period along the stretch between the SW angle and the *porta principalis sinistra* unless for part of this length a shallow gully led westwards into the drain just mentioned (see pp. 109–10).

(c) In the southern *retentura* (FIG. 52) on the east side of the fort a drain ran along the outer edge of the *via sagularis*, and at least in the area of Trench E I was stone-lined where it passed through metalling (p. 92). Indeed, the length beneath the *via decumana* had been abandoned and filled in during the life-time of the Antonine I fort. This stretch of drain was in alignment with the contemporary drain in the northern *retentura* (see below) but had its fall in the opposite direction, towards the south, from 121.25 ft. O.D. (36.96 m) at the north face of Trench E I to 121.00 ft. (36.88 m) at the south face. Unfortunately in Trench F I the drain had been destroyed by later post-holes and no level could be established.

Along the south side of the Central Range (p. 55) and of this side of the *retentura* a large plank-lined drain accompanied the inner edge of the southern *via sagularis* and had a fall towards the east, from 117.99 ft. O.D. (35.96 m) in Trench V II to 117.52 ft. (35.85 m) in T I. Thus both the eastern and southern drains converged on the SE angle of the fort where there must have been an outfall beneath the rampart.

Two gutters were found in this quarter of the fort, one running down the centre of a street separating Buildings X and XI, and one in the *via quintana*. A large U-shaped gutter accompanied the south wall of the Bath-building (p. 99), and a stone-lined drain was found near the corner of the Central Range; it ran obliquely out towards the rampart (p. 55).

(d) In the northern *retentura* a plank-lined drain accompanied the inner edge of the eastern *via sagularis* (FIG. 34; PL. XXII B). In Trench 1973 I the level of its base was 119.30 ft. O.D. (36.36 m). As mentioned above, this drain, although on the opposite side of the *via sagularis*, was in alignment with the drain in the southern *retentura*, the street itself having been laid on a different line. But the fact that the connection below the *via decumana* between the two parts of the drain had later been blocked, and knowledge that the level in Trench 1973 I was 1.95 ft. (0.59 m) lower than the drain in E I, suggest that there was a watershed at the *via decumana* (just as at the *via praetoria*) and that in the northern *retentura* the fall was to the north. This conclusion is confirmed by observation that along the northern side of the *retentura* (FIG. 34) the drain did not continue round to an outfall at the *porta principalis dextra*: instead a drain began outside the north end of Building III and fell eastwards, from 118.72 ft. O.D. (36.18 m) at its terminus to 117.77 ft. (35.90 m) at the east end of the length excavated. This is 1.53 ft. (0.47 m) lower than the drain in Trench 1973 I and we must conclude that both drains converged to an outfall through the NE angle of the fort as indicated on FIG. 34.

Somewhere outside the north end of Building IV a new drain began, for in Trench 1982 H I (FIG. 34) a narrow U-shaped gully, here only 10 in. (0.25 m) deep was seen at the inner edge of the *via sagularis* (p. 61). The base lay at *c*. 122.40 ft. O.D. (37.31 m) and the gully no doubt connected with the standard plank-lined drain which, further to the west, bordered the Central Range (FIG. 25) in Trench 1986 V I. The floor of this lay at 120.89 ft. (36.58 m) and it doubtless continued westwards to share an outfall beneath the *porta principalis dextra* with the corresponding drain in the *praetentura* (see above).

A gutter was found accompanying the west edge of the *via quintana* (FIG. 34).

Antonine II

A new set of perimeter drains was installed. (a) In the south *praetentura* (FIG. 62) near the *porta praetoria* a drain was found on the outer side of the *via sagularis* in Trench S III (p. 113). It

30. The drain continued through Trench L III, but here it had been recut in the Antonine II period, so that the level of its floor (119.47 ft. = 36.41 m) here is strictly relevant only to the Antonine II drain.

evidently began just north of this trench, for its depth on entering the trench was only 2 in. (0.05 m). The fall was to the south; the floor of the drain at the south edge of the Trench lay at 122.00 ft. O.D. (37.18 m). Further south, in Trench L III, there was no sign of a drain on the outer side of the street: unless the two are distinct – a possibility discussed on p. 113 – the drain must have passed under the *via sagularis* between the two Trenches, to reappear in L III on the street's inner edge, here in a re-cutting of its Antonine I predecessor (p. 113). In Trench L III the floor of the drain lay at 119.47 ft. O.D. (36.41 m). At the corner of the street the drain evidently turned east and reappeared along the inner edge of the southern *via sagularis*. In Trench R II the floor lay at 118.45 ft. (36.10 m) and in M I it had sunk to 118.27 ft. (36.05 m). Near the east side of the latter Trench the course of the drain appeared to be curving south to pass under the street, no doubt heading for an outfall at the *porta principalis sinistra*.

(b) In the northern *praetentura* a corresponding drain ran along the inner edge of the western *via sagularis* (FIG. 42). It began within Trench B I at a point *c.* 18 ft. 6 in. (5.64 m) north of the junction with the *via praetoria*; here it was only 2 in. (0.05 m) deep, but sank to 6 in. (0.15 m) at the north edge of the Trench. The level of the base here was 122.70 ft. O.D. (37.40 m), and in Trench A II the level was the same; but clearly the fall must have been to the north. The drain did not turn to run along the inner side of the northern *via sagularis*, but either accompanied the outer side to an exit at the *porta principalis dextra* or else outflowed beneath the rampart near the angle. The former alternative is the more likely, for otherwise the water would have accumulated in the fort's inner ditch.

In the area of Trench A II the drain had been supplemented at some stage by a ditch 1.2 m wide and 0.6 m deep (p. 79), which had been dug along the outer edge of the street; it was not traced elsewhere.

(c) Along the south side of the Central Range and of the south *retentura* no perimeter drain was provided. The only drains found were (i) a large stone-lined drain running obliquely towards the rampart in Trench 1986 V II (FIG. 30); this was a reconstruction of a drain already built in the previous period (p. 55). From soil signs it appeared to have crossed the *via sagularis* just west of the Trench (p. 56). (ii) a U-shaped gutter along the outer side of the Bath-building (p. 99). Along the east side of the south *retentura*, however, a large plank-lined drain was present (p. 95), accompanying the inner side of the *via sagularis* (FIG. 53; PL. XXXI A). A gutter led into it from the corner of Building VIII. This drain continued under the *via decumana* to connect with the similar large drain in the northern *retentura*, and in both areas there was evidence for careful levelling of the base of the original trench with a layer of make-up to create a steady fall. But, as in the previous period, there was a watershed at the *via decumana*: the southern drain had a fall to the south as the figures on pp. 95–6 show, and it must have run to an outlet through the rampart near the SE angle.

(d) In the northern *retentura* the eastern perimeter drain (FIG. 35) continued on the same alignment as in the southern *retentura*. In Trench 1973 II the surface of its layer of make-up lay at 118.30 ft. O.D. (36.06 m), and in Trench 1985 N II the base of the drain was at 117.70 ft. (35.87 m). The fall was therefore to the north, and in the absence of any drain connecting with it along the north side of the fort it must have made an outfall below the rampart near the NE angle (FIG. 35). A new drain, however, began on the north side of Building IV, presumably with a fall to the west. Its remains in Trench 1982 H I had been badly damaged by a demolition-pit, but a very large capping-stone lay in the remains of the Trench. No level could be taken but the bottom was thought to lie at about 121.50 ft. O.D. (37.03 m). From here the drain continued along the north side of the Central Range (FIG. 27), where a plank-lined drain with stone kerbs (p. 51) was found outside Building A in Trench V I (PL. XXI A). Its base lay at 120.33 ft. O.D. (36.68 m). No doubt it reached an outfall at the *porta principalis dextra*.

Barrack Floors

The nature of the floors within the barracks was often elusive; they seem often to have been the plain earth surface, perhaps once covered with rushes or hay. In the Flavian fort an earth floor is noted on p. 60. In the Antonine forts floors composed of thin spreads of gravel, sometimes

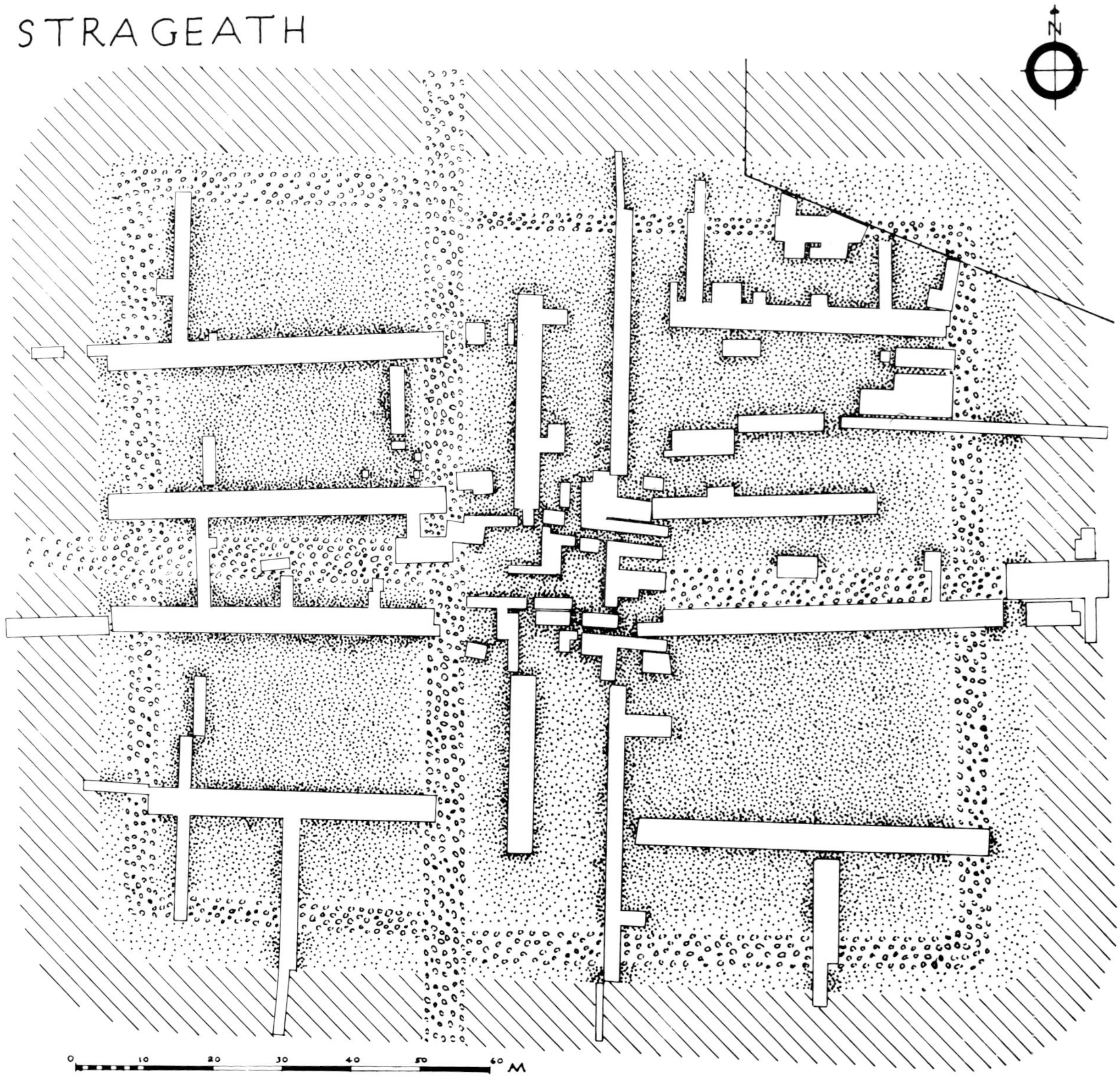

FIG. 65. Strageath: the areas excavated.

combined with scatters of flat stones and amphora sherds, were noted in several buildings (see Index, s. v. 'floors'), and were best seen where they had sunk into underlying pits. A floor of fine sandy loam was recognised in Building XII of the Antonine I fort, and this fort also yielded a unique floor of pebbles set in hard pink clay in one of the officer's rooms in Building VIII (p. 76).

The Street-systems in the forts

The main streets of the Flavian fort (*viae principalis*, *praetoria* and *decumana*) were well metalled with gravel over a foundation of river boulders. The suggestion has been made (p. 117) that these streets may have been laid down by legionaries who were brought to construct the ramparts. But of the minor streets between buildings only that dividing Buildings III and IV showed any trace of metalling (p. 60). This absence of metalling on minor streets, and the notable failure to provide street-drains, are curious features of the Flavian fort.

Both defects were rectified in the two second-century forts. In the Antonine I fort only the street between Buildings V and VI was unmetalled – a fact which, if not due to later disturbance, may suggest that Building V in reality faced on to the *via principalis*, despite the dimensions of the *contubernia* which suggest the opposite (p. 74). Otherwise, only the alleys separating the backs of buildings remained unmetalled, even when as wide as 2.75 m (as with the space between Buildings X and XI (FIGS. 52, 67).)

The *via sagularis* in each of the Antonine forts varied considerably in width around the circuit. In the Antonine I fort a width of 4.27–4.6 m was maintained from the *porta praetoria* round to the *porta principalis dextra* on the north side; but beyond this the street widened to 7.62 m along the north side of the *retentura*, as if allowing for increased traffic towards the workshops in this area. From the *porta praetoria* southwards the street was also 4.27 m wide; but along the south side of the *praetentura* it narrowed to 2.74 m, and at the north-west corner of the Bath-building the width was reduced to only 1.48 m. It seems clear that neither much wheeled traffic nor movement of men in large numbers were anticipated along the south side of the fort: the *porta principalis: sinistra* led only down into the boggy southern side-valley. The main thoroughfares for both traffic and marching men were the *porta praetoria* and the *porta principalis dextra*. The other two gates led nowhere in particular, and this implies that the purpose of the fort was not primarily an all-round local tactical command but a concern with the road and bridge and with the control of the regions to which these gave access.

In the Antonine II fort the *via sagularis* maintained a somewhat more even width, ranging between 3.66 m along the south side of the *praetentura*, 4.25–5.18 m on the east side of the *retentura* and 5.33 m along the west side of the south *praetentura*. Only on the north side of the *retentura* did it narrow to 2.13 m, and this may have been because of the encroachment of an *intervallum* building (p. 63). A bottleneck only 1.52 m wide remained at the north-west corner of the Bath-building.

GENERAL CONCLUSION

The successive forts at Strageath throw interesting light on the problems of frontier garrisons. Only in the Antonine I period does Strageath appear to have held a 'normal' garrison consisting of a single unit, apparently a *cohors quingenaria equitata*. In both the Flavian and Antonine II periods the garrison consisted of all or most of one unit and a vexillation of another. In both these periods the position evidently called for a more powerful force than a single quingenary unit; but probably because the available milliary units – few in number – were already engaged elsewhere, a composite force consisting of elements of two *cohortes equitatae* was installed. It is interesting to note that, despite this, only one *praetorium* was provided; there was to be but a single military commander even if for some administrative purposes the men of the fragmented unit were still regarded as attached to their original headquarters. It is also interesting to note that in all periods there was a need for cavalry as well as a strong force of infantry.

Now that the chronological gap between the Antonine I and II occupations of Scotland has been shown to be very brief, some modern writers have tended to regard the two periods as little more than a single episode in the history of the North. The results at Strageath show that this is a false view. The fort, including its defences, was totally rebuilt and a completely different and more powerful garrison was installed. The Antonine II fort represents a new view of military requirements in Strathearn.

Finally, anomalies in the number of *contubernia* in barracks of all three periods suggest not only that the respective units were under strength when they built their accommodation, but also that restoration to full strength was not anticipated in the foreseeable future. The first conclusion is not surprising if we are correct in supposing that the forts were built in the autumn after a campaign; but the second has a wider bearing on Roman policy for recruitment and replenishment of garrisons, and on the efficiency of their military organisation. That the internal buildings were indeed the work of the auxiliary garrisons, even in the Flavian period, has been argued on p. 117.

TABLE III

STRAGEATH : FLAVIAN BARRACKS

Dimensions in metres as restored

Building	Length	Width: (including veranda where present)	Width: percentage of length	Officers' Block: length	Officers' Block: width	Officers' Block: percentage of length to length of complete barrack	Officers' Block: area (m²)	Officers' Block: area as percentage of barrack area (less veranda)	Contubernia: number of	Contubernia: overall length	Contubernia: width less veranda where present	Front Room (internal) Depth	Front Room (internal) Width	Front Room (internal) Area (m²)	Rear Room (internal) Depth	Rear Room (internal) Width	Rear Room (internal) Area (m²)
I	47.85	8.54	17.85	19.50	12.20	40.75	237.90	49.56	8	28.35	8.53	3.66	3.36	13.40	3.80	3.36	12.77
III	47.40	8.69	18.33	10.70	8.54	22.57	91.38	22.62	10	35.97	8.69	3.80	3.36	12.77	3.80	3.36	12.77
IV	47.54	8.54	17.96	11.28	8.54	23.73	96.33	23.87	10	35.97	8.54	3.51	3.36	11.79	3.96	3.36	13.31
VI	43.43	8.23	18.95	12.20	8.23	28.09	100.40	33.16	6 (+1)	30.20	6.70	1.52	3.66	5.56	4.27	3.66	15.63
VII	42.67	9.46 –	22.17 –	12.20	10.67	28.59	130.20	33.84	7	29.56	8.08 –	2.75	3.66	10.06	5.18 –	3.66	18.96 –
		10.68	25.03								9.14				4.27		15.63
IX	45.87	9.14	19.92	18.29	8.84	39.87	161.68	45.54	8 (+ 1)	27.58	7.01	2.89	2.74	7.92	2.89	2.74	7.92
X	46.79	9.60	20.52	12.80	7.32	27.36	93.70	26.57	10 (+ 1)	33.98	7.62	3.01	2.74	8.25	3.01	2.74	8.25
XI	46.48	10.97	23.60	14.10	8.53	30.34	120.27	30.38	10	32.31	8.53	3.81 –	2.74	10.44 –	3.66 –	2.74	10.03 –
												2.74		7.51	4.11		11.26
XII	46.18	9.37	20.29	12.19	9.37	26.40	114.22	33.22	10	33.83	9.45 +	2.74 –	3.01	8.25 –	(a) 4.27	3.01	12.85
											7.77	3.66		11.02	(b) 3.35		10.08
XIII	47.55	8.23	17.30	12.20	8.23	25.66	100.40	26.16	9	34.44	8.23	one 2.44	4.27	10.42	4.27	4.27	18.23
												six 2.44	3.35	8.17	4.27	3.35	14.30
												two 3.96	3.35	13.27	3.05	3.35	10.22
XIV	47.55	6.93	14.57	12.20	6.86	25.66	83.70	25.87	9	34.60	6.93	eight 1.68	3.35	5.63	3.96	3.35	13.27
												one 1.68	4.27	7.17	3.96	4.27	16.91
XV	46.33	10.97	23.68	12.34	10.06	26.63	124.10	31.32	8	33.07	8.23	1.52	2.74	4.16	5.48	2.74	15.02

TABLE IV

STRAGEATH : ANTONINE I BARRACKS

Dimensions in metres as restored

Building	Length	Width	Width: percentage of length	Officers' Block: length	Officers' Block: percentage of length to length of complete barrack	Officers' Block: area (m^2)	Officers' Block: area as percentage of whole barrack	Contubernia: number of	Contubernia: overall length	Front Room: internal Depth	Front Room: internal Width	Front Room: internal Area (m^2)	Rear Room Depth	Rear Room Width	Rear Room Area (m^2)
V	41.75	7.3	17.48	12.80	30.66	93.44	30.66	10	28.95	3.05	2.44	7.44	3.35	2.44	8.17
VII	42.67	7.9	18.51	12.80	29.99	101.10	29.99	10	29.56	3.97	2.44	9.69	3.05	2.44	7.44
VIII	42.98	7.0 –	16.29	13.70	31.87	100.01	31.83	7	29.26	2.44 –	4.27	10.42 –	2.14 –	4.27	9.14 –
		7.62	17.73							3.66		15.63	4.27		18.23
X	44.20	9.75	22.06	13.12	29.68	127.92	29.68	10	31.09	3.43	2.74	9.40	5.18	2.74	14.19
XI	43.59	9.91	22.73	11.27	25.85	110.30	25.53	10	32.31	3.05	2.90	8.84	5.56	2.90	16.12
XII	42.52	9.60	22.58	11.89	27.96	114.14	27.96	10	30.63	3.96 –	2.74	10.85 –	4.27	2.74	11.70
										4.42		12.11			
XVI	42.67	8.53 –	19.99	13.41	31.43	114.40	30.36	7	29.26	3.66	4.27	15.63	4.57	4.27	19.51
		9.14	21.42												
XVII	42.67	7.32	17.15	13.72	32.15	100.40	32.14	7 or 8	29.26	4.57	4.27	19.51	1.52	4.27	6.49

TABLE V

STRAGEATH : ANTONINE II BARRACKS

Dimensions in metres as restored

Building	Length	Width	Width: percentage of length	Officers' Block: length	Officers' Block: percentage of length to length of complete barrack	Officers' Block: area (m²)	Officers' Block: area as percentage of whole barrack	Contubernia: number of	Contubernia: overall length	Front Room: internal			Rear Room		
										Depth	Width	Area (m²)	Depth	Width	Area (m²)
I	44.20	10.37	23.46	18.90	42.76	195.99	42.76	6	24.99	3.96	3.96	15.68	4.88	3.96	19.32
II	45.72	7.02	15.35	13.70	29.96	96.17	29.96	10	31.70	3.05	2.74	8.36	3.05	2.74	8.36
IV	44.50	7.30	16.40	13.41	30.13	105.94	32.61	10	30.99	3.05	2.50	7.62	3.05	2.05	7.62
V	46.00	10.80	23.48	14.60	31.74	157.70	31.74	9	31.09	3.66	2.75 –	10.06 –	5.80	2.75 –	15.95 –
											3.66	13.39		3.66	21.23
VI	46.30	9.80	21.17	13.40	28.94	131.30	28.94	8	32.90	seven 3.05	3.66	11.16	seven 5.50	3.66	20.13
										one 3.05	4.88	14.88	one 5.50	4.88	26.84
VII	47.24	9.15	19.37	18.59	39.35	189.60	43.86	10	28.65	3.66	2.44 –	8.93	4.57	2.44 –	11.15 –
											2.75	10.06		2.75	12.57
VIII	46.18	7.92 –	17.15 –	15.24 or	33.00	121.91 or	32.72 or	10 or	30.48 or	2.44	2.74	6.69	4.57	2.74	12.52
		8.23	17.82	12.50	27.06	100.00	26.83	11	33.83						
IX	46.18	7.92 –	17.15 –	13.41	29.04	120.55	30.89	10	32.61	Contubernium length			Contubernium width		
		8.99	19.46							7.01 to 7.92				2.74	
X	46.02	9.75 –	21.19	15.54 or	33.76	142.04 or	32.70 or	10	30.48	3.50 –	2.74	9.59 –	3.96 –	2.74	10.85 –
		9.14	19.86	12.34	26.81	112.79	25.96			3.81		10.44	4.72		12.93
XI	42.37	10.06	23.74	15.85	37.41	159.40	37.41	8	26.52	5.49	3.00	16.47	4.11	3.00	12.33
XII	42.06	11.80 –	28.05	14.63	34.78	172.60	36.87	8	27.43	5.79	3.00	17.37	4.57	3.00	13.71
		10.47	24.89					8	26.82	3.66	3.00 –	10.98 –	4.27	3.00 –	12.81 –
XIII	41.00	9.14	22.29	14.02	34.19	128.10	34.18				3.35	12.26		3.35	14.30

PART II: THE FINDS

IX. THE COINS

(identified by Professor Anne Roberton, Dr Richard Reece and Andrew Burnett)

	EMPEROR	COIN	RIC. NO.	CONTEXT
1.	Republican?	Denarius	–	77 A I 8
2.	Mark Antony 32–1 BC	Denarius	Crawford 544/18	78 B III 4
3.	Mark Antony 32–1 BC	Denarius	Crawford 544	85 N III 16
4.	? Mark Antony 31 BC	Denarius	Crawford 544	82 G I 20
5.	? Mark Antony *c.* 31 BC	Denarius	legend illegible	83 L II 11
6.	Nero AD 66	As	I^2 312/13	82 G I 20
7.	Vitellius AD 69	Denarius	$I^2$62	75 P XLII 9
8.	Vespasian AD 70–2	Denarius	? as 39	81 F II 8
9.	Vespasian AD 71 or 72/3	As	497 or 747	73 II 2
10.	Vespasian AD 72 – early 73	Dupondius	739	76 K I 4
11.	Vespasian AD 72 – early 73	Dupondius	740	76 K I 23
12.	Vespasian AD 73	Denarius	as 43	81 F II 26
13.	Vespasian AD 74	Denarius	77	78 B V 3
14.	Vespasian AD 71	As	494	77 A I 64
15.	Vespasian AD 69–79	Denarius	as 5	80 E II Pit 1
16.	Vespasian	Denarius		77 A I 8
17.	Flavian (probably Vespasian)	As		77 A I 8
18.	Titus AD 73 (after July)	Dupondius	(Vesp.) 649	76 H I 12
19.	Titus AD 77–8	Dupondius	(Vesp.) 777 (b)	76 K I 13A
20.	? Titus AD 77–8	As	(Vesp.) 784	79 D VI 4
21.	Domitian AD 77–8	As	(Vesp.) 724	73 I 14
22.	Domitian AD 84	As	242 A	77 A I 64
23.	Domitian AD 85	Dupondius	293	77 A I 64
24.	Domitian AD 85	As	as 301 (b)	81 F I 14
25.	Domitian AD 85	As	301 (a)	79 D III 5
26.	Domitian AD 86	As	335	78 B V 4
27.	Domitian A.D. 81–96	As	highly corroded	79 DV–VI+
28.	Domitian ?	Denarius		73 II 33A
29.	1st century	As	highly corroded	80 E II 14
30.	Trajan AD 103–11	Sestertius	492	77 A II 31
31.	Trajan	Sestertius	illegible	81 F II 21
32.	Hadrian AD 119–28	Denarius	127a	76 H II 3
33.	Hadrian AD 117–28	As		78 B I 5
34.	Hadrian AD 117–38	Sestertius	Reverse uncertain	82 G I 15
35.	Hadrian AD 134–8	Denarius	Reverse uncertain	81 F I 18
36.	Hadrian AD 134–8	Sestertius	970	82 G I 20
37.	? Hadrian	As		78 B III 3
38.	Late 1st century/early 2nd century (Hadrian ?)	As		77 A I 18
39.	Probably Trajanic or Hadrianic (from size)	Sestertius	illegible	84 S I 5
40.	Antoninus Pius AD 138–61	Denarius	Copper core of plated forgery, as BMC iii Pius No. 244	85 N III 4
41.	Illegible	As		84 S I 5
42.	Anonymous (prob. Domitian – since the context is a Flavian demolition-layer.	Quadrans	II, p. 216, No. 2	79 D I 18
43.	Non-Roman. Scots turner or bodle of Charles I or II			74 K I 2

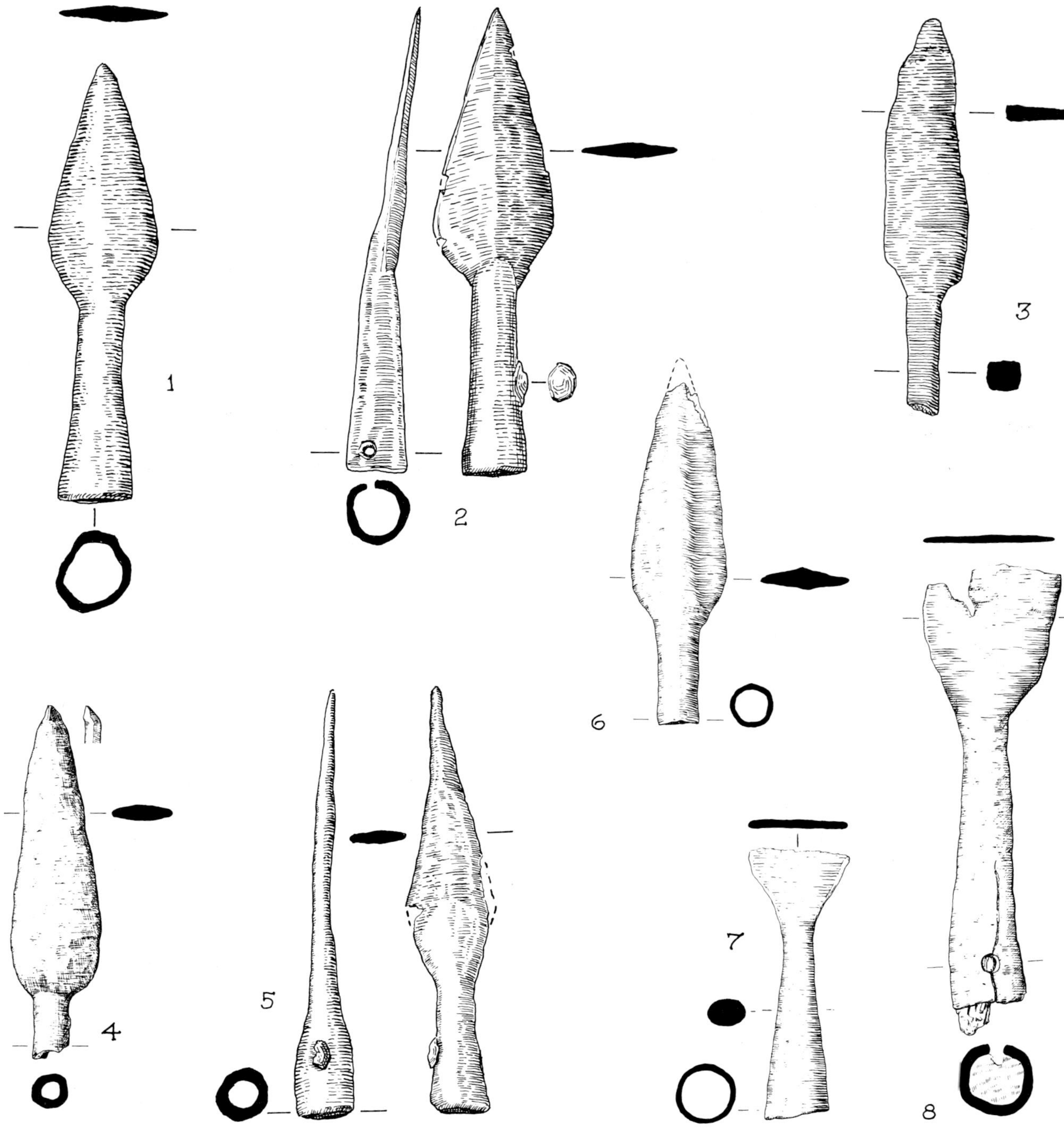

FIG. 69. Iron spears (½).

X. THE OBJECTS OF METAL AND JET[1]

By Francis Grew and S.S. Frere

Spearheads and ferrules (all iron)

The site yielded a total of 14 spearheads. At least 6 of these, and possibly as many as 9, have leaf-shaped blades of very similar dimensions: a length of *c.* 80–100 mm, and a width of *c.* 25–35 mm. These would be useful either for throwing or for impaling people on the ground – an action commonly depicted on first-century cavalry tombstones. Two of the remaining spear-heads have longer leaf-shaped blades but essentially are similar to the last group, while a third (No. 11) has an exceptionally broad blade. It is possible that a weapon such as this would be used principally by an infantryman in hand-to-hand combat. The final two blades are of unusual forms, and may in fact have been used as catapult bolts.

(a) *Small/medium leaf-shaped blades*
1. 1985 N I 11, demolition-layer, Flavian Building III.
2. 1979 D II 4, demolition-layer, Antonine I Central Range Building A.
3. 1983 L I 11, occupation-layer, Antonine I Building XVI.
4. 1978 B III 4, occupation-layer, Antonine I Building V.
5. 1979 D II 6, occupation-layer, Antonine I Central Range Building VI.

Not illustrated: heavily corroded complete spearhead, measuring *c.* 140 mm overall and probably very similar in proportions and form. 1981 F I 8, demolition-layer, Antonine I Building IX.

6. Median rib. 1977 A I 8, demolition-layer, Antonine I Building V or VI.
7. 1978 B I 20. Flavian demolition-layer south of Building VIII.
8. 1977 A I 8. Antonine I demolition-layer, Building V or VI. Traces of wood in the socket. The head is very corroded and it is not clear whether corrosion has given the blade its indented shape or whether this is the original form. If the latter is so the object would resemble a group from Vindolanda which, it has been suggested, may have been the tips of standards.

(b) *Large leaf-shaped blades*
9. 1977 A I 8, demolition-layer, Antonine I Building V or VI.
10. 1974 P XXX 10, demolition-layer, Antonine I Principia.
11. 1980 E I 18, demolition-layer, Flavian Building IX.

(c) *Other forms*
12. 1978 B I 5, occupation-layer, Antonine I Buildings VI, VII or VIII.
13. 1980 E II 14, demolition-layer, Flavian Building XII.

(d) *? Pila*
14. 1974 G I 21.
15. 1974 G I 8.

(e) *Ferrules/spear butts*
Few ferrules can definitely be attributed to spears, except perhaps those with a knob terminal (No. 16). These seem to have been found almost exclusively on military sites. No. 17 comes from a very thick shaft – possibly a lance of similar proportions or even larger than that to which spearhead No. 11 once belonged.

1. Francis Grew had written the text for Nos. 1–51 and notes on many other pieces before pressure of other duties forced him to leave the completion of the report to S.S.F.

16. 1976 H II 6, demolition-layer, Flavian Building III.

Not illustrated: a second example, very similar. 81 F II (20).

17. 1974 P VIII 2, courtyard gravel, Antonine Principia.

Arrowheads (iron) (FIG. 71)

Three examples of trefoil tanged arrowheads were found.

18. 1980 E II 15, demolition-layer, Flavian Building XI.
19. 1985 R I 9, granary-trench, Flavian Building XVI, but probably intrusive from Antonine I Building XVII above.

Not illustrated (tang and tip missing): 1985 N III 3, demolition-layer, Antonine I Building VIII.

Three examples of tanged arrowheads with square (Nos. 20, 21) or triangular (No. 22) cross-sections.

20. 1980 E II 11, occupation-layer, Antonine I Building XII. Possibly, however, this is an awl, see under No. 192.
21. 1980 E I 16, Antonine I occupation layer between Building IX and the *via sagularis*.
22. 1980 E II 15, demolition-layer, Flavian Building XI.

Catapult bolts (iron) (FIG. 71)

23. 1976 H I 7, demolition-layer, Antonine I Building III.
24. 1983 L I 11, occupation-layer, Antonine I Building XIV.

Sword scabbard fittings (Nos. 25, 27 copper alloy: No. 26 iron) (FIG. 71)

25. Scabbard chape, possibly for the cavalry *spatha*.
1978 B I 40, Flavian western *via sagularis*.
26. Scabbard chape from *spatha*, similar to No. 22,
but in iron. 1984 S II 2, demolition-layer, Antonine I Building XV.
27. Mount in dolphin form affixed to the scabbard back for attachment to the belt or baldric. Probably a 2nd-century type. 1982 G I 20, occupation-layer, Flavian Buildings I-II.

Body armour (copper alloy) (FIG. 72)

28. Buckle from the *lorica segmentata*. 1982 G I 28, demolition-pit in Antonine I Building I.

Not illustrated: two further examples:
1979 D V 15, Central Range south, wall-trench between Flavian Buildings C and D.
1980 E II 14, demolition-layer Flavian Building XIL.

Horse-harness (all copper alloy) (FIG. 72)

Fragments from sets of horse-harness of the type well-known from Xanten, Doorwerth, Fremington Hagg and other sites. All probably Flavian in date.

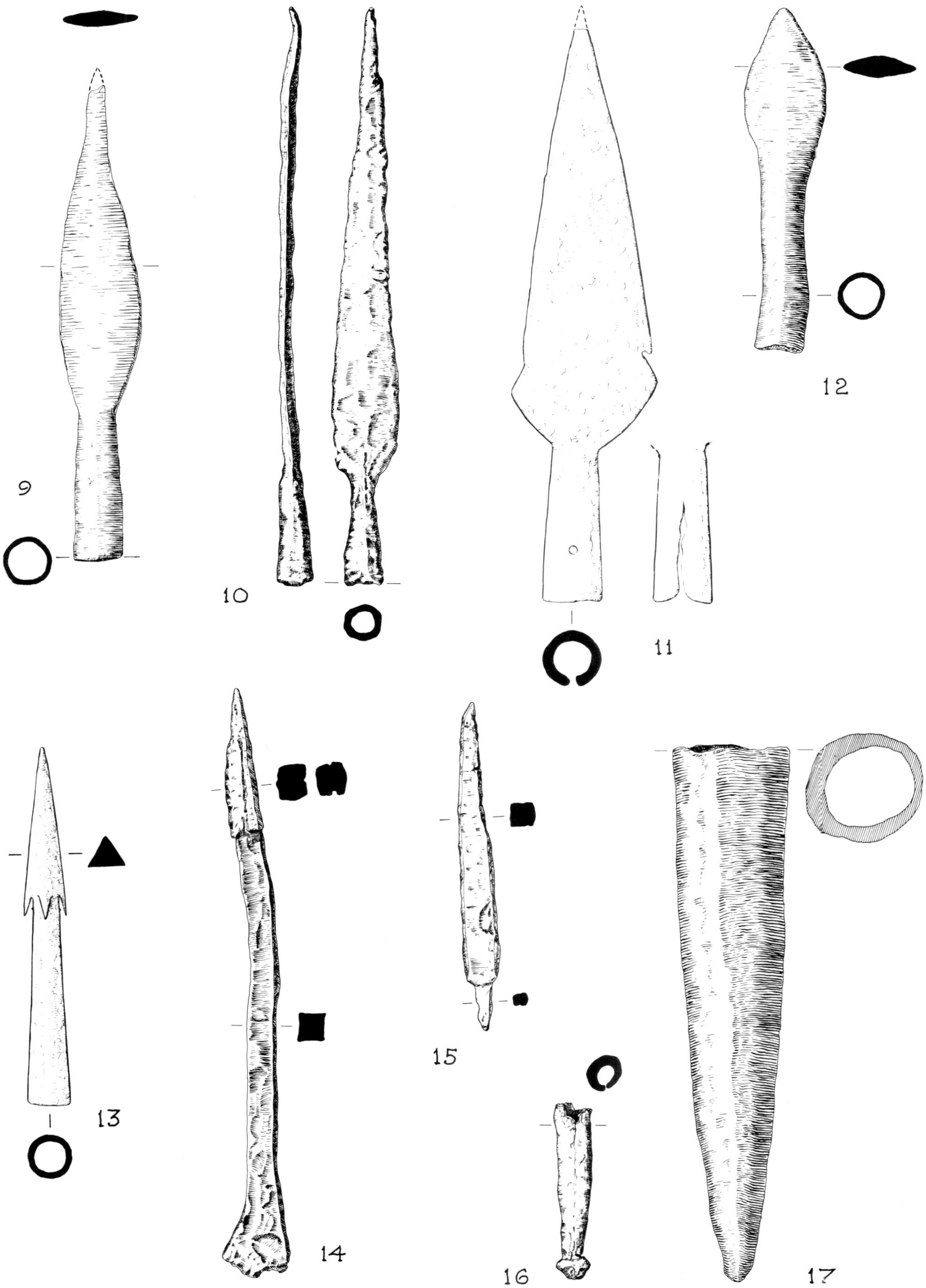

FIG. 70. Iron spears and ferrules (½).

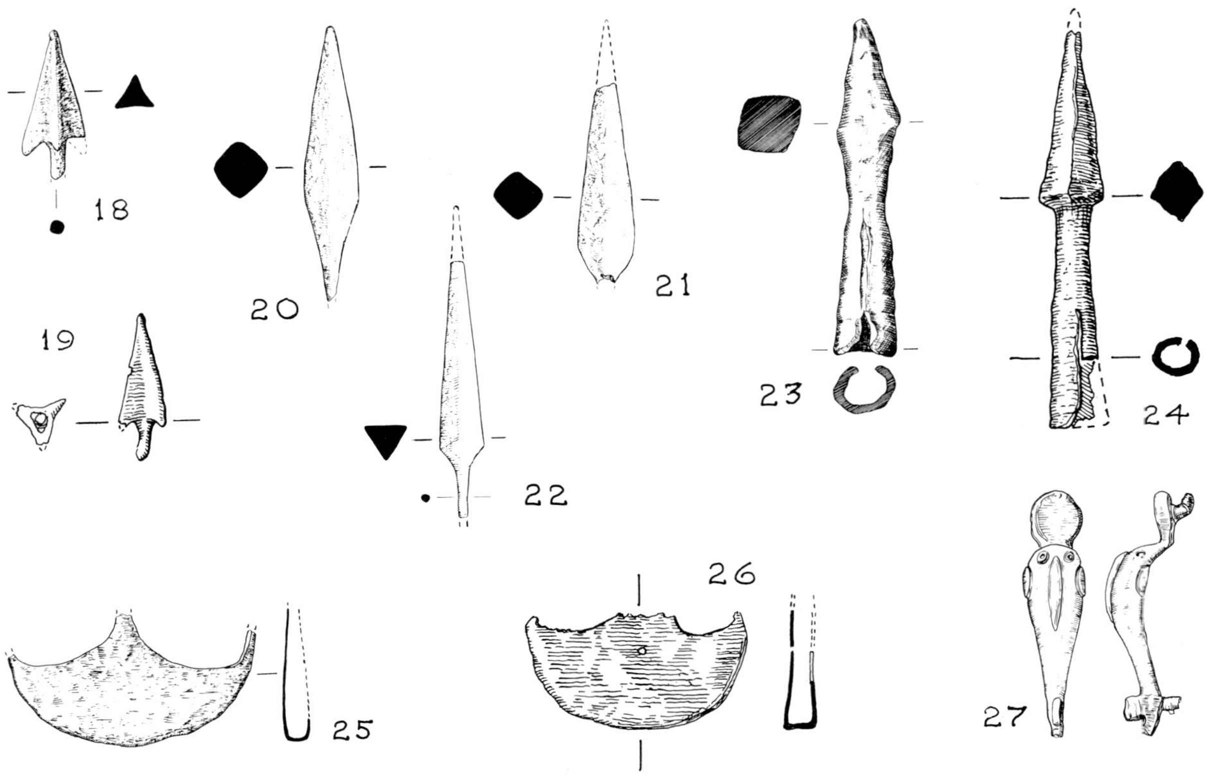

FIG. 71. Iron arrowheads (18–21), catapult-bolts (bronze) (23, 24), and scabbard-chapes (25, 26). Bronze scabbard-fitting (27) ($\frac{1}{2}$). In the captions, 'bronze' is used in the traditional, non-specific, sense.

(a) *Circular bosses*

Type 1: silvered with engraved and niello-inlaid decoration.

29. 1981 F II 11 occupation-layer, Antonine I Building XI. Analysis shows the metal to be brass.
30. 1982 G I 20, occupation-layer, Flavian Building III. Traces of notching around the circumference.
31. 1978 B III 4, occupation-layer, Antonine I Building V, with No. 32. A groove surrounds the central dome-headed pin.

Not illustrated: three further examples

1976 H II 8, demolition-pit in Flavian Building III. Apparently from the same mould as No. 29.
1982 G I 18, demolition-layer, Antonine I Building II.
1986 T I 3, demolition-layer, Antonine I Building X.

Type 2: plain silvered with bold concentric rib.

32. 1978 B III 4, occupation-layer, Antonine I Building V, with No. 31. At the back, two strap-holders: these were originally made as four prongs, to which flat strips were soldered.

(b) *Clips for attaching straps to bosses*

33. 1976 H I 12, occupation-layer, Antonine II Building I.

34. 1976 H II 12, demolition-layer, Flavian Building III. Two pairs of stud-holes, surrounded by grooves. The pairs are separated by a moulding of one broad and two narrow transverse ribs.
35. 1973 II 2, ploughsoil over Flavian Building I.
36. 1981 F I 24, wall-trench, Flavian Building IX or X. Above the knob are faintly-engraved lines, perhaps once inlaid.

Not illustrated: four further examples

1976 H I 15, Flavian occupation-layer, Building III. Similar to No. 34.
1977 A I, unstratified. Similar to No. 34.
1977 A I 8, demolition-layer, Antonine I Buildings V, VI, VII. Fragment.
1981 F I 17, occupation-layer, Antonine I Building X.

(c) *Strap-end, ball-ended* (and see Nos. 43–5)
37. 1981 F I 18, demolition-layer, Flavian Building IX. At the top, below the break, are two countersunk perforations.

(d) *Rectangular mounts*
Type 1: engraved and niello-inlaid
38. 1979 D VIII 4, Central Range north, occupation-layer, Antonine II *praetorium*. Broken, but perhaps once symmetrical. The centre has two pairs of mouldings joined by four engraved transverse lines, possibly once inlaid.

Type 2: plain, with prominent ribbed central moulding.
39. 1977 A 1 7, occupation-layer, Antonine II Buildings V and VI.

Not illustrated: six further fragments from clips or mounts

1973 II 29, Pit 2. Antonine I demolition-pit.
1977 A I 8, demolition-layer, Antonine I Buildings V, VI, VII.
1977 A I 12, Flavian wall-trench, Building VI.
1977 A I 38, Antonine I post-pit, Building VI.
1978 B I 19, occupation-layer, Flavian Building VII.
1981 F I 17, occupation-layer, Antonine I Building X.

(e) *Pendants* (FIG. 73)
Type 1: silvered with engraved and niello-inlaid decoration
40. 1982 J 5, occupation-layer, Flavian Building IV.

Not illustrated: Part of another similar to No. 40 but with prong on the back. 1986 V II 6, Flavian demolition-layer, Central Range Building D.

Type 2: lunate, with additional small pendant
41. 1982 G II 6, wall-trench, Flavian Building IV.

(f) *Strap-terminals and apron-mounts* (all copper alloy)
Type 1: keyhole-shaped terminal
42. 1980 E II 11, occupation-layer, Antonine I Building IX. The rectangular plate terminates at the bottom in one broad and two narrow transverse mouldings: beyond are the remains of a (?) keyhole-shaped aperture. The back is flat but recessed for a strap-end held by two prongs, apparently separately soldered, and burred over at the ends. The front is tinned and there are remains of niello-inlaid leaves at the square end.

Type 2: ball-ended (see also No. 37)

43. 1980 E II 8, Antonine I Street XI/XII. Face overlaid with silver sheet. The niello inlay is mainly missing from the incised decoration. At the back of the top are the traces of a single prong probably soldered on but now missing.

44. 1980 E I 13, north wall-trench, Antonine I Building X. Face tinned but otherwise undecorated. On the back a recessed ledge for the strap, part of which survives, and two prongs (broken).

45. Similar but not silvered. 1973 II 3, unstratified over Flavian Building I.

(g) *Miscellaneous belt- or strap-fittings* (all copper alloy)

46. 1981 F II 8, Antonine I demolition-layer, Building XI. Open-work belt-mount, probably second-century.

47. 1985 R I 5, demolition-layer, Antonine I Building XVII. Plain sub-rectangular belt-mount, probably second-century.

48. 1979 D III 5, wall-trench, Antonine I Building V. Enamelled belt-mount, probably second-century. Around the edge is a scored groove. The central panel is divided into three squares, each subdivided into four triangles and carrying a central 'flower'. The 'flowers' and the lines dividing the cells are reserved. The triangular cells are filled with opposing pairs of red (to the sides) and green (probably originally blue) enamel. Four prongs at the back (two broken): these have been filed to shape but are not clenched.

49. 1979 D V 5, Central Range south, wall-trench, Antonine I Building C. Plain silvered or tinned boss perhaps from horse-harness and probably Flavian. Perforations at centre and near one edge.

Other Bronze Objects

Vehicle Fittings (FIG. 74) (all copper alloy)

50. 1986 V I 1. Lower topsoil in Central Range over Antonine I Building B and Antonine II Building A (pp. 50, 51). Griffon mount with wings outstretched in flight. Slight corrosion has resulted in the loss of the edges of the wings, ears and crest. The underside of the wings carries stylized plumage although the tops are plain, suggesting that it was intended to be viewed from beneath. Similar grooving along the mane, on the ears and crest. The object has been repaired: a hole on the upper surface behind the mane contains the remains of a rivet, presumably to fix it to the end of a horizontal shaft, and traces of a second hole, never perforated, exist diametrically opposite on the underside. Later a thin bronze plate with two prongs has been soldered to the back, attached to which is a strip of iron curved to form a socket for a vertical staff. Such objects were used to decorate the shafts and other parts of vehicles: see J.M.C. Toynbee and A. Wilkins, *Britannia* xiii, 245–51. The Strageath griffon may be compared with that recently discovered at the fort of Trawscoed (J.L. Davies, *Britannia* xviii (1987), 277–8); but the Strageath griffon was later reused with its attachment in a different plane. The date is probably Antonine I (p. 51).

51. 1986 V I 5, Antonine I occupation in Central Range, Building B. Terret or harness-ring. A free-running trace was held in the upper ring, while the lower was held in place by straps. The lower ring is broken and heavily tainted with iron corrosion. The terret is of the type where the lower ring is in a plane at right-angles to that of the upper ring: cf. Webster *Arch. Journ.* cxv (1958) 88 No. 175 (Margidunum). Others have it in the same plane, cf. Webster *ibid.*, No. 252, and Curle, *Newstead*, pl. LXXV, 12.

52. Number not used.

53. 1979 D II 6. Antonine I occupation-layer, Central Range between Buildings A and B (p. 49). Drawn with the aid of X-ray photographs. Object of unidentified purpose, possibly part of a vehicle- or furniture-fitting, or conceivably part of a curved *cornu* or signal-horn. It is made of two tubes inserted into a junction-sleeve; one tube appears to

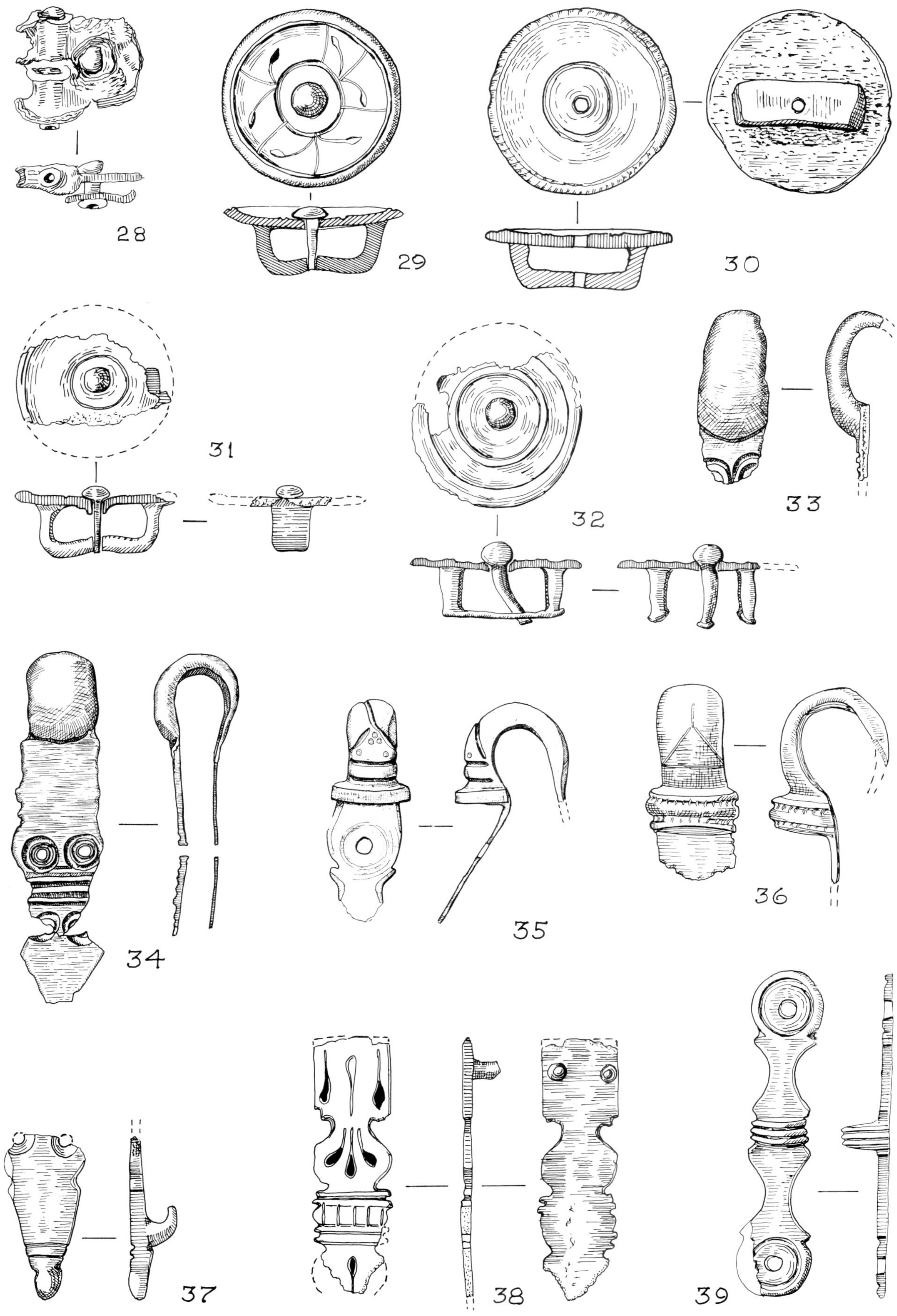

FIG. 72. Items of armour and horse-harness, all of bronze (1/1).

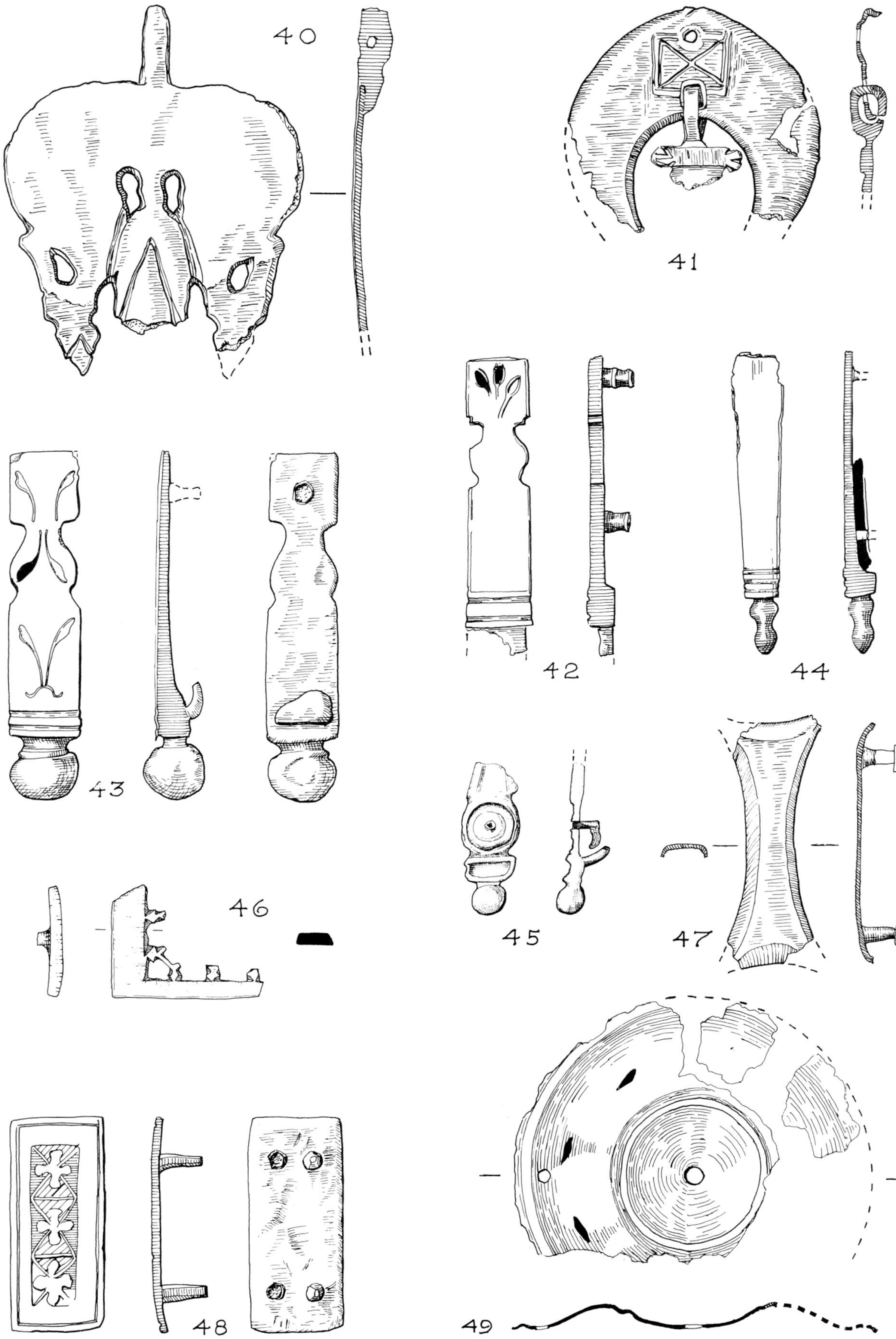

FIG. 73. Items of harness, all bronze (1/1).

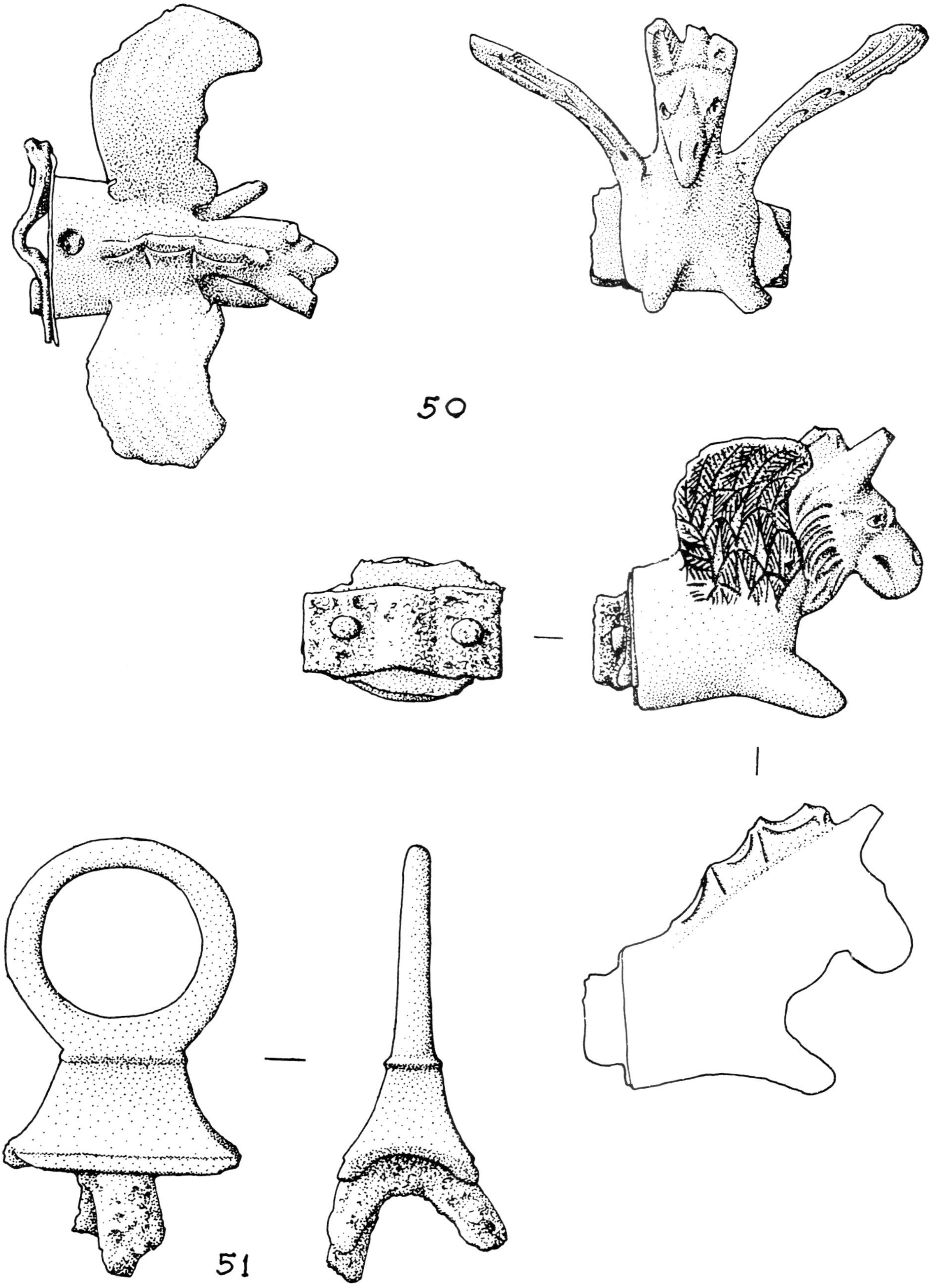

FIG. 74. Griffon-terminal and terret-ring, both bronze (1/1).

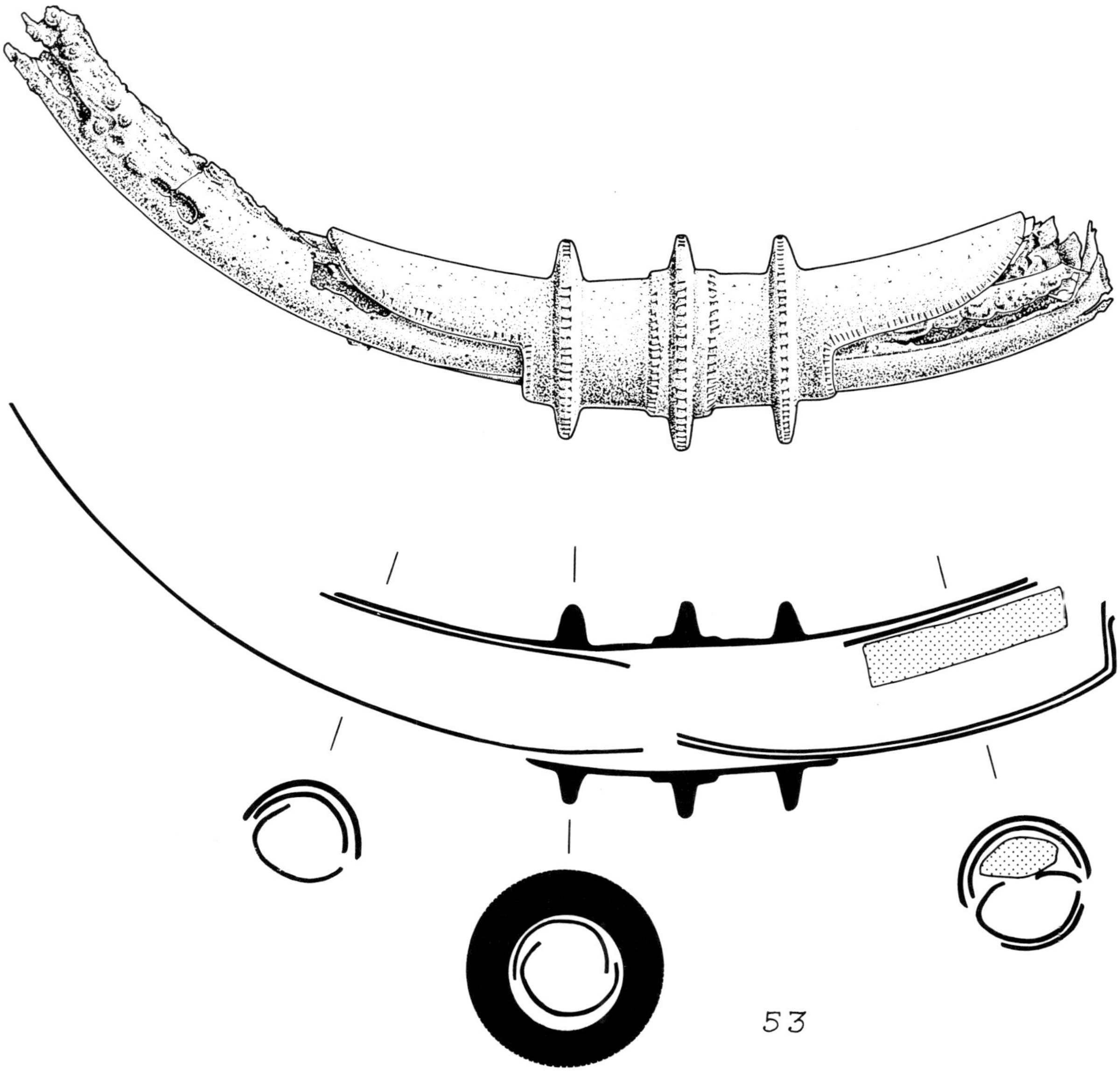

FIG. 75. Fragment of bronze tubing with junction-slieve (1/1).

have an additional cover along the top. The sleeve is decorated with three notched discoidal mouldings; similar incisions run along the edges of the sleeve. The form of construction suggests that the object was originally almost circular, for the gentler curve, e.g. of a chair leg, such as that illustrated by Espérandieu from Langres (*Recueil* iv No. 3361) could be made in one piece; moreover the legs of both chairs and folding stools normally have a rectangular cross-section (see for example the folding stool from Nijmegen, Liversidge, *Furniture in Roman Britain* (1955), pls. 40, 41).

Brooches (all copper alloy) (FIG. 76)

54. 1973 II 21, Antonine I occupation, Building I. Knee brooch.

55. 1981 F II 1, old ploughsoil over Antonine II Building XII. Part of a head-stud brooch: the stud has a ring of red enamel surrounding a centre of uncertain colour, possibly blue. Below is the beginning of a strip of inlay consisting of red triangles forming lozenges from which the colour is lost. The shoulders of the brooch are grooved and contain traces of red enamel. Six complete turns of the spring survive. The clasp retaining the spring is broken away.

56. 1985 N III 3. Antonine I demolition-layer, Building VIII. Trumpet brooch.

Not illustrated: fragments of another trumpet brooch from 1978 B V 3, Antonine II occupation-layer, Building V. The trumpet head and parts of a six-turn spring survive; it is broken just above the central moulding, but possible signs of an acanthus leaf can be seen.

57. 1986 V II 13, Antonine I occupation, Central Range south, Building C. Circular plate brooch, originally tinned or silvered around the rim and on the solid triangles dividing the enamelled cells. These are alternately a well-preserved brilliant royal blue (black on drawing) and a decayed greenish enamel, possibly once red.
58. 1979 D V 3, Antonine I occupation, Central Range south, Building C. Penannular brooch. The pin is circular in section but is hammered flat to make its loop.

Bosses and Studs (all copper alloy) (FIG. 76)
59. 1981 F II 33, Antonine I filling of water-tank in Building XII. Enamelled disc. Within a broad reserved ring is a circle of green (? originally blue) enamel around one of red enamel. Outside the ring is a seven-pointed star, each 'point' having curved edges: within one of these 'points' contain green (? blue) enamel around a dot of a different colour. The back is slightly concave and shows remains of a single, large prong (broken off); this is slightly off-centre and the object may be from a button-and-loop dress-fastener (cf. J. Oldenstein, *BRGK* lvii (1976), Taf.55 No. 675) rather than from a stud.
60. 1981 F II 8, Antonine I demolition-layer Building XI. Enamelled stud or dress-fastener head, as No. 59, with off-centre stub of prong at the back. The face shows an eagle. The eagle's body, wings, head, feet and crest are reserved against an enamelled background which is mainly decayed but may originally have been red (surviving areas shaded on drawing). The eye and various markings on the body are also enamelled. Below the body is a reserved double-curved feature of which the significance is obscure.
61. 1981 F I 22, Antonine I occupation, Building X. Lion-headed finial, much corroded. The mane is indicated by tooled grooves. A (?) peg of charcoal is retained in the filling at the back. The diameter at *c.* 30 mm is greater than those of the lion-headed studs from the casket-burials at Puckeridge (18–25 mm) (C. Partridge, *Skeleton Green*, 312, 314), which also had bronze spikes for attachment, as on Nos. 62–4 below. It seems possible, therefore, that No. 61 was not affixed to a casket but covered the end of, for example, the arm of a chair.
62. 1977 A I 11, Demolition-pit A, Flavian Building V. Stud in form of a Medusa's head. The eyes have hollow pupils, lids above and folds below. The sides are slightly turned over at the back where a round-sectioned rivet is soldered on; the end is hammered over a washer. Thickness of original wood *c.* 6 mm.
63. 1981 F I 16, Antonine I demolition-layer, Building X. Stud in the form of a lion's head. The mane is shown by shallow incisions, and the whiskers and curve of the nose by engraved lines. The eyes were deeply drilled, with an engraved line above and below. The back is quite clean with no indication of the means of attachment; but associated with No. 63 was a fragment from the rim of a stud with a prong at the back: possibly therefore No. 63 is not complete and was held by two rivets one on either side.
For lion-headed studs from caskets see Partridge, *Skeleton Green*, cited under No. 61.
64. 1984 S I 2, Antonine I demolition-layer, Building XIII. Fragment as No. 63 with iron pin. Thickness of original wood at least 7.5 mm, but the pin is probably broken.
65. 1984 S V 3, Antonine I demolition-pit, Building XVII. Part of lobate disc. Similar discs frequently decorate *loricae segmentatae*, but these always seem to have a plain rim around the lobes. No. 65 is therefore probably a decorative stud-head, cf. J. Oldenstein, *BRGK* lvii (1976), Taf. 57, Nos. 704–9.
66. 1980 E I 17, Flavian occupation-layer, Building X. Stud with notched rim. cf. No. 100.
67. 1983 L I 11, Antonine I Street XIV/XVI. Dome-headed stud, with circular-sectioned pin.
68. 1982 J 5, Flavian occupation, Building IV. Dome-headed stud with square-sectioned pin.
69. 1981 F II 18, silting above sunk filling of Antonine I Pit 2. Cast conical boss. There is no sign of a pin for attachment, the inside being filled with replaced wood. Such bosses are

found on cavalry helmets (Russell Robinson *Armour of Imperial Rome*, 94–5) but could have a variety of other decorative purposes, cf. the Richborough casket (J.P. Bushe-Fox, *Richborough* iv pl. XLVII), similarly lacking pins.

70. 1973 II 2, old ploughsoil over Flavian Building I. With No. 35 and so more probably associated with armour.

Parts of Vessels (all copper alloy) (FIG. 77)

71. 1986 N III 4, Antonine I demolition-layer, Building VIII. Handle of bronze jug. The angle of axis is uncertain.

72. 1980 E II, old ploughsoil. Handle and rim of bronze saucepan, somewhat bent. Unusual form. The end of the handle is missing; it joins the side of the vessel at a short rim *c.* 3 mm high with a quarter-round moulding below, and then a shelf, perhaps a lid-seating, before the side turns downwards towards the base.

73. 1980 E II 7, Antonine I demolition-layer, Buildings XI, XII. Fragment of the base of a saucepan, probably No. 72 near which it was found. Inside the footstand are three concentric mouldings.

74. 1986 V II 14, Flavian occupation-layer, Central Range, Building D. Openwork handle, perhaps of a key.

75. 1981 F II 8, Antonine I demolition-layer, Building XI. Saucepan handle, traces of a tinned surface remain. Raised ribs surround the suspension-hole and circular head, and other ribs, notched and bordered by grooves, run the length of the handle. For the type of vessel see M.H.P. den Boesterd, *The Bronze Vessels in the Rijksmuseum G.M. Kam* pls. I, II.

76. 1981 F I 30, Antonine I post-pit, Building X. Part of similar tinned saucepan-handle. Some notches inside part of the circumference rib.

Miscellaneous objects (all copper alloy)

77. 1978 B I 20. Flavian demolition-layer in front of Building VIII. Heavy cast collar with a raised rim around the central hole. The back is flat with no evident means of attachment. Overall diameter 42 mm, diameter of hole 22 mm.

78. 1984 S III 10, Flavian demolition-layer, Building XVI. Bronze drop-handle (attachments missing). Possibly a helmet-handle: although often much more elaborately made, simple versions such as No. 78 are known, cf. L. Allason-Jones and R. Miket, *Cat. of Small Finds from S. Shields Roman Fort*, 164–167. However, use on a casket cannot be ruled out.

79. 1986 T I 12, Flavian wall-trench, Building X. Heavy bronze casting. Height 6.5 mm, diameter 21.5 mm, diameter of aperture 4.5 mm. Possibly part of a crest-attachment from a helmet.

80. 1980 F I 18, Flavian demolition-layer, Building IX. Crushed bell with remains of iron clapper.

Not illustrated: another from 1980 E II 14, Flavian demolition-layer, Building XII. Trapezoidal handle, with round aperture, soldered on. Iron attachment for missing clapper.

81. 1978 B I 5, Antonine I occupation-layer, Building VII. Scalpel handle with stub of iron blade. cf. Wheeler, *London in Roman Times* pl. XXXVIII, 1; Künzl, *BJ* 182 (1982), 1–131 *passim.*

82. 1980 E II 11, Antonine I occupation-layer, Buildings XI, XII. Slide-bolt of tumbler-lock. For suitable keys see Nos. 134, 135.

Not illustrated: another, similarly with six perforations; 1976 H I 17, Flavian wall-trench, Building II.

83. 1973 II 7, Flavian wall-trench, Building I. Slide-bolt of tumbler-lock with perforations differently arranged.

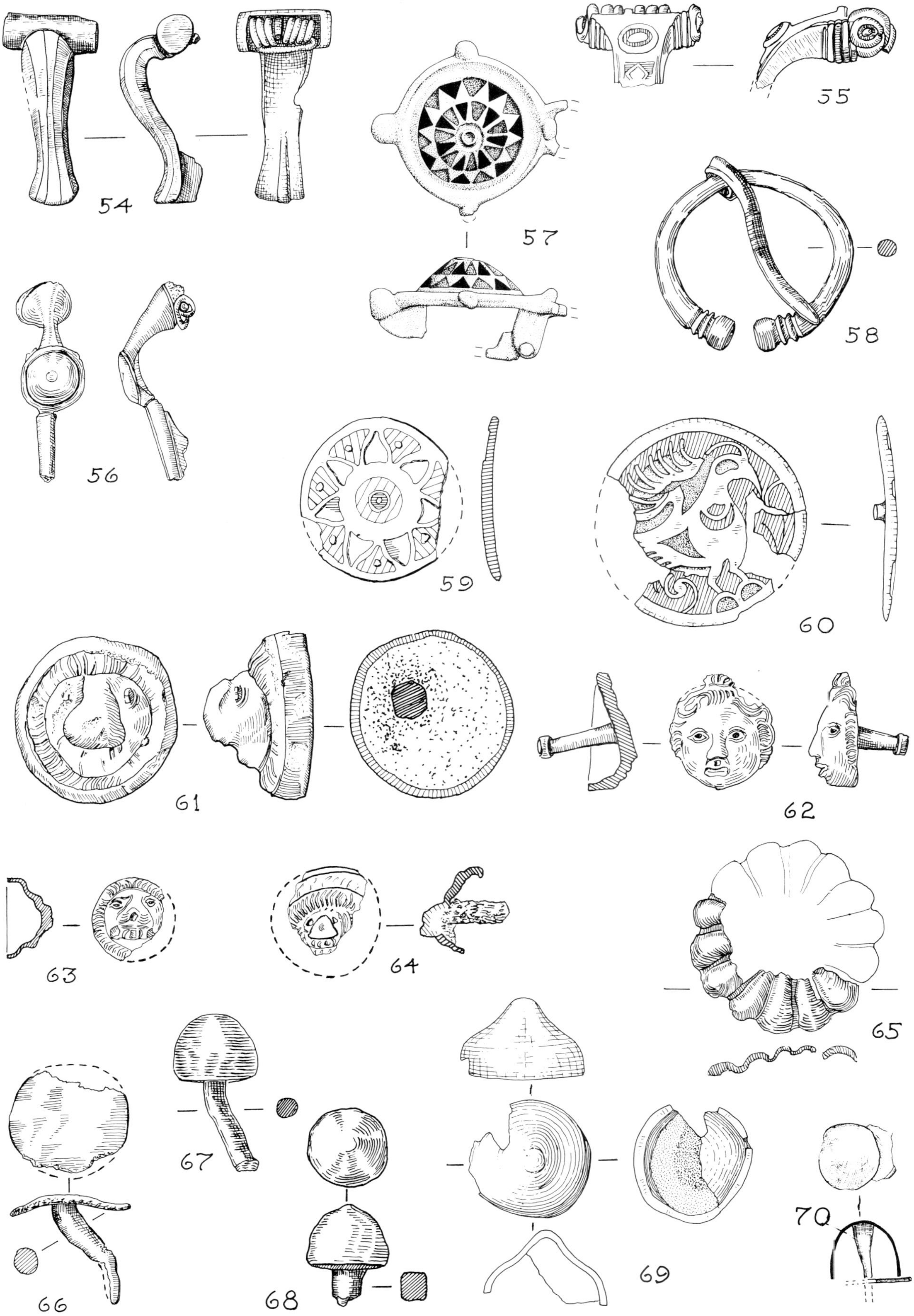

FIG. 76. Bronze brooches and studs (1/1).

84. 1982 G I 15, Antonine I occupation-layer, Building I. Damaged casting, rather heavy for a harness pendant. Perhaps part of a dress-fastener, or perhaps part of the handle-attachment of a bucket.

85. 1978 B I 5, Antonine I occupation-layer, Building VII. Button-and-loop dress-fastener approximating to Wild's class Va (*Britannia* i (1970), 139–40).

86. 1978 B V 4, Antonine I occupation-layer, Building V. Bronze strip, expanded in the middle for a rivet-hole 6 mm in diameter, and bent through a right-angle at (?) both ends, where the one surviving arm has a second rivet-hole. The object resembles the support for a modern scales pan.

87. 1984 S I 17, from Flavian metal-working hearth in Building XIII. Part of steelyard beam with grooves for the weight at 4.5–5.5 mm intervals and a number of irregular incisions in the lower side. On the side is engraved the figure IV.

88. 1985 N II 2, unstratified over Antonine II *via sagularis*. Part of unidentified object.

89. 1986 V I 5, Antonine I demolition-layer, Central Range Building B. Bronze hinge-socket.

90. 1982 G I 6, Antonine II occupation-layer, Building I. Probably part of a belt-buckle.

91. 1977 A I 3, Antonine II demolition layer, Buildings V , VI. Perhaps a strap-end. Heavily leaded cast bronze, surface possibly tinned. The edges are corroded. The back is flat, but the front is slightly recessed below a groove, and has a rivet-hole at the bottom. Inside are traces of (?) decayed leather. At the top a rectangular loop.

92. 1979 D III 2, Antonine II occupation-layer, Building V. Bronze washer.

93. 1977 A II 12, Antonine I demolition-layer, Building VIII. Plain rectangular mount, *c.* 48 by 22 mm, now bent but probably flat originally. It is pierced by two flat-headed rivets the ends of which are hammered flat over two very crude washers and give a thickness of 3.5 mm for the vanished supporting material. The thickness, for instance, of the Doncaster shield (*Britannia* ix (1978), 249) was *c.* 10 mm, so that No. 93 is more likely to have been fixed to leather.

94. 1973 III 22, *via decumana* metalling. Part of a heavy curving rod, thicker at one end than at the other. Possibly from a drop-handle.

95. 1984 S V 2, Antonine I demolition, Building XVII. Heavy bronze hinge-pin.

96. 1982 G II 2, Antonine II occupation, Buildings III, IV. Harness-ring with scalloped edge.

97. 1978 B I 5, Antonine I Street VI/VII. Thick cast bronze collar, diameter 17 mm, width 13 mm, thickness 2 mm. A pair of grooves borders each edge. For a somewhat similar collar from Baginton see *T. Birmingham and Warwicks. A.S.* lxxxv (1972), 76 fig. 24, No. 43.

98. 1981 F II 20, Flavian occupation, Building XI. Bronze finger ring. The circular bezel is decorated with a four-lobed 'flower' in yellow enamel within areas of red enamel.

99. 1981 F I 4A, Antonine II demolition-material in perimeter drain. Iron finger-ring ($\frac{1}{2}$). The bezel is hollowed to hold a gem-stone now missing.
For another iron finger-ring with gem still present see p. 179, No. 4.

100. 1978 B I 10, Antonine I *via sagularis*. Stud with wide slightly-domed head and traces of notching around the edge. On the back are remains of an iron strip or sheet. Square-sectioned pin. cf. No. 66.

Objects of Silver (FIG. 79)

101. 1977 A II 40, Flavian wall-trench, Building VIII. Silver buckle: a plain ring with traces of a bronze pin.

102. 1978 B I 39, Antonine I demolition-pit, Building VII. Silver ball-headed pin. The shank is soldered into a socket in the head.

Objects of Jet (FIG. 79)

103. 1975 G IV 6, Antonine I street in *porta decumana*. Portion of jet bangle.

104. 1975 P XLI 16, Antonine I demolition-layer, *principia*, Rooms 1, 4, Portion of jet bangle.

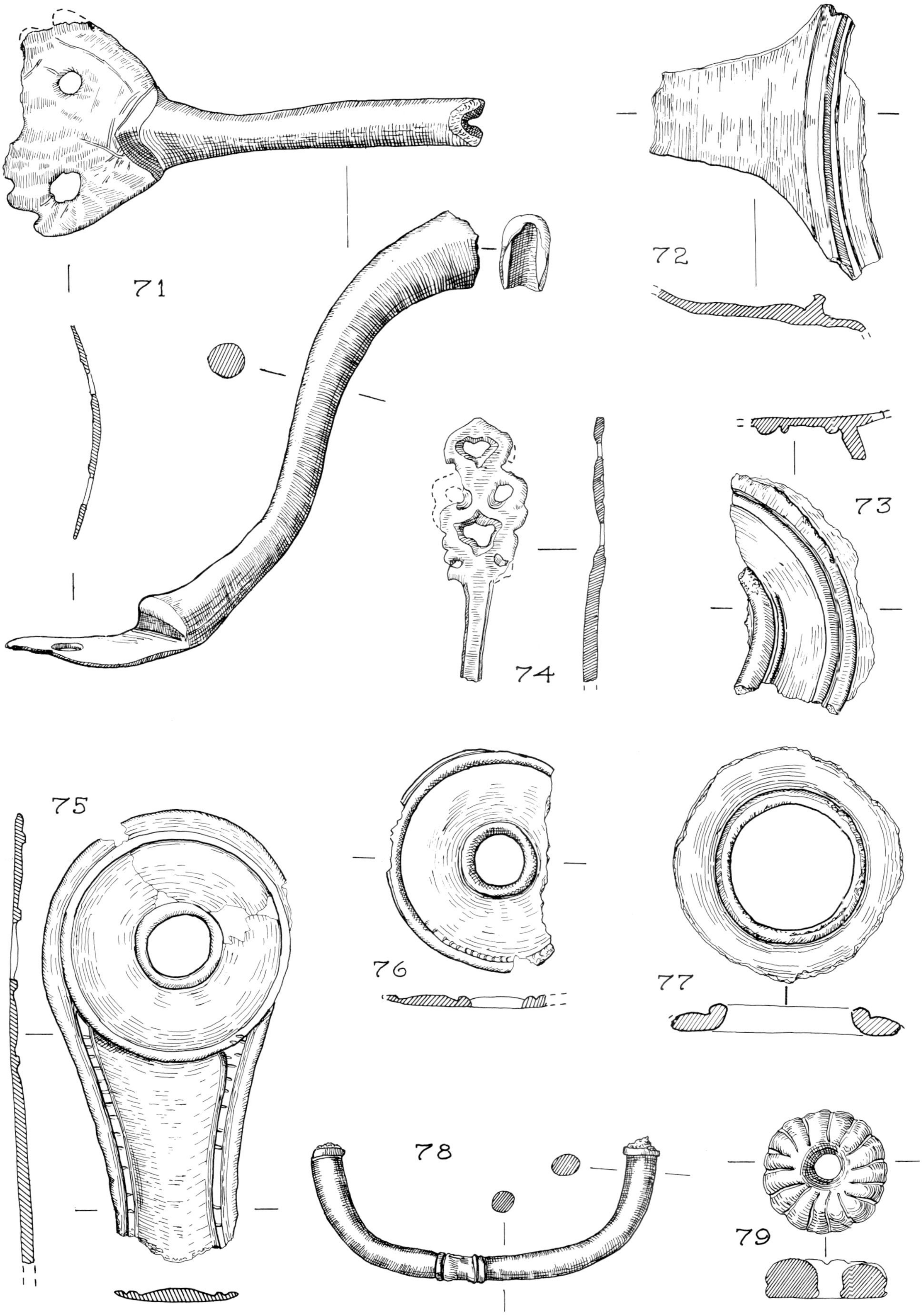

FIG. 77. Miscellaneous bronze objects (1/1).

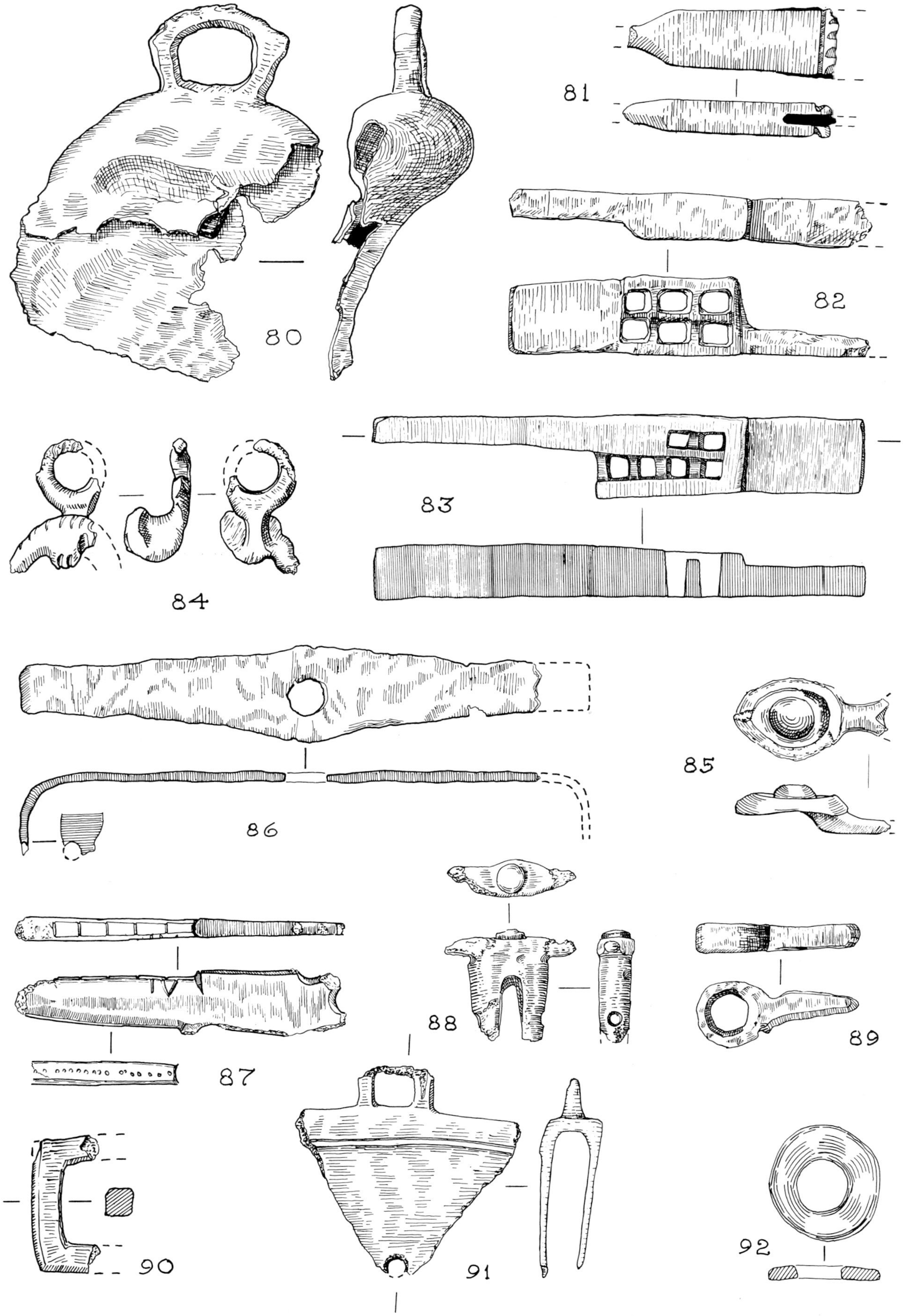

FIG. 78. Bronze objects (1/1).

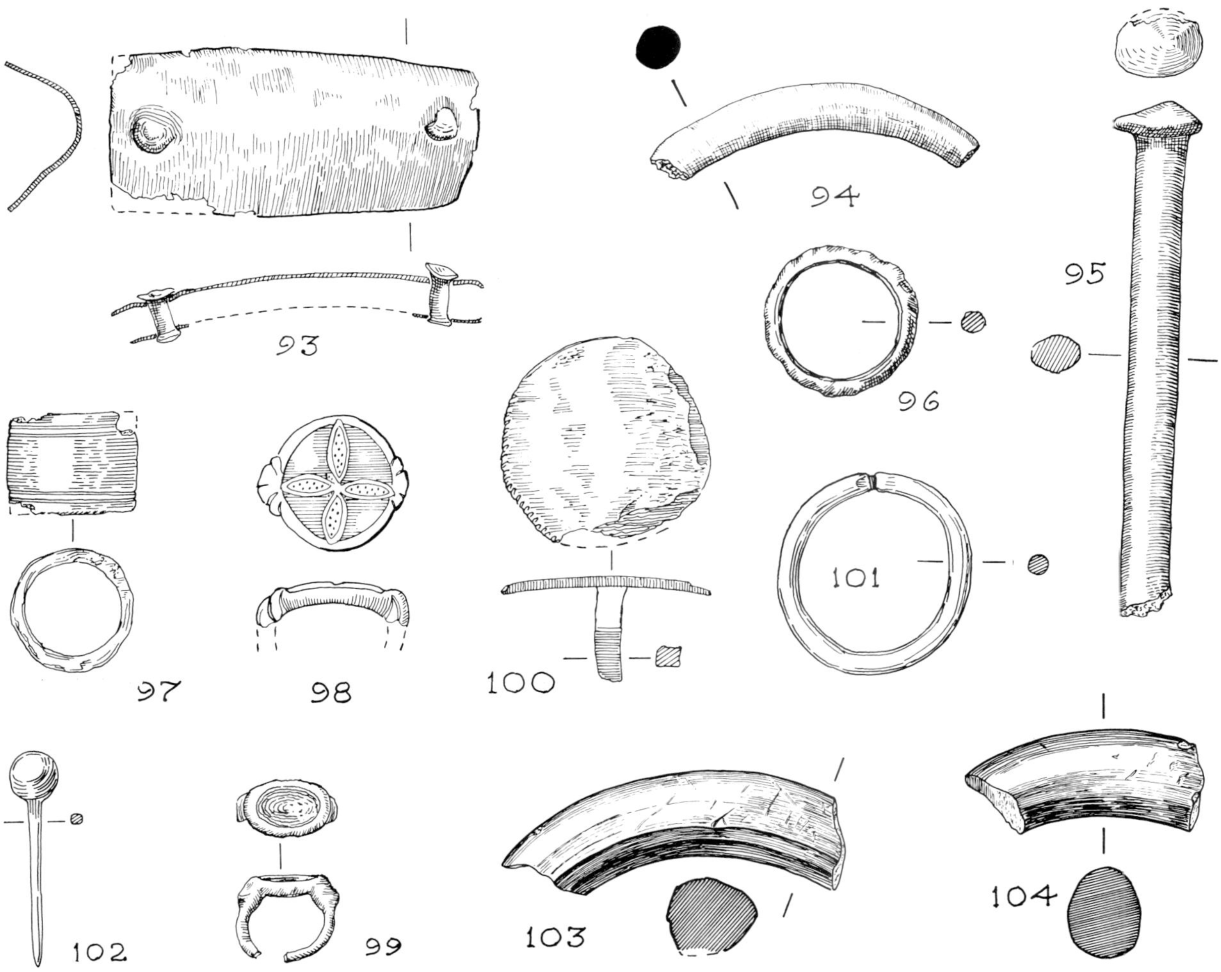

FIG. 79. Miscellaneous bronze objects (93–7, 100), finger-rings of enamelled bronze (98) and iron (99), silver buckle and pin (101, 102) and jet bangles (103–4) (All 1/1 except 99 (½)).

Objects of Lead (FIG. 80)

105. 1984 S III 10, Flavian demolition-layer, Building XVI. Lead weight, 30.81 gm. Incised inscription II. The weight, however, is the equivalent of only one *uncia* (27.3 gm).
106. 1974 P V Trench 2, Flavian wall-trench, *principia*, basilica. Lead weight similarly inscribed.
107. 1978 B I 5, Antonine I occupation-layer, Building VIII. Thin pierced lead disc or weight.
108. 1985 R I 5, Antonine I demolition-layer, Building XVII. Pierced lead disc or weight. 8.07 gm.
109. 1984 S V 2, Antonine I demolition-layer, Building XVII. Pierced lead disc or weight. 19.14 gm.

Compare the pierced stone discs with similar weight-range (p. 188, FIG. 99).

110. 1981 F I 17, Antonine I occupation-layer, Building X. Grey-ware jar with substantial lead rivet in place.
111. 1974 P XXXII 5, post-hole of Antonine II *principia*. Lead rivet.
112. 1984 S I 15, metal-worker's hearth, Antonine I, Building XV. Lead object.
113. 1978 B III 12, Antonine I demolition-pit, Building VI. Lead steelyard-weight, iron suspension-loop missing. IIII inscribed on lower side. Weight 401.1 gm.
114. 1978 B III 4, Antonine I occupation-layer, Building V. Lead steelyard-weight with iron suspension-loop. Weight 1218.7 gm.

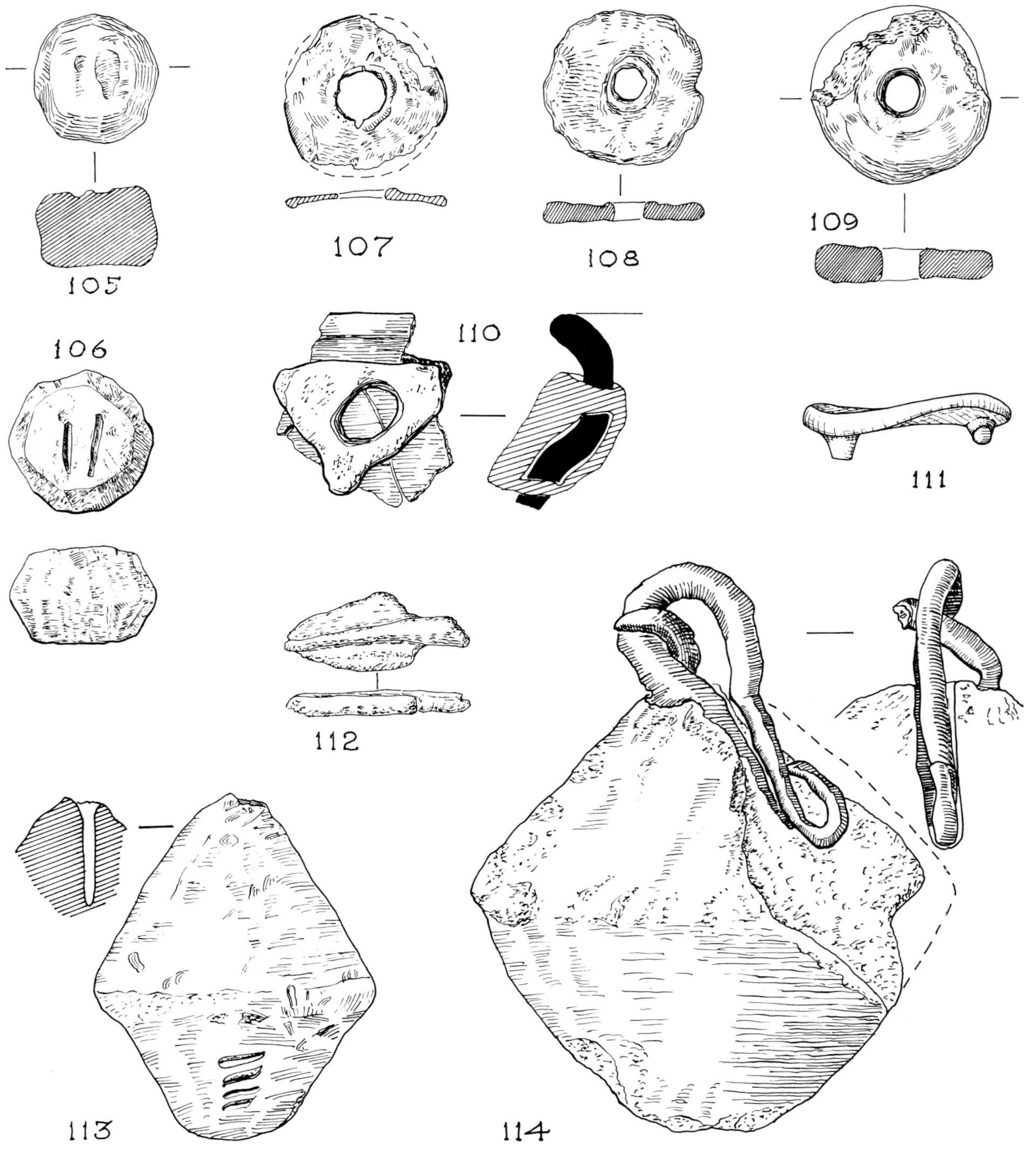

FIG. 80. Objects of lead (1/1).

Not illustrated: a small hemispherical lead weight, diameter 20 mm, from the same context as No. 114, with indications of a former bronze casing.

Other Objects of Iron

Iron Scythe and Bar (FIG. 81)

115. Scythe (¼). From 1980 E I 26, demolition-deposit in Flavian drain (p. 88), with lead pig (FIG. 93), four iron ingots (FIG. 92) and three axes (FIG. 82). Overall length 68 cm, maximum width of blade 9 cm. There is a single rivet-hole at the junction of blade and tang, and the blade is strengthened in this area by a midrib. Although the length is some

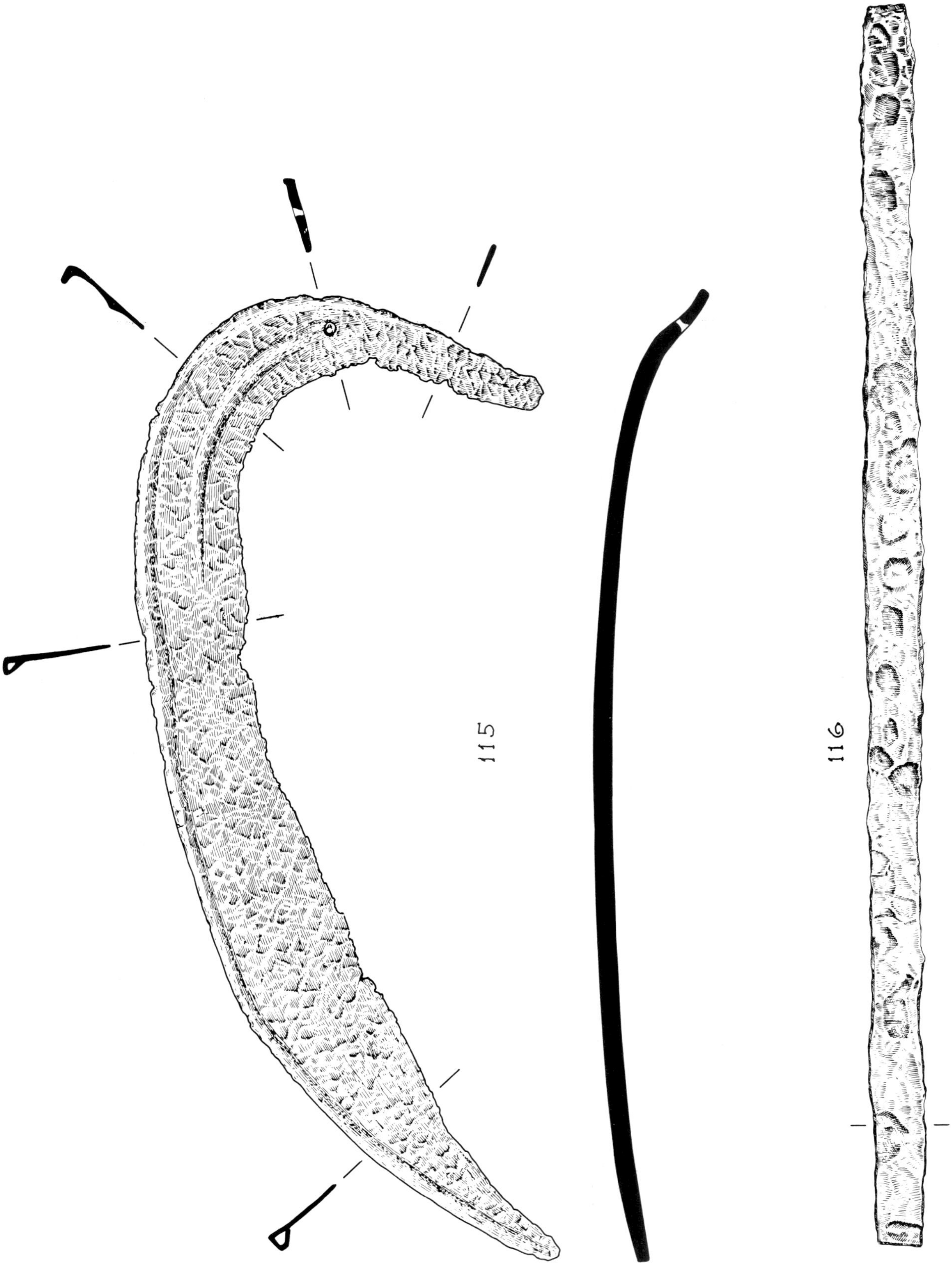

FIG. 81. Iron scythe and iron bar (1/4).

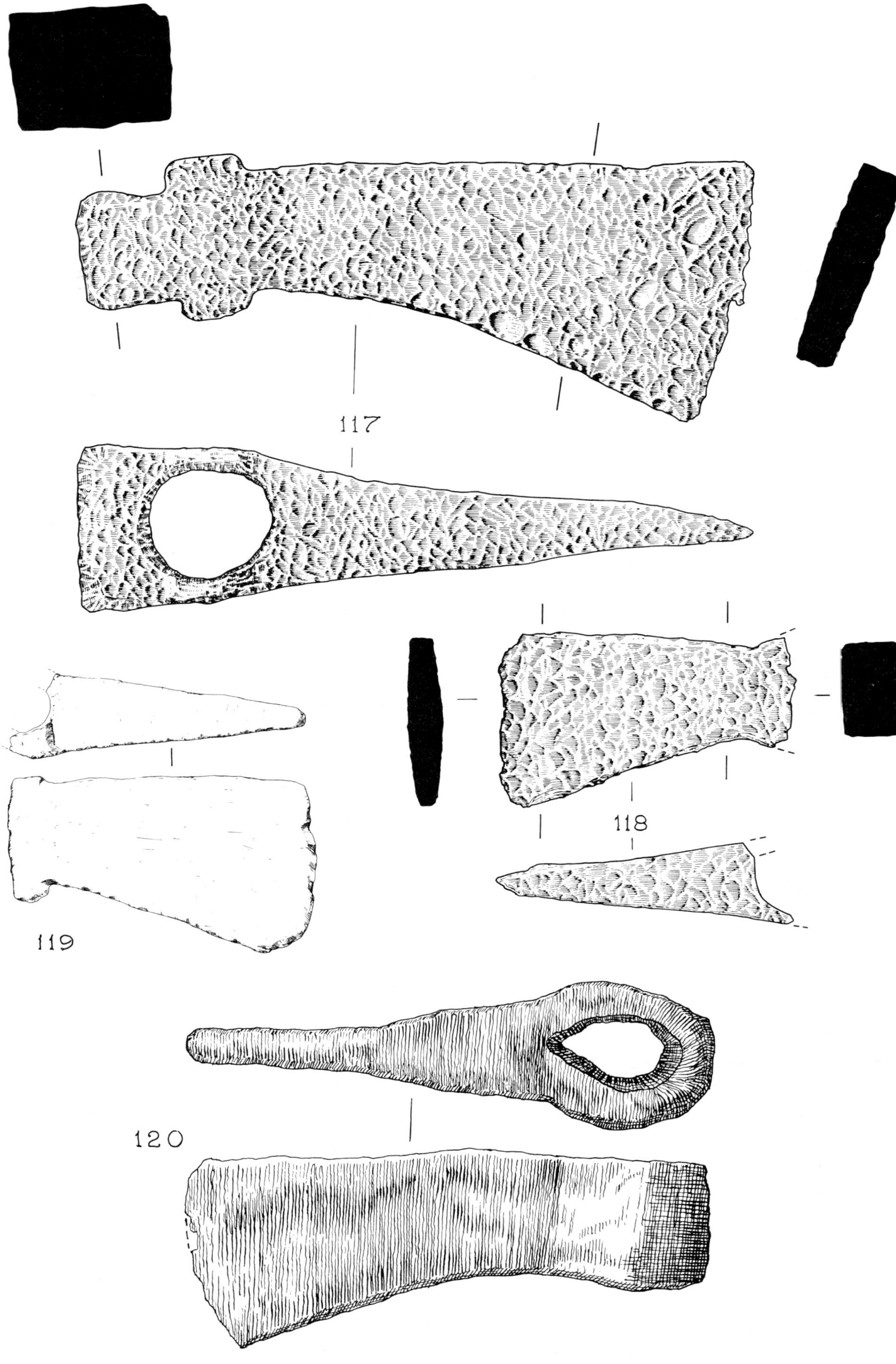

FIG. 82. Iron axes ($\frac{1}{2}$).

20 cm shorter than the smallest of the four contemporary scythes found at Newstead (Curle, *Newstead*, 284), the implement is of the same type (cf. Manning, B.M. *Cat.*, 49–50), which was widely used by the army.

116. Iron bar (¼). From 1974 P XXX 10, demolition-layer in front of the Antonine I *principia*. Length 84.4 cm, width 3.5 cm, thickness 1.4 cm. This perhaps represents the first working up of an ingot preparatory to use in manufacture.

Iron Axes (FIG. 82)

117. 1980 E I 26, demolition-deposit in Flavian drain (p. 88), with lead pig (FIG. 93), four iron ingots (FIG. 92), scythe (No. 115 above) and axes Nos. 118, 120. Axe with lugs round the eye and rectangular butt: cf. Manning, CW^2 lxvi (1966) 11–13.
118. Broken axe-blade, context as No. 117, and probably possessing lugs.
119. 1973 II 2, Antonine II demolition-layer over Building I. Broken axe-blade of same type as No. 117.
120. Axe with rounded butt, same context as No. 117.

Not illustrated: another complete axe, similar to No. 117, from 1979 D II 6, Antonine I occupation-layer, Central Range between Buildings A and B, with No. 53.

Other Iron Tools (FIG 83)

121. 1976 H III, spade-iron found standing vertical in Antonine II post-hole of Building II (p. 64) and evidently abandoned when the handle broke off during demolitions. Manning's Type 2A (B.M. *Cat.*, 44).
122. Spade iron, from 1975 P XLV 1, old ploughsoil over the basilica of the Antonine II *principia*. Manning, Type 1D.
123. Trowel, from 1977 A II 12, Antonine I demolition-layer, Building VIII. Manning, Type III (Newcastle *Cat.*, 27)
124. Farrier's Butteris (broken). From 1980 E II 19, Antonine I construction-trench, Building X. Tool used for paring horses' hooves before shoeing.
125. Fragment of saw, from 1978 B I 5, Antonine I occupation-layer, Building VIII. There is a single rivet-hole for affixing the handle: the piece is probably therefore from a bow or frame-saw. Teeth, which appear to be set, occur at *c.* 4 mm intervals (7 points to the inch).

Not illustrated: another smaller fragment of saw from 1975 P XLI 8, demolition-layer, Antonine I *principia*, Room 1.

126. Small anvil. From 1980 E II 15, Flavian demolition-layer, Building XI. The stem is pierced by a small hole like the tool described by Manning (Newcastle *Cat.* No. 63) as a mason's wedge. However, there was no employment for masons at Flavian Strageath. The head is intentionally shaped rather than expanded by hammering. The object is taken to be a small bench-anvil for use by smiths or carpenters: the hole is too small for this to be a hammer.
127. Table- or couch-leg, or possibly part of a candelabrum, broken at each end. From 1980 E I 19, Flavian occupation-layer, Building VIII. For similar objects see Manning, CW^2 lxvi (1966), 27 Nos. 36, 37; B.M. *Cat* No. P7.
128. Shears. From 1979 D III 3, Antonine I occupation-layer, Building VII. Although used elsewhere for such purposes as cloth-cutting or sheep-shearing (Manning, B.M. *Cat.*, 34), at Strageath a more likely function would be trimming horses' coats or even shaving the rampart-face; but it is possible that some elementary tailoring took place among the garrison.
129. Shears blade or large knife. From 1978 B I 3, Antonine II occupation-layer, Building VII.
130. Knife. From 1980 E II 7, Antonine I demolition-layer, Buildings XI, XII. An iron ring from the sheath remains *in situ* near the point.

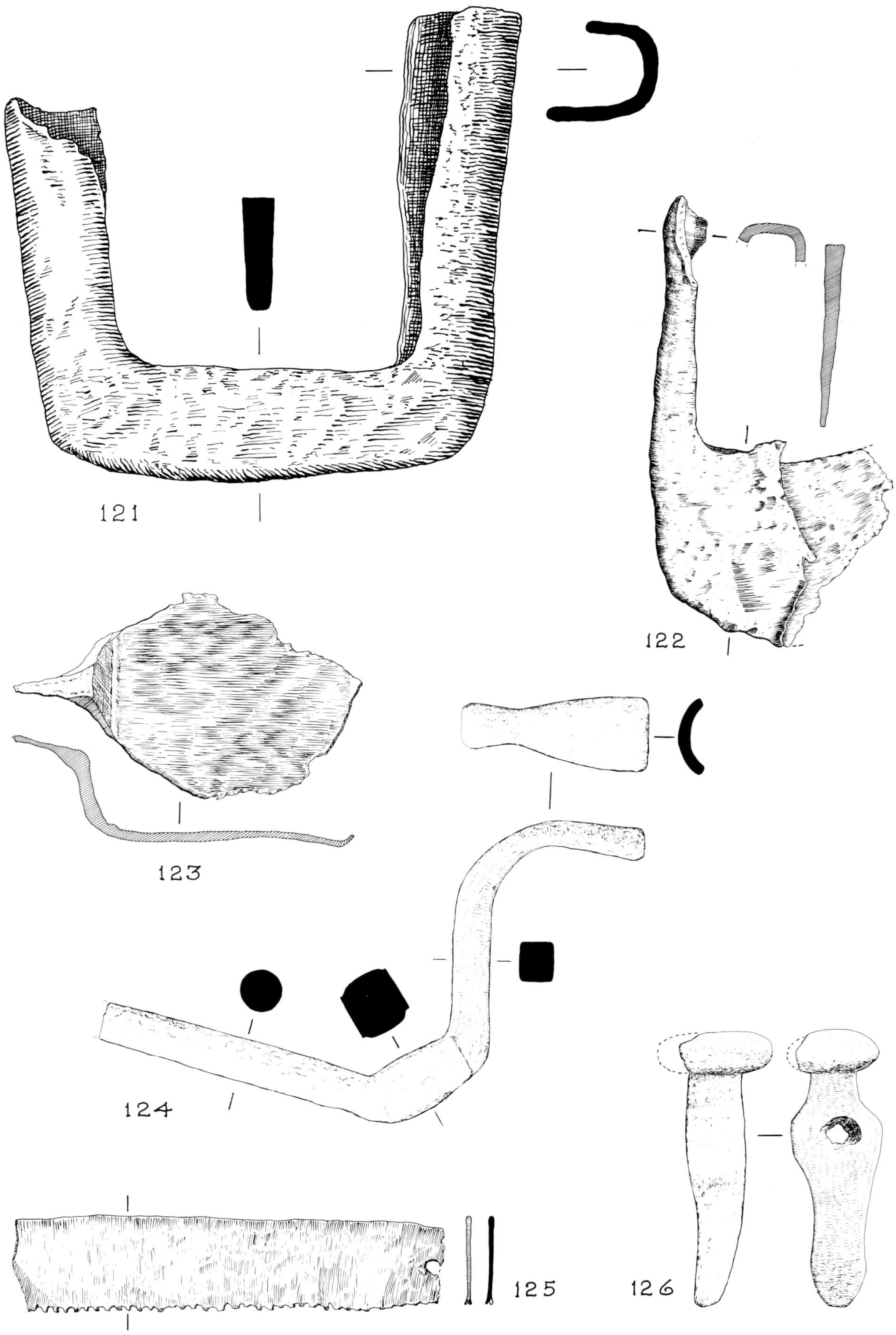

FIG. 83. Iron tools ($\frac{1}{2}$).

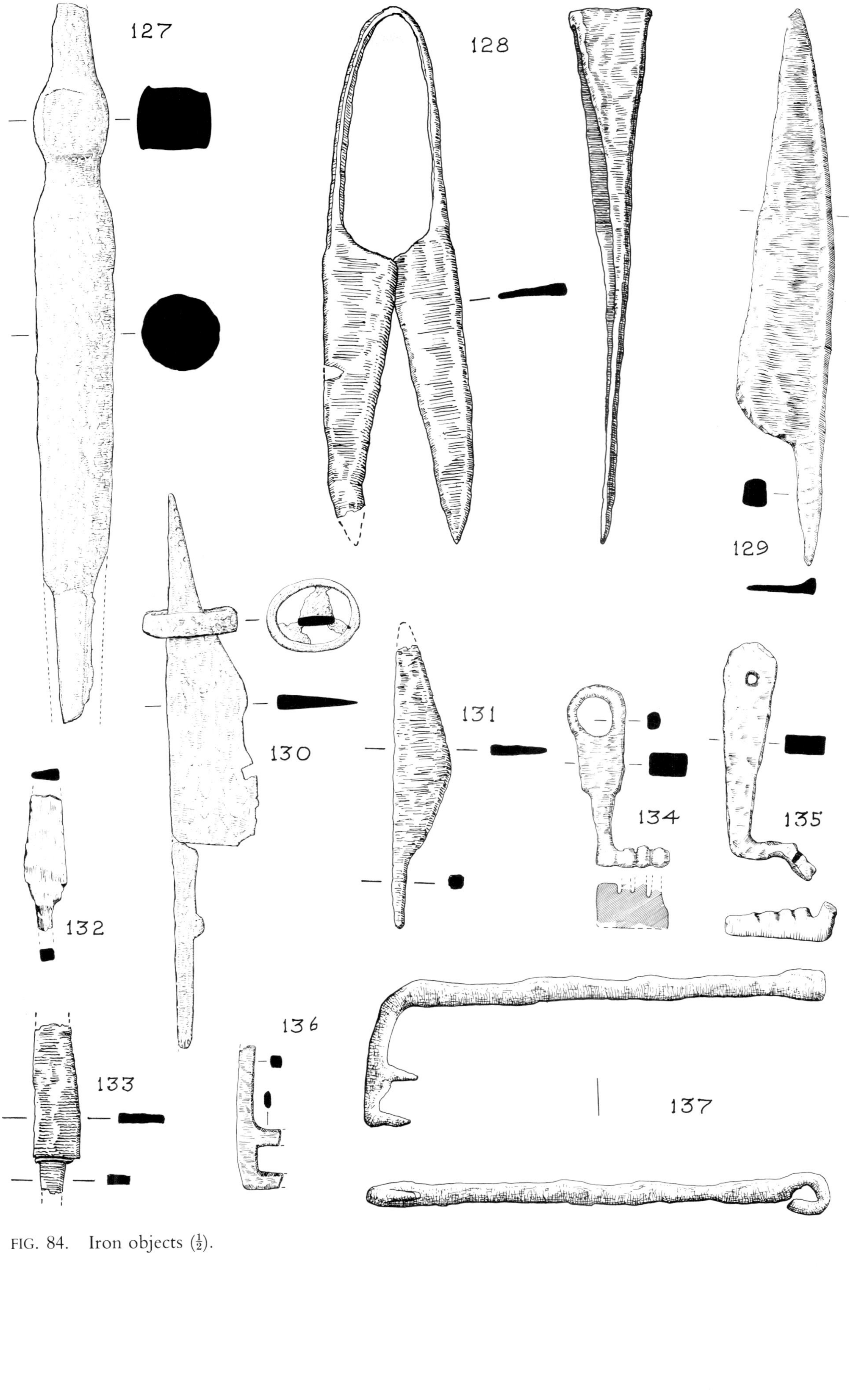

FIG. 84. Iron objects ($\frac{1}{2}$).

131. Knife. From 1981 N II 7, Antonine I occupation-layer, Building I.
132. Knife. From 1973 I 2, Antonine II silting in the *intervallum* area.
133. Knife. From 1980 E II 15, Flavian demolition-layer, Building XI. A bronze band lies at the junction of blade and tang.
134. Key. From 1977 A I 8, Antonine I demolition-layer, Buildings V, VI. This is Manning's slide-key Type 1 (B.M. *Cat.*, 92) for moving the tumblers retaining the slide-bolt in a tumbler-lock, cf. Nos. 82, 83.
135. Key. From 1976 H I 11, Antonine I occupation-layer, Building II. Slide-key of Type 2.
136. Fragment of lift-key, cf. No. 137. From 1977 A II 23A, Antonine I pit, *intervallum* space.
137. Key. From 1985 N III 6, Antonine I demolition-layer, Building VIII. Drawn from an X-ray photograph. An example of Manning's lift-key (B.M. *Cat.*, 90, fig. 25.2) for raising the tumblers clear of the bolt.
138. Parts of a tumbler lock case. From 1980 E I 8, Antonine II demolition-layer, Building VIII. There are two fragments, one (138B) being part of the corner of the case with a vertical rivet in the angle. The other (138A) is a plate to which are corroded three pins side by side. These are probably the pins which descended into corresponding holes in the bolt to hold it in the locked position, but which could be raised to free the bolt by a slide-key such as Nos. 134, 135.
139. Part of barb-spring padlock. From 1973 II 28, Antonine I demolition-pit 2. One barb remains, the other is broken off. A key inserted from the left over these springs would compress them, enabling the bolt to be withdrawn to the right by means of the split pin. cf. Manning, B.M. *Cat.*, 95.
140. Fragment of lift-key. From 1976 H I 5, Antonine I demolition-layer, Building III. For this type of key cf. Manning, B.M. *Cat.*, 90.
141. (?) Lift-key. From 1977 A I 64. Flavian demolition-pit C, Building V. Square-sectioned bar with suspension-loop at one end and fragment of another loop at the other end. It is drawn reconstructed as a lift-key, but the identification is not certain.
142. Ox-goad. From 1973 II 2, Antonine I demolition-layer, Building I. See No. 143.
143. 1981 F II 22, Flavian occupation-layer, Building XI. Although objects such as Nos. 142–4 have usually been identified as ox-goads, R.E. Birley has recently shown that some are in reality pen-nibs. Small and delicate examples such as Nos. 143–4 may be taken to be nibs; but No. 143 is too large and long for anything but a goad.
144. (?) Pen-nib. From 1973 II 2, Antonine I demolition-layer, Building I. For comment see No. 143.
145. 1973 II 2, as No. 144. Small looped spike.
146. Chisel. From 1977 A I 8, Antonine I demolition-layer, Buildings V, VI, VII. Broad-bladed firmer chisel with square tang (broken).
147. Mortice chisel. From 1985 N III 2, Antonine I demolition-layer, Building VIII. A stout circular shaft, 10 mm in diameter, has a slightly expanded head and a bevelled blade 6 mm wide. For chisels of Manning, B.M. *Cat.*, 20–24.
148. 1977 A I 47, Antonine I demolition-pit F. Z-shaped fragment, perhaps from a farrier's rasp or carpenter's float. For these see Manning, B.M. *Cat.*, 28, 61.
149. 1985 N I 16, Flavian latrine-pit, Building II. Handle with well-wrought spiral terminal, resembling a modern window peg-stay. The terminals of hipposandals normally have loops of only one twist; No. 149 is more elaborately decorative and, if not a window- or shutter-stay, is perhaps the terminal of a chair- or table-leg.
150. Small rake-tine. From 1976 H I 5, Antonine I demolition-layer, Buildings II, III.
151. Large rake-tine. From 1973 I 14, Antonine I demolition-layer in the *intervallum*.
152. Four rake-tines found together in 1975 G II 9, Antonine II gate-post pit, *porta decumana*. For a well-preserved rake see Curle, *Newstead*, pl. LXI. 7; there, seven slightly curving tines, *c.* 4 cm apart, were held in a wooden clog over which the tops of their tangs were bent to hold them. At Strageath the tangs have been broken off. Cf. Manning, B.M. *Cat.*, 59.

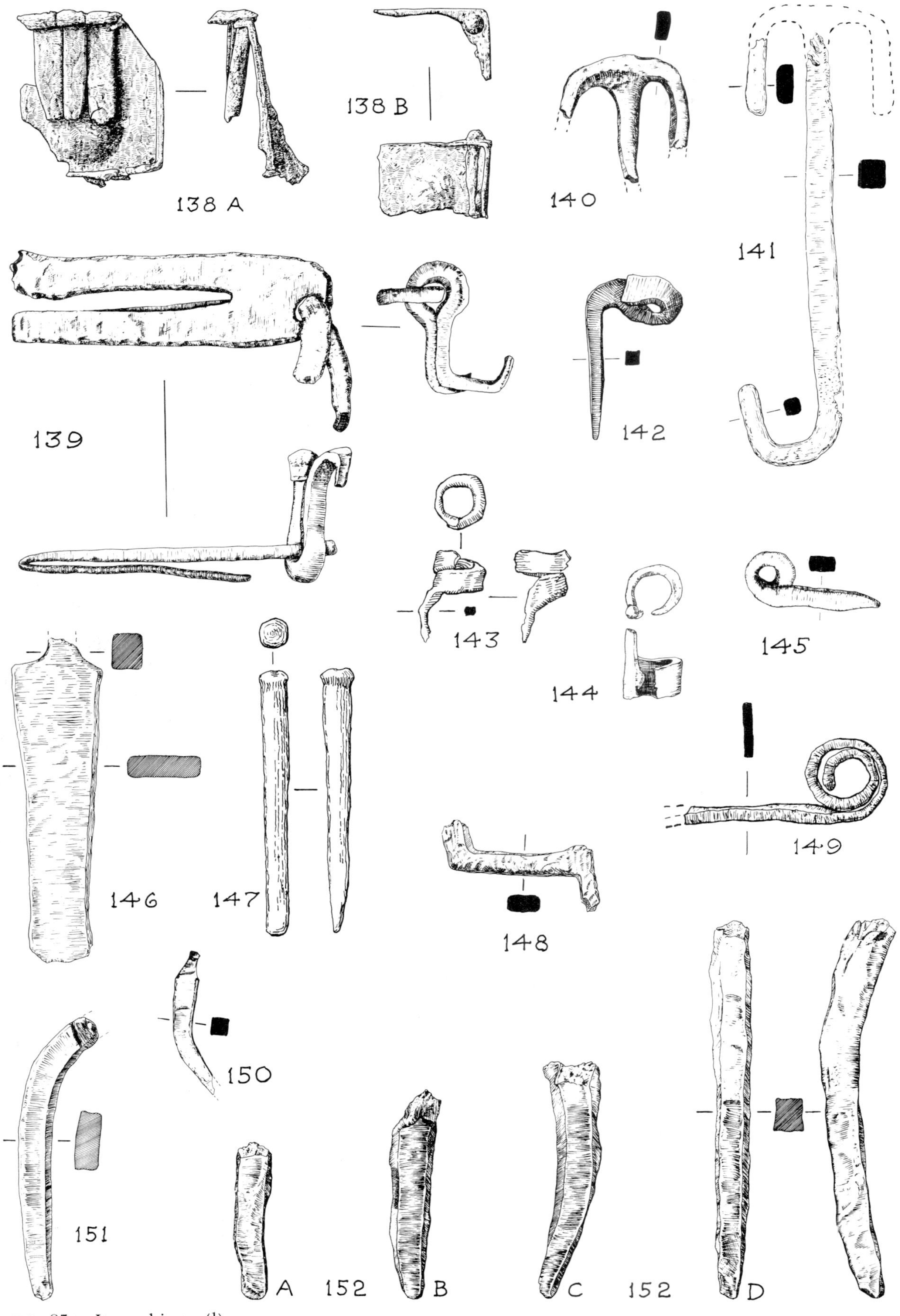

FIG. 85. Iron objects ($\frac{1}{2}$).

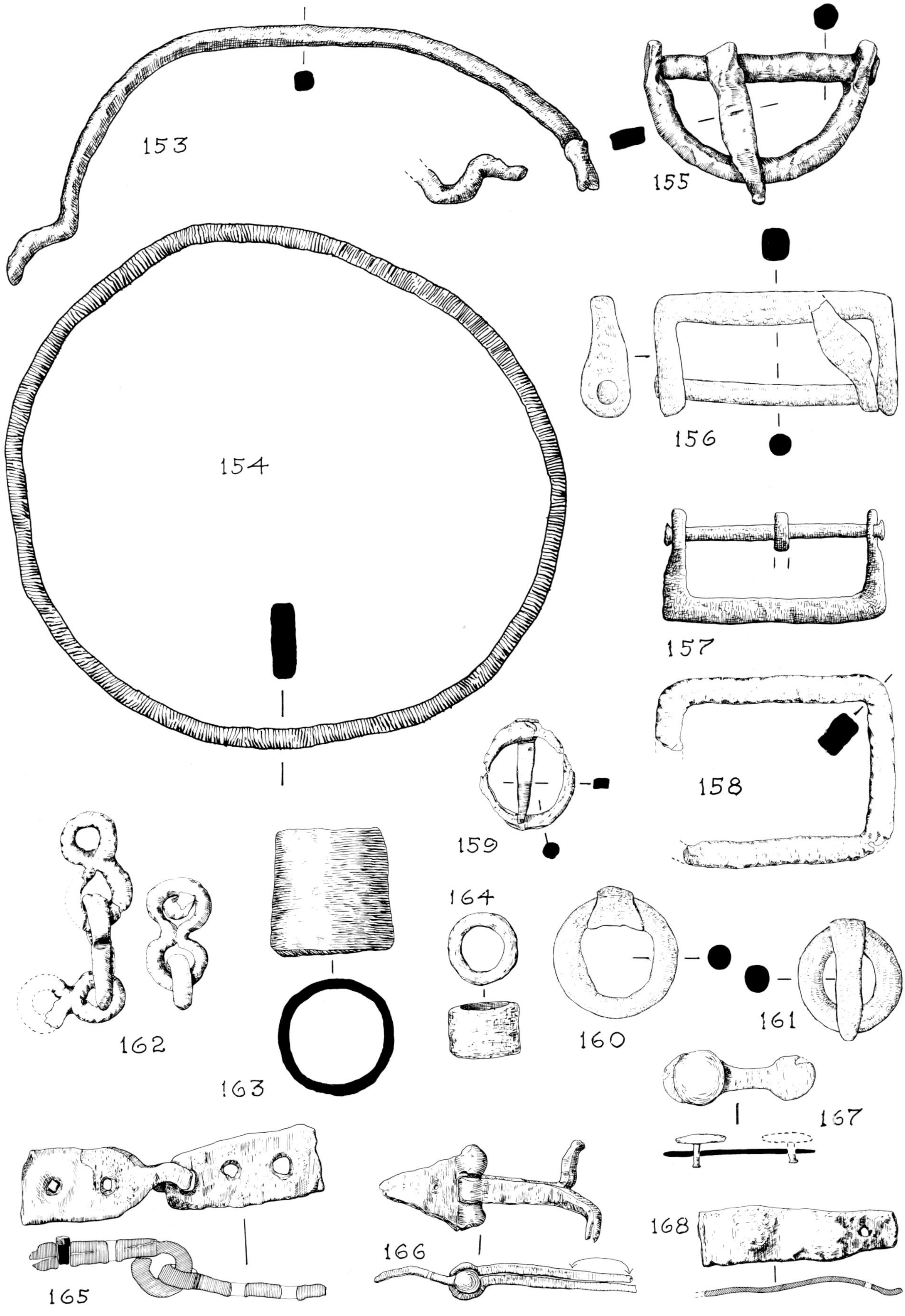

FIG. 86. Iron objects (½).

Other iron objects (FIG. 86)

153. Bucket-handle, somewhat bent. From 1973 II 28, Antonine I demolition-pit 2.

154. Bucket-hoop. From 1978 B VI 20, Flavian demolition-layer, in front of Building VIII. Internal diameter *c.* 175–180 mm.

Buckles: Nos. 155–161

155. Large D-shaped buckle. From 1976 H I 8, Antonine I demolition-layer Buildings II, III.

156. Large oblong buckle. From 1980 E II 11, Antonine I occupation-layer, Buildings XI, XII. Flattened tongue.

157. As No. 156. From 1986 T I 3, Antonine I demolition-layer, Building X. Drawn from X-ray photograph. Tongue broken off.

158. (?) Remains of rectangular buckle. From 1973 IV 4, Antonine II *via sagularis*. Cf. L. Allason-Jones and R. Miket, *Cat. of Small Finds from S. Shields Roman Fort* 292, No. 5.43.

159. Circular buckle. From 1973 II 2, Antonine I demolition-layer, Building I.

160. Circular buckle. From 1979 D II 4, Antonine I demolition-layer, Central Range, Building A. Of the tongue only the fold remains.

161. Circular buckle. From 1981 F I 8, Antonine I demolition-layer, Building IX.

162. Fragments of chain. From 1973 I 12, Antonine I demolition-layer, *intervallum*. Figure-of-eight links.

163. Plain reinforcement collar. From 1978 B I 5, Antonine I occupation-layer, Building VIII. Diameter diminishes from 44 to 40 mm; length 45 mm. Cf. S.S. Frere, *Verulamium Excavations* i, 188. No. 125.

164. Smaller similar collar. From 1978 B III 4, Antonine I occupation-layer, Building V. Diameter 25 mm, height 17 mm.

165. Loop-hinge. From 1977 A II 5c, Antonine II furnace in *intervallum*. Neither plate is complete; each has two perforations, and one still retains part of a square-sectioned nail. Cf. Manning, B.M. *Cat.*, 126.

166. Small hinge. From 1977 A II 12, Antonine I demolition-layer, Building VIII. A triangular plate with one perforation is linked to a split pin. If the bends of this pin are original, the panel to which it was affixed was *c.* 25 mm thick.

167. Thin band expanded at each end, where remains of flat-headed bronze studs held it in position probably on leather, since the pins give a thickness of *c.* 3 mm. Perhaps therefore a belt-plate. Length 55 mm. From 1977 A II Pit 5, Flavian demolition-pit, Building VIII.

168. Binding or hinge-fragment with single perforation. From 1975 P XLV 1, old ploughsoil over the basilica of the Antonine II *principia*.

169. Binding. From 1977 A I 12, Flavian wall-trench, Building VI. The bar has been bent double but is drawn in restored form. A plate with two perforations ends in a loop perhaps once joining another plate at right-angles like *Richborough* v, pl. LVII No. 288. Vehicle-fitting, or possibly part of a door-hinge.

170. 1977 B I 2, old ploughsoil over Antonine II Street III/IV. Reinforcement-bar of D-section with perforation at one slightly expanded end. Width 12 mm, thickness 4 mm. This closely resembles the hand-grip of the Doncaster shield (*Britannia* ix (1978), 249 with fig. 4) which was 17 mm wide and 10 mm thick.

171. 1977 A II 17, Antonine I occupation-layer, Building VIII. Double-spiked loop, cf. Manning, B.M. *Cat.*, 130.

172. 1977 A I 25, Flavian demolition-pit A, Building V. Thin sheet forming a loop. Part of a hinge or buckle-plate ? Cf. S.S. Frere, *Verulamium Excavations* iii, fig. 42, No. 97.

173. 1981 F I 25, Flavian wall-trench, Building X. Bolt and spike. The bolt, which has a domed head, fits closely through a loop in the spike. Length of bolt 182 mm, diameter 12 mm. Length of spike 250 mm. The size of the spike suggests association with a substantial timber. The object is more probably from a cart than a building.

174. 1976 H I 10, Antonine I post-hole, Building IV. Folded sheet in two parts. Length 174 mm. Perhaps from a spade-iron (cf. Nos. 121, 122).

175. 1981 F I 2, old ploughsoil over Antonine II, Building VIII. T-cramp, length 110 mm. Though normally associated with masonry buildings such as baths, Nos. 175 and 176 evidently served a function in timber architecture.

Not illustrated: others from:
1974 G I 15, Antonine II extension to rampart, *porta decumana*.
1977 A II 5, Antonine II furnace.
1978 B I 41, turf bedding of Flavian *via sagularis*.
1984 S III 4, Antonine I perimeter drain.

176. 1973 II 25. Antonine I demolition, Building II. T-cramp, broken.
177. 1984 S III 10, Flavian demolition-layer, Building XVI. Heavy rectangular loop.
178. 1982 J 7. Flavian demolition-pit, Building IV. Hook, length 55 mm.
179. 1980 E I 3, old ploughsoil over Antonine II Building VIII. Drop-hook (?), fragmentary.
180. 1983 L II 14, Antonine I demolition-pit C. The object was bent double, but has been drawn in restored form. Door-fastening. The bar is hinged at one end on a split pin and curved upwards at the other; a loop on the other side received a bolt or padlock.
181. 1980 E II 11, Antonine I occupation-layer, Building XII. Drop-handle or part of buckle.
182. 1982 F I 8, Antonine I demolition-layer, Building IX. Drop-handle retained by split pins. Drawn from X-ray photographs.
183. 1985 R I 5, Antonine I demolition-layer, Building XVII. Hinge formed by two interlocked loops. Drawn from X-ray photographs.
184. 1985 N III 4, Antonine I demolition-layer, Building VIII. Small iron strap-hinge. Drawn from X-ray photograph. Cf. Manning, B.M. *Cat.*, 126–7.
185. 1980 E I 16, Antonine I occupation, Building IX. Meat-hook. Cf. J.W. Brailsford, *Hod Hill* i, pl. XII, No. K 42.
186. 1985 N III 4, Antonine I demolition-layer, Building VIII. Meat-hook.
187. 1981 F I 17, Antonine I occupation-layer, Building X. Perhaps part of a small axe.
188. 1980 E I 19, Flavian occupation-layer, Building IX. L-shaped tie with one perforation in the longer arm.
189. 1980 E II 11, Antonine occupation, Building XII. Nail hook: oblong-sectioned shank with angled projection from the head, hooked at the end. For a similar object cf. I.A. Richmond, *Hod Hill* ii, fig. 59 C 6c.
190. 1977 A I 22, Flavian demolition-pit A, Building V. Curving strip, width 53 mm. Diameter *c.* 100 mm. Perhaps part of a bucket-hoop.
191. 1979 D II 6, Antonine I occupation-layer, Central Range, Building A. Plain length of strap.
192. 1980 E II 11, Antonine I occupation-layer, Building XII. Perhaps a Leather-worker's awl, cf. Manning, B.M. *Cat.*, 40–3; it has, however, also been included among the arrowheads (No. 20).
193. 1973 II, Post-hole 48. Antonine II post-hole, Building I. Large joiner's dog with broad flat top, 41 mm wide.
194. 1981 F I 4, Antonine II perimeter drain. Fragment of strap.
195. 1973 II 17, Flavian occupation-layer, Building I. Fragmentary wall-hook. Cf. Manning, B.M. *Cat.*, 129.

Joiner's Dogs (with 193), used for joining timbers (FIG. 89)
196. 1983 L I 11, Antonine I occupation-layer, Building XVI.
197. 1981 F I 8, Antonine I demolition-layer, Building IX.
198. 1977 A II 9, Antonine II perimeter drain.
199. 1978 B I 5, Antonine I occupation-layer, Building VIII.
200. 1985 R I 6, Antonine I demolition-layer, Building XVII.
201. 1973 II 3, Flavian occupation-layer, Building I.

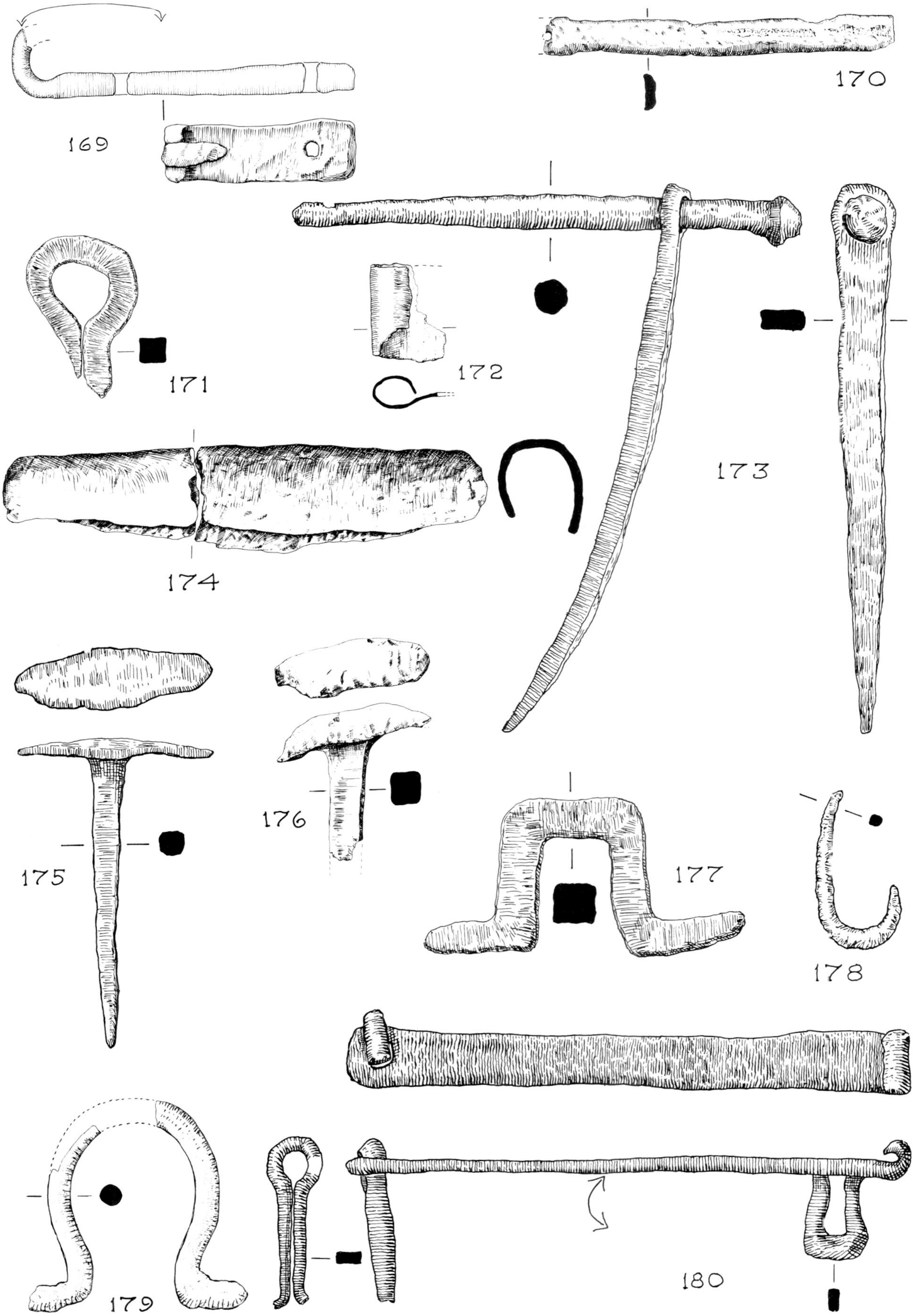

FIG. 87. Iron objects (½).

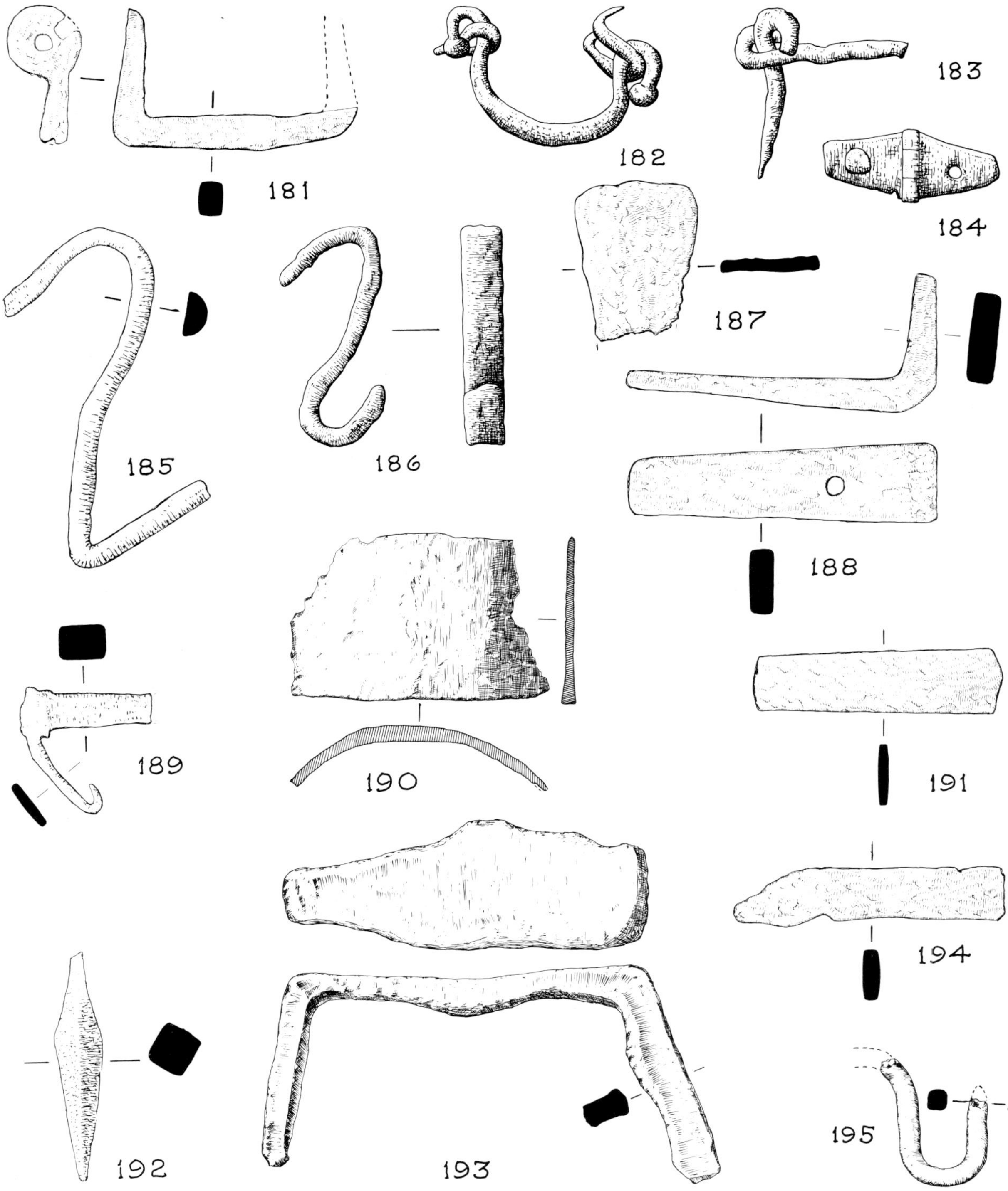

FIG. 88. Iron objects ($\frac{1}{2}$).

202. 1978 B I 3, Antonine II occupation-layer, Building VII. In this example the arms are only 10 mm apart; perhaps therefore intended for suspension, rather than joining timbers.

203, 204. 1978 B I 5, Antonine I occupation-layer, Building VIII.

205. 1980 E II 7, Antonine I demolition-layer, Buildings XI, XII.

Harness Rings (FIGS. 89)

206. 1973 II 2, Antonine I demolition-layer, Building I.

207. 1975 P XLIV 4, Street south of Antonine II *principia*.

208. 1975 P XLIV 5, Antonine II metalling of *principia* courtyard.

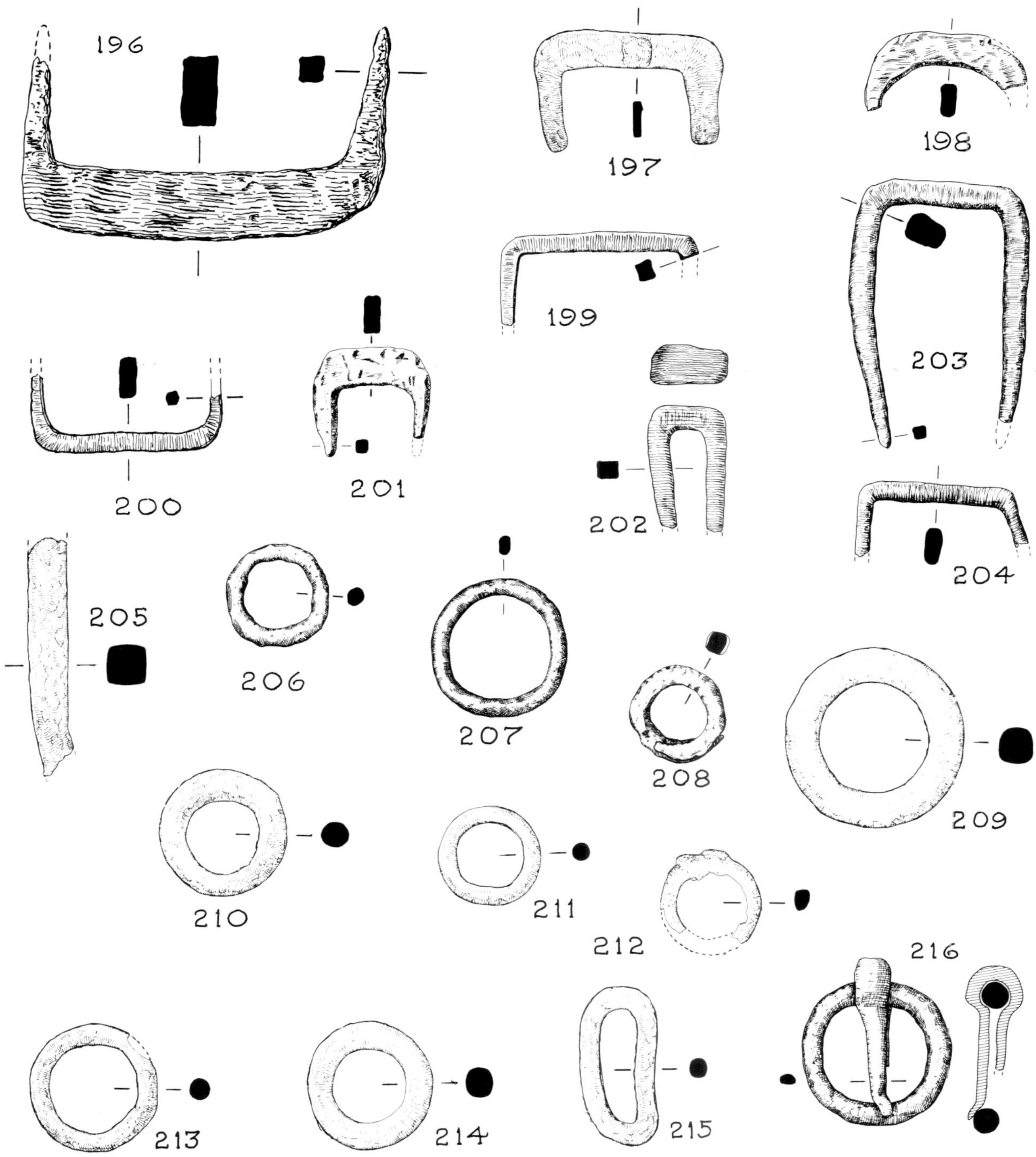

FIG. 89. Iron objects ($\frac{1}{2}$).

209. 1980 E I 17, Flavian occupation-layer, *intervallum* area.
210. 1980 E I 20, Flavian occupation-layer, Building IX.
211. 1981 F I Post-hole 5, Antonine II post-hole, Building VIII.
212. 1980 E II 15, Flavian demolition-layer, Building XI.
213. 1979 D II 4, Antonine I demolition-layer, Central Range, Building A.
214. 1981 F I 22, Antonine I occupation-layer, Building X.

215. Chain-link. From 1980 E II 10. Antonine I demolition-layer, Buildings XI, XII.
216. Double-spiked loop. From 1978 B I 5, Antonine I occupation-layer, Building VIII. Cf. Manning, B.M. *Cat.*, 130. The spikes have become folded back over the ring and one is broken off.

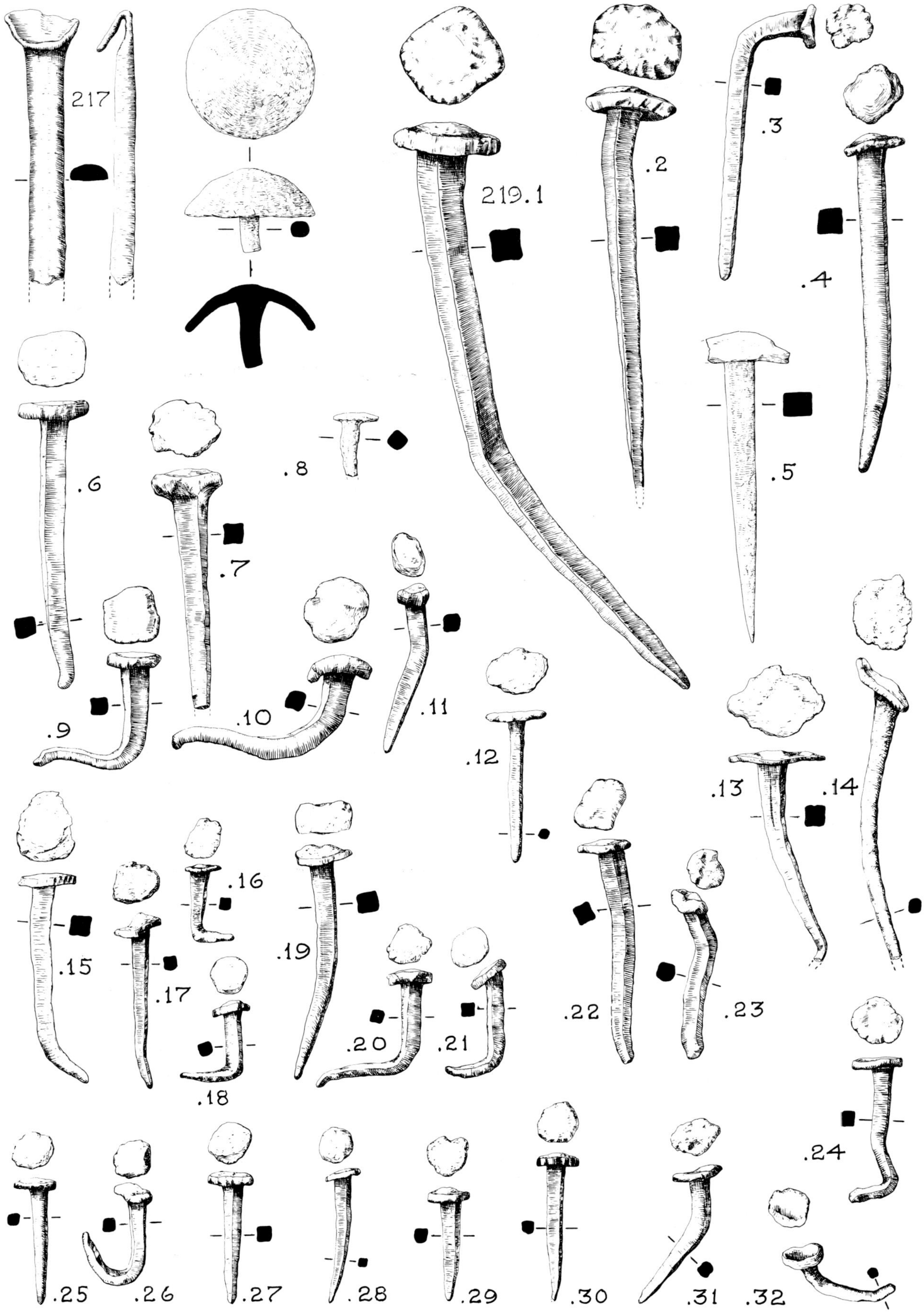

FIG. 90. Iron objects (½).

217. 1973 II 3, Flavian occupation-layer, Building I. Object with D-sectioned stem narrowing to a (?) blade now bent back. In shape it resembles the (?) shield-grip, No. 170, but has no perforation in the flattened area. The D-section makes it unlikely to be a chisel.

Nails: 218–219 (FIG. 90)

218. Dome-headed nail of Manning Type 8 (B.M. *Cat.*, 135).

219.1,2. Nails of Manning Type 1A (B.M. *Cat.*, 134), lengths 225 and *c.* 150 mm. Both came from the *porta decumana*: 219.1 from 1974 G I 27, filling of Antonine I gate-post; 219.2 from 1974 G I 14, Antonine I demolition-layer.

219.3–219.32. Nails of Manning Type 1B.

219.3 1973 I 12, Antonine I demolition-layer in the *intervallum*. Length 105 mm, bent on withdrawal.

219.4 1973 I 17, Antonine II occupation-layer in the *intervallum*. Length 120 mm.

219.5 1980 E I 19, Flavian occupation-layer, Building IX with Nos. 188, 218. Length 110 mm.

219.6 1973 II 4, Antonine II perimeter drain. Length 100 mm.

219.7. 1973 II 14, Antonine II *via sagularis*. Length 85 mm (broken).

219.8–32. Nails of various lengths, many bent with the claw-hammer during demolition. Nails of these sizes and type occurred in very large numbers in layers of all periods in every building.

Shoes (FIG. 91)

220. 1980 E II 21, filling of wall-trench of extension to Antonine II *principia* Drawn from X-ray photographs. Remains of sole *c.* 220 mm long with five rows of hobnails and extra clusters near the toes, suggesting repair. No leather survives, the pattern of nails being held together by rust.

221. 1973 II 1, make-up of Antonine II perimeter drain. Fragment showing clenched hobnails.

Not illustrated: fragments of another from 1973 A I 31, make up of Antonine II ovens in *intervallum*.

222. 1982 G I 20, Flavian occupation, Buildings I, II.

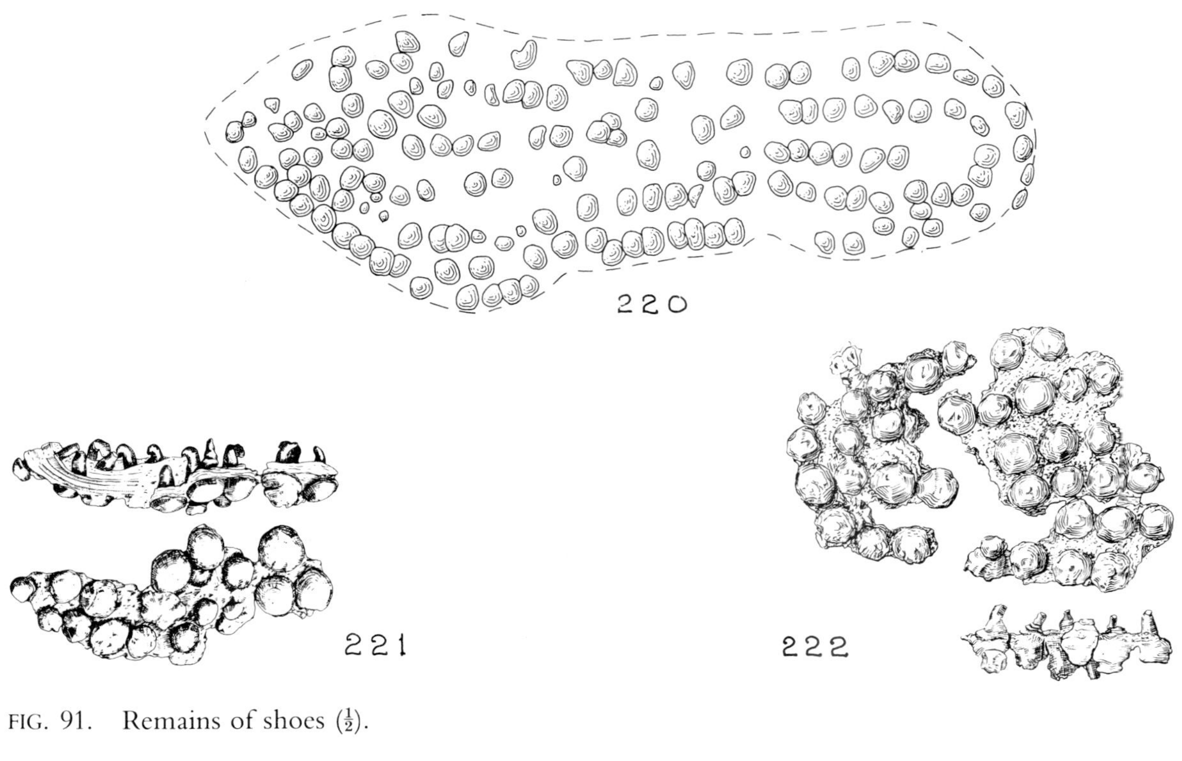

FIG. 91. Remains of shoes ($\frac{1}{2}$).

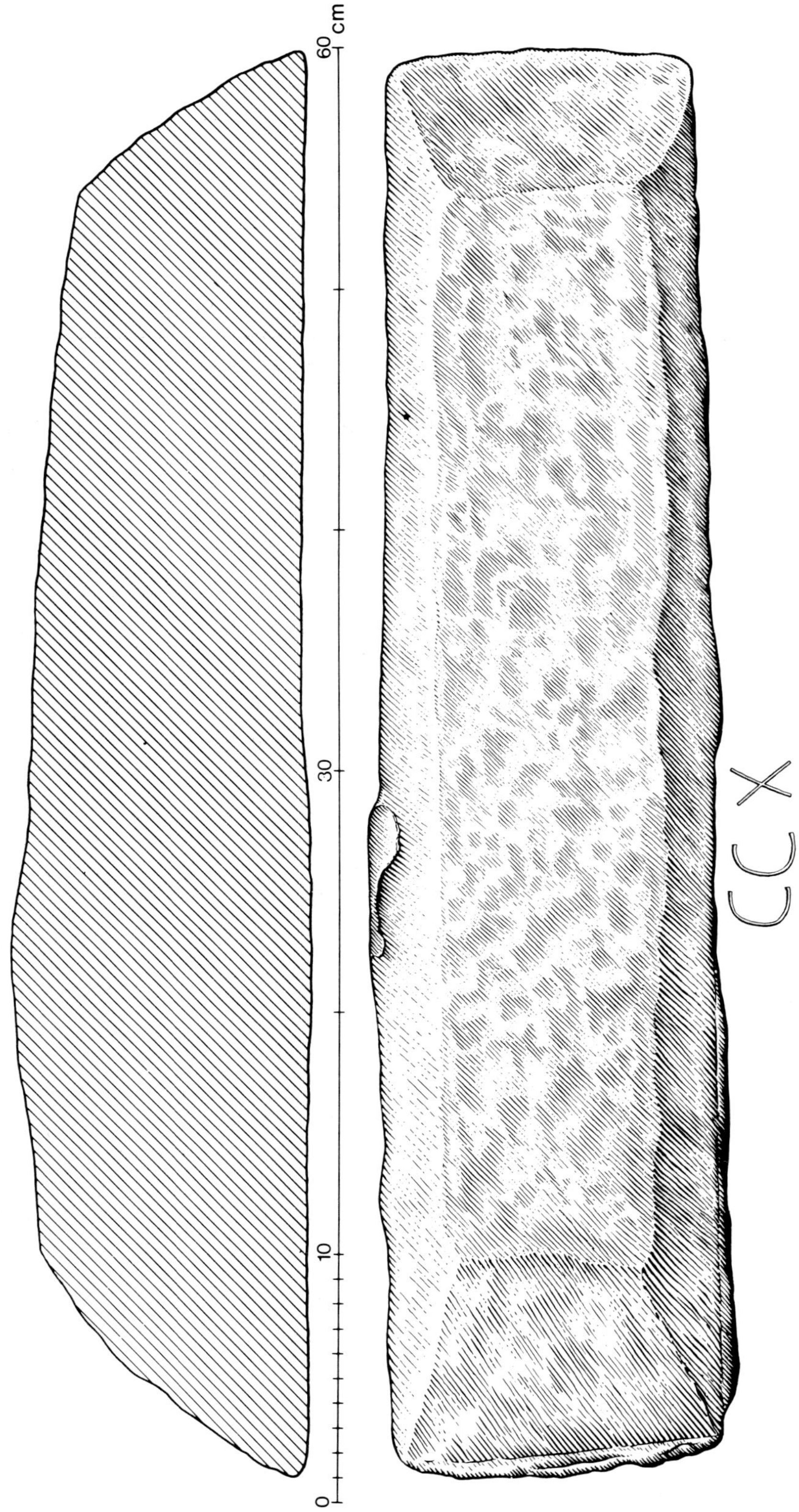

FIG. 92. Lead pig (1/3): Crown copyright reserved.

XI. THE LEAD PIG

Lead pig of normal shape (FIG. 92). 80 E I 26. Flavian drain near *porta decumana* (p. 88). Face 450 by 90 mm, base 590 by 147 mm, height 125 mm. Weight 68.5 kg (151.02 English pounds) = 209.2 Roman pounds, reckoning 327.45 g to the *libra*. The pig has been conserved by Mr Richard Welander in the Ancient Monuments Laboratory at Edinburgh; he reports that it was hoped to recover traces of an inscription on the upper surface; but repeated attempts, using electrolytic cleaning and consolidative techniques, failed to highlight any such details. It seems certain that there was no original inscription, and that the uneven surface apparent before cleaning was not due to a hidden inscription but to a poor moulding surface.

On the underside the engraved figures **CCX** were recorded; these presumably indicate the original weight of 210 Roman pounds. The minimal loss of weight (0.8 *libra*, less than 0.5%) implicit in these figures is presumably attributable to surface corrosion; when found, all surfaces were spongy. It cannot be considered sufficient to suggest that an original cast inscription once existed but has been lost through chiselling or excessive corrosion of the upper surface.

This is only the third lead pig ever to have been recorded in Roman Scotland. The first was found in 1774 in a deep pit or burial-shaft at the fort of Bertha (*RIB* ii, 2404, 70). It weighed only 73 lbs (33.1 kg) and was thus either exceptionally small or part-used.[1] The second was dug up at Kirkintilloch on the Antonine Wall (*RIB* ii 2404.69) in *c.* 1825; like the Strageath pig it carried a record of weight but no moulded inscription.

Tylecote[2] records six pigs weighing less than 100 lb (45 kg) out of a total of 48 of which the weight is known; the two lightest are one of *c.* 50 lb (22.7 kg) from Bruton, Somerset, and one of 76 lb (34.5 kg) from Bristol. The Strageath ingot, however, at 151.02 lbs is only 7.8 lb (3.54 kg) below average weight.

The composition of the pig was examined by Dr Noel Gale who writes as follows.

'The lead isotope composition —

$208_{Pb}/206_{Pb}$,	$208_{Pb}/206_{Pb}$,	$206_{Pb}/204_{Pb}$)
2.09109	0.85350	18.233

shows that the lead did *not* come from the Mendips, Flintshire or Derbyshire. There is a distressing lack of precise modern isotope analyses of lead ores in Britain; but from the little that there is, possible sources seem to be in County Durham or in the Lake District around the Vale of Newlands (*c.* 9 km SW of Keswick).'

This is an important but surprising result. The central Lake District shows no evidence of Roman occupation as early as Agricola. If the lead comes from Co Durham or Alston or somewhere in southern Scotland, it would be additional evidence from the very swift exploitation of mineral resources in the wake of military advance.[3]

NOTES

1. R. Stuart, *Caledonia Romana* (1845), 203; Ed. 2 (1852), 206. He refers to Cant's edition of H. Adamson, *The Muses' Threnodie* (Perth, 1774), pp. 21, 25 when other discoveries in a series of deep shafts eroded on the river bank outside the fort of Bertha are recorded shortly before 1774; but the lead pig is not mentioned.
2. R.F. Tylecote, *Metallurgy and Archaeology* (London, 1962), 82 ff.
3. For this see S.S. Frere *Britannia, A History of Roman Britain* (3rd edition, 1987), 276–7.

XII. THE IRON BILLETS

By Rod Clough

Four iron billets or ingots (FIG. 92) were found in the filling of a Flavian drain-trench (p. 88) at the east end of Trench E I (80 E I 26), where they were associated with an iron scythe-blade and axeheads together with a lead pig (pp. 158, 161, 175).

The billets when received were encrusted with corrosion products which included mineralised traces of organic material. They were photographed, measured, and two of the four bars were selected for metallographic analysis.

Two small V-shaped segments were removed from bars 2 and 4 (TABLE 1) and then mounted and polished using standard metallographic techniques and their microstructure was studied in the etched and unetched condition. The etchant used was Nital (2% nitric acid in alcohol).

Unetched, slag inclusions of varying size were evident. The smaller inclusions aligned themselves parallel to the surface indicating the direction of working. The slag was typical of the bloomery process with wustite and fayalite being the predominant mineral phases, along with a small proportion of glassy phase.

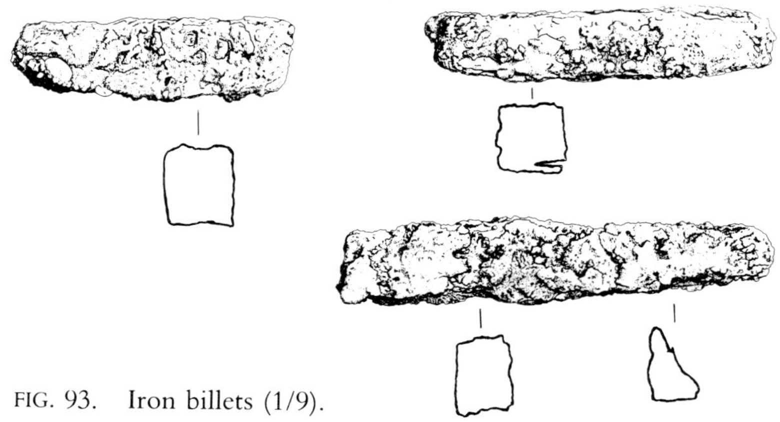

FIG. 93. Iron billets (1/9).

The two billets revealed a similar microstructure on etching. Both samples showed large ferrite grains expected from air-cooling of the finished product. Grain size along with carbon content was variable; the structure ranged from pure ferrite to the eutectoid pearlite, indicating a carbon content from 0.0 – 0.3%.

Microhardness tests were carried out on a Vickers instrument using a 500g load. The microhardness ranged from VH120–150, which is in the region expected from a low-carbon iron.

The weights of the billets (TABLE 1) were within the range of bloom weights typical for Roman bloomery furnaces.[1] From this together with their general morphology and microstructure, it would appear that these billets were the result of rough forging of the bloom in preparation for later reworking into various artefacts.

TABLE VI

APPROXIMATE DIMENSIONS AND WEIGHTS OF THE BILLETS

	Dimensions	*Weight*
1.	30 cm × 6.5 cm × 6.5 cm	7.3 kg
2.	36 cm × 6 cm × 6 cm (narrowing each end to 4 cm × 4 cm	5.7 kg
3.	45 cm × 6 cm × 7 cm (narrowing each end to 3 cm × 3 cm)	6.9 kg
4.	34 cm × 6 cm × 6 cm (narrowing each end to 5 cm × 5 cm)	7.4 kg

1. R F Tylecote, 'Furnaces, Crucibles and Slags', p. 22, in *The Coming of the Iron Age*, Ed. Theodore A Wertime and James D Muhly, Yale University Press, London 1980.

XIII. BAKED-CLAY SLING-BULLETS
(FIG. 94, PL. XXXVIII B)

Groups of baked-clay sling-bullets were found in two separate buildings in the Antonine I fort (pp. 50, 111) in addition to a single example each from the centurion's quarters in Building XVII (Trench 1985 R II 8) and the Antonine I *principia* (74 P I 4). A selection is illustrated in PL. XXXVIII B and FIG. 94.

A. *Building XV*

In the portion of this Building examined in Trench 1983 L I (FIG. 61) the occupation-layer (11) yielded 35 examples, of which ten were complete, the remainder having lost segments from their surfaces or having been broken in half. The complete examples ranged in weight from 34.5 gm

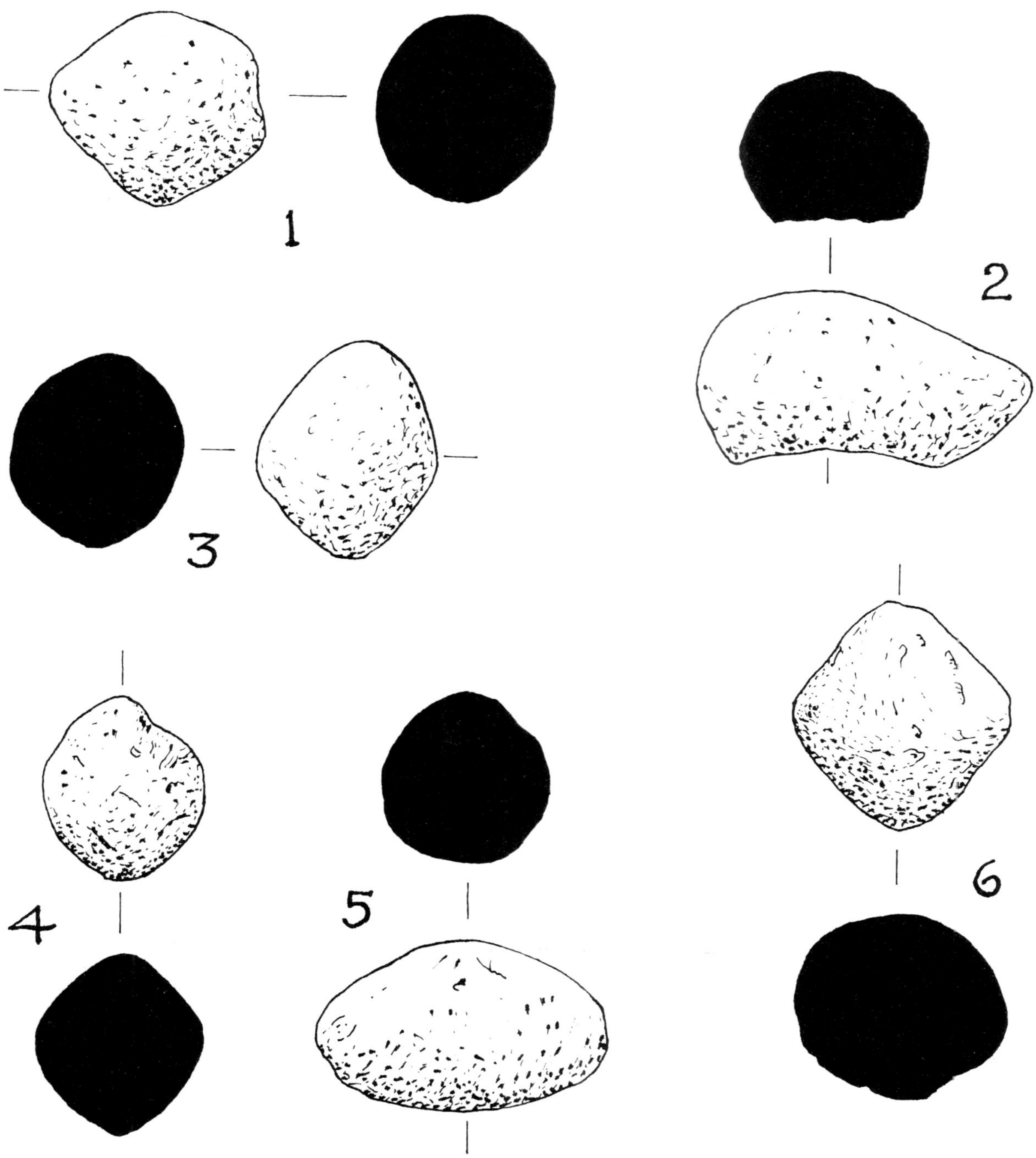

FIG. 94. Baked clay sling-bullets (1/1).

down to 22.3 gm. A further ten examples were recovered from the demolition-layer (L I 5) in the same building. Of these six were complete and ranged in weight from 30 gm down to 18.5 gm. The average weight of all the complete examples in both layers was 28.47 gm. They fall into two classes: (a) with an oval outline and (b) with a double-cone outline. The former weigh *c.* 10 gm more than the latter.

Thirteen further sling-bullets were found in the occupation-layer near the northern end of Building XV in Trench 1984 S I 5, and three more in the Antonine I demolition-layer (1984 S II 2) over the north end of Building XVI, whether they had perhaps been scattered during demolition from the adjoining building.

B. *Central Range, Building B*

Twenty-three similar bullets were found scattered over the south end of Building B in the northern part of the Central Range of the Antonine I fort (FIG. 25). Their distribution is shown on FIG. 26. The same two types were represented.

The number of bullets recovered suggests that they had been stored – and perhaps even manufactured (in view of the many flawed examples) – in both buildings. See further p. 128 and note 27 there.

XIV. THE GEMSTONES (PLS. XXXVII, XXXVIII)

By Martin Henig

1. From 78 B III 3: Antonine I occupation-layer in Building XIV (PL. XXXVII A). Pale orange cornelian. Flat upper face. Shape F1. Chipped on left side and upper face. Dimensions 12.5 × 11 × 2 mm. Remains of iron corrosion on back of stone and within cut areas suggest that the gem was set in an iron ring.
Publ. M. Henig in Rodwell 1980, 93–4 pl. 5.1.
Device: Above a ground-line Cupid approaches a shrine upon a rock, right, his body slightly bent in obeisance. Behind him a female figure wearing a long tunic supports with both hands an offering upon her head. This consists of a tray or basket containing five fruits. Damage to the upper face has removed all but a tiny part of the shrine (above the rocks).

Cupids are frequently portrayed making offerings at shrines, for example on a cornelian from Bath (Henig 1978, No. 114). See also examples in collections at Vienna (Zwierlein-Diehl 1979, No. 1339) and Aquileia (Sena Chiesa 1966, No. 317). The motif is related to other sacro-idyllic themes showing satyrs, maenads and rustic votaries before shrines of Priapus (Guiraud 1974; Henig 1978, Nos. 493–4; Maaskant-Kleibrink 1978, Nos. 347, 491).

The physical appearance of the gem and its style of execution suggest a date in the late first century A.D..

2. From 83 L I 5: Antonine I demolition-layer over Building XV (PL. XXXVII B). Intaglio: olive green jasper, shot through with two black veins, and set in an iron ring.
Ring: hoop incomplete. External diameter 29.5 mm; internal diameter 18 mm; width across bezel 14 mm. Ring Type III.
Intaglio flat with bevelled edge, shape F4; upper face 9 × 8 mm expanding to 11 × 8.5 mm. The gem depicts a goatherd wearing a skin coat, leaning on his staff, watching a goat browsing on a tree. Type as Henig 1978, No. 500 (from Hacheston, Suffolk), Maaskant-Kleibrink 1978, No. 653. Similar gems show herdsmen (?) with their hounds beside trees, e.g. Henig 1978, No. 498. See Guiraud 1982, on gems such as these which portray an idyllic countryside – 'cette vision d'une nature aimable, aménagée, où le berger est un élément du décor au même titre que l'arbre, sont liées à la glyptique elle-même qui est un art de luxe et un art urbain' (p. 45).

Late first century A.D..

3. From 80 E I 3: Antonine II occupation-layer, Building VIII, end room (PL. XXXVIII A).
Nicolo glass intaglio. Flat upper face, bevelled sides. Shape F4.
Dimensions 8 × 6.5 × 1.5 mm.
Device: Ganymede, nude apart from Phrygian cap, stands to the front. He faces left towards the cup (?) which he holds in his right hand. His left arm rests against his *pedum*. His stance is relaxed with his left leg crossed over his right leg. There is a short ground line.

Such representations of Jupiter's cupbearer are well-known and we may note a late Roman marble statuette from Carthage (Gazda 1981); perhaps the stance is dervied from representations of the Praxitelean Apollo Sauroktonos (Horster 1970, 83–91, pls. XVII–XIX).

There are nicolo glass representations of Ganymede from Silchester (Henig 1978, No. 476) and Lockleys, Welwyn (ibid. No. App. 76). Unlike Nos. 1–2, this intaglio is likely to be contemporary with the Antonine occupation of the site.

4. From 1981 F I 25: Flavian demolition-deposit in centurion's quarters, Building IX (PL XXXVIII B).
Nicolo glass intaglio, set in an iron ring.

Ring: corroded. External diameter 17 mm; internal diameter 16 mm; width across bezel 15 mm. Ring Type III.
Intaglio flat with bevelled edge, F2 or F4; upper face *c.* 9 × 8 mm expanding to 12 × 10 mm.

The intaglio depicts a warrior in corselet and tunic standing towards the front. An impression shows him with his right leg bent at the knee and his *sagum* billowing out on his left side. He holds a trophy in his left hand, supporting it on his left shoulder. He seems to hold a spear in his right hand but there is a crack in the glass at this point. There is an exact parallel in glass at Göttingen (Gercke 1970, No. 356. cf. also No. 357): this is in an old collection and without provenance or date. However, a very similar figure appears on a chalcedony intaglio from the Agricolan supply-base at Red House, Corbridge which, like the Strageath gem, is set in an iron ring (Henig 1978, No. App. 156 and idem in Hanson *et al.* 1979, 68 and 70 pl. IX b). I have suggested that the subject is either Mars or his son Romulus.

While it is possible that Nos. 1 and 2 were lost in Antonine times (though they may be residual), in all probability they were cut in the Flavian period and reflect the widespread hopes for renewal amongst the literate classes in the period, after the Civil Wars of 68–70. Gems 1 and 2 demonstrate that the interests and expectations even of men serving in the army were not necessarily different from civilians living in Italy. Gem 4, however, does allude to the needs of the Roman soldier for protection from danger.

The use of iron for the two surviving rings and the trace of iron on the back of one of the loose gems suggests what we would in any case have expected, that they belonged to men lower in rank than the *primus pilus* (in the legions) or the prefect (in the auxiliary regiments). In all likelihood they were the signets of ordinary soldiers.

XV. HAND-MILLS (FIGS. 95–97)

By S.S. Frere

Jacobi's study of the hand-mills from the Saalburg[1] showed that there were two sizes of military hand-mill, a smaller type (diameter *c.* 40 cm) owned in common by each *contubernium* and a larger one (diameter 66–81 cm) by the century as a whole. He quotes inscriptions on querns, such as *C(enturia) C. Rufi* (from Wiesbaden) or *C(enturia) Virei* (from Mainz) which attest the latter, while the Saalburg itself yielded a stone bearing the inscription *Con(tubernium) Brittonis* as an example of the former.[2] The likely association between each centurial barrack and a bread-oven in the *intervallum*[3] suggests that the centurial quern was used to grind flour for the main bread issue, and that the querns of the *contubernia* produced flour for items of individual taste.

Strageath has yielded no examples of the centurial size of millstone, although No. 4 with a diameter of 48.2 cm is exceptionally large for one of *contubernium* size. One lower stone of the smaller (*contubernium*-type) size (No. 15) was found, apparently *in situ*, on the cobbled floor of an Antonine II *contubernium* in Barrack X (p. 98). But quern-stones are easily moved and some types are easily broken. When only fragments are found they are often likely to be residual in their contexts, as is certainly true of portions used as packing-stones in post-holes; but to judge from the frequency of fragments in occupation-layers, lava querns must often have broken in use. Dating the querns is therefore not always a simple matter.

The majority of quern-stones found at Strageath were of Niedermendig lava, imports from the Rhine valley; but this rock fractures so easily, or crumbles under adverse conditions of soil, that few are capable of illustration. A second, smaller group of querns was made from rocks or erratics of local origin; these were all recovered from Antonine contexts, but one (No. 16) may be of Flavian manufacture. A few lava querns may still have been reaching Strageath in the Antonine II period, but the majority are Flavian, with some attributable to the Antonine I period. In the Flavian period there was evidently an enormous export of Niedermendig querns to the Army in Britain.

I. Querns of Niedermendig Lava

Although the number of measurable stones is not statistically significant, such upper stones as can certainly be dated to the Flavian occupation (FIG. 95, Nos. 1–3) have a greater thickness than those examples which on other grounds may be assigned an Antonine date. The figures are as follows:-

Flavian: No. 1, 13.7 cm; No. 2, 8.2 cm; No. 3, 9.7 cm.
Antonine I: No. 7, 6.8 cm; No. 8, 6.2 cm.
Antonine II: No. 11, 5 cm; No. 12, 7 cm.

The upper surfaces of the lower stones (Nos. 4–6, 10, 13) are furnished with radiating grooves to engage the corn-grains, and so are the grinding surfaces of the upper stones (Nos. 1–3, 7–9). But grooves were generally cut also on the upper faces of the upper stones (Nos. [1, 2], 3, 7, 8, [9]) and again round the circumference of both types of stone (Nos. 1, 2, [3], 4, [5], 6, [7], 8, [10], [13]). This is a decorative rather than a functional feature. The grooves were evidently cut with repeated but controlled blows from a hammer and small punch. Their comparatively good state of preservation shows that none of the querns had suffered excessive wear.

The lava querns were of differing sizes; the largest diameter (No. 4, a lower stone) is 48.2 cm, the smallest (No. (c)) is *c.* 25 cm.

1. *Saalburg Jahrbuch* iii (1912) 79–95; cf. L.A. Moritz, *Grain-mills and Flour in Classical Antiquity* (Oxford, 1958), pp. 116, 124.
2. *Saalb. Jahrb.* iii (1912), p. 21, Taf. V, 40.
3. cf. L. Pitts and J.K. St Joseph, *Inchtuthil, The Legionary Fortress* (1985), 200.

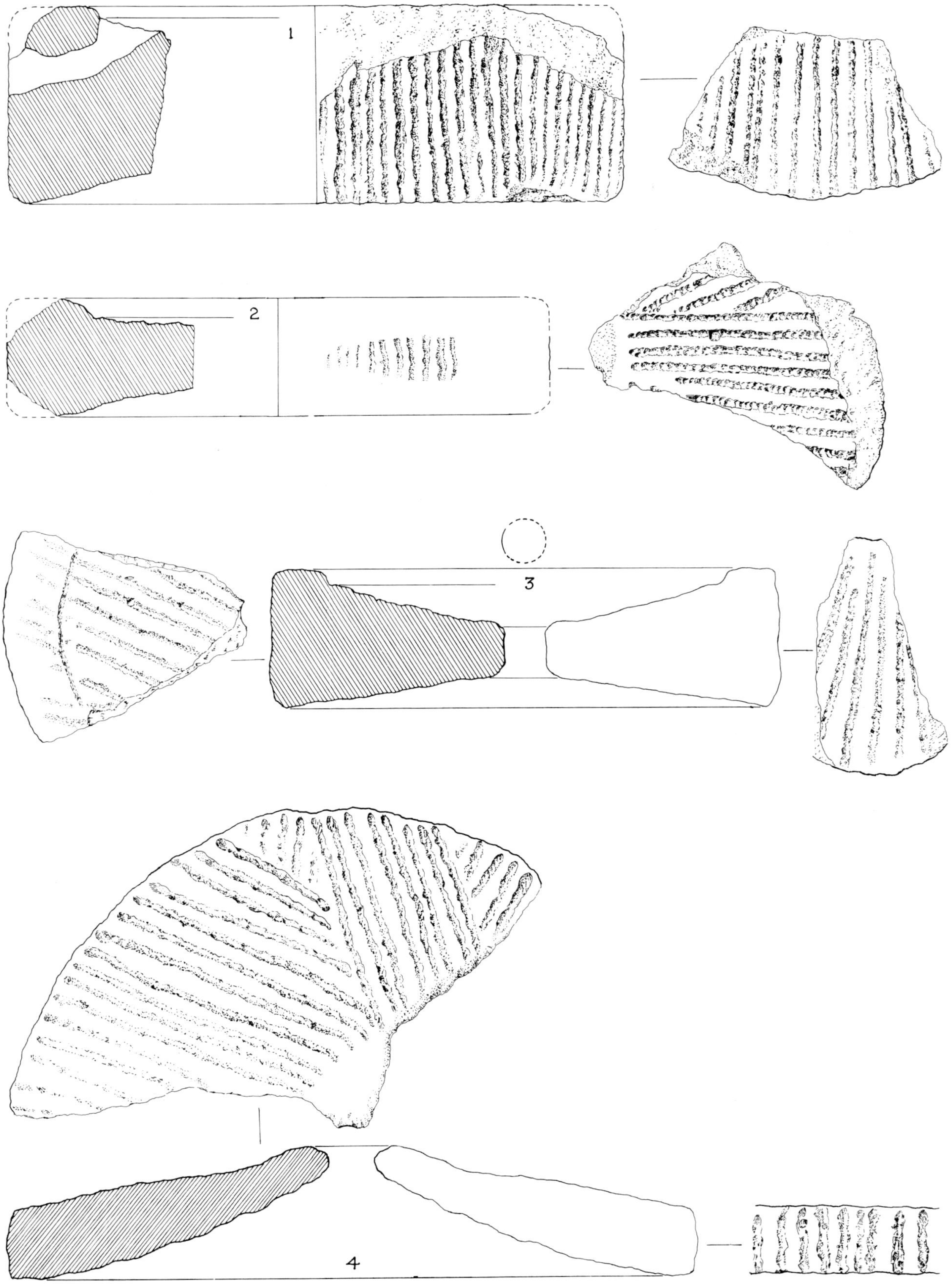

FIG. 95. Hand-mill stones of Niedermendig lava (1/4).

A. *Flavian upper stones*

1. From 1981 F II 26: packer in Antonine I post-hole. Height, 13.7 cm, diameter 43 cm. Radial tooling on upper surface (*not illustrated*) as on lower (*right*) but more shallowly cut, leaving a rough surface. Transverse hole for handle. The upper surface forms a shallow dished hopper surrounded by a low collar.
2. From 1984 S I 5: interface of Flavian demolition-layer and Antonine I occupation. Height, 8.2 cm; diameter *c.* 38 cm. Groups of tooled grooves obliquely arranged on lower (grinding) surface (*right*) and more shallowly on upper surface (*not illustrated*) except on the raised rim. Vertical tooling on circumference (*centre*).
3. From 1983 M I 19; reused in kerb of Antonine I *via sagularis*. Height 9.7 cm, diameter 35.8 cm. Oblique tooling on upper surface (*left*), continued over rim. Radial tooling on lower (grinding) surface (*right*). Vertical lines of tooling on circumference, very worn (*not illustrated*).

Not illustrated

(a) 1978 B VI 19: Flavian occupation-layer. Very worn piece of upper stone with no grooves surviving. Thickness at edge 5.5 cm; width of rim 5 cm; top surface recessed 0.5 cm below the rim.

(b) 1978 B I 43: Flavian wall-trench. Fragment of edge of (?) upper stone with lower surface ground flat. Vertical tooling round circumference.

B. *Flavian lower stones*

4. From 1982 J 26: incorporated in make-up laid down over the sunken top of a Flavian demolition-pit to support the Antonine I *via quintana*. Height 9.0 cm; diameter 48.2 cm. Groups of tooled grooves obliquely arranged on upper (grinding) surface; vertical tooling on circumference (*right*).
5. From 1984 S III 10: Flavian demolition-layer. Height 7.7 cm; diameter 40.4 cm. Irregular group of radial tooling on grinding surface with another group arranged obliquely on the left. Vertical tooling on circumference (*not illustrated*).
6. From 1978 B III 16: Antonine I construction-trench. Small fragment with grooves on grinding surface (*above*) and on circumference. Thickness, 5.6 cm.

Not illustrated

(c) 1978 B I 19: Flavian occupation-level. Large piece of lower stone. Thickness at edge, 5.5 cm, thinning to 5 cm nearer centre. Diameter, *c.* 25 cm. Grinding surface tooled as No. 4. The under-surface is ground flat in a zone *c.* 6 cm wide round the edge for stability, the remainder left rough under the rise.

C. *Antonine I upper stones*

7. From 1983 L II 4: Antonine I occupation-layer. Height 6.8 cm; diameter 38.8 cm. Slightly diagonal tooling on upper surface (*left*), continued over rim; radial on lower (grinding) surface (*right*). The circumference once bore vertical tooling but much has been lost through wear or weathering (*not illustrated*).
8. From 1983 S VI 18: Antonine I pit. Height 6.2 cm; diameter 41 cm. The upper face (*left*) has radial tooling on the rim and groups of tooling at right-angles on face. Vertical tooling on circumference (*right*). Irregular radial tooling on lower (grinding) surface (*right, lower*).
9. (FIG. 97). From 1978 B III 4: Antonine I occupation-layer. Small fragment with remains of rounded socket for handle, outer edge broken away. Faint traces of tooling on top, vertical tooling round circumference (*neither illustrated*).

D. *Antonine I lower stone*

10. (FIG. 96). From 1982 G I 15: Antonine I occupation-layer. Height 6.2 cm; diameter 34.7 cm. Upper (grinding) surface bears groups of tooling arranged obliquely. Slight traces of vertical tooling (*not illustrated*) survive on the circumference, which has suffered from

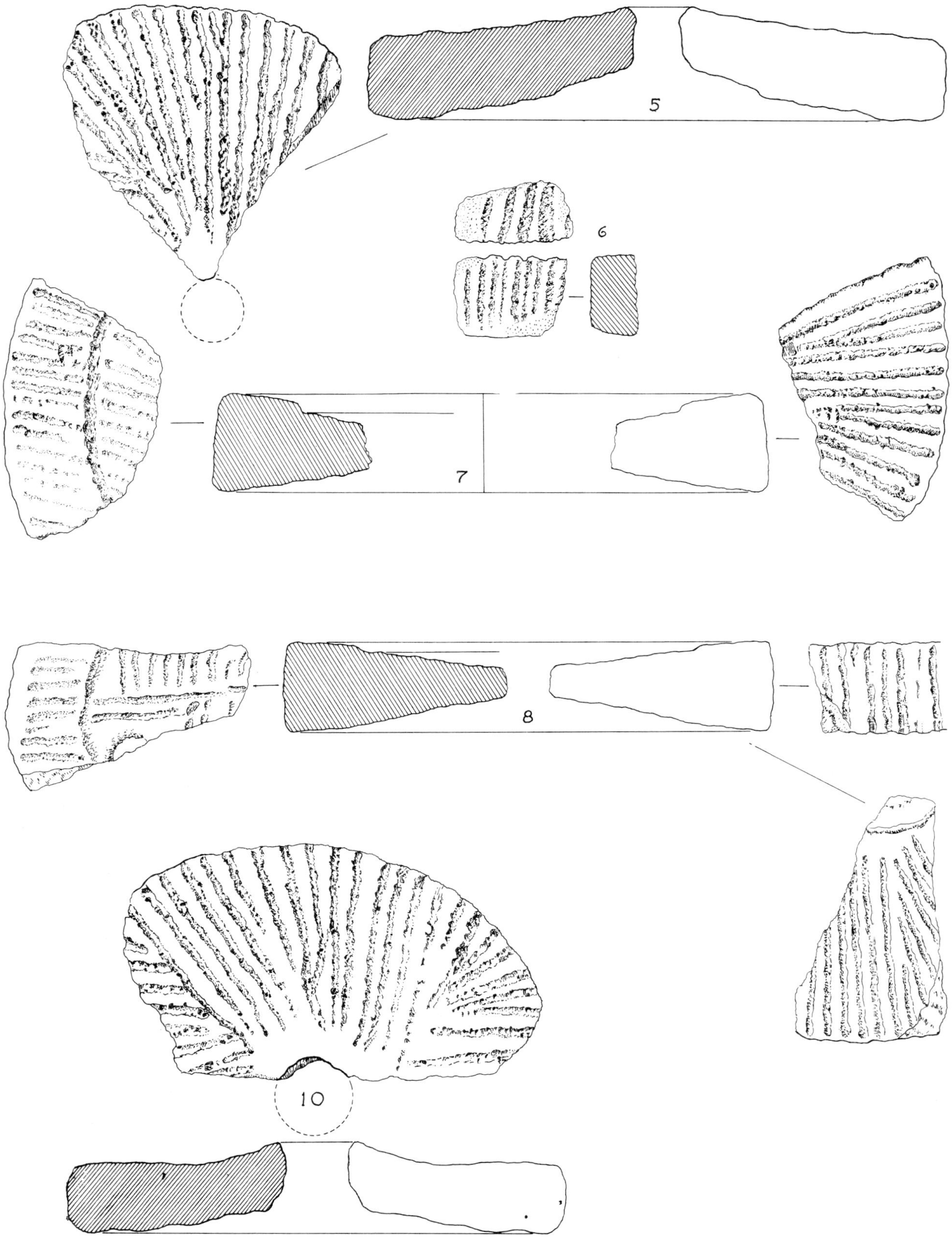

FIG. 96. Hand-mill stones of Niedermendig lava Nos. 5–8 and 10 ($\frac{1}{4}$). For No. 9 see FIG. 97.

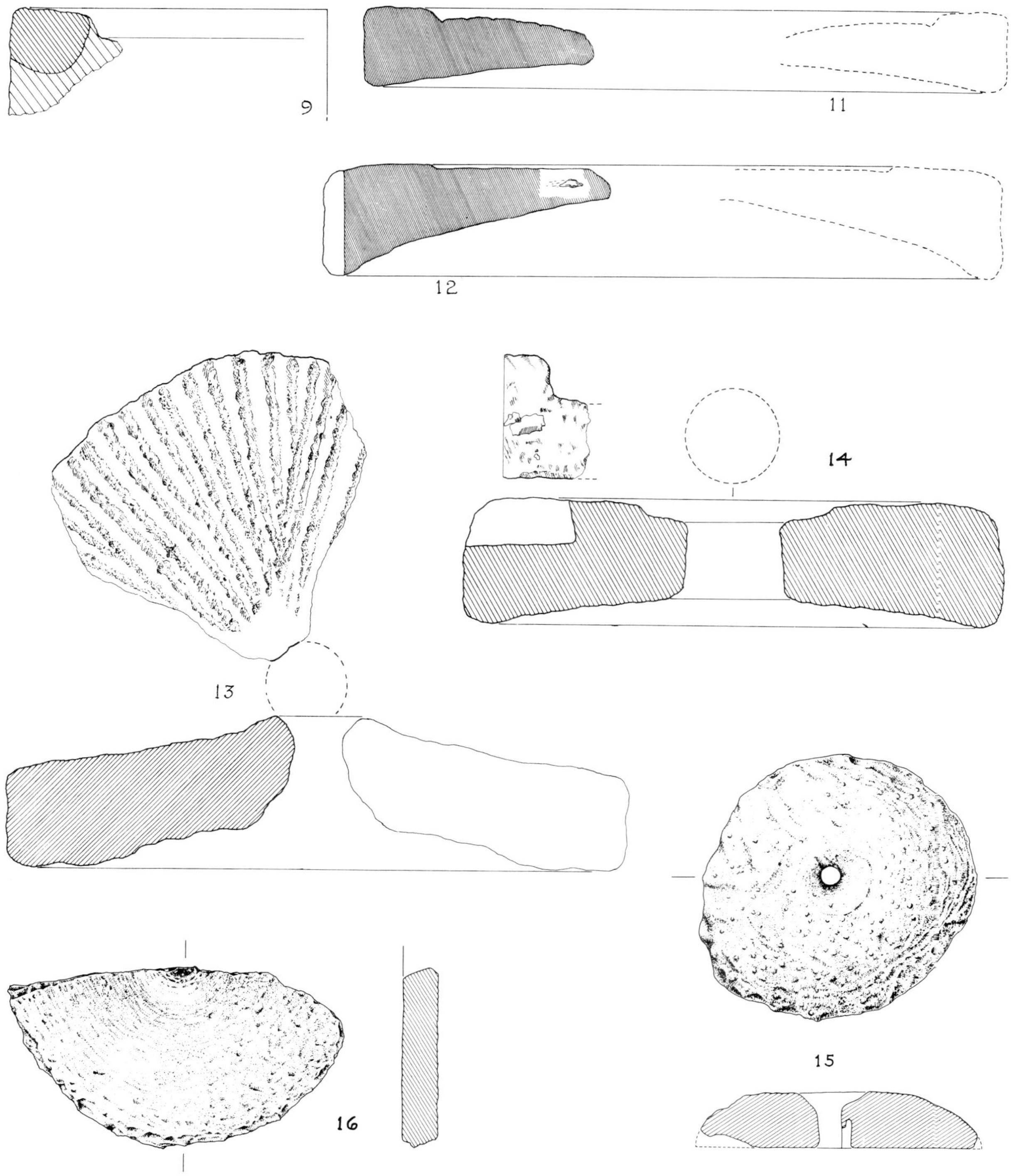

FIG. 97. Hand-mill stones Niedermendig lava Nos. 9, 11–14 (1/4), Nos. 15 and 16 of local stone (1/8).

flaking. A zone 5 cm wide is ground flat at the edge of the under-surface for stability (cf. No. (c) above).

Not illustrated

(d) 1978 B I 21: lower filling of Antonine I Pit A. Lower stone, similar to No. 5. Thickness at edge 4 cm: at centre, 5 cm. Irregular radial grooves on grinding surface, and very weathered vertical grooves on circumference.

(e) 1975 P XLI 20: large fragment on Antonine I floor in *principia*. Lower stone. Diameter *c.* 42 cm. Thickness at edge 4.2 cm; thickness at 13 cm from edge, 3.8 cm.

E. *Antonine II upper stones* (FIG. 97)

11. From 1977 A I 10: upper filling of Pit B. Height 5 cm; diameter 41 cm.
12. From 1977 A II 7: Antonine II floor. Height 7 cm; diameter 43.4 cm. This stone retains part of a chase for the rynd, still containing remains of iron; and carries in the circumference a vertical chase 3 cm wide and 1.3 cm deep as seating for a handle.

F. *Antonine II lower stone*

13. From 1981 F I 20: silt from rampart. Height 9.8 cm; diameter 39.8 cm; not quite circular in outline. Radial tooling on upper (grinding) surface. Vertical tooling (*not illustrated*) on circumference.

II. Querns of local origin

14. From 1981 F II 1: disturbed Antonine II demolition-layer. Nearly half an upper stone (not quite circular in outline) in a brown conglomerate rock with pebble inclusions. Height 8.0 cm; diameter 34.6 cm. Part of a horizontal socket 3 cm deep for the handle survives in the upper surface (cross-section *above*). The surfaces are fairly rough except in the central hole, which is smooth.
15. From 1980 E II 4 (scale ⅛): *in situ* on cobbled floor of the end *contubernium* in Antonine II Barrack X (FIG. 53). Height, 7 cm; maximum diameter, 37 cm. The rock is a coarse-grained garnet-mica-schist containing both muscovite and biotite micas. The rock is common among the metamorphic rocks in Perthshire and to give a close provenance is consequently impossible.[4]
16. From 1980 E II post-hole 52 (scale ⅛): in east wall of Antonine I Building XII. Height, 4.6 cm; diameter, *c.* 44 cm. An orange-coloured granite, probably of Lower Old Red Sandstone age and originating in Aberdeenshire; but it may have been a glacial erratic.[4] The context of this quern suggests a Flavian origin.

4. Thanks are due to Mr G.H. Collins for determining the source of Nos. 15 and 16.

XVI. OTHER OBJECTS OF STONE (FIGS. 98, 99)

By S.S. Frere and Fiona Roe

1. From 1984 S III 13: Antonine I *via sagularis* (so of Flavian origin). Thick lump of red sandstone with squared edges (left and top in FIG.): the lower edge is rough and may have been broken after use. The top surface has been worn smooth and slightly concave (see PL. XXXIX A) by the sharpening of knives or weapons which have also created some transverse grooving.
2. From 1973 II 21: Flavian demolition-layer. Slab of red sandstone with highly polished surface, the result of use for sharpening knives or swords.
3. From 1979 D III 8: Antonine I wall-trench. Piece of buff sandstone, left side squared, upper and lower edges broken. Both faces are smooth, particularly the upper one (figured). A deep groove has been cut down the centre of each face, possibly with a view to separation into two hones. A hone broken vertically beside similar grooves (1981 F I 1) confirms this interpretation.
4. From 1978 B VI 20: Flavian demolition-layer. Piece of red sandstone with smooth unscratched surfaces. Although resembling a hone in outline, it carries shallow wide grooves *c.* 3 cm from each end on all four faces; these appear to have been made deliberately rather than as a result of wear, since the section remains square. Perhaps a hone grooved for attachment to a belt.
5. From 1973 I 31: among remains of Antonine ovens behind rampart. Spherical ball of granite. The shape may be caused by wear in the river, but its transport to the fort suggests intended use as a sling bullet. Another similar from 1977 A I 7, Antonine II occupation-layer (**No. 5A**).
6. From 1978 B I 19: Flavian demolition-layer. Slab of red sandstone broken on three sides; used for sharpening. The upper surface is smoothed and carries scratch-marks near the edge. Several other examples from the fort.
7. From 1981 F II 1: Base of topsoil, so (?) from Antonine II demolition-layer. Roundel of red sandstone, grooved near the edge of the upper surface which is smoother than the lower. Perhaps a trivet.
8. (*not illustrated*). From 1976, unstratified. Piece of red sandstone, water-worn, with incised marks.
9. (FIG. 99). From 1973 II 2: lower ploughsoil. Stone hone, well worn; broken across one end. Fiona Roe writes: 'The material is micaceous sandstone, buff-coloured and fairly fine-grained. Probably a Coal-Measures sandstone obtainable from the midland valley of Scotland or from northern England.'
10. (FIG. 99). From 1976 H II 6: Antonine II floor. Sandstone hone used on all six sides. Length (broken) 8 cm, sides 4 by 4 cm.
11. (*not illustrated*). From 1977 A II 31: Antonine I occupation-layer, Building VIII. Hone of micaceous schist measuring *c.* 11 cm by 3 by 4 cm, worn in all four faces. Dalradian.
12. (*not illustrated*). From 1979 D VII 13. Flavian post-hole, Central Range Building C. Highly polished fragment of siltstone or phyllite; length 8.1 cm, sides 1.8 by 1.9, tapering to 0.9 cm. Fiona Roe writes that it is likely to come from the Dalradian.

Shaft-hole implement (broken)

From 1986 T I 9, Antonine Bath-building (*not illustrated*). Part of a shaft-hole implement with hour-glass perforation; the stone is split in half longitudinally and damaged round the circumference. The surviving surface is worn and relatively flat, curving down towards the edge; it is roughly oval in shape but with one side comparatively straight. Diameters 14.2 and 12 cm; surviving thickness 2 cm. Outer diameter of shaft-hole 4.2 cm; inner, 2 cm.

It is made from a very rough flaking micaceous schist which on macroscopic examination can be seen also to contain chlorite and garnet. The most probable derivation is from the Dalradian schists, obtainable north of the Highland Boundary Fault and less than 10 miles from the site. We are grateful to Fiona Roe for identifying the stone.

Probably of prehistoric date.

Pierced stone discs (FIG. 99)

These are hardly likely in this context to be spindle whorls, and No. 14 is somewhat irregular for that purpose. Perhaps they are weights connected with fishing. We are grateful to Fiona Roe for geological determinations.

13. 1980 E I 19: Flavian occupation-layer in space between Buildings IX and X. Weight: 4.94 gm. Dark grey siltstone, possibly from the Dalradian Aberfoyle slates.
14. 1978 B I 5: Antonine I occupation-layer in Building VI. Weight: 5.83 gm. Grey, banded siltstone, possibly Old Red Sandstone.
15. 1978 B I 4: silt over Antonine II *intervallum*. Weight: 4.45 gm. Buff-coloured, slightly micaceous siltstone, possibly from the Lower Old Red Sandstone.
16. 1981 F I 22: Antonine I occupation-layer in Building X. Old red sandstone. Weight: 28.29 gm.

Another (*not illustrated*) from 1986 T I 3, demolition layer of centurion's quarters, Antonine I Building X. Weight: 14.87 gm. Buff/pink-coloured siltstone with some iron staining. This may derive from the Lower Old Red Sandstone.

There is a possibility that all these discs belong to the Antonine I occupation, for the findspot of No. 13 is only just below (and just outside the wall of) Antonine I Building X, from which also came No. 16. All seem to be made from naturally worn pebbles of varied fine-grained slightly micaceous sandstones which could perhaps have been collected fairly locally from the river Earn.

Glazed Stones

Two pieces of burnt and glazed stone were found in the Antonine II levels of the southern block of the Central Range. Dr Julian Henderson kindly examined them and sent the following report.

Stones can become glazed, or are covered by a vitreous layer, under a variety of circumstances. The chemical requirements for this to occur are a supply of alkali (wood ash), a supply of silica (normally quartz or sand in the crucible or silica-rich stones in the environment) and heat. These conditions are satisfied during almost any high-temperature industrial process. The production of metals such as bronze, iron or brass would provide high temperatures, silica and an alkali source. The general term used to describe these industrial slags is **fuel ash slags**. These slags are chemically distinct from man-made glasses; the composition of glass adhering to glass-making or glass-working crucibles has its own distinctive characteristics, having been manufactured deliberately using a specific recipe for the time and place it was made. The two artefacts submitted for chemical analysis were of interest because of the possibility that they might have resulted from a glass industry at the site.

1. *Bluish glazed stone* (1986 V II 11, Antonine II occupation-layer, Central Range, Southern Block).

The qualitative x-ray fluorescent analysis of the translucent glassy surface of this stone revealed elemental peaks reflecting the formation of a glass: silica, potassium oxide, sodium oxide and minor or trace levels of alumina and magnesium oxide. In addition, relatively high levels of copper and zinc were detected. This composition suggests that brass was made at or near the site and that this fuel ash slag resulted from debris associated with the industry interacting with the hot surface of the silica-rich stone in an environment in which a plant ash provided the alkali for glass formation (probably in or near a furnace).

2. *Green glazed stone* (1986 V II 2, Antonine II occupation-layer, Central Range, Southern Block).

The same major compositional characteristics were detected as found in specimen no. 1 above but copper and zinc were absent from this sample. The principle chemical characteristic of this

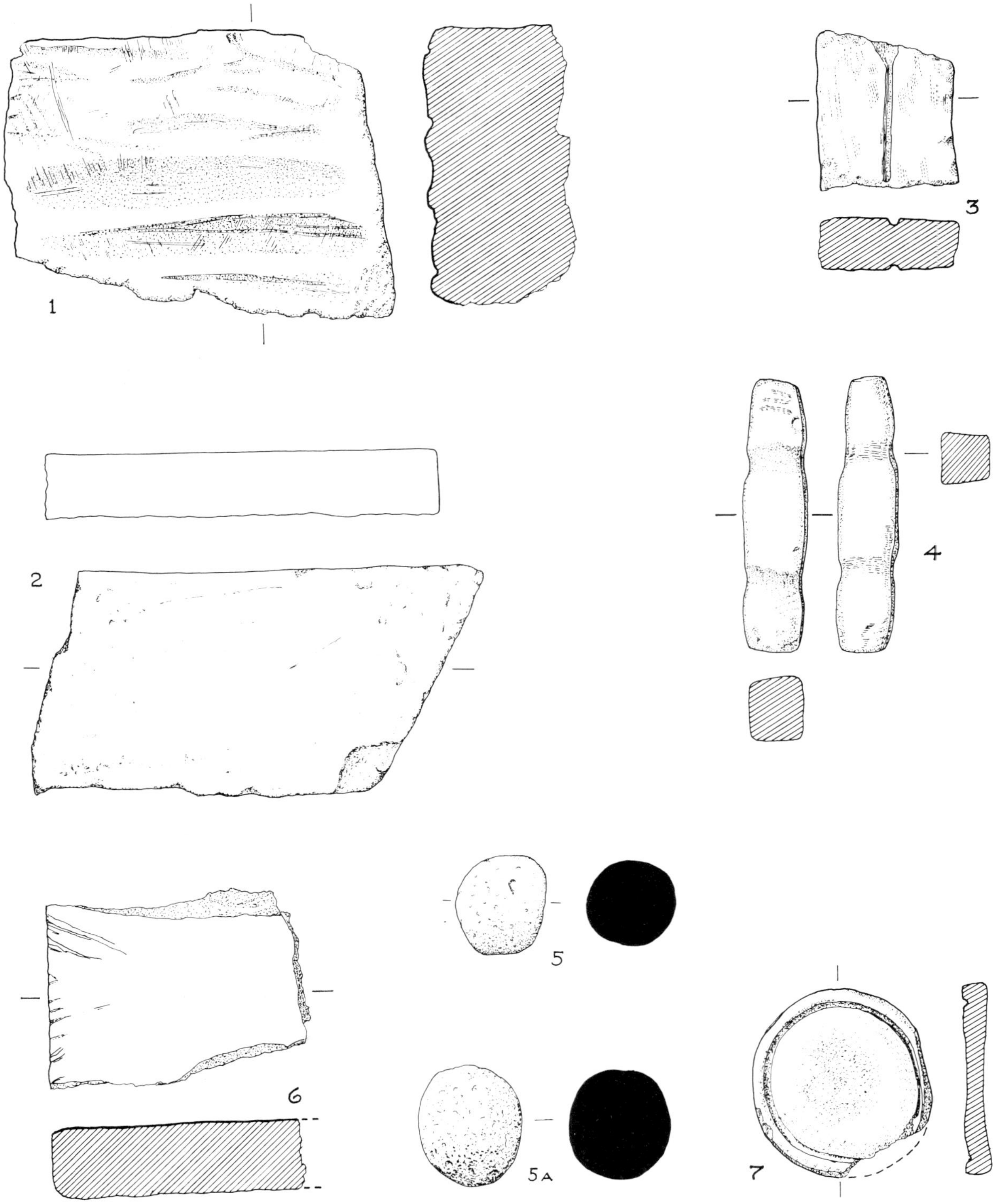

FIG. 98. Other stone objects, Nos. 1–7 ($\frac{1}{3}$).

glass was high barium. The results obtained using x-ray fluorescence analysis (XRF), a surface technique, suggested that the barium was present in the glass as a result of interaction with the underlying rock surface. However the XRF analysis of the unglazed rock surface failed to reveal the presence of barium. Nevertheless the presence of barium in the glass layer could still have resulted from an interaction between the glass and a localised inclusion of barytes immediately below the site of glass formation.

In order to examine this hypothesis in more detail a section was cut through the rock and the barium-rich glass. The sectioned surface was then coated with carbon and examined using a scanning-electron microscope with an energy-dispersive analytical attachment. The sectioned surface was analysed using analytical spots of 3 microns and atomic contrasts observed at magnifications of up to × 5000. A chemical examination of the rock and the covering barium-rich glass revealed that no barium was detectable in the underlying rock. The presence of barium in the glassy fuel-ash slag is therefore difficult to explain.

Pierced discs of baked clay (FIG. 99)

17. 1981 F I 17: Antonine I occupation-layer in Building X. Disc made from the base of a vessel in BB2 ware.
18. 1973 II 2: lower ploughsoil. Disc of baked clay.

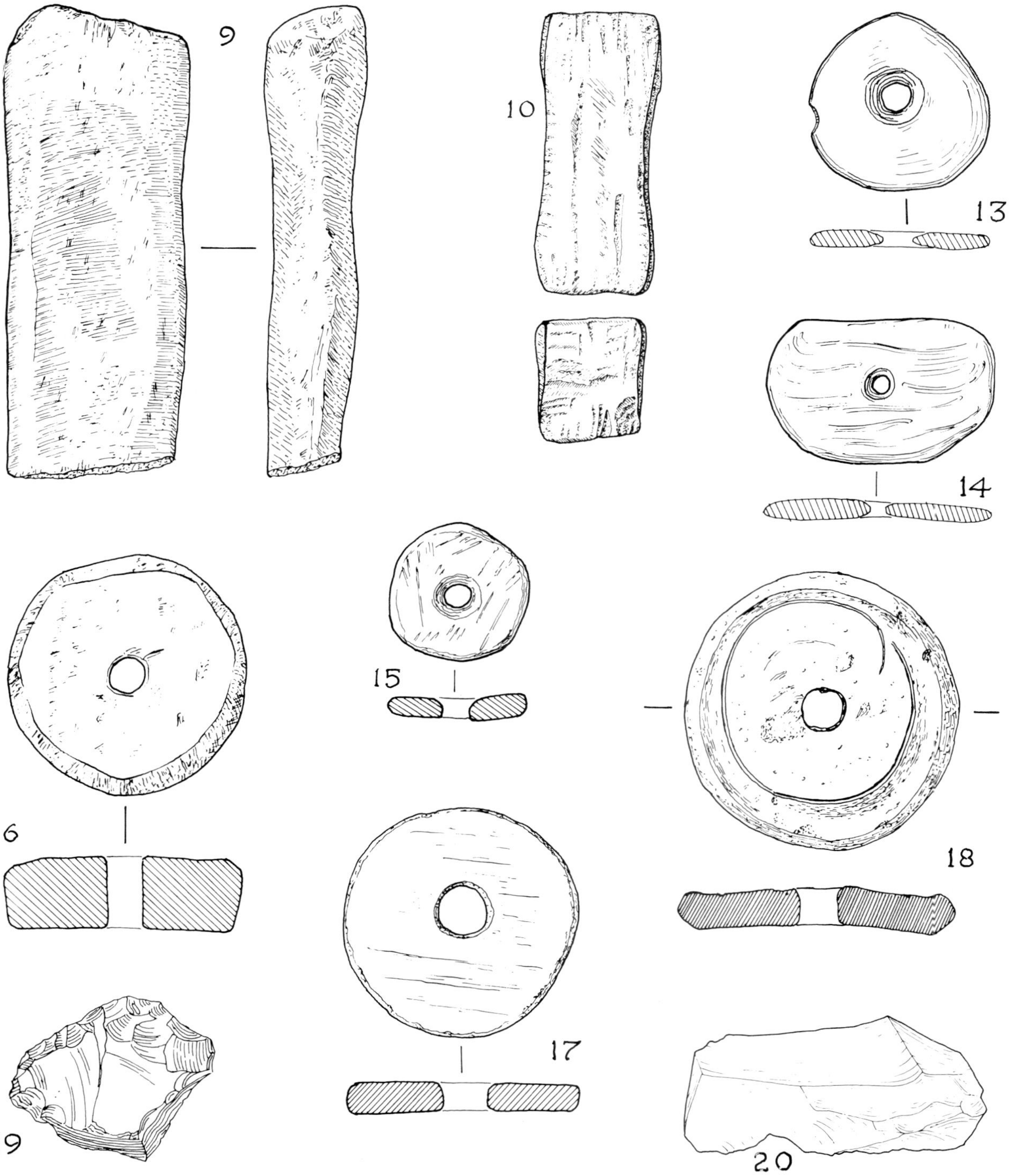

FIG. 99. Objects of stone (9–16), baked clay (17–18) and flint (19–20) (½). For Nos. 19–20 see p. 270.

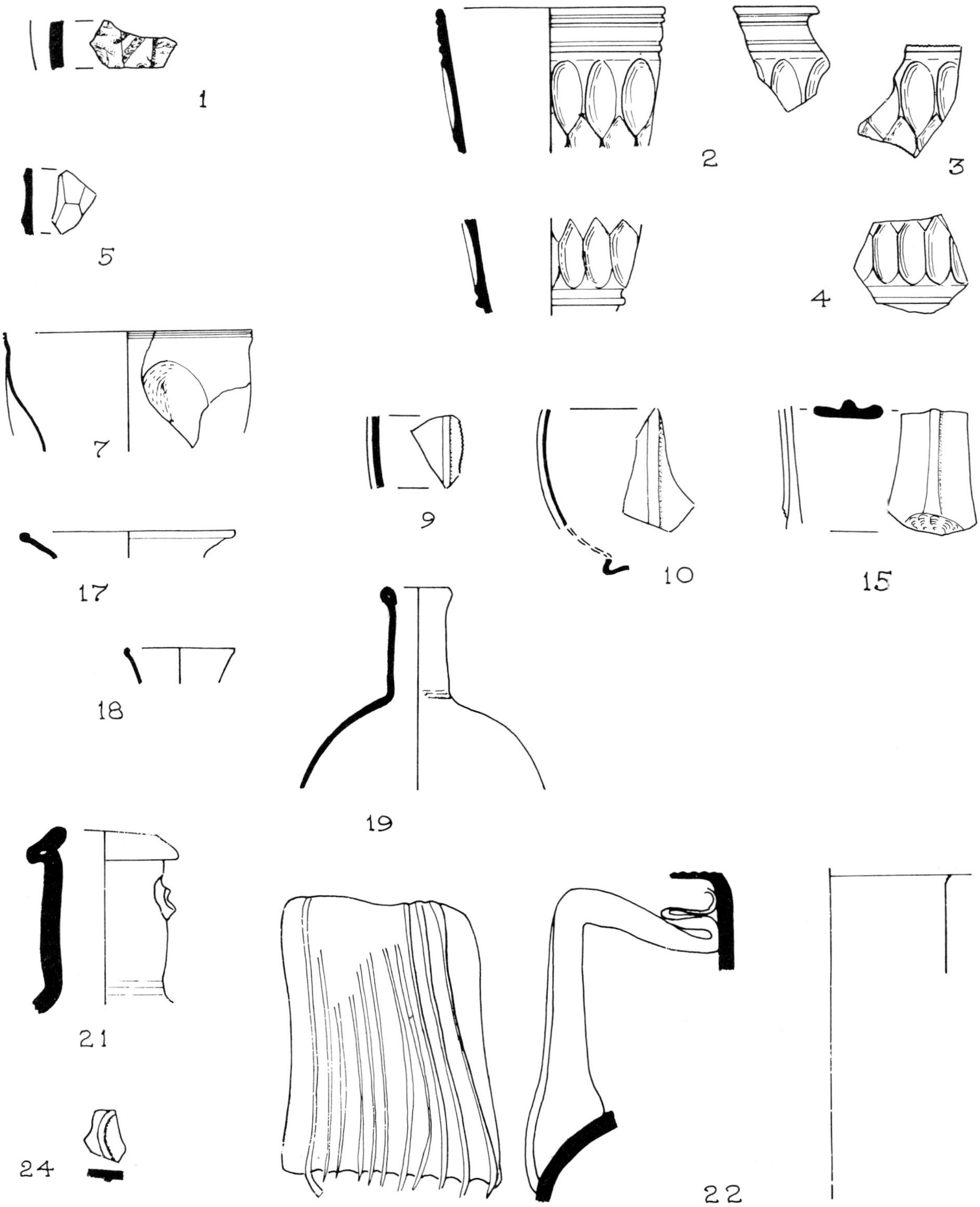

FIG. 100. The Glass Vessels ($\frac{1}{2}$) (*Drawn by Jennifer Price*)

XVII. THE ROMAN GLASS

By Jennifer Price

The excavations produced 436 fragments of Roman glass. Of these, 271 came from vessels and 115 from window panes, the remaining 50 being objects, including 34 frit beads. All the window glass and most of the vessel glass was bluish green (204 fragments), though polychrome (1), dark blue (4), yellowish brown (1), yellowish green (1), greenish colourless (7) and colourless (7) pieces were also found.

The vessel glass has been divided into two principal categories – (a) tablewares, and (b) household wares and containers. Among the tablewares at least ten vessels have been recognised. These are a polychrome bowl, three colourless and one greenish colourless drinking cups, a minimum of four dark blue, yellowish brown, yellowish green and bluish green jugs, and a bluish green globular-bodied jar or jug with open pushed-in base ring. Among the household wares and containers, which are all bluish green, there are at least three flasks and a small jar, one perhaps with indents on the body, as well as 175 bottle fragments. It has been difficult to establish the minimum number of bottles; there may be as few as seven or eight, though it is likely that many more are represented by the surviving fragments. An almost equal number of square and cylindrical bottles occurred in the assemblage (68 and 71 fragments respectively), and there is at least one hexagonal bottle.

The dates of production of the vessel types found at Strageath range from the early or mid first century to the second century, and it is likely that more of them were in use during the Flavian occupation of the fort than in the Antonine phases. This may indicate that less glass was present during the Antonine occupation, perhaps reflecting a change in the pattern of use of glass on military sites, or it may simply mean that there was an organised collection of broken glass for cullet in the later period, but not in the first century. It is interesting that a few vessel fragments (Nos. 3, 9, and 21) show some signs of re-working after breakage, as their edges have been grosed. Of these, No. 3 and possibly No. 9 are from late first-century vessels.

Polychrome pillar-moulded bowls (**No. 1**) are unlikely to have been made much after *circa* A.D. 55–60, and nearly all strongly coloured glass becomes less common from the Flavian period onwards, though yellowish green and yellowish brown vessels, usually jugs (cf. **Nos. 9 and 15**), continue in use into the early second century, and a few specimens are known from mid second-century deposits. Two of the colourless drinking cups (**Nos. 2–4 and 5**), and the greenish colourless one (**No. 7**) were made in the late first or early second century, while the third colourless cup (**No. 6**), an early to mid second-century form, would have been in production during the Antonine period.

The flasks and small jar (**Nos. 17–20**) cannot be closely dated, as they occur at many different dates within the late first and second centuries. Square bottles are also very commonly found on almost all sites occupied from the Neronian period to the end of the second century, but cylindrical bottles (and probably hexagonal bottles as well) disappear early in the second century, and so they are likely to belong to the Flavian phase of occupation.

The objects are also very likely to have been produced in the first or second century, though few are closely dated. It is difficult to assign precise dates to plano-convex counters or gaming pieces or frit melon beads unless they are found in closed contexts (pp. 200 and 202) as they occur on very many sites of different periods. The dating of the glass beads is more widespread; an unusual globular specimen (No. 6) was found in a Flavian pit, the small distorted cube-shaped bead (No. 7) is a type customarily associated with late Roman deposits, and the remaining five (Nos. 8–12), which were found together, are types which were mostly produced in the Iron Age.

The window glass all came from cast panes. Most pieces have rounded edges, though some (see **No. 26**) have grosed edges. Cast window glass was produced in the first and second and perhaps in the early third century.

The only fragment of cast vessel glass comes from a translucent purple *pillar-moulded bowl* with opaque yellow marbling (**No. 1**). Pillar-moulded bowls (Isings 1957, Form 3) are found very widely in the Roman world and occur on many sites in Britain. They were produced in polychrome and brightly monochrome glass, as well as in bluish green glass. The polychrome and brightly-coloured pillar-moulded bowls, in common with most other polychrome and brightly-coloured cast and blown glass, appear to have gone out of production during the Neronian period (see the discussions of this change in production in Harden and Price 1971, 320–3; Price and Cool 1985, 41).

Polychrome bowls are found principally in Claudian and Neronian contexts and are becoming quite rare by the early Flavian period. They have occasionally been noted on military sites in northern Britain established in the Flavian period, as at the St Mary's Abbey site, York (unpublished), Corbridge (Charlesworth 1959a, 36), Newstead (Curle 1911, 272), and Camelon (unpublished), as well as on native sites such as Stanwick (unpublished), Traprain Law (Curle 1931–32, 291 and 358; Stevenson 1954–56, 216) and (?) Tealing (Thorpe 1939–40). This fragment from Strageath is the most northerly find of a polychrome pillar-moulded bowl, apart from the piece said to come from an earth house at Tealing in Angus, and fragments of bluish green bowls are also very scarce in the region north of the Forth-Clyde isthmus apart from a few pieces at Inchtuthil (Price 1985, 304–5), although these continued in production in the early Flavian period.

This colour combination has not often been noted, and it may sometimes have been mistaken for dark brown with opaque yellow. In Britain, similar fragments are known from Mancetter (Price and Cool forthcoming), Spong Hill and Camelon (both unpublished).

Three colourless fragments with *facet-cut decoration* (**Nos. 2–4**) come from a truncated conical beaker, and No. 5 comes from a second example. Colourless glass does not occur in Claudian or early Neronian contexts in Britain, but as polychrome and strongly coloured glass disappeared it became popular, and from the Flavian period onwards was almost always used for tablewares. Cut decoration of various kinds became common at the same time, and facet-cut vessels occur in many parts of the Roman world during the Flavian-Trajanic period. They are fairly frequent finds in Britain (see Price 1985, 303 for a list of fragments from sites occupied in the Flavian period in northern Britain).

Oliver (1984) has recently examined the range of early Roman facet-cut glass, and has noted that there are two principal truncated conical cup forms, tall and short, and that the glasses divide into two groups, one where the facet-cut zone is raised above the level of the undecorated areas near the rim and base, and the second, which has a ridge or wheel-cuts defining ribs above and below the facet-cut zone, which is often, though not always, flush with the undecorated zones.

The Strageath beaker (Nos. 2–4) belongs to Oliver's group 2, and is broadly comparable with a beaker from Salter's Hall, Walbrook, London (Charlesworth 1959a, 42, pl. I, 3; Oliver 1984, 57, No. 91) both in the shape and in the wheel-cut lines on the undecorated areas near the rim and on the lower body. It is, however, difficult to provide close parallels for the style of facet-cutting. The Walbrook beaker also has very large oval facet-cuts in quincunx on the upper body, but only one row of vertical ovals on the lower body; and a small body fragment from the Agricolan supply-base at Red House, Corbridge has similar large oval facets below a horizontal rib (Charlesworth 1979, 58, fig. 20, 1).

The body fragment (**No. 5**) is too small for the certain identification of either the shape of the beaker or the pattern of facet-cutting, though the straight horizontal terminals on the elongated diamond-shaped facets are similar to those on the beaker fragment from Birrens (as illustrated by Ward 1903, fig. 10) and on a small body fragment from the amphitheatre at Caerleon (Wheeler and Wheeler 1928, pl. 34, 6), among many others.

No. 6 is also a small colourless body fragment, but there is little doubt that it has come from a cylindrical or biconical drinking cup with wheel-cut linear decoration. Until comparatively recently these vessels were rarely noticed, chiefly because they have generally been found in very small fragments. It is now becoming increasingly clear that several versions of these cups were in common use in Britain during the early to mid second century. Published examples from many sites, such as Hardknott (Charlesworth 1959b, fig. 3), Verulamium (Charlesworth 1972, fig. 77, 43), Towcester (Price 1980, fig. 14, 4) and Felmongers, Harlow (Price 1987, 188–91, fig. 2, 8–14) show a wide range of body shapes and bases and base-rings.

The date of production of the greenish colourless indented fragment from a cup with wheel-cut lines below the rim (**No. 7**) is more difficult to determine. It is closely comparable with a fragmentary colourless cup from a mid-first century deposit at the bottom of Well 1 at Richborough (Bushe-Fox 1926, 49, pl. 19, 8), except that the Strageath cup has a slightly curved rim; but similar vessels from later first- or early second-century deposits have not been noted in Britain. A colourless indented beaker found in a stone coffin on the Mount, York is thought to date from the third century (Harden 1962, 140, pl. 66, HG180), which suggests that the vessel form was long-lived.

Nos. 9–16 are small pieces from a group of jugs and jars, though it is not always possible to be certain of the precise vessel forms represented. Long-necked jugs with angular handles and globular or conical bodies (Isings 1957, Forms 52 and 55) and globular bodied jars (Isings 1957, Form 67 c) are found only in the regions north of the Alps, with particular concentrations in the lower Rhineland, central and northern France and Britain. They were all produced during the last third of the first and first quarter of the second century, and in Britain at least, some of the jugs continued in use until after the middle of the second century, as at Park St., Towcester (Price 1980, 65–6, fig. 15) and Felmongers, Harlow (Price 1987, 193–5, fig. 3, 20).

Fragments of these vessels are common finds on most Flavian and early second-century sites in Britain, and some complete examples, usually from burials, are also known. Conical jugs may have ribbed or undecorated bodies, and simple concave bases, as at Radnage, Buckinghamshire. (Harden *et al* 1987, No. 68), Grange Road, Winchester (Harden 1967), or Turriff, Aberdeenshire (Thorpe 1933–34), or open base-rings and concave bases, as at Lower Runhams, Lenham, Kent (Monkton 1979, 120. fig. 3), the Bartlow barrows, Ashdon, Essex (Gage 1834, 5, pl. 2, 1), and Park St., Towcester (Price 1980, 65–6, fig. 15). Globular and discoid jugs usually have ribbed bodies, and always have open base-rings and concave bases. They have not been noted as often as conical ones, perhaps because they do not occur in many burials and the body fragments are often indistinguishable from those of globular jars. Examples are known from Littlington, Cambridgeshire (Fox 1923, 189 and 217, pl. 25, 4), Shefford, Bedfordshire (Fox 1923, 213 and 216, pl. 26, 2), and Enfield (Price 1977, 155–58, fig. 27, 2).

Globular jars have wide mouths and vertical folded 'collar' rims, but otherwise their bodies and bases are similar to the globular jugs discussed above. Although some examples with undecorated bodies are known, as in the east cemetery, Wroxeter (Haverfield and Taylor 1908, 240, fig. 32), most have ribbed bodies. These vessels are also frequently found on Flavian to early second-century sites in Britain, both at settlements and in burials, but as yet there is little evidence that they continued in use after this time, except at Park St., Towcester (Price 1980, 66, fig. 16). Finds in closely dated contexts have come from sites such as Verulamium (Charlesworth 1972, 205–6, fig. 76, 25–26), Richborough (Bushe-Fox 1932, 84, pl. 15, 57) and the Lunt, Baginton (Charlesworth 1975, 39, pl. 10a).

Small jars with rims similar to **No. 17** are commonly found in the western provinces in the first to mid second centuries, and they occur on many sites in Britain. There is some evidence that jars of this kind were being made at the second-century glass-working site at Mancetter, Warwickshire (Price and Cool forthcoming). For the most part they occur only in small fragments, but substantially complete examples, sometimes with indented sides (cf. No. 8), are known from Lower Runhams, Lenham (Monkton 1979, 120, fig. 2), and Felmongers, Harlow (Price 1987, 195–6, fig. 3, 23–25).

Nos. 18–20 come from small flasks or unguent bottles. Nos. 18 and 20 are too small for the vessel form to be identified, but No. 19 is a robust, rather carelessly made globular-bodied vessel with a folded rim and short neck. The form is related to the ovoid and globular flasks or unguent bottles found in first- and second-century contexts (Isings 1957, Form 16; see also the discussion of the fragment from Inchtuthil – Price 1985, 307, fig. 93, 10), though exact parallels are hard to find. A long-necked vessel with similar body was found in the Bartlow barrows, Ashdon, Essex (Gage 1836, 304, pl. 33, 4), and a somewhat similar example is known from York (Harden 1962, fig. 89, H.G.49).

It is usual to find that fragments of bluish green containers account for a sizable proportion of the total number of vessel fragments on Romano-British sites of first- and second-century date.

The finds from Strageath illustrate this point well, as 175 out of 271 fragments (64.5%) came from bottles. The two principal body shapes of these bottles are square and cylindrical (Isings 1957, Forms 50 and 51), but hexagonal (**No. 23**) and rectangular versions are also known. Square and cylindrical bottles are extremely common in many parts of the Roman world, particularly the western provinces, and they occur on some sites in Britain from the Claudian period onwards, though they became very popular as containers for liquid and semi-liquid substances from the later Neronian period onwards. Cylindrical bottles appear to have been as common as square bottles in the Flavian period and early years of the second century, as both are found on virtually all the Flavian military sites in northern Britain; but they disappear completely thereafter, leaving square bottles as the main container form used for the rest of the second century.

The Strageath fragments are not large enough for the sizes and proportions of the bottles to be established, though the dimensions of the cylindrical fragment (**No. 22**) are comparable with the tall narrow examples from Newstead (Curle 1911, fig. 36) and Inchtuthil (Price 1985, 307, fig. 94,11). It is curious that only one decorated base fragment from a square bottle (No. 24) was recovered during the excavations.

In the first and second centuries **window glass** was usually made by casting, that is, pouring hot glass into rectangular trays probably made of wood or stone (see Boon 1966 and Harden, 1974). This produced window panes which have thick rounded edges, flat, matt and sometimes pockmarked under-surfaces and shiny uneven upper surfaces. The use of trays to determine the shape of the panes must have allowed window panes to be made to fit their apertures, but it is noteworthy that some panes were also cut down from larger pieces, as these have grosed edges. This finish can be seen on No. 27, and is also visible on two of the four sides of the pane from the bath-house at Garden Hill, Hartfield (Harden 1974).

Window glass appears around the middle of the first century A.D. and becomes increasingly common on Flavian and later military sites, as well as in villas and town buildings. Very little is known about glazed windows in military buildings, though it seems probable that the commandant's house would have had some, and there is frequently some evidence that the windows in rooms of the fort bath-house, especially in the *caldarium*, were glazed. Fragments of matt/glossy window panes were found in most seasons of excavation at Strageath, but the greatest concentration (see No. 25) came from the eaves-drip drain of the bath-house in use in the second Antonine phase of occupation; some these pieces were affected by heat.

The **glass objects** consist of counters or gaming pieces and beads, apart from one small disc with two convex faces (p. 200 and PL. XL A). This is bluish green with a thin layer of opaque red glass on one of the curved faces, and may be a ring bezel, though precise parallels have been difficult to find.

The counters or gaming pieces (p. 200) are the usual 'black' and white plano-convex discs which occur on British sites throughout the Roman period, and are particularly frequent on first- and second-century military sites. As a rule they are found as single finds or in small groups, and it is not possible to establish whether they were used for accounting or as playing pieces, but some larger groups are also known, as at Ravenglass, where seven glass and 119 bone discs were found on the floor of a barrack-block, having been kept together in a container, perhaps of cloth or leather (Potter 1979, 75–6). These are thought to have been used for a board game (Turner 1979), as are the sets of black and white discs found in burials, as at Grange Road, Winchester (Biddle 1967, 244–5, fig. 9) and Ospringe (Whiting *et al* 1931, pl. 56).

The glass beads fall into three groups. No. 6 (FIG. 102, PL. XL A) is rather unusual. It is globular, made in dark blue glass with six prominent translucent green eyes surrounded by opaque yellow arranged in an irregular horizontal band round the centre. Both the bead form and the eye decoration are recorded in Guido's section on Iron Age beads of continental origin or inspiration (Guido 1978, 46–71), though they do not occur on one bead. The colours of the eyes and surrounds are apparently rare in Britain, though Guido (1978, 49–50, 107–110) has listed class three annular beads with green eyes at several sites, such as Whitton, Glamorgan, Gussage Down, Dorset, South Harting, Sussex, Atworth, Wiltshire, and Barbury Castle, Wiltshire, and annular beads with eyes ringed with opaque yellow have been noted from the Marne region, as at

Recy Voie Chantereine. One from Newstead has a blue and yellow striped eye also ringed with opaque yellow (Curle 1911, pl. 91,12).

No. 7 is a small and distorted square-sectioned bead of a type which is usually found in later Roman contexts (Guido 1978, 96 and 212–5, fig. 37,7). A few examples have, however, been noted on military sites with first- and second-century occupation, as at Templeborough, Yorkshire, Great Chesters, Northumberland, and South Shields: so it is possible that at least some of these beads were made at that time.

Nos. 8–12 are small opaque yellow discoid beads which were found close together. These beads are found in pre-Roman Iron Age contexts in many parts of Britain; in Scotland they have been recorded in brochs, forts and crannogs and there is a concentration of them in the Culbin Sands (Moray) area, where they may have been made. A few have also been noted in Roman contexts on native sites, as at Traprain Law and Castle Hill, Dalry, and Guido (1978, 73–6, 179–82, fig. 24) has suggested these beads were produced from around 250 B.C. to around A.D. 50. It is noteworthy that a few examples have come from military sites in northern England, as at South Shields, Corbridge, Halton Chesters and Housesteads, but Guido did not note any from the Roman forts in Scotland.

The thirty-four frit melon beads (p. 202) are typical of the large numbers found in first- and second-century contexts in many parts of the western provinces. Similar beads also occur in the later Roman period, but they are not so common at that time. They were produced in many different sizes and are found on virtually all military sites in Britain. The Strageath melon beads are closely comparable in their sizes and state of preservation with specimens found at Newstead (Curle 1911, Pl. 91, Nos. 2, 4, 7, 9, 14, 15, 22, 27–29, 33 and 34).

CATALOGUE OF THE ROMAN GLASS

Cast vessel

1. 1978 B III 4: Antonine I occupation, Building V. Body fragment, Pillar-Moulded bowl. Translucent purple ground, opaque yellow streaks and chips. Very little weathering. Part of convex curved side, one prominent vertical rib. Inside surface ground and wheel-polished, outside shiny. Dimensions 13.5 by 26 mm; thickness (side) 4.25 mm. Pre-Flavian.

Blown vessels

Facet-cut decoration

2. 1981 F I 17: Antonine I occupation, Building X. Rim fragment, truncated conical drinking cup. Colourless. Very little weathering; very few small bubbles. Vertical rim, edge cracked off and ground smooth, straight side tapering inwards. Outside surface ground away to leave raised moulding at rim, and horizontal rib above row of large vertical oval facet-cuts. Horizontal wheel-polishing marks on ground surfaces, vertical polishing marks in facets. Present height 34 mm; rim diameter 74 mm; thickness 2.75 mm. Flavian-Trajanic.

3. 1978 B I 7: Antonine II street VI/VII. Body fragment, truncated conical drinking cup. Colourless. Very little weathering; very few small bubbles. Part of straight side tapering inwards. Outside surface ground away to leave horizontal rib above two rows of closely-set large vertical oval facet-cuts; second row arranged to form diamonds or hexagons. Horizontal wheel-polishing marks on ground surfaces, vertical polishing marks in facets. Reworked (grosed) broken surfaces at horizontal rib and across facets indicating secondary use for fragment. Present height 37 mm; thickness 3 mm. Flavian-Trajanic.

4. 1978 B I 19: Flavian occupation, Building VIII. Lower body fragment, truncated conical drinking cup. Colourless. Very little weathering, very few small bubbles. Part of straight side tapering inwards. Two rows of closely-set large vertical oval facet-cuts; below this the outside

surface is ground away to leave horizontal rib. Horizontal wheel-polishing marks on ground surfaces, vertical polishing marks in facets. Present height 33 mm; thickness 3.5–5.5 mm. Flavian-Trajanic.

5. 1978 B III (3): Antonine II occupation, Building V. Body fragment, truncated conical drinking cup. Colourless. Dull; very few small bubbles. Small part of straight side. Three rows of closely-set long vertical oval facet-cuts arranged in quincunx to produce hexagons. Vertical polishing marks in facets. Dimensions 21 by 13 mm; thickness 2.25–2.75 mm. Flavian-Trajanic.

Linear cut decoration
6. 1984 S I (14): Flavian wall-trench, Building XIII (*not illustrated*). Body fragment, drinking cup. Colourless. Strain cracks, otherwise little weathering; very few small bubbles. Part of slightly convex curved side expanding out. Three narrow horizontal wheel-cut lines in band. Dimensions 20.5 by 14.5 mm; thickness 1–1.25 mm. Flavian-Trajanic.

Linear cut decoration and indents
7. 1978 B I 5: Antonine I occupation, Building V. Rim fragment, indented drinking cup, greenish colourless. Very little weathering; some bubbles. Small curved rim, edge cracked off and ground, convex curved side. Two closely-set narrow horizontal wheel-cut lines at rim, parts of two deep oval indents on body. Dull in cut area, vertical tool mark in indent. Present height 39 mm; rim diameter 80 mm; thickness 0.5–1.5 mm.

Indented decoration
8. 1983 L III 7: Antonine I occupation, *intervallum* space (*not illustrated*). Body fragment, indented vessel. Blue-green. Little weathering; some small bubbles. Part of curved side with oval indent. Dimensions 19 by 29.5 mm; thickness 1.5 mm.

Ribbed decoration
9. 74 P III 5: Antonine I wall-trench, *principia* Room 6. Body fragment, conical jug (?). Yellow-green. Dull; few small bubbles. Part of slightly convex curved side, narrow vertical rib. One edge grosed. Dimensions 22 by 15 mm; thickness 2–2.75 mm.

10. 78 B I 5: Antonine I occupation, Building VII; B I 13; Antonine I occupation, Building VIII; and 78 B I 19: Flavian occupation, Building VIII. Eighteen body and one base fragments, some joining, globular jar or jug. Blue-green. Little weathering; bubbles throughout. Part of convex curved side with broad vertical ribs, open pushed-in base ring. Present height (largest fragment) 57 mm; thickness 0.4–1.25 mm.

11. 73 II Trench 5: Flavian wall-trench, Building I (*not illustrated*). Ribbed body fragment. Blue-green. Little visible weathering; heat affected; few small bubbles. Part of distorted convex curved side with one rib. Dimensions 29 by 24 mm; thickness 0.8–1.8 mm.

12. 73 II 3: unstratified (*not illustrated*). Ribbed body fragment. Blue-green. No visible weathering; few bubbles. Part of convex curved side with one rib. Dimensions 17.5 by 11 mm; thickness 1 mm.

Undecorated
13. 1985 N II 4: Antonine II *via sagularis* (*not illustrated*). Lower body and base fragment, jar or jug (?). Dark blue. Dull; some bubbles. Part of wide lower body tapering in to constriction above open base-ring (missing). Present height *c.* 12 mm; thickness 2 mm.

14. 1977 A I 50: Antonine I demolition debris in mouth of Pit C (*not illustrated*). Handle fragment, jug (?). Dark blue. Dull; bubbly. Very small part of ribbon handle with vertical ribs. Dimensions 14 by 12 mm.

Also (*not illustrated*):
a. 1975 P XLI Posthole 10: Flavian post-hole, *principia*, Room 3; chip. Dark blue. Dimensions 6 by 5.5 mm.
b. 1986 V II 5: Antonine I drain, Central Range, South; body fragment. Dark blue. Dimensions 18 by 16 mm.

15. 1982 H I 2: Antonine II occupation, Building IV. Handle fragment, jug. Yellow-brown. Little weathering; bubbly. Lower part of angular ribbon handle with central rib. Present height 40 mm; maximum width 29.5 mm.

16. 1983 L I 5: Antonine I demolition, Buildings XIV, XV (*not illustrated*). Three joining fragments, lower body and base, conical jug (?). Pale green. Little weathering; some small bubbles. Straight side expanding out above concave base (missing). Present height *c.* 22 mm; base diameter *c.* 140 mm; thickness 2–2.5 mm.

17. 1982 G I 26: Antonine I demolition, Building II. Rim fragment, jar. Blue-green. Dull; small bubbles. Folded rim, edge rolled in, funnel mouth tapering inwards. Present height 9 mm; rim diameter 70 mm; thickness 1.25 mm.

18. 1979 D V 2: Antonine I demolition, Central Range, Building C. Rim fragment, flask or jug (?). Pale blue-green. Little weathering; small bubbles. Folded rim, edge rolled in, funnel mouth tapering in. Present height 12 mm; rim diameter 36 mm; thickness 0.8 mm.

19. 1977 A III 5: Flavian pit on western berm. Two joining fragments, rim, neck and body, globular flask. Blue-green. No weathering; black streaks and specks. Folded rim, edge bent out, up, in and flattened inside, short cylindrical neck, tooling marks at junction with wide convex curved body. Present height 66 mm; rim diameter 24 mm; thickness 1–2.5 mm.

20. 1984 S III 1: Antonine II occupation, Building XIII (*not illustrated*). Rim fragment, flask or unguent bottle (?). Blue-green. Dull; small bubbles. Small part of rolled rim, edge bent out, up and flattened. Present height 6 mm; rim diameter *c.* 40 mm; thickness 2 mm.

Bottles

21. 1977 A I 22: Flavian filling, Pit A. Rim and neck fragment, bottle. Blue-green. Dull; bubbles. Folded rim, edge bent out, up and in, and flattened diagonally, short cylindrical neck, tooling marks at junction with shoulder. Scar from upper attachment of handle on neck below rim; horizontal wear marks around neck. Broken edges of neck grosed (?). Present height 52 mm; rim diameter 52.5 mm; thickness 6.5 mm.

Also (*not illustrated*):
a. 1978 B III 10: Antonine I demolition, Building V; rim fragment, as 21.

22. 1977 A II 37A: Antonine I occupation, *intervallum* space. Rim, neck, shoulder and handle fragment, cylindrical bottle. Blue-green. Little visible weathering; some bubbles. Part of underside of folded rim, wide cylindrical neck, convex curved sloping shoulder, straight-sided upper body with cylindrical section. Broad angular reeded ribbon handle applied to shoulder and attached to neck below rim, 11 points pulled down on shoulder. Present height 115 mm; neck diameter *c.* 70 mm; thickness 4.5–6 mm.

Also (*not illustrated*):
a. 1977 A I 3: Antonine II demolition, Buildings V and VI; neck fragment, bottle.
b. 1977 A II 7: Antonine II floor, Building VII, handle fragment, bottle.

23. 1974 P II 3: Antonine I occupation, *principia*, Room 10 (*not illustrated*). Body fragment,

hexagonal bottle. Blue-green. Dull; some bubbles. Small part of two faces with angle. Wear marks on angle. Dimensions 28 by 29 mm; thickness 3 mm.

24. 1977 A I 20: Antonine II make-up over Pit C. Base fragment, square bottle. Blue-green. Dull, strain cracks; bubbles. Concave base, one raised concentric circle. Dimensions 17 by 14 mm; thickness 4 mm.

Window glass

25. 1986 T I 9: Antonine II bath-house eaves-drip drain. Thirty-eight fragments, some joining. Blue-green. No weathering (some pieces affected by heat). Upper surface shiny, uneven with depressions near edge, lower surface matt, pockmarked, with some evidence of striations in mould. Edges rounded. No evidence for method of holding window pane in frame. Dimensions (largest fragment) 177 by 218 mm; thickness 1.5–5 mm.

26. 1983 L II 1: Antonine II occupation, Buildings XVI, XVII. Fragment. Blue-green. No weathering. Upper surface shiny, lower surface matt and pockmarked. Two edges and right-angle at corner grosed. No evidence for method of holding window pane in frame Dimensions 54 by 41 mm; thickness 3.5 mm.

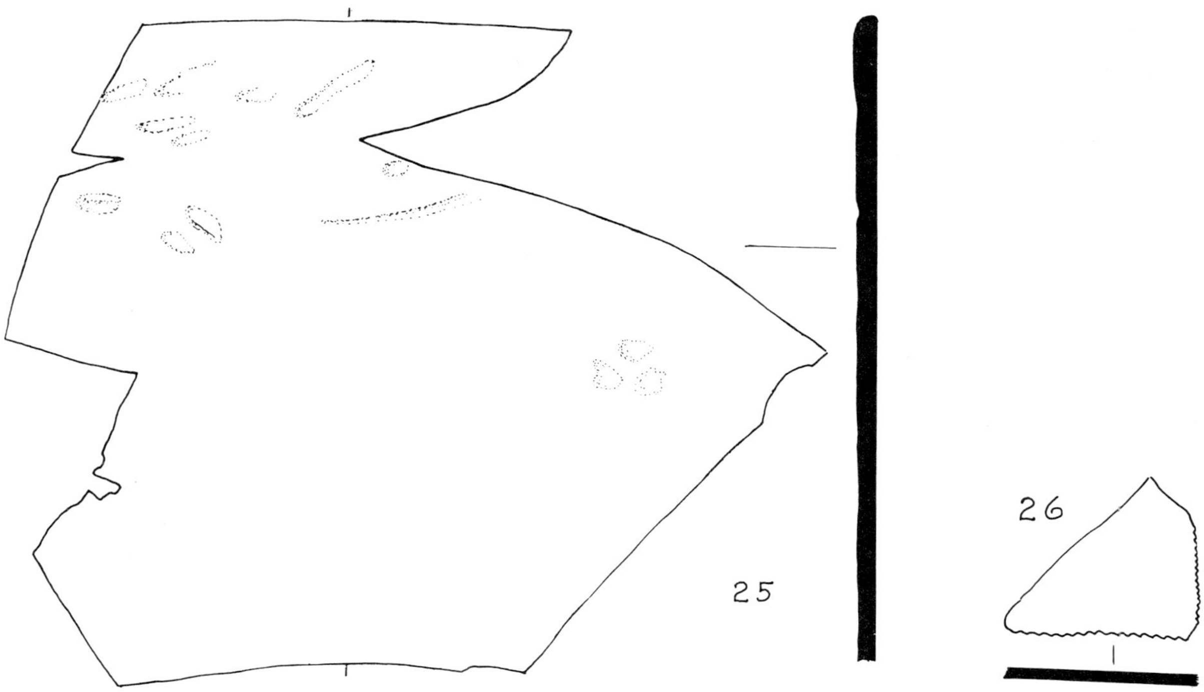

FIG. 101. Window-glass (½) (*Drawn by Jennifer Price*);

Other objects of glass

Glass gem-stone (PL. XL A)
1979 D III Extension, 16: Flavian occupation-layer Building V. Circular translucent bluish green glass gemstone from the bezel of a finger-ring. The lower surface retains an opaque buff deposit containing minute pieces of red glass which may be the remains of the paste cement which once held it in place. Diameter 11 mm.

Glass gaming counters (FIG. 102)

1. From 1978 B I: unstratified. Blue-black glass. Diameter 20 mm.
2. From 1974 P XI 4: Antonine I demolition-layer in *principia*. White glass. Diameter 18 mm.

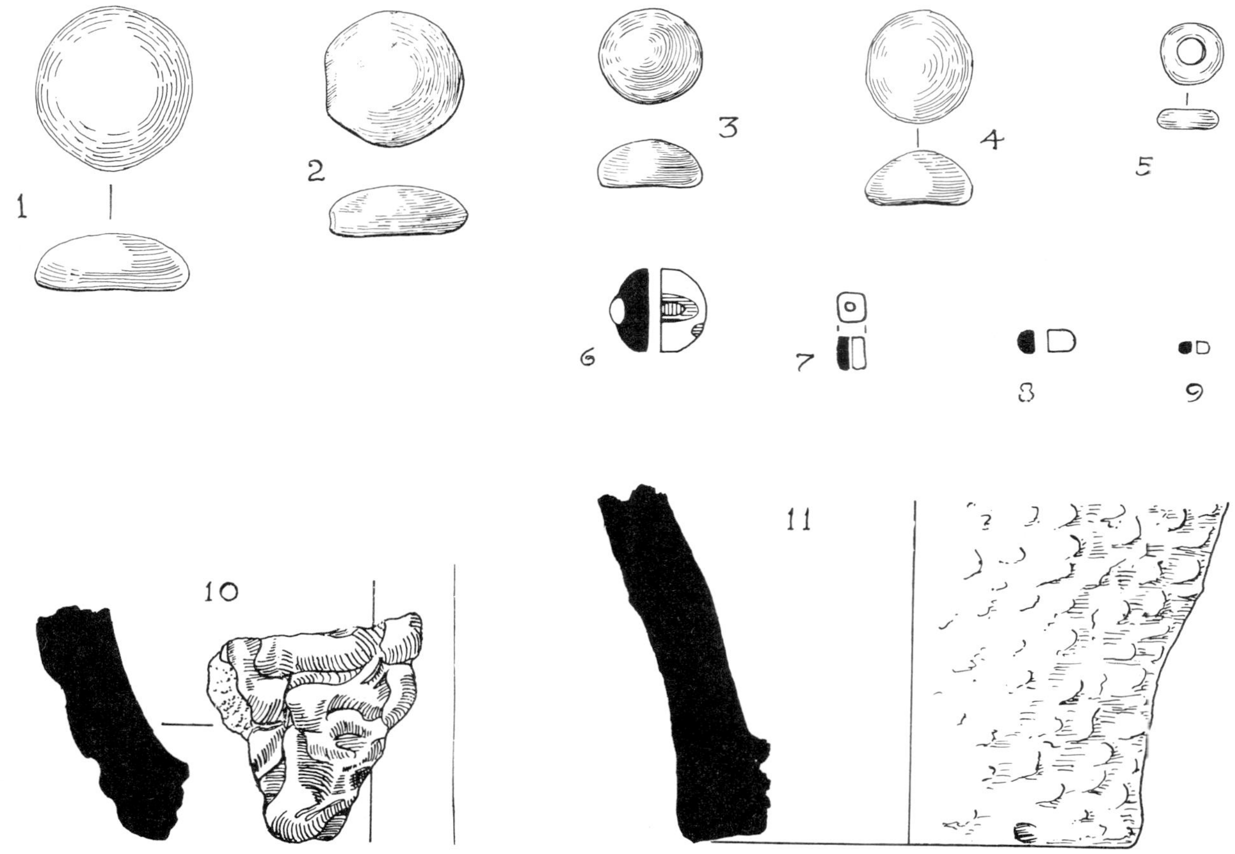

FIG. 102. Glass gaming-counters and beads, and clay crucibles (½).

3. From 1973 I 49: charcoal deposit on back of rampart. Blue-black glass. Diameter 14 mm.
4. From 1978 B III 4: Antonine I occupation-layer. White glass. Diameter 14 mm.

Not illustrated: blue-black glass

(a,b) 1978 B III 4 (two): Antonine I occupation. Diameters 15 mm, 16 mm (oval). With. Nos. 4 and (h).
(c) 1979 D VI 4: Antonine I occupation, Central Range, Building C. Diameter 13 mm.
(d) 1981 F II 1: unstratified. Oval, 17 by 15 mm.
(e) 1984 S III 4: Antonine I demolition layer in Building XVII. Diameter 15 mm. With No. (t).

Not illustrated: white glass

(f) 1974 P XXX 1: unstratified above *principia*. Diameter 16 mm.
(g) 1977 A I 9: Antonine I occupation. Diameter 13 mm.
(h) 1978 B III 4: Antonine I occupation. Diameter 20 mm. With. Nos. 4 and (a), (b).
(i) 1978 B V 4: Flavian demolition. Diameter 16 mm.
(j, k) 1979 D III 3 (two): Postholes, Antonine I, Building V. Diameters 14, 15 mm.
(l) 1979 D III 6: Antonine I wall-trench, Building V. Diameter 18 mm.
(m) 1979 D III 7: Antonine I wall-trench, Building V. Diameter 13 mm.
(n) 1979 D VI 3: Antonine I demolition, Central Range, Building C. Diameter 12 mm.
(o) 1979 D VIII 2: Antonine I demolition, Central Range, Building A. Fragment.
(p) 1981 F II 31: Antonine I demolition-pit 2. Diameter 20 mm (oval).
(q) 1982 J 1: ploughsoil. Diameter 20 mm.
(r) 1984 S I 1: unstratified. Diameter 12 mm.
(s) 1984 S I 10: Antonine I demolition-pit. Oval, 17 by 15 mm.
(t) 1984 S III 4: Antonine I demolition-layer in Building XVII. Broken; diameter 18 mm. With No. (e).

It is noteworthy that almost all the counters come from Antonine I deposits.

Glass Beads (FIG. 102, PL. XL A)

5. 1983 L II 4: Antonine I occupation, Building XVII. Opaque light yellow glass. Diameter 8.5 mm.
6. 1980 E II Pit 1: Flavian (PL. XL A). Globular bead. Translucent dark blue ground, six opaque yellow 'eyes' with translucent green centres. Dull. Large perforation. Height 11 mm; maximum diameter 12.5 mm; perforation diameter 4 mm.
7. 1978 B III 3: Antonine II occupation, Building V (PL. XL A). Small square-sectioned bead. Opaque bright blue. Rather distorted. Length 4 mm; sides 3.5 by 3.8 mm.
8. 1985 R II 5: Antonine I demolition, Building XVII (PL. XL A). Fragment, annular bead. Opaque yellow. Approximately 50% of bead. Flattened upper and lower surfaces. Large perforation. Height 3 mm; diameter 7.5 mm; perforation diameter 2.8 mm.
9. 1985 R II 5: context as No. 8 (PL. XL A). Small annular bead. Opaque yellow. Flattened upper and lower surfaces. Very small perforation. Height 1.9 mm; diameter 4.5 mm.
10. (*not drawn*). 1985 R II 5: context as No. 8 (PL. XL A) Small annular bead. Opaque yellow. Flattened upper and lower surfaces. Very small perforation. Height 2 mm; diameter 4.2 mm.
11. (*not drawn*) 1985 R II 5: context as No. 8 (PL. XL A) Small annular bead. Opaque yellow. Flattened upper and lower surfaces. Very small perforation. Height 1.75 mm; diameter 5 mm.
12. (*not drawn*). 1985 R II 5: context as No. 8 (PL. XL A) Small annular bead. Opaque yellow. Flattened upper and lower surfaces. Very small perforation. Height 1.8 mm; diameter 4.8 mm.

Frit Melon Beads (*not illustrated*)

1. 1973 I 2: unstratified fragment.
2. 1973 II 2: unstratified fragment.
3. 1973 II 11: make-up, Antonine II drain. Fragment.
4. 1974 P VIII 4: Flavian occupation in *principia*. Fragment.
5. 1975 G IV 22: Antonine I deposit, *porta decumana*. Fragment.
6. 1977 A II 17: Antonine I occupation, Building VIII. Diameter 11 mm.
7. 1977 A II 8A: Antonine II occupation, Building VII. Diameter 16 mm.
8. 1977 A II 12: Antonine I demolition, Building VIII. Diameter 13 mm.
9. 1977 A II 26B: Antonine I drain. Diameter 28 mm.
10. 1978 B V 6: Flavian demolition-pit, Building V. Fragment.
11. 1978 B VII 4: Proto-Flavian granary-trench. Diameter 14 mm.
12. 1979 D III 4: Flavian occupation, Building V. Diameter 15.5 mm.
13. 1979 D V 17: Flavian pit. Fragment.
14. 1980 E I 16: Antonine I occupation-layer between Building IX and the *via sagularis*. Diameter 22 mm.
15. 1980 E I 19: Flavian occupation, Building X. Fragment.
16. 1980 E II 11: Antonine I occupation, Building XI. Diameter 10 mm.
17. 1980 E II 14: Flavian demolition, Building XII. Diameter 16.7 mm.
18. 1981 F II 11: Antonine I occupation, Building XI. Fragment.

19,20. 1981 F II 20 (two): Flavian occupation, Building XI. Diameters 18 and 20 mm.

21. 1981 F II 26: Antonine I demolition layer, Building XII. Fragment.
22. 1982 G II 8: Antonine II demolition, Building IV. Fragment. Diameter *c.* 25 mm.
23. 1983 L I 5: Antonine I demolition, Buildings XIV, XV.
24. 1983 M I 22A: Antonine I demolition deposit in *intervallum* area.
25. 1984 S I 2: Antonine I demolition, Building XIII.
26. 1984 S I 10: Antonine I filling of Pit E.

27. 1984 S III 5: Antonine I demolition layer, *intervallum* area.
28. 1985 R I 5: Antonine I demolition, Building XVII. Fragment.
29. 1986 V I 1: topsoil.
30. 1986 V I 2: Antonine I demolition, Central Range, Building B.
31. 1986 V I 5: Antonine I demolition, Central Range, Building B.
32,33 1986 V II 13 (two): Antonine I demolition-pit, Central Range, Building C.
34. 1986 V II 14: Flavian wall-trench, Central Range, Building D.

XVIII. THE CRUCIBLES

(FIG. 102 Nos. 10, 11)

10. From 1984 S I 6: Antonine I post-hole in Building XV. Small fragment near the base of a crucible. Smooth grey interior surface, exterior rusticated and burnt black; finer smoother paste than No. 11, fired grey.
11. From 1983 L II 3: Antonine I occupation, Building XVI. Base angle of crucible. Rough whitish granular paste; fired light grey outside and dark grey inside.

XIX. LIST OF SAMIAN SHERDS

By S.S. Frere and B.R. Hartley

The samian found during the excavations was identified by Mr. B.R. Hartley and is listed below. The decorated sherds which are illustrated on FIGS. 105–6 are indicated thus: D1, D2 etc. and the samian potters' stamps (S1, S2 etc.) are illustrated on FIG. 104. Mr Hartley's comments on these pieces follow the list.

Context	*Samian*
1973	
I, 2, old ploughsoil	33, C.G. Antonine
11, over Antonine II rampart	Dish, S.G. Flavian
17, debris over Antonine II ovens	15/17 or 18 footing (burnt), S.G. Flavian 31 (heavily burnt), Antonine
18, Antonine I, intervallum	37 (**D1**), C.G., with scroll in the Cerialis-Cinnamus style, *c.* A.D. 140–170
37, inner ditch	18/31 stamped by Carillus ii (**S1**), S.G., *c.* A.D.. 70–85
46, Antonine II oven	31, C.G. Antonine
II, P-h 48, Antonine II post-hole	29, rim, S.G., *c.* A.D. 70–85
2, old ploughsoil	35, S.G. grooved footring as if 27, Flavian
	27, very large, C.G.; Hadrianic-Antonine
	27, late Montans ware, early Antonine
	31, C.G., early Antonine
	Curle 15, C.G., perhaps Les Martres-de-Veyre, Hadrianic-Antonine
	Curle 15 or Curle 23, C.G. Antonine
11, packing for Antonine II perimeter drain, so residual from Antonine I	37 (**D2**) (riveted), stamp of Cinnamus (**S2**). C.G., A.D. 150–180
12, Antonine II wall-trench	37, sherd of Cinnamus bowl (**D2**)
	31, C.G., in very pale fabric such as Quintilianus and associates sometimes used. Early Antonine
17, filling of Antonine I water-tank	37, sherd of, Cinnamus bowl (**D2**).
21, Antonine II wall-trench	31, C.G., Antonine
III 25, Antonine II wall-trench	Cup, heavily burnt sherd, (?) C.G.
IV 6, Antonine I demolition	29 (**D3**), S.G., *c.* A.D. 70–85
1974	
G I 9, Antonine II street	eroded sherd, S.G.
25, silt from rampart	18/31 or 31, C.G. (Les Martres-de-Veyre), *c.* A.D. 130–150
	31 (burnt), C.G., Antonine 18/31, C.G., Hadrianic-Antonine dish, two sherds (burnt), probably C.G., Antonine
P II P-h 9 Flavian principia	18, first-cent. Lezoux ware

Context	Sherd
3A, Flavian demolition, principia	Flake, S.G., Flavian (?)
4 (as 3A)	sherd of the f.18 in P-h 9.
P X 5, Flavian demolition	Inkwell (three burnt sherds), S.G., Flavian (cf. P XIII 9 below)
P XIII 4, Antonine II demolition	Flake, S.G. Flavian (?)
9, Flavian demolition	Inkwell base (burnt), S.G. Flavian, probably same vessel as in P X 5.
P XXXI 1, topsoil	30 or 37 rim, C.G., Hadrianic or Antonine
1976	
H I 2, ploughsoil	31, C.G. Antonine
5, Antonine I demolition	18/31 or 31, C.G., Hadrianic or Antonine
8, (as 5)	18/31 S.G., stamp of Chresimus (**S3**), *c.* A.D. 120–145; graffito Rufius on underside (FIG. 134, No. 13).
10, Antonine I post-hole	31, C.G., early Antonine
11, Flavian demolition	29, S.G., *c.* A.D. 75–85
16, Flavian wall-trench	Dish, S.G., Neronian or early Flavian
19, Flavian demolition-pit	29 (**D4**), S.G., *c.* A.D. 70–85
H II 1, ploughsoil	30 or 37, S.G. The inscribed circle around the centre of the base is not uncommon on f.30. Flavian
H III 3, Antonine II floor	18/31 or 31, C.G., Hadrianic or early Antonine.
K I 9, Antonine II demolition	31 (burnt) C.G. Antonine, probably not earlier than *c.* A.D. 160
13, Antonine I make-up	27 (burnt), first-cent. Lezoux ware. Flavian.
	29 (**D5**), S.G., perhaps by Gallicanus, *c.* A.D. 55–70
28, Antonine I floor	footring (burnt and eroded), ? S.G.
1977	
unstratified	29 footring, S.G., Flavian
A I 3, Antonine II demolition	67, S.G. Flavian
	31 (burnt) C.G., stamp, probably of Certus (**S4**), *c.* A.D. 140–170.
7, Antonine II occupation	18 (heavily burnt), S.G., Flavian
8, Antonine I demolition	15/17 (?R), S.G., Flavian
10, top filling of Antonine I demolition-pit B	30 or 37 base, S.G., Flavian
11, Antonine I demolition-pit A	37 S.G. (**D6**), ovolo of (?) Crucuro, Flavian
18, Antonine I demolition-pit B	37, S.G., scroll decoration, from a worn mould, *c.* A.D. 75–90
20, Antonine II demolition	30 or 37 rim (burnt), S.G. Flavian
	37 (flake), S.G. S-shaped gadroons closed the decoration below. Flavian
	18, S.G., Neronian or early Flavian
	flake, S.G., Flavian (?)
25, Flavian demolition-pit A	37, S.G. The ovolo occurs in the Pompeii hoard of A.D. 79. *c.* A.D. 75–90
33, Flavian wall-trench	37, S.G. Flavian
34, Flavian post-pit	Curle 11 flange, S.G. Flavian

64, Flavian demolition-pit C	15/17, 18 and 67 (**D7**), all S.G. and Flavian
	18, first-cent. Lezoux ware
A II P-h 10 Antonine I post-hole	18/31 with rivet-hole, C.G., Antonine
6, Antonine *via sagularis*	18/31, C.G., Hadrianic or early Antonine
7, Antonine II floor	18/31, C.G. (Les Martres-de-Veyre), Hadrianic-Antonine
	Scrap, C.G., Hadrianic or Antonine
7A, as 7	18/31, C.G., Hadrianic or early Antonine
12, Antonine I demolition	18R, S.G. Flavian
	Flat dish in pale fabric with dull brown glaze. Probably late Montans ware, *c.* A.D. 120–145
12B, as 12	29, flake, S.G. Flavian
	33, C.G., Antonine
16, Antonine I occupation	29 (**D8**), S.G. *c.* A.D. 70–85.
20, Flavian occupation	27, S.G., Flavian.
23, 23A, Antonine I occupation	67 (**D9**, **D10**) S.G., Flavian
35, Flavian demolition	35/36 rim, S.G., Flavian
1978	
Unstratified	37, base, S.G., Flavian
	18 and flake of decorated ware, both S.G., Flavian
B I 4, Antonine II demolition	15/17 or 18, S.G., Flavian
5, Antonine I occupation	flake, S.G., Neronian or early Flavian
	18/31, C.G., Hadrianic-Antonine
13, as 5	27, S.G., Flavian
	36, S.G., Flavian
16, Antonine I intervallum drain	15/17 or 18R, S.G., Flavian
19, Flavian occupation	flake from unstamped dish (? 36), Flavian
41, turf bedding of Flavian *via sagularis*	Bowl, probably Curle 11, S.G., Flavian
B II 3, old ploughsoil	Rim, probably 30 or 37, S.G., Flavian
5, Antonine I occupation	18/31R, C.G., Hadrianic-Antonine
17, Antonine I floor	Dish or bowl, C.G., Hadrianic or early Antonine
B III 3 Antonine II occupation	37 (**D11**), S.G., with four-pronged tongue to ovolo. *c* A.D. 70–90.
4, Antonine I occupation	37, S.G., probably with wreath closing the decoration. Flavian
	18, S.G., Flavian
	27, S.G., Neronian or early Flavian
	29 (**D12**), S.G. *c.* A.D. 70–85
10, Flavian demolition-pit	27, S.G., Flavian
B IV 4, Antonine I pipe-trench	37, C.G., style of Arcanus of Lezoux *c.* A.D. 125–145 (see under **D13**)
B VI 20, Antonine I demolition	37, C.G., with unusual ovolo, only otherwise known on a bowl in the style of Cettus, from Camelon. The fabric is consistent with origin at Les Martres-de-Veyre, where Cettus worked. *c.* A.D. 135–160

Context	Sherds
1979	
D I 8, Antonine I demolition	37 (**D14**), C.G., style of Cinnamus. *c.* A.D. 150–180
D II 4, Antonine I demolition	enclosed vessel, perhaps 72, C.G., *c.* A.D. 150–200
6, Antonine I occupation	enclosed vessel, probably inkwell, S.G., Flavian
13, Antonine I post-hole	33, C.G. (probably Les Martres-de-Veyre), Hadrianic-Antonine
D III 3, Antonine I floor, and 4, Flavian occupation	two fragments of the same 27, S.G., Flavian
6, Antonine I wall-trench	18, S.G., Flavian
	37, S.G., Flavian
7, Antonine I post-pit	29 (rim), S.G. Flavian
	37, S.G., Flavian
	37 (**D15**), zonal decoration, S.G., *c.* A.D. 70–85
	18, S.G. Flavian
	18/31R, C.G., Hadrianic or early Antonine
8, as 7	27g, S.G. stamp of Vitalis (**S5**), Flavian
10, Flavian wall-trench	18R (heavily burnt), S.G. Flavian
D V 4, Flavian occupation	27 (two), S.G., Flavian
17, Antonine I make-up over Flavian water-tank	18/31 Tq, C.G., Hadrianic-Antonine
D VI 3, Antonine II occupation	29 (rim), 30 or 37 (rim), and scrap, all S.G., Flavian
11, Antonine I demolition	18, S.G., Flavian
14, Antonine I demolition-pit	29 (rim), S.G., *c.* A.D. 70–85
18, as 14	flake (burnt), probably 29, S.G., Flavian
D VII 6, Antonine I occupation	18/31 or 31, C.G., Hadrianic or early Antonine
1980	
Unstratified	33, C.G., Antonine
	18/31R (three large fragments), C.G., Hadrianic-Antonine
Outer ditch on south side of fort, exposed by levelling	37, S.G., Flavian
E I 3, Antonine II occupation	eroded scrap, S.G., (?) Flavian
8, Antonine I demolition	31, C.G.; high quality of glaze suggests early Antonine date
	36, without barbotine on rim. Almost certainly late Montans ware and *c.* A.D. 120–145
11, Antonine I *via sagularis*	31, C.G. Antonine
12, Antonine I demolition-pit (Pit 9)	enclosed vessel, two burnt fragments, probably inkwell. S.G., Flavian
18, Flavian demolition	Flake, S.G., Flavian
27, Antonine II perimeter drain	18/31 or 31, C.G. (Les Martres-de-Veyre), Hadrianic-Antonine
	18/31 or 31, C.G., probably Antonine

	30 or 37 rim, grooved for mending, C.G., Antonine
	37, C.G. (see under **D16**), scroll decoration in the manner of Cinnamus and associates. Below the decoration is part of a stamp which is in the mould:] Ḷ I M, perhaps a stamp of Paullus iv (3f) who was loosely associated with Cerialis and Cinnamus. See **S6, D16** *c.* A.D. 140–170
	37, (**D17**) two fragments of bowl in the style of Secundus of Lezoux, *c.* A.D. 150–180
32, Flavian wall-trench	30 or 37 (rim), S.G., Flavian
Antonine make-up over Pit 2	37 (**D18**) in style of Criciro of Lezoux. *c.* A.D. 135–160
E II 1, ploughsoil	Flake (burnt), S.G., (?) Flavian
	37 (**D19**), C.G., ovolo only, of Cinnamus. *c.* A.D. 150–170
	37 (**D20**), Antonine
	37, C.G., Antonine
14, Flavian demolition	36, S.G., Flavian
	Bowl (Curle 11?), S.G., Flavian
	15/17 or 18, S.G., Flavian
	18 (heavily burnt), S.G., Flavian
Ext.14, Antonine I occupation	18/31R, C.G., Hadrianic or early Antonine
15, Flavian demolition	46 (having rim of Curle 15 type), S.G., Flavian
19, Antonine II gully	36, S.G., Flavian
1981	
F I 2, old ploughsoil	37 (**D21**), C.G., *c.* A.D. 140–160
3, Antonine II *via sagularis*	37 (**D22**), C.G., *c.* A.D. 140–165
4, Antonine II perimeter drain	18/31 or 31 (two fragments) with rivet-hole, possibly early Antonine
	37 (rim, burnt). The pale fabric and internal grooving suggest late Montans ware, *c.* A.D. 120–145
	37 (**D23**), C.G. (burnt). *c.* A.D. 140–175
4A, lower fill of Antonine II drain	37 (rim), C.G., grooved for mending, Antonine
7, Antonine II occupation	37 (rim), S.G., Flavian
11, Antonine II street	35/36, S.G., Flavian
	Flake, S.G., Flavian
	Decorated fragment, probably C.G. and Hadrianic
	Two flakes, C.G., Antonine
17, Antonine I occupation	18/31 or 31, C.G., early or mid Antonine
22, as 17	Flake (burnt), probably S.G. and Flavian
23, surface of Flavian *via sagularis*	Scrap of decorated ware (burnt), probably 37 C.G. and Antonine
29, Antonine I demolition-pit (Pit 1)	Flake of decorated ware, probably S.G. and Flavian
	Flake, S.G., Flavian
Ph 44, Antonine I post-hole	37 (**D24**), C.G., Style of Criciro, *c.* A.D. 135–160

Context	Sherds
F II 3, Antonine II street	Dish, S.G., Flavian
8, Antonine I demolition	31, C.G., Antonine
	37 (rim), probably late Montans ware and *c.* A.D. 120–145
	27, C.G., *c.* A.D. 130–150
18, post-Antonine silting of Pit 2	Flakes (two), S.G., (?) Flavian
	35/36 (rim), S.G., Flavian
	18/31 or 31 (two), C.G., Hadrianic-Antonine
	37, C.G. Hadrianic or early Antonine
26, Antonine I demolition	31 (heavily burnt rim), C.G., Antonine
	30 or 37 rim, S.G., Flavian
	18R with rivet-holes, Flavian
1982	
G I 9, Antonine II demolition	Flake, S.G., Flavian
15, Antonine I occupation	Flake, S.G., Flavian
	29 (?), burnt flake (**D25**), S.G., *c.* A.D. 70–85
	Bowl, C.G., Antonine
	37 (**D26**), C.G., *c.* A.D. 150–180
G II 1, old ploughsoil	15/17. S.G., Flavian
H I 3, Antonine demolition-pit	18/31 (burnt), E.G. The orange fabric and red glaze point to origin at La Madeleine. That centre's products are the only East Gaulish wares to reach Scottish military sites at all frequently (Hartley, *Britannia iii* (1972), 31). *c.* A.D. 130–160
6, Antonine I occupation	18/31R, C.G. illegible stamp. Hadrianic-Antonine
H III 6, Antonine I occupation	37 (**D27**), C.G., *c.* A.D. 130–150.
J 1, old ploughsoil	Dish in pale fabric, perhaps late Montans ware and *c.* A.D. 120–145
	18/31, C.G., Hadrianic or early Antonine
11, Antonine II drain	33, burnt, almost certainly C.G., early or mid Antonine
1983	
L I 5, Antonine I demolition	Scraps (two), S.G., Flavian
	Scrap (?37), S.G., (?) Flavian
	37 (**D28**), panel decoration, S.G., Flavian
	37, S.G., with large winding scroll, Flavian
	30 or 37 (base, heavily burnt), S.G., Flavian
	18/31, C.G. (Les Martres-de-Veyre), *c.* A.D. 130–150, unworn footring
	18/31, C.G., Hadrianic-Antonine
	31 (two), C.G., Antonine
11, Flavian demolition/Antonine I occupation	37 (**D29**), S.G., ovolo only *c.* A.D. 75–95
	67, S.G., Flavian
	sherd of uncertain form, S.G., Flavian
	37 (**D30**), ovolo 2 of Potter X 6, *c.* A.D. 125–150.

	37, S.G., with slight traces of cursive signature below decoration. Flavian
	27, S.G., Flavian
13, Antonine I demolition-pit (Pit A)	31, C.G., Antonine
L II 1, Antonine II occupation	18/31, C.G., Hadrianic-Antonine
3, Antonine II *via sagularis*	18/31 or 31, C.G., stamp of Lallus (**S7**) and graffito (FIG. 134, No. 12). *c.* A.D. 150–165.
	Scrap, S.G. (?)
4, Antonine I occupation	15/17 or 18, S.G., Flavian, probably Vespasianic
	31 (burnt), C.G., Antonine
	37, C.G., almost certainly ovolo 1 of Cinnamus, A.D. 150–180. Another sherd of this vessel in 85 R I 5.
15, as 4	15/17 or 18, S.G., Flavian
	Scrap, S.G., Neronian-Flavian
L II/III, 3, Antonine II *via sagularis*	31, C.G., Antonine
	Scrap, S.G., Flavian
M I 18, Antonine I demolition	18, S.G., Flavian
24, Antonine I occupation	37 (**D31**), S.G., Flavian
1984	
S I 1, old ploughsoil	27 (slightly burnt), S.G., Flavian
	Flake, S.G., Flavian
2, Antonine I demolition	18, 27 and two flakes, all S.G., Flavian
	30 or 37 (rim), C.G., Antonine
3, Antonine II post-hole	18, S.G., Flavian
4, over Antonine II *via principalis*	29 (**D32**), S.G., A.D. 65–80
	Flakes (three), S.G.
5, Flavian demolition	27, S.G., Neronian or early Flavian
	27, S.G., Flavian
	36, S.G., Flavian
	18 R, S.G., Flavian
	Fragment, S.G., Flavian
	Scrap, S.G., (?) Flavian
6, Antonine I post-holes	18, S.G., Flavian
	27 (two), S.G., Flavian
	Uncertain form, S.G., Flavian
	Flakes (three), S.G., Flavian
	37 (**D33**), style of Cinnamus *c.* A.D. 150–180
16, Flavian occupation	18 (two), S.G., Flavian
	18 (?R), S.G., Flavian
	27 (burnt), S.G., Flavian
S II 12, Antonine I demolition	18, S.G., Flavian
13, Flavian demolition	18, first-cent Lezoux ware (**FIG. 103**)
	33, S.G., Flavian

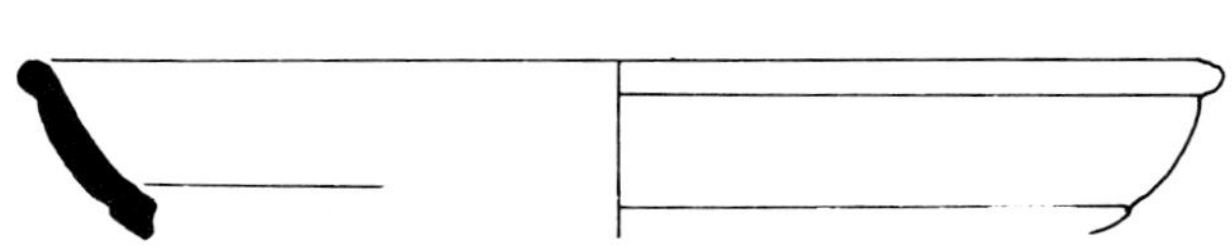

FIG. 103. First-century Lezoux samian dish, form 18 (½).

S III 4, Antonine I demolition	37, C.G., with ovolo of Attianus, *c.* A.D. 130–150
	27, S.G., Flavian
	30 or 37 (rim, burnt), C.G., Antonine
7, Antonine I post-hole	31 (heavily burnt), two rivet-holes. C.G., Antonine, probably same vessel as in S III 12
10, Flavian demolition	Flakes (three), S.G., Flavian
	37, S.G. with zone of festoons at base. Flavian
	30 or 37 (rim, burnt), S.G., Flavian
11, Flavian wall-trench	15/17 or 18 (slightly burnt), S.G., Flavian
12, Antonine I demolition-pit	37, Montans ware, Antonine
	31 (heavily burnt), Antonine: see S III 7.
15, Flavian *via sagularis*	37, S.G., Flavian
	30 or 37 (rim, different vessel), S.G., Flavian
S V 2, Antonine I demolition	37 (**D34**), Montans, Hadrianic-Antonine
1985	
N I 3, old ploughsoil	Decorated bowl, S.G., Flavian
N II 3, old ploughsoil	37 C.G., scroll decoration, Antonine
7, Antonine I occupation	15/17 or 18 R, S.G., Flavian
N III 3, Antonine I demolition	? decorated bowl, S.G., Flavian
4, as 3	33 (two), C.G., Antonine
	Dish, late Montans ware, (?)Hadrianic–Antonine
6, Antonine I demolition	18/31R, C.G., early to mid Antonine
8, Antonine II perimeter drain	18/31 or 31, C.G., Hadrianic-Antonine
9, Antonine I occupation	18/31, C.G., Hadrianic-Antonine
	37 (**D35**), *c.* A.D. 140–165
R I 5, Antonine I demolition	Scrap, S.G., (?) Flavian
	37, C.G., almost certainly ovolo 1 of Cinnamus, *c.* A.D. 150–180: another sherd of this vessel in 83 L II 4
	30 or 37 (rim), C.G., Antonine
R II 5, Antonine I demolition	30 or 37 (rim), C.G., second century
7, Antonine I perimeter drain	Scrap, C.G. second century
R III 3, Antonine I demolition	Flake, S.G., (?) Flavian
1986	
T I 3, old ploughsoil	18/31 or 31, C.G. (Les Martres-de-Veyre), early to mid Antonine
	18/31, C.G., Antonine
	31 (burnt), C.G., Antonine
	Scrap, S.G., Flavian
	29, S.G., with festoons in lower zone, *c.* A.D. 70–85
V I 5, Antonine I demolition	Flake, S.G., (?) Flavian
8A Antonine I post-hole	18, S.G., Flavian
V II 2, Antonine II occupation	29 (**D36**), S.G., *c.* A.D. 70–85
	38, C.G., Antonine
6, Antonine I occupation	Knorr 78 (**D37**), S.G., *c.* A.D. 75–95
	?27, scrap, S.G. Flavian
	33, C.G., Hadrianic-Antonine

XX. SAMIAN POTTERS' STAMPS AND DECORATED WARE.

By B.R. Hartley

Potters' Stamps

S1. 1973 I 37. Carillus ii of La Graufesenque on Form 18 from a die originally giving stamps reading **CARILLFE** (Die la), but gradually deteriorating until the reading became **CARILLI**, as here. Similar examples have been recorded from Caersws, Rottweil and from the Nijmegen fortress, as well as La Graufesenque. Stamps from the original version of the die seem to be mainly late Neronian, and the devolved version is not likely to be later than the 70s or early 80s of the first century. *c.* A.D. 70–85.

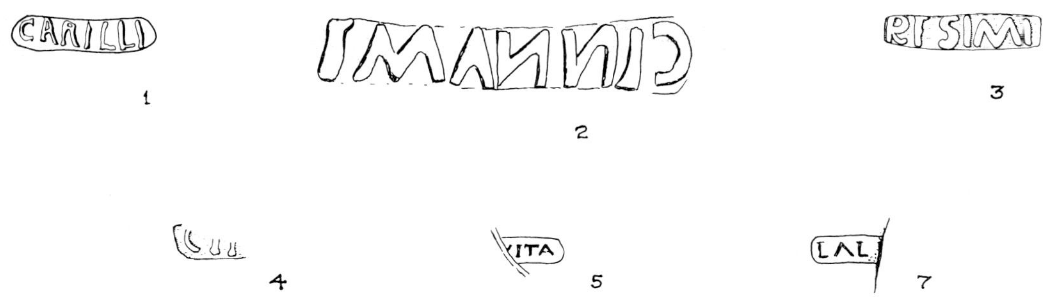

FIG. 104. The samian potters' stamps (1/1).

S2. 1973 II 11. Cinnamus ii of Lezoux on Form 37 stamped **CINNAMI** ret. (Die 5b), with the common decorated-ware stamp of Cinnamus which is abundantly represented in Scotland. See D 2.

S3. 1976 H I 8. Chresimus of Montans on Form 18/31. The full stamp is **C-RESIMI** (Die 4d). Curiously enough, although many stamps of Chresimus have been recorded from Montans and western France in general, this particular one has 14 examples in Britain, though only one in Gaul (at Le Mas d'Agenais). In Scotland it is recorded from Inveresk (twice) and Traprain Law.

The dating of such late Montans products depends largely on their presence in the Second Fire deposits at London, as well as in the Antonine occupation of Scotland (especially at Inveresk, where there was no Flavian site). It has therefore been natural to suppose that the Scottish examples belonged to the Antonine I occupation. It is useful now to have confirmation for the first time (cf. D34). This stamp may be dated *c.* A.D. 120–145.

S4. 1977 A I 3. Certus ii(?) of Lezoux on Form 18/31 or 31 **CII[RTIMA]** (Die 2b), a stamp only otherwise known from Carlisle and Milhamport (Gloucs). The evidence for this potter is slight, but there is nothing in his records that conflicts with an Antonine date.

S5. 1979 D III 8. Vitalis ii of La Graufesenque on Form 27g, reading **VITA** (Die 31k). This is not one of Vitalis's common stamps, and it has only previously been recorded from London and Nijmegen, all three stamps being on Form 27. There is no doubt of basic Flavian date.

S6. (*not illustrated*) 1980 E I 27. Paullus iv? of Lezoux on Form 37. The stamp was impressed in the mould below the decoration and reads]ḶIM retr. This fits well with Paullus iv's Die 3f, often used on moulds, including examples from Lezoux also stamped under the decoration. Paullus was associated with Cinnamus and Cerialis and used the 'Cerialis-Cinnamus' ovolo (Hartley 1972, p.34). For comments on the decoration see D17.

It is likely that Paullus began to work under Hadrian, in view of his relatively common use of Form 27. However, at least one of his moulds survived long enough to produce a bowl found in the Wroxeter Gutter deposit (Atkinson 1942, p.134). As the Wroxeter bowl was stamped with Die 3f, the Strageath sherd is not necessarily residual in an Antonine II deposit. *c.* A.D. 140–170.

S7. 1983 L II 3. Lallus of Lezoux on Form 18/31 or 31, reading LAL[LI.M] (Die 2a). This stamp is known from a pit-group of complete pots at Alcester assignable to the 150s (soon to be published). It is also recorded from Aquincum and Tác where it should be earlier than the Marcomannic wars. *c.* A.D. 150–165.

Decorated Ware

D1. 1973 I 18. Form 37, Central Gaulish, with the Cinnamus-Cerialis ovolo and a scroll of the kind used by Cerialis and Cinnamus in their associated work. It is useful to have another example of a Cerialis-Cinnamus bowl from an Antonine I context. *c.* A.D. 140–170.

D2. 1973 II 11, 12 and 17. Form 37, Central Gaulish, with a rivet-hole and a stamp of Cinnamus (see S2). The panelled decoration is in the fully developed Cinnamus style with Ovolo 1 (Rogers B223). The panels are: a) Osiris (O.413) over a lozenge (Rogers U33); bi) lion (D.753) in a festoon over bii) Cupid with missing left hand (D.236); c) candelabrum (Rogers Q43) over basket supporting dolphins (Rogers Q58); d) medallion with Victory (D.474) between a dolphin (D.1057) and a cantharus (Rogers T15). The next panel should have been a repeat of a), but the potter's stamp replaces the Osiris. *c.* A.D. 150–180. As all three contexts are Antonine I, this bowl gives extremely useful confirmation of the introduction of the standard Cinnamus style by A.D. 150 or soon after.

D3. 1973 IV 6. Form 29, South Gaulish, with a scroll in the upper zone. The decoration is too slight to assign to a potter, but the bowl must belong to the period A.D. 70–85, to judge by its coarse nature.

D4. 1976 H I 19. Form 29, South Gaulish, with a panel of small heart-shaped leaves of the kind used by many Flavian potters cf. Hartley 1985, fig. 98, D4 (Inchtuthil). *c.* A.D. 70–85.

D5. 1976 K I 13. Form 29, South Gaulish, with scrolls in the upper and lower zones. There are some general similarities to the work of Gallicanus of La Graufesenque and some contemporaries. The bowl is likely to have been one which survivied abnormally long in use. *c.* A.D. 55–70.

D6. 1977 A I 11. Form 37, South Gaulish. The ovolo has a straight three- pronged tongue, and is almost certainly one used at La Graufesenque by Crucuro. *c.* A.D. 75–95.

D7. 1977 A I 64. Form 67, South Gaulish. Pots of this form are notoriously difficult to date, partly because the decoration, as here, is often extremely limited in nature.

D8. 1977 A II 16. Form 29, South Gaulish. Part of the upper zone with a conventional scroll of the kind common in the Flavian period e.g. at Inchtuthil (Hartley 1985, fig.98, D24), though there on form 37. There are closer parallels on form 29 at Buxton and at Camelon (FX116). *c.* A.D. 70–85.

D9–10. 1977 A II 23, 23A. Both Form 67, South Gaulish, with banal decoration similar to D8, though all are from different jars. Flavian.

D11. 1978 B III 3. Form 37, South Gaulish, with an ovolo having both a four-pronged tongue and narrow core. Although this ovolo has not been recorded on signed or stamped bowls, it is common in Flavian contexts, having been recorded from Catterick, at least twice in recent work at Camelon and from Period II at Verulamium (Hartley 1972a, p.229, D44, where the implication that the ovolo was used by Crucuro and M. Crestio should be deleted). The maker's name is unknown, though some bowls with this ovolo do have connexions with C. Iulius Sa–. *c.* A.D. 70–90.

D12. 1978 B III 4. Form 29, South Gaulish. A large winding scroll in the lower zone has a symmetrical conventional plant, partly disguised by being cut away by the fluting under the decoration. Similar devices were used by several Neronian-Flavian and Flavian potters, such as Lucceius, Rufinus and Severus, but the closest parallels are on bowls stamped by Cotto (Knorr 1919, Taf.27) and Cosius Rufinus (Knorr 1952, Taf.16C), who both used the central spear-like element. *c.* A.D. 70–85.

D13. 1978 B IV 4 (*not illustrated*). Form 37, Central Gaulish, noted as in the style of Arcanus of Lezoux, but there is no drawing, apparently. This piece is of considerable interest, as it is the only instance of Arcanus's work from Scotland. His activity was entirely, or predominantly Hadrianic.

D14. 1979 D I 8. Form 37, Central Gaulish. The large double medallion contains Venus and pillar (D.184) typical, when used in this way, of the standard Cinnamus style (Stanfield & Simpson 1958, pl.159, 34. *c.* A.D. 150–180.

D15. 1979 D III 7. Form 37, South Gaulish. This kind of zonal decoration is represented at Inchtuthil (Hartley 1985, p.318, D24) and in the Pompeii Hoard (Atkinson 1914, pls. IX–XIII, 49, 52 and 40). *c.* A.D. 70–85.

D16. 1980 E I 27 (*not illustrated*). Form 37, Central Gaulish, with a simple large vine-scroll in the manner of Sacer, Attianus and the Cerialis-Cinnamus group. See **S6**.

D17. as last. Form 37, Central Gaulish. Two sherds from the same bowl in the style of Secundus v of Lezoux. The two concentric double-medallions, the beaded borders without masks at the junctions and the use of the small dolphin (D.1057 variant), often only partly impressed, as a 'filler' are all characteristic. The sea-monster (D.36) and the small goat (D.889) were often used by him. His work is about equally represented in Scotland and on Hadrian's Wall (Hartley 1972, 33). *c.* A.D. 150–180.

D18. 80 E I, make-up over Pit 2. Form 37, Central Gaulish. The ovolo (Rogers B12) and the bird (O.2295A) are both characteristic of Criciro (cf. Stanfield & Simpson 1958, pl.117,2). Criciro's work is common in Scotland and also on Hadrian's Wall, where it probably appeared first before the Antonine evacuation and was still current when reoccupation came in A.D. 158 or so. *c.* A.D. 135–160.

D19. 80 E II 1. Form 37, Central Gaulish, with Ovolo 3 of Cinnamus (Rogers B143), also used by Sacer, and conceivably his work here, in view of the small, neat beads. *c.* A.D. 130–170.

D20. as last. Form 37, Central Gaulish. The fragmentary figures appear to be the seated Diana (D.68) and hare (D.950a), a combination perhaps suggesting a member of the Cinnamus group. Antonine.

D21. 1981 F I 2. Form 37, Central Gaulish. The Vulcan (D.39) combined with the nature of the relatively large beads suggests the work of the Cerialis-Cinnamus group. *c.* A.D. 140–160.

D22. 1981 F I 3. Form 37, Central Gaulish. This looks like a typical Cerialis-Cinnamus bowl in view of the lozenge (Stanfield & Simpson 1958, pl.161, 56, perhaps Rogers U5), border terminal and ring. *c.* A.D. 140–165.

FIG. 105. Decorated samian vessels (½).

D23. 1981 F I 4. Form 37, Central Gaulish, in Cerialis-Cinnamus or Cinnamus style. The figures are Perseus (D.146) over Pan mask (D.675). *c.* A.D. 140–175.

D24. 1981 F I Ph 44. Form 37, Central Gaulish, with a panel junction-mask characteristic of Criciro, who also used the caryatid whose arm shows (D.657) cf. Stanfield & Simpson 1958, pl.117. See **D18**.

D25. 1982 G I 15. Form 29? South Gaulish, a burnt flake. If truly a Form 29, then from the lower zone. The tassels with leaves at the panel corners are reminiscent of Flavian examples of form 37, though they were also used by some earlier potters. *c.* A.D. 70–85.

D26. as last. Form 37, Central Gaulish. Part of a large scroll with a leaf (Rogers J15) used only on bowls in the standard Cinnamus style. *c.* A.D. 150–180.

D27. 1982 H III 6. Form 37, Central Gaulish. The ovolo is not in the normal Antonine repertoire and agrees with the fabric and glaze in suggesting Hadrianic manufacture. The likely candidate is Sacer or one of his associates (cf. Rogers B14).

D28. 1983 L I 5. Form 37, South Gaulish. The left panel has part of the man with scroll (Hermet 1936, pl.20, 136) used at La Graufesenque by many Flavian potters. Neither it nor the saltire help to identify the maker. Flavian.

D29. 1983 L I 11. Form 37, South Gaulish. The ovolo is a distinctive one only used, so far as is known to me, by M. Crestio, whose Flavian date is not in doubt. *c.* A.D. 75–95.

D30. as last. Form 37, Central Gaulish, with an ovolo (Rogers B32) used by Stanfield and Simpson's X–6 and by Mapillus and Pugnus, whose early work was influenced by X–6. *c.* A.D. 125–150.

D31. 1983 M I 24. Form 37, South Gaulish. The ovolo has a four-pronged tongue and wide core and seems to be the one used by Crucuro and M. Crestio. *c.* A.D. 75–95.

D32. 1984 S I 4. Form 29, South Gaulish. Both the festoon and the small leaf were used by Passenus in his later work (Knorr 1952, Taf.49D). *c.* A.D. 65–80.

D33. 1984 S I 6. Form 37, Central Gaulish. A bowl with a large winding scroll in the manner of Cinnamus with leaves Rogers J153 and H52. The former seems only to have been used on the standard Cinnamus bowls. *c.* A.D. 150–180.

D34. 1984 S V 2. Form 37, Montans. This substantial piece is a useful addition to the late Montans decorated ware from Scotland. The ovolo occurs on bowls stamped by Attillus (Bushe-Fox 1932, pl.xxx, 1), and has also been noted from Mumrills (Hartley 1972, p.44). As often with the late bowls from Montans, the figure-types are reduced copies of ones current earlier at La Graufesenque. Here we have devolved versions of a Victory (D.481), the satyr with grapes (D.323), and perhaps a variant of the drunken Bacchus (D307). The same spirals and dagger-like leaves are on a waster of Form 37 with a mould-stamp of Attillus from Montans, and the arcade supports are on another bowl with this ovolo from Wilderspool.

It is useful to have added evidence of the use of the late Montans bowls in the Antonine I period in Scotland. *c.* A.D. 120–145.

D35. 1985 N III 9. Form 37, Central Gaulish, with the Cerialis-Cinnamus ovolo (Rogers B144) and the lion attacking a boar (D.778), much used on Cerialis moulds. *c.* A.D. 140–165.

D36. 1986 V II 2. Form 29, South Gaulish. The scroll of the upper zone has a slightly unusual arrangement. The bird in the lower part is D.1009. The rather high out-turned rim suggests a date *c.* A.D. 70–85.

D37. 1986 V II 6. Knorr 78, South Gaulish. The arrangement in panels, and the details approximate to those used on contemporary bowls of forms 30 and 37. *c.* A.D. 75–95.

Comments

As at Inchtuthil and Ardoch, the samian ware from the Flavian occupation of the fort at Strageath consists mainly of small scraps, and remarkably few of those considering the extent of the excavation. The contrast with Camelon is great, especially when the material from the recent work (as yet unpublished) is taken into account. It is likely that the answer lies in army discipline, which obviously required the removal of rubbish from the interiors of fortresses and forts. At Camelon much of the area where rubbish was dumped outside the fort was also excavated, and there were not only many more larger sherds than at the other two sites, but also frequent instances of many fragments of the same bowl.

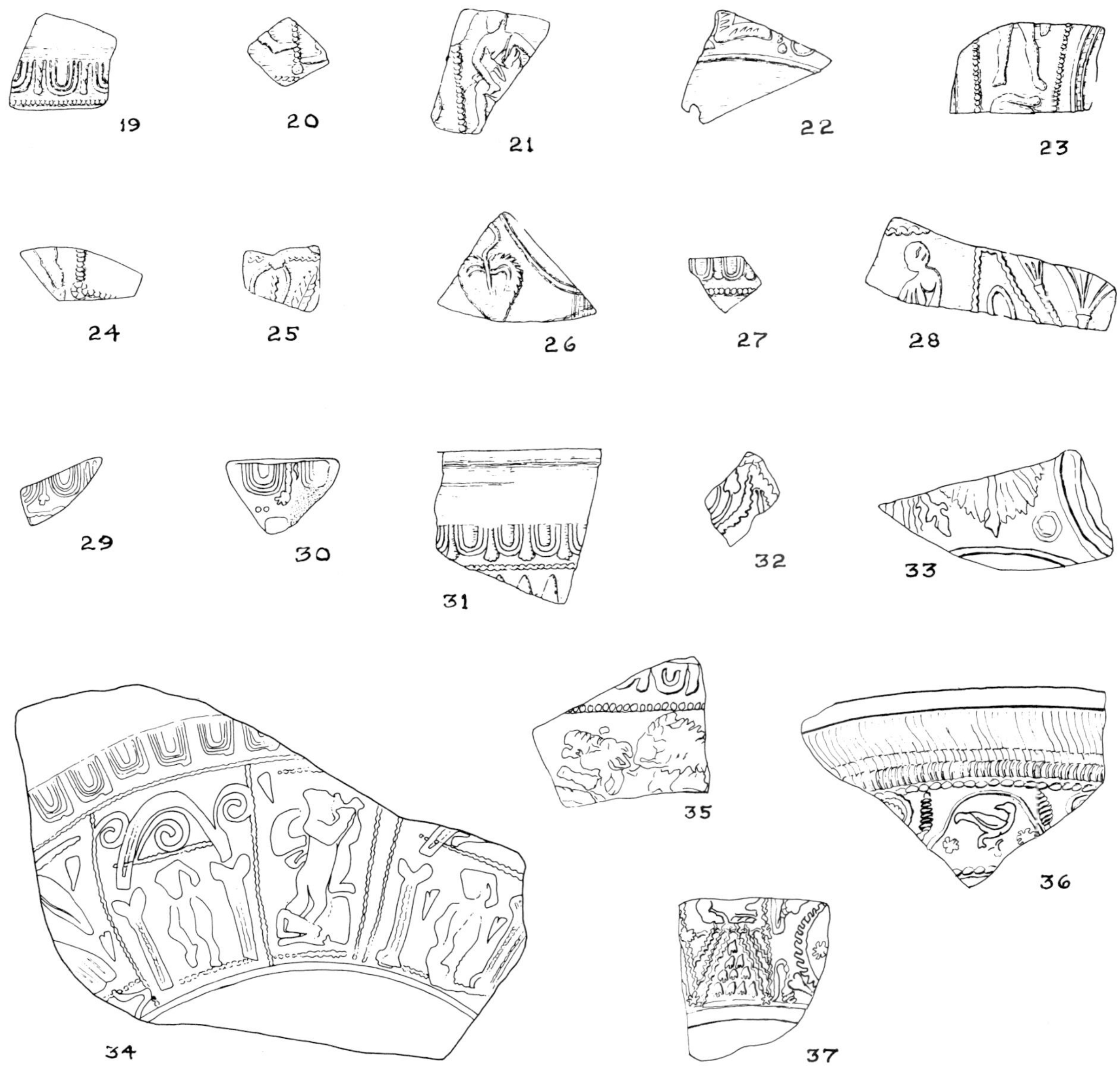

FIG. 106. Decorated samian vessels ($\frac{1}{2}$).

Despite those differences, the statistics of the relatively small numbers of sherds from Camelon, Inchtuthil and Strageath are of some interest. The ratios for forms 29 and 37 at the three sites (taking only the old material from Camelon) are:

Camelon 29:23 (1.26) Inchtuthil 20:16 (1.25) Strageath 18:15 (1.20)

Here is a strong indication that all three sites were founded and evacuated more-or-less simultaneously, particularly in view of the rate at which the older form 29 was being replaced by form 37 in the 80s of the first century. It will be instructive to compare the ratios eventually with the decorated ware from Elginhaugh.

More subjectively, there does seem to be one difference between the three sites. It has been said of Inchtuthil that there is a total absence of anything pre-Flavian in the decorated samian and an extreme rarity of pots likely to belong to the early 70s (Hartley 1985, p.322). Both at Camelon and Strageath there seems to be a higher proportion of old bowls, some pre-Flavian or early Flavian, others of the early or mid 70s. At first sight this could be taken as a chronological indication suggesting that Inchtuthil was founded slightly later. But the differences in foundation dates could only be very slight on any interpretation of events and another explanation must be sought for this phenomenon. It seems highly likely that the Inchtuthil legion carried stocks of samian with it, ready for a new issue to all who wished to have it. The auxiliary units may be supposed to have brought their pots in use to the new stations with them.

The first-century samian from Strageath is almost all from La Graufesenque and is entirely consistent with evacuation of the site in the later 80s. Once more, as at Camelon and Inchtuthil, there is a complete absence of the latest exported products of La Graufesenque such as appear in quantity at Newstead. One point gained is the presence of first-century samian from Lezoux. This has also now been recorded at Camelon, and while the pots may have been survivals at both sites, there is clearly a hint that export may have continued rather later into the 70s than is usually presumed.

There are few surprises among the second-century material. What there is matches closely with the range established for the Antonine Wall and indeed the Antonine occupation of Scotland in general (Hartley 1972, 15 f). As usual, the work of Cerialis-Cinnamus and Cinnamus is predominant, while all of the major potters who began work later in the Antonine period, such as Advocisus, Paternus, Casurius or Doeccus are absent, as is East Gaulish samian, apart from a single sherd from La Madeleine (cf. Hartley 1972, p.31).

Late Montans ware appears several times, and both it and the standard Cinnamus style are firmly attested more than once in Antonine I deposits.

XXI. THE LIST OF MORTARIA

(Dates and Sources identified by K.F. Hartley)

Note: Vessels attributed to '(?) Pas de Calais' are of Hartley, Group II (K.F. Hartley in J. Dore and K. Greene (eds.), *Roman Pottery Studies in Britain and Beyond* (BAR Supplementary Series No.30 (Oxford, 1977), 5–15), or Gillam, type 238. 'Northern Britain' includes Northern England and Scotland. In this list, where no date is given, sherds attributed to Northern Britain should be considered second-century, Verulamium region probably first-century and Colchester second-century.

Context	*Date*	*Source*
1973		
I 2, scrap	(?) 2nd cent.	(?) Colchester
I 3, sherds (No. 61)	2nd cent.	Northern Britain
sherd		Verulamium region
I 12	Antonine	Mancetter/Hartshill
I 14	Antonine	Mancetter/Hartshill
	130–170	(?) Colchester
	Flavian or Flavian-Trajanic	Verulamium region
I 18	70–100	(?) Pas de Calais
I 39, scrap	65–100	(?) Pas de Calais
(No. 2)	pre A.D. 90	Gaul
I 50 (No. 24)	Flavian	Verulamium region
II 1	Flavian	Verulamium region
II 2, scrap	(?) 2nd cent.	(?) Colchester
scrap		Northern Britain
	Flavian	Verulamium region
	60–90	Verulamium region
	70–100	(?) Pas de Calais
(No. 15)	Flavian/Trajanic heavily burnt	Gaul: cf. Bushe-Fox type 26/30
base, see II 28	Flavian	
	(?) Flavian	(?) Northern Britain
(No. 47)	130–170	Colchester
II 3		Northern Britain
	60–90	Verulamium region
II 4 (No. 44)	almost complete, riveted, well-used. Stamp (FIG. 115, No. 20). 130–170. Antonine II context	Colchester
II 21 (No. 13)	70–100	(?) Pas de Calais
(No. 35)	(?) Flavian	(?) Northern Britain
base sherd	Flavian	Gaul
II P-h 22	Flavian	Verulamium region
II 25 B (No. 40)	early to mid-Flavian	Same (unidentified) source as II 28.
spout	see II 28	
II 27, sherd		(?) Northern Britain
II P-h 27	(?) Flavian, heavily burnt	
II 28 (No. 38)	prob. early to mid Flavian: translucent white grits.	unidentified source

	Other sherds in II 2, II 25 B, II 29	
II 29	See II 28	
III 3	Flavian	Verulamium region
III 4	Flavian	Verulamium region
III 9 (two vessels)	Flavian	Verulamium region
IV 6	70–100	(?) Pas de Calais
1974		
G I 26, sherd		unidentified
P II 3, spout fragment burnt		unidentified
P III 3 (No. 81)	2nd cent.	Verulamium region
P IV 4 (No. 64)	2nd cent.	probably North Britain
P VI 4	(?) Flavian	Verulamium region
P XIII 2	130–170	Colchester
P XIII P-h 2A, burnt	probably 1st century	unidentified
P XXXII 3, burnt	2nd cent.	Mancetter/Hartshill
1975		
G V 2 (No. 7)	70–100	Gaul
P XLIII 3	70–110	Verulamium region
1976		
H I 4 (No. 19)	65–95	Verulamium region
three sherds from (?) two vessels		Gaul
H I 5	70–100	Verulamium region
H I 8 (three)	70–100	(?) Pas de Calais
	70–110	probably Verulamium region
base		Northern Britain
rim fragment		probably Northern Britain
H I 9A	2nd cent.	Colchester
H I 10	70–100	(?) Pas de Calais
H I 11	70–100	(?) Pas de Calais
	130–170, stamp (FIG. 115, No. 21)	Colchester
H I 12 (No. 74)	160–200	style of Bellicus, Corbridge.
	joins with sherd in K I 15	
H I 13, flange fragment	probably 130–170	probably Colchester
H I 18	2nd cent.	Colchester
H I 23	2nd cent.	probably Colchester
H I 24 (No. 6)	70–100	(?) Pas de Calais
H II 3	70–110	Verulamium region
H II 4, sherd	2nd cent.	Northern Britain
spout fragment	probably 2nd cent.	probably Northern Britain

H II 6A rim sherd (No. 46)	130–170	Colchester
	2nd cent.	(?) Colchester
H III 2, base	140–200	probably Colchester
	70-100 (burnt)	Verulamium region
H III 3, flange fragment, burnt	2nd cent.	Colchester
flange fragment	2nd cent.	Mancetter/Hartshill
H III 8, base fragment	2nd cent.	Colchester
sherd	1st cent.	uncertain
H III 9 (No. 25)	Flavian	Verulamium region
rim fragment	70–100	(?) Pas de Calais
K I 8 (No. 76)	and see K I 9 A.D. 160–200	NE England, perhaps by Bellicus of Corbridge.
K I 9	large sherd of K I 8	
	70–100	(?) Pas de Calais
K I 15	flange of H I 12 (q.v.)	Corbridge
	70–95	Verulamium region
K I 25 (No. 26)	Stamp of Sollus (FIG. 115, No. 12): 60–100	Verulamium region
K I 27, Flange chip	130–170	Colchester
K I 28, burnt		(?) Verulamium region
rim fragment, burnt	2nd cent.	(?) Mancetter/Hartshill
sherd	2nd cent.	NW England or Scotland
K I 29	130–170	Colchester
base		(?) Colchester
K I 30, rim fragment	probably 60–90	Verulamium region

1977

A I 1, base		Verulamium region
base	probably 70–100	probably (?) Pas de Calais
A I 2 (No. 16)	well worn; counter-stamp of Albinus (FIG. 115, No. 1, A.D. 60–90	Verulamium region
(No. 65)	with large joining sherd in A I 8, cf. A I 3	Northern Britain
Stamp (FIG. 115, No. 16)., burnt	2nd cent.	Northern Britain
A I 3 (No. 45), burnt	140–170	Colchester
(No. 60) rim sherd	probably part of No. 65 above	Northern Britain
rim sherd		Verulamium region
sherds, burnt (No. 51)	(?) 2nd cent.	(?) Colchester
A I 6 (No. 14)	70–100	(?) Pas de Calais
flange fragment		probably Colchester
spout	(?) Flavian	Verulamium region
spout		probably Colchester
A I 7 (No. 27), burnt	Flavian	Verulamium region
three sherds	2nd cent.	Colchester
A I 8 (No. 32)	70–110	Verulamium region
(No. 10)	70–100	(?) Pas de Calais

	sherd also in A I 9	
sherd of spout	joins stamped vessel No. 65 in A I 2	Northern Britain
flange	70–100	probably Verulamium region
sherds	probably 70–100	probably (?) Pas de Calais
flange sherd	part of unidentifiable herringbone stamp (No. 23): 140–170	Colchester
A I 9 sherd of No. 65 in A I 8, above		
flange	2nd cent.	Colchester
spout fragment		probably Northern Britain
A I 10, rim sherd, burnt	probably 2nd cent.	
A I 11 spout fragment		Verulamium region
A I 19, flange	70–100	(?) Pas de Calais
flange		Northern Britain
A I 20, sherd		(?) Colchester
sherds, (two vessels), burnt		Verulamium region
A I 29 (No. 42)	unusual shape, probably Flavian	unidentified
A I 54 (No. 33)	70–100	Verulamium region
(No. 22)	70–100	Verulamium region
sherd, worn		Verulamium region
A I 57, base		Verulamium region
A I 64 (No. 34), burnt	70–100	Verulamium region
(No. 41), internal scoring (mica in fabric)	Flavian	unidentified source
burnt	late 1st-early 2nd cent.	Verulamium region
burnt	probably Flavian	Verulamium region
sherd		origin uncertain
sherd		Verulamium region
A II 7A (No. 50)	140–170	Colchester
A II 8 (No. 43)	140–170	Colchester
A II 12 (No. 54)	135–170	Mancetter/Hartshill
stamp of Sarrius (FIG. 115, No. 10)		
flange sherd	Flavian	Verulamium region
(No. 70)	with edge of stamp (FIG. 115, No. 17)	probably Scotland
A II 14 A	probably 70–100	probably (?) Pas de Calais
A II 16	Flavian	Verulamium region
A II 20	70–100	(?) Pas de Calais
worn base		Northern Britain
A II 26 (No. 66)	2nd cent.	Northern Britain
A II 39	140–170	Colchester

1978

B I 3 (No. 67)	2nd cent.	Northern Britain
	140–170	Colchester
	2nd cent.	Northern Britain
flange	70–100	Verulamium region
sherds, two	2nd cent.	Colchester

B I 5 sherd		Verulamium region
flange, (tip missing) (No. 59)	2nd cent.	Northern Britain
spout fragment	2nd cent.	Northern Britain
flange fragment	140–170	Colchester
rim fragment	Flavian	Verulamium region
B I 7 flange fragment	70–100 (joins B I 13)	Verulamium region
B I 12	mid 2nd cent.	Mancetter/Hartshill
B I 13, sherd	joins B I 7	
(No. 28)	Flavian	Verulamium region
B I 19	Flavian	Verulamium region
B I 45	probably 2nd cent.	probably Northern Britain
B II 5 (No. 58)	150–220 (with sherd in B VI 19)	Mancetter/Hartshill
sherd	with sherd in B II 8	Northern Britain
B II 8, sherd	see B II 5	
B III 3, sherd		Verulamium region
base sherd	2nd cent.	Mancetter/Hartshill
B III 4, flange		Northern Britain
spout fragment	2nd cent.	Mancetter/Hartshill
B III 11, worn sherd		Verulamium region
B III 15, rim fragment	probably Flavian	Verulamium region
B VI 19, sherd of No. 58	(B II 5) 150–220	Mancetter/Hartshill
B VI 25, sherd		unidentified

1979

D I 1, very heavily burnt	uncertain	probably Verulamium region
D I 2 (No. 5)	70–100	(?) Pas de Calais
D I 4	70–100	Verulamium region
flange fragment (heavily burnt)	70–100	Verulamium region
base fragment (heavily burnt)	70–100	Verulamium region
D I 7 burnt	probably Flavian	uncertain
D II 4, two joining sherds	uncertain	uncertain
D II 6 (No. 68)	probably Antonine	probably Northern Britain
base sherd	uncertain	probably an import
D III 2, base fragment	70–100	Verulamium region
D III 3 (No. 79)	Antonine	(?) NE England
D V 5, sherd	uncertain	Import
D VI 2	probably Flavian	Verulamium region
D VI 3, two joining fragments		Northern Britain
D VI 5, flange fragment	70–100	Verulamium region
D VII 3, flange fragment	70–100	Verulamium region

flange fragment, weathered	2nd cent.	probably Mancetter/Hartshill
D VII 5 heavily worn, heavily burnt ,	70–100	Verulamium region
D VII 6 (No. 1),	40–60	probably an import
heavily burnt	probably Antonine	Mancetter/Hartshill
(No. 55), burnt		Midlands
D VII 9, base fragment	uncertain	uncertain
D VII 10, heavily burnt	70–100	Verulamium region

1980

unstratified, Outer Ditch, South side of fort	stamp (FIG. 115, No. 18), 2nd cent.	Lincoln or Mancetter/Hartshill
ibid. (No. 73)	Antonine	perhaps Scotland
ibid., sherd	Flavian or Trajanic	probably Verulamium region
E I 1, heavily burnt (No. 80)	140–200	probably Verulamium region
	140–180	Colchester
E I 15 (No. 78)	with stamp MA[(FIG. 115, No. 8) Antonine	North-eastern England.
flange, burnt	probably Flavian	uncertain
E I 16, sherds of two vessels	70–100	Verulamium region
E I 18, flange probably part of Albinus bowl, E I 20		
E I 19, sherd of Albinus bowl, E I 20		
E I 20 (No. 23), some sherds heavily burnt	Albinus counter-stamp 60–90 (FIG. 115, No. 2)	Verulamium region
flange fragment	probably Flavian	probably an import
E I 21 (No. 8), three joining sherds	70–100	(?) Pas de Calais
E I 23 (No. 75), heavily burnt and worn	probably Antonine	NE England or Scotland
burnt	uncertain	probably Northern Britain
E I 26, (associated with lead pig) (No. 29)	70–100, style of Albinus	Verulamiun region
(No. 30), two joining sherds	Flavian, stamp of Sexti Valerii (FIG. 115, No. 13). 50–90	Verulamium region
two joining sherds	uncertain	uncertain
E I 30, sherds of two vessels, burnt and worn	70–100	Verulamium region
E I 32, sherd joining Albinus bowl, E I 20 (No. 23)		
E II 1	Antonine, stamp of Loccius Pro[. . . (FIG. 115, No. 7), perhaps from vessel in E II 14	Mancetter/Hartshill
E II 7, base fragment probably from Albinus bowl in E I 20 (No. 23)		Verulamium region
rim sherd: others in E II 8, E II Pit 2	2nd cent.	Colchester
flange (No. 69)	2nd cent.	NW Britain

E II 8, flange – fragment: see E II 7	2nd cent.	Colchester
E II 10 (No. 48)	130–170	Colchester
probably same vessel as in E II Pit 1 (No. 53) rim, heavily burnt	Antonine	uncertain
E II 11 (No. 17)	60–90	Verulamium region
	140–180	probably Colchester
flange, burnt	70–100	Verulamium region
E II 12, two flange fragments, one joining vessel in E II 14, other probably same vessel	Antonine	Mancetter/Hartshill
E II 13, perhaps part of vessel in 81 F II 8	140–180	Colchester
E II 14 (No. 63)	Antonine	Northern Britain, possibly Scotland
rim fragment and sherds: see also E II 12,	not before 150	Mancetter/Hartshill
E II 19 (No. 77), almost complete	stamp probably of Marcus. Mid 2nd cent. (FIG. 115, No. 9)	probably Corbridge
E II P-h 3 (Antonine II) (No. 82)	uncertain	uncertain
E II Pit 1 rim	55–85	Gaul: Hartley Group 1
spout fragment	Flavian	Verulamium region
(No. 53)	herringbone-stamp No. 24 130–170	Colchester
sherd from vessel in E II 14		Mancetter/Hartshill
E II Pit 2, sherd from vessel in E II 7, E II 8		Colchester

1981

F I 2, flange fragment	Antonine	Mancetter/Hartshill
F I 6	70–100	Verulamium region
F I 7, flange fragment, burnt	probably Antonine	NW England or Scotland
base fragment, burnt, worn	probably Flavian	Verulamium region
F I 8	140–180	Colchester
F I 9, flange tip		Verulamium region
flange of very large vessel	uncertain	uncertain: probably an import
fragments: different vessel from E I 21	70–100	(?) Pas de Calais
F I 11 (No. 62)	Antonine	Northern Britain, possibly Scotland
F I 13 (No. 39), heavily worn	uncertain	uncertain
F I 18, spout fragment, burnt	70–100	(?) Pas de Calais
F I 22, flange fragment	70–100	Verulamiam region
flange fragment, burnt	probably Flavian	uncertain
flange fragment	probably 70–100	probably (?) Pas de Calais
F I 23, two base fragments	probably 140–180 but possibly 70–100	Colchester (?) Pas de Calais

F I 25, burnt	perhaps 70–100	perhaps (?) Pas de Calais
F I 29, flange fragment	70–100	(?) Pas de Calais
flange fragment	Antonine	Mancetter/Hartshill
F I P-h 52, base sherd	130–170	Colchester
F II 1 (No. 56), unusual form	130–165	Mancetter/Hartshill
(No. 72)	Antonine	Scotland
F II 8 (No. 56), two sherds from vessel in F II 1	Mancetter/Hartshill	
(No. 52), other sherds in 80 E II 13	140–180	Colchester
flange fragment	probably 130–170	probably Colchester
two sherds	probably 130–170	probably Colchester
three sherds	2nd cent.	probably Northern Britain
base fragment, worn	uncertain	uncertain
spout, heavily burnt	2nd cent.	uncertain
two sherds, burnt	either 70–100 or 130–170	(?) Pas de Calais Colchester
F II 9	140–180	Colchester
F II 11, heavily worn, burnt	60–90	Verulamium region
burnt	140–180	Colchester
flange fragment	uncertain	uncertain
sherd	uncertain	probably import
F II 18, spout fragment	135–170	Mancetter/Hartshill
rim fragment (No. 49)	140–180	Colchester
F II 20	70–100	(?) Pas de Calais
F II 26 (No. 31)	probably 70–100	probably Verulamium region

1982

G I 1	stamp of Austinus (FIG. 115, No. 6) Antonine	Carlisle Area
G I 6 (No. 4), heavily burnt	stamp]D.M. FIG. 115, No. 15) Flavian	Probably Gaul
G I 14 flange fragment	140–180	Colchester
G I 15 (No. 36), burnt	probably Flavian	possibly Scotland
two sherds	Antonine	Mancetter/Hartshill
body sherd (different)	Antonine	Mancetter/Hartshill
flange (different)	130–160	Mancetter/Hartshill
flange fragment, burnt (different)	Antonine	Mancetter/Hartshill
three burnt sherds	uncertain	uncertain
base fragment	1st cent.	Verulamium region
(No. 37)	presumably Antonine	Northern Britain
G I 18 (No. 57), over half the vessel	stamps of Sarrius (FIG. 115, No. 11) 135–170	Mancetter/Hartshill
(No. 9) four sherds of vessel of unusual form	70–100	cf. Hartley Groups I, II. (?) Pas de Calais
G II 1, heavily burnt	Flavian	probably an import
G II 3 (No. 20) slightly burnt	stamp of Albinus 60–90 (FIG. 115, No. 3)	Verulamium region
G II 4, burnt	probably Antonine	Northern Britain

G II 12 (No. 21), burnt	stamp of Albinus (FIG. 115, No. 4) (different vessel from G II 3) A.D. 60–90	Verulamium region.
H I 4 (No. 11)	70–100	(?) Pas de Calais
H II 3 (No. 12), unusual form	70–100	cf. Hartley Group II, (?) Pas de Calais
J 5, (No. 18), heavily burnt	60–90	Verulamium region
(No. 3), burnt	60–90	Hartley Groups I/II (?) Pas de Calais
J 11, base fragment	uncertain	Scotland
J 12 (No. 71)	probably Antonine	probably Scotland

1983

L I 5	herringbone stamp (FIG. 115, No. 22) 130–170	Colchester
two sherds	70–100	(?) Pas de Calais
three sherds, different vessel	70–100	(?) Pas de Calais
sherd	1st cent.	Verulamium region
L I 7, two rim-sherds from vessel with rivet-hole in L I 11	70–100	(?) Pas de Calais
base sherd	2nd cent.	NW England or Scotland
L I 10, base sherd, heavily worn	probably 1st cent.	Verulamium region
rim sherd	probably 2nd cent.	NW England or Scotland
L I 11, sherd	1st cent.	Verulamium region
two sherds, very well worn		Verulamium region
rim sherd	60–90	Verulamium region
	70–100	(?) Pas de Calais
base sherd	2nd cent.	NW England or Scotland
rim with rivet-hole	70–100	(?) Pas de Calais
L II 4, base sherd	130–170	Colchester
sherd	2nd cent.	Midlands, probably Mancetter/ Hartshill
sherd	2nd cent.	NW England or Scotland
two sherds, well worn	probably 2nd cent.	NW England or Scotland
L II 8	130–170	Colchester
L II 17, rim sherd, well worn	probably 60–90	Verulamium region
M I 19, rim	Gillam type 237 Flavian	Scotland
M I 22 B	130–170	Colchester

1985

N I 3, sherd, burnt	2nd cent.	Midlands
N I 5, rim sherd	70–100	(?) Pas de Calais
N I 6, flange sherd	130–170	Colchester

N I 11, rim and heavily worn body sherd	Flavian	Verulamium region
N I 15, sherd	probably after 130	Mancetter/Hartshill
N II 3, sherd	(?) 130–170	(?) Colchester
N II 4, two vessels	130–170	Colchester
N II 6	70–100	(?) Pas de Calais
N III 3, three joining rim sherds	2nd cent.	Colchester
N III 3) sherds of N III 4) one vessel	130–170	Colchester
N III 4, spout fragment	probably 60–90	Verulamium region
N III 10, rim sherd	probably Antonine	probably Lincolnshire
N III 11, sherd	130–170	Colchester
N III 21, base	Flavian	Verulamium region
N III 23, base, burnt	2nd cent.	uncertain
R I 5, base	130–170	Colchester
two rims sherds from one vessel and one from another	130–170	Colchester
R II 5	stamp: 2nd cent. (FIG. 115, No. 19)	Lincolnshire

1986

T I 2	sherd from same Mancetter vessel as in T I 3	
T I 3, three pieces of incomplete rim	Antonine	Mancetter/Hartshill
	stamp probably of Q Valerius Veranius 70–100 (FIG. 115, No. 14)	
sherd	70–100	(?) Pas de Calais
sherd	Antonine	probably Scotland
T II 3, pink ware	70–100	(?) Pas de Calais
T II 5, raetian ware, burnt	Antonine	Scotland
V I 1, base, very worn	Antonine	(?) Corbridge
V I 2, two sherds, burnt	Antonine	Probably Scotland
V I 4	65–100	(?) Pas de Calais (Gillam type 238, variant)
V I 8A	probably same vessel as in V I 1	
V II 2	70–100	Verulamium region
V II 3	2nd cent.	Mancetter/Hartshill
rim chip	2nd cent.	Colchester
V II 6	Flavian	Verulamium region
sherd	Flavian	Import, Hartley Group I or II
V II 12	70–100	(?) Pas de Calais
V II 13, incomplete rim	2nd cent.	possibly Scotland

We owe a considerable debt of gratitude to Mrs K.F. Hartley, who has regularly examined and commented upon the mortarium fragments recovered over the years at Strageath, and has enabled the above list to be compiled. Fragments which could be associated with others as belonging to individual mortaria, either by joins or through individual traits, have been treated as single units in the statistics discussed below, but no concerted attempt has been made to group sherds into individual vessels; moreover, the long duration of the excavation made it impracticable to attempt the matching of sherds from successive seasons. There were, however, indications (as for instance in the appearance of a number of mortarium sherds in the *principia*) that sherds from broken vessels had sometimes been dispersed over a wide area.

In the absence of reliable deductions about the original numbers of whole vessels, the assumption has been made that breakage was essentially uniform: the collection of mortarium sherds is treated as a sample which may provide an indication of the main sources of these vessels and of the varying importance of the sources in the first- and second-century occupations of the fort. For this purpose the two Antonine occupations have been grouped together both because the time-span is insufficient to yield significant differences between them and because plough-damage to the upper levels of the fort has greatly magnified the normal problems of residuality. It may be noted, however, that a virtually complete and well-worn vessel from the Colchester kilns (FIG. 111, No. 44), bearing a herring-bone stamp (FIG. 115, No. 20) and mended with rivets, was found in the final filling of an Antonine II drain (p. 63).

From TABLE VII it will be seen that in the Flavian period the two chief – and almost exclusive – sources of supply were the kilns of the Verulamium region in southern Britain and those of North-western Gaul (? Pas de Calais). Although manufacture of mortaria had already been started in Scotland in the Flavian period, products from Scotland and from Northern England were arriving at Strageath in only insignificant quantity during that period. The picture here is very different from the one established at the Flavian legionary fortress at Inchtuthil: there the manufacture of mortaria and other pottery was established locally, and the proportions of mortaria from the Verulamium region and from the Continent is far lower.[1] Whether or not Inchtuthil was intended to become a source of supply for auxiliary forts in its region, that position had not yet been reached when northern Scotland was evacuated.

TABLE VII
THE MORTARIA: PERCENTAGES OF SOURCES

FIRST-CENTURY SHERDS (Total 142)			SECOND-CENTURY SHERDS (Total 142)			TOTAL ASSEMBLAGE (Total 335)	
Verulamium region		53.47			1.41		28.66
(?) Pas de Calais		31.94					13.73
Other Gaulish Imports		4.17					1.79
Imports, no source identified		2.08					2.09
Others, no source identified		5.55			2.11		6.27
Northern Britain	1.39			12.68		10.45	
		2.78					
Scotland	1.39			4.93		3.28	
			N W England or Scotland	6.34		2.69	17.91
					26.76		
			NW England	2.11		1.19	
			NW England or Scotland	0.70		0.30	
			Colchester		46.48		19.70
			Mancetter/Hartshill		21.13		8.95
			Midlands		0.70		0.30
			Lincolnshire		1.41		0.60
TOTAL		99.99%			100%		100%

1. L.F. Pitts and J.K. St Joseph, *Inchtuthil, the Legionary Fortress* (London, 1985), 330–2.

In the Antonine period Verulamium-region products had almost disappeared from the available stores: only two sherds of certainly Antonine date from this source were found. Nor are there any Continental imports. In this period the two chief individual sources of supply were Colchester and the Mancetter/Hartshill factories; but it is also very striking that when the totals from various sources in Northern England and Scotland are added together they account for 26.76% of the market. This is an indication of the progress of economic development in the North during the Hadrianic and Antonine periods, although that development was no doubt largely the result of military initiatives. The presence of two vessels from Lincolnshire, one of them stamped, (FIG. 115, No. 19), is interesting; the mortaria from this source, however, are not unusual at sites in Scotland although always present only in small quantity.

XXII. THE ILLUSTRATED MORTARIA (FIGS. 107–14)

By S.S. Frere and K.F. Hartley

(For reference to Hartley Groups I and II see K.F. Hartley in J.N. Dore and K. Greene (eds.), *Roman Pottery Studies in Britain and Beyond* (BAR Supplementary Series No. 30 (Oxford 1977), 5–15; for references to Gillam see J.P. Gillam, *Types of Roman Coarse Pottery Vessels in Northern Britain* (3rd edition, Newcastle upon Tyne, 1970); and to Bushe-Fox see J.P. Bushe-Fox, *Excavations at Wroxeter in 1912* (Oxford, 1913), 77).

A. First-century Imports or Probable Imports from the Continent (FIG. 107)

1. From 1979 D VII 6. Early wall-sided mortarium. Smooth hard cream-coloured ware, heavily burnt. A.D. 40–60. Probably an import. Although a typically Claudio-Neronian product, examples were sometimes long-lived. Another vessel of this type from Scotland is recorded at Camelon (information from K.F. Hartley).
2. From 1973 I 39. Hard buff ware: dark and light grey grits. A.D. 65–90. Gaul.
3. From 1982 J 5. Finely granular cream-coloured ware, burnt: grey, white and black grits. A.D. 60–90. Hartley Groups I–II. (?) Pas de Calais.
4. From 1982 G I 6, with stamp]D.M. (see p. 241, **stamp No. 15**; *q.v.* for description of fabric); heavily burnt. Flavian, probably from Gaul.
5. From 1979 D I 2 (lip of flange damaged). Smooth yellow-buff ware: grey-white grits. A.D. 70–100. Hartley Group II. (?) Pas de Calais.

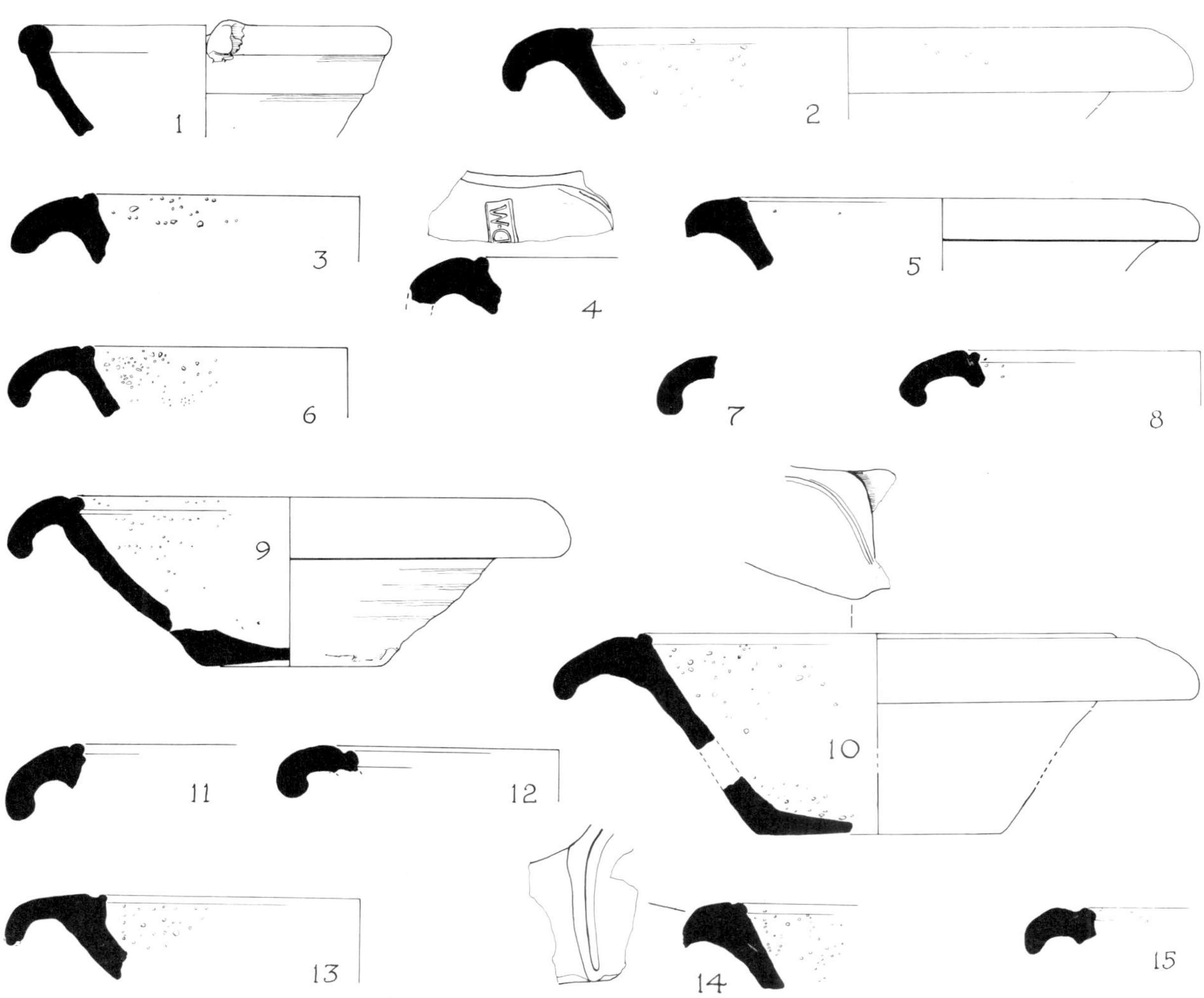

FIG. 107. First-century imported Mortaria (1/4).

6. From 1976 H I 24. Hard yellow-buff ware: dark and light grey and white grits. A.D. 70–100. Gillam 238; Hartley Group II. (?) Pas de Calais.
7. From 1975 G V 2: diameter *c.* 31 cm. Yellow-buff ware: grey and white grits. Flavian. Gaul.
8. From 1980 E I 21. Hard cream-coloured ware: white and grey grits. Hartley Group II, style of Q. Valerius Veranius. A.D. 70–100. (?) Pas de Calais.
9. From 1982 G I 18. Smooth hard cream-coloured ware: grey, dark, and a few reddish grits. Four sherds, heavily worn. Unusual form, Hartley Groups I/II. A.D. 70–100. (?) Pas de Calais.
10. From 1977 A I 8. Buff ware: grey and white grits. Gillam 238. A.D. 70–100. (?) Pas de Calais.
11. From 1982 H I 4. Yellow-buff ware. Hartley Group II. A.D. 70–100. (?) Pas de Calais.
12. From 1982 H II 3. Hard cream-coloured ware: reddish and small dark grits on rim. Unusual form, variety of Hartley Group II. A.D. 70–100. (?) Pas de Calais.
13. From 1973 II 21. Hard buff ware: light and dark grey grits. Tip of flange missing. A.D. 70–100. (?) Pas de Calais.
14. From 1977 A I 6. Smooth yellow-buff ware: grey and white grits. Flange incomplete: fragment of spout. Gillam 238. A.D. 70–100. (?) Pas de Calais.
15. From 1973 II 2. Heavily burnt. Flavian-Trajanic. cf. Bushe-Fox type 26/30. Gaul.

B. **First-century Mortaria from the Verulamium Region** (FIGS. 108–9)

16. From 1977 A I 2, with counter-stamp F.LVGVDV of Albinus (p. 239, **stamp No. 1**). Hard rather finely granular cream-coloured ware (with pink core): grey, white, brown and reddish grits. Well worn. A.D. 60–90.
17. From 1980 E II 11. Hard finely granular yellow-buff ware. One large flint grit on the outside; rim stained dark underneath. Probably burnt. A.D. 60–90.
18. From 1982 J 5, flange broken. Hard rather finely granular buff ware: grey, white and light brown grits. Heavily burnt. A.D. 60–90.
19. From 1976 H I 4. Hard granular buff ware. Burnt. One white grit present. A.D. 65–95.
20. From 1982 G II 3, with part of the name-stamp of Albinus (p. 239, **stamp No. 3**). Hard rather finely granular yellow-buff ware: white and grey grits. Slightly burnt. A.D. 60–90.
21. From 1982 G II 12, with part of the name-stamp of Albinus (p. 239, **stamp No. 4**). Hard rather finely granular buff ware, blue-black core: grey grits. Burnt. A.D. 60–90.
22. From 1977 A I 54. Ware as No. 20: light grey grits. A.D. 70–100.
23. From 1980 E I 20 with counter-stamp F.LVGVDV of Albinus (p. 239, **stamp No. 2**). Hard finely granular buff ware: grey and white grits. Some sherds heavily burnt: one sherd with vitrification attached in fire. A.D. 60–90.
24. From 1973 I 50. Hard rather finely granular buff ware. Burnt. Flavian.
25. From 1976 H III 9. Hard very finely granular yellow-buff ware: white and grey grits. Flavian.
26. From 1976 K I 25 with stamp of Sollus (p. 241, **stamp No. 12**). Hard rather finely granular buff ware. Flavian.
27. From 1977 A I 7. Ware as No. 26: translucent white grits. Burnt. Flavian.
28. From 1978 B I 13. Hard rather granular buff ware, smoothed surface: dark and light grey grits. Flavian.
29. From 1980 E I 26. Hard rather finely granular buff ware, grey core: grey, white and red-brown grits. Style of Albinus. A.D. 70–100.
30. From 1980 E I 26, with fragmentary stamp of Sextus Valerius (p. 241, **stamp No. 13**). Granular greyish-cream fabric with abundant well-sorted quartz and sparse red-brown inclusions: flint and quartz grits. Flavian.
31. From 1981 F II 26. Fine cream-coloured fabric with pink core and much quartz tempering. Some red-brown as well as quartz particles appear on the inner surface, but this is probably

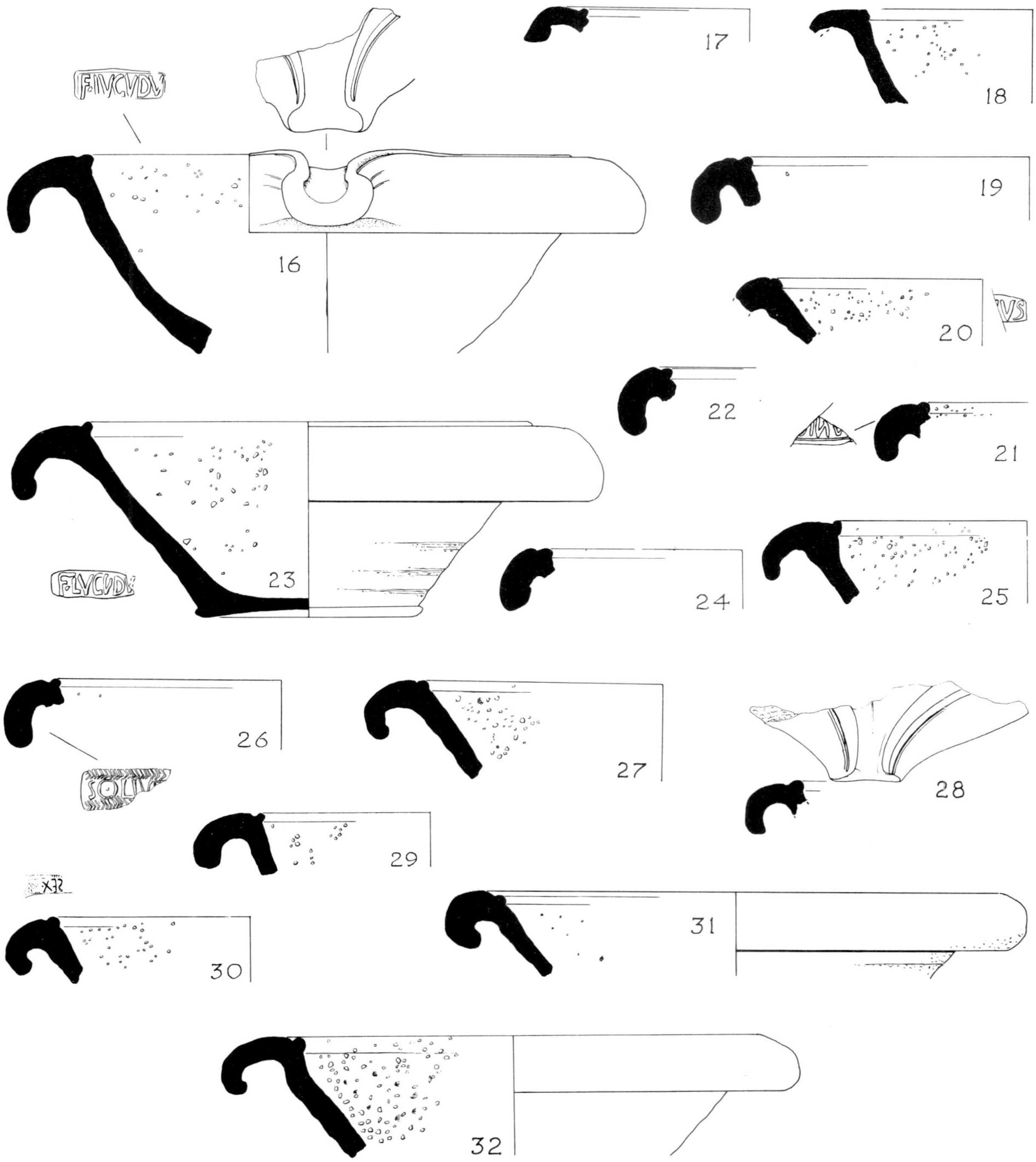

FIG. 108. First-century Mortaria from the Verulamium region (1/4).

tempering rather than trituration grits. The fabric is made granular by these additions. Probably A.D. 70–100. Probably Verulamium region.

32. From 1977 A I 8. Hard rather finely granular yellow-buff ware, grey core: translucent white and light brown grits. A.D. 70–110.
33. From 1977 A I 54. Hard rather finely granular yellow-buff ware: dark and light grey grits. A.D. 70–100.
34. From 1977 A I 64. Ware as No. 33: translucent grey and white grits. Burnt. A.D. 70–100.

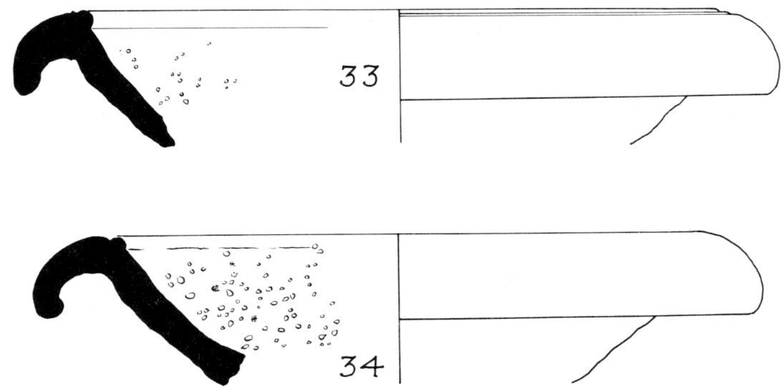

FIG. 109. First-century Mortaria from the Verulamium region (1/4).

C. **First-century or probably First-century Mortaria from Northern Britain** (Nos. 35, 37), **Scotland** (No. 36) **and Uncertain Origin** (Nos. 38–42) (FIG. 110)

35. From 1973 II 21. Smooth buff ware, orange-buff core: grey and white grits. (?) Flavian. (?) Northern Britain.
36. From 1982 G I 15. Flange fragment burnt throughout. Soft red-brown fabric with black core. Probably Flavian. Possibly Scotland (but condition too bad for certainty).
37. From 1982 G I 15. Brownish buff fabric with grey core: grey, dark and a few reddish grits. Date uncertain: possibly Antonine. Northern Britain.
38. From 1973 II 28. Hard buff slightly micaceous ware, grey core: translucent white grits and one grey. Probably early to mid Flavian. Source unidentified (see No. 40).
39. From 1981 F I 13. Slightly sandy cream-coloured fabric: red-brown and quartz grits. Heavily worn. Date and source uncertain.
40. From 1973 II 25B. Smooth hard buff ware with traces of reddish slip: small translucent grits. Early to mid Flavian. Same unidentified source as No. 38.
41. From 1977 A I 64. Hard finely granular buff ware, small grey and white grits. Burnt. Flavian. Source unidentified.
42. From 1977 A I 29. Buff ware, mainly burnt black: grey grits. Unusual form. Probably Flavian. Source unidentified.

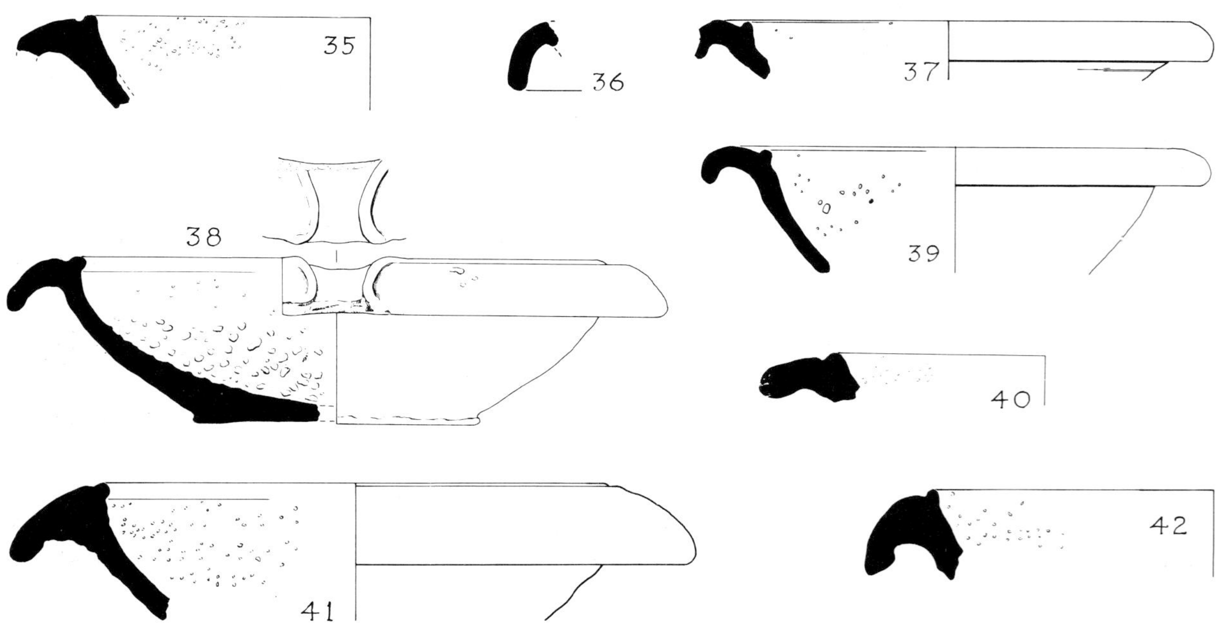

FIG. 110. First-century Mortaria from northern Britain (1/4).

D. **Second-century Mortaria from the Colchester Kilns** (FIG. 111)

43. From 1977 A II 8. Smooth yellow-buff ware: grey and white grits. A.D. 140–170. Colchester.
44. From 1973 II 4: demolition deposit in Antonine II drain (p. 63). Almost complete through broken and riveted vessel with **stamp No. 20** (p. 242), *q.v.* for description of fabric): a few white, grey and red grits remaining. Well worn. A.D. 130–170.
45. From 1977 A I 3. Smooth yellow-buff ware: grey and white grits. Burnt. A.D. 140–170. Colchester.
46. From 1976 H II 6A. Hard finely granular cream-coloured ware: grey and white grits. A.D. 130–170. Colchester.
47. From 1973 II 2. Smooth buff ware, orange core: white and grey grits. A.D. 130–170, but probably late in the series. Colchester.
48. From 1980 E II 10. Rather finely granular buff ware, much abraded: white and grey grits. Possibly from same vessel as No. 53. A.D. 130–170. Colchester.
49. From 1981 F II 18. Incomplete rim-section. Smooth yellow-buff ware: white and grey grits. Burnt. A.D. 140–180. Colchester.
50. From 1977 A II 7A. Hard yellow-buff finely granular ware: large white and grey grits, many missing. A.D. 140–170. Colchester.
51. From 1977 A I 3. Base sherd with one lead rivet *in situ* and one empty rivet-hole. Smooth light reddish ware, cream-coloured slip: brown and grey grits. (?) Colchester.
52. From 1981 F II 8. Yellow buff ware, orange core: grey and white grits. A.D. 140–180. Colchester.
53. From 1980 E II Pit 1, with fragment of stamp (p. 242, **No. 24**). Yellow-buff ware: grey and white grits. Worn. A.D. 130–170. Colchester.

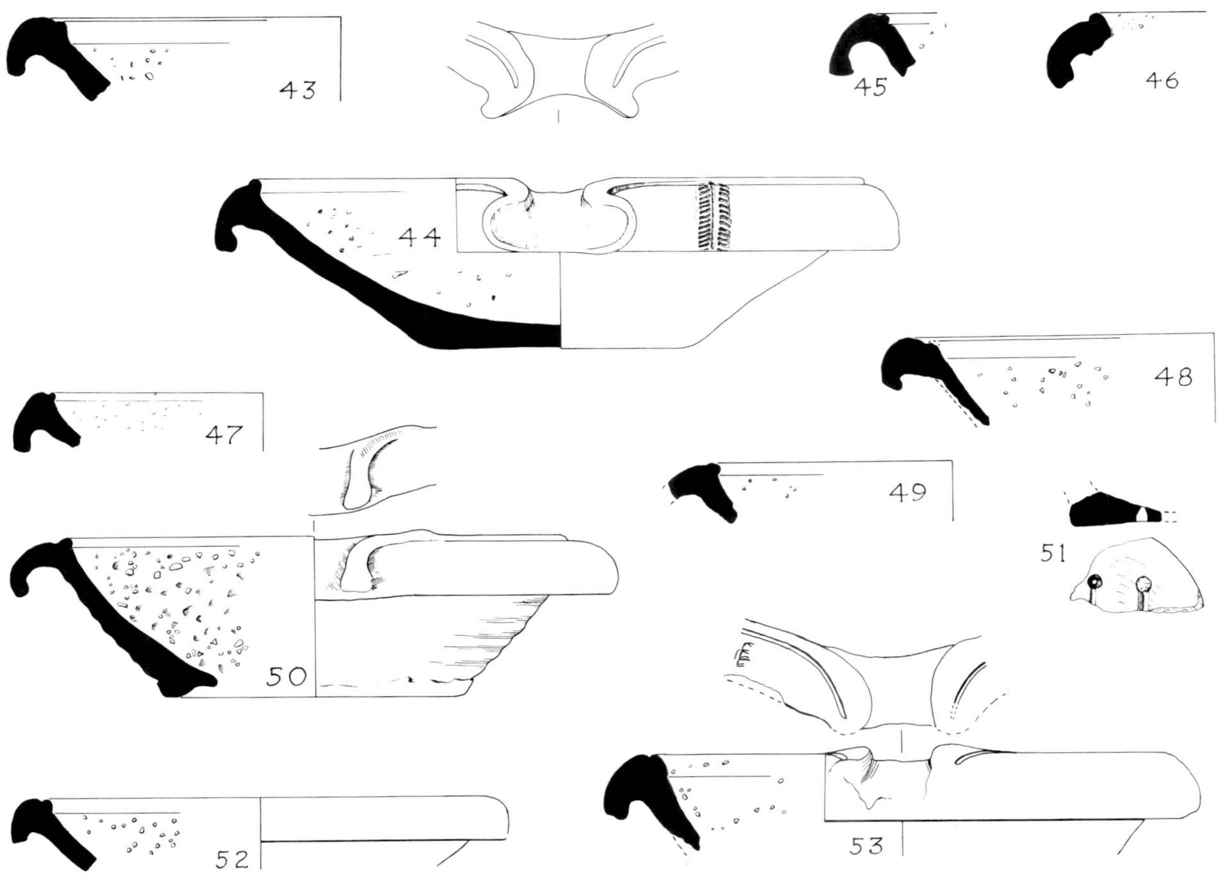

FIG. 111. Second-century Mortaria from Colchester (1/4).

E. **Second-century Mortaria from Mancetter/Hartshill** (FIG. 112)

54. From 1977 A II 12, with fragmentary stamp of Sarrius (p. 240, **stamp No. 10**). Smooth hard creamy-white ware with thick slightly pinkish core: brown grits. A.D. 140–170. Mancetter/Hartshill.
55. From 1979 D VII 6: tip of flange missing. Smooth hard cream-coloured ware: brown (and one white) grits. Burnt. Probably Antonine. Mancetter/Hartshill.
56. From 1981 F II 1. Unusual form with distal bead on flange. Smooth cream-coloured ware: black ironstone-like grits. A.D. 130– 165. Midlands.
57. From 1982 G I 18, with stamps of Sarrius (p. 240, **stamp No. 11**). Over half the vessel, broken. Smooth creamy-white ware: red-brown and black grits. A.D. 135–170. Mancetter/Hartshill.
58. From 1978 B II 5. Wall-sided mortarium in hard cream-coloured ware, smoothed surface: grey grits, some as tempering. A.D. 150–220. Mancetter/Hartshill(?).

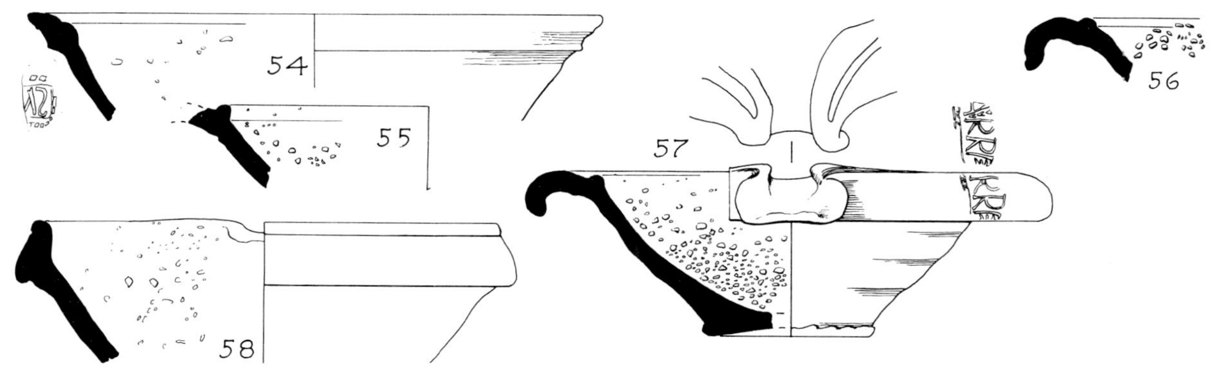

FIG. 112. Second-century Mortaria from Mancetter/Hartshill (1/4).

F. **Second-century Mortaria from Northern Britain** (FIG. 113)

59. From 1978 B I 5: tip of flange missing. Smooth light reddish ware, grey core; trace of cream slip. Second century. Northern Britain.
60. From 1977 A I 3. Smooth hard orange-buff ware, cream slip. Perhaps part of No. 65. Second century. Northern Britain.
61. From 1973 I 3: broken flange. Pinkish-buff ware: grey and white grits. Northern Britain.
62. From 1981 F I 11. Hard orange-brown ware, cream slip: quartz tempering and quartz, black and brown grit. Antonine. Northern Britain, possibly Scotland.
63. From 1980 E II 14. Abraded sherd. Smooth orange-buff to light reddish ware: white grits. Antonine. Northern Britain, possibly Scotland.
64. From 1974 P IV 4. Smooth hard reddish-buff ware, traces of cream slip: grey and white grits. Well worn. Burnt. Second century. (?) Northern Britain.
65. From 1977 A I 2 with twice-impressed stamp (p. 241, **stamp No. 16**, *q.v.* for description of fabric). Northern Britain.
66. From 1977 A II 26. Smooth light reddish ware, grey core, trace of cream slip: white and grey grits. Second century. Northern Britain.
67. From 1978 B I 3. Smooth hard ware burnt grey. Second century. Northern Britain.
68. From 1979 D II 6. Two joining pieces of small bowl-like vessel. Orange-red fabric: quartz grit. Probably Antonine. Probably Northern Britain.

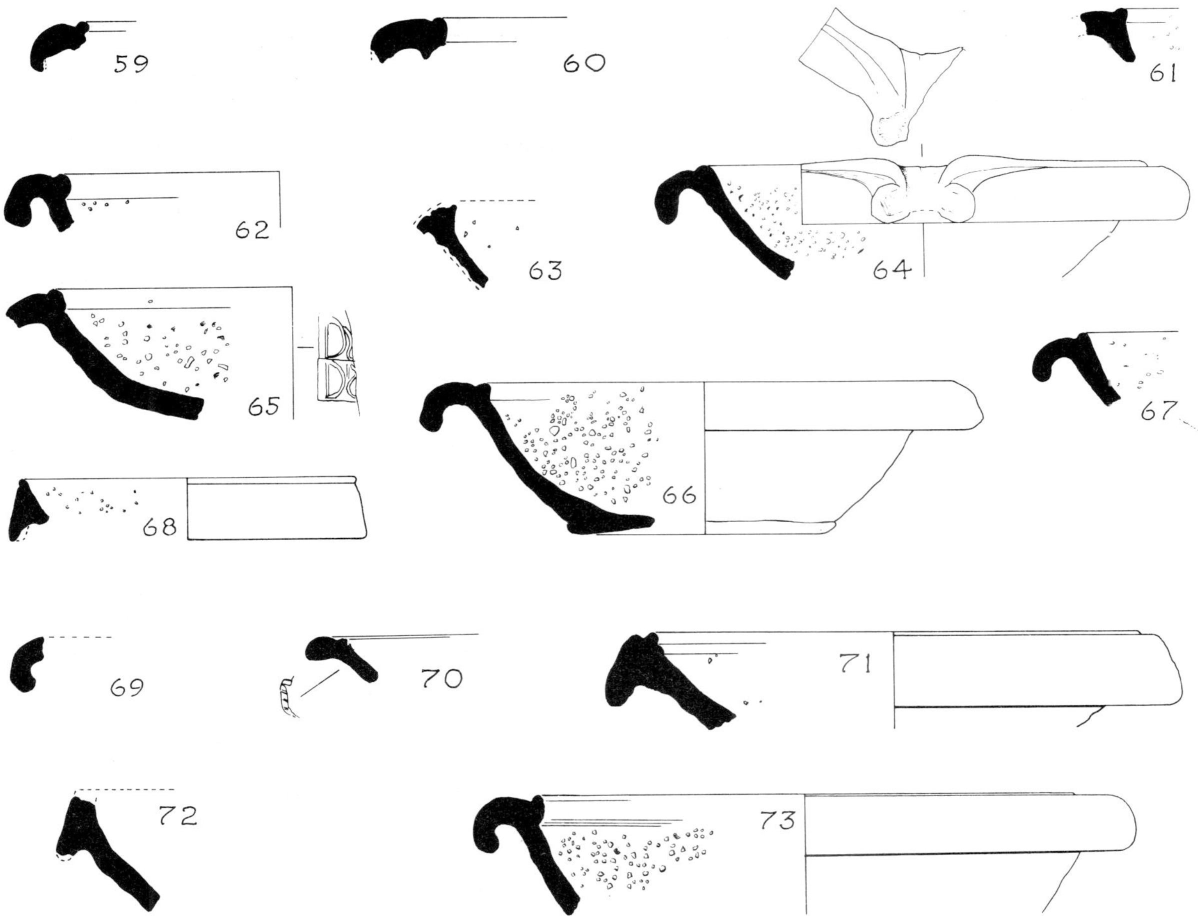

FIG. 113. Second-century Mortaria from northern Britain (1/4).

G. **Second-century Mortaria from North-west Britain** (No. 69) **and Scotland** (Nos. 70–73)

69. From 1980 E II 7. Red-brown ware with traces of cream slip. Second century. North-western Britain.
70. From 1977 A II 12, with fragment of stamp (p. 241, **stamp No. 17**, *q.v.* for description of fabric). Probably Scotland.
71. From 1982 J 12. Pinkish-brown fabric with self-coloured slip: quartz and occasional red-brown grits. Probably Antonine. Probably Scotland.
72. From 1981 F II 1. Flange broken. Hard finely granular reddish-buff ware. Grey core: white grits. Burnt. Perhaps a mortarium and if so certainly made in Scotland. Antonine.
73. From 1980, outer ditch in south side of fort. Hard rather finely granular reddish ware, deep cream-coloured slip: grey, brown and white grits. Antonine. Perhaps Scotland.

H. **Mortaria from North-eastern England** (FIG. 114)

74. From 1976 H I 12. Smooth hard orange-buff ware: grey and white grits. A.D. 150–200. Style of Bellicus, Corbridge.
75. From 1980 E I 23. Smooth light reddish ware, grey core, cream slip: grey grits. Worn. Heavily burnt. Probably Antonine. Probably North-eastern England or Scotland.
76. From 1976 K I 8. Hard buff finely granular ware: large brown, white and grey grits. A.D. 160–200. North-eastern England: style of Bellicus of Corbridge.

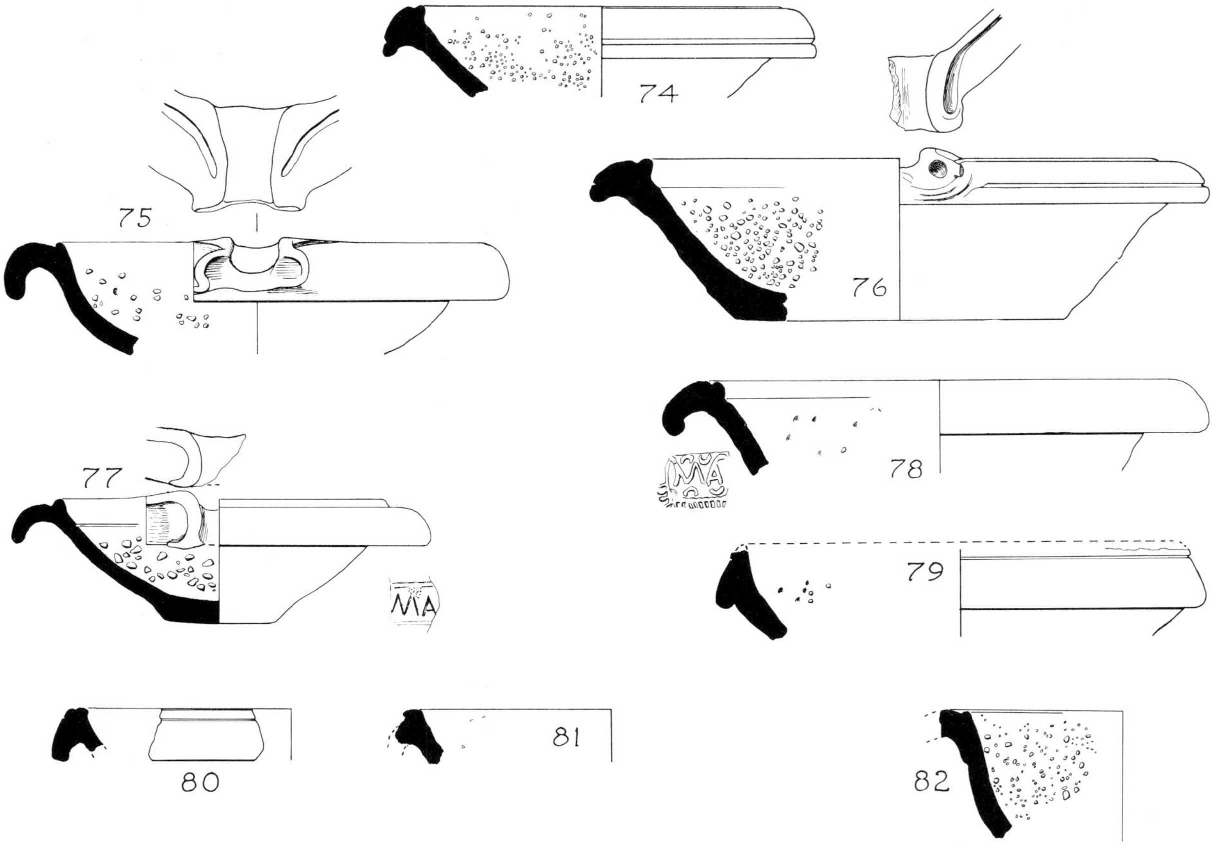

FIG. 114. Second-century Mortaria from north-eastern England (Nos. 74–79) and from the Verulamium region (80–82) (1/4).

77. From 1980 E II 19, with stamp MA[(p. 239, **stamp No. 9**). Almost whole vessel: soft orange fabric with ill-sorted sub-angular quartz and occasional black inclusions; cream slip: opaque quartz grit. The stamp is probably of Marcus. Probably Corbridge.
78. From 1980 E I 15, with stamp MA[(p. 239, **stamp No. 8**, *q.v.* for description of fabric). Antonine. North-eastern England.
79. From 1979 D III 3. Hard whitish ware: brown and white grits. Top of bead missing. North-east England, perhaps Corbridge.

I. **Second-century Mortaria from the Verulamium Region** (Nos. 80, 81) **and Source Unknown** (No. 82)

80. From 1980 E I 1. Unusual form, heavily burnt. Greyish-cream fabric with dark core, and possibly a slip. A.D. 140–200. Probably Verulamium region.
81. From 1974 P III 3. Flange broken. Hard finely granular buff ware: dark grey grit. Second century. Verulamium region.
82. From 1980 E II Post-hole 3. Flange broken. Smooth hard cream-coloured ware: red-brown and some grey grits. Date and source unknown.

XXIII. THE MORTARIUM STAMPS

(FIG. 115)

By K.F. Hartley

1. 77 A I 2. LVGVDV. Flange fragment in granular cream fabric with pink core (FIG. 108, No. 16). The stamp is from the same die-type as Frere 1972, fig. 145, No. 6.
2. 80 E I 20 and E I 19 joining E I 32. F.LVGVDV. A heavily worn mortarium (FIG. 108, No. 23) in basically similar fabric with vitrification on E I 20. The stamp is identical to No. 1 except that the top bar of the F is extended and joins the top of the L. It always appears with the same name die as No. 1 and the changes could possibly be the result of deterioration and trimming of the die having taken place.
3. 82 G II 3. Albin]VS. On a burnt mortarium with incomplete rim-section (FIG. 108, No. 20). The stamp is from the same name-die as Frere 1972, fig. 145, No. 5; this name die was regularly used in conjunction with the dies producing the above counterstamps (Nos. 1 and 2).
4. 82 G II 12. Alb]IN[us, N reversed. Stamp impressed diagonally across the rim of a mortarium which has been fired to cream at the surface but has a very thick blue-black core (FIG. 108, No. 21). The stamp is from the same die as Frere 1972, fig. 145, No. 3.
5. (*Not illustrated*). Unstratified: Part of a letter, probably F, impressed diagonally across the flange. The flange fragment is burnt grey throughout. This cannot be fully identified without further study but it is probably the first letter of an F.LVGVDV counterstamp; it is not the counterstamp used with the above name stamp (No. 3).

These stamps are all name or counterstamps of Albinus and represent 4–5 vessels. More than 360 mortaria of Albinus have been recorded from sites throughout Roman Britain. This total is about three times larger than for any other known mortarium potter. All but one to three of his mortaria are in fabric entirely typical of the important potteries adjacent to Watling Street in the area between Verulamium and Brockley Hill. At least two and perhaps three of his mortaria are in one of two other differing fabrics; at least one of these is most unlikely to have been produced in the Verulamium region and may indicate that Albinus moved to this region at an early stage in his career after starting it elsewhere, probably at Colchester. Albinus worked in the period A.D. 60–90. For some further details of his work see Frere 1972, 371–2 and Frere 1984, 281–2.

6. 82 G I 1. Ploughsoil, unstratified. A broken stamp from a die of Austinus which probably gave AUSTIN/MANV when completely impressed. Austinus almost certainly began his working life at Wilderspool (Hartley & Webster 1973, 95–7), and later moved to the Carlisle region; he may also have worked in Scotland where 20 of his 51 mortaria have been found. His activity fell within the period A.D. 120–165. He is perhaps the only mortarium potter to have used '*manu*' ('by the hand of') in his stamps.
7. 80 E II 1. Ploughsoil, unstratified. A broken retrograde stamp of Loccius Pro..; his name is always abbreviated and should doubtless be expanded to something like Loccius Probus or Proculus. He worked at Mancetter, Warwickshire within the period A.D. 130–165. Eleven of his mortaria have been found in Scotland and 24 from sites in the Midlands and north of England, excluding his production site.
8. 80 E I 15. Antonine I demolition-layer. Hard orange-brown fabric with some ill-sorted quartz and (?) iron slag inclusions and traces of cream slip; trituration grit consists of quartz and red-brown material (FIG. 114, No. 78). Worn. An incompletely impressed stamp, MA[, from a die which gives MARF. Other stamps from the same die are known from Cramond in Scotland and Catterick; Chesters; Vindolanda; and Corbridge (three). The distribution and the rim-profiles would fit production within the period A.D. 120–160. He worked in north-east England in the Bainesse/Corbridge area.
9. 80 E II 19. (?) Antonine II gully. About three-quarters of the vessel survives (FIG. 114, No. 77). The fragmentary and very faint stamp reads MA[, and it can be attributed to Marcus.

FIG. 115. The Potters' stamps on Mortaria ($\frac{1}{2}$).

Other stamps from the same die are known only from Corbridge (five), where he probably worked. A.D. 120–160.

10. 77 A II 12. Antonine I demolition-layer. A faint, broken stamp preserving the final S of a stamp of Sarrius from a die which gives the name with one R, reversed S at beginning and end, and with an extra stroke attached to the V, giving it the appearance of a reversed N. On a mortarium with incomplete rim-section (FIG. 112, No. 54).

11. 82 G I 18. Antonine I demolition-pit. Over half of a mortarium (FIG. 112, No. 57) in creamy white fabric with black and red-brown trituration grit. The stamps from both sides survive, though both are broken; they are from the most commonly-used die of Sarrius and read **SARRI** with decorative motifs between some of the letters.

Sarrius was the most productive mortarium potter stamping mortaria in the second century and is of quite exceptional interest for other reasons. His main workshops were at Mancetter and Hartshill in Warwickshire but he opened a secondary workshop at Rossington Bridge (report forthcoming), and the possibility of a third one in Scotland is now being considered. Both of the Strageath mortaria are from his Midland workshops, which he probably kept functioning throughout the period when he was producing mortaria in northern Britain. There are now 16 of his Midland mortaria and at least 24 of his northern products recorded from Scotland; from sites in England there are 9 mortaria from his Rossington Bridge workshop and 82 from his Midland workshops, excluding finds from the kiln-sites. The number of his mortaria from Antonine deposits in Scotland leaves no doubt of his primarily Antonine date; two stamps of his are known from sites on Hadrian's Wall, at Birdoswald (Richmond & Birley 1930, 188, fig. 13, No. 2 on 187, described as illiterate, in Period 1a, A.D. 125–140); (the Strageath stamp No. 10 is from the same die); and at Housesteads (information P. Moffat). A stamp from Verulamium is recorded from a deposit dated about A.D. 155/160 (Frere 1972, 378, No. 35). The evidence as a whole supports a date of A.D. 135–170 for his activity.

12. 76 K I 25. A broken stamp from the most commonly-used die of Sollus. More than 100 of his mortaria are now known from sites throughout Britain, including four from Brockley Hill in the Verulamium region, where he may have worked, and four from Loudon Hill (1–2), Newstead (two), and Strageath in Scotland. His rim-profiles are consistently early and a date of A.D. 60–100 is reasonably certain for his work (cf. FIG. 108, No. 26).
13. 80 E I 26. Diameter 31 cm. Two joining fragments from a mortarium (FIG. 108, No. 30), made in the Verulamium region. The fragmentary stamp, reading **SEX[** (retrograde), is from a die which gives SEX.VA.IV possibly followed by S. This man was one of at least five potters who shared the same *praenomen* and *nomen*, Sextus Valerius, indicating that they were the freedmen of one master. They all worked at Colchester but this man at some point had a workshop in the Verulamium region. Their work falls within the period A.D. 50–90.
14. 86 T I 3. A spout and flange fragment in fine-textured, yellowish-cream fabric, which is partly crazed; some tiny quartz and rare red-brown and black inclusions are just visible at x10 magnification; none of the inside surface survives. The fragmentary stamp is in poor condition but is almost certainly from the top right-hand corner of a stamp of Q. Valerius Veranius, which reads **VERANI** when completely impressed. The fabric and rim are typical of the work of Veranius and several other potters who worked in the same tradition. Veranius's production can be dated A.D. 65/70–100. For further details of his distribution and evidence for his date, see Hartley 1977, 8 and 10; it is now clear that he and other potters producing similar mortaria worked entirely on the Continent and there is some evidence to suggest that their potteries were in the Pas de Calais area.
15. 82 G I 6. Fragment from a rim-profile (FIG 107, No. 4), which is either of Hartley Group I type or a variant of that type (Hartley 1977); in micaceous, very fine-textured brown fabric with browner core; no inclusions visible except for rare red-brown material; no trituration grit survives. The fragmentary stamp which reads **]D.M**, is otherwise unrecorded. The mortarium is almost certainly an import from Gaul and is certainly first-century in date.
16. 77 A I 2. Antonine II demolition-layer. Two joining fragments from a mortarium (FIG. 113, No. 65) with incomplete rim-section; hard, fine-textured, orange-brown fabric with some quartz and rare red-brown inclusions, and trituration grit of similar material; there are traces of cream slip. Worn. Two stamps have been impressed close together and both are broken; they may read **]SCI** or **]SD** retrograde but no other examples are recorded. The mortarium can be attributed to a workshop in northern Britain; it is undoubtedly second-century.
17. 77 A II 12. Antonine I demolition-layer. Diameter 24–25 cm. Small fragment in fine-textured, drab, orange-brown fabric with dark grey core and rare quartz inclusions; the trituration grit included quartz and there are traces of a buff-cream slip. Only the border survives of a stamp which is almost certainly unrecorded elsewhere. This rim-profile in

conjunction with this fabric may reasonably be taken to indicate production in Scotland in the second century.

18. 1980, from exposure of the most southerly ditch on the south side of the fort, cut by agricultural operations. Flange fragment in softish fine-textured white fabric with rare red-brown and quartz inclusions. This fragmentary stamp has been recorded only once before, at Aldborough, Yorks. The latter stamp, though still incomplete shows]**ARQ**[in large letters with Q upside down. In fact it is impossible to know which way up the stamp is intended to be and it may be the work of a semi-literate potter. The fabric points to production at either Lincoln or Mancetter, the former perhaps the more likely. The profile fits a second-century date.
19. 85 R II 5. Antonine I demolition-layer. Diameter 24 cm. Rim fragment in micaceous, fine-textured, pale brown fabric with occasional red-brown inclusions; no trituration grit survives. Slightly burnt. The stamp is almost complete but it is not possible to interpret it with any assurance; it could include . . .**ANDINF**, with AN and NF ligatured, but it may be the stamp of a semi-literate potter. Other stamps from the same die have been noted from Winterton (Stead 1976, 122, No. 8), and Lincoln and production may be attributed to the Lincoln area in the second century.
20. 73 II 4. Demolition-filling of Antonine II drain (p. 63). An almost complete mortarium (FIG. 111, No. 44), well-worn and riveted; in soft, pale brownish-cream fabric. The herringbone-type stamp from the same die as Hull 1963, fig. 60, No. 30 is the commonest produced in the second-century potteries at Colchester.
21. 76 H I 11. Antonine I: trodden into Flavian demolition-layer. A mortarium in generally similar fabric to No. 20, with a herringbone-type stamp from the same die as *ibid.*, No. 33.
22. 83 L I 5. Antonine I demolition-layer. Mortarium in yellowish-cream fabric of powdery texture with surface beginning to craze; some quartz and flint inclusions. The herringbone-type stamp is from the same die as *ibid.*, No. 38.
23. (*Not illustrated*). 77 A I 8. Antonine I demolition-layer. A herringbone-type stamp on a Colchester mortarium; stamp too fragmentary for identification.
24. (*Not illustrated*, but see FIG. 111, No. 53). 80 E II Pit 1 + E II 10. Antonine I demolition-layer. Four fragments from a Colchester mortarium; stamp too fragmentary for identification.

These mortaria and their herringbone-type stamps are typical of mortaria sent to Scotland in considerable quantities during the Antonine occupation (Hull 1963, 114–16). For details of their total distribution see MacIvor, Thomas and Breeze 1978–80, 261–4 and Thomas (forthcoming) on Inveresk.

XXIV. THE OTHER POTTERY

By Anne Anderson

The coarse pottery is presented as a series of types. Because of the high proportion of sherds of Flavian vessels in residual contexts the division between Flavian and Antonine forms has had to rely on typological rather than stratigraphical considerations since many of the recognisably early types were found in Antonine I or II contexts. Where possible a firm indication of date is given; but particularly in the case of coarse-ware jars, distinction of Flavian from Antonine forms is sometimes difficult; for forms assigned a Flavian date, however, there is often at least one stratified piece from a Flavian context among other (residual) examples. When a vessel has a Flavian context, that context is stated, other examples being given just one star for an Antonine I context or two stars for one in Antonine II.

The period concerned is too short for typological distinctions to be made between Antonine I and Antonine II vessels, but vessels with an Antonine II context are distinguished with two stars, and in Section B their contexts are described.

A. FIRST-CENTURY OR PROBABLY FIRST-CENTURY POTTERY

Ring-Necked Flagons, Flavian (FIG. 116)

Flagons were rarely found at Strageath, and with the possible exception of No. 7 all are Flavian. What form of vessel was used instead in the Antonine forts is impossible to decide; only six Antonine contexts yielded flagon-sherds, none of them diagnostic. Only one example of a bronze jug (FIG. 77, No. 71) was found, so that, although this did come from an Antonine I context, there is very little indication that such vessels were used as substitutes.

1. Two upper rings defined by narrow ridges. Hard white finely granular ware.
   1977 A I 47.*
2. Rim and four lower smaller rings. Smooth hard buff ware.
   1973 III 9.**
3. Rim and two other rings of the same size. Smooth reddish-buff ware.
   1974 P XI 5, Flavian occupation layer, *principia* Also (*not illustrated*):
   1977 K I 18, Flavian demolition-layer, Building IV.
   1979 D III 2.**
4. Rim and four lower rings. Buff ware, finely granular with orange to buff core.
   1981 F II 10.*
5. Narrow ring below the rim. Smooth burnished light red ware.
   1982 G I 24, Flavian wall-trench, Buildings I-II.
6. Rim and three equal-sized lower rings. Smooth light reddish-buff ware.
   1976 H I 8.*

Plain Flagon

7. Cupped, slightly moulded rim. Smooth light grey-buff ware.
   1973 II 2.*

Unguent Jar (FIG. 116)

8. Evenly rilled sides, pedestal base. Hard light reddish finely granular ware with a buff slip.
   1977 A II 17.* Also (*not illustrated*):
   1983 L II 11.*

Poppy-head Beakers

(a) (*not illustrated*). Upright neck, Gillam type 70.
   1983 L I 11.*
   1984 S II 17.*

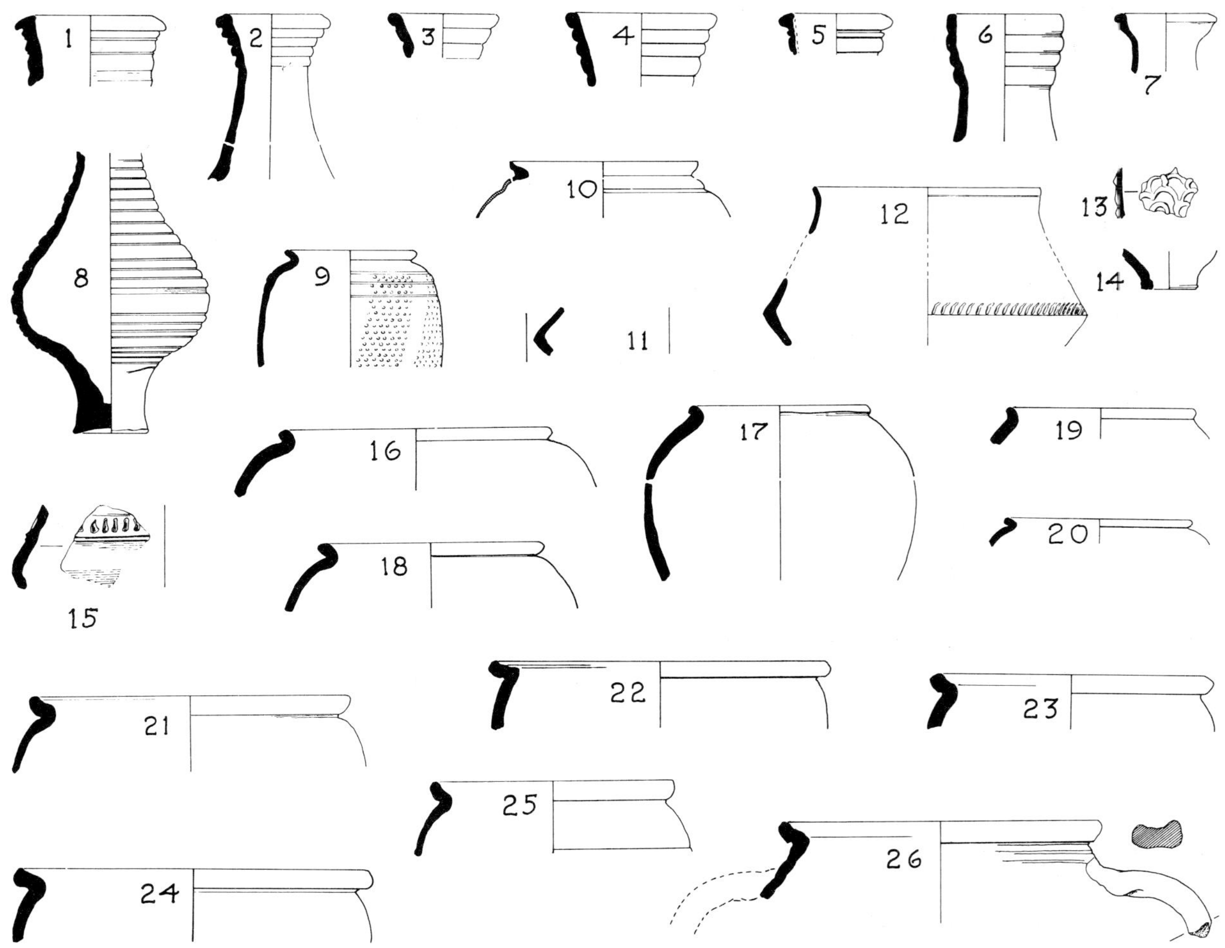

FIG. 116. Flavian Flagons, Unguent Jar, Beakers and Jars (¼).

(b) (*not illustrated*). Beaded rim. Fine light grey-buff ware with buff core.
1985 L II 14.*

Beaker with barbotine dots (FIGS. 116)

9. Small everted rim, three slight shoulder-grooves. Fine hard light grey ware; possible slip on surface.
77 A I 7.**

Beakers, Flavian (FIG. 116)

10. Mica-dusted beaker, cupped rim and shoulder-groove. Very fine buff ware with grey core.
1975 P XLI 15, Flavian demolition-layer in the *principia*, with added shoulder-sherd from P XLI 12, Flavian wall trench, *ibid.*
11. Biconical beaker. Fine micaceous grey ware, burnished.
1979 D III 2.** (Also (*not illustrated*):
1979 D III 3.*
1981 F II 20, Flavian occupation-layer, Building XI.
12. Biconical beaker with rouletting. Fine burnished grey ware.
1981 F II 20, Flavian occupation-layer, Building XI.

13–14. Colour-coated beaker with barbotine scale. Fine orange-buff ware, red-brown coating on both surfaces. Pre-Flavian import (?)
1977 B I 2.*
1977 B I 3.*

15. Beaker with impressed decoration at base of neck. Very fine smooth cream ware similar to Lyon ware. (?) Import.
    1983 L II 4.★

Jars, Flavian (FIG. 116)

(a) *Bead-rim*

16. Hard grey burnished ware.
    1976 H I 16, Flavian wall-trench, Building II. Also (*not illustrated*):
    1977 A II 43, Flavian occupation-layer, Building VIII.
    1978 B I 19, Flavian occupation-layer, Building VII.
    1983 L I 11.★
17. Small bead-rim. Smooth micaceous burnished grey ware.
    1977 A I 9.★ Also (*not illustrated*):
    1977 A II 43, Flavian occupation-layer, Building VIII.
18. 1977 A I 64, Flavian demolition-pit, Building V.
19. Smooth micaceous burnished light grey ware.
    1978 B III 15.★
20. Smoothly burnished light grey ware.
    1981 F II 20, Flavian occupation-layer, Building XI. Also (*not illustrated*):
    1982 H I 6.★

Lid-seated Jars, Flavian (FIG. 116)

21. Grey burnished ware.
    1973 II 2.★ Also (*not illustrated*):
    1973 II 3, Flavian occupation-layer, Building I.
    1977 A II 23, Flavian demolition-pit.
    1977 A I 8.★
22. Grey burnished ware.
    1982 G I 18.★
23. Burnished reddish-buff ware, Gillam type 103.
    1977 A I 14, Flavian occupation-layer, Buildings V, VI.
24. Burnished reddish-buff ware.
    1977 A I 37, Flavian wall-trench, Building VII.
25. Burnished reddish-buff ware.
    1981 F II 31.★ Also (*not illustrated*):
    1984 S I 5.★

Honey Jar (FIG. 116)

26. Buff coarse ware.
    1985 N II 7.★

Rusticated Jars, Flavian (FIG. 117)

27. Two shallow shoulder-grooves, Gillam type 97. Hard light grey to buff ware, light grey core.
    1979 D V 8.★
28. Single shoulder-groove, Gillam type 98. Hard light grey micaceous ware, surfaces light grey to buff; burnished rim and shoulder.
    1975 P XL 16.★
29. As No. 28.
    1977 A II 3.★★

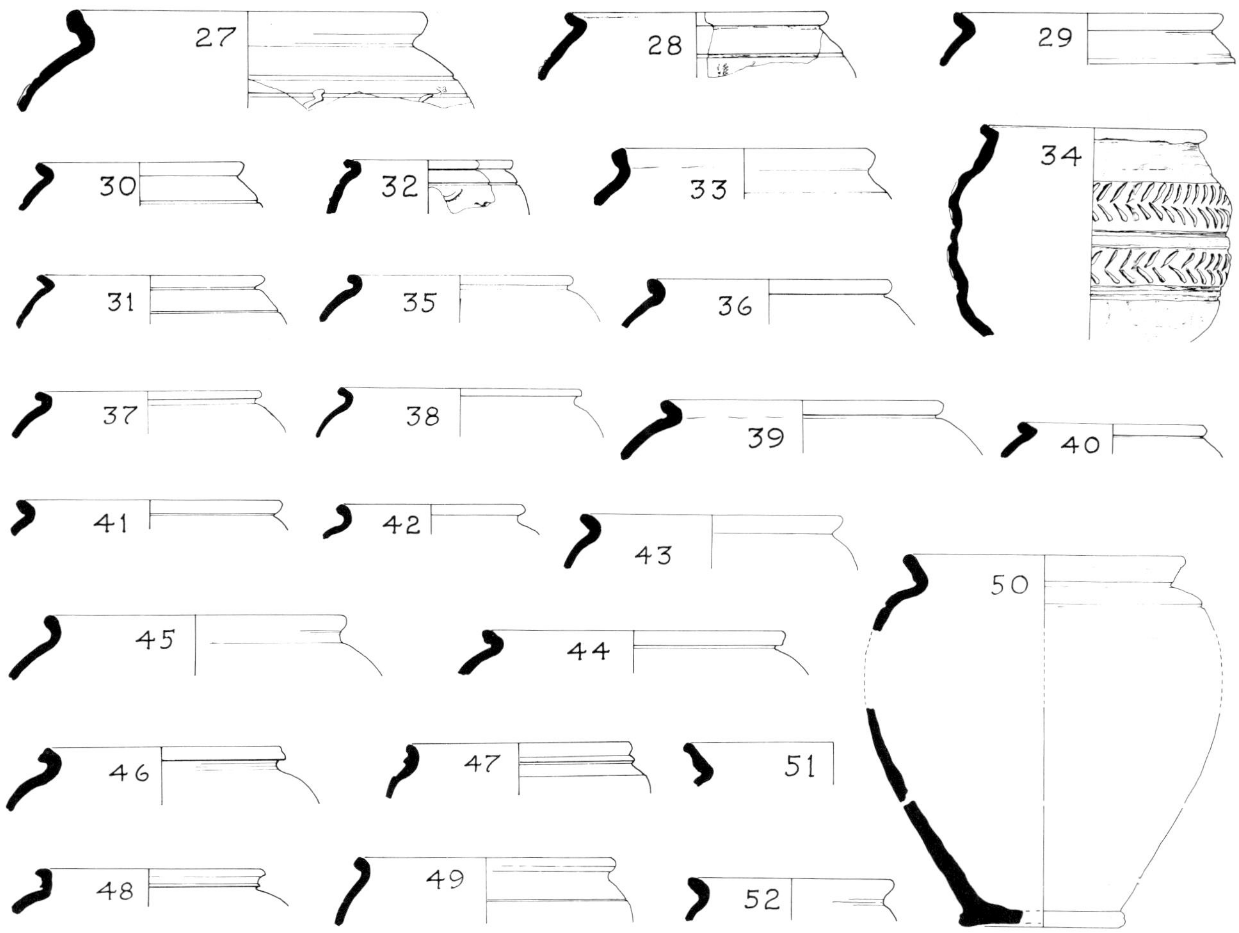

FIG. 117. Flavian Jars (¼).

30. Smooth yellow-buff micaceous ware, grey core.
1977 A I 8.★ Also (*not illustrated*):
1977 A II 16.★
1979 D III 2.★★
1979 D V 3.★
1980 E I 15.★
1981 F II 20, Flavian occupation-layer, Building XI.
1981 F II 25.★★
1981 F II 26.★
31. Fine burnished grey ware, single shoulder-groove.
1981 F II 28. Flavian wall-trench, Building XI.
32. Grey ware.
1976 H I 11, Flavian demolition-layer, Building II. Also (*not illustrated*):
1981 F II 19.★★
1983 L I 11.★
1983 L II 2.★★
1984 S I 5.★
33. Smooth hard light grey ware, burnished black slip, the same fabric as No. 35. Probably rusticated.
1977 A II 12.★
34. Herringbone decoration; hard granular dark grey ware with darker grey surfaces.
1985 R II 7.★★

High-shouldered Jars (FIG. 117)

35. Rounded rim. Fine hard light grey ware, burnished.
 1973 I 2.* Also (*not illustrated*):
 1977 A II 16.*
36. 1985 N II 7.*
37. As No. 35. Fine light grey ware. Inside of rim bevelled.
 1981 F II 11.*
38. 1981 F II 20, Flavian occupation-layer, Building XI.
39. Smooth hard light grey ware, dark burnished slip.
 1977 A II 12.*
40. Outside of rim bevelled. Buff ware with grey core, burnished.
 1977 A I 47.*
41. Buff ware.
 1977 A I 47.*
42. Burnished buff ware.
 1978 B I 5.*
43. Smooth orange-buff ware, burnished.
 1980 F II 15, Flavian demolition-layer, Building XI.
44. Hard grey ware, rim slightly grooved.
 1976 H I 18, Flavian demolition-pit, Building II.
45. Hard finely granular light grey ware.
 1978 B III 4.*
46. Hard finely granular grey ware, rim slightly grooved.
 1979 D VI 11, Flavian demolition-layer, Central Range, Building C. Also (*not illustrated*):
 1979 D VI 3.*

High-shouldered Jars with moulded rim, Flavian (FIG. 117)

47. Hard orange-buff ware, light grey slip. Upright rim with neck-cordon.
 1982 G I 24, Flavian wall-trench, Buildings I, II.
48. Fine micaceous grey ware, burnished.
 1982 J 5, Flavian occupation-layer, Building IV. Also (*not illustrated*):
 1983 L II 4.*
 1984 S I 16, Flavian occupation-layer, Buildings XIII, XIV.
49. Burnished light grey ware.
 1981 F II 11.*
50. Smooth hard light grey-buff ware, burnished. Everted rim, shoulder groove and moulded base. Gillam type 101.
 1973 II 2.*
51. As No. 50. 1973 II 18.** Also (*not illustrated*):
 1973 II 20.*
 1980 E II 2, ploughsoil.
52. Hard light grey-buff ware, darker burnished slip. Everted rim.
 1977 B I 3.*

Necked Jars with narrow mouth (FIG. 118)

53. Hard finely granular grey ware with buff surfaces. Rounded rim.
 1979 D VII 12, Flavian wall-trench, Central Range, Building C.
54. Hard finely granular dark grey ware with buff core. Burnished. Rounded rim.
 1980 E I 18, Flavian demolition-layer, Building IX. Also (*not illustrated*):
 1981 F I 8.*
55. Light reddish-buff burnished ware. Rounded rim.
 1976 H I 6.*

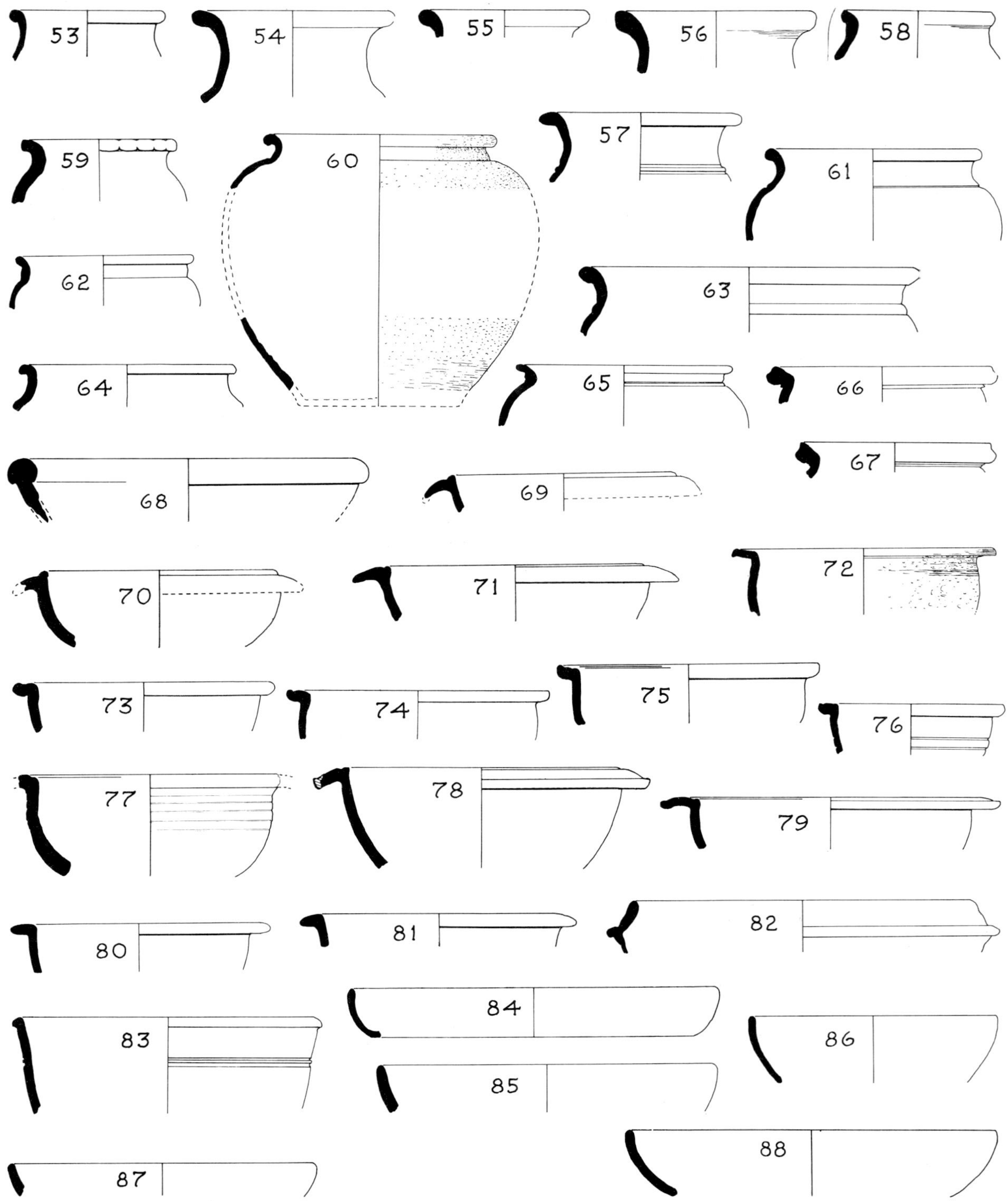

FIG. 118. Flavian Jars (53–67), Bowls (68–83) and Dishes (84–88) (¼).

56. Hard light grey ware. Squared rim.
1974 P III 3.★★
57. Smooth light reddish burnished ware. Rounded rim and shoulder-cordon.
1981 F I 7.★★
58. Smooth burnished light grey ware. Rounded rim, thickened neck.
1977 A I 44.★★
59. Smooth deep yellow-buff ware. Rim slightly frilled.
1977 A I 8.★

Necked Jars with wide mouth, Flavian (FIG. 118)

60. Hard grey granular ware. Curved everted rim.
1974 G I 28, Flavian demolition-layer in *porta decumana*. Also (*not illustrated*):
1977 A I 12, Flavian wall-trench, Building VI.
61. Smooth hard grey ware. Rounded everted rim and shoulder-groove.
1980 E II 14, Flavian demolition-layer, Building XII.
62. Finely granular orange-buff ware, burnished. Rounded rim, thickened neck. 1981 F II 1, ploughsoil. Also (*not illustrated*):
1981 F II 8.*
63. Finely granular light reddish ware with grey core; burnished. Rounded rim, shoulder-cordon.
1976 H II 3.** Also (*not illustrated*):
1984 S V 2.*
64. Smooth light grey-buff micaceous ware. Square rim and beginning of a shoulder-cordon.
1979 D III 2.**
65. Hard light grey ware, darker surfaces. Everted rim, thickened neck with groove.
1977 A II 18.*

Jars with moulded rims (FIG. 118)

66. Hard burnished buff ware.
1974 P III 3.**
67. Hard finely granular buff ware, burnished.
1976 K I 4.**

Bowls (FIG. 118)

68. Smooth hard burnished grey ware. Thick rounded rim.
1982 G II 4.*
69. Smooth cream-coloured ware, orange core, burnished.
1980 E I 16.*
70. Hard burnished finely granular micaceous grey ware.
1982 J 5, Flavian occupation-layer, Building IV.
71. Smooth hard deep cream-coloured ware.
1983 M I 24.*

Reeded-rim Bowls, Flavian (FIG. 118)

72. Very coarse granular dark grey to buff ware. Curved side.
1973 II 25 B.* Also (*not illustrated*):
1976 K I 32, Flavian occupation-layer, Building IV.
73. Finely granular brown-buff ware with grey core; burnished. Shallow groove in rim.
1978 B III 3.** Also (*not illustrated*):
1982 H II 3.*
74. Fine sandy orange ware. Single groove on rim.
1985 R II 5.*
75. Finely granular orange-buff ware, burnished. Two grooves on rim.
1979 D II 4.*
76. Finely granular micaceous grey-buff ware; burnished surfaces. Single groove on rim; two girth-grooves.
1978 B I 5.* Also (*not illustrated*):
1978 B I 13.*
77. Smooth micaceous light orange ware. Multiple fine girth-grooves.
1978 B VI 20, Flavian demolition-layer in front of Building VIII.

78. Smooth hard buff ware with grey core. Gillam type 215.
1980 E II 11.★ (rim restored from following unfigured piece). Also (*not illustrated*):
1981 F I 4 B.★★
79. Smooth fairly hard finely granular ware with a little mica. Two shallow grooves on rim.
1986 T I 3.★

Flat-rimmed Bowls, Flavian (FIG. 118)

80. Smooth dark grey ware, burnished.
1980 E I 18, Flavian demolition-layer, Building IX. Also (*not illustrated*):
1983 L II 4.★
81. Smooth buff ware, mica-coated.
1982 H I 7, Flavian occupation-layer, Building IV.

Flanged Bowl, Flavian (FIG. 118)

82. Smooth burnished light grey ware. Plain inturned rim, small flange.
1974 P XIII 4.★

Hemispherical Bowl, Flavian or Antonine (FIG. 118)

83. Grey ware. Small bead rim, straight wall with two grooves; perhaps imitating samian form 37.
1985 N III 12.★

Dishes, Flavian (FIG. 118)

84. Finely granular light reddish burnished ware. Curved wall and plain rim.
1982 G I 10.★ Also (*not illustrated*):
1983 L II 2.★★
1984 S III 10, Flavian demolition-layer, Building XVI.
85. Finely granular light reddish-buff ware, burnished.
1974 P XIII 4.★★
86. Burnished grey ware. Deeper example.
1981 F I 2, old ploughsoil.
87. Ware as No. 85.
1975 G IV 22.★
88. Ware as No. 85.
1976 H III 7, Flavian demolition-layer, Building III.

B. ANTONINE POTTERY

In this section vessels from Antonine I contexts are again distinguished by one star. Vessels from Antonine II contexts are marked with two stars and a description of the context.

Bag-shaped Beakers (FIG. 119)

89. Cornice rim. Fine orange ware, grey core, dark grey colour-coating. Clay roughcasting. Product of Colchester.
1973 II 2.★

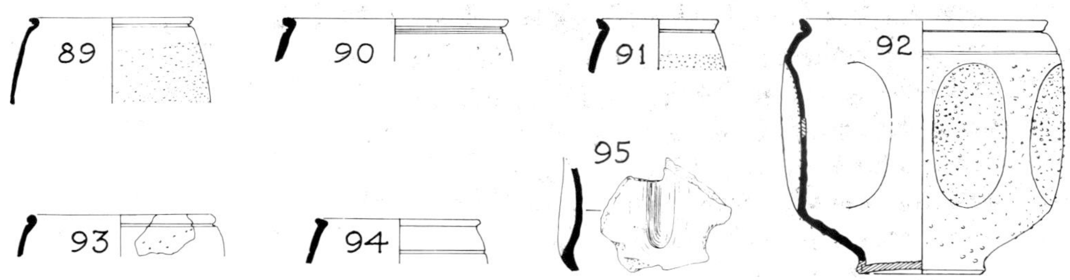

FIG. 119. Antonine bag-shaped and indented Beakers ($\frac{1}{4}$).

90. Cornice rim. Orange-buff ware with grey colour-coating. Clay roughcasting. Product of Colchester.
1981 F II 8.*

91. Cornice rim. Fine white ware, orange to light grey colour-coating. Fine clay roughcasting. Product of Cologne.
1979 D I 4.* Also (*not illustrated*):
1976 H I 17, in Flavian wall-trench, Building II; presumably intrusive.

92. Cornice rim, indented beaker with shoulder-groove. Fine orange-buff ware, grey colour-coating. Clay roughcasting.
1980 E I 27.** Antonine II demolition deposit in perimeter drain. Also (*not illustrated*):
1980 E I 4, ploughed-down rampart.
1980 E I 15.*

93. Cornice rim. Orange ware with dark brown colour-coating. Fine clay roughcasting. Product of northern Gaul.
1985 N III, unstratified.

94. Cornice rim and shoulder-groove. Fine burnished light grey ware.
1981 F II 29.*

95. Indented bag-shaped beaker. Rather coarse burnished grey ware.
1973 II 2.*

Black-Burnished 1 Ware: Jars (FIG. 120)

Bead-rim jars, Gillam type 118.

96. Burnished lattice.
1973 II 4.** Antonine Ii perimeter drain.

97. 1981 F II 11.*

Everted-rim Jars: thick neck, burnished lattice, Gillam type 130.

98. 1973 II 25 B.* Also (*not illustrated*):
1977 A II 26 A.*
1977 A I 8.*
1979 D V 2.*
1980 E II 15, Flavian demolition-layer, intrusive.
1981 F I 17.*
1981 F I 25, Flavian wall-trench, intrusive.
1981 F II 4.** Antonine II occupation-layer, Central Range, Building D.
1982 J 6.*

99. 1976 H II 5.*

100. 1981 F II 26.*

101. 1976 H I 8 A.*

102. 1986 T I 3.*

103. Burnished arc on rim, graffito on lip (p. 268, No. 14). Gillam type 120.
1978 B I 5.*

104. 1985 R I 5.* Burnt red.

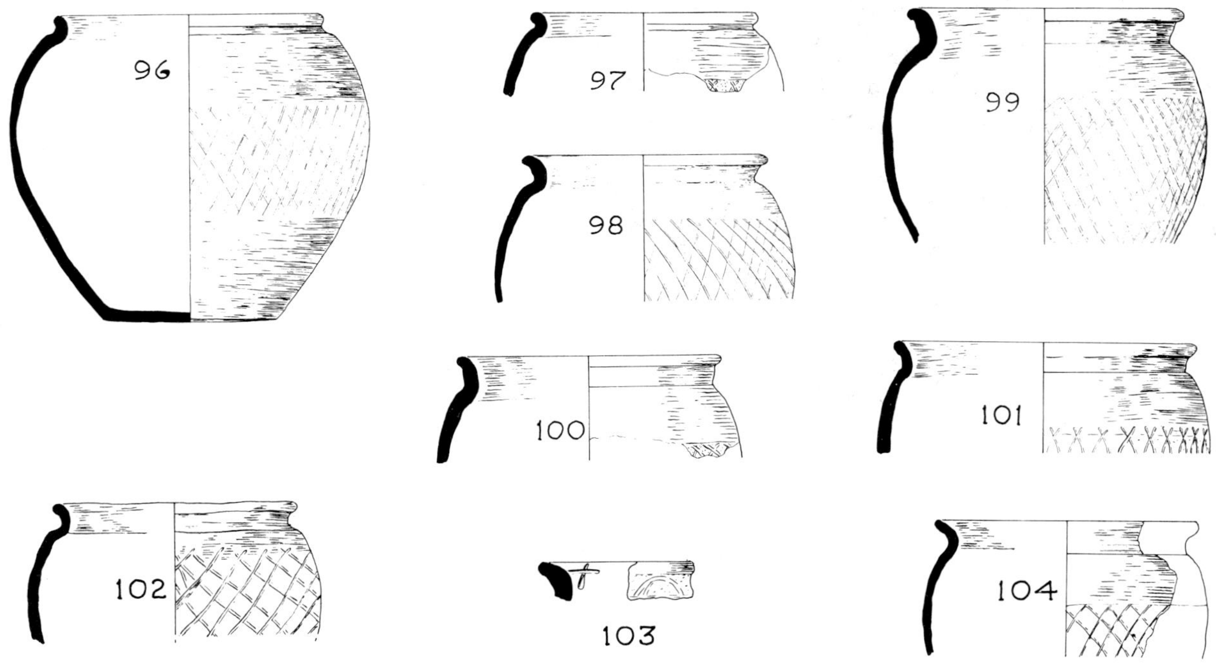

FIG. 120. Black-Burnished 1 Ware Jars (¼).

Black-Burnished 2 Ware: Jars (FIG. 121)

Bead-rim Jar

105. Thick rim slightly beaded. Burnished lattice.
1977 A II 18,* 26.*

Everted-rim Jars

106. Fine everted rim. Gillam type 137–9.
1973 II 11.** Make-up in Antonine II perimeter drain.

107. 1985 N II 7.* Also (*not illustrated*):
1975 P XLI 2,** Antonine II demolition-layer, *principia*.
1975 P XLIV 6,** Antonine II construction-trench, *principia*.
1977 A II 7 C,** Antonine II layer in *intervallum*.
1977 A II 26.*
1977 A II 26 A,* 26 B.*

108. Wide burnished lattice.
1973 I 3, old ploughsoil. Also (*not illustrated*):
1973 II 2.*
1973 II 29.*

109. 1985 R II 5.*

110. Undercut rim, Gillam type 139.
1976 H I 8.* Also (*not illustrated*):
1977 A II 6.*

111. Undercut rim.
1973 III 2.* Also (*not illustrated*):
1976 K I 6.*
1976 K I 8.*
1976 K I 13.*
1977 A I 3.** Antonine II demolition-layer, Buildings V, VI.
1978 B I 14.*

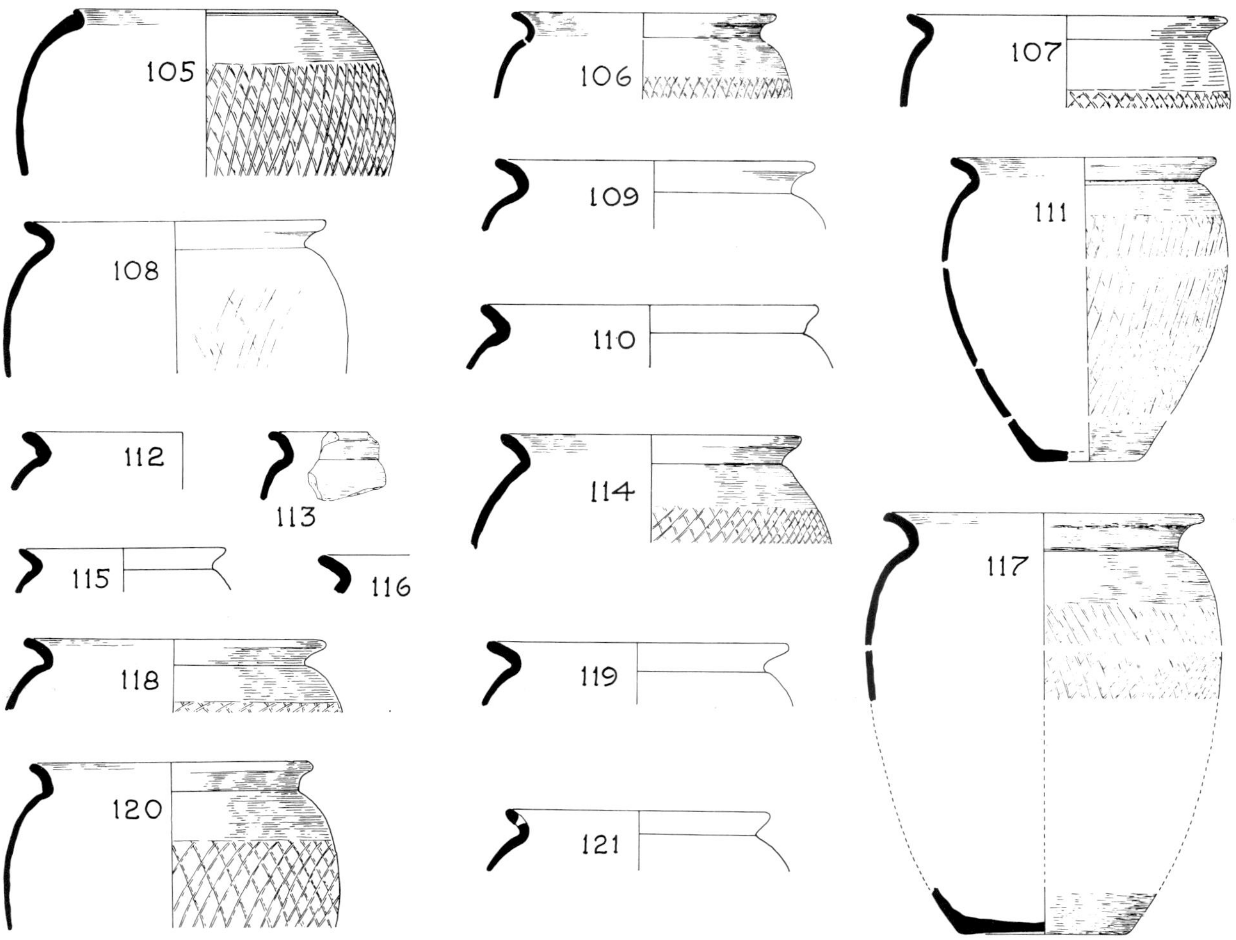

FIG. 121. Black-Burnished 2 Ware Jars (¼).

1978 B I 39.★
1980 E I 27.★★ Antonine II perimeter drain, upper filling.
1981 F II 26.★

112. Undercut rim.
1977 A II 35, Flavian demolition-layer (intrusive).

113. 1973 I 12.★

114. Straighter rim.
1978 B I 5.★ Also (*not illustrated*):
1980 E I 16.★

115. 1982 H I 3.★★ Antonine II demolition-pit over drain.

116. 1976 H I 4.★ Also (*not illustrated*):
1976 H I 5.★
1976 H I 11, Flavian demolition-layer (intrusive).
1977 A II 18.★
1979 D II 3,★★ Antonine II occupation-layer, Central Range, Building A.

117. Curved rim, Gillam type 143.
1974 G I 25,★★ Antonine II demolition-layer, *porta decumana*. Also (*not illustrated*)·
1974 G I 12,★★ Antonine II *via decumana*.

118. 1985 R II 7,★★ Antonine II perimeter drain.

119. 1985 R II 5.★

120. Upright rim.
1985 N III 12.★

121. Rim with perforation.
1980 E I 31,★★ Antonine II drain from Building VIII.

Grey Ware Imitations of Black-Burnished Ware 1 and 2 Jars (FIG. 122)

122. Hard finely granular light grey ware, closely imitating BB1. Burnished lattice.
1981 F II 11.★

123. Hard grey ware with lighter core. Short everted rim. Closely imitating BB2.
1978 B I 16.★ Also (*not illustrated*):
1978 B I 33, Flavian wall-trench (intrusive).
1983 L II 4.★

124. Hard grey ware with darker surfaces. Thick everted rim.
1977 A II 26 A.★

Everted-rim Jars, Antonine (FIG. 122)

125. Hard finely granular light grey ware, smooth burnished surfaces.
1980 E II 4,★★ Antonine II floor, Building IX.

126. Smooth hard orange-buff ware, burnished.
1978 B I 13.★ Also (*not illustrated*):
1978 B I 19, Flavian occupation-layer (intrusive).

127. Finely granular grey to buff ware, burnished except on neck.
1978 B I 20, Flavian demolition-layer in front of Building VIII (intrusive).

Miscellaneous Jars (FIG. 122)

128. Smooth light reddish ware. Upright rim with internal ledge.
1977 A II 25.★

129. Lid-seated jar. Hard finely granular dark grey burnished ware.
1976 K I 27, Flavian demolition-layer, Building IV, but perhaps intrusive from Antonine layer above.

130. Thick round rim. Fine burnished light grey ware.
1979 D VI 4.★

131. Smooth hard burnished grey ware, worn, with lighter core.
1978 B I 33, Flavian wall-trench, Building VII.

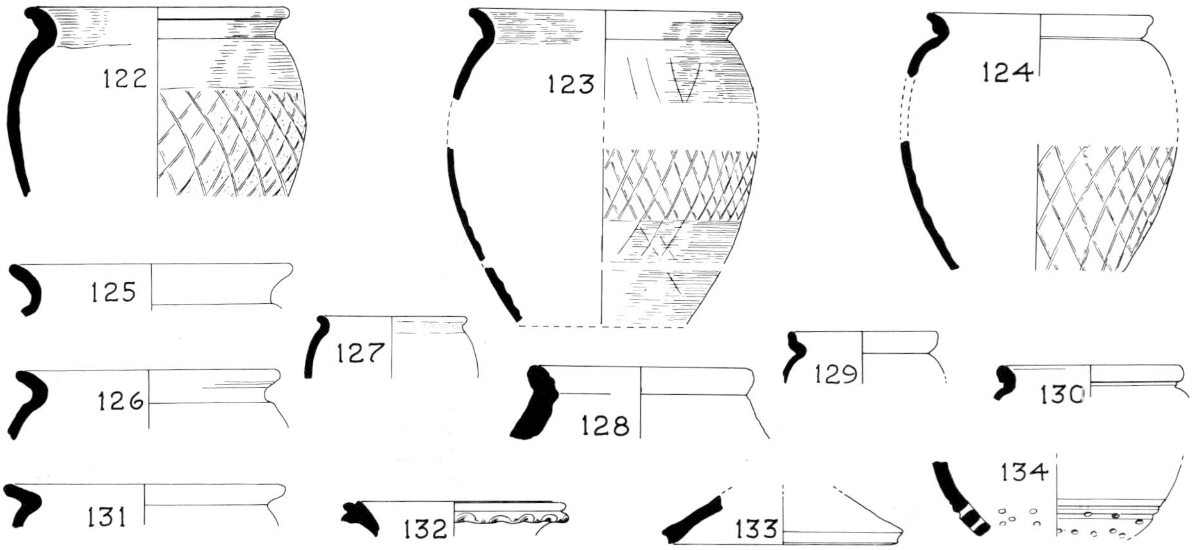

FIG. 122. Antonine Jars: imitation BB1 and 2 Jars (122–4), Everted-rim Jars (125–7), and Miscellaneous Jars (128–31). Tazza (132), Lid (133) and Strainer (134) (¼).

Tazza (FIG. 122)

132. Finely granular buff ware, frilled rim.
1977 A II 27, Flavian *via sagularis*.

Lid (FIG. 122)

133. Hard finely granular pink-buff ware with partly grey core. 1986 V I 2.*

Strainer (FIG. 122)

134. Smooth burnished light grey ware, buff core. Unevenly-spaced perforations.
1981 F II 8.*

Bowls in Black-Burnished 1 Ware (FIG. 123)

135. Bead rim, burnished lattice decoration.
1985 N I 7.*
136. Wide sloping rim, burnished lattice.
1982 G I 15.*
137. Wide level rim. Burnished lattice decoration and zig-zag lines below base.
1976 K I 8.*
138. Wide flat rim, burnished diagonal lines.
1981 F II 8.*
139. Wide flat rim, burnished loop.
1981 F II 8.*
140. Wide flat rim, lattice decoration. Very deep bowl.
1980 E I 8,** Antonine II demolition-layer, Building VIII.
141. Deep bowl, lattice decoration.
1985 N III 12.*
142. Moulded rim, lattice decoration.
1986 V I 12, *intervallum*, unstratified.
143. Moulded rim, burnished loops.
1977 A I 3,** Antonine II demolition-layer, Buildings V, VI, Also (*not illustrated*):
1977 A I 8.*
1978 B I 12.*

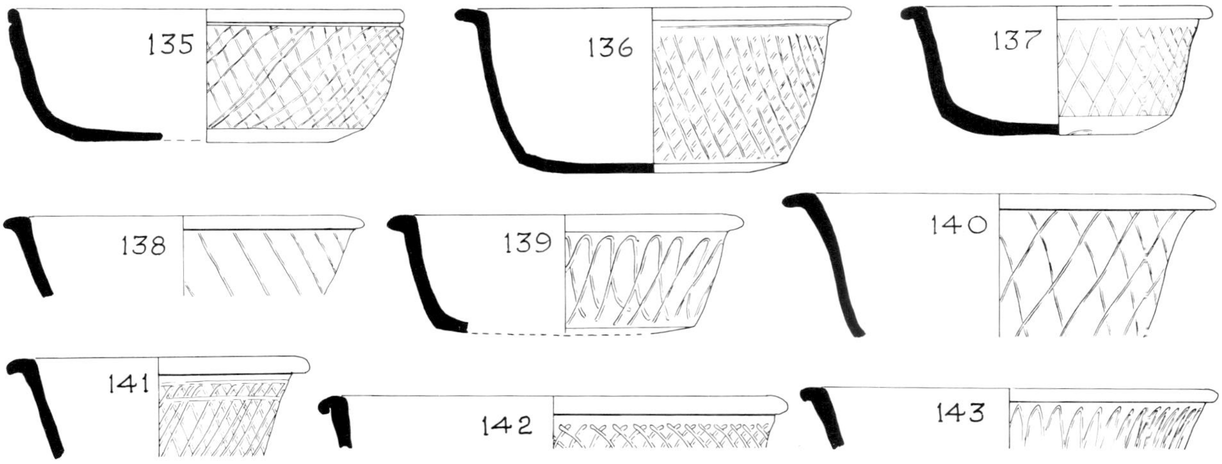

FIG. 123. Black-Burnished 1 Ware Bowls ($\frac{1}{4}$).

Bowls in Black-Burnished 2 Ware (FIG. 124)

144. Large triangular-shaped rim, undecorated.
1975 P XLVI 2.*
145. Undecorated.
1976 H I 11, Flavian demolition-layer (intrusive).
146. 1976 H I 11, as above.
147. Burnished lattice decoration.
1978 B II 15.*
148. Small to medium triangular rim, Gillam type 222. Burnished lattice decoration. Deep bowl, rounded at base.
1982 H I 3,** Antonine II demolition-pit over perimeter drain.
149. As No. 148,** Ibid.
150. Medium-sized rim, lattice decoration.
1976 H III 4.* Also (*not illustrated*):
1978 B I 5.*
1979 D II 7.*
1980 E II 7.*
1981 F II 3,** Antonine II *via quintana*
151. 1985 R II 5.*
152. Medium-sized rim, perforation below rim.
1985 N III 12.*

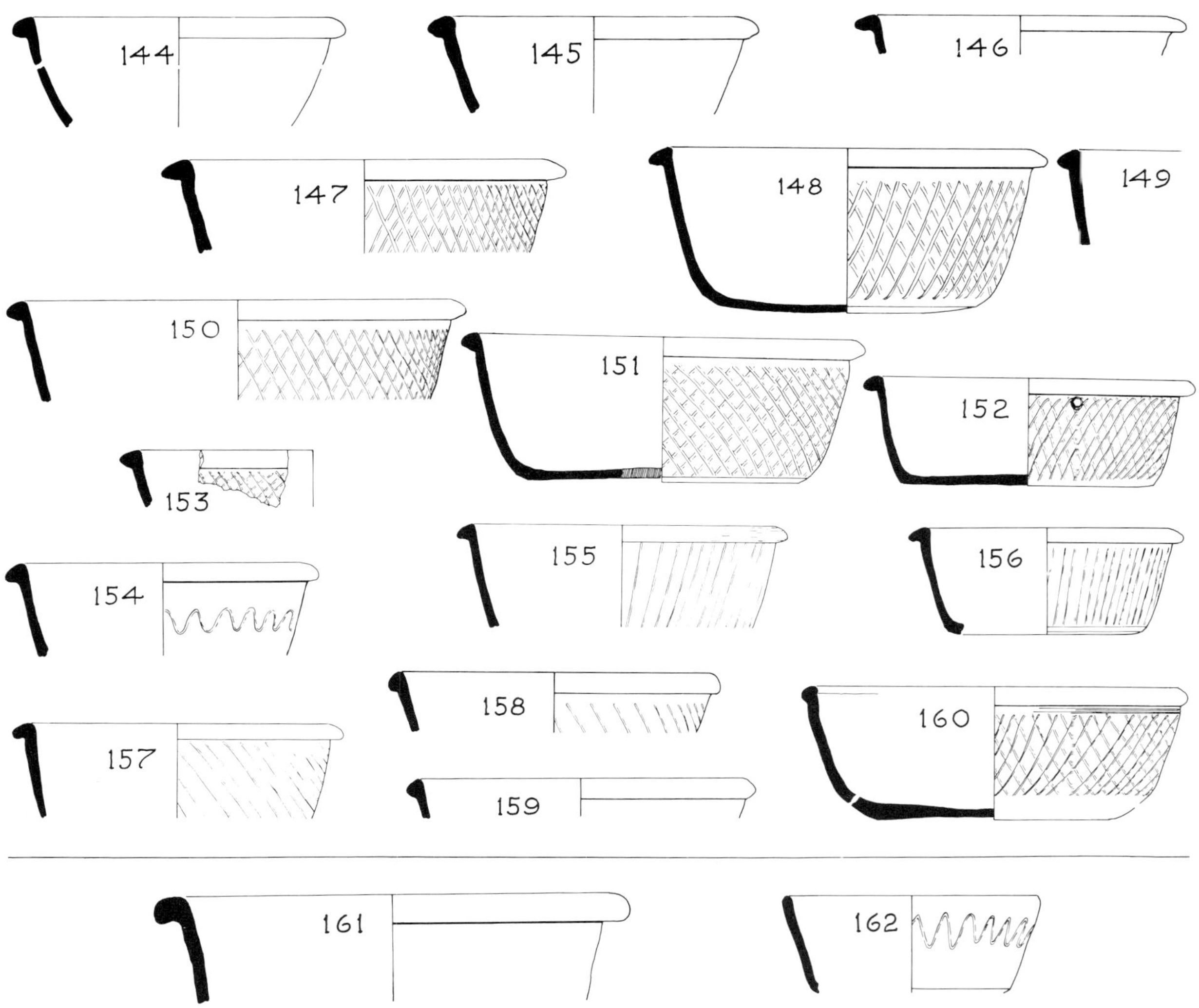

FIG. 124. Black-Burnished 2 Ware Bowls (144–160) and imitations (161–2) (¼).

153. 1985 N II 12.★
154. Medium-sized rim, burnished wavy line. Gillam type 223.
1980 E II Pit 1, 3,★★ Antonine II make-up over Flavian pit.
155. Almost straight burnished lines.
1973 II 2.★ Also (*not illustrated*):
1976 K I 10.★
1981 F I 11,★★ Antonine II street.
1982 H I 8, ploughed-down rampart.
156. 1977 A II 12.★ Also (*not illustrated*):
1977 A I 7,★★ Antonine II occupation-layer, Building V.
1977 A II 26.★
1978 B I 5.★
157. Diagonal burnished lines.
1974 P XXXII 5,★★ post-hole, Antonine II *principia*. Also (*not illustrated*):
1976 H I 8.★
158. 1976 K I 24, Flavian wall-trench, Building IV (intrusive).
159. Small triangular rim, undecorated.
1978 B I 3,★★ Antonine II occupation-layer, Building VII.
160. Lattice decoration. Chamfered base.
1985 N III 12.★

Bowls imitating BB1 or 2 forms (FIG. 124)

161. Large square rim; finely granular grey ware, burnished but undecorated.
1979 D II 7.★
162. Small deep bowl, plain rim, burnished wavy line. Possibly Black-Burnished 2 ware.
1977 A II 6.★ Also (*not illustrated*):
1977 A II 12.★
1977 A II 31.★

Dishes in Black-Burnished 1 Ware (FIG. 125)

163. Bead rim, straight sides.
1980, from outer ditch on south side.
164. Small flat rim, sloping sides, undecorated.
1981 F I 13.★ Also (*not illustrated*):
1981 F I 17.★
165. Wide flat rim, sloping sides, burnished lattice.
1980 E II 1, old ploughsoil.
166. Wide flat rim, chamfered base, burnished lattice.
1981 F II 26.★
167. Similar to No. 166, burnished wavy lines on base.
1985 R II 7,★★ Antonine II perimeter drain.
168. Flat inward-tilted rim, slightly chamfered base, undecorated.
1981 F II 8.★

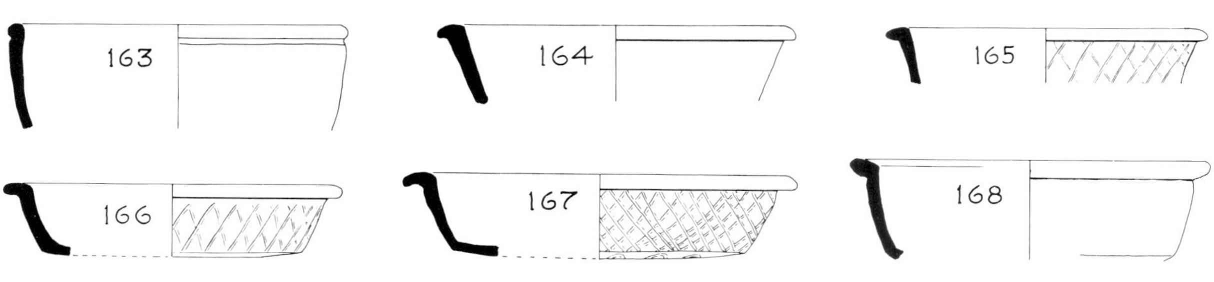

FIG. 125. Black-Burnished 1 Ware Dishes ($\frac{1}{4}$).

Dishes in Black-Burnished 2 Ware (FIG. 126)

169. Curving sides and plain rim, undecorated.
1976 H I 4.★ Also (*not illustrated*):
1976 H I 11, Flavian demolition-layer (intrusive).

170. Straight sides, plain rim, Gillam type 328. Burnished lattice and horizontal burnished lines.
1980 E I 16.★

171. 1981 F II 8.★

172. Straight sides, plain rim, burnished wavy line.
1976 H I 14, Flavian wall-trench, Building II (intrusive). Also (*not illustrated*):
1980 E II 13.★
1981 F I 11,★★ Antonine II street.
1982 G I 15.★

173. As No. 172, with chamfered base.
1977 A II 26.★

174. 1980 E II 11.★ Also (*not illustrated*):
1982 G I 3, silt from rampart.

175. 1977 A I 10,★★ Antonine II make-up over Antonine I demolition-pit. Also (*not illustrated*):
1984 S V 2.★

176. As No. 175 with burnished double wavy line and horizontal lines.
1980 E I 43.★

177. Bead rim, burnished lattice, Gillam type 318.
1973 III 2.★

178. Bead rim, burnished wavy lines.
1973 II 2.★

179. Medium-sized triangular rim, curved sides, undecorated.
1973 II 2.★

180. Medium-sized triangular rim, curved sides, burnished lattice.
1973 II 4,★★ Antonine II perimeter drain. Also (*not illustrated*):
1976 K I 2,★★ Antonine II demolition-layer, Building IV.
1980 E I 18, Flavian demolition-layer, Building IX (intrusive).
1981 F I 8.★
1981 F I post-hole 58.★

181. 1973 II 11,★★ Antonine II make-up in perimeter drain. Also (*not illustrated*):
1973 II 3, Flavian occupation, Building I (intrusive).
1974 P XIII 4.★
1977 A I 54.★
1977 A II 18.★

182. Medium-sized triangular rim, curved sides, chamfered base, burnished lattice.
1977 A II 8,★★ with graffito on rim. Antonine II street. Also (*not illustrated*):
1977 A II 12★ (three examples).

183. 1980 E I 27,★★ Antonine II perimeter drain, upper fill. Also (*not illustrated*):
1981 F II 8.★

184. 1977 A II 14A,★★ with Amphora-urinal in *via sagularis*. Also (*not illustrated*):
1978 B I 5.★
1979 D II 4.★
1980 E II 7.★
1980 E II 10.★
1981 F I 2, old ploughsoil.
1981 F I 4,★★ Antonine II perimeter drain.
1981 F I 8.★

185. 1979 D II 4.★

186. Very fine burnished lattice.
1976 H II 3,★★ Antonine II floor, Building II.

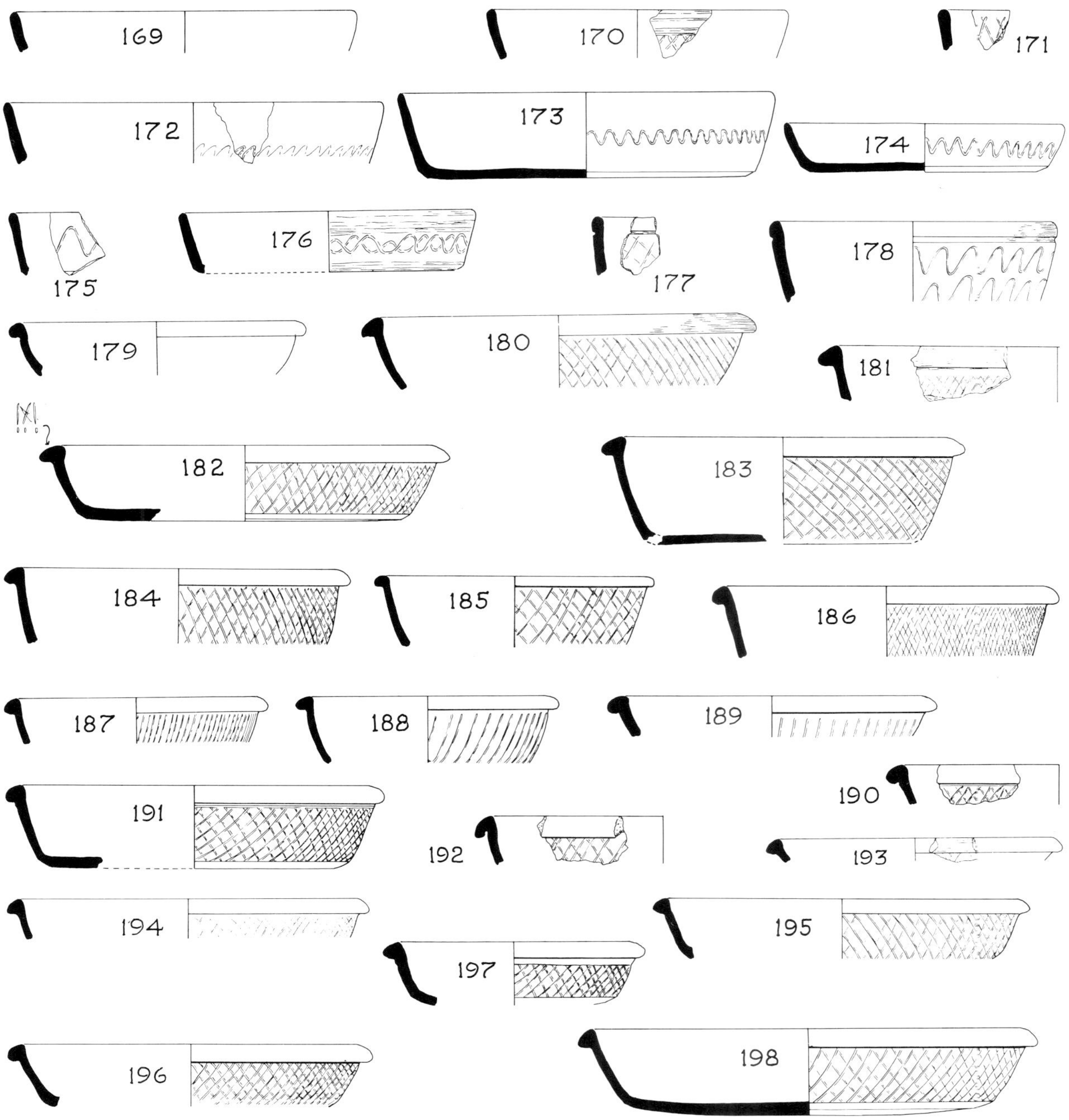

FIG. 126. Black-Burnished 2 Ware Dishes (¼).

187. Medium-sized triangular rim, curved sides, burnished diagonal lines.
1976 H I 8.* Also (*not illustrated*):
1979 D I 4.*

188. Similar to No. 187, more widely-spaced diagonal burnished lines.
1977 A I 16.* Also (*not illustrated*):
1980 E II 1, old ploughsoil.
1981 F II 8.*
1981 F II 18,** silting over Antonine I demolition-pit 2.

189. 1981 F II 8.*

190. Medium-sized triangular rim undercut by a groove; burnished lattice.
1978 B I 3,** Antonine II occupation-layer, Building VII.

191. As No. 190, with chamfered base.
1978 B I 4,** silt over Antonine II *intervallum*.

192. Undercut downward-sloping rim, burnished lattice.
1978 B I 5.*
193. Small triangular rim, curved sides, burnished lattice.
1973 III 2.*
194. Similar to No. 193.
1974 P III post-hole 8.* Also (*not illustrated*):
1977 A I 19,** Antonine II street.
1977 A I 57, in top of Flavian demolition-pit C.
1977 A II 7,** Antonine II floor, Building VII.
1977 A II 8,** Antonine II street.
1977 A II 12.*
1978 B I 3,** Antonine II occupation-layer, Building VII.
1978 B III 3,** Antonine II occupation-layer, Building V.
1978 B III 9.*
195. Similar to No. 194, with chamfered base.
1975 G VI 2, fallen rampart-turves. Also (*not illustrated*):
1976 K I 2,** Antonine II demolition-layer, Building IV.
1977 A II 12.*
1981 F II 22, Flavian occupation-layer, Building XI (intrusive).
1983 L III 10,** Antonine II perimeter drain.
1984 S III 10, Flavian demolition-layer, Building XVI (intrusive).
196. Similar to No. 195.
1981 F II 10.*
197. 1986 V II 3.*
198. 1978 B I 12.* Also (*not illustrated*):
1980 E I 15.*
1981 F I 9.*
1982 G I 3, ploughed-down rampart.
1982 G I 15.*
1982 J 7, Flavian demolition-pit, Building IV (intrusive).
1982 J 10, Flavian occupation-layer, Building IV (intrusive).

Imitations of Black-Burnished 1 and 2 Dishes (FIG. 127)

(a) *Imitations of BB1*
199. Small flat rim, straight sides, flat base. Smooth hard micaceous light grey-buff ware, burnished. 1978 B I 8,** Antonine II *via sagularis*. Also (*not illustrated*):
1978 B I 19, Flavian occupation-layer, Building VII (intrusive).
200. Wide flat rim. Hard burnished finely granular grey ware with lighter core.
1978 B I 13.*
201. Wide flat rim, sloping sides. Hard burnished grey-buff ware with grey core.
1981 F I 11,** Antonine II street.
202. Wide flat rim, sloping sides, flat base. Hard burnished grey ware.
1981 F II 8.*
203. Wide flat rim. Burnished buff ware, finely granular, with orange core.
1981 F II 10.*

(b) *Imitations of BB2*
204. Medium-sized triangular sloping rim, curved sides. Smooth burnished light grey ware with buff core.
1977 A II 12.*
205. Similar to No. 204. Hard finely granular grey ware, smooth buff surface.
1981 F II 8.*

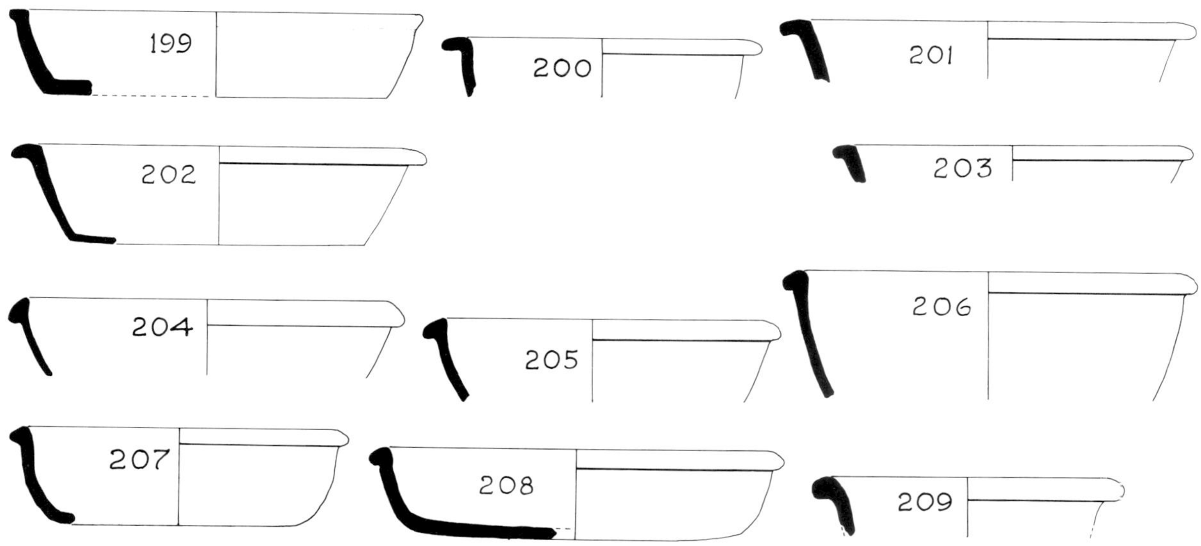

FIG. 127. Imitations of Black-Burnished 1 Ware Dishes (199–203), and of BB2 dishes (204–9) ($\frac{1}{4}$).

206. Burnished buff ware with light grey core.
1981 F II 11.*
207. Medium-sized triangular rim, curved sides, flat base. Burnished buff ware, light grey core.
1979 D II 4.*
208. Light grey ware with traces of lighter slip.
1981 F II 10.* Also (*not illustrated*):
1982 H II 7.*
209. Smooth hard burnished light grey ware.
1978 B I 3,** Antonine II occupation-layer, Building VII.

THE AMPHORAE By S.S. Frere

Dressel 20 (FIGS. 128–130)

By far the most frequent amphora sherds to be found at Strageath were those of the Spanish amphora, Dressel form 20. Large sherds from these vessels were frequently used for patching floors, and fragments of necks or handles were sometimes employed as packers in post-holes. Such large vessels when broken yield so many otherwise featureless sherds that it is impossible to reckon the total number of vessels in use; but fragments were recorded from over 90 different contexts. The great majority came from Antonine deposits, but there are five examples of first-century type or date (Nos. 212–14, 217, 221).

This type of amphora was apparently used primarily for the transport of olive oil – used in cooking, lighting and in the Baths; but the empty vessel was often used for secondary purposes. One example from a Flavian context (1980 E II 15, demolition of Building XI) had had its rim and neck intentionally removed; and the lower half of another (No. 211) was buried in the *via sagularis* of the Antonine II fort with its base knocked off for use as a urinal.

210. 1978 B I 12,* reconstructed from parts of three amphorae in the Antonine I perimeter drain. Graffiti on rim and handle (p. 268, No. 17).
211. 1977 A II 14 A.** Lower half of vessel set in the Antonine II *via sagularis* as a urinal (p. 80).
212. 1977 A I 64, Flavian demolition-pit C in Building V. For type see D. Peacock and D.

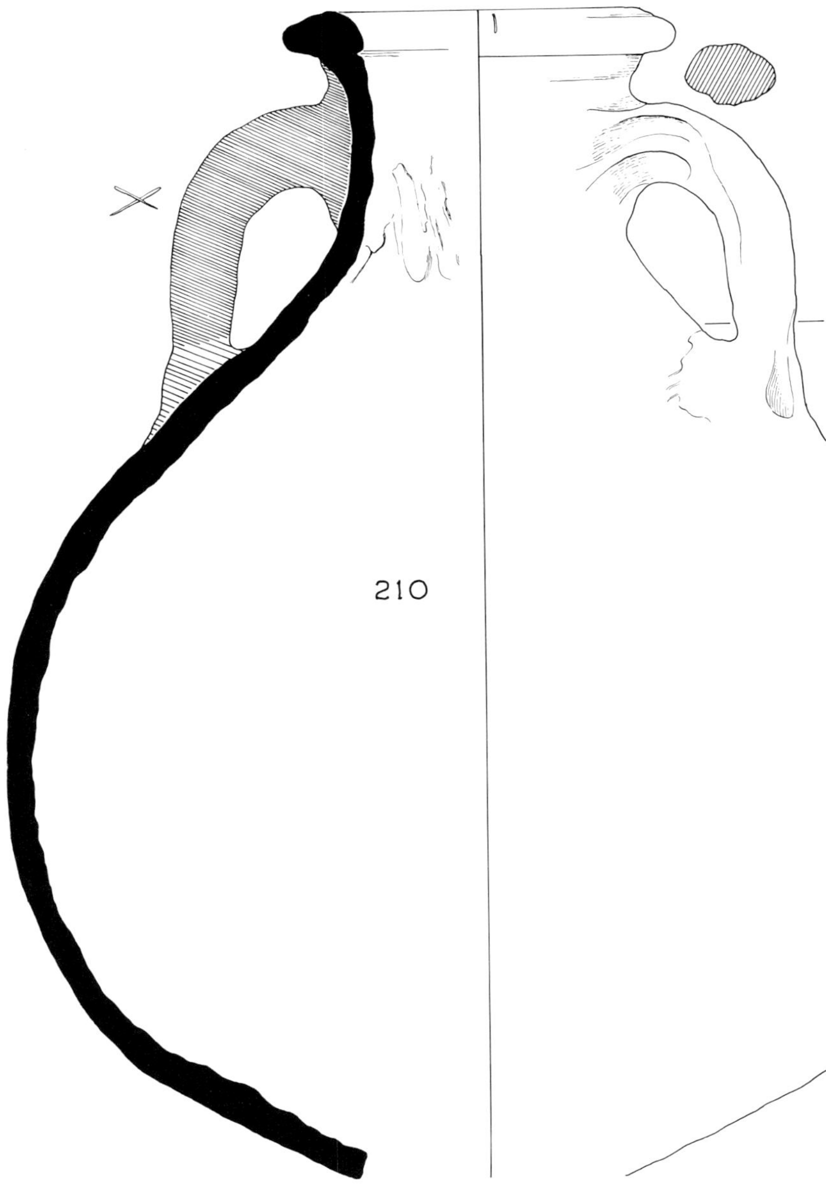

FIG. 128. Amphora of Dressel form 20 ($\frac{1}{4}$).

Williams, *Amphorae and the Roman Economy* (1986), fig. 65.23. Graffito on rim (p. 000, No. 15).

213. 1981 F II 26.★ Flavian type, residual; cf. Peacock and Williams, fig. 65.17–18.
214. 1973 I 3, old ploughsoil. Flavian type, residual; cf. Peacock and Williams, fig. 65.18.
215. 1978 B II 3.★★ Antonine II occupation-layer, Building VII; cf. Peacock and Williams, fig. 66.32.
216. 1981 F I 8.★ Graffiti, XI on handle, XII on shoulder (FIG. 133, No. 3). Stamp C.TY.C (FIG. 132, No. 2).
217. 1978 B II 27, Flavian wall-trench bounding east side of area in front of Building VIII; cf. Peacock and Williams, fig. 65.14–16.
218. 1973 II 25.★ cf. Peacock and Williams, fig. 66.26.
219. 1975 P XLIII 3.★★ Antonine II make-up, *principia*.
220. 1975 P XLII 3 A.★
221. 1976 H III post-hole 2, packing of Antonine I post-hole, Building III, so Flavian (residual).
222. 1981 F II 8.★ Graffito IVLIA on rim, incised with the base of the letters towards the outside (FIG. 133, No. 5).

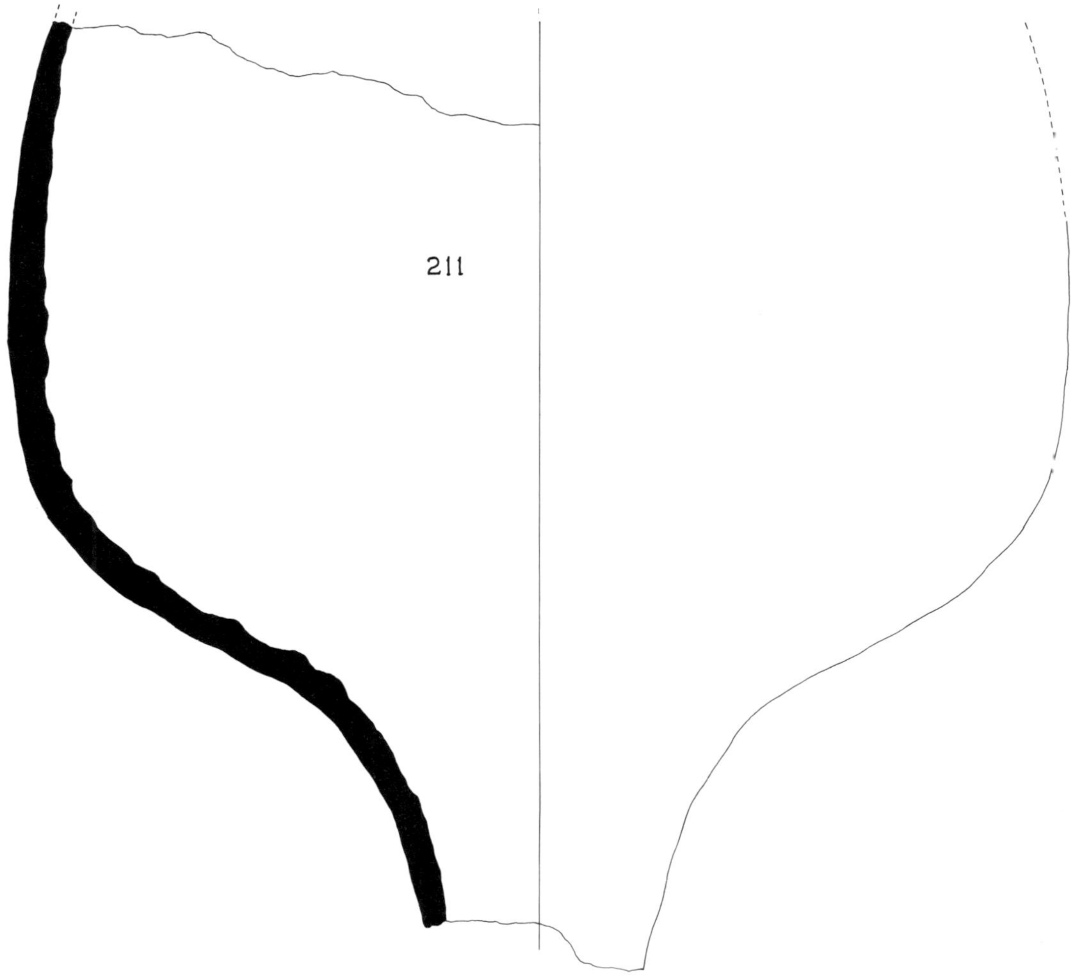

FIG. 129. Lower half of Dressel form 20 amphora used as a urinal in the Antonine II *via sagularis* (p. 80) ($\frac{1}{4}$).

223. 1974 P III post-hole 9,★★ Antonine II *principia*.
224. 1979 D II 3,★★ Antonine II occupation, Central Range, Building A.
225. 1973 II post-hole 14.★
226. 1979 D II 3★★ with No. 224. Basal spike with plug.

Other Types of Amphora (FIG. 131)

Compared with the numerous amphorae bringing olive oil to the fort (Dressel 20, above), those definitely used for transporting wine were curiously few in number. Those noted comprise two examples of Pélichet 47 and fifteen of Dressel 2–4. Amphorae of Camulodunum form 186 are thought to have carried fish sauce; fourteen examples were noted. According to Peacock and Williams (*Amphorae in the Roman Economy* (1986), 121, 123) their production did not outlast the early second century and so at Strageath they should belong to the Flavian period of occupation; but many were in residual contexts. They were notably concentrated in two areas, the southern end of (Flavian) Building V (seven examples) and in Trench 1976 H I at (Flavian) Buildings II and III.

227. 1986 V II 13, Flavian occupation-layer, Central Range, Building C. Pélichet 47, southern France, wine amphora.
228. 1985 R II 7,★★ Antonine II perimeter drain. Unidentified type. Buff fabric with dark grey surfaces.

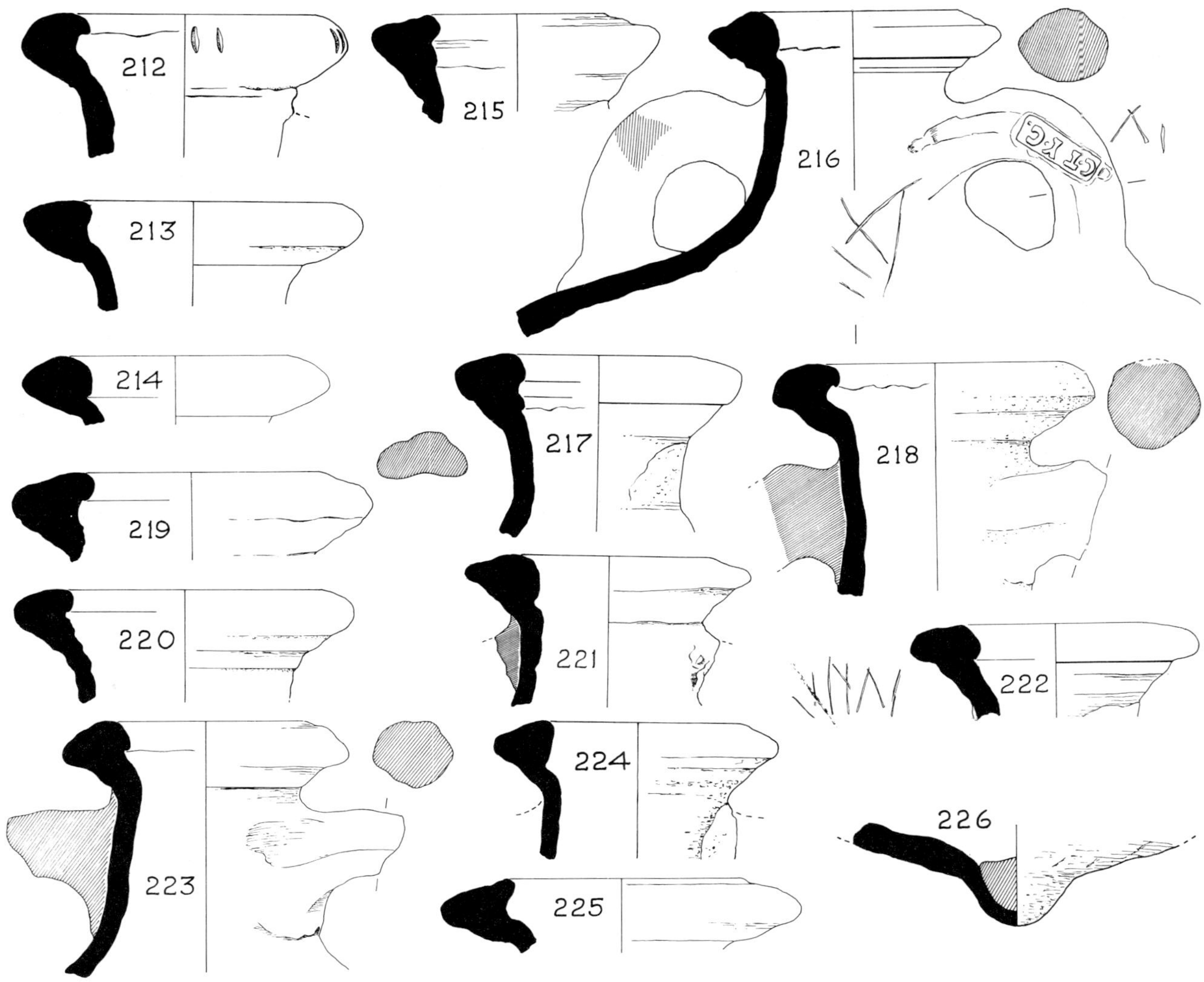

FIG. 130. Amphorae of Dressel form 20 ($\frac{1}{4}$).

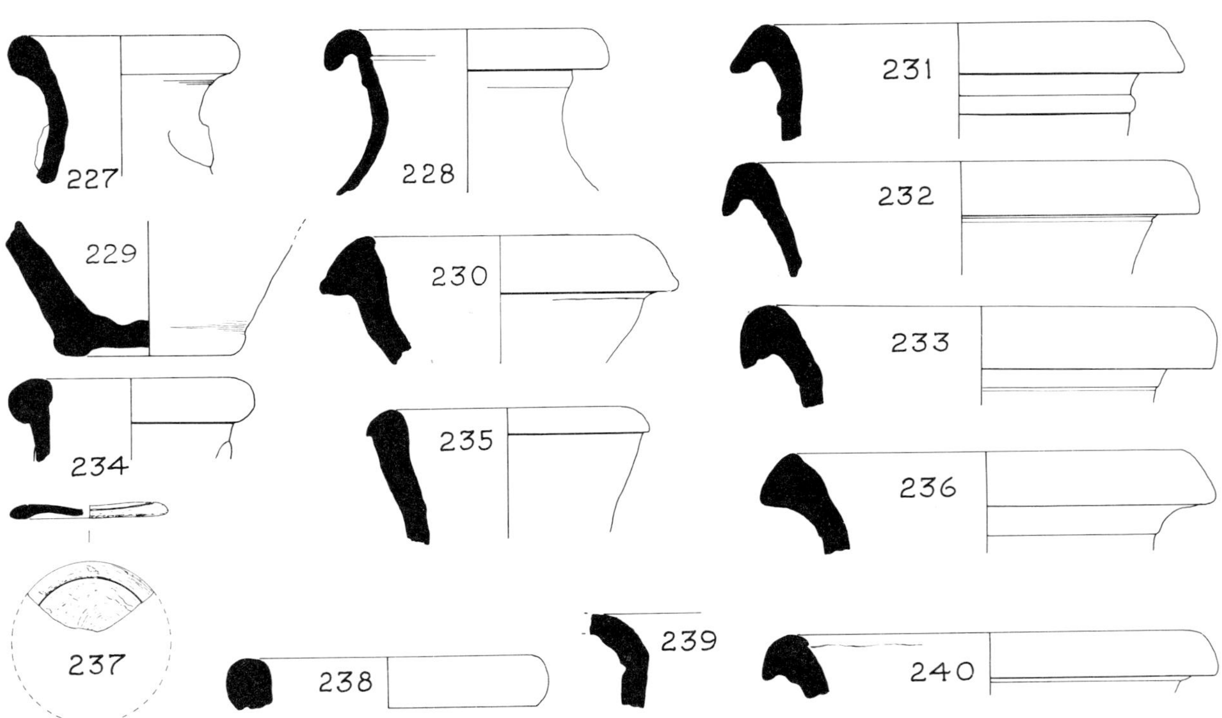

FIG. 131. Amphorae of other types ($\frac{1}{4}$).

229. 1976 H III 6, Flavian demolition-layer, Building III; base, (?) Pélichet 47, cf. No. 227.
230. 1981 F I 8,* Dressel 7–11. Fish sauce; Spanish.
231. 1978 B III 3,** Antonine II occupation-layer, Building V. Camulodunum 186 C. Fish sauce.
232. 1978 B III 6,* Antonine I occupation-layer, Building V. Camulodunum 186 C. Fish sauce.
233. 1978 B III 15,* Antonine I construction-trench, Building V, so Flavian (residual). Camulodunum 186 C. Fish sauce.
234. 1979 D II 6,* Dressel 2–4. Wine.
235. 1978 B III 4,* Dressel 2–4. Wine.
236. 1978 B IV 4,* Antonine I pipe-trench, *via praetoria*, so probably Flavian (residual). Camulodunum 186 A. Fish sauce.
237. Amphora lid, cf. D. Atkinson, *Wroxeter 1923–7* (1942), 288 No. A 14. 1979 D III 7,* Antonine I construction-trench, Building V.
238. 1976 H I 8,* Dressel 2–4. Wine.
239. 1976 H I 8,* Camulodunum 186, lip broken. Fish sauce.
240. 1978 B III 4,* Antonine I occupation-layer, Building V. Camulodunum 186 C. Fish sauce.

XXV. AMPHORA STAMPS (FIG. 132)

1. **AGRICOL[**. From 1979 D I 4, Antonine I occupation-layer. Callender[1] No. 51, there dated to the second half of the first century.
2. **C.TY.C.** From 1981 F II 8, Antonine I demolition-layer. On handle of Dressel 20, cf. FIG. 130 No. 216. Callender No. 494, there dated mid second-century.
3. **CMF** (or **E**). From 1978 B I 45, Flavian pit. cf. Callender No. 389. On handle, probably Dressel 2–4.
4. **M ↑ S ↑ ST**. From 1974 P XIII post-hole 1: post-hole packing in Antonine. II *principia* (and thus of Antonine I origin). On wall of a (?) Dressel 2–4 vessel. Callender No. 1181, there dated before 161.
5. **Q[**. From 1981 F II 26, Antonine I demolition-layer. On handle of Dressel 20.
6. **PO[**. From 1977 A I 8, Antonine I demolition-layer. Perhaps POR(tus) C.P.R., Callender No. 1370, 3a, there provisionally dated to the second half of the first century. Near base of handle. (Dr. 20).
7. **R.SAEN**. From 1981 F I 17, Antonine I occupation-layer. Perhaps P]R.SA͡EN[I, Callender No. 1159 (1), there dated 80/90–130/40.
8. **SNR** (or **SN͡ER**). From 1973 II 25, Antonine I occupation-layer. cf. Callender No. 1641, there dated 140–180.
9. **M. FELICIS** (?). From 1976 H I 13, Antonine I occupation-layer. Very weathered stamp on handle, apparently also partly clogged with clay. Reading uncertain, but possibly **M. FELICIS**, Callender No. 1085(b).

1. M.H. Callender, *Roman Amphorae* (Oxford, 1965).

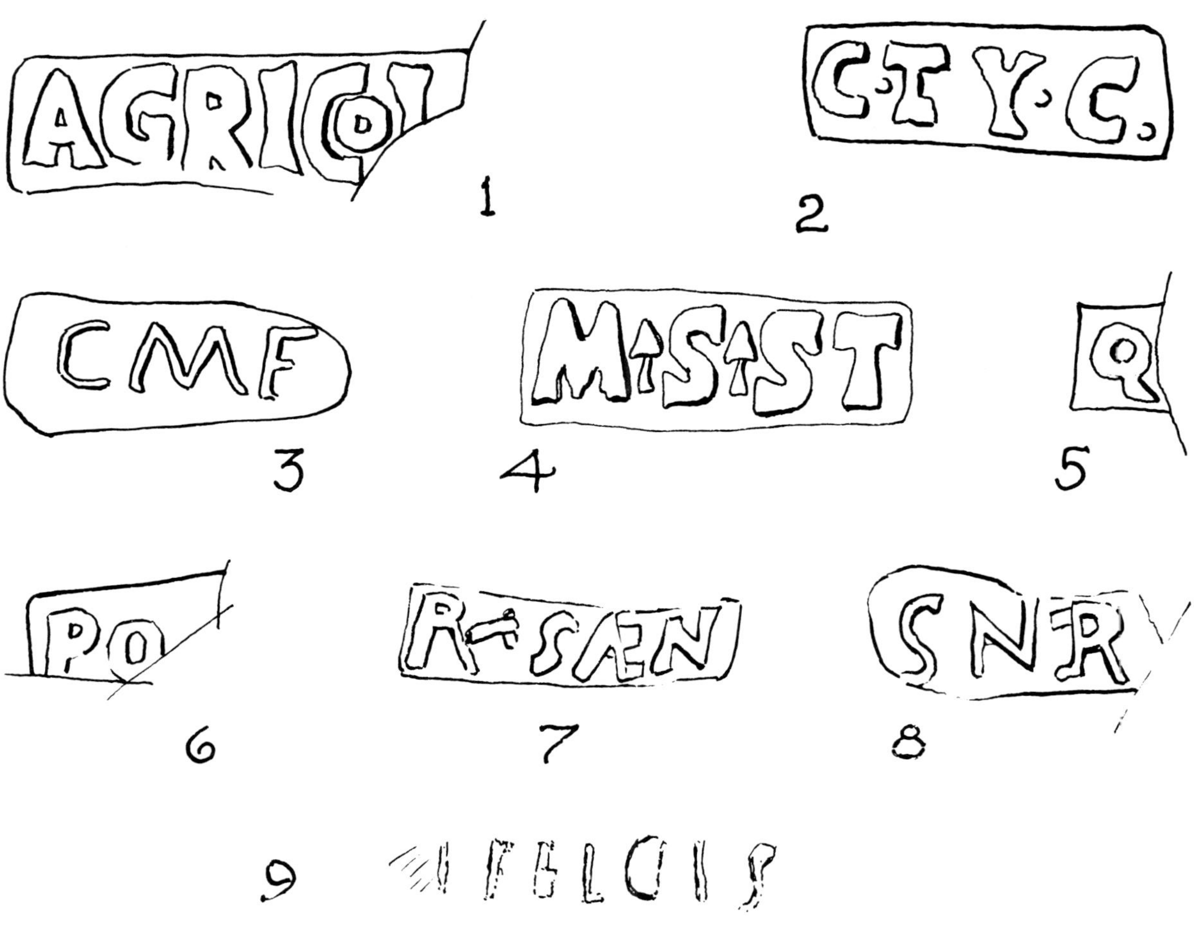

FIG. 132. The Amphora Stamps (1/1).

XXVI. GRAFFITI[1] (FIGS. 133–4)

1. MAI incised on buff amphora sherd. From 1976 H II 3, floor of Antonine II barrack. *Britannia* ix (1978), 482, No. 71.
2. AIV incised on thin sherd of dark orange-brown (?) jug. From 1974 P XI 5, Flavian occupation-layer in *principia*.
3. XI incised on handle, XII on body of Dressel 20 amphora, see FIG. 130, No. 216. From 1981 F I 8, Antonine I demolition-layer.
4. XI[incised on Dressel 20 amphora sherd. From 1982 H II, unstratified.
5. IVLIA on rim of Dressel 20 amphora, incised with the base of the inscription towards the lip of the vessel, cf. FIG. 130, No. 222, From 1981 F II 8 Antonine I demolition-layer, Building XI.
6.]TPV[incised on two joining sherds of a buff jug. From 1985 N I 11, Flavian demolition-level below Antonine I *via sagularis*. *Britannia* xvii (1986), 450, No. 83.

1. The help of Dr R S O Tomlin is gratefully acknowledged.

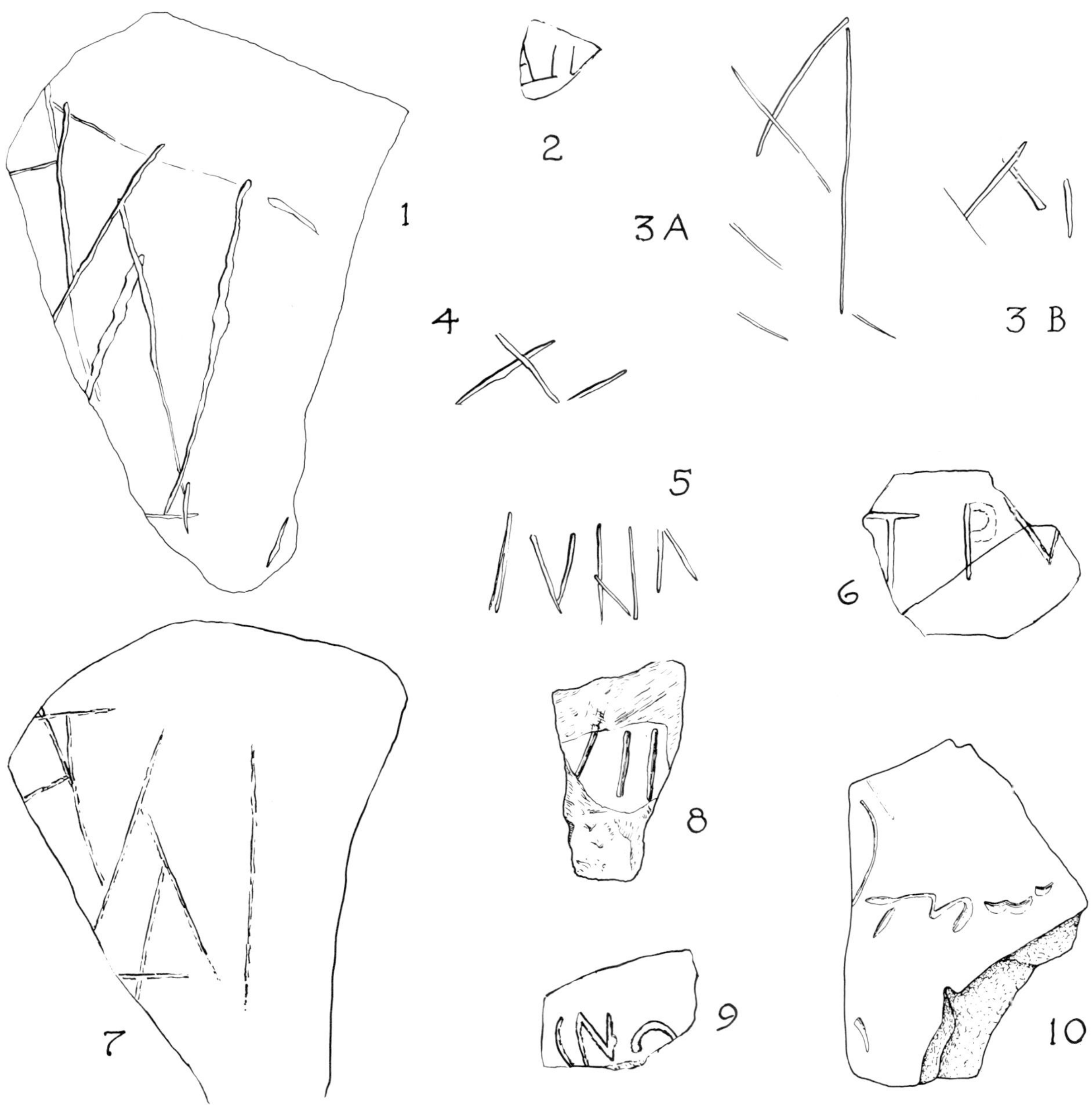

FIG. 133. The Graffiti Nos. 1–10 (½).

7. From 1976 H III 9, Flavian wall-trench. Graffito faintly scratched on body of a Dressel 20 amphora. Dr R S O Tomlin suggests that it may read NΛ within an oblong frame.
8.]ṾII[incised on amphora sherd. From 1975 P XLI 11 among Dressel 20 sherds packing wall-trench in Antonine II *principia*.
9.]INO[incised on amphora sherd. From 1983 L I 11, Antonine I occupation-layer. *Britannia* XV (1984), 348, No. 66.
10.]ITVṚẠ[. . .]. .[. .] incised in cursive letters before firing on an amphora sherd. Dr Tomlin writes that the exaggerated height of the I suggests that it was the initial letter. There may have been a space after the last letter. From 1983 L II 10, filling of Antonine II drain.
11. . . .]ÇΛRITỌ[. . . incised in clumsy capitals on a sherd of amphora, Dressel 20. Perhaps the personal name Carito, for Charito which is well attested as a cognoman. From 1986 V II 3, Antonine I occupation.
12. Perhaps ṢTẠTII, incised on underside of a samian f. 18/31 or 31 stamped LAL[LVS (FIG. 104, No. S7). Elongated letters of which only the bottom half is preserved: the reading, by Dr Tomlin, assumes vertical distortion and that the cross-strokes of S and T are lost. From 1983 L II 3, Antonine II *via sagularis*.
13. RVFIVS incised on underside of samian bowl, form 18/31 stamped by Chresimus (FIG. 104, No. 3). A.D. 120–145. From 1976 H I 8, Antonine I demolition-layer.
14. (FIG. 120, No. 103). X incised on inside of rim of jar. From 1978 B I 5, Antonine I occupation-layer.
15. (FIG. 130, No. 212). II incised twice on rim of Dressel 20 amphora. From 1977 A I 64, Flavian demolition-pit C, Building V.
16. (FIG. 126 No. 182). X in frame incised on a BB2 dish. From 1977 A II 8, Antonine II street.
17. (FIG. 128, No. 210). I on rim and X on handle of a Dressel 20 amphora. From 1978 B I 12, Antonine I perimeter drain.

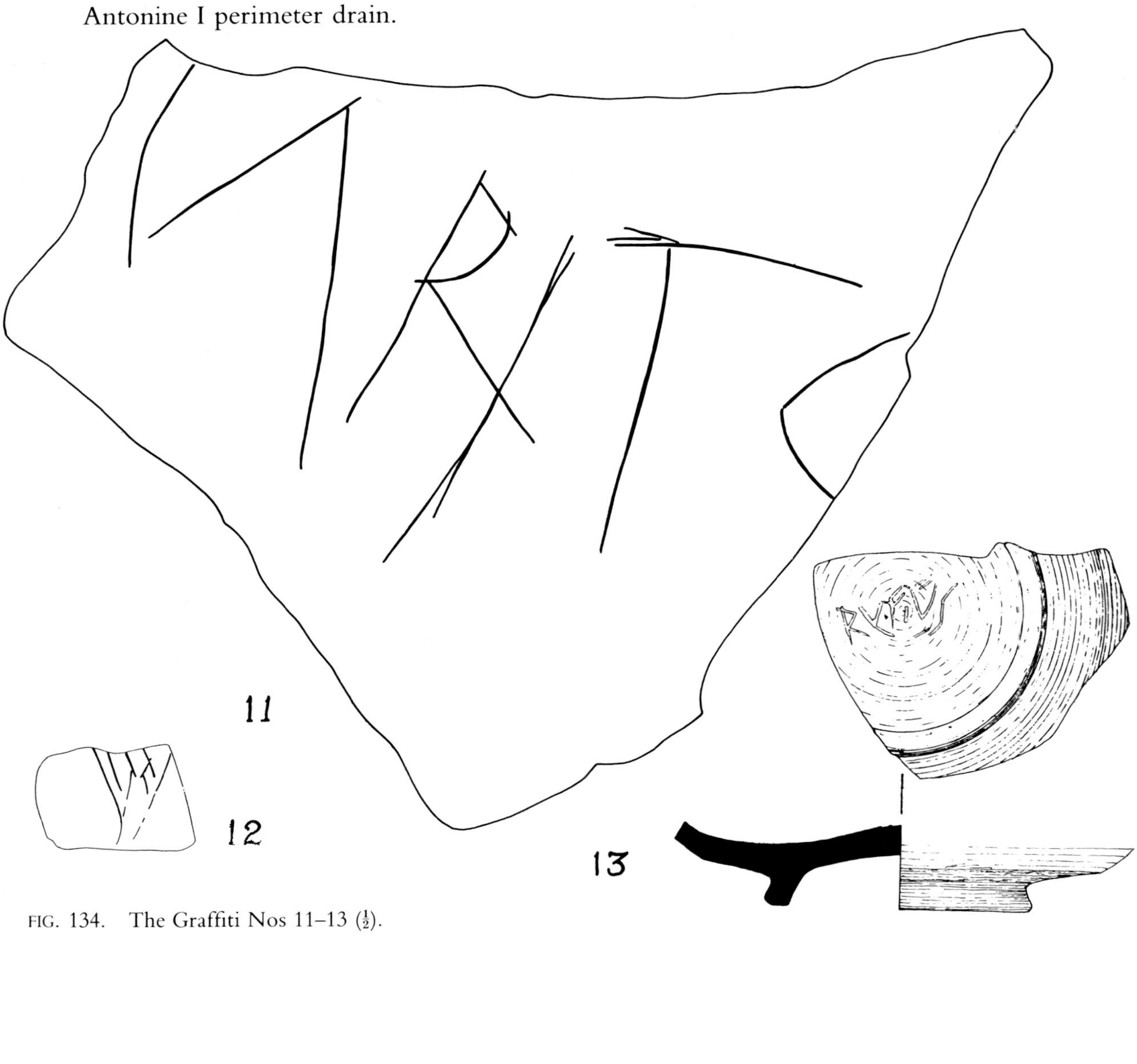

FIG. 134. The Graffiti Nos 11–13 (½).

XXVII. THE PREHISTORIC POTTERY

(FIG. 135)

By S.S. Frere

Although there is evidence (p.272) that the surroundings of the fort had already been cleared to some extent of woodland, and that the plateau may have been used for grazing and cultivation (pp.17–18) from a nearby settlement, no pre-Roman structures were encountered in the excavations. But three prehistoric sherds were found in residual contexts.

1. Body-sherd of coarse pottery with profuse grits: thickness 13 mm, reddish-brown exterior surface, inside surface and core black. From 1977 A I 9, Antonine I occupation-layer in the *praetentura*. The sherd was examined by Mr. T. Cowie, who writes: 'assessment of such a featureless sherd can only be made on the basis of fabric, for which the closest comparisons would appear to be among some Neolithic assemblages, as at North Mains, Strathallan. Very cautiously therefore, it may be suggested that the sherd derives from near the base of a coarse Neolithic vessel, with a possible date in the earlier third millenium (in radiocarbon years).'
2. Thick flat rim, slightly curved below, suggesting perhaps a bowl form. Hard sandy ware with flecks of mica but few grits. Brown exterior surface, black interior surface and core. From 1986 V I 5, Antonine I demolition-layer in the north block of the Central Range.
3. Flat rim of possible situla-shaped jar. Ware similar to No. 2 but with large grits of rock, up to 3 mm across, protruding through the surfaces. The sherd thickens at the base of the neck as if for an angle. From 1986 V I 13A, top of Flavian wall-trench in the north block of the Central Range.

Nos. 2–3 would appear to date from the earlier half of the first millenium B.C. and suggest that clearance and use of the plateau had occurred several centuries before the arrival of Agricola's army.

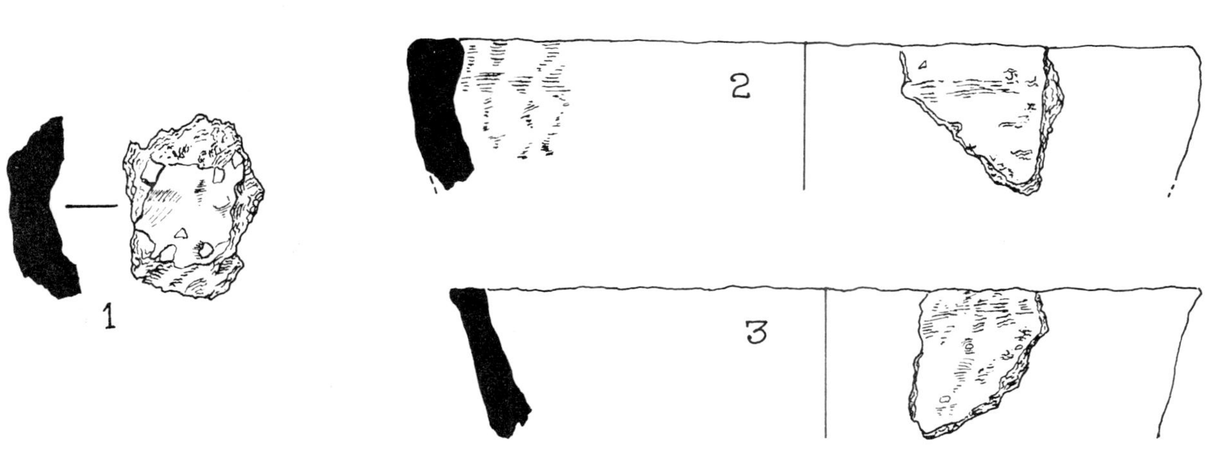

FIG. 135. The Prehistoric pottery ($\frac{1}{2}$)

XXVIII. FLAKED FLINT
By Jean MacDonald

As mentioned on p. 8, the site of the fort yielded a few scattered flint flakes. Five are here described.

1. (FIG. 99, p. 191 No. 19). From 1973 I 3, scraper.
2. (FIG. 99, p. 191 No. 20). From 1979 D IV 1: flaked flint.
3. From 1973 I 21. Blade-like flake with two roughly parallel ridges, the distal end terminating in a hinge fracture. Prepared platform. Flaking suggests manufacture from a two-platform core. Damage to both edge and distal end. Some sandy material adheres to bulbar face. Opaque; honey/grey; a few inclusions. 1. 34 mm; w. 25 mm; th. 6 mm.
4. From 1973 I 25. Flake, roughly triangular section. Bulb and distal end broken off. Probably struck. Some sandy material adheres to the dorsal face. Translucent; reddish-brown. 1. 18 mm; w. 10 mm; th. 3 mm.
5. From 1973 II 2. Blade-like flake with scalene triangular section and plain striking platform. Distal end broken off. Slightly rough surface; opaque; light grey/buff with slight brown staining and cortication at bulbar end. 1. 38 mm; w. 20 mm; th. 9 mm.

Discussion

The flakes are not distinctive enough to be datable without context, but a possibly Neolithic sherd is noted on p. 269. No pre-Neolithic sites seem to be known in the area round Strageath[1] but there are a number of Neolithic and later prehistoric sites in Strath Earn, with a concentration within a few kilometres of Strageath.[2] Topographically, the closest comparison with Strageath comes from North Mains, Strathallan, where a henge, a round barrow, two ring-ditches, later burials and undated features were excavated in 1978–79. The Strathallan sites lay about 3.2 km downstream from Strageath, on the same gravel terrace on the south bank of the River Earn, at about 35 m. above sea level. The prehistoric features, dated from the early third millennium bc to the early 1st millennium bc, produced 142 pieces of flaked flint and other stone. Buried soil under the henge bank (dated late third millennium bc) and the barrow (dated early to mid second millennium bc) had apparently been cultivated and grazed, like the buried soils beneath the turf ramparts at Strageath. Romans and Robertson found a close resemblance between the soils at Strathallan and Strageath and consider they had similar histories of land use, though the Strageath soils were presumably something, like 1700–1800 years later than those at Strathallan. Romans and Robertson concluded that Strageath, like Strathallan, enjoyed a combination of soil and level terrain that was almost ideal for the agriculture of the time and was managed so as to maintain a stable agricultural system.[3] All this must raise the possibility of a prehistoric site in the vicinity of Strageath.

The source of the flint used at Strageath is uncertain. Scotland has no known sources of flint *in situ* but deposits of flint pebbles occur, usually near the coast or on beaches.[4] Caroline Wickham-Jones has suggested that the Strathallan flint was collected from a local source, such as alluvial gravels,[5] and this seems a likely source for the Strageath flint.

1. Morrison, A., *Early Man in Britain and Ireland* (1980) 154–71, fig. 7.8. Hulme, P.D. and Shirriffs, J. 'Pollen analysis of a radiocarbon-dated core from North Mains, Strathallan, Perthshire' *P.S.A.S.* 115 (1985), 109.
   Lawson, T. and Bonsall, C. 'Early settlement in Scotland: the evidence from Reindeer Cave, Assynt' *Quaternary Newsletter* No. 49 (June 1986) 1– 7.
2. For instance: Henshall, A.S., *The Chambered Tombs of Scotland* 2 (1972) 475–6, Map 3. Burl, A., *The Stone Circles of the British Isles* 190–202, fig. 32. Maxwell, G.S., 'Recent aerial survey in Scotland', *The Impact of Aerial Reconnaissance on Archaeology* (CBA Res. Rep. No. 49, 1983), 27–40, figs. 23, 30.
3. Barclay, G.J. *et al.*, 'Sites of the third millennium bc to the first millennium ad at North Mains, Strathallan, Perthshire' *P.S.A.S.* 113 (1983), 122–281.
   Romans, J.C.C. and Robertson, L., 'The general effects of early agriculture on the soil profile', *The Impact of Aerial Reconnaissance on Archaeology* (CBA Res. Rep. No. 49, 1983) 136–41.
4. Wickham-Jones, C.R. and Collins, G.H., 'The sources of flint and chert in northern Britain' *P.S.A.S.* 109 (1977–78) 7–21.
   Wickham-Jones, C.R. 'The procurement and use of stone for flaked tools in prehistoric Scotland' *P.S.A.S.* 116 (1986) 1–10.
5. Wickham-Jones, C.R. in Barclay, G.J. *et al.* (cited in note 3), 164.

XXIX. BURNT WOOD
By Camilla Dickson and Caroline Cartwright

1. Parts of some burnt planks were found on the surface of the Flavian *via decumana* near the East Gate (80 I 29, see p. 88). A sample was transported to the Department of Botany, Glasgow University, where Dr Camilla Dickson reported as follows:

Two parts of a carbonised plank of *Quercus* sp. (oak). One part is now *c.* 20 cm broad, 15 cm long and 1.5–1.8 cm thick; the other *c.* 17 × 20 × 1.8 cm. The estimated diameter of the wood used for the plank is at least 25 cm, based on a maximum measurable circumference of 3 cm. In the middle of the wood the annual rings run parallel and at the edges curve round at right angles to the faces of the board. This indicates that the wood was plain or slash-sawn. The rings are about 2–3 mm apart in the middle and 1–1.5 mm at the edges, the normal reduction in annual increment as the tree increased in girth. This relatively fast rate of growth produces hard strong timber; the best for structural work.'

2. Fifteen pieces of charcoal were kindly identified by Caroline Cartwright at the London Institute of Archaeology as follows:

84 S IV 22: upper filling of Flavian west ditch, sealed by Antonine I road. 1 sample of *Quercus* sp. (oak).
84 S IV 22: as above. 1 sample of *Corylus* sp. (hazel).
84 S V 3: Antonine I demolition-pit. 1 sample of *Corylus* sp. (hazel).
84 S I 5: Antonine I occupation-layer. 1 sample of *Corylus* sp. (hazel).
84 S II 3: Antonine I street. 1 sample of *Corylus* sp.
84 S II 13: Flavian demolition-layer. 1 sample *Corylus* sp.
86 V I 5: Antonine I demolition-layer. 2 samples of *Corylus* sp. 4 samples of *Fraxinus* sp. (ash).
86 V I 6: Antonine I drain. 1 sample of *Corylus* sp.
86 V 1 5: Flavian latrine pit. 1 sample of *Corylus* sp.
86 V II 2: Antonine II demolition-layer. 1 sample of *Fraxinus* sp.
86 V II 3: Antonine I demolition-layer. 1 sample of *Corylus* sp.
86 V II 6: Antonine I occupation-layer. 1 sample of *Corylus* sp.
86 V II 13: Flavian occupation-layer. 1 sample of *Quercus* sp. (oak).
86 V II 12: Flavian occupation-layer. Large sample of branch-sized fragments of *Betula* sp. (birch).

With the exception of the 86 V II 12 *Betula* sp. samples, most of the contexts have yielded charcoal fragments with stem diameters relating to twig-sized material. In some cases measurement of stem diameters was impossible because of high fragmentation.

XXX. ANIMAL BONES

Soil conditions at Strageath were such that no bone whatever survived except for a few minute fragments which had been burnt in demolition bonfires. A selection of these was examined by Annie Grant who was able to report only that they included fragments of long bones, ribs and vertebrae, but that none could be identified to species.

XXXI. POLLEN ANALYSIS FROM THE WEST RAMPART

In September 1984, when excavation of a section through the West Rampart (Trench 1984 S IV, pp. 20–21) had been completed, the site was visited by members of the staff of the Ancient Monuments Laboratory, Edinburgh, under whose supervision pollen samples were taken and the same day removed to Edinburgh. A column of samples was cut from the turves of the Flavian rampart and another from the Antonine I rampart in front of it. The following report was received in April 1988.

Rampart Pollen Samples

By Simon Butler

Two sets of samples were submitted from Strageath, one set relating to the Flavian rampart and one to the Antonine I rampart. A pilot analysis was commissioned with the aim of assessing the potential information available from pollen work on these samples. On receipt of the samples, however, it was discovered that all the numbers had worn off so that it was impossible to ascertain their stratigraphic relationships. All that remained therefore were two sets of samples, one identifiably Flavian and the other Antonine, but no information concerning the stratigraphic position of each sample within either of these two ramparts. A random selection of 9 samples were nevertheless examined – five from the Flavian rampart and four from the Antonine. This was done in order to assess pollen preservation at Strageath and, if possible, to compare and contrast pollen assemblages from the two periods of rampart construction despite the absence of stratigraphic control within each rampart.

Methods

Known quantities of Lycopodium spore tablets were added to measured volumes of soil from each sample in order to allow subsequent calculation of pollen concentrations. All samples were boiled in 10% NaOH and then sieved at 150 microns and 10 microns, with swirling and retention of the 10–150 micron size class. After staining, dehydration and mounting in silicone oil, the material was examined at × 400 magnification. Pollen counts were continued until 400–500 total land pollen (excluding Filicales, *Polypodium, Pteridium*, and *Sphagnum*) were identified in each sample. However, in some cases very low pollen concentrations meant that these sums could not always be achieved in the time available for analysis (see FIG. 136 for actual pollen sums attained). A small number of cereal-sized grass pollen grains were encountered and these were assigned on the basis of size measurements to the 'Hordeum Type' catagory of Anderson (1979). It should be borne in mind that this catagory includes some wild grasses in addition to cultivated barley.

RESULTS

1 . *Flavian Rampart Material.*

Herb pollen consistently dominates in all the spectra at between 60% and 75% of the pollen sum. Of these herbs, Gramineae (Grass family) is always the best represented taxon, with the single exception of sample F5 where it is replaced by Cyperaceae (Sedge Family). Of the remaining herbs a large proportion are types which often occur in association with man's presence. Tree and shrub pollen, at some 25%–40% of the pollen sum, indicates some woodland presence also, with *Quercus* (Oak), *Alnus* (Alder) and Coryloid (probably Hazel rather than Bog Myrtle) as the prevalent tree or shrub types.

It therefore seems from these pollen data that before the turves were incorporated into the Flavian rampart local woodland was already much reduced, so that the site appears to have been located in an area that had already undergone some clearance. Before their use as rampart material

Strageath ramparts

Percentage pollen data. Sum excludes spores *(Filicales, Polypodium, Pteridium, Sphagnum)* and unidentified

n.b. Absence of stratigraphic control

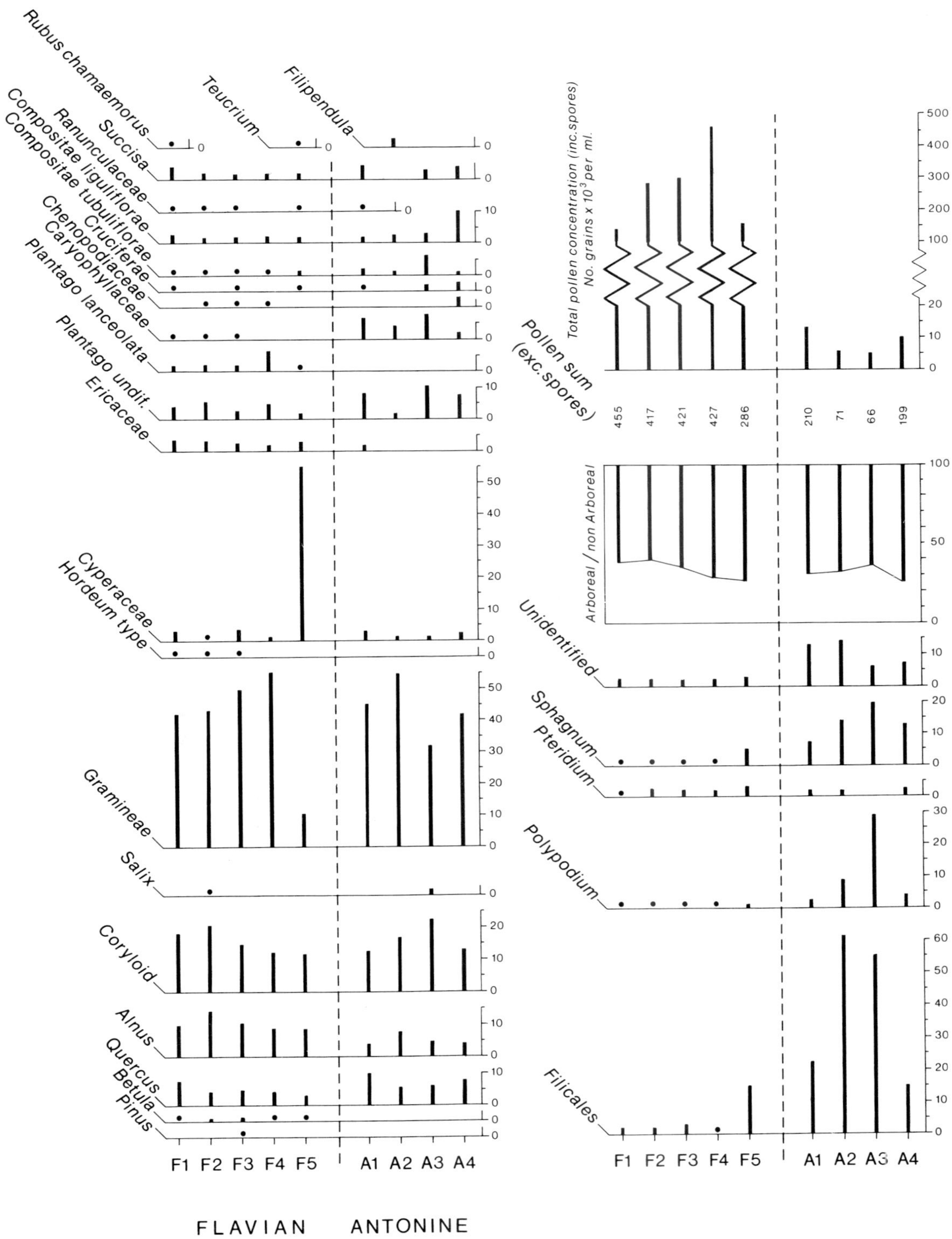

FIG. 136. Pollen Analysis Diagram.

the turves supported a largely grassland flora in which the presence of *Plantago lanceolata* (Ribwort Plantain), Compositae (Tubuliflorae, Daisy family) and Ranunculaceae (Buttercup family) could indicate grazing. At the same time it would appear that Barley (*Hordeum* type) perhaps was being cultivated nearby, and the pollen of Cruciferae (Cabbage, Mustard, Cress etc.), Chenopodiaceae (Goosefoot family) and Caryophyllaceae (Pink family) may be associated with this.

2. *Antonine Rampart Material.*

There is a very striking difference between the two ramparts in the total concentration of pollen within the soil, with the Antonine samples containing far lesser amounts of pollen per unit of soil. The condition of the pollen is also worse, with up to 14% of the sum being totally unidentifiable. In terms of pollen composition, herb types again dominate the spectra at 65%–75% of the pollen sum, and Gramineae is again the best represented taxon. The same variety of herb types as found in the Flavian material tend to be represented, but with increased frequencies for some taxa, particularly Caryophyllaceae, Compositae (Tubuliflorae) and Cruciferae. The relative proportions of the different tree or shrub types remains largely unchanged, while there is a striking increase in the frequency of fern (Filicales and *Polypodium*) and *Sphagnum* spores.

If seen as representing landscape change, the differences in pollen content between the Flavian and Antonine material would perhaps suggest that the meadows and fields of pre-Agricolan times were not subsequently maintained, and were allowed to become overgrown with ferns and weeds. To some extent this might be seen as consistent with Boyd's (1984) suggestion of a decline in grazing pressure with, or soon after, the Agricolan campaign in central Scotland. However, it must be pointed out that the pollen in the Antonine rampart material at Strageath is scarce and poorly preserved, and could be giving a misleading impression. Thus, it is possible that much of the difference between Flavian and Antonine samples results to some extent from the different preservation or concentration characteristics of the two sample sets. For example, higher frequencies of fern spores are often encountered in deteriorated pollen spectra, where their resistance to corrosion or abrasion may explain the relative abundance. The apparent absence of *Plantago lanceolata* in the Antonine samples could very likely reflect the difficulty in speciating poorly preserved *Plantago* pollen, so that they all get recorded as *Plantago* undifferentiated. The apparent absence of *Hordeum* Type pollen could simply reflect the low pollen sums attained in the Antonine rampart material, while the much higher sums of the Flavian samples allowed the occassional cereal-sized grain to be encountered. It remains difficult to explain, however, why the Antonine rampart pollen should be so much more scarce and have suffered greater deterioration then the Flavian rampart pollen. Indeed, it may be that the lower pollen concentration values result less from post-depositional decay of pollen, which might be expected to act similarly on both ramparts, and more from depositional effects such as vegetational change and/or changes in contemporary soil surface characteristics and rates of soil formation.

Conclusion

A methodological caution has to be expressed in concluding this brief analysis from Strageath. Both Dimbleby (1985) and Boyd (1985) have pointed out that in suitably acid soils where faunal mixing of pollen is reduced, a 'graduated pollen stratigraphy' may exist in the soil. This means that pollen at different depths in an excavated soil profile will relate to different time periods. At Strageath each of the fossil turves, having been cut from an ancient soil profile at the time the ramparts were built, might therefore contain such a pollen stratigraphy relating to the millennia leading up to the constructional event. As a result, an absence of stratigraphic control on the pollen samples leads to uncertainty over their age. The quality of information from pollen analysis might have been improved had field sampling retrieved complete vertical sequences of the excavated profiles.

INDEX

PLATES

(*Photo: Colin Martin*)

PL. 1. The fort and annexes from the north west, with the river Earn in the background.

(*Photo: Colin Martin*)

PL. II. The fort and annexes from the south west.

(*Photo: University of Cambridge*)

PL. III. The annexes from the south, with part of the fort to the right.

PL. IV. The fort, looking east, 1962.

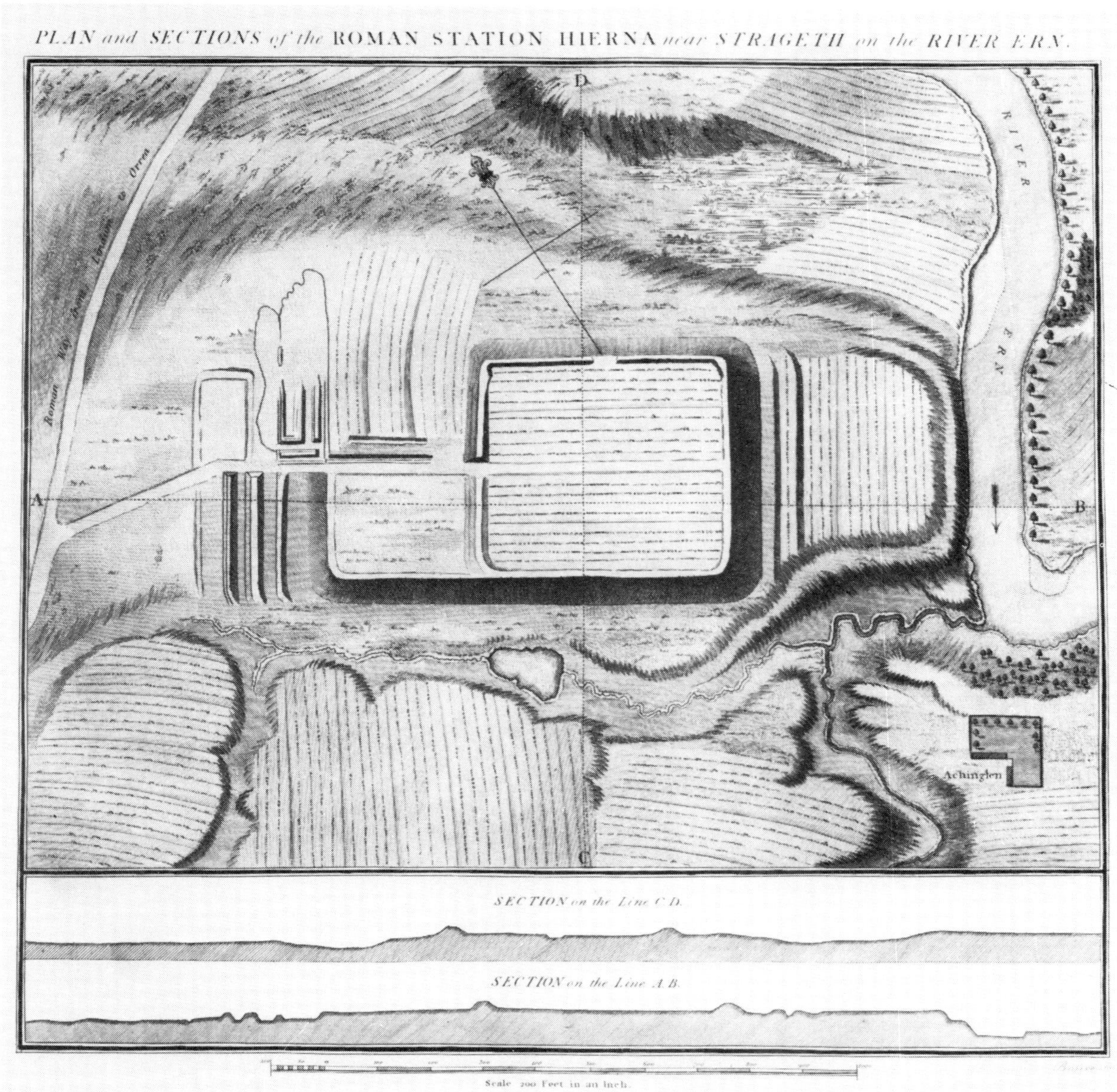

PL. V. General Roy's plan of Strageath, *c.* 1760.

(*Photo: University of Cambridge*)

PL. VI A. Vertical aerial view of the fort, 1962: the narrow street round the *principia* is visible. North to the left.

(*Photo: R. Goodburn*)

PL. VI B. Trench for an obstacle on the berm between ditches III and IV on the east side of the fort (p. 15). What may be a second, oblique, trench was much disturbed by rabbits. Scale in feet.

PL. VII A. The 1973 trench through the east defences, looking west (p. 15). Behind the two ditches lie (a) the timber strapping at the base of the Antonine I rampart and (b) the Flavian rampart with strapping at a higher level. Scales in feet.

PL. VII B. The Flavian rampart partly cut back, with the Antonine I addition in front resting on remains of timber strapping (p. 17). Scales in feet.

(Photo: R. Goodburn)

PL. VIII. The eastern defences (p. 17): The Flavian turf rampart with the Antonine I and II additions in front, the latter partly overlying Ditch I. Scale in feet.

(*Photos: R. Goodburn*)

PL. IX A. The eastern defences: the turf front of the Antonine I rampart (right), with the Antonine II rampart beyond, partly overlying Ditch I. Scale in feet.

PL. IX B. The eastern defences: the front of the Flavian rampart (left) overlying mineralised remains of timber strapping; the Antonine I front in centre and on right (p. 19). Scale in feet. cf. PL. X A

(*Photos: R. Goodburn*)

PL. X A. The eastern defences looking north: detail showing a discontinuity in the turfwork marking the front of the Flavian rampart rising at an angle of 67° (p. 17). Scale in feet.

PL. X B. The eastern defences looking north: vertical back of the Flavian rampart with stones of Antonine II oven (left) and black ash overlying laid turves of a Flavian *ascensus* (p. 17). Scale in feet.

PL. XI A. The eastern defences: detail of front turves of the Antonine I rampart-front in section, looking south. Scales in feet.

PL. XI B. The same: turves in plan (p. 19).

(*Photos: A. Scott Anderson*)

PL. XII A. The western defences: vertical rear face of the Flavian rampart, here built of dark turves, overlying marks of timber strapping (p. 20) with dark silt to right: Trench 1977 A II. Scales in feet.

PL. XII B. The western defences, Trench 1977 A III: The Antonine I rampart (right) and Antonine II rampart (left). cf. FIG. 9, p. 20.

(*Photos: J.J. Wilkes*)

PL. XIII A. The western defences: the Flavian rampart (right) and Antonine ramparts in section, looking north in Trench 1984 S IV. (p. 21) Scale in feet.

PL. XIII B. The western defences: Trench 1984 S IV. Antonine I rampart (left) with metalled street beyond, sealed by Antonine II rampart. Scales in feet.

(*Photo: J.J. Wilkes*)

PL. XIV A. The western defences: the inner (clay-lined) face of the Flavian ditch partly excavated, looking north in Trench 1984 S IV; the ditch is sealed by an Antonine I street and the Antonine II rampart. Scale in feet.

(*Photo: R. Goodburn*)

PL. XIV B. The *via decumana* just behind the East Gate (Trench G I), looking east. The Flavian and Antonine I streets are both sealed by falls of turf and then by Antonine II metalling (foreground and near top of section). (p. 29 and see FIG. 15, Section C–D). Scales in feet.

PL. XV A. North side of the East Gate, 1974 Trench G I, looking west, showing Antonine I street-surface and threshold-slot (p. 30), with upper filling of passage-trench and turf of rampart to the right. Scale in feet.

PL. XV B. Similar view showing the Flavian street-surface with the stone packing of the Antonine I passage-trench to right. The large post-hole at bottom right marks the front of the Antonine I rampart (see FIG. 14). Scales in feet.

(*Photos: R. Goodburn*)

PL. XVI A. North side of East Gate, Trench G I, looking north-east, showing Antonine I street and threshold-slot (p. 30): at top lies a post-hole of the Antonine II gate. Scales in feet.

PL. XVI B. East Gate, Trench G I: hearth on Antonine I berm beneath Antonine II rampart (p. 30). Scales in feet.

(*Photos: R. Goodburn*)

PL. XVII A. South side of East Gate, Trench 1975 G IV, looking west (p. 29), showing Flavian street-surface (right) cut by Antonine I post-pit (right) and stone-packed post-holes of the Antonine I, southern passage-wall (centre). The Flavian gravel spread extends left beneath the rampart (p. 27). Scales in feet.

PL. XVII B. South side of East Gate, Trenches G IV (left) and G II (right), showing Flavian street-surface (background) and stone-packed trench of Antonine I passage-wall. View from south. Scales in feet.

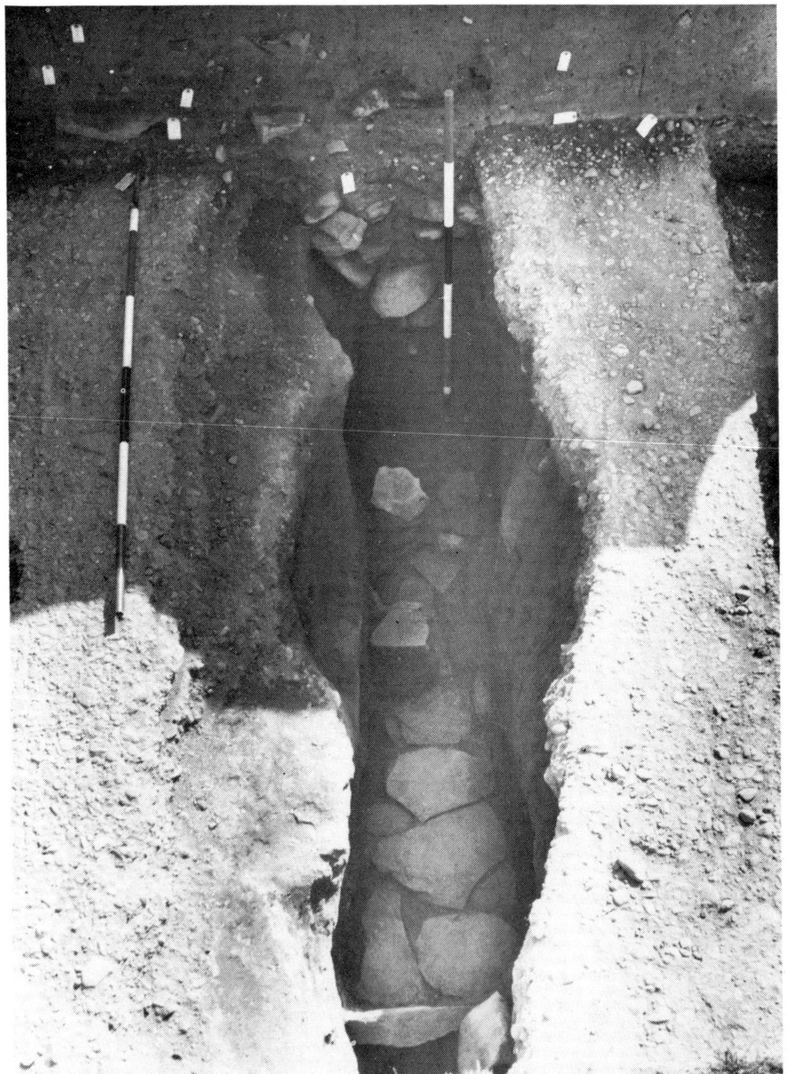

PL. XVIII A. The East Gate. Trench of southern passage-wall of the Flavian gate emptied to show base-plate stones at bottom (p. 27). The stone-packed Antonine I trench, less deep on the same line, is seen in section (background). View from west. Scales in feet.

PL. XVIII B. The same, detail.

(*Photos: R. Goodburn*)

PL. XIX A. South side of East Gate, Trench G II looking west (p. 29), showing the East end of the deep Flavian passage-wall trench (centre) and Flavian threshold trench (right): the stone-packed Antonine I trench continues in foreground. Scales in feet.

PL. XIX B. The same, looking north-east.

(*Photos: R. Goodburn*)

PL. XX A. The *principia*, Trench P XLIV looking north, showing the external north wall-trench of the Flavian building and the east wall-trench of its Room 2 (foreground), with the north wall-trench of the Antonine I *principia* beyond it. To north lies a large natural rock (p. 8), beyond which lies street-metalling cut by the north wall-trench of the Antonine II building. Scales in feet.

PL. XX B. The *principia*, Trench P II, looking east: south external wall of the Antonine I building (left) and of the Antonine II building (centre), with the rocky foundation for narrow Antonine II street (right), overlying a wider Antonine I metalling. Scale in feet.

(*Photos: J.J. Wilkes*)

PL. XXI A. The Central Range (North): Antonine I (right) and Antonine II drains in Trench 1986 V I, looking west (pp. 50–51). Scale in feet.

PL. XXI B. The Central Range (South): *via sagularis* and stone-lined drain (pp. 55–6) showing sandstone (Antonine I) construction overlain by rebuild in rough boulders. View from south. Scale in feet.

(*Photo: R. Goodburn*)

PL. XXII A. The northern *retentura*: general view of Trench 1973 II, North Extension, from the west showing three large Antonine I post-holes with two Flavian wall-trenches of Building I beyond: in the background the Antonine II drain and *via sagularis* (p. 63).

(*Photo: A. Scott Anderson*)

PL. XXII B. The northern *praetentura*. Part of Flavian Building VI in Trench 1977 A I, looking north. Scales in feet.

PL. XXIII A. The northern *retentura*. View of Flavian Buildings I–IV in Trench 1982 G I–II, looking east. Scales in feet.

PL. XXIII B. The northern *retentura*, Trench 1973 I, looking east. In foreground two Antonine I stone-packed post-holes and drain cut through the Flavian *via sagularis*: in background, stones of Antonine II oven.

PL. XXIV A. The northern *praetentura*. General view of Trench 1977 A II from the west. In foreground the Flavian *via sagularis* and two granary trenches of Flavian Building VIII.

PL. XXIV B. The northern *praetentura*. Antonine II furnace in Trench 1977 A II, looking north (p. 80). Scale in feet.

PL. XXV A. The northern *praetentura*. The Antonine II *via sagularis* from the south-west in Trench 1977 A II, showing the amphora-urinal *in situ* (foreground) and Antonine II drain beyond. Scales in feet.

PL. XXV B. The amphora-urinal, detail (p. 80). Scale in feet.

(*Photos: A. Scott Anderson*)

PL. XXVI A. The northern *praetentura*, Trench 1977 A II, looking north. Kerb-stones of the Antonine I *via sagularis* with remains of Antonine II metalling to right and also above in section. Antonine II drain on right. Scale in feet.

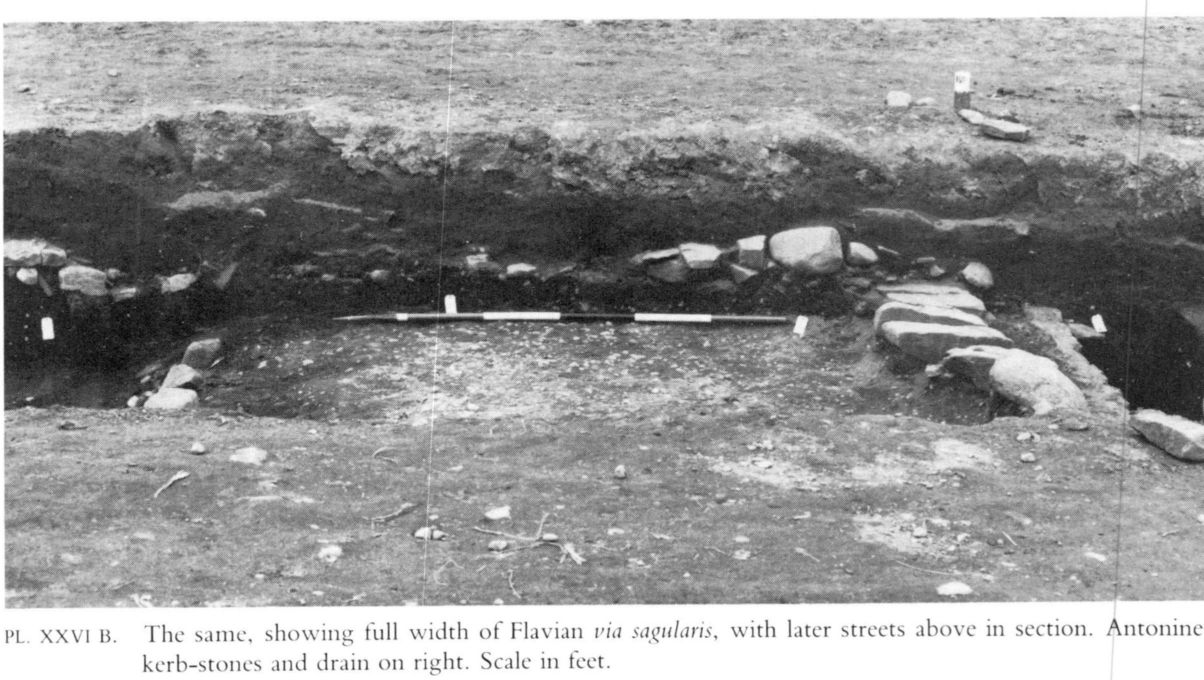

PL. XXVI B. The same, showing full width of Flavian *via sagularis*, with later streets above in section. Antonine I kerb-stones and drain on right. Scale in feet.

(*Photos: A. Scott Anderson*)

PL. XXVII A. The northern *praetentura*. Street between Antonine II Building V (right) and VI (left); looking north in Trench 1977 A I. In the foreground the metalling is concealed by sinkage into Antonine I demolition-pit B (p. 78). Scales in feet.

PL. XXVII B. The northern *praetentura*, Trench 1977 A I, looking north east. The *via principalis* (right) is flanked by the wall-trench of Flavian Building V, to left of which are post-holes of Antonine I Building V. In background lies Flavian demolition-pit C. Scales in feet.

(*Photos: A. Scott Anderson*)

PL. XXVIII A. The northern *praetentura*, Trench 1977 A I, looking south. Metalling of street dividing Antonine II Buildings V and VI sinking into underlying Antonine I demolition-pit B (p. 78): Antonine I post-holes (formerly sealed by the street) to left. Scale in feet.

PL. XXVIII B. The southern *retentura*: east end of Trench 1980 E I, looking north. Flavian lead pig *in situ*, with Antonine I stone-lined drain to right (pp. 88, 92). Scale in feet.

(*Photo: A. Scott Anderson*)

PL. XXIX A. The southern *retentura*: Trench 1980 E II, looking east. Post-holes of Antonine II Building X: note lower stone of quern *in situ*, in left foreground (p. 98). Scales in feet.

(*Photo: J.J. Wilkes*)

PL. XXIX B. The southern *retentura*. Part of Antonine II Building IX in Trench 1981 F I, looking south. Scales in feet.

(*Photo: A. Scott Anderson*)

PL. XXX. The southern *retentura*. General view of Trench 1980 E I, looking east. Antonine II *via sagularis* in background, partly subsided into Flavian pit below. Two large kerb-stones this side of it mark the line of the Antonine II drain. In left foreground the edge of the *via decumana*, interrupted by the site of Trench 1973 III.

PL. XXXI A. The southern *retentura*, Trench 1981 F I, looking north. The Antonine II drain with *via sagularis* to right. Postholes of Antonine I Building IX on left. Scale in feet.

PL. XXXI B. The southern *praetentura*. General view of Trench 1983 L looking west and showing Antonine II buildings. Scales in feet.

(*Photos: J.J. Wilkes*)

PL. XXXII A. The southern *retentura*, Trench 1981 F II looking south. Subsidence of Antonine II street-metalling into Antonine I demolition-pit 2. See p. 98 and FIG. 56, Section P–Q. Scales in feet.

PL. XXXII B. The same in section of Demolition-pit 2. Scale in feet.

(*Photos: J.J. Wilkes*)

PL. XXXIII A. The southern *retentura*. Trench 1986 T I across the Bath-house (p. 98). View looking north. Scales in feet.

PL. XXXIII B. Section across the Bath-house, looking south. Note the turf-filled trench accompanying the north wall (p. 99). Scales in feet.

PL. XXXIV A. The southern *praetentura*: Trench 1983 I, III, looking south-east, showing the kerb of the western Antonine I *via sagularis* protruding from beneath its Antonine II successor. Part of Flavian granary-trench in Building XVI beyond. Scales in feet.

PL. XXXIV B. The southern *praetentura*, Trench 1983 M I looking south, showing rows of Antonine II post-holes in Building XII (p. 114). Scales in feet.

(*Photos: J.J. Wilkes*)

PL. XXXV A. The southern *praetentura*. Post-pit of Antonine I granary in Trench 1984 S I (p. 110). Scale in feet.

PL. XXXV B. The southern *praetentura*, Trench 1984 S II. Hearth in Antonine I Building XVI (p. 111). Scale in feet.

(*Photo: S.S. Frere*)

PL. XXXVI A. The southern *praetentura*, Trench 1984 S III, looking south. The kerb of the Antonine I *via sagularis* with Antonine II metalling extending over it and sinking into the filling of the Antonine I drain. (p. 113).

(*Photo: J.J. Wilkes*)

PL. XXXVI B. The southern *praetentura*. Antonine I oven in Trench 1983 M I (p. 108). Scale in feet.

(*Photos: R.L. Wilkins*)

PL. XXXVII A. Intaglio No. 1 and (right) impression (p. 179). Scale 4:1.

PL. XXXVII B. Intaglio No. 2 in iron ring, two views (p. 179). Scale 4:1.

(*Photos: R.L. Wilkins*)

PL. XXXVIII A. Intaglio No. 3 (p. 179). Scale 4:1.

PL. XXXVIII B. Intaglio No. 4 in iron ring and (right) impression (p. 179). Scale 4:1.

(*Photo: R.L. Wilkins*)

PL. XXXIX A. Sharpening Stone (p.187, No. 1). Scale *c.* 1:2.

PL. XXXIX B. Baked Clay Sling-Bullets, all from Antonine I Building XV except bottom right, which is from Antonine I Building XVII (p.177). Scale 1:2.

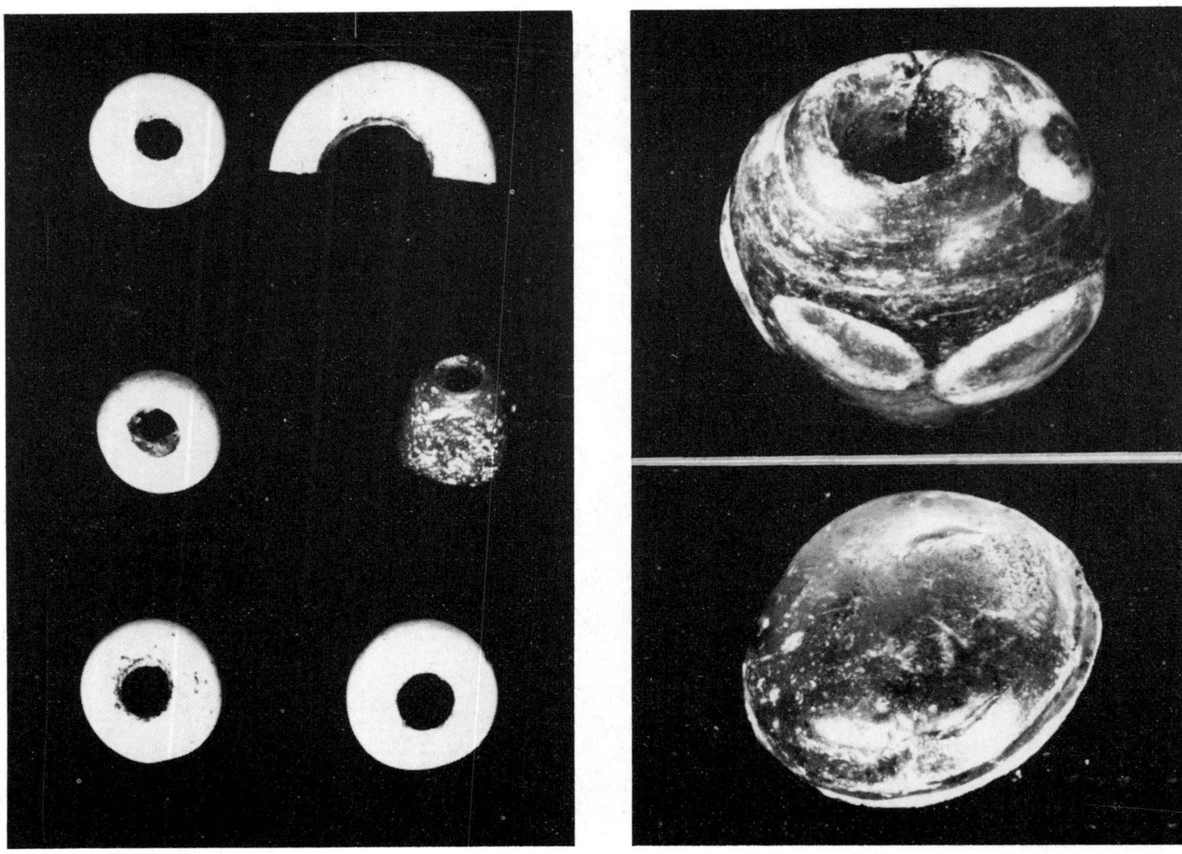

(*Photo: Henry*)

PL. XL A. Glass Beads (p.202). I, Left, (Left to right) Nos. 9, 8, 10, 7, 12, 11. II, Top right, polychrome bead No. 6 (p.202). III, Bottom right, Glass 'gem' stone (p.200). Scale 4:1.

(*Photo: S.S. Frere*)

PL. XL B. Strageath, view from the south-west. The annexes lie in the left background beyond a fold in the fields, with the rise of the fort's west rampart visible in the darker field and the rest of the fort in the light area, background right.